Eighth Edition

Purchasing and Supply Chain Management

KENNETH LYSONS
MA, MEd, PhD, Dipl.PA, Ac.Dip.Ed.,
DMS, FCIS, FCIPS, FInst M, MILT

BRIAN FARRINGTON
BSc(Econ), MSc, PhD, FCIPS

PEARSON

Harlow, England • London • New York • Boston • San Francisco • Toronto • Sydney • Auckland • Singapore • Hong Kong
Tokyo • Seoul • Taipei • New Delhi • Cape Town • São Paulo • Mexico City • Madrid • Amsterdam • Munich • Paris • Milan

Pearson Education Limited
Edinburgh Gate
Harlow
Essex CM20 2JE
England

and Associated Companies throughout the world

Visit us on the World Wide Web at:
www.pearson.com/uk

First published 1981 Macdonald & Evans Limited
Second edition 1989 Longman Group UK Limited
Third edition 1993 Longman Group UK Limited
Fourth edition 1996 Pitman Publishing, a division of Pearson Professional Limited
Fifth edition 2000 Pearson Education Limited
Sixth edition 2003 Pearson Education Limited
Seventh edition 2006 Pearson Education Limited
Eighth edition 2012 Pearson Education Limited

© Macdonald & Evans Limited 1981
© Longman Group Limited 1989, 1993
© Pearson Professional Limited 1996
© Pearson Education Limited 2000, 2012

ISBN 978-0-273-72368-4

British Library Cataloguing-in-Publication Data
A catalogue record for this book is available from the British Library

Library of Congress Cataloging-in-Publication Data
Lysons, Kenneth.
   Purchasing and supply chain management / Kenneth Lysons, Brian Farrington. – 8th ed.
      p. cm.
   ISBN 978-0-273-72368-4 (pbk.)
1. Purchasing. 2. Business logistics. I. Farrington, Brian. II. Title.
   HF5437.L97 2012
   658.7'2–dc23
                                                              2011040039

10 9 8 7 6 5 4 3 2
16 15 14 13 12

Typeset in 10/12pt Sabon by 35
Printed and bound in Great Britain by Ashford Colour Press Ltd, Gosport, Hampshire

Brian Farrington dedicates this book to the memory of Kenneth Lysons, acknowledging all the support he had from his devoted wife, Audrey and their family.

This book is also dedicated to:

Joyce
Joanne
Sandra
Suzanne
Claire
Jake
Lucy
Spencer

The support of Stephen Ashcroft and Ray Gambell, colleagues of Brian, with specific research is warmly acknowledged.

Contents

Preface   xvi
Acknowledgements   xvii
Publisher's acknowledgements   xviii
Plan of the book   xix

Part 1   Introduction and strategy   1

1   What is purchasing?   3

Learning outcomes   3
Key ideas   3
Introduction   3
1.1   Perspectives on purchasing   4
1.2   Definitions   5
1.3   The evolution of purchasing   9
1.4   Purchasing and change   16
1.5   World class purchasing   17
1.6   The status of purchasing and supply management (PSM)   19
Case study   26
Discussion questions   27
Past examination questions   27
References   28

2   Strategy and strategic procurement   30

Learning outcomes   30
Key ideas   30
Introduction   31
2.1   Strategic thinking   31
2.2   What is strategy?   32
2.3   Strategy development   34
2.4   Levels of organisational strategy   37
2.5   Corporate strategy   38
2.6   Growth strategies   38
2.7   Business-level strategy   41
2.8   Strategic management   44
2.9   Strategic analysis   44
2.10   Important environmental factors   45
2.11   Internal scrutiny   49
2.12   Strategy formulation   51
2.13   The evaluation of alternative strategies   56
2.14   Strategy implementation   67
2.15   Post-implementation evaluation, control and review   71
2.16   Strategic purchasing and supply chain process models   73

Case study   76
Discussion questions   77
Past examination questions   78
References   79

3   Logistics and supply chains   81

Learning outcomes   81
Key ideas   81
Introduction   82
3.1   What is logistics?   82
3.2   Materials, logistics and distribution management   83
3.3   Reverse logistics   88
3.4   Supply chains   89
3.5   Supply chain management (SCM)   92
3.6   Supply chain vulnerability   97
3.7   SCM and logistics   98
3.8   Value chains   98
3.9   Value chain analysis   103
3.10   Supply chain optimisation   106
3.11   Supply chains and purchasing   109
Case study   112
Discussion questions   113
Past examination questions   114
References   114

4   Structure and supply chains   117

Learning outcomes   117
Key ideas   117
Introduction   118
4.1   Organisational structures   118
4.2   New type organisations   125
4.3   Networks   126
4.4   Factors in configurations   134
4.5   Lean organisations   138
4.6   Agile organisations and production   140
4.7   Supply and value chain mapping   144
Case study   148
Discussion questions   149
Past examination questions   150
References   150

5   Purchasing structure and design   153

Learning outcomes   153
Key ideas   153
Introduction   154
5.1   Business environmental factors and purchasing structures   154
5.2   Purchasing as a functional department   156

5.3	Horizontal organisations and processes	157
5.4	Teams	159
5.5	Cross-functional purchasing	160
5.6	Some problems of cross-functional teams	161
5.7	Cross-organisational teams	162
5.8	Divisional purchasing structures	162
5.9	Centralised purchasing	164
5.10	Decentralised purchasing	165
5.11	Purchasing in multi-plant organisations	166
5.12	Evolving purchasing structures	169
5.13	Organisational change	170
	Case study	174
	Discussion questions	175
	Past examination questions	176
	References	176

6   Purchasing procedures and supporting tools | 178

	Learning outcomes	178
	Key ideas	178
	Introduction	178
6.1	The sequence and impact of purchasing procedures	179
6.2	Analysing a procurement process	180
6.3	E-commerce, e-business, e-SCM and e-procurement	181
6.4	The evolution of e-procurement models	184
6.5	Electronic data interchange (EDI)	185
6.6	E-hubs, exchanges, portals and marketplaces	189
6.7	E-catalogues	192
6.8	E-auctions	195
6.9	Reverse auctions	196
6.10	E-payment	200
6.11	Low-value purchases	202
6.12	Purchasing manuals	203
6.13	Supplier manuals	205
6.14	Legal aspects of purchasing	206
	Case study	210
	Discussion questions	211
	Past examination questions	212
	References	212

Part 2   Strategy, tactics and operations 1: purchasing factors | 215

7   Supplier relationships | 217

	Learning outcomes	217
	Key ideas	217
	Introduction	217
7.1	Relationship purchasing and purchasing relationships	218
7.2	The contrast between transactional and relationship purchasing, taking account of contractual requirements	218

7.3	Collaborative business relationships	218
7.4	Relationship formation	221
7.5	Models of supplier relationships	223
7.6	Practical considerations of supplier relationship management	229
7.7	The termination of relationships	232
7.8	Further aspects of relationships	234
	Case study	235
	Discussion questions	236
	Past examination questions	236
	References	237

8   Purchasing: product innovation, supplier involvement and development   238

	Learning outcomes	238
	Key ideas	238
8.1	Innovation and *kaizen*	240
8.2	Environmentally sensitive design	243
8.3	Purchasing and new product development	246
8.4	Early supplier involvement (ESI)	248
8.5	Advantages and problems of ESI	250
8.6	Supplier development	251
8.7	Supplier associations (SA)	254
	Case study	256
	Discussion questions	257
	Past examination questions	258
	References	258

9   Specifying and managing product quality   260

	Learning outcomes	260
	Key ideas	260
9.1	What is quality?	261
9.2	Quality systems	263
9.3	The importance of TQM	263
9.4	Specifications	268
9.5	Alternatives to individual specifications	272
9.6	Standardisation	275
9.7	Variety reduction	279
9.8	Quality assurance and quality control	280
9.9	Tests for quality control and reliability	280
9.10	The cost of quality	293
9.11	Value management, engineering and analysis	293
	Case study	305
	Discussion questions	305
	Past examination questions	307
	References	308

10   Matching supply with demand   309

	Learning outcomes	309
	Key ideas	309
10.1	Inventory, logistics and supply chain management	309

10.2	Reasons for keeping inventory	310
10.3	Inventory classifications	310
10.4	Scope and aims of inventory management	311
10.5	Some tools of inventory management	312
10.6	The economics of inventory	317
10.7	Inventory performance measures	318
10.8	Safety stocks and service levels	319
10.9	The right quantity	322
10.10	The nature of demand	323
10.11	Forecasting demand	324
10.12	'Push' and 'pull' inventories	329
10.13	Independent demand	330
10.14	Dependent demand	334
10.15	Just-in-time (JIT)	334
10.16	Materials and requirements planning (MRP)	341
10.17	Manufacturing resource planning (MRP II)	345
10.18	Enterprise resource planning (ERP)	347
10.19	Supply chain management systems	349
10.20	Distribution requirements planning (DRP)	349
10.21	Vendor-managed inventory (VMI)	351
10.22	Purchasing and inventory	354
	Case study	354
	Discussion questions	355
	Past examination questions	356
	References	357

11	**Sourcing and the management of suppliers**	**358**
	Learning outcomes	358
	Key ideas	358
11.1	What is sourcing?	359
11.2	The sourcing process	360
11.3	Sourcing information	361
11.4	Analysis of market conditions	361
11.5	Directives	363
11.6	E-sourcing	365
11.7	Locating suppliers	365
11.8	Supplier assessment	366
11.9	Supplier approval	374
11.10	Evaluating supplier performance	375
11.11	Policy issues in sourcing	378
11.12	The supplier base	379
11.13	Outsourcing	380
11.14	Outsourcing manufacturing	381
11.15	Outsourcing services	386
11.16	Drivers of outsourcing	388
11.17	Types of outsourcing	388
11.18	Benefits of outsourcing	388
11.19	Problems of outsourcing	389

11.20	Handling an outsourcing project	390
11.21	Sub-contracting	392
11.22	Partnering	393
11.23	Intellectual property rights and secrecy	403
11.24	Support for marketing	404
11.25	Intra-company trading	405
11.26	Local suppliers	406
11.27	Purchasing consortia	406
√11.28	Sustainability	407
11.29	Sourcing decisions	408
11.30	Factors in deciding where to buy	410
Case study		412
Discussion questions		413
Past examination questions		414
References		415

12	Managing purchase prices	417
Learning outcomes		417
Key ideas		417
12.1	What is price?	418
12.2	The buyer's role in managing purchase prices	418
12.3	Supplier pricing decisions	426
12.4	The supplier's choice of pricing strategy	428
12.5	Price and cost analysis	430
12.6	Competition legislation	433
12.7	Collusive tendering	435
12.8	Price variation formulae	436
Case study		438
Discussion questions		440
Past examination questions		441
References		442

Part 3	**Strategy, tactics and operations 2: buying situations**	**443**
13	Contrasting approaches to supply	445
Learning outcomes		445
Key ideas		445
Introduction		446
13.1	Industrial products	446
13.2	Capital investment items	446
13.3	Capital expenditure	447
13.4	Factors to be considered when buying capital equipment	448
13.5	Controlling the acquisition of capital equipment	449
13.6	New or used equipment	450
13.7	Financing the acquisition of capital equipment	452
13.8	Selecting suppliers of capital equipment	456
13.9	Evaluating capital investments	458
13.10	The buyer and capital investment purchases	461

13.11   Production materials   462
13.12   Raw materials   462
13.13   Futures dealing   464
13.14   Methods of commodity dealing   467
13.15   Purchasing non-domestic gas and electricity   470
13.16   Energy regulation   470
13.17   Energy supply chains in the UK   470
13.18   Markets   471
13.19   Pricing   472
13.20   Procuring energy contracts   473
13.21   Energy consultants and management   476
13.22   Component parts and assemblies   476
13.23   Consumables   477
13.24   Construction supplies and bills of quantities   478
13.25   Purchasing services   480
Case study   487
Discussion questions   489
Past examination questions   490
References   492

14   Buying from overseas   493

Learning outcomes   493
Key ideas   493
14.1   Terminology   494
14.2   Motives for buying from overseas   494
14.3   Sources of information for overseas suppliers   495
14.4   Overcoming challenges when sourcing overseas   496
14.5   Incoterms   500
14.6   Ocean shipping terminology   505
14.7   Customs and excise   506
14.8   Transport systems, costs and considerations   507
14.9   Freight agents   509
14.10   Methods of payment   512
14.11   Countertrade   514
14.12   The true cost of overseas buying   517
14.13   Buying capital equipment overseas   517
14.14   Factors in successful overseas buying   519
Case study   520
Discussion questions   520
Past examination questions   521
References   522

Part 4   Strategy, tactics and operations 3: negotiation, support
         tools and performance   523

15   Negotiation   525

Learning outcomes   525
Key ideas   525

Introduction   526
15.1   Approaches to negotiation   529
15.2   The content of negotiation   529
15.3   Factors in negotiation   533
15.4   The negotiation process   537
15.5   Pre-negotiation   538
15.6   The actual negotiation   543
15.7   Post negotiation   549
15.8   What is effective negotiation?   550
15.9   Negotiation and relationships   550
15.10   Negotiation ethics   552
Case study   556
Discussion questions   557
Past examination questions   558
References   559

16   Support tools   560

Learning outcomes   560
Key ideas   560
16.1   Tendering   561
16.2   Debriefing unsuccessful tenderers   564
16.3   Post-tender negotiation (PTN)   565
16.4   Application of costing techniques   566
16.5   Lifecycle costing   566
16.6   Target costing   571
16.7   Absorption costing   573
16.8   Activity-based costing (ABC) and management   577
16.9   Standard costing   582
16.10   Budgets and budgetary control   584
16.11   Learning curves   584
16.12   Project management   589
16.13   Scheduling   591
16.14   Operational research (OR)   599
Case study   602
Discussion questions   602
Past examination questions   604
References   605

17   Purchasing research, performance and ethics   606

Learning outcomes   606
Key ideas   606
17.1   Purchasing research   606
17.2   Purchasing performance evaluation   611
17.3   Accounting approaches   613
17.4   The purchasing management audit approach   616
17.5   Benchmarking and ratios   621
17.6   Integrated benchmarking   628
17.7   Management by objectives (MBO)   631

17.8   Miscellaneous approaches applicable to measuring purchasing
        performance   632
17.9   Purchasing ethics   632
17.10   Some ethical issues relating to suppliers   633
17.11   Ethical codes and training   636
17.12   Ethical decisions   640
17.13   Purchasing and fraud   640
17.14   Environmental aspects of purchasing   647
Case study   657
Discussion questions   657
Past examination questions   659
References   659

*Appendix 1: Code of professional ethics – Chartered Institute of
Purchasing and Supply (CIPS) (Approved by the CIPS Council,
11 March 2009)*   662
*Appendix 2: Principles and standards of ethical supply management
conduct (ISM) (Adopted May 2008)*   664

Definitions, acronyms and foreign words and phrases   665
Index of names and organisations   670
Subject index   675

Supporting resources

Visit **www.pearsoned.co.uk/farrington** to find valuable online resources

For Instructors:
- Comprehensive Instructor's Manual containing teaching tips and notes on case studies for each chapter
- Downloadable PowerPoint slides containing figures from the book

For more information please contact your local Pearson Education sales representative or visit **www.pearsoned.co.uk/farrington**

Preface

Within a short time of the seventh edition being published, Dr Kenneth Lysons sadly passed away. He had dedicated his professional life to influencing the role and impact of purchasing. The fact that this book is now in its eighth edition is testimony to his foresight, diligence and ability to explain complex matters in such a way that all levels of the purchasing profession can identify with.

Dr Brian Farrington has accepted the role of lead author for the eighth edition. In this regard there are some important points to make.

1 The publisher's research showed that, broadly, the content of the book should remain the same. The book's intended purposes of providing a comprehensive input supporting those engaged in professional studies and providing practitioners with reference materials, meets defined needs.

2 Dr Farrington has used the resources of Steve Ashcroft and Ray Gambell to assist in the considerable research that was undertaken. Both are professional colleagues in Brian Farrington Ltd, a specialist consultancy and training company.

3 The eighth edition remains true to the principles and rigour of Dr Lysons, although much of the content has been refreshed and brought up to date, taking due account of developments in purchasing and supply chain management.

4 A greater balance of private and public sector practices has been included. There are practices that are transferable.

5 As a textbook, coverage is provided of the syllabus of the Chartered Institute of Purchasing and Supply at both the Foundation and Professional stages. The book should be useful to students taking the examinations of the Institute of Logistics and Transport and first and higher degrees in Business Strategies and Management, which contain Purchasing and Supply Management Elements.

There are countless opportunities for the purchasing profession. There are unprecedented challenges even as this edition was being finalised. The world economy is in a serious downturn, there are supplier financial failures, energy costs are spiralling, environmental considerations are paramount, the public sector is in a funding crisis and the consequences of the world banking and financial crisis are still being played out. Purchasing needs to have a strategic role in which it influences long-term business decisions. Without question, purchasing is rapidly becoming a profession requiring an extensive range of skills and knowledge, embracing technical, financial, contractual, logistics, psychology, negotiations and strategic business inputs.

The names of people and organisations used in the case studies are, and are intended to be, fictitious and any similarity to real people and organisations is entirely accidental.

Acknowledgements

Dr Farrington is indebted to many organisations and people who gave their valuable time sharing real life experiences. There are too many to name, but the support of David Stanley (University of Manchester), Stephen Barnes (Chief Executive, Pendle Borough Council), Doug Bridson (ex-Scottish Power), Brian Gibson (Sefton MBC), Sandy Duckett (Standard Life) and Julie Muscroft (Walker Morris) deserve special mention.

The Chartered Institute of Purchasing and Supply kindly gave permission to use questions set at the Foundation and Diploma Stage examinations and to quote from publications written for the Institute by Kenneth Lysons.

Brian Farrington places on record the assistance and support given by Steve Ashcroft and Ray Gambell. They are business colleagues and personal friends. Inevitably, authors have to sacrifice some family life when producing books of this magnitude. Brian's wife, Joyce, has displayed patience, support and the ultimate belief that the book's success is a family achievement. She is right!

Sandra Small has project managed the production of the manuscript with impeccable diligence. She has coped with the stress of meeting deadlines in an admirable way. Thank you!

Without the encouragement, drive and enthusiasm of Rufus Curnow and Mary Lince at Pearson it is unlikely that the book would have come to fruition. To them, a very personal thanks.

Publisher's acknowledgements

We are grateful to the following for permission to reproduce copyright material:

Figures

Figures 1.4, 1.5 from *Improving Purchase Performance*, Pitman (Syson, R. 1992) pp. 254–5; Figure 2.12 adapted from Purchasing must become supply management, *Harvard Business Review*, Sept/Oct, pp. 109–17 (Kraljic, P. 1983); Figure 2.16 from Rob Atkins and Bracknell Forest (UK) Borough Council; Figure 2.18 adapted from http://www.cips.org/Documents/Resources/PSM_model_Feb03.pdf; Figures 3.14, 3.15 adapted from Integrated materials management: the value chain redefined, *International Journal of Logistics Management*, 4(1), pp. 13–22 (Hines, P. 1993); Figures 3.16, 3.17 from Bourton Group, Half delivered: a survey of strategies and tactics in managing the supply chain in manufacturing businesses, 1997, pp. 26–7; Figure 4.7 from *Industrial Technological Development: A Network Approach*, Croom Helm (Hakansson, H. 1987); Figure 4.9 from New organizational forms for competing in highly dynamic environments, *British Journal of Management*, 7, 203–18 (Craven, D.W., Piercy, N.F. and Shipp, S.H. 1996); Figure 6.10 from *The CIPS E-procurement guidelines: measuring the benefits*, CIPS; Figure 12.8 from *Review of the UK's Competition Landscape* (National Audit Office); Figure 15.4 adapted from *Marketing by Agreement: A Cross-cultural Approach to Business Negotiations*, Wiley (McCall, J.M., and Norrington, M.B. 1986); Figure 15.5 adapted from Effect of delivery systems on collaborative negotiations for large-scale infrastructure projects, *Journal of Management in Engineering*, April 2001, 105–21 (Pena-Mora, F., and Tamaki, T.).

Tables

Table 4.2 from An initial classification of supply networks, *International Journal of Operations and Production Management*, 20(6) (Lamming, R., Johnsen, T., Zheng, J. and Harland, C. 2000); Table 4.4 from New organizational forms for competing in highly dynamic environments, *British Journal of Management*, 7, 203–18 (Craven, D.W., Piercy, N.F. and Shipp, S.H. 1996).

In some instances we have been unable to trace the owners of copyright material, and we would appreciate any information that would enable us to do so.

Plan of the book

Part 1 Introduction and strategy					
Chapter 1 What is purchasing?	Chapter 2 Strategy and strategic procurement	Chapter 3 Logistics and supply chains	Chapter 4 Structure and supply chains	Chapter 5 Purchasing structure and design	Chapter 6 Purchasing procedures and supporting tools

Part 2 Strategy, tactics and operations 1: purchasing factors					
Chapter 7 Supplier relationships	Chapter 8 Purchasing: product innovation, supplier involvement and development	Chapter 9 Specifying and managing product quality	Chapter 10 Matching supply with demand	Chapter 11 Sourcing and the management of suppliers	Chapter 12 Managing purchase prices

Part 3 Strategy, tactics and operations 2: buying situations	
Chapter 13 Contrasting approaches to supply	Chapter 14 Buying from overseas

Part 4 Strategy, tactics and operations 3: negotiation, support tools and performance		
Chapter 15 Negotiation	Chapter 16 Support tools	Chapter 17 Purchasing research, performance and ethics

Part 1

Introduction and strategy

Chapter 1

What is purchasing?

Learning outcomes

This chapter aims to provide an understanding of:

- the scope and influence of purchasing
- the stages of purchasing development and future trends in purchasing development
- factors influencing the internal and external status of purchasing.

Key ideas

- Purchasing as a function, process, supply or value chain link, a relationship, discipline and profession.
- Definitions of purchasing and procurement.
- The evolution of purchasing and supply management (PSM) from a reactive transactional to a proactive strategic activity.
- Globalisation, information technology, changing production and management philosophies as factors in the evolution of purchasing.
- Characteristics of purchasing in the future and world class purchasing.
- Leverage, focus and professionalism as factors contributing to the status of purchasing within a particular organisation.
- Purchasing as a change agent.

Introduction

There is no one definition of Purchasing as will be shown later in this chapter. Neither is there a term to describe the activity of committing expenditure. It is variously referred to as Purchasing, Buying, Procurement, Materials Management, Supply Chain Management, Purchasing and Supply Chain Management and Sourcing Management. For consistency, the term Purchasing is used throughout the book. Where other terms are used they will be defined.

The thrust of this book is to advance the view that purchasing applied at world class standards has a focus on strategy, risk management, decision making, innovative supply chain creation, financial prudence, high ethical standards and finding sustainable solutions for long-term supply needs.

1.1 Perspectives on purchasing

The study of purchasing can be approached from several perspectives. Such perspectives include those of function, process, link in the supply or value chain, relationship, discipline and profession.

1.1.1 Purchasing as a function

In management studies, a 'function' is often defined as a unit or department in which people use specialised knowledge, skills and resources to perform specialised tasks. A function is also what a resource is designed to do, so, for example, the function of a pen is to make a mark. A distinction can therefore be made between the *purchasing function* and the *purchasing department*. The former, in a business context, involves acquiring raw materials, components, goods and services for conversion, consumption or resale. The latter is the organisational unit responsible for carrying out this function. In too many organisations, purchasing remains an inconsequential clerical function that has little influence on third-party expenditure. In contrast, other organisations have created integrated structures to cope with design, source selection, purchasing, logistics and long-term product support.

1.1.2 Purchasing as a process

A *process* is a set of sub-processes or stages directed at achieving an output. The various tasks or stages can be depicted as a process chain. Thus, as with Figure 1.1, purchasing can be depicted as a process chain leading to the acquisition of supplies.

The link in the purchasing process chain is information. The challenge for purchasing is to manage information at all phases of the process chain and ensure every stakeholder is informed on the current status. A comprehensive knowledge management system is essential.

1.1.3 Purchasing as a link in the supply or value chain

Supply and value chains are discussed in Chapter 3, where it is shown that, in his value chain model, Porter[1] regards procurement as one of four support activities that contribute to the competitive advantage of a business. Purchasing within a manufacturing business will link with production, warehousing and transportation. This may be contrasted

Figure 1.1 The purchasing process chain

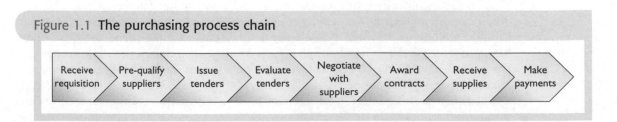

| Receive requisition | Pre-qualify suppliers | Issue tenders | Evaluate tenders | Negotiate with suppliers | Award contracts | Receive supplies | Make payments |

with purchasing in a construction business where the link will be with architects, quantity surveyors, project managers, site agents and commissioning staff.

1.1.4 Purchasing as a relationship

The ability of purchasing to create, and maintain, relationships is a significant challenge. The strength of internal relationships will be a key factor in dealing with negative impressions of purchasing, such as processes taking too long and arguments about price. The strength of external relationships with suppliers will be an influence on the quality of contract performance. The creation of effective partnering arrangements requires the investment of resources. As Ford *et al.*[2] observe:

> The main issue facing managers is no longer about 'buying the right products at the right time at the right price' but of handling and developing relationships with key suppliers over long periods.

1.1.5 Purchasing as problem-solving

The following is the view of the IMP (Industrial Marketing and Purchasing Group):[3]

> Customers are not looking for a product from a manufacturer. Instead they seek a solution to a problem from a supplier. Business purchases are problem driven. A problem may relate to the customer's need to carry out its basic activities efficiently and economically. Examples include the problems of wastage of material, poor utilisation of staff or an unacceptable failure rate in components. We refer to these as problems of 'rationalisation'. A problem can also arise for positive reasons such as when a company is trying to develop relationships with new customers or enhance the performance of a product. We refer to these as problems of 'development'.

1.1.6 Purchasing as a discipline

A discipline is a branch of knowledge, an area of study. The academic content of purchasing lacks the clearly defined focus associated with other fields of study, such as mathematics, economics and law, and draws heavily on other subjects to build its knowledge base. Such subjects include accounting, economics, ethics, information technology, law, management accounting, operational research, marketing, management and psychology. Purchasing as a sub-area of study is often included in wider-ranging courses, including logistics management, operations management and marketing. The discussion of purchasing as a field of study in its own right is continued in section 1.6.3, later in this chapter.

1.1.7 Purchasing as a profession

Purchasing is a profession when practised at the highest level. In broad terms it has failed to establish itself as a profession that holds the same regard as doctors, architects, lawyers and chemists. This is discussed further in section 1.6.3.

1.2 Definitions

Day[4] has rightly pointed out that 'no definition can wholly incorporate the demands placed on a purchasing team's set of skills'. Situational diversities, such as strategic importance, amount of spend contribution to profitability, supplier relationships and the recognition given to purchasing in a particular organisation, mean that any definition of purchasing is open to criticism. Apart from integrated definitions, such as materials, logistics and supply management, some definitions are considered below.

1.2.1 The classic definition of purchasing

This defines the objectives of purchasing as:

> To buy materials of the right quality, in the right quantity from the right source delivered to the right place at the right time at the right price.

Some criticisms of this definition centre on the difficulties associated with the word 'right'.

■ What is 'right' is contingent on a particular organisation or situation.

■ In practice, some of the above 'rights' are irreconcilable and a particular 'right' can only be obtained by trading off another. Thus, it may be possible to obtain the right quality but not at the right price. In practice, the right suppliers are often, but not necessarily, the busiest and also the most expensive.

The above definition is outmoded as it implies that purchasing is:

■ *reactive rather than proactive* – that is, purchasing is a service activity buying what it is instructed to buy rather than one that takes the initiative in helping to determine purchasing policies

■ *transactional rather than relational* – that is, purchasing is primarily concerned with the mechanics of order placing on a one-off basis rather than the establishment, where appropriate, of long-term, collaborative supplier relationships

■ *tactical rather than strategic* – that is, purchasing is focused on short-term buying rather than on contributing to the achievement of long-term corporate goals.

A much more recent definition of purchasing (Winthrop.edu[5]) is 'Purchasing is the process of procuring the proper requirement, at the time needed, for the lowest possible costs from a reliable source.'

1.2.2 Purchasing as procurement

Procurement is a wider term than purchasing and has been defined as[6]:

> 'Procurement is the process of acquiring goods, works and services, covering both acquisitions from third parties and from in-house providers. The process spans the whole lifecycle from identification of needs, through to the end of the useful life of an asset. It involves options appraisal and the critical "make or buy" decision.' This definition was included in the 'National Procurement Strategy for Local Government, October 2008'.

1.2.3 Purchasing as organisational buying

Organisational buyers have been defined by Marrian[7] as:

> Those buyers of goods and services for the specific purpose of industrial or agricultural production or for use in the operation or conduct of a plant, business, institution, profession or service.

Table 1.1 A typology of organisational buyers

Types of organisation	Characteristics	Examples
Industrial/producer organisations	Purchase of goods and services for some tangible production and commercially significant purpose	Manufacturers: primary (extractive) producers – agriculture, forestry, fishing, horticulture, mining
Intermediate organisations	Purchase of goods and services for resale or for facilitating the resale of other goods in the industrial or ultimate consumer markets	Distributors, dealers, wholesalers, retailers, banks, hotels and service traders
Government and public-sector organisations	Purchase of goods and services for resale or use by organisations providing a service, often tangible, and not always commercially significant at national, regional and local levels	Central and local government, public utilities
Institutions	Purchase of goods and services for institutions that buy independently on their own behalf	Schools, colleges, hospitals, voluntary organisations

Organisational buyers are, therefore, those who buy on behalf of an organisation rather than for individual or family use or consumption. Organisational buyers can, as shown in Table 1.1, be considered to belong to one of four buying groups, each of which can be further subdivided.

Some of the categories in Table 1.1 may overlap. Thus, in the National Health Service, some supplies may be bought centrally by government agencies, regionally by health authorities and locally by hospitals themselves.

1.2.4 Purchasing as supplier management

Supplier management may be defined as:

> That aspect of purchasing or procurement concerned with rationalising the supplier base and selecting, coordinating, appraising the performance of and developing the potential of suppliers and, where appropriate, building long-term collaborative relationships.

Supplier management is a more strategic and cross-functional activity than 'purchasing', which is transactionally and commercially biased. The relationship between procurement purchasing and supplier management is shown in Figure 1.2.

1.2.5 Purchasing as external resource management

The following is the view of Lamming:[8]

> The new strategic function will probably not be called purchasing – that is much too limited a word. The connotations of purse strings and spending money have no relevance to the setting up and management of strategic interfirm relationships. This task is concerned with ensuring the correct external resources are in place to complement the internal resources. Perhaps 'external resource managers' is a term that future purchasing managers will adopt.

Figure 1.2 The relationship between procurement, supplier management and purchasing

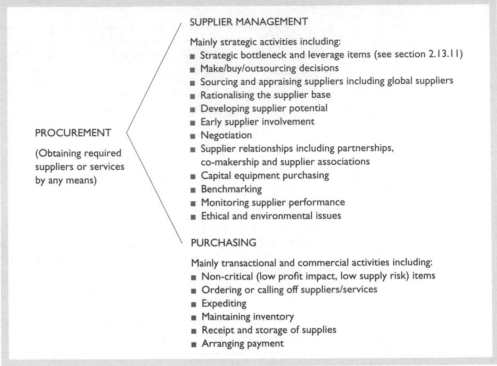

The perspective of external resource management is also adopted by van Weele,[9] who defines purchasing as:

> Obtaining from external sources all goods and services which are necessary for running, maintaining and managing the company's primary and support activities at the most favourable conditions.

Against these definitions, it may be held that 'external resources' includes people, the recruitment and management of whom, as individuals, is primarily a human resource management responsibility. Services provided by people collectively, as in outsourcing or the procurement of facilities, may, of course, fall within the purchasing remit. As a staff manager, the purchasing executive will also be responsible for the management of internal resources.

1.2.6 A composite definition

In spite of its inadequacies, the term 'purchasing' is used in the title of this book as it is still retained in the names of both the British Chartered Institute of Purchasing and Supply (CIPS) and the journals such as *The European Journal of Purchasing Management*. The following definition of purchasing is offered as including aspects discussed above:

The process undertaken by the organisational unit that, either as a function or as part of an integrated supply chain, is responsible for procuring or assisting users to procure, in the most efficient manner, required supplies at the right time, quality, quantity and price and the management of suppliers, thereby contributing to the competitive advantage of the enterprise and the achievement of its corporate strategy.

The significant words or terms in the above definition are the following:

■ *Processes* – the chain or sequence of activities involved in procuring supplies.

■ *Organisational unit* – this may be a department, team, cost or profit centre responsible for all purchasing activities under the control of a designated manager. An alternative term might be 'responsibility centre'.

■ *Function* – a discrete organisational unit.

■ *Integrated supply chain* – refers to the absorption of formerly discrete organisational units, such as purchasing, production and sales, into a continuous flow of interaction.

■ *Procurement* – as stated above, is the process of obtaining goods or services by any means.

■ *Assisting users to procure* – refers to the increasing practice of negotiating contracts with one supplier for a range of items, such as office supplies. Users can then order their requirements directly online, using a procurement card. It also refers to advice given by purchasing as part of a purchasing team.

■ *The most efficient manner* – the elimination, so far as possible, of all non-value-adding activities in the purchasing process.

■ *Quality, quantity, time and price* – these concepts are discussed in appropriate chapters of this book.

■ *The management of suppliers* – this is defined above and, as stated, is sometimes regarded as a support activity distinct from the actual procurement of supplies.

■ *Competitive advantage* – is a special edge that enables an organisation to deal with market and environmental forces better than its competitors do. Purchasing power and well-developed supplier relationships are two ways in which an organisation may obtain competitive advantage over its competitors.

■ *Corporate strategy* – the aims and objectives of an enterprise together with the means by which these are to be achieved. Functional strategies such as a purchasing strategy should be related to corporate strategy.

1.3 The evolution of purchasing

Purchasing represents a stage in the evolution of civilised human relationships as it enables a desired object to be obtained by trading rather than conquest, plunder or confiscation. It is a very ancient activity. A cuneiform clay tablet excavated at El-Rash Shamra, northern Syria, dated about 2800 BC, carries an inscription that, roughly translated, reads: 'HST to deliver 50 jars of fragrant smooth oil each 15 days after [a starting date] and during the reign of AS. In return he will be paid 600 small weight in grain. This order will continue indefinitely until the purchaser or his son removes his consent.'

The evolution of purchasing can be analysed in seven periods.

Period 1: The early years (1850–1900)

Some observers define the early years of purchasing history as beginning after 1850. Evidence exists, however, that the purchasing function received attention before this date. Charles Babbage's book on the economy of machinery and manufacturers, published in 1832, referred to the importance of the purchasing function. Babbage also alluded to a 'materials man' responsible for several different functions. Babbage wrote that a central officer responsible for operating mines was 'a materials man who selects, purchases, receives, and delivers all articles required'.

The greatest interest in and development of purchasing during the early years occurred after the 1850s – a period that witnessed the growth of the American railroad. By 1866, the Pennsylvania Railroad had given the purchasing function departmental status, under the title of Supplying Department. A few years later, the head purchasing agent at the Pennsylvania Railroad reported directly to the president of the railroad. The purchasing function was such a major contributor to the performance of the organisation that the chief purchasing manager had top managerial status.

The comptroller of the Chicago and Northwestern Railroad wrote the first book exclusively about the purchasing function, 'The Handling of Railway Supplies – Their Purchase and Disposition', in 1887. He discussed purchasing issues that are still critical today, including the need for technical expertise in purchasing agents along with the need to centralise the purchasing department under one individual. The author also commented on the lack of attention given to the selection of personnel to fill the position of purchasing agent.

Period 2: Growth of purchasing fundamentals (1900–1939)

The second period of purchasing evolution began around the turn of the twentieth century and lasted until the beginning of the Second World War. Articles specifically addressing the industrial purchasing function began appearing with increasing regularity outside the railroad trade journals. Engineering magazines in particular focused attention on the need for qualified purchasing personnel and the development of material specifications.

Purchasing gained importance during the First World War because of its role in obtaining vital war materials. This was due largely to purchasing's central focus of raw material procurement during this era (versus buying finished or semi-finished goods). Ironically, the years during the First World War featured no publication of any major purchasing books. Harold T. Lewis, a respected purchasing professional during the 1930s through the 1950s, noted that there was considerable doubt about the existence of any general recognition of purchasing as being important to a company. Lewis noted that from the First World War to 1945, at least a gradual if uneven recognition developed of the importance of sound procurement to company operation.

Period 3: The war years (1940–1946)

The Second World War introduced a new period in purchasing history. The emphasis on obtaining required (and scarce) materials during the war influenced a growth in purchasing interest. In 1933, only nine colleges offered courses related to purchasing. By 1945, this number had increased to 49 colleges. The membership of the National Association of Purchasing Agents increased from 3,400 in 1934 to 5,500 in 1940 to 9,400 in the autumn of 1945. A study conducted during this period revealed that 76 per cent of all purchase requisitions contained no specifications or stipulation of brand. This suggested that other departments within the firm recognised the role of the purchasing agent in determining sources of supply.

Period 4: The quiet years (1947–mid-1960s)

The heightened awareness of purchasing that existed during the Second World War did not carry over to the post-war years. John A. Hill, a noted purchasing professional, commented about the state of purchasing during this period: 'For many firms, purchases were simply an inescapable cost of doing business which no one could do much about. So far as the length and breadth of American industry is concerned, the purchasing function has not yet received in full measure the attention and emphasis it deserves.'

Articles began appearing during this period describing the practices of various companies using staff members to collect, analyse and present data for purchasing decisions. Ford Motor Company was one of the first private organisations to establish a commodity research department to provide short-term commodity information. Ford also created a purchase analysis department to give buyers assistance on product and price analysis.

Period 5: Materials management comes of age (mid-1960s–late 1970s)

The mid-1960s witnessed a dramatic growth of the materials management concept. Although interest in materials management grew during this period, the historical origins of the concept date back to the 1800s. Organising under the materials management concept was common during the latter half of the nineteenth century in the US railroads. The combined related functions such as purchasing, inventory control, receiving and stores were under the authority of one individual.

The behaviour of purchasing during this period was notable. Purchasing managers emphasised multiple sourcing through competitive bid pricing and rarely viewed the supplier as a value-added partner. Buyers maintained arm's length relationships with suppliers. Price competition was the major factor determining supply contracts. The purchasing strategies and behaviours that evolved over the last half-century were inadequate when the severe economic recession of the early 1980s and the emergence of foreign global competitors occurred.

Period 6: The global era (late 1970s–1999)

The global era, and its effect on the importance, structure, and behaviour of purchasing, has already proved different from other historical periods. These differences include the following:

- Never in our industry history has competition become so intense so quickly.
- Global firms increasingly captured world market share from domestic US companies, and emphasised different strategies, organisational structures and management techniques compared with their American counterparts.
- The spread and rate of technology change during this period was unprecedented, with product lifecycles becoming shorter.
- The ability to coordinate worldwide purchasing activity by using international data networks and the World Wide Web (via Intranets) emerged.

This intensely competitive period witnessed the growth of supply chain management. Now, more than ever, firms began to take a more coordinated view of managing the flow of goods, services, funds and information from suppliers through end customers.

Managers began to view supply chain management as a way to satisfy intense cost and other improvement pressures.

Period 7: Integrated supply chain management (beyond 2000)

Purchasing and supply chain management today reflects a growing emphasis concerning the importance of suppliers. Supplier relationships are shifting from an adversarial approach to a more cooperative approach with selected suppliers. The activities that the modern purchasing organisation must put in place are different from just a few years ago. Supplier development, supplier-design involvement, the use of full-service suppliers, total-cost supplier selection, long-term supplier relationships, strategic cost management, and integrated Internet linkages and shared databases are now seen as ways to create new value within the supply chain. Purchasing behaviour is shifting dramatically to support the performance requirements of the new era.

It is possible to reach three conclusions about this new era. First, the reshaping of the role of purchasing in the modern economy is underway in response to the challenges presented by worldwide competition and rapidly changing technology and customer expectations. Second, the overall importance of the purchasing function is increasing, particularly for firms that compete in industries characterised by worldwide competition and rapid change. Third, purchasing must continue to become more integrated with customer requirements, as well as with operations, logistics, human resources, finance, accounting, marketing, and information systems. This evolution will take time to occur fully, but the integration is inevitable.

The authors have adapted the above from an article in *Solar Energy Market Express*.[10] For a more detailed exposition of professional development and published literature Fearon[11] details it in his historical evolution of the purchasing function.

Reck and Long[12] have identified four strategic stages of development that purchasing must pass through to become a competitive weapon in the battle for markets (see Table 1.2).

Reck and Long[13] also identify the effect at each of the four stages of 12 non-operational development variables, as shown in Table 1.3.

Other attempts to trace the evolution of purchasing are those of Syson[14] and Morris and Calantone[15] who each identify three stages. Syson refers to 'the changing focus of purchasing as it evolves from a purely clerical routine activity to a commercial stage in which the emphasis is on cost savings and finally a proactive strategic function concerned with materials or logistics management.' Morris and Calantone differentiate between (i) clerical, (ii) 'asset management' and profitability and (iii) 'core-strategic' function stages.

Jones,[16] however, criticises the above approaches on two grounds. First, they are non-operational and merely indicate the stage of development of purchasing activity, the criteria for which may differ from one procurement organisation to another. Second, the models have a restricted number of development measurement variables. In an attempt to remedy those deficiencies Jones suggests a five-stage development model using 18 measurement criteria. The five stages of purchasing development measured on a scale of 1–5 are shown in Table 1.4.

The purchasing profile shown in Figure 1.3 enables the stage of development reached by a particular organisation to be identified and assessed on a scale of 1–5. The profile also indicates areas where further development is required, as measured in the 18 criteria shown in Figure 1.3. Appropriate strategies to meet identified shortcomings can then be devised.

Table 1.2 Strategic stages of the development of a purchasing function

Stage	Definition and characteristics	
Stage 1 Passive	Definition	Purchasing function has no strategic direction and primarily reacts to the requests of other functions
	Characteristics	■ High proportion of time on quick-fix routine operations ■ Functional and individual communications due to purchasing's low visibility ■ Supplier selection based on price and availability
Stage 2 Independent	Definition	Purchasing function adopts the latest purchasing techniques and processes, but its strategic direction is independent of the firm's competitive strategy
	Characteristics	■ Performance based primarily on cost reduction and efficiency disciplines ■ Coordination links are established between purchasing and technical disciplines ■ Top management recognises the importance of professional development ■ Top management recognises the opportunities in purchasing for contribution to profitability
Stage 3 Supportive	Definition	The purchasing function supports the firm's competitive strategy by adopting purchasing techniques and products, which strengthen the firm's competitive position
	Characteristics	■ Purchasers are included in sales proposal teams ■ Suppliers are considered a resource, with emphasis on experience, motivation and attitude ■ Markets, products and suppliers are continuously monitored and analysed
Stage 4 Integrative	Definition	Purchasing's strategy is fully integrated into the firm's competitive strategy and constitutes part of an integrated effort among functional peers to formulate and implement a strategic plan
	Characteristics	■ Cross-functional training of purchasing professionals and executives is made available ■ Permanent lines of communication are established with other functional areas ■ Professional development focuses on strategic elements of the competitive strategy ■ Purchasing performance is measured in terms of contribution to the firm's success

Source: Adapted from Reck, R. F. and Long, B., 'Purchasing: a competitive weapon', *Journal of Purchasing and Materials Management*, Vol. 24, No. 3, 1998, pp. 2–8

Table 1.3 Stage characteristics – Reck and Long's development model

Characteristics (variable)	Passive	Independent	Supportive	Integrative
Nature of long-range planning	None	Commodity or procedural	Supportive of strategy	Integral part of strategy
Impetus for change	Management demands	Competitive parity	Competitive strategy	Integrative management
Career advancement	Limited	Possible	Probable	Unlimited
Evaluation based on	Complaints	Cost reduction and supplier performance	Competitive objectives	Strategic contribution
Organisational visibility	Low	Limited	Variable	High
Computer systems focus	Repetitive	Techniques	Specific to concern	Needs of concern
Sources of new ideas	Trial and error	Current purchasing practices	Competitive strategy	Interfunctional information exchange
Basis of resource availability	Limited	Arbitrary/affordable	Objectives	Strategic requirements
Basis of supplier evaluation	Price and easy availability	Least total cost	Competitive objectives	Strategic contributions
Attitude towards suppliers	Adversarial	Variable	Company resource	Mutual interdependence
Professional development focus	Deemed unnecessary	Current new practices	Elements of strategy	Cross-functional understanding
Overall characteristics	Clerical function	Functional efficiency	Strategic facilitator	Strategic contributor

Table 1.4 Purchasing development stages and performance capabilities

Stage of development	Capabilities	Estimated organisational contribution
Stage 1 Infant	Fragmented purchasing	None or low
Stage 2 Awakening	Realisation of savings potential	Clerical efficiency. Small savings via consolidation 2–5 per cent
Stage 3 Developing	Control and development of purchasing price/negotiation capabilities	Cost reduction 5–10 per cent
Stage 4 Mature	80/20 recognised Specialist buyers Cost reductions Commencement of supplier base management	Cost reduction 10–20 per cent Acquisition costs 1–10 per cent
Stage 5 Advanced	Devolution of purchasing Strong central control Supply chain management	Cost reduction 25 per cent Cost of ownership Acquisition cost and supply chain management 30 per cent + Leverage buying Global sourcing Understanding and practice of acquisition cost and cost of ownership

Figure 1.3 Purchasing profile analysis

Measurement area	Stage of development				
	1 Infant	2 Awakening	3 Developing	4 Mature	5 Advanced
Activity breakdown analysis					
Purchasing organisational structure					
Purchasing services					
Function position in the business					
Extent of training/ development of buyer					
Relative remuneration levels					
Measurement of purchasing performance					
Standard of information systems					
Computer technology					
Standard of operating procedures					
Interface development (buying centre)					
Buying process involvement					
Buyer characteristics/ development					
Degree of purchasing specialism					
Supplier interface development					
Policy on ethics					
Hospitality					
Quality of buyer/supplier relationship					

1.4 Purchasing and change

There are a number of drivers influencing and demanding changes in purchasing, including those detailed in the following sections.

1.4.1 The challenge to manage escalating costs in purchasing goods and services

In 2008 a number of pressures on costs manifested themselves. Not the least of these has been the rapidly increasing cost of oil, feeding its way into most supply chain costs. The related impact on the cost of living and consequent demands for wage increases are signs of potentially troubling times. The traditional emerging economies supplying, for example, the retail sector cannot escape the pressure on costs. Adding to this is the impact of difficulties in the financial services sector, making the cost of capital a factor in investment decisions and the availability of working capital.

1.4.2 The public sector focus on driving out inefficiencies in public expenditure

Some of the greatest changes in purchasing in the 1990s and first decade of the twenty-first century have been in public expenditure. The large amounts of spend in central and local government have been tackled through aggregation. While significant improvements have been made there remain challenges to further improve value for money. It can be postulated that procurement will have to adapt across departmental boundaries and that classic silos of purchasing will have to be abolished.

1.4.3 The increasing trend to outsource manufacture and services

There has been a rapidly growing trend to outsource a wide range of manufacturing and service delivery. This trend has challenged purchasing departments to improve their handling of tender processes, due diligence, negotiation with different cultures, managing outsourced contracts and applying open book methodologies. Purchasing is not immune from outsourcing actions.

1.4.4 The recognition that purchasing is a significant contributor to corporate efficiency

Enlightened organisations have recognised that purchasing can contribute to corporate efficiency. An example is long-range business planning which requires input on long-range costs, availability of strategic materials and supplies, supply chain developments and trends in service delivery, for example, voice recognition technology as an anti-fraud measure.

1.4.5 The positive impact of global sourcing

It may be argued that the retail sector has developed a long-standing expertise in global sourcing and coping with long-range supply issues. Their challenge includes responding to fashion changes and a cycle of product selection for the seasons of the year. The challenge for other buyers is their ability to find excellent suppliers wherever they are in the world. International airlines have used global sources to provide equipment and services. The change for purchasing includes how to structure their organisation. It is not uncommon for retailers to set up a purchasing organisation in the Far East.

1.4.6 The enhanced use of information technology and e-procurement

The IT revolution has impacted on purchasing. What developments lie ahead? The drivers for change in purchasing must surely include the objective of eradicating paper. In a recent procurement each tender document weighed in excess of six kilograms. The resultant tenders were heavier! Secure networks that facilitate a whole electronic procurement system, through to payment, is a far reaching objective for the global economy. E-procurement is in its infancy with relatively few reverse auctions, electronic tendering and knowledge storage and gathering is far from developed.

1.4.7 The redressing of purchasing power

Many suppliers have grown by acquisition and have assumed to themselves a power that has affected buyer's pricing, output allocation and other restrictions. The purchasing profession has been relatively unsuccessful in countering this power by forming effective buying clubs, although the public sector has taken significant initiatives in setting up consortia.

1.4.8 The challenge to outdated traditional practices

It is always difficult to look within. The purchasing profession itself must challenge outdated traditional practices. A movement from transactional operations to strategic activities would be desirable in many organisations. Defensive posturing that involves keeping stakeholders in the dark by denying them access to information, for example, the status of tendering processes, is unprofessional. An effective challenge to traditional practices would be useful in the construction sector where quantity surveyors handle the complete purchasing cycle to the total-exclusion of procurement specialists.

1.5 World class purchasing

The term 'world class' was popularised by the book *World Class Manufacturing* by Schonberger[17] published in 1986. Schonberger defined world class manufacturing as analogous to the Olympic motto 'citius, altius, fortius' (translated as faster, higher, stronger). The world class manufacturing equivalent is continual and rapid improvement.

Twelve characteristics of world class supplier management were identified by the Center for Advanced Purchasing Studies,[18] namely the following:

- *Commitment to total quality management (TQM).*
- *Commitment to just-in-time (JIT).*
- *Commitment to total cycle time reduction.*

■ *Long-range strategic plans* that are multidimensional and fully integrated with the overall corporate plan, including the organisation's supply strategy, and related to customers' needs.

■ *Supplier relationships*, including networks, partnerships and alliances. Relationships include such matters as supply base rationalisation and the segmentation of suppliers as 'strategic', 'preferred' and 'arm's length'. Relationships with strategic suppliers include a high level of trust, shared risks and rewards, sharing of data and supplier involvement in product improvement.

■ *Strategic cost management* – this involves a total life acquisition approach to evaluating bids and the use of IT to support a paperless and seamless purchasing process across the whole supply chain.

■ *Performance measurements*, including regular benchmarking with and across industries. Performance measures are developed in consultation with customers, other organisational units and suppliers.

■ *Training and professional development*, including identification of required skills for higher-level purchasing posts and the maintenance of employee skills inventories.

■ *Service excellence* – purchasing is proactive, anticipates customers' needs and demonstrates flexibility.

■ *Corporate social responsibility*, especially regarding ethical, environmental and safety issues and support of local suppliers.

■ *Learning* – world class purchasing recognises that learning and education are critical factors in continuous improvement.

■ *Management and leadership* – although listed last, this is probably the key factor. Purchasing executives earn and enjoy top management support and recognise the importance of transformational change. Such leaders have vision, foster open communications, treat others with respect and develop the potential of both their staff and suppliers.

Ultimately, world class purchasing depends on obtaining world class suppliers. World class suppliers will tend to mirror the characteristics of world class purchasing listed above. Research reported by Minahan[19] indicates that, to be considered 'world class' suppliers must excel in such areas as competitive pricing, quality and lead times, these attributes are 'just the price of entry to get into the game'. The research identified the following three characteristics of world class suppliers:

■ *continuous improvement* – world class suppliers have a formal and proven commitment to achieve year-on-year products and process improvements

■ *technology and innovation* – world class suppliers are technology leaders in their respective industries, providing customers with next-generation technologies and a 'leg-up' on their competition

■ *adaptability* – world class suppliers are willing to invest in new equipment, develop new technologies and rework their businesses to better support the strategies of their customers.

World class supplier management is therefore concerned with:

■ searching for suppliers with the above characteristics or the potential to achieve them

- providing such suppliers with specifications of the purchaser's expectations relating to products and services and agreeing how supplier performance will be measured against expectations

- recognising outstanding supplier performance by such means as the award of long-term contracts and sharing the benefits of collaborative innovation or performance that enhance the purchaser's competitiveness.

Strategic purchasing partnerships are partnerships of equals in which suppliers are regarded as a source of the competitive edge responsible for a major share of product costs. As Saunders[20] rightly observes:

> For a firm to reach world class standards in serving its own customers, it is vital to achieve world class standards in controlling its network of suppliers.

1.6 The status of purchasing and supply management (PSM)

Within a particular organisation the status of PSM is influenced by leverage, focus and professionalism.

1.6.1 Leverage

Traditionally, leverage of purchasing has been focused on enhancing profitability. This is relevant in a manufacturing or purchase for resale context, but is irrelevant for purchasing in a central and local government environment where purchasing has a direct impact on the quality of public services being offered. The same can be said of purchasing goods and services for the National Health Service.

The greatest scope for savings lies in the areas of greatest expenditure. For many organisations these areas are labour and materials. Labour is usually outside the scope of purchasing unless outsourcing activities are being considered. Within this context, outsourcing call centres to the Far East has reduced some labour costs by more than 20 per cent for European-based organisations. Similarly, when labour is outsourced within Europe under TUPE (Transfer of Undertakings Protection of Employment) regulations, labour costs have also been reduced by more than 20 per cent. This is achieved by finding smarter ways of working and redeploying the labour to other roles. There is also the factor of the labour becoming more productive by using advanced IT systems. These cost improvements require a short-term investment by the new provider of services.

Expenditure on materials and services that are purchased from third parties is where professional buyers must demonstrate their effectiveness in obtaining value for money. The benefits can be highlighted in organisations driven by the profit motive. It is the case that:

- assuming other variables remain constant, every pound saved on purchasing is a pound of profit

- for many reasons, such as increased defects or poorer deliveries, a pound off the purchase price does not necessarily represent a pound of profit

- when purchases form a high proportion of total costs, a modest saving on bought-out items will result in a similar contribution to profits as would a substantial increase in sales; so, as shown below, a 4 per cent reduction in purchase costs makes the same contribution to profits as a 20 per cent expansion in turnover.

SALES			
Then	Now	Increase	Extra profit
£	£	%	£
100,000	120,000	20	2000 (assuming 10 per cent on turnover)
PURCHASING			
50,000	48,000	−4 (i.e. a saving)	2000

This argument must, however, be used carefully.

- Cost reduction can be counter-profitable if the result is lower quality or higher expenditure on production.
- The total cost of ownership (TCO) approach emphasises that not just the purchase price but also all costs associated with the acquisition, use and maintenance of an item should be considered.
- As the proportion of expenditure on supplies and the complexity of bought-out items varies widely from organisation to organisation, it follows that there will be a corresponding variance in the contribution of purchasing to profitability.

The profit contribution may be low, for example, in the pharmaceutical industry where the ingredients of a patent medicine can be insignificant compared with the costs of marketing the product. Conversely, it will be significant in the motor vehicle industry where the proportion of material costs to total factory costs will be high.

Purchasing as a factor in profitability is likely to be critical where:

- bought-out items form a high proportion of total expenditure
- short-run prices fluctuate
- judgements relating to innovation and fashion are involved
- markets for the finished product are highly competitive.

Purchasing will be less critical, though still important, where:

- bought-out items form a small proportion of total expenditure
- prices are relatively stable
- there is an absence of innovation in operations.

Within non-manufacturing organisations the savings resulting from value-for-money efficiency purchasing may allow increased expenditure in other areas.

1.6.2 Focus

Syson[21] states that the position of purchasing within a particular organisation depends on whether the focus of the function is transactional, commercial or strategic. Each of

Figure 1.4 Positioning graph strategies/policies

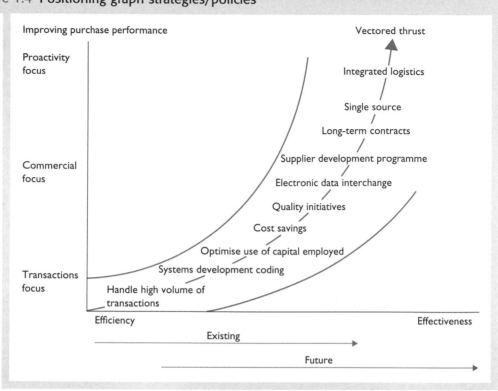

these foci is appropriate to sustaining commercial advantage for different types of enterprise: 'in terms of effectiveness, the key question is whether the correct focus exists. In terms of efficiency, how well are the key tasks discharged?' Over time, the focus of purchasing may, as shown in Figures 1.4 and 1.5, change from transactional to a procedure perspective. The more purchasing becomes involved in commercial and strategic areas, the greater will be its effectiveness and consequent standing within the organisation.

In Figures 1.4 and 1.5 it will be noticed that as PSM moves from a transactional to a pro-activity focus, performance measures also change from efficiency to effectiveness.

Efficiency is a measure of how well or productively resources are used to achieve a goal.

Effectiveness is a measure of the appropriateness of the goals the organisation is pursuing and of the degree to which those goals are achieved.

Syson[22] refers to the level of the purchasing department, implying that the level at which purchasing is placed in a hierarchical structure reveals its status within that company. From a different perspective, broadly similar considerations will apply in determining the recognition given to purchasing by other supply chain members.

A somewhat different approach to determining the internal status of purchasing is provided by the three laws propounded by Farmer:[23]

1 Purchasing increases in perceived importance in direct relationship with the reduction in length of the product lifecycle times.

Figure 1.5 Positioning graph: measures of performance.

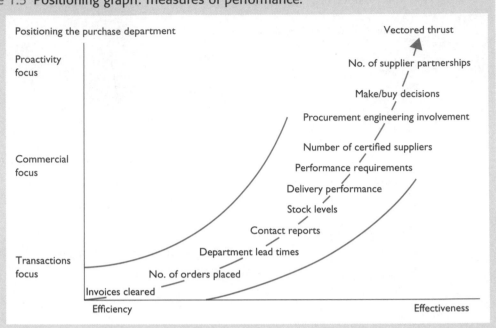

2 Purchasing is perceived to be important when the business concerned interfaces significantly with a volatile market(s).

3 Purchasing is important whenever the organisation concerned spends a significant proportion of its income on purchasing goods and services in order to allow it to do business.

Empirically, the importance of purchasing both organisationally and within the supply chain is indicated by structural and influential factors.

Structural factors

These include:

- the job title of the executive responsible for PSM
- to whom and at what level the executive in charge of PSM reports
- the total spend for which PSM is responsible
- the financial limits placed on PSM staff to commit the undertaking without recourse to higher authority
- the committees on which PSM staff are represented.

Influential factors

Ibarra[24] has identified network centrality, power and innovative involvement as important influential factors in the determination of status.

Network centrality, like format authority, implies a high position in a status hierarchy and also varying degrees of access to and control over valued resources. As stated in section 3.2.1, purchasing is frequently a key activity in materials management. Purchasing is also central in supply chains, as indicated in section 3.11.

Power may be considered from two aspects: the sources of power and the use of power. The sources of power are briefly considered in section 4.1.4. The use of power may be defined as the ability to affect outcomes.

The executives in charge of PSM may have all the five sources of power identified by French and Raven in section 4.1.4. Executives also derive power from having access to information or occupying a boundary-spanning position that links organisations' internal networks to external suppliers and information sources.

Innovative involvement, as Ibarra shows, may be either administrative or technical and may itself be an indicator of power as any change in the status quo requires an individual to use power and mobilise support, information and material resources to overcome resistance to change. Persons with a high position in the organisation are more likely to be successful innovators than those further down with less or little power.

Technical innovators are directly related to the primary work activity of an organisation and include the introduction of new products, services and production technologies.

Administrative innovations involve changes in structure and administrative processes and are more directly related to internal management than the other types of innovation. Kanter's[25] observation that 'corporate entrepreneurs have often to pull in what they need for their innovation from other departments or areas, from peers over whom they have no authority and who have the choice about whether or not to ante up their knowledge, support or resources to invest in or help the innovator' is of relevance to both supply chain management and the centrality of purchasing within it.

The status of PSM in any organisation depends on two key factors. First, the ability to impact positively on the bottom line of corporate strategic planning and, second, recognition by PSM of the value of its contribution to profitability and competitive advantage and being able to market that contribution to top management and other supply chain members.

1.6.3 Professionalism

As long ago as 1928, Carr-Saunders[26] made a distinction between professionalism and professionalisation. *Professionalism* is traditionally associated with certain attributes, including:

- skill based on theoretical knowledge
- prolonged training and education
- demonstration of competence by means of tests and examinations
- adherence to a code of professional ethics.

Professionalisation is associated with the development of associations that seek to establish minimum qualifications for entrance to a professional practice or activity, enforce appropriate rules and norms of conduct among the members of the professional group and raise the status of the professional group in the wider society. Thus, attempts to raise the external perception of purchasing have included:

- the establishment of institutions concerned with promoting the concept of 'professional' purchasing, such as the Chartered Institute of Purchasing and Supply (CIPS) in the UK and the Institute of Supply Management (ISM) in the USA (in 2004, over

42 national purchasing associations were affiliated to the International Federation of Purchasing and Materials Management)

■ the development of undergraduate and postgraduate courses with a purchasing content

■ the establishment of 'chairs' in purchasing or logistics at some universities

■ research into PSM and related fields

■ the publication of textbooks and specialist journals relating to purchasing, such as *Supply Management (UK), European Purchasing Management* and the *International Journal of Purchasing and Supply Management,* as well as, in the logistics field, *Logistics Focus* and the *International Journal of Logistics*

■ published codes of ethics (see Appendices 1 and 2).

Notwithstanding the enhanced status of purchasing in the UK by the granting in 1992 of a Royal Charter to the Institute of Purchasing and Supply, the occupation has to surmount difficulties in its quest for professional status.

Such difficulties include:

■ no regulation of entry – it is not necessary to have a professional qualification in purchasing to enter the occupation

■ purchasing practitioners are at all levels of evolution, so those with only an operational or transactional knowledge of purchasing might experience difficulty in moving to strategic purchasing

■ limited powers to enforce ethical standards.

The general problem, however, is what constitutes the academic content. Purchasing is a hybrid subject that draws heavily on other disciplines to build its knowledge base. Such disciplines include accounting, economics, ethics, information technology, marketing, management and psychology.

Even the study of subjects such as negotiation can be enhanced by knowledge of the approaches to negotiation in such fields as politics and industrial relations.

Cox[27] regards much contemporary academic work relating to procurement as 'unscientific', characterised by uncritical accounts of what purchasing practitioners do, untheoretical research and the development of 'fads and short-term fixes'. Such academic work is often regarded as irrelevant by purchasing practitioners. Cox therefore calls for a proactive, scientific approach to the academic study of purchasing. He believes that such an approach will involve the use of systematic theory to provide general laws and the application of deductive and inductive reasoning to respectively 'construct optional procurement strategies based on 'fit for purpose' awareness of business and market processes and indicate the optional role for procurement in business'.

The change in emphasis from purchasing as a reactive administrative activity to one that is proactive and strategic has resulted in numerous lists of the skills and attributes that purchasing staff should possess in order to maximise their contribution to the achievement of organisational goals. Two typical surveys in the USA are those by Kolchin[28] and Giunipero and Pearcy.[29]

The first of these studies, based on the responses of a large sample of American purchasing executives, identified the following ten subjects as the most important to purchasers in the year 2000:

1 total cost analysis

2 negotiation strategies and techniques

3 supplier/partner management

4 ethical conduct

5 supplier evaluation

6 quality techniques

7 purchasing strategy and planning

8 price/cost analysis

9 electronic data interchange

10 interpersonal communication.

The second study, based on a review of relevant literature and a rating by 136 purchasing/ supply management professionals identified 32 skills required of a world class purchaser. These skills were categorised under seven headings:

1 strategic

2 process management

3 team

4 decision making

5 behavioural

6 negotiation

7 quantitative

Examples of strategic, behavioural and quantitative skills are:

Strategic skills	Behavioural skills	Quantitative skills
Strategic thinking	Interpersonal/communication	Computational
Supply base research	Risk-taking/entrepreneurship	Technical
Structuring supplier relationships	Creativity	Blueprint reading
Technology planning	Inquisitiveness	Specification development
Supplier cost targeting		

One further writer, Whittington,[30] has stated that 'the buying task as we know it will disappear . . . Organisationally purchasing will often find itself in a place called "distribution functionality" or "strategic supply" located where the customer is'. She also believes that the purchasing professional of the future will be concerned with three types of tasks:

- *facilitating* that is, team leadership and providing the 'proper blending and use of all necessary skills'

- *contract negotiating and developing* that is, purchasing people – this will still be required – to write and negotiate advantageous contracts for the organisation

- *technical expertise (computer skills)* that is, the challenges of purchasing on the Net and funding products in the world of cyberspace as well as other EDI tasks.

This view is supported by Lamming (see section 1.2.5) and others. In the Kolchin study referred to above, almost two-thirds of the respondents believed that the designation of purchasing would change. The three most cited new names were 'supply management', 'sourcing management' and 'logistics'.

Case study

Eagersaver.com

Eagersaver.com was established in 2005 by the CEO Colette Bevan as an online comparison site primarily focused on car insurance and related products. Since then it has grown, both organically and by acquisition of other companies into an organisation that now compares home insurance, legal insurance, pet insurance, travel insurance, life insurance and accident insurance. It has diversified into other comparison services in financial products, travel services and utilities. It has moved offline with the opening of call centre activities and a TV shopping channel. The company's turnover is £100m.

The managing director Dirk Bradfield now wishes to float the company on the stock exchange and following a due diligence exercise by Colette's corporate advisors she has been advised to 'professionalise the procurement activities throughout the group'. The due diligence uncovered the following facts:

- There are five locations within the UK, situated at Chester, Edinburgh, Sheffield, Bristol and Cardiff. They work independently and only one location has a purchasing manager (TV shopping channel).
- The largest spend across the group is on marketing (£12m online and £8m TV).
- Marketing is centrally managed by the marketing director.
- Most other procurement is undertaken by service heads including IT and agency staff.
- Numerous media companies are engaged often without competition.
- The same or similar products and services are procured from different suppliers.
- There is a range of prices paid for the same product or service, some ranging by ±30%.
- Most contracts are under the vendor's terms and conditions and in some cases there are verbal arrangements.
- The company has outgrown many of its original suppliers who are finding it difficult to cope with demand and there are instances where contract performance has slipped.
- The chief executive is responsible for many of these problematic relationships based upon personal friendship at the inception of the company.

Tasks

You have been appointed into the new position of group procurement director and have a meeting arranged with Colette to discuss the way forward. In considering your plan, how specifically would you deal with:

1 structuring the procurement activities?

2 rationalising the product and supply chain?

3 managing the marketing director who states corporate expenditure is his budget and he will decide who has the last say on contract awards?

4 managing the expenditure attributed to other service heads?

Discussion questions

1.1 In certain organisations the functional approach to purchasing has decided advantages. Consider the extent to which this statement is true.

1.2 Taking one example of 'an important purchase' in your organisation, prepare a flow chart showing the processes involved in procuring that purchase. Can you then identify the decision points?

1.3 Supply chain management was initially developed by the wholesale and retail sectors. What, in your opinion, can other sectors learn from wholesale and retail operators?

1.4 Purchasing has long been transfixed with the six 'rights'. Do you agree that they are not portraying purchasing in a positive light?

1.5 Consider the four stages of the development of the purchasing function identified by Reck and Long. State, with reasons, the stage reached by purchasing in your organisation.

1.6 If purchasing is to increase its influence in an organisation what do you believe that it must do?

1.7 If purchasing believes in change, how can that be squared with placing long-term contracts?

1.8 Many purchasing actions are conducted electronically. What do you foresee as the next major development in this regard? When you answer this, think about reverse auctions and their impact on negotiation of price and cost.

1.9 Would it be true that when purchasing is effectively organised and operated the balance of power can never be with a supplier?

1.10 Is purchasing a commercial or a technical function?

1.11 Would you believe that the contemporary academic scrutiny of purchasing has had any impact on the operational development of purchasing?

1.12 It is often alleged that purchasing is under-resourced. Why is this? How would you decide on an appropriate staffing resource to manage purchasing?

Past examination questions

1 (a) Describe **five** examples of behaviour by a purchasing officer that may be perceived as being unethical.
  (b) Explain why it is important for purchasing staff to act ethically.
  (c) Discuss **two** ways that culture can affect international purchasing
    CIPS, *Understanding the Purchasing Environment*, May 2009

2 (a) Define the term 'competitive advantage'.
  (b) Describe **three** typical ways in which 'competitive advantage' may be achieved.
    CIPS, *An Introduction to Purchasing Strategy*, November 2009

3 Improvement to the purchasing cycle is an important consideration for purchasing managers.
   (a) Identify **five** stages of a purchasing cycle of your choice.
   (b) Suggest how each stage identified for (a) could be improved or made more efficient.

   CIPS, *An Introduction to Purchasing Strategy*, November 2008

4 Explain with the aid of a diagram how experience might lower the cost of purchasing.

   CIPS, *An Introduction to Purchasing Strategy*, November 2007

References

1 Porter, M. E., *Competitive Advantage*, Free Press, 1985

2 Ford, D., Gadde, L-E., Hakansson, H. and Snehota, I., *Managing Business Relationships*, 2nd edn, John Wiley, 2003, p. 92

3 IMP (Industrial Marketing and Purchasing Group): www.impgroup.org

4 Day, M. (ed.) in Farmer D. and Day, M. (eds), *Handbook of Purchasing Management*, 3rd edn, Gower, 2002, Introduction, p. 2

5 Winthrop University, Rock Hill, SC 29733, USA: www.winthrop.edu

6 National Procurement Strategy For Local Government, October 2008

7 Marrian, J., 'Market characteristics of industrial goals and buyers', in Wilson, A. (ed.), *The Marketing of Industrial Products*, Hutchinson, 1965, p. 11

8 Lamming, R., 'The future of purchasing: developing lean supply', in Lamming, R., and Cox, A., *Strategic Procurement Management in the 1990s*, Earlsgate Press, 1985, p. 40

9 Van Weele, A. J., *Purchasing Management*, Chapman & Hall, 1994, p. 9

10 *Solar Energy Market Express*

11 Fearon, Harold, Center for Advanced Purchasing Studies, Emeritus

12 Reck, R. F. and Long, B., 'Purchasing a competitive weapon', *Journal of Purchasing and Materials Management*, Vol. 24, No. 3, 1998, p. 4

13 Reck, R. F. and Long, B., as 12 above

14 Syson, R., *Improving Purchasing Performance*, Pitman, 1992, pp. 254–5

15 Morris, N. and Calantone, R. J., 'Redefining the purchasing function', *International Journal of Purchasing and Materials Management*, Fall, 1992

16 Jones, D. M., 'Development models', *Supply Management*, 18 March, 1999. The authors are particularly grateful to Dr Jones for the use of Figures 1.6 and 1.7

17 Schonberger, R. J., *World Class Manufacturing: The Next Decade: Building Power, Strength and Value*, Free Press, 1986

18 Carter, P. L. and Ogden, J. A., *The World Class Purchasing and Supply Organisation: Identifying the Characteristics*, Center for Advanced Purchasing Studies, University of Arizona

19 Minahan, T., 'What Makes a Supplier World Class?', *Purchasing On Line*, 13 August, 1988

20 Saunders, M., *Strategic Purchasing and Supply Chain Management*, Pitman, 1994, p. 11

21 Syson, R., as 14 above

22 Syson, R., as 14 above

23 Farmer, D., 'Organisation for purchasing', *Purchasing and Supply Management*, February, 1900, pp. 23–7

24 Ibarra, H., 'Network centrality, power and innovation involvement, determinants of technical and administrative power', *Academy of Management Journal*, Vol. 36 (3), June, 1993, pp. 471–502

25 Kanter, R. M., 'When a thousand flowers bloom' in Staw, B. M., and Cummings, L. L. (eds), *Research in Organisational Behaviour*, Vol. 10, 1988, p. 189

26 Carr-Saunders, A. M. and Wilson, P. A., *The Professions*, Oxford University Press, 1928

27 Cox, A., 'Relational competence and strategic procurement management', *European Journal of Purchasing and Supply Management*, 1996, Vol. 2 (1), pp. 57–70

28 Kolchin, C., 'Study reveals future educational and training trends', *NAPM Insights*, July, 1993

29 Giunipero, L. C. and Pearcy, D. H., 'World class purchasing skills: an empirical investigation', *Journal of Supply Chain Management*, 2000, Vol. 36 (4), pp. 4–13

30 Whittington, E., 'Will the Last Buyer Please Stand Up!', Proceedings NAPM 84 Annual Conference, May 1999

Chapter 2

Strategy and strategic procurement

Learning outcomes

With reference, where applicable, to business and procurement this chapter aims to provide an understanding of:

- the origins and development of strategic theory
- corporate, business and functional/operating strategies
- strategy development using Mintzberg's ten schools
- strategic management
- business growth strategies
- strategic analysis
- strategic purchasing and purchasing strategy
- strategy formulation – rational planning or incremental
- the evaluation of alternative strategies
- strategy implementation
- the post implementation, evaluation, control and review of strategies.

Key ideas

- Mintzberg, Johnson and Scholes and the definitions of strategy.
- Mintzberg's ten schools of strategic development.
- Rational planning, incremental and emergent views of strategy.
- Growth, stability, combination and retrenchment strategies.
- Strategic purchasing and purchasing strategy.
- Environmental and internal scanning to strengthen strategic formulation and challenge.
- Linking procurement strategies to corporate strategic objectives.
- Critical success factors.
- Vision and mission statements and business, purchasing and supply objectives.
- Lifecycles, scenario planning, cost–benefit, profitability and risk analysis as approaches to the evaluation of strategies.
- Portfolio planning with special reference to Kraljic and Kamann.
- Policies and strategy implementation plans.
- The CIPS procurement and supply chain model.

Introduction

There are continuous challenges to public and private sector organisations. These challenges require strategic thinking and planning. It is not unusual, in large organisations, to find a strategic planning function operating at corporate level. It is less usual to find a corporate procurement function, actively contributing to the strategic planning of the whole organisation. Some essential considerations are shown in Figure 2.1.

We will now consider strategic thinking.

Figure 2.1 Procurement strategy – some essential considerations

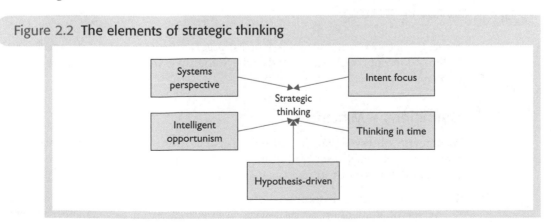

2.1 Strategic thinking

Five elements that make up strategic thinking – as identified by Liedtka[1] – are shown in Figure 2.2.

Figure 2.2 The elements of strategic thinking

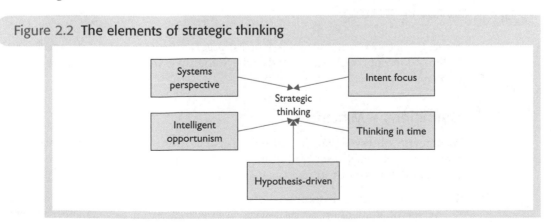

The characteristics of each of the five elements are discussed in a fine paper by Lawrence,[2] as follows.

1 *Systems perspective* – A 'system' is a set of independent and interrelated parts that is dependent for survival on its environment. Strategic thinking, from a systems perspective, requires an understanding of:

- the external, internal and business ecosystem in which the organisation operates (an ecosystem in a business context is a network of interrelated enterprises that may cross a variety of industries) and managing within such an ecosystem requires the ability to think strategically about the position of the enterprise within it and the relationships and alliances with the enterprises that it comprises
- how corporate, business and functional strategies relate vertically to the external environment and horizontally across departments, functions, suppliers and buyers;
- interrelationships between the individual parts of the system
- individual roles within the larger system and how individual behaviour impacts on other parts of the system and the final outcome.

2 *Intent focus* – Strategic thinking is concerned with the identification of goals and devising strategies for their achievement.

3 *Intelligent opportunism* – Strategic thinking is 'openness to new experiences which allows one to take advantage of alternative strategies that may emerge as more relevant to a rapidly changing business environment'.

4 *Thinking in time* – Strategic thinking is concerned with 'bridging the gap' between current reality and future intent. Thus, when current resources and capabilities are insufficient, the organisation must bridge the gap by making the best of what is available. 'By connecting the past with the present and linking this to the future, strategic thinking is always "thinking in time".'

5 *Hypothesis driven* – Strategic thinking accommodates both creative and analytical thinking. Hypothesis *generation* poses the creative question 'What if . . . ?' Hypothesis *testing* follows up with the critical question 'If . . . , then' and evaluates the data relevant to the analysis. Taken together and repeated, this process allows an organisation to pose a variety of hypotheses without sacrificing the ability to explore novel ideas and approaches.

2.2 What is strategy?

Strategy, derived from the Greek word *strategia*, means 'generalship' and is primarily a military concept that, since the end of the Second World War, has been used in a business context.

2.2.1 Definitions – Mintzberg

Mintzberg[3] observes that the word strategy 'has long been used implicitly in different ways even if it has been traditionally used in only one'. He therefore provides five different definitions of strategy as plan, ploy, pattern, position and perspective.

1 As a *plan*, strategy is some sort of consciously intended course of action, a guideline (or set of guidelines) to deal with a situation. From this perspective, strategy is

concerned with how leaders try to provide organisational direction and predetermined courses of action. It is also concerned with cognition (knowing) or how plans or intentions are initially conceived in the human brain.

2 As a *ploy*, strategy is a specific manoeuvre intended to outwit an opponent or competitor.

3 As a *pattern*, strategy is a stream of actions demonstrating consistency in behaviour, whether intended or not intended.

4 As a *position*, strategy is a means of locating an organisation in an environment. The positional approach sees strategy as 'a mediating force by which organisations find and protect their positions or "niches" in order to meet, avoid or subvert competition in the external environment'.

5 As a *perspective*, strategy is a concept or ingrained way of perceiving the world. Mintzberg points out that 'strategy in this respect is to the organisation what personality is to the individual' – that is, distinct ways of working deriving from the culture or ideology of the undertaking that become the shared norms, values and determinants of the behaviour of the people who collectively form the organisation.

Mintzberg's five definitions help us to avoid attaching simplistic meanings to strategy. As he observes:[4]

> Strategy is not just a notion of how to deal with an enemy or set of competitors in a market . . .
>
> A good deal of confusion . . . stems from contradictory and ill-defined uses of the term strategy. By explicating and using various definitions we may thereby enrich our ability to understand and manage the processes by which strategies form.

2.2.2 Definitions – Johnson and Scholes

Johnson and Scholes[5] identify eight characteristics of strategy that include most of those described above:

1 strategy is likely to be concerned with the *long-term* direction of an organisation

2 strategic decisions are normally about trying to achieve some *advantage* for the organisation over its competitors

3 strategic decisions are likely to be concerned with the *scope* of an organisation's activities

4 strategy can be seen as the *matching* of the resources and activities of an organisation to the environment in which it operates – sometimes known as the strategic *fit*

5 strategy can also be seen as *building on* or '*stretching*' an organisation's resources and competences to create opportunities to capitalise on them

6 strategies may require major *resource changes* for an organisation

7 strategic decisions are likely to affect *operational decisions*

8 the strategy of an organisation is affected not only by environmental forces and resources availability but also the *values and expectations* of those who have *power* in and around the organisation.

By combining the above characteristics, Johnson and Scholes provide the following definition:

> Strategy is the *direction* and *scope* of an organisation over the *long term* which achieves *advantage* for the organisation through its configuration of resources within a changing *environment* and to fulfil *stakeholder* expectations.

2.3 Strategy development

2.3.1 Mintzberg's ten schools

Mintzberg *et al.*[6] have identified ten 'schools' that have appeared at different stages in the development of strategic development, which they classify under three headings: prescriptive, descriptive and configuration.

Prescriptive schools are concerned with how strategies *should* be formulated, rather than how they actually are. Mintzberg's three prescriptive schools are shown in Table 2.1.

Table 2.1 Mintzberg's prescriptive schools of strategy formation

Designation	Strategy formation process
The design school	Strategy making as a process of *conception* – that is, abstract thinking or reflective activity. Strategy making is an acquired, not a natural or intuitive, skill and must be learned formally
The planning school	Strategy formation as a *formal* process – that is, a course of action or procedures
The positioning school	Strategy formation as an *analytical* process – that is, strategy formation is the selection of generic, specifically common, identifiable positions in the marketplace based on analytical calculations

Descriptive schools are concerned with representing how, in reality, strategies are formulated rather than how they 'ought' to be made. Mintzberg's six descriptive schools are shown in Table 2.2.

The *configuration school* emphasises two aspects of strategy. The first describes 'organisational states' and their surroundings as *configurations*. An organisation 'state' implies entrenched behaviour. Configurations are therefore relatively stable clusters of characteristics relating to a particular school. Thus, 'planning' is predominant in mechanistic conditions of relative stability and 'entrepreneurship' in more dynamic configurations of start-up and turnaround. The configuration school, therefore, can integrate the preceding nine schools as it recognises that each school represents a particular configuration contingent on its time and context.

The second aspect is concerned with *transformation*. The configuration school sees strategy formation as a process of transformation or 'shaking loose' entrenched behaviour so that the organisation can make the transformation or development to a new state or configuration. The key to strategic management, therefore, is to sustain stability but periodically recognise the need for change to a new configuration.

Table 2.2 **Mintzberg's descriptive schools of strategy formation**

Designation	Strategy formation process
The entrepreneurial school	Strategy formation as a *visionary* process – that is, strategy exists in the mind of the leader as a vision of the organisation's long-term future
The cognitive school	Strategy formation as a *mental* process – that is, strategy formation takes place in the mind of the strategist as a process of perceiving, knowing and conceiving the environment in an objective way, distinct from emotion or volition
The learning school	Strategy formation as an *emergent* process of learning over time, in which, at the limit, formulation and implementation become indistinguishable
The power school	Strategy formation as a process of *negotiation* – that is, strategy is shaped by political games involving transient interests and coalitions of those holding internal or external power who seek to arrive at a consensus on strategy by means of persuasion, bargaining and sometimes direct confrontation
The cultural school	Strategy formation as a *collective* process – that is, strategy formation is a process of social interaction based on beliefs and understandings shared by organisational members
The environmental school	Strategy formation as a *reactive* process – that is, adapting to the environment rather than by initiating changes in the environment

2.3.2 Rational planning and incremental and emergent views

Rational planning encompasses all Mintzberg's prescriptive schools and is the traditional view of strategy formation based on the economist's concept of a rational economical person. The rational economical person is assumed to:

- make decisions to maximise returns
- consider all the alternatives
- know the costs and consequences of all the alternatives
- allow decisions to be made by a single person
- order consequences according to a fixed preference.

Such planning normally involves two stages:

1 summarising external and internal strengths and weaknesses, opportunities and threats (SWOT analysis) and identifying goals or objectives that can be translated into measurable targets

2 identifying the means by which such goals can be achieved and specifying appropriate plans.

Lawrence[7] states that traditional notions of strategic planning have been attacked on the ground that such planning 'often takes an already agreed upon strategic direction and helps strategists decide how the organisation is to be configured and resources allocated to realise that direction'. Fahey and Prusak[8] regard this predisposition to focus on the past and the present rather than on the future as one of the 11 deadly sins of knowledge management. Other criticisms are that:

■ planning is overly focused on analysis and extrapolation rather than creativity and invention

■ planners rarely know all the available alternatives and, therefore, have a limited ability to process information

■ rational planning assumes a stable environment, yet, when the environment changes, strategic priorities also change.

Incremental and emergent views encompass Mintzberg's descriptive and configuration schools and emphasise that strategies may be formulated over time and implemented step by step.

Logical incrementalism is primarily associated with Charles Lindblom[9] who also referred to this approach as 'muddling through'.

In this view, managers make incremental changes as they learn from experience. Intelligent or strategic opportunism or the managerial ability to stay focused on long-term objectives while retaining the flexibility to cope with short-term problems and opportunities has already been identified in section 2.1 above as an essential element of strategic thinking. Waterman[10] states that, in leading organisations, managers 'sense opportunity where others can't, act while others hesitate and demur when others plunge'.

Such considerations led Mintzberg to develop the concept of *emergent strategies*. Such strategies evolve in an organisation without being consciously intended or formulated as managers learn from and respond to work situations.

As Mintzberg observes:[11]

> Managers who craft strategy do not spend much time in reading reports or industry analyses. They are involved, responsive to their materials, learning about their organisation and industries through personal touch. They are also sensitive to experience, recognising that while individual vision may be important, other factors may determine strategy as well.

An example of emergent strategy is provided by the Japanese Honda Company.

Honda attempted to enter the United States' motorcycle market in 1959. It had four machines: a 50cc Supercub and larger 125cc, 250cc and 305cc models. The initial annual target was 6000 machines, with each model representing approximately 25 per cent of the total number. The sales value was, of course, heavily weighted towards the larger bikes.

Little effort was made to sell the 50cc machines, which were regarded as unsuitable for the US market where everything was big and luxurious. The larger machines, however, developed oil leaks and clutch failures as they were being driven harder and longer than they were in Japan.

The 50cc model attracted attention when used by Honda staff to ride around Los Angeles on errands. Due to the faults in the larger models, Honda had to sell more of the smaller 50cc machines to raise funds. Supported by the slogan 'You meet the nicest people on a Honda', the 50cc model proved popular with people who had not previously bought motorcycles. By 1965, Honda had captured 63 per cent of the US motorcycle market.

The Honda story illustrates the general principle that successful strategies need not be clearly formulated in advance. Such strategies can just *emerge*. An emergent strategy may therefore be defined as:

A strategy developed out of a pattern of behaviour not consciously imposed by senior management.

2.3.3 Strategic drift

This refers to situations in which organisational strategies fail to develop in line with gradual changes in the environment. Ultimately, if left unchecked, the long-term consequence of strategic drift is business failure.

Perseverance with strategies that are no longer relevant to the environment may be due to the fact that, when faced with pressures to change, managers tend to minimise uncertainty by turning to that which is known and familiar. This often results in slow, incremental changes building on existing knowledge skills and routines when what is required is rapid, transformational change.

The main symptoms of strategic drift are:

- a homogenous culture – established routines, little questioning, resistance to new ideas
- major political barriers to change, such as resistant, dominant leaders, stakeholder conflict, 'concrete ceilings'
- introspection – lack of sensitivity to environmental and competitive factors
- deteriorating relative performance, market share or profits.

The prevention of strategic drift requires strategies to question their taken-for-granted assumptions and beliefs with a view to fostering critical debate on the relevance of current strategies.

2.4 Levels of organisational strategy

As shown in Figure 2.3, in a typical large, diversified business, strategies are formulated, evaluated and implemented at three levels.

For non-diversified undertakings and those with only one line of business, corporate and business strategies are normally synonymous.

Figure 2.3 **Levels of organisational strategy**

2.5 Corporate strategy

Generally, corporate strategies are concerned with:

- determining what business(es) the enterprise should be in to maximise profitability
- deciding 'grand' strategies (see below)
- determining the 'values' of the enterprise and how it is to be managed
- coordinating and managing major resources and relationships between the enterprise, its markets, competitors, allies and other environmental factors
- deciding on business locations and structures.

Because corporate strategies provide long-term direction, they change infrequently.Corporate strategies are usually less specific than those at lower levels and, consequently, are more difficult to evaluate.

'Grand' or 'master' strategies referred to above fall into four categories: growth, stability, combination and retrenchment.

2.6 Growth strategies

These are adopted when an organisation seeks to expand its relative market share by increasing its level of operations. Growth strategies can be classified as shown in Figure 2.4.

2.6.1 Integration strategies

Vertical integration strategies reflect the extent to which an organisation expands *upstream* into industries that provide inputs (*backward integration*), such as a car manufacturer acquiring a steel rolling mill, or *downstream* (*forward integration*) into industries that distribute the organisation's products, such as a car manufacturer acquiring a car distribution chain.

Figure 2.4 **Growth strategies**

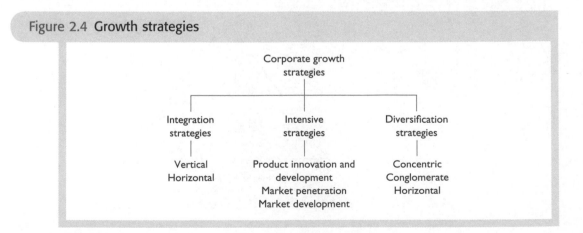

Backward integration

Backward integration seeks to ensure continuity of supplies by owning or controlling suppliers. David[12] has identified the following conditions that might cause an organisation to adopt a backward integration strategy, all of which have purchasing and supply applications:

- when an organisation's present suppliers are especially expensive, unreliable or incapable of meeting the firm's needs for parts, components, assemblies or raw materials
- when the number of suppliers is few and the number of competitors is many
- when an organisation competes in an industry that is growing rapidly (in a declining industry, vertical and horizontal strategies reduce an organisation's ability to diversify)
- when an organisation has both the capital and human resources needed to manage the new business of supplying its own raw materials
- when the advantages of stable prices are particularly important (this is a factor because an organisation can stabilise the cost of its raw materials and the associated price of its product via backward integration)
- when present suppliers have high profit margins, which suggest that the business of supplying products or services in the given industry is a worthwhile venture
- when an organisation needs to acquire a needed resource quickly.

A further important factor may be:

- to reduce dependence on suppliers of critical components.

Forward integration

Forward integration can:

- avoid dependence on distributors who have no particular allegiance to a particular brand or product and tend to 'push' items that yield the highest profits
- provide production with stable, continuous and predictable demand requirements
- provide cost savings by eliminating intermediaries or distributors.

Some disadvantages of vertical integration include:

- difficulties in balancing capacity at each stage of the supply chain as the efficient scale of operation of each link in the supply chain can vary, so, when internal capacity is inadequate to supply the next stage it will be necessary to supply the deficiency by buying out and, conversely, excessive capacity gives rise to the need to dispose of the surplus
- high investment in technology and development may inhibit innovation and change due to the need to redesign, retool and retrain.

Backward or forward integration often call for highly diversified skills and abilities, such as manufacturing, transport and distribution, which require different business capabilities.

For the above reasons, many manufacturers – particularly in car and food manufacture – have abandoned vertical integration in favour of:

- outsourcing
- tiering

- long-term partnerships or joint-venture agreements with suppliers
- *Keiretsu* strategies (*Keiretsu* is the Japanese word for 'affiliated chain' and such chains are comprised of mutual alliances that extend across the entire supply chain of suppliers, manufacturers, assemblers, transporters and distributors)
- the creation of virtual companies that use suppliers on an 'as needed' basis.

Horizontal integration

Horizontal integration focuses on expanding operations by acquiring other enterprises operating in the same industry or merging with competitors. Examples of horizontal integration are mergers, acquisitions and takeovers aimed at:

- reducing competition
- increasing economics of scale
- transferring and integrating resources and competences.

2.6.2 Intensive strategies

These are termed 'intensive' because they are 'vigorous' efforts to improve an organisation's competitive position in relation to its competitors.

- *Product innovation and development* seeks to increase sales by improving present products or services or developing new ones. Purchasing can contribute to this strategy in such ways as advising on specifications, value management and suggesting alternative materials, components and production methods.
- *Market penetration* seeks to enhance the market share for existing products or services by greater marketing efforts.
- *Market development* seeks to increase the demand for a product by discovering new uses for it or introducing it into new geographical areas.

2.6.3 Diversification strategies

These seek to reduce dependence on a single industry or product. Such strategies may be:

- *concentric* – that is, adding new, but related, products to the existing range
- *conglomerate* – that is, adding new, unrelated products or services
- *horizontal* – that is, adding new, unrelated products or services for existing customers, such as a car distributor offering insurance.

The current trend is away from diversification and in favour of 'sticking to the knitting', or concentrating on the core business.

2.6.4 Stability, combination and retrenchment strategies

Stability focuses on maintaining the present course of action and avoiding, so far as possible, major changes. It is not necessarily a 'do nothing' approach but a considered decision that the present way of working is the most appropriate in a given situation.

Combination is the simultaneous adoption of several strategies according to the needs of a particular aspect of a business. Thus, in a divisionalised organisation, a strategic decision may be to pursue a growth strategy in some divisions and one of stability in others.

Retrenchment, or defensive, strategies are clearly the opposite of those focusing on growth. Typical retrenchment strategies include:

- *harvesting* – maximising short-term profits and cash flow while maintaining investment in a product flow
- *turnaround* – attempting to restructure operations to restore earlier performance levels
- *divestiture* – selling off one or more units of an enterprise to raise cash or concentrate on core activities
- *liquidation* – the decision to cease business and dispose of all assets.

2.7 Business-level strategy

A strategic business unit (SBU) has been defined[13] as:

> An operating unit or planning focus that groups a distinct set of products or services that are sold to a uniform set of customers facing a well-defined set of competitors.

Generally business strategies are concerned with:

- coordinating and integrating unit strategies so that they are consonant with corporate strategies
- developing the distinctive competences and competitive advantages of each unit
- identifying product market niches and developing strategies for competing in each
- monitoring products and markets so that strategies conform to the needs of product markets at their current state of development.

The selection of a business strategy involves answering the strategic question 'How are we going to compete in this particular business area?'

Two approaches to business-level strategy are the competitive strategy of Michael Porter[14] and the adaptive strategy of Miles and Snow.[15]

2.7.1 Porter's competitive strategy

Competitive strategies are based on some combination of quality, service, cost and time. Porter's typology identifies three strategies that can be used to give SBUs a competitive advantage.

- *Cost leadership* – operating efficiencies so that an organisation is the low-cost producer in its industry. This is effective when:
  - the market is comprised of many price-sensitive buyers
  - there are few ways to achieve product differentiation
  - buyers are indifferent regarding brands (Coke *v* Pepsi)

  Some potential threats to this strategy are that:
  - competitors may imitate this strategy, thus driving profits down
  - competitors may discover technological breakthroughs
  - buyer preferences may be influenced by differentiating factors other than price (see also section 3.9.1).

- *Differentiation* – attempting to develop products that are regarded industry-wide as unique (see also section 3.9.2).
- *Focus* – concentration on a specific market segment and within that segment attempts to achieve either a cost advantage or differentiation. Because of their narrow market focus, firms adopting a focus strategy have lower volumes and therefore less bargaining power with their suppliers.

2.7.2 Miles and Snow's adaptive strategy

Adaptive strategies are based on the premise that an organisation should formulate strategies that will allow each of its SBUs to adapt to its unique environmental challenges. Four major strategies are identified:

- *defender* – this emphasises output of reliable products for steady customers and is appropriate for very stable environments
- *prospector* – this emphasises a continuous search for new market opportunities and innovation and is appropriate for dynamic environments with untapped customers
- *analyser* – this emphasises stability while responding selectively to opportunities for innovation and is appropriate for moderately stable environments
- *reactor* – this is really no strategy as reactors respond to competitive pressures by crisis management.

2.7.3 Functional strategies

These are concerned with the formulation of strategies relating to the main areas or activities that constitute a business – purchasing, finance, research and development, marketing, production/manufacturing, human resources and logistics/distribution.

Functional strategies are expected to derive from and be consistent with corporate and business strategies and are primarily concerned with:

- ensuring that the skills and competencies of functional specialists are utilised effectively
- integrating activities within the functional/operating area, such as purchasing and marketing
- providing information and expertise that can be utilised in the formulation of corporate and business strategies.

The selection of functional strategies involves answering the strategic question 'How can we best apply functional expertise to serve the business needs of the SBU or organisation?'

Strategic purchasing and purchasing strategy

Strategic purchasing is the linking of purchasing to corporate or business strategies.[16] Some comparisons between purchasing at the corporate and functional levels are shown in Table 2.3.

Some purchasing decisions, such as those relating to the acquisition of capital equipment, outsourcing and entering into long-term partnership alliances, are generally made at the corporate/business level, often on the basis of information or recommendations from

Table 2.3 Purchasing strategy at corporate and functional levels

Corporate/business level	Functional/operational level
Formulated at higher levels in the hierarchy	Taken at lower levels in the hierarchy
Emphasise purchasing effectiveness	Emphasise purchasing efficiency
Based on widespread environmental scanning. Some of this information will be communicated upwards from functional level	Based on information from a more limited environmental scanning. Some information obtained from suppliers etc. may be communicated upwards
Corporate strategy must be communicated downwards	Integrated with corporate strategies so far as these are communicated and understood
Focused on issues impacting future long-term procurement requirements and problems	Focused on issues impacting current tactical procurement requirements and problems

purchasing at functional or operational levels. As stated in Chapter 1 the extent to which purchasing is involved in the formation of organisational strategies is largely dependent on the extent to which purchasing is perceived by top management as contributing to competitive advantage. The purchasing executive who reports directly to the chief executive is clearly in a stronger position to influence organisational strategy than one lower in the hierarchy who reports to a materials or logistics manager. Irrespective of their level of reporting, purchasing staff should seek to contribute to corporate strategy by the provision of intelligence on the basis of which decisions can be made and to competitive advantage by improving the effectiveness of the function.

Kraljic[17] states that a company's need for a supply strategy depends on:

- the strategic importance of purchasing in terms of the value added by the product line and the percentage of materials in total costs
- the complexity of the supply market, gauged by supply scarcity, pace of technology and/or materials substitution, entry barriers, logistics cost or complexity and monopoly or oligopoly condition.

Kraljic claims that:

> By assessing the company's situation in terms of these two variables, top management and senior purchasing executives can determine the type of supply strategy the company needs both to exploit its purchasing power vis-à-vis important suppliers and reduce its risk to an acceptable minimum.

2.7.4 Purchasing strategy

Purchasing strategy relates to the specific actions that purchasing may take to achieve the objectives of the business. Some examples are shown in Table 2.4.

2.7.5 Global purchasing strategy

This is discussed in Chapter 14.

Table 2.4 Purchasing strategy examples

Situation	Solution
A manufacturing company keeps failing to win work in the Far East because they cannot guarantee 'local content' by purchasing goods in the local Far East market	Revision of purchasing strategy to include sourcing study in the Far East with the deliberate aim of purchasing at least 30 per cent of goods in Far East market
An international airline with a 'Buy British' strategy is not providing internationally competitive sources of supply, thereby reducing financial operating margins	Revision of purchasing strategy to actively research international supply markets and locate new sources that offer competitive prices and world-class supply
Corporate purchasing failing to meet the specific needs of Strategic Business Units where each SBU Managing Director is accountable for R.O.C.E.	Revision of purchasing strategy and organisation to create SBU purchasing whose sole focus will be the SBU profitability

2.8 Strategic management

Strategic management, as shown in Figure 2.5, refers to the processes of strategic analysis, formulation, evaluation, implementation, control and review.

Figure 2.5 The cycle of strategic management

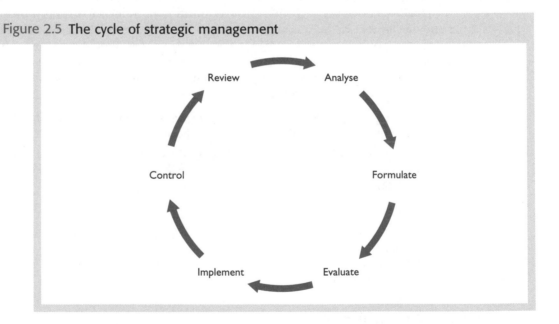

2.9 Strategic analysis

A useful definition is:[18]

> Developing a theoretically informed understanding of the environment in which the organisation is operating together with an understanding of the organisation's interaction with its

environment in order to improve organisational efficiency and effectiveness by increasing the organisation's capacity to deploy and redeploy its resources intelligently.

The tools of strategic analysis include environmental scanning, Porter analysis, scenario analysis, organisational appraisal, critical success analysis, gap and SWOT analysis.

2.9.1 Environmental scanning

Some writers regard 'the environment' as relating to all factors relevant to strategic management that are outside the boundaries of a particular organisation. Others think of the environment as encompassing both external and internal environments.

Environmental scanning has been described as 'a kind of radar to scan the world systematically and signal the new, or unexpected, the major and minor'.[19] Choo[20] states that organisations monitor their environments to:

> understand the external forces of change so that they may develop effective responses which secure or improve their position in the future. They scan to avoid surprises, identify threats and opportunities, gain competitive advantage and improve short-term and long-term planning.

2.9.2 Scanning methods

Scanning can be:

- *passive* – for example, reading a quality newspaper or professional journal
- *active* – such as desk or field research in which attention is focused on information relating to a specific industry or task
- *electronic* – this uses a field intelligence agent (FIA), which is comprised of a data-base, knowledge base, reasoning engine and data-mining unit. FIAs provide environmental information from multiple sources, comment on environmental trends and changes and enable users to ascertain whether or not current assumptions are valid or new patterns have emerged.

2.10 Important environmental factors

Important external environmental factors relating to the strategy of an organisation are sector, industry and macro-environmental.

2.10.1 Sector

Sector relates to whether the enterprise is located in the private, public or voluntary sectors of the economy.

The *private sector* includes single traders, partnerships and companies owned by private investors as opposed to the government. There is a wide variety of such undertakings that can be loosely classified according to their primary function into:

- *primary*, or extractive, organisations, such as agriculture, mining, fishing
- *secondary*, or manufacturing and assembly, organisations, such as food or car manufacturers

- *tertiary*, or distributive, organisations, concerned with the physical distribution of goods from producers to consumers, such as transport, wholesalers, retailers or providers of services, such as schools, hospitals.

The *public sector* is comprised of the national government, local government, government-owned and controlled agencies and corporations and monetary institutions, such as the armed forces and the National Health Service.

The *voluntary sector* describes bodies that are independent of government and business and are non-profit making, such as charities and churches.

Because of the wide variety of enterprises, some writers prefer to use the term 'organisational' in preference to 'corporate' strategy. Sector factors influence strategic management both at the organisational and functional levels.

At both levels, strategy is influenced by the underlying philosophy of the sector. Thus, what is known as the public–private paradox emphasises that, while business and government have much in common, ultimately they are different. Public-sector and private-sector purchasing members of staff, for example, do many of the same things and are both increasingly focused on competitiveness. There are, however, substantial differences that, as shown in Table 2.5, help to determine their respective purchasing strategies.

Table 2.5 Comparison of some public-sector and private-sector factors relating to procurement strategies

Factor	Public sector	Private sector
Aims	To provide the end users, members of the general public, with what they need when they need it and at the best value for money	To provide the enterprise with supplies that will enable it to achieve competitive advantage via positioning, cost and differentiation
Profit	Value for money spent irrespective of profit	Value for money spent commensurate with and as a contribution to profitability
Accountability	Purchasing officers in central and local government are accountable and subject to audits for the spending of public money	Private purchasing is accountable to the shareholders or owners of the undertaking for the spending of private money
Transparency	In the context of public purchasing, transparency refers to the ability of all interested parties to know and understand how public procurement is managed	In the context of private purchasing, the requirement for transparency is confined to those directly concerned, such as customers, suppliers and similar stakeholders
Procedures	In the interests of transparency, public procedures are characterised by: - well-defined regulations and procedures open to public scrutiny, such as standing orders, EU directives - clear standardised tender documents and information - equal opportunity for all in the bidding process	Fewer standardised procedures and greater flexibility on the part of purchasing staff to make unilateral strategic decisions than in the public sector

2.10.2 Industry

An industry can be defined as a group of companies within a sector offering products or services that are close substitutes for each other.

Rivalry among competitors is central to the forces contributing to industrial competitiveness. It is important to understand, therefore, the environmental factors that contribute to the attractiveness and competitiveness of an enterprise within the industry.

The five forces model devised by Michael Porter is by far the most widely used model to evaluate industry attractiveness.

Porter's five forces model

Reference has already been made to Porter's competitive strategy (section 2.7.1). Porter's five forces model is shown in Figure 2.6.

Figure 2.6 illustrates Porter's main principles.

■ In any industry, five competitive forces dictate rivalry between competitors and the generic industry structure. These forces are the main players (competitors, buyers, suppliers, substitutes and new entrants), their interrelationships (the five forces) and the factors behind those forces that help to account for industry attractiveness.

■ In aggregate, the five forces determine industry profitability because they directly influence the prices an enterprise can charge, its cost structure and investment requirements.

■ No enterprise can successfully perform at above average level by endeavouring to be all things to all people. Management must therefore select a strategy that will give the business a competitive advantage. As stated earlier, Porter argues that there are only three generic strategies that can be used, singly or in combination, to create a defensible position or outperform competitors: cost leadership, differentiation and focus on a particular market niche.

A critique of Porter's five forces model

Porter's model has been criticised on several grounds, including the following.

■ *Changed economic conditions* – Porter's theories relate to the economic situation of the 1980s, characterised by strong competition, inter-enterprise rivalry and relatively stable structures. They are less relevant in today's dynamic environment in which the Internet and e-business applications have the power to transform entire industries.

■ *Identification of new forces* – Downes[21] has identified digitalisation, globalisation and deregulation as three new forces that influence strategy.

  – *Digitalisation* – putting data into digital form for use in a digital computer – has provided all players in any given market with access to more information, thus enabling even external players to change the basis of competition.

  – *Globalisation* enables businesses to buy, sell and compare prices globally. Competitive advantage can be derived from cooperation, ability to develop strategic alliances and manage extensive global networks for the mutual advantage of buyers and sellers.

  – *Deregulation* – that is, a much reduced involvement of central government in the control of such industries as airlines, banking and public utilities.

Figure 2.6 Porter's analysis of industrial structure in his five forces model

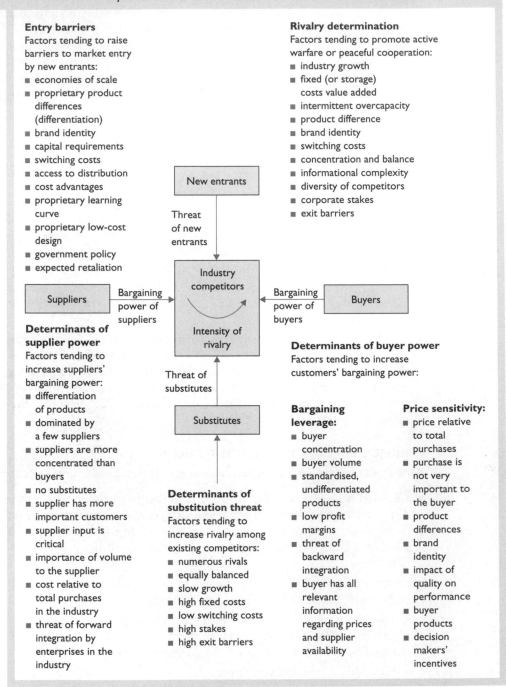

Entry barriers

Factors tending to raise barriers to market entry by new entrants:

- economies of scale
- proprietary product differences (differentiation)
- brand identity
- capital requirements
- switching costs
- access to distribution
- cost advantages
- proprietary learning curve
- proprietary low-cost design
- government policy
- expected retaliation

Rivalry determination

Factors tending to promote active warfare or peaceful cooperation:

- industry growth
- fixed (or storage) costs value added
- intermittent overcapacity
- product difference
- brand identity
- switching costs
- concentration and balance
- informational complexity
- diversity of competitors
- corporate stakes
- exit barriers

New entrants

Threat of new entrants

Industry competitors

Intensity of rivalry

Suppliers — Bargaining power of suppliers

Bargaining power of buyers — Buyers

Threat of substitutes

Substitutes

Determinants of supplier power

Factors tending to increase suppliers' bargaining power:

- differentiation of products
- dominated by a few suppliers
- suppliers are more concentrated than buyers
- no substitutes
- supplier has more important customers
- supplier input is critical
- importance of volume to the supplier
- cost relative to total purchases in the industry
- threat of forward integration by enterprises in the industry

Determinants of substitution threat

Factors tending to increase rivalry among existing competitors:

- numerous rivals
- equally balanced
- slow growth
- high fixed costs
- low switching costs
- high stakes
- high exit barriers

Determinants of buyer power

Factors tending to increase customers' bargaining power:

Bargaining leverage:

- buyer concentration
- buyer volume
- standardised, undifferentiated products
- low profit margins
- threat of backward integration
- buyer has all relevant information regarding prices and supplier availability

Price sensitivity:

- price relative to total purchases
- purchase is not very important to the buyer
- product differences
- brand identity
- impact of quality on performance
- buyer products
- decision makers' incentives

Downes states that the foremost differences between what he terms the 'Porter world' and 'the world of new forces' is information technology (IT). The old economy used IT as a tool for implementing change. Today, technology has become the most important driver of change.

The three forces of digitalisation, globalisation and deregulation have effectively removed the barriers to industrial entry and enabled new competitors and new ways of competing to develop at an accelerated speed.

■ *Relationships* – Porter's wording 'bargaining power of suppliers and buyers' suggests adversarial relationships. Current thinking regards suppliers as partners, the relationships with them needing to be nutured and strengthened so that they become resources based on lasting friendly relationships derived from performance and integrity. Outsourcing relationships may enhance both the efficiency and effectiveness of purchasing.

Nevertheless, Porter's work should still be closely studied by purchasing professionals as it provides perspectives on how suppliers may regard their customers and, conversely, how customers may regard their suppliers.

2.10.3 Macro-environmental factors

These are the changes in the political, economic, social, technological, environmental and legal environments that directly or indirectly affect the organisation, both sector and industry-wise, as well as nationally and globally. The list of each of these factors, which can be recalled by the mnemonic PESTEL, is long. Typical examples are:

■ Political – the role of government, that is, regulator or participator, political ideology
■ Economic – gross domestic product (GDP), labour rates, monetary and fiscal policies
■ Social – social trends, socio-economic groupings, value systems, ethics
■ Technological – changes, rates of technological change, costs and savings, patents
■ Environmental – 'Green' considerations, disposal of products, atmospheric factors
■ Legal – laws relating to competition, employment, the environment, consumer protection.

2.11 Internal scrutiny

This, in effect, is the internal scanning of resources, culture, value chains, structure and critical success factors.

2.11.1 Resources

Resources commonly identified are money, physical facilities and human and IT resources.

■ *Money* enables an organisation to have the maximum choice between alternatives. An important aspect of money is liquidity or ready availability. Too much money tied up in plant or stocks may limit the ability of an enterprise to take advantage of opportunities.

■ *Physical facilities* include plant and machinery. Important strategic factors are location, life, flexibility or alternative uses and the dangers of obsolescence. Such factors influence decisions regarding whether to buy or hire facilities or outsource certain operations.

■ *Human resources* include the specialised competences of the workforce and how easily specific attributes can be acquired or replaced. A further factor is the extent to which human resources can be replaced by technology. Non-availability of resources may limit the achievement of corporate goals and lead to the search for alternative means of acquiring them, such as via partnership agreements or outsourcing. Other resources, including patents and reputation, may provide an organisation with a competitive advantage over rivals in the same industry.

■ *IT resources* facilitate rapid communication between the organisation and its external contacts, including suppliers and customers, in addition to being a source of intelligence.

2.11.2 Culture

Culture is 'the way things are done round here'. More formally, culture is the system of shared values, beliefs and habits within an organisation that interacts with the formal structure to produce behavioural norms. A very simple structure of culture at the operational level is that purchasing staff should never keep sales representatives waiting. Representatives who cannot be seen with the minimum of delay should be informed so that their time is not unduly wasted. Culture is an important aspect of strategy because, if a supportive culture does not exist or cannot be cultivated, strategy changes can be difficult to implement. A model of the elements that comprise the culture web of an organisation is shown in Figure 2.7.

Figure 2.7 Culture web of an organisation

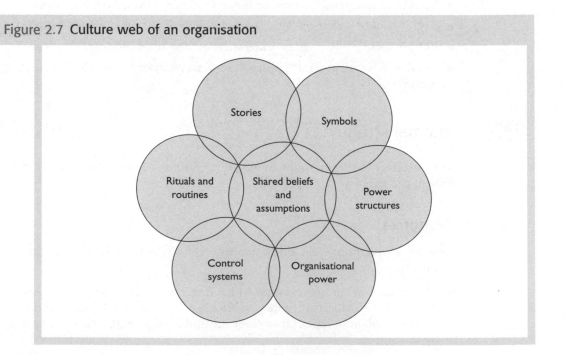

2.11.3 Value chains and structure

These are dealt with in Chapters 3 and 4 respectively.

2.11.4 Critical success factors (CSFs)

A CSF has been defined as:[22]

> An element of organisational activity which is central to its future success. Critical success factors may change over time and may include such items as product quality, employee attitudes, manufacturing flexibility and brand awareness.

In the design of new products, the early involvement of suppliers may be a critical success factor.

CSFs are linked to key tasks and priorities. *Key tasks* are what must be done to ensure that each critical success factor is achieved. *Priorities* indicate the order in which key tasks are performed.

Some critical success factors relating to purchasing strategies include:

- total quality management
- smaller supply bases
- just-in-time deliveries
- total cycle time reduction
- supplier relationships
- total cost management
- e-purchasing
- performance management
- training and development of purchasing staff
- service to internal customers
- environmental, product safety and ethical standards.

Research shows that undertakings possessing strengths in their critical success factors outperform their rivals.

2.11.5 Resources available but not owned

These are resources that can be acquired by means of lease, hire, consultancy agreements, outsourcing, joint ventures, partnerships and shared use arrangements.

2.12 Strategy formulation

As we have seen, strategies can be formulated by a process of rational planning or may emerge incrementally. These two approaches are sometimes presented as conflicting, based on the concept that strategic planning is inimical to creative thinking. Instead, however, the two approaches should be seen as complementary. A great enterprise such as the Second World War Normandy landings in 1944 could not have been accomplished without creative thinking involving vision, creativity and incremental learning based on constantly changing intelligence. Such thinking, however, had to become operationalised by means of strategic thinking. As Lawrence[23] observes:

> The essential point . . . is that strategic thinking and strategic planning are both necessary and none is adequate without the other, in an effective strategy making regime. The real challenge is how to transform today's planning process in a way that incorporates, rather than undermines strategic thinking.

Strategy formulation at corporate, business and functional levels relates to the:

- formulation of a vision statement
- preparation of a mission statement
- derivation of objectives
- application of SWOT analysis.

2.12.1 Vision statements

Vision, from a strategic aspect, has been defined as:[24]

> A mental representation of strategy created or at least expressed in the head of the leader. That vision serves both as an inspiration and a sense of what needs to be done.

Such a vision is often the starting point for strategy formulation. The vision must, however, be communicated to others in a mission statement.

A vision statement articulates a realistic, credible and positive projection of the future state of an organisation or functions or operations within that operation.

A typical vision statement for the purchasing activity might be:

> To develop, as part of an integrated supply chain, world class purchasing strategies, policies, procedures and personnel to ensure that, by means of effective sourcing, competitive advantage is achieved by, for example, lowered supplies costs, commensurate with quality, shortened supply cycles and good supplier relationships.

Dr Charles Handy, an acknowledged management guru, associated effective leader behaviour with an ability to develop a vision. He set out five conditions, which in his view need to be met, if visionary leadership is to be effective. These are:

1 The vision has to be different. It has to be a new story, almost a dream.
2 The vision has to make sense, be challenging but capable of being achieved.
3 It must be understandable and stick in people's minds.
4 The leader must exemplify the vision by his or her behaviour and display commitment.
5 To be successful, the vision has to be a shared one.

The vision statement of Harley-Davidson Inc. reads:

> Harley-Davidson, Inc. is an action-orientated, international company, a leader in its commitment to continuously improve our mutually beneficial relationships with stakeholders (customers, suppliers, employees, shareholders, governments and society). Harley-Davidson believes the key to success is to balance stakeholders' interests through the empowerment of all employees to focus on value-added activities.

2.12.2 Vision and mission statements

Vision and mission statements are sometimes considered to be synonymous, but Campbell and Yeung[25] point out some differences.

- Vision refers to a future state, 'a condition that is better than now'.
- When a vision is achieved, a new vision needs to be developed, but a mission can remain the same.
- A vision is associated with a goal, whereas a mission is associated with a way of behaving.

The mission statement answers the question 'What is our business?' It is the sense of purpose provided by a mission statement that helps in both strategy formulation and maintaining the focus of strategic plans.

At the operating level, a mission statement should indicate the following:

- The aims of the function or operation. These should be carefully considered and reflect the needs and expectations of both internal and external customers. Aims, especially at the organisational level, may be narrowly or broadly defined. A building society may define its mission narrowly as to provide mortgages to prospective house purchasers. More broadly, this purpose is to provide financial services. Similarly, for a film company, 'to provide entertainment' is a broader aim than 'to make films'.
- How the aims will be achieved.
- The basis of internal and external relationships.
- The link with organisational strategies.

2.12.3 Objectives

Objectives are explicit statements of the results the organisation wishes to achieve. Corporate and business objectives are medium-term to long-term, strategic and general and usually cover growth, profitability, technology, products and markets. Functional or operational objectives are short-term, tactical and specific. Thus, 'elements of strategy at a higher management level become objectives at a lower one.'[26]

As we saw earlier, the classic definition of the overall purchasing task is:

> To obtain materials of the right *quality* in the right *quantity* from the right *source* delivering to the right *place* at the right *time* at the right *price*.

As you will also recall, this definition is somewhat simplistic for the following reasons:

- the term 'right' is situational – each company will define 'right' differently
- what is 'right' will change as the overall purchasing context and environment change
- the above rights must be consistent with corporate goals and objectives from which functional/operating goals and objectives are derived
- in practice, some rights are irreconcilable – for example, it may be possible to obtain the right quality, but not the right price as 'the best suppliers are often the busiest but also the dearest'.

Table 2.6 Purchasing and corporate objectives

Business objectives	Purchasing and supply objectives
A statement of the position the organisation is aiming for in its markets, including market share	The objective of providing the quantity and quality of supplies required by the market share and market positioning objectives
A key objective of, say, moving out of speciality markets and entering volume markets	A key objective of developing new, larger suppliers and materials flow systems more geared to larger numbers of fewer parts while keeping the total inventory volume low
A key objective to build new businesses that will generate positive cash flow as well as reasonable profits	Contribute to cash flow improvement by means of lower average inventory and by negotiating smaller delivery lots and/or longer payment terms
A plan to develop some specific new products or services	A plan to develop appropriate suppliers
An overall production/capacity plan, including an overall policy on make or buy	A plan to develop systems that integrate capacity planning and/or purchase planning, together with the policy on make or buy and partnering relationships
A plan to introduce a cost reduction programme	A plan to introduce supplies standardisation, supplier reduction programmes and e-procurement
A financial plan, setting out in broad terms how the proposed capital expenditure is to be financed, together with an outline timescale and an order in which the objectives need to be achieved	A financial plan, setting out broadly the profit contribution expected from purchasing and supply, together with the time in which it should be achieved and the priorities of the objectives

Purchasing objectives have therefore to be balanced according to overall corporate strategy and requirements at a given time.

An alternative definition of the key purpose for the purchasing and supply chain, derived for the UK Purchasing and Supply Lead Body for National Vocational Qualifications by the University of Ulster, is:

> To provide the interface between customer and supplier in order to plan, obtain, store and distribute as necessary, supplies of materials, goods and services [m, g, s] to enable the organisation to satisfy its external and internal customers.

As shown in Table 2.6, purchasing objectives derive from corporate objectives.

Short-term objectives are those set for a short period – one year, say – so that actual achievement can be measured against the original objectives, distinguishing between factors relating to attainment or non-attainment for which the purchasing activity and its staff can be held accountable. The technique of management by objectives is discussed in section 17.7.

Figure 2.8 SWOT matrix

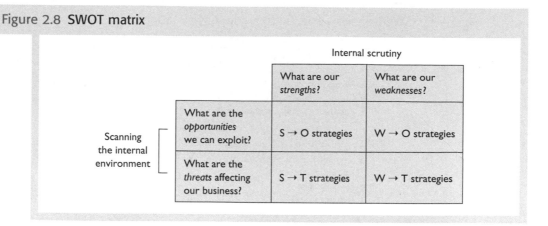

2.12.4 SWOT analysis

Environmental scanning and internal scrutiny described earlier in this chapter provide the intelligence for a SWOT (strengths, weaknesses, opportunities and threats) analysis. Figure 2.8 indicates that some form of SWOT analysis or matrix is an essential preliminary step in the formulation of strategies designed to convert the inspirations expressed in vision and mission statements into realities and ensure that the objectives are achieved.

In Figure 2.8:

- *S → O strategies* are those that seek to utilise organisational strengths to exploit external opportunities
- *W → O strategies* are those that seek to rectify organisational weaknesses so that external opportunities can be exploited
- *S → T strategies* are those that utilise organisational strengths to reduce vulnerability to external threats
- *W → T strategies* establish defensive plans to prevent organisational weaknesses from being highly vulnerable to external threats.

SWOT analysis can be undertaken at all three organisational levels – corporate, business and functional. An example of a SWOT analysis leading to some possible W → T strategies is where the organisation is under some threat as the manufacture of a major product requires the purchase of a highly sensitive material for which there is a high demand and few suppliers. In such a case, the SWOT/TOWS matrix may be used, as shown in Figure 2.9.

SWOT analysis has been criticised on the grounds that, in practice, such exercises are often poorly structured, hastily conducted and result in vague and inconsistent lists of subjective factors reflecting the interests and prejudices of the proposers. Such criticisms can be countered by:

- *making the analysis a group process* in which the free flow of ideas is encouraged
- *the use of qualifiers* requires the movers of statements for inclusion in the analysis to give reasons, so, instead of just saying 'too much reliance on one supplier', the proposer would be required to add 'because the supplier takes our business for granted and we are possibly paying more than necessary'.

Figure 2.9 SWOT analysis applied to a supplies situation

STRENGTHS	WEAKNESSES
■ Purchasing power ■ Regular demand ■ Purchasing probity and goodwill	■ Highly sensitive imported material
THREATS	OPPORTUNITIES
■ Competition for the material from competitors ■ Few suppliers ■ Exchange rates	■ Alternative materials ■ Possibility of vertical integration with a supplier ■ Outsourcing ■ Partnerships ■ Virtual company formation

2.13 The evaluation of alternative strategies

In a given situation, there are normally several alternative strategies that are available. The aim is to evaluate several strategic options – including a 'do nothing' or 'do the minimum' option, which, where appropriate, may be included, even if it is unacceptable in operational terms.

Rumelt[27] identifies four principles that can be applied to strategic evaluation:

- *consistency* – the strategy must not present mutually inconsistent policies
- *consonance* – the strategy must represent an adaptive response to the external environment and the critical changes occurring within it
- *advantage* – the strategy must provide for the creation and/or maintenance of a competitive advantage in the selected area of authority
- *feasibility* – the strategy must neither overtax available resources nor create insoluble problems.

An alternative set of criteria is that a given strategy should, first, meet the requirements of a given situation, second, provide sustainable competitive advantage and, third, improve company performance.

2.13.1 Methods of strategy evaluation

There are several possible approaches to choosing a strategy that meets the above criteria. Porter's positional approach to strategy formation is simply the selection of one of three generic positions based on an analysis of the organisation's position in the environment.

Other important approaches include lifecycle analysis, scenario planning, return analysis, profitability analysis, risk analysis, resource deployment analysis, non-financial factor appraisal and portfolio planning and analysis.

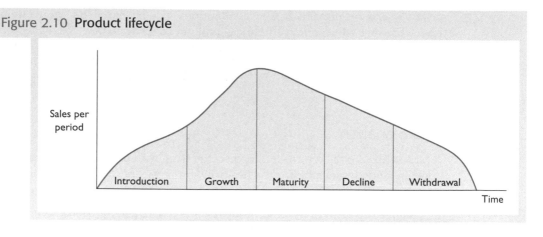

Figure 2.10 **Product lifecycle**

2.13.2 Lifecycle analysis

This is based on the concept that all products in their original, unmodified form have a finite lifespan, as shown in Figure 2.10.

The product lifecycle or Gopertz curve plots the actual or potential sales of a new product over time and shows the stages of development – growth, maturity, decline and eventual withdrawal. Important aspects of product lifecycles are:

- *their length* – from development to withdrawal, which may be short with products subject to rapid technological advances
- *their shape* – not all products have the same shape to their curve; so-called high learning, low learning, fashion and fad products have different curves reflecting different marketing strategies
- *the product* – this can vary depending on whether the product lifecycle applies to a *class* (that is, the entire product category or industry), a *form* (that is, variations within the class) or a *brand*.

From the strategic aspect, the lifecycle approach has become increasingly important for the following reasons:

- *environmental factors* – such as the relative environmental performance of a product, as in the case of purchasing packaging, paper and the subsequent management of waste
- *durability factors* – such as competition between substitute commodity products – aluminium and steel in the car industry, for example
- *obsolescence* – with regard to capital equipment, which may be a factor in deciding to adopt an outsourcing strategy
- *changing demand* – this concept of the product lifecycle helps marketing managers to recognise both that products may need to be continually changed to prevent sales decline and that there is a need to formulate marketing strategies to stimulate demand; this strategy may impact purchasing strategies, such as how far in advance to place orders for materials or components that are likely to change.

2.13.3 Scenario planning

Scenario planning consists of developing a conceptual forecast of the future based on given assumptions. Thus, by starting with different assumptions, different future scenarios can be presented. The assumptions can be based on the examination of trends relating to economic, political and social factors that may affect corporate objectives and supply and demand forecasts. Planning therefore involves deciding which scenario is most likely to occur and devising appropriate strategies for it. An example is examining how the prices of sensitive commodities change in the scenarios of glut and shortage.

2.13.4 Return analysis

Return analysis – the returns likely to accrue from the adoption of a particular strategy – may be done by such means as cost–benefit analysis or profitability analysis.

Cost–benefit analysis may be defined as:

> A comparison between the costs of the resources used, plus any other costs imposed by an activity (such as pollution, environmental damage) and the value of the financial and non-financial benefits derived.

Cost–benefit analysis often involves a consideration of trade-offs. Thus, when considering which of several alternative materials or components to use, a number of cost–benefit trade-offs need to be considered. Generally, increased quality means increased prices and, ultimately, increased costs. The decision on which to specify must therefore attempt to balance the interrelationships of cost, quality and projected selling prices with company objectives relating to sales quantities and profitability.

2.13.5 Profitability analysis

This uses a number of ratios to measure the ability of the business to make a profit, including:

- *sales growth* indicates the percentage increase (or decrease) in sales between two time periods – that is:

$$\frac{\text{Current year's (or other period) sales} - \text{Last year's sales}}{\text{Last year's sales}}$$

and if overall costs and inflation are on the rise, then a related increase in sales should be expected; if not, this is an indication that prices are not keeping up with costs

- *costs of goods sold to sales* gives an indication of the percentage of sales used to pay for expenses that vary directly with sales – that is:

$$\frac{\text{Cost of goods sold}}{\text{Sales}}$$

- *gross profit margin* indicates profit earning on products without consideration of selling and administrative overheads – that is:

$$\frac{\text{Gross profit}}{\text{Total sales}}$$

- *net profit margins* indicate how much profit comes from every £1 of sales – that is:

$$\frac{\text{Net profit}}{\text{Total sales}}$$

■ *return on assets* indicates how effectively assets are used to provide a return – that is:

$$\frac{\text{Net profit}}{\text{Total assets}}$$

Profitability analysis can also include such measures as return on capital employed (ROCE), payback and discounted cash flow, referred to in Chapter 13.

2.13.6 Risk analysis

From a strategic perspective, a risk is something that may have an impact on the achievement of objectives.

Risks can be assessed from three standpoints:

■ *The likelihood of the risk being realised* – a realised risk is known as an issue and, as such, must be dealt with.

■ *The impact of risk* – thus the breakdown of a JIT contract may have quantitative and qualitative consequences. *Quantitative* consequences include the costs of a breakdown in production, obtaining substitute supplies and, possibly, funding a new supplier. *Qualitatively*, the reputation of the purchasing activity may be adversely affected by sourcing from an unreliable supplier.

■ *The costs and benefits of taking steps to reduce either the risk or its impact* should the risk become an issue. Risks from a strategic viewpoint do not always have a negative connotation. Risks present opportunities to be embraced, such as global sourcing, as well as dangers to be avoided.

Some approaches to the reduction and control of strategic risks include the following:

■ *Decision support modelling and information systems* – these software programs use information from both internal and external sources to support decision making.

■ *Probability analysis* – this determines the probability of a risk occurring on a scale of 0 to 1. The probability of an event can be computed by the formula:

$$\frac{\text{Number of ways an outcome could occur}}{\text{Total number of outcomes}}$$

Thus the probability of obtaining the number 3 when rolling a six-sided dice is:

$$\frac{1}{6} \text{ or } 0.167$$

In the real world, the calculation of probability is often impossible due to insufficient data. Even when it can be done, statistical conclusions should be supported by some form of qualitative assessment. From experience we know that a dice can be rolled six times without a 3 occurring once.

■ *Sensitivity analysis* – this is used to determine how 'sensitive' a strategy is to changes in the assumptions on which it is based. Such analysis questions or challenges each of the assumptions underlying the strategy and determines how sensitive the desired or predicted outcome is to each assumption. Essentially sensitivity looks at the question of 'What if . . . ?' when a variable is different from that originally expected. Thus, except for the initial purchase price, all data relating to the purchase of a capital asset such as life, return on investment and cost of maintenance are estimates.

Any estimate, however, is subject to error. Sensitivity analysis identifies an error range for the various estimated values over which the purchase will be acceptable. While sensitivity analysis of each variable, such as the estimated life of the asset, will be reduced by obsolescence resulting from improved technology, it does provide a tolerance factor for estimation errors by providing upper and lower ranges for selected variables.

- *Hedging* is a method of minimising investment risk, particularly in the contexts of investment management and commodity dealing. The financial tools most frequently used for hedging are forward buying, futures and options. Collectively, these tools are known as *derivatives*. Hedging is discussed further in section 13.13.4.

- *Satisficing* – this is a concept introduced by Cyert and March[28] who argue that managers do not attempt to discover every alternative. When managers satisfice, they choose acceptable solutions based on the information available to them rather than trying to make the optimum decision.

2.13.7 Resource deployment analysis

Resource deployment analysis is the assessment of the likely effect on key resources of adopting a particular strategy. Thus, a decision whether or not to adopt an outsourcing strategy with regard to a support service will be preceded by an analysis of the effects on tangible and intangible resources, including finance, human resources, competitive advantage and growth.

2.13.8 Non-financial factor appraisal

When making strategic decisions, it is important to consider such non-financial aspects as:

- enhancement (or otherwise) of the organisational image
- effects on suppliers, customers, competitors and the general public
- environmental and ethical factors
- the likelihood of change, development, obsolescence
- staff and union reaction to the strategy
- ethical implications of the proposed strategy.

2.13.9 Portfolio planning and analysis

Portfolio planning and analysis aim to assist with strategic decisions as to where to invest scarce organisational resources among a number of competing business opportunities. This approach is analogous to an investment manager deciding which shares to buy with the aim of creating a portfolio designed to meet a given investment strategy, such as achieving growth or providing income.

2.13.10 The BCG portfolio

One of the most popular portfolio approaches is the Boston Consulting Group (BCG) matrix. This approach to strategy formulation, analyses business opportunities according to market growth rate and market share. As shown in Figure 2.11, based on these criteria, businesses can be categorised as:

Figure 2.11 Corporate strategies within the BCG matrix

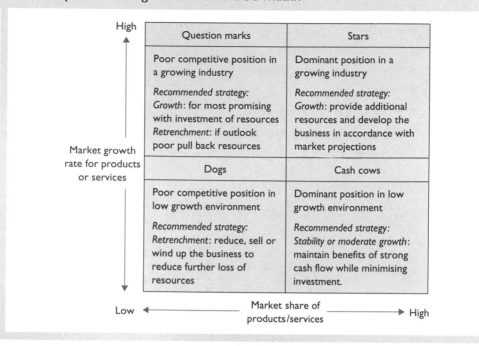

- *stars* – businesses with high market share and high growth
- *cash cows* – businesses with high market share and low growth
- *question marks* – businesses with low market share and high growth
- *dogs* – businesses with low market share and low growth.

The BCG matrix can be used to decide what strategy(ies) to adopt at all three strategic organisational levels: corporate, business and functional/operational.

2.13.11 Purchasing portfolio management

In 1983, Kraljic[29] introduced the first portfolio approach for use in purchasing and supply management, although a similar 'matrix' was described by Fisher[30] in 1970. Kraljic's starting premise is that:

> Threats of resource depletion and raw materials scarcity, political turbulence and government intervention in supply markets, intensified competition and accelerating technological changes have ended the days of no surprises. As dozens of companies have learned, supply and demand patterns can be upset virtually overnight.

The Kraljic portfolio aims to guide managers so that they can recognise the weakness of their organisation and formulate strategies for guarding against supplies disruption. Kraljic states that the *profit impact* of a given supply item can be defined in terms of:

- volume purchased
- percentage of total cost
- impact on product quality or business growth.

Supply risk for that item is assessed in terms of availability:

- availability
- number of suppliers
- competitive demand
- make-or-buy opportunities
- storage risks
- substitution opportunities.

These profits and risk factors enable all purchased items to be assigned to one of the four quadrants shown in Figure 2.12.

Figure 2.12 The Krajic portfolio matrix (adapted)

Purchasing importance and profit impact of a given supply item measured against criteria such as cost of materials, total costs, volume purchased	Leverage products (Examples: steel plate and sections)	Strategic products (Examples: assemblies, gear boxes, engines, optics)	Balance of power in purchaser/supplier relationship
High	■ Relatively large share of product price ■ Small change in price has large impact on profit Risk small as: ■ many alternative suppliers ■ substitution possible Buyer-dominated segment Competitive bidding	■ Together with leverage products can account for 80% of turnover ■ Small changes in price will have an immediate and significant impact on costs Risk significant due to high dependence on supplier Balance of power may differ between purchasers and suppliers. Performance-based partnership	
	Non-critical (routine) products (Examples: standard office supplies, MRO items, fasteners, consumables)	Bottleneck products (Examples: natural flavours, vitamins, pigments)	
Low	■ Can require up to 80% of purchasing activity for 20% of purchasing turnover ■ Low product/high administrative cost No risk due to: ■ many alternative suppliers ■ large product variety Reduce number of suppliers Use systems contracting and e-procurement solutions	■ Relatively limited in value but danger of sudden price rises High risk due to: ■ few, if any, alternative suppliers ■ suppliers may be technology leaders Supplier-dominated segment Secure long- and short-term supply Seek alternative suppliers	
	Low (many suppliers) ← Supply risk measured against such criteria as short- and long-term availability, number of potential suppliers, structure of supply markets → High (one or few suppliers)		

Nellove and Söderquist[31] state that all portfolio approaches to procurement involve three common steps:

1 analysis of the products and their classification
2 analysis of the supplier relationships required to deliver the products
3 action plans to match product requirements to supplier relationships.

Thus, the steps for the use of the matrix in Figure 2.12 are:

- list all purchases in descending value order
- analyse the risk and market complexity of each purchase
- position each item on the matrix accordingly
- periodically, decide whether or not to move a particular purchase to an alternative quadrant.

The aims and possible tasks associated with each quadrant are shown in Table 2.7.

Gelderman and van Weele[32] point out that 'in general little is known about *the actual use* of purchasing portfolio models or how purchasing professionals position commodities and suppliers into the portfolio and develop strategies from its use'. To gain insights into such issues, we interviewed a limited number of executives and purchasing professionals employed by a large Dutch chemical company. The interviewees were selected for their experience in the use of portfolio models in actual purchasing situations. Their findings in relation to the company DSM may be summarised as follows.

Basic

- Generally matrix movements follow a clockwise pattern from bottleneck to non-critical; non-critical to leverage; leverage to strategic.
- DSM works on the principle that the non-critical and bottleneck quadrants should be as empty as possible.

Bottleneck items

For processed materials, a key question is whether standardisation is possible, permitting movement to the leverage quadrant.

Where standardisation is not possible, approaches reported are:

- capacity deals, concentrating purchases with one supplier
- obtaining a better bottleneck position by reducing supply risk on the one hand and obtaining a better negotiating position on the other
- 'staying in the corner and making the best of it' by keeping stocks, hedging, broadening the specification, searching for alternative suppliers and so on.

Many non-critical (MRO) and equipment items are 'bottleneck' due to overspecification. Less complicated and more generic specifications allow 'pooling' of purchases across units/groups and consequent movement from the bottleneck quadrant to the non-critical one and/or non-critical to the leverage quadrant.

Non-critical items

At DSM, the main products are office supplies and services. As stated above, the main considerations influencing movement to the leverage quadrant are standardisation and pooling. Where pooling is not an option, purchase cards are useful for individual non-strategic commodities.

Table 2.7 Aims, tasks and information associated with each procurement focus

Procurement focus	Aims	Main tasks	Required information
Leverage aims (high profit impact, low supply risk)	■ Obtain best short-term deal ■ Maximise cost savings	■ Ensure suppliers are aware that they are in a competitive situation ■ Group similar items together to increase value and quality for quantity discounts ■ Utilise blanket orders but keep contract terms relatively short (1–2 years) ■ Search for alternative products/suppliers ■ Negotiate value-added arrangements – VMI, JIT, storage ■ Consider moving into strategic quadrant	■ Good market data ■ Short-term to medium-term demand planning ■ Accurate vendor data ■ Price/transport rate forecasts
Strategic items (high profit impact, high supply risk)	■ Maximise cost reductions ■ Minimise risk ■ Create competitive advantage ■ Create mutual commitment to long-term relationships	■ Prepare accurate forecasts of future requirements ■ Carefully analyse supply risk ■ Seek long-term supplier/partnering agreements (3–5 years) with built-in arrangements for continuous improvement and performance measurement ■ Consider joint ventures with selected suppliers and customers to gain competitive advantage ■ Take prompt action to rectify slipping performance ■ Possibly move purchasing back into leverage quadrant until confidence restored	■ Highly detailed market data ■ Long-term supply and demand trend information ■ Good competitive intelligence ■ Industry cost curves
Non-critical (routine) items (low profit impact, low supply risk)	■ Reduce administrative procedures and costs ■ Eliminate complexity ■ Improve operational efficiency	■ Simplify requisitioning, buying and payment ■ Standardise where possible ■ Consolidate and buy from consortia ■ Encourage direct ordering by users/internal customers against call-off contracts ■ Use e-procurement ■ Consider clustering into leverage quadrant	■ Good market overview ■ Short-term demand forecast ■ Economic order quantity ■ Inventory levels
Bottleneck items (low profit items, high supply risk)	■ Reduce costs ■ Secure short-term and long-term supply	■ Forecast future requirements as accurately as possible ■ Consolidate purchases to secure leverage ■ Determine importance attached to purchases by supplier ■ See if specification measures – buffer stocks, consigned stocks, transportation ■ Search for alternative products/supplies ■ Contract to reduce risk	■ Medium-term demand/supply forecasts ■ Very good market data ■ Inventory costs ■ Maintenance plans

Leverage items

DSM distinguishes between 'strategic partnerships' and 'partnerships of convenience'.

Only a limited number of supplies qualify for movement from the leverage to the strategic quadrant, which is feasible when:

- the supplier has proper capabilities for co-design
- the purchaser (DSM) is prepared to spend time on supplier development
- the purchaser has sufficient levels of trust in the supplier at all organisational levels.

When a supplier does not qualify as a strategic supplier, the focus is on efficiency and cost reduction rather than design optimisation.

Partnerships can be either technology (joint venture, co-development, concurrent engineering) or logistics-driven (JIT). The latter are regarded as 'partnerships of convenience' or tactical solutions to tactical problems and reside in the leverage quadrant.

Strategic items

Successful strategic partnerships are rare and DSM policy is to reduce or restrict dependence on the supplier involved. Partnerships, over time, may become unsatisfactory or the supplier does not wish to be involved in joint development.

With underachieving partners, DSM may adopt such approaches as supplier development, making the product less complicated and developing new suppliers.

Conclusions

While recognising the limitation of their investigation, Geldermann and van Weele concluded that:

- the portfolio approach is helpful in positioning commodities/supplies in different matrix quadrants
- the pre-eminent value of the approach is in helping purchasing practitioners to move commodities/suppliers around specific quadrants to reduce dependence on specific suppliers
- the Kraljic portfolio is 'an effective tool for discussing visualising and illustrating the possibilities of differentiated purchasing strategies . . . it is a powerful tool for coordinating purchasing strategies among various, fairly autonomous business units'.

In addition, the Kraljic categories provide a useful way of classifying purchases by total spend under each heading.

There are various modifications or variants to the Kraljic matrix, of which possibly the best-known one is that of Bensaou.[33] One objection to purchasing portfolio models is that they do not take account of the supplier's perspective. Using the complexity of the supply market (ask yourself, 'In practice are there many or few suppliers?') and the complexity of the buyer markets ('Many or few buyers?'), Kamann[34] has developed the alternative matrix shown in Figure 2.13.

Figure 2.13 identifies four classifications of products:

- *generic items* – standardised commodities
- *tailorised items* – items produced using flexible technology – mass customisation
- *proprietary products* – brand names, such as Microsoft
- *custom design* – the real one-to-one relationships.

Figure 2.13 The buyer's market from the supplier's perspective

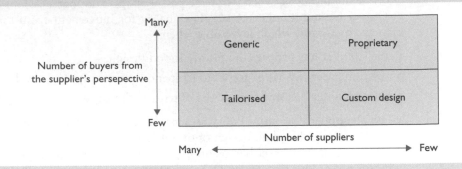

Figure 2.14 The Kamann cube

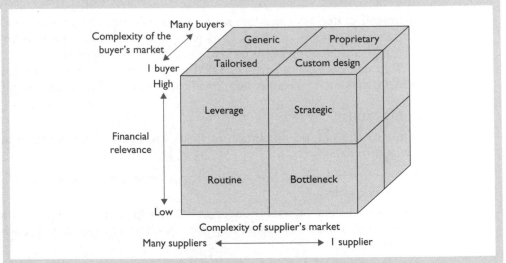

By combining the Kamann and Kraljic matrices, we obtain a cube, as shown in Figure 2.14. This cube reflects both the complexity of the supplier's market (from the purchasing perspective) and the buyer's market (from the supplier's perspective).

Kamann observes, inter alia, the following.

■ *Parts of the strategic and bottleneck items belong to the proprietary column (one monopolistic or very few oligopolistic suppliers and many buyers)* – the chances of getting adapted product specifications for such items are therefore small. This is especially true for smaller buyers, who may deal with agents rather than directly with producers.

■ *Many companies differentiate between various types of leverage items in their supplier strategy* – a food multinational, for example, differentiates between simple products (such as potatoes) and more complicated products (such as a complete meal). For complicated products, joint value analysis, involving customers and suppliers, is used to standardise products across markets and producers.

■ *Purchasing procedures* – generic, tailored and proprietary items can be well integrated. Custom design requires many face-to-face contacts. Suppliers can be categorised as:

Figure 2.15 Co-developer relationships

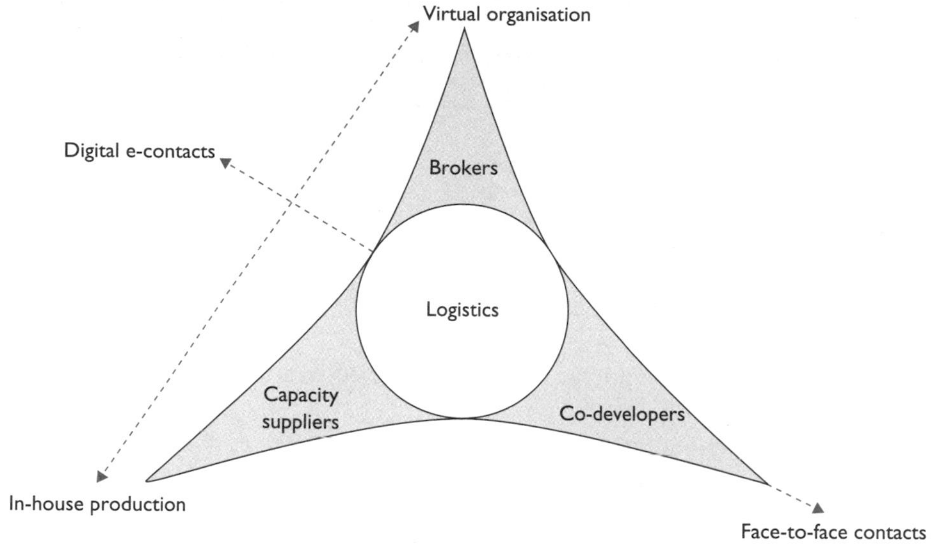

- *brokers* – potentially virtual organisations that just redistribute orders, organise and collect leveraged buying power, combined with spot buying on the Internet
- *capacity suppliers* – actually produce goods and services
- *codevelopers* – concerned with product development and design requiring much face-to-face contact and long-term relationships. Logistics is 'the glue that blends the business processes of brokers, capacity suppliers and codevelopers'. These relationships are depicted in Figure 2.15.

2.14 Strategy implementation

Strategy implementation is concerned with converting a strategic plan into action and doing what needs to be done to achieve the targeted strategic goals and objectives. The principal differences between strategy formulation and strategy implementation are shown in Table 2.8.

Strategy implementation should be seen as a learning process from which all organisational levels can benefit.

2.14.1 The main stages of strategy implementation

1 Communicate strategic plans to all who have not been involved in their formulation. Good communication helps to avoid negative reactions, particularly where strategies involve significant change.
2 Obtain commitment from those concerned. This involves disclosure and discussion in consultative processes, such as meetings and team briefings.
3 Framing policies and procedures.

Table 2.8 Contrasts between strategy formulation and implementation

Strategy formulation	Strategy implementation
The positioning of forces before the action	Management of forces during the action
Focuses on effectiveness	Focuses on efficiency
Is primarily an intellectual process	Is primarily an operational process
Requires good initiative and analytical skills	Requires special motivation and leadership skills
Requires coordination of a few individuals	Requires coordination of many people

4 Setting operational targets and objectives and ensuring that these are related to corporate objectives.
5 Assigning responsibilities and commensurate authority to individuals and teams for the achievement of objectives.
6 Changing organisational structures, where necessary.
7 Allocation of resources and agreeing budgets.
8 Providing employees with required training.
9 Constantly monitoring the success or otherwise of strategies and making required revisions.

Resource allocation and policies are important aspects of the above activities. Organisational structures are considered in Chapter 4 and procedures in Chapter 6.

2.14.2 Resource allocation

In most organisations the financial, physical, human and technological resources allocated to a function/activity will be reduced to quantitative terms and expressed in budgets or financial statements of the resources needed to achieve specific objectives or implement a formulated strategy.

2.14.3 Policies

Policies are instruments for strategy implementation. A policy is:

> a body of principles, expressed or implied, laid down to direct an enterprise towards its objectives and guide executives in decision making.

Policies are mandatory and must be adhered to by all people and activities throughout the organisation.

It is useful to consider the advantages of policy generally and policies for purchasing specifically.

The advantages of policies

At corporate, functional and operational levels, policies have the following advantages:

■ corporate policies provide guidelines to executives when formulating functional and operating strategies

- policies provide authority based on principle and/or precedent for a given course of action
- they provide a basis for management control, allow coordination across organisational units and reduce the time managers spend making decisions
- they provide management by exception, providing guidelines for routine actions, so a new decision is required only in exceptional circumstances
- they lead to uniformity of procedures and consistency in thought and action.

Purchasing policies

Typical examples include the following:

- Ethical purchasing policy (Vodafone)

  It is the policy of the Board of Vodafone Group Plc that local operating companies should only deal with suppliers of goods or services that comply with Vodafone's ethical standards. These ethical standards will form the Code of Ethical Purchasing ('CEP'). It is each supplier's responsibility to establish procedures to comply with this code. Breaching the CEP will result in an immediate termination of the relationship or in a detailed corrective action plan to be agreed with the supplier.

- Purchasing policy (Carnegie Mellon University)

  The goal of purchasing policies and procedures is to provide reasonably priced, high-quality goods and services to end users, while preserving organisational, and financial and civic accountability.

- Environmental purchasing policy (Yorkshire Wolds and Coast Primary Care Trust)

  In pursuit of the organisation's objectives relating to sustainability, we recognise the critical need to act as a role model, by carrying out purchasing activities in an environmentally responsible manner. We will therefore:

  - Comply with all relevant environmental legislation;
  - Encourage and persuade suppliers to investigate and introduce environmentally friendly processes and products;
  - Educate our suppliers concerning the organisation's sustainable development strategy;
  - Ensure that, where appropriate, environmental criteria are used in the award of contracts;
  - Specify, wherever possible and reasonably practicable within the financial constraints operating within a cash limited public service, the use of environmentally friendly materials and products;
  - Ensure that suppliers' environmental credentials are considered in the supplier appraisal process;
  - Ensure that consideration is given to inclusion, within all specifications, of a facility for potential suppliers to submit prices for environmentally alternatives; and
  - Ensure that appropriate consideration is given to the costs and benefits of environmentally friendly alternatives.

- Basic purchasing policy (Toyota Boshoku)

  1 Open and fair transactions

  We provide all companies with an opportunity to participate in conducting transactions in an open, equitable, and impartial manner, regardless of whether the party is Japanese or foreign. Supplier selection is based on fair comparisons and an overall consideration of reliability, product quality, technical capabilities, costs, and assurance of delivery schedules, and numerous other aspects.

2 Mutual developments through mutual trust

Our approach is to strive for mutual development with our suppliers through our business transactions. We think it is important to build good, long-term relationships, consider reliable, long-term relationships through close communications with our suppliers.

3 Promotion of 'green purchasing'

So that we may pass along a rich, abundant environment to succeeding generations. Toyota Boshoku intends to make purchasing of environmentally sound products a priority issue as part of an overall stance that requires us to make efforts to procure safe parts and materials. We are taking steps to promote green purchasing to help create a recycling-based society.

4 Promotion of local purchasing as a good corporate citizen

Aware of the company's role as a member of the local community Toyota Boshoku aims to develop and contribute to society as a good corporate citizen. In our expansion overseas, we shall act as a local enterprise in promoting purchasing from other companies in the immediate area so as to contribute to the local community.

5 'Law-abidingness' and maintaining 'Confidentiality'

- We shall adhere to all laws and social norms that bear on our purchasing activities.
- We shall exercise all due care in handling confidential information obtained through mutual purchasing activities.

Policy statements can be written in relation to virtually every aspect of purchasing activity. Other important areas for which policy statements may be prepared include:

- purchasing authority – who may purchase and limitations on authority
- use of purchasing cards
- purchase of capital equipment
- environmental policies
- disposal of waste and surplus
- purchasing from SMEs and local purchasing
- e-procurement
- ethical policies.

In general, the purchasing policies of individual organisations should conform to three basic principles:

- purchasing policies should aim to select and procure, in an economically rational manner, the best possible goods and services available
- suppliers worldwide should be eligible to participate in procurement transactions on open, fair and transparent principles and easy-to-understand, simple procedures
- purchasing transactions have an important contribution to make to society worldwide – for example, corporate purchasing practices should consider the effective preservation of natural resources and protection of the environment.

Purchasing policies are usually specified in a purchasing manual that is regularly revised. The policies may be varied to meet an exceptional situation, such as a breakdown in supplies, but this should only be done on the authority of the executive who has ultimate responsibility for purchasing.

2.14.4 An example of a strategy implementation plan

An example of a public-sector organisation plan is shown in Figure 2.16.[35] The 11 headings of the plan can easily be adapted to the requirements of a private-sector enterprise.

2.15 Post-implementation evaluation, control and review

This is concerned with verifying the degree to which implemented strategies are fulfilling the mission and objectives of the organisation. Evaluation differs from control. Post-implementation evaluation can apply the principles listed in section 2.12 above. Spekman[36] states that the objective of evaluation is to enable procurement managers to understand both the process and result of strategic planning and offers the following list of evaluation criteria:

- *Internal consistency*
  - Are the procurement strategies mutually achievable?
  - Do they address corporate/division objectives?
  - Do they reinforce each other? Is there synergy?
  - Do the strategies focus on crucial procurement issues?
- *Environmental fit*
  - Do the purchasing strategies exploit environmental opportunities?
  - Do they deal with external threats?
- *Resource fit*
  - Can the strategies be carried out in the light of resource constraints?
  - Is the timing consistent with the department's and/or business's ability to adapt to the change?
- *Communication and implementation*
  - Are the strategies understood by key implementers?
  - Is there organisational commitment?
  - Is there sufficient managerial capability to support effective procurement planning?

The control process involves four stages, as shown in Figure 2.17. Setting standards is not easy, owing to the multitude of possibilities.

Normally, specific performance standards can be grouped under four headings:

- service to internal and external customers
- contributors to the competitive advantage of other elements in the supply chain
- staff effectiveness and efficiency
- financial measures – that is, cost reductions, conformity to budgets.

Performance measurement, as applied to the purchasing function, is considered in Chapter 17.

Johnson and Scholes[37] state that, in reviewing strategic options, it is important to distinguish between three interrelated aspects of any strategy. The typical purchasing strategies/tactics or contributions for each of the three aspects of strategic development are shown in Table 2.9.

Figure 2.16 An example of a strategy implementation plan

Aims

To support the achievement of the council's key objectives and allow concentration of more resources, both financial and staff time, on delivering core tasks. This will be done by securing best value for money, reducing or managing risk and modernising related business processes by adopting best practice procurement techniques for all bought-in external goods and services.

Objectives

1 Take a *strategic overview* of corporate procurement.
  ■ Undertake portfolio analysis to identify key spend areas and supplies.
  ■ Identify scope for aggregation of demand into large/corporate contracts.
  ■ Identify scope for collaborative arrangements.
  ■ Identify the procurement community within BFBC.
  ■ Create procurement performance measures against agreed baseline.
  ■ Prepare an annual report to the executive board.
2 Establish procurement as specific element in *corporate and departmental planning process*.
  ■ Incorporate council's procurement strategy and this implementation plan into the council's annual policy and performance plan.
  ■ Establish procurement strategy/plan for each individual department as part of annual service plans.
  ■ Review plans annually in normal planning process.
3 Adopt a commercial approach, in line with *best value principles*, to all procurement decisions.
  ■ Evaluate all bids on quality as well as whole life costs whenever appropriate.
  ■ Review procurement processes and contract regulations (and keep them under review).
  ■ Prepare process guide in the form of a procurement manual and best practice toolkit with standard documentation and procedures to help department staff.
  ■ Ensure, in addition, that departments have access to professional advice/involvement wherever needed.
4 Development scope for *e-procurement*.
  ■ Forge links with neighbouring authorities to identify scope for collaborative procurement and establishment of local e-marketplace.
  ■ Ensure new contracts incorporate requirements for e-trading wherever possible.
  ■ Identify scope for e-tendering and e-auctions.
5 Commit to principles of *sustainability and ethical procurement* where these can be achieved within the terms of best value principles.
  ■ Develop appropriate best practice guidance with staff.
6 Simplify *business processes*.
  ■ Establish framework agreements for high-volume/low-value goods and services.
  ■ Prepare process guide in the form of a procurement manual and best practice toolkit with standard documentation and procedures to help departmental staff.
  ■ Ensure effective interfaces with other council systems and processes.
7 Improve *communications* with markets.
  ■ Publish annual procurement plan/programme of forthcoming contracts.
  ■ Identify markets that do not deliver optimum performance and seek to develop/manage them to better effect.
  ■ Identify opportunities for greater partnerships working/collaboration with suppliers/markets.
  ■ Initiate development programme with major suppliers and partners.
8 Ensure availability of appropriate *training and guidance* for all staff involved in procurement (including schools).
  ■ Undertake procurement skills gap analysis.
  ■ Develop training programme, buying in expertise as required.
  ■ Prepare procurement guidance reference manual covering principles and processes and summarised mini guide.
  ■ Prepare detailed best practice toolkit with standardized documentation.
9 The *organisation of procurement* will remain unchanged but:
  ■ Improve communications with staff and schools.
  ■ Develop feedback system for identifying lessons learnt from individual procurement exercises and sharing best practice.
  ■ Ensure clarity in all guidance issued (use plain English).
10 Ensure all suppliers are treated fairly and openly in the awarding of council contracts.
  ■ Prepare ethical code as part of procurement manual and integrate with council's code of conduct.
11 Commit to *continuous improvement* of all procurement practices and procedures.
  ■ Regularly review contracts regulations, procurement manual and toolkit.
  ■ Initiate benchmarking review of procurement and refresh biannually.
  ■ Establish and monitor key performance indicators for procurement.

Figure 2.17 **Steps in the control process**

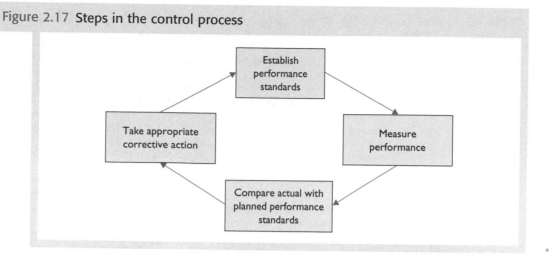

2.16 Strategic purchasing and supply chain process models

2.16.1 What are models?

Models are representations of real objects or situations. A model aeroplane, for example, is a representation of the real thing. Physical replicas are referred to as *iconic models*. Alternatively, we can have models that are physical in form but do not have the same appearance as the things that they purport to represent. These are known as *analogue models*. A thermometer, which represents temperature, is an analogue model. Today, computers are used to simulate situations and provide answers to 'What if . . . ?' questions. In general, models can be classified as:

- *mathematical* – these represent a problem by a system of symbols and mathematical relationships or expression (the formulae used in Chapter 9 are of this type)
- *non-mathematical* – these can take the form of charts, diagrams and similar visual representations that communicate information.

2.16.2 The CIPS procurement and supply management model

Much of what has been discussed in this chapter is admirably summarised in the CIPS procurement and supply management model.[38] This is a generic representation of an organisation and shows where purchasing and supply management fit into it at both strategic and operational levels. The model shows where the organisation's purchasing and supply management strategy fits in, too, what it covers and how it can be implemented. The model shows the high-level stages of purchasing and supply management activity and the key steps at each stage. The model can also be used by purchasing and supply management practitioners to explain to colleagues where their role fits into their organisation and what it covers.

The overall CIPS model is shown in Figure 2.18.

Table 2.9 Typical aspects of purchasing strategies, tactics or contributions to corporate development strategies

Aspects of strategic development	Typical purchasing strategies/tactics contributions
Generic strategy (the basis on which the organisation will compete or sustain excellence)	
Cost leadership	Lower purchase costs achieved by consolidation of purchases, single sourcing, global procurement. Reduction in costs of purchasing system and administration. Value for money spent. Logistical contributions to competitive advantage. Buying sub-assemblies in lieu of components, etc.
Differentiation	Involvement of suppliers in product design and development, value analysis, total quality management, alternative materials. Stimulation of technological developments in one supplier market, etc.
Focus	Location of specialist suppliers, make-or-buy decision for specialist components, subcontracting, outsourcing, etc.
Alternative strategy directions in which the organisation may choose to develop	
Do nothing	
Withdrawal	Running down/disposal of inventory. Negotiating contract cancellations, etc.
Consolidation	Moving to standard/generic materials/components to increase potential use. Negotiation of limited period contracts, etc.
Market penetration	Provision of information regarding competitors, price volatility, unused capacity in the supplier market. Negotiation of contracts with options for increased supply or stocking of inventory at suppliers, etc.
Product development	Liaison with design and production. Partnership sourcing; supplier appraisal. Negotiation regarding ownership of jigs and tools for bought-out items. Timing of supply deliveries. MRP II. Value engineering, etc.
Market development	Liaison with marketing. Partnership sourcing, specifying packaging and shipping instructions. Identification of vital points in the supply/value chain
Diversification	Supply considerations, such as effect on set-up costs and productions runs. Purchasing quantity considerations. Promotion of interchangeability of materials and components, etc.
Alternative methods by which any direction of development may be advanced	
Internal development	Organisational aspects of purchasing. Recruitment or development of purchasing staff. Integration of purchasing into materials management or logistics
Acquisition	Corporate level issues relating to: ■ backward integration – activities concerned with securing inputs, such as raw materials by acquisition of supplies ■ forward integration – activities concerned with securing outputs, such as acquisition of distribution channels, transport undertakings, etc. ■ horizontal integration – activities complementary to those currently undertaken, such as consortia, franchising, licensing or agency and outsourcing agreements

Figure 2.18 The CIPS procurement and supply management model

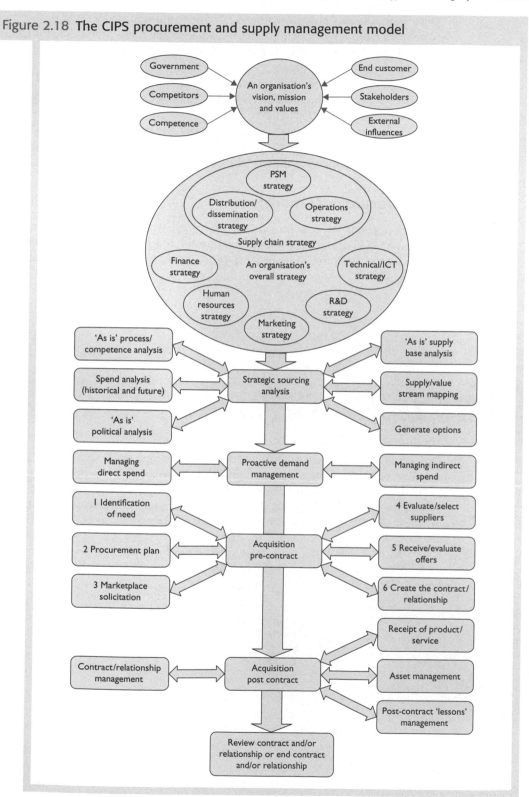

The model shows how organisational vision, mission, values and corporate strategy are derived from environmental factors, such as the government, customers, competitors, stakeholders and other external influences, and an evaluation of organisational competences.

The model also shows how purchasing strategies interface with and are related to other organisational functions/activities such as R&D, finance, marketing and technical ICT strategies.

The aspects of procurement indicated under the headings of strategic sourcing analysis, proactive demand management and acquisition pre-contract and post contract are dealt with in appropriate chapters of this book.

2.16.3 Other procurement models

Other purchasing models include the Ministry of Defence's acquisition management system (AMS), the supply chain operations reference (SCOR) and the European Federation of Quality Management (EFQM) model. All these can be accessed on the Internet.

Case study

Equipment Installations Ltd

Equipment Installations Ltd (EIL) are a UK-based company who install robotic production line equipment for specialist industries. Strategically, the company sources from ROBOCO Inc. in the United States. Deliveries from the US can take from 6 to 12 weeks depending on available production capacity. EIL quote a 26-week lead time to include for the variables indeliveries from the United States and to cover installation time. EIL are never late on commissioning the equipment. Forty per cent of sales are to Euro zone countries who insist on euro pricing. A typical installation selling for €1m would include $800,000 of equipment and £300,000 labour. With exchange rates of $1.6638/£ and €1.1025/£ the economics are as follows:

	Original currency	Exchange rate originally	Sterling equivalent
Sales	€1,000,000	1.1025	£907,029
Cost of sales			
Equipment	$800,000	1.6638	£480,827
Labour	£300,000	1	£300,000
Profit/(Loss)		13.9%	£126,202

However, only six months later the deal is not viable as can be seen in the table below:

	Original currency	Exchange rate 6 months later	Sterling equivalent
Sales	€1,000,000	1.214	£823,723
Cost of sales			
Equipment	$800,000	1.4896	£537,057
Labour	£300,000	1	£300,000
Profit/(Loss)		(1.6%)	(£13,334)

Tasks

1 Identify a strategy for each of the equipment and labour cost elements of the transaction that will mitigate the risk of loss.

2 What financial factors would you need to take into account in implementing these strategies?

3 How would you seek to overcome the problem of a variable delivery date from the US and hence an unknown exchange rate?

Discussion questions

2.1 Define 'strategy' and link the definition to a purchasing strategy within your organisation.

2.2 How do you think that a purchasing strategy can be directly linked to the organisation's strategy and long-term business plan?

2.3 If you were faced with the proposition that a purchasing strategy is irrelevant because market forces will always dictate where the balance of power is at any time, how would you explain that while market forces are at work a purchasing strategy is essential?

2.4 (a) What from the standpoint of strategic 'fit', is the relationship between (1) opportunities in the business environment and (2) resources and competencies?
   (b) What strategy(ies) might you adopt if you have recognised a good opportunity in the environment that you can't exploit because of lack of resources?

2.5 Prepare simple diagrams of vertical and horizontal integration for:
   (a) food production
   (b) book production.

2.6 Thinking about the organisation in which you are employed or have knowledge of, list up to three examples under each of the following headings:
   – key strengths
   – key weaknesses
   – key opportunities
   – key threats.

2.7 If a strategic supplier to an organisation encounters any of the following what impact will it have on a purchasing strategy?
   – taken over by a competitor
   – closes a major manufacturing plant in the UK and transfers production to the Far East
   – goes into administration
   – announces it will cease supplying goods within the next three months because they are not profitable.

2.8 Choo points out that organisations engage in environmental scanning to understand the forces of change. What should purchasing departments undertake to ensure they monitor in supply markets to understand the forces of change?

2.9 Macro-environmental factors impact on purchasing strategies. Using the PESTEL approach what steps should a purchasing operation take to ensure it monitors the legal impact on its strategies?

2.10 Could you recommend a formal approach to risk management in a purchasing context? When you put your thoughts together, consider:
   – short-term risks
   – long-term risks
   – supply market risks
   – own business generated risks.

2.11 In Kraljic's purchasing portfolio, under which headings 'leverage', 'routine' and 'bottleneck' would you place the following items?
   (a) chemical supplies for glass manufacture
   (b) steel
   (c) cleaning materials
   (d) security services
   (e) bottling equipment for a brewery.

2.12 Your sales director has said that your products are now uncompetitive in world markets and a cost reduction of 20 per cent is required on purchased goods and services. The existing purchasing strategy is such that only European suppliers are used. How would you approach the existing strategy and formulate an alternative?

Past examination questions

1 (a) Describe **two** key risks which a procurement function may face in the current economic climate.
  (b) Outline an appropriate action which could be taken to reduce these risks.
                    CIPS, *An Introduction to Purchasing Strategy*, May 2010

2 Describe **five** problems that an organisation which is said to have 'monopoly power' causes for a buyer in that market.
                    CIPS, *The Business Environment for Purchasing and Supply*, November 2007

3 (a) Explain how each of the following factors may affect an organisation:
    (i) economic factors
    (ii) political factors
    (iii) technological factors
    (iv) social factors.

(b) Outline **three** ways in which environmental or 'green' pressure groups seek influence government policy.

CIPS, *Analysing the Supplier Market*, May 2009

4 The 'Supply Positioning Model' (Kraljic Matrix) is often quoted and used in order to analyse the purchases of an organisation.
   (a) Construct and label the 'Supply Positioning Model Diagram'.
   (b) Explain **two** ways in which this type of analysis might help an organisation.
   (c) Describe **two** actions that are typically taken regarding purchasing strategy as a result of this type of analysis.

CIPS, *Introduction to Purchasing Strategy*, May 2009

References

1 Liedtka, J. M., 'Strategic thinking; can it be taught?', *Long Range Planning*, Vol. 31 (1), 1998, pp. 120–9

2 Lawrence, E., 'Strategic thinking', paper prepared for the Research Directorate Public Service Commission of Canada, 27 April, 1999

3 Mintzberg, H., 'Five Ps for strategy' in Mintzberg, H., Lampel, J., Quinn, J. G. and Ghoshal, S. *The Strategy Process*, Prentice Hall, 2003, pp. 3–10

4 As 3 above, p. 9

5 Johnson, G. and Scholes, K., *Exploring Corporate Strategy*, 6th edn, Prentice Hall, 2002, pp. 4–10

6 Mintzberg, H., Ahlstrand, B. and Lampel, J., *Strategy Safari*, Prentice Hall, 1998, pp. 1–21

7 As 2 above

8 Fahey, L. and Prusak, L., 'The eleven deadliest sins of knowledge management', *California Management Review*, Vol. 40, spring, 1998

9 Lindblom, C., *The Intelligence of Democracy*: *Decision Making Through Mutual Adjustment*, Free Press, 1965

10 Waterman, R. H., *The Renewal Factor*, Bantam Books, 1987

11 Mintzberg, H., 'Crafting Strategy' in Mintzberg *et al.*, as 3 above, p. 147

12 David, F. R., *Concepts of Strategic Management*, Macmillan, 1991, p. 4

13 Hax, A. C. and Majluf, N. S., *The Strategy Concept and Process*, Prentice Hall, 1999, p. 416

14 Porter, M., *Competitive Strategy: Techniques for Analysing, Industries and Competitors*, Macmillan, 1980

15 Miles, R. E. and Snow, C. C., *Organisational Strategy, Structure and Process*, McGraw-Hill, 1978

16 Carr, A. S. and Smeltzer, L. R., 'An empirically based definition of strategic purchasing', *European Journal of Purchasing and Supply Management*, Vol. 3, 1997, pp. 199–207

17 Kraljic, P., 'Purchasing must become supply management', *Harvard Business Review*, Sept/Oct, 1983, p. 110

18 Worral, L., 'Strategic analysis: a scientific art', Occasional paper No. OP001/98, University of Wolverhampton, 27 May, 1998

19 Brown, A. and Weiner, E., *Supermanaging: How to Harness Change for Personal and Organisational Success*, Mentor Books, 1985, p. ix

20 Choo, C. W., 'Environmental scanning as information seeking and organisational learning', *Information Research*, Vol. 7, No. 1, October, 2001

21 Downes, L., 'Beyond Porter' in *Context Magazine*, available at: www.contextmag.com/archives/199712/technosynthesis.asp

22 ICMA, *Management Accounting 2000: Official Terminology*: www.icmacentre.ac.uk

23 As 2 above

24 As 6 above, p. 124

25 Campbell, A. and Yeung, S., 'Creating a sense of mission' in De-luit, B. and Meyer, R., *Strategy: Process, Content, Context*, West Publishing, 1994, pp. 153–4

26 As 16 above

27 Rumelt, R. P., 'Evaluating business strategy' in Mintzberg *et al.*, as 3 above, p. 81

28 Cyert, K. and March, J., *Behavioural Theory of the Firm*, Prentice Hall, 1963

29 As 17 above, pp. 109–17

30 Fisher, L., *Industrial Marketing: An Analytical Approach to Planning and Execution*, Brandon Systems Press, 1970

31 Nellove, R. and Söderquist, K., 'Portfolio approaches to procurement', *Long Range Planning*, Vol. 33, 2000, pp. 245–67

32 Gelderman, C. J. and van Weele, A. J., 'Strategic direction through purchasing portfolio management: a case study', *International Journal of Supply Chain Management*, Vol. 38, spring, 2002, pp. 30–8

33 Bensaou, M., 'Portfolio of buyer–supplier relationships', *Sloan Management Review*, summer, 1999, pp. 35–44

34 Kamann, D. and Jan, F., 'Extra dimensions to portfolio analysis', paper presented at the IPSERA meeting London, Ontario, Canada, 1999

35 This figure is reproduced by kind permission of Rob Atkins and the Bracknell Forest (UK) Borough Council

36 Spekman, R. E., 'A strategic approach to procurement planning', *Journal of Purchasing and Supply Management*, spring, 1989, pp. 3–9

37 Johnson, G. and Scholes, K., *Exploring Corporate Strategy Text and Cases*, 3rd edn, Prentice Hall, 1993, pp. 203–43

38 CIPS, procurement and supply management model. Full details of this model are shown on the CIPS website: www.cips.org

Chapter 3

Logistics and supply chains

Learning outcomes

This chapter aims to provide an understanding of:

- the origin and scope of logistics and impact on a business
- materials logistics and distribution management
- reverse logistics
- supply chains and supply chain management (SCM)
- supply chain vulnerability
- value chains
- value chain analysis
- supply chain optimisation
- supply chains and their relationship to modern purchasing.

Key ideas

- Military and non-military logistics to support operations at optimum cost.
- The scope of materials and physical distribution management (MM and PDM).
- Total systems management, trade-offs, cooperative planning and manufacturing techniques as important logistics concepts.
- Reverse logistics to deliver value from waste and recycling.
- Networks, linkages, processes, value and the ultimate 'customer' as key supply chain characteristics.
- Infrastructure, technology, strategic alliances, software and human resource management (HRM) as key supply chain enablers.
- External and internal supply chain risks.
- Porter's value chain model.
- Hines's value chain model.
- Cost and differentiation as a means to competitive advantage.
- Objectives and factors in supply chain optimisation.
- The influence of the supply chain concept on traditional purchasing practices and the need for partnering behaviour.

Introduction

Purchasing is increasingly considered within the wider context of supply chains. Logistics, however, is a much older term. It is therefore appropriate that the present chapter should begin with a consideration of logistics.

We next define the terms 'supply chain' and 'supply chain management' (SCM) and identify some types of supply chains, the processes that comprise supply chain management and the enablers via which SCM is implemented. An aspect of SCM that has only recently received serious attention is supply chain vulnerability.

The chapter ends with a consideration of supply chain optimisation, the impact of SCM on traditional purchasing and some contributions of purchasing to the supply chain management field.

3.1 What is logistics?

3.1.1 Military logistics

The supply chain approach developed from logistics. Logistics, initially a military term dating from the Napoleonic Wars, refers to the technique of moving and quartering armies – that is, quartermasters' work. The scope of logistics in a military sense is reflected in the definition adopted by NATO:[1]

The science of planning and carrying out the movement and maintenance of forces. In its most comprehensive sense the aspects of military operations which deal with:

(a) design and development, acquisition, storage, transport, distribution, maintenance, evacuation and disposition of materiel (materiel: equipment in its widest sense including vehicles, weapons, ammunition, fuel, etc.);

(b) transport of personnel;

(c) acquisition of construction, maintenance, operation and disposition of facilities;

(d) acquisition or furnishing of services; and

(e) medical and health service support.

NATO also distinguishes between two important aspects of logistics: acquisition logistics and operational logistics (Figure 3.1).

The importance of military logistics is apparent from a consideration of the enormous problems relating to the supply of the Allied forces involved in the D-Day invasion of Europe in the Second World War, the Falklands War of 1982 or the invasion of Iraq in 2003.

3.1.2 Non-military applications of logistics

Non-military applications of logistics, although generally less complicated, still cover the same ground, as indicated by the following definitions:

Logistics is the total management of the key operational functions in the supply chain – procurement, production and distribution. Procurement includes purchasing and product development. The production function includes manufacturing and assembling, while the distribution function involves warehousing, inventory, transport and delivery.[2]

Logistics is the process of managing both the movement and storage of goods and materials from the source to the point of ultimate consumption and the associated information flow.[3]

Figure 3.1 The scope of military logistics

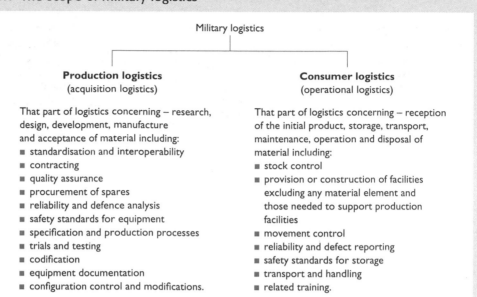

Source: NATO, *Logistics Handbook*, 1997, paragraph 104

Logistics is that part of the supply chain process that plans, implements and controls the efficient, effective flow and storage of goods, services and related information from the point of origin to the point of consumption in order to meet the customers' requirements.[4]

3.2 Materials, logistics and distribution management

As shown in Figure 3.2, logistics is comprised of both materials management and physical distribution management.

3.2.1 Materials management

Materials management (MM) is concerned with the flow of materials to and from production or manufacturing and has been defined as:[5]

> The planning, organisation and control of all aspects of inventory embracing procurement, warehousing, work-in-progress and distribution of finished goods.

Some aspects of MM that may be included under the heading 'Materials flow' are listed in Table 3.1.

The factors influencing the activities assigned to MM include the following:

- purchasing is frequently the 'key' activity
- production planning and control may be assigned to MM or the manufacturing function where this is separate – the former tends to apply when production is materials orientated, such as in an assembly factory; the latter when production is machine/process orientated.

Figure 3.2 Scope of logistics management

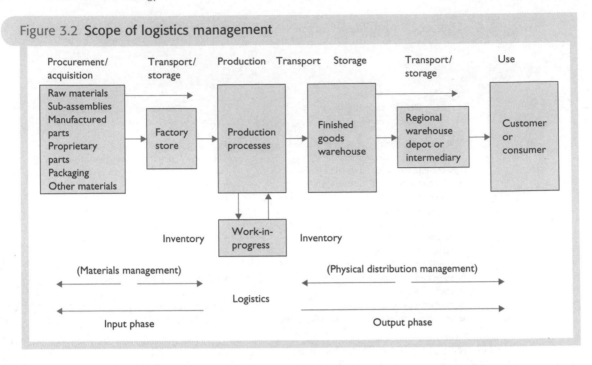

Table 3.1 Materials flow activities

Materials flow	Typical activities
Planning	Preparation of materials budgets, product research and development, value engineering and analysis, standardisation of specifications
Procurement	Determining order quantities, processing works and stores requisitions, issuing enquiries, evaluating quotations, supplier appraisal, negotiation, placing contracts, progressing deliveries, certifying payments, vendor rating, supplier and contract management
Storage	Stores location, layout and equipment, mechanical handling, stores classification, coding and cataloguing, receipt of purchased items, inspection, storage or return, stock and store safety and security, stock integrity and rotation, stores environment management, issuing to production, providing cost data, stock records and verification, recycling or disposal of obsolete, surplus or scrap material
Production control	Forward ordering arrangements for materials, preparing production schedules and sequences, issuing orders to production, emergency action to meet material shortages, make-or-buy decisions, quality and reliability feedback and adjustment of supplies flow to production line or sales trend

3.2.2 Physical distribution management

Physical distribution management (PDM) is often considered to be concerned with the flow of goods from the receipt of an order until the goods are delivered to the customer. An alternative view, adopted in this text, is that, whereas MM is concerned with the *input* phase of moving bought-out items, such as raw materials and components from suppliers, to production, PDM relates to the *output* phase of moving finished goods from production departments to finished goods stores and then through appropriate channels of distribution to the ultimate consumer.

The main activities associated with PDM are inventory control, warehousing and storage, materials handling, protective packaging and containerisation and transportation. Developments such as just-in-time (JIT), where both producers and distributors carry a few hours' stock and rely on their suppliers to meet their production or sales requirements, have greatly enhanced the importance of PDM.

The perspective of the logistician is that 'what flows can be made to flow faster'. From this standpoint, the logistician studies the costs incurred by the enterprise, beginning with the initial input factor, time spent on the production process and terminating when the customer pays for the product or service received. The longer the time spent at each stage of the process, the higher the costs incurred. A reduction in the time taken at any stage will provide an opportunity for cost reduction, which can, in turn, lead to a reduction in price. Alternatively, where products are built to order, a shorter lead time, can also allow a provider to raise prices for the time sensitive customers.

3.2.3 Some important logistics concepts

Total systems management

Total systems management emphasises a total rather than a limited departmental viewpoint. Total systems management has been facilitated by the availability of IT. Functions or groups of processes or activities with a total system may be regarded as subsystems.

Trade-offs

A trade-off is where an increased cost in one area is more than offset by a cost reduction in another, so that the whole system benefits. This may give rise to interdepartmental conflicts owing to different objectives. Also known as sub-optimisation as the organisation's optimal outcome can be achieved by departments sacrificing or reducing some of their individual goals. Thus, purchasing may advocate bulk purchases of materials to secure larger supplier discounts. This policy might be opposed by finance because of money tied up in working capital and in inventory because of the increased cost of warehousing. Conflicts should be settled on the basis of which policy yields the greatest trade-off. Similarly, purchasing may have to consider whether or not the security of supply consequent on having a number of suppliers is offset by the economies resulting from single-source buying. Thus, the effects of trade-offs may be assessed according to their impact on total systems costs and sales revenue. Higher inventory costs, for example, may result from increased stocks, yet quicker delivery may increase total sales revenue. Obtaining information for computerised exchange requires the breaking down of functional barriers that protect departmental 'territory' and discourage information sharing.

Cooperative planning

This can work forwards to customers and backwards to suppliers. The change from product-orientated to customer-orientated supply chains and, thus, faster supply resources, can provide customers with alternatives such as make to stock, make to order and finish to order. Conversely, from the inward supply side, effective, cooperative planning may relate to zero defects, on-time delivery, shared products and information exchanges relating to such matters as shared specifications, design support, multiyear commitments and technology exchange. Overall, both suppliers and customers can benefit from reduced costs of inventory, capacity, order handling and administration. Cooperative planning utilises, as appropriate, manufacturing and scheduling techniques, including the following:

- *Manufacturing techniques*
  - computer-aided design (CAD)
  - computer integrated manufacture (CIM)
  - flexible manufacturing systems (FMS)
  - materials requirement planning (MRP)
  - manufacturing resources planning (MRP II)
  - optimised production technology (OPT)
  - strategic lead time management (STM)
- *Scheduling techniques*
  - just-in-time (JIT)
  - materials requirement planning (MRP)
  - manufacturing resources planning (MRP II)
  - enterprise resource planning (ERP).

This can be explained by the cost–value curve shown in Figure 3.3.

1 The lowest cost value is at the procurement stage when supplies are purchased.
2 During transportation of supplies, value remains low because little capital is invested until raw materials and components enter production – the only costs incurred relate to acquisition and holding.
3 The curve becomes steeper as raw materials and components are gradually incorporated into the final product. This is because of accumulated manufacturing costs and increasing interest costs that reflect the value of capital invested.

Figure 3.3 **The added value aspect of logistics**

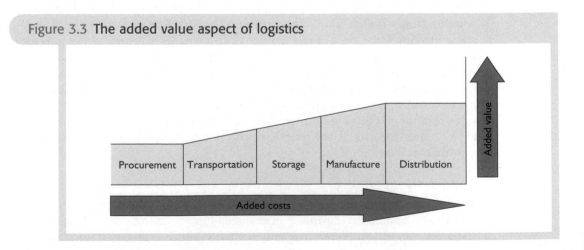

Figure 3.4 **Materials, products and information flows across an organisation**

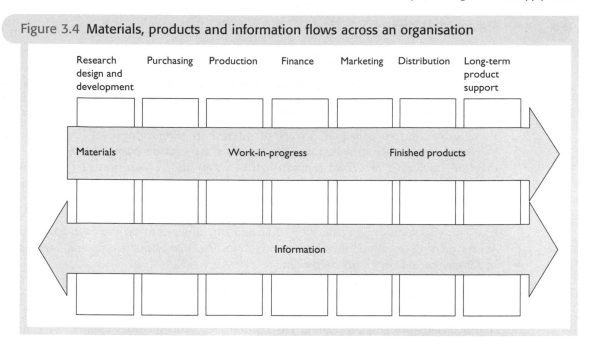

4 The curve becomes flatter (but not flat) at the end of the production process because no more manufacturing costs apply. The value added in distributing must exceed its cost at the macro level otherwise the manufacturer would supply an ex-works product. However, on an item basis they may choose to add a figure for distribution that is less than its unit cost. This increased value may be seen in the form of greater total sales. At this stage the invested capital is at its highest value and the cost of stocking finished goods instead of selling them involves higher opportunity costs than holding the initial supplies. This shows why the logistician is, if anything, more concerned with PDM than MM as the potential for cost reduction is the highest at this point of the total supply chain. Cost reduction by speeding flows of materials, work-in-progress and finished products is not the only concern of the logistician. Logistics management involves two flows. The first, as stated above, is the flow of materials and work-in-progress across the organisation to the ultimate customer. The second, as shown in Figure 3.4, is a reverse flow of information, in the form of orders or other indicators on which future demand forecasts can be based. Such forecasts, as Gattorna stated, can in turn 'trigger replenishment orders which produce inventories at distribution centres. These orders influence production schedules which, in turn, help to determine the timing and quantities with which raw materials are procured.'

Logistics management may be regarded as a subsystem of the larger enterprise or a system of which purchasing, manufacturing, storage and transportation are sub-systems. In essence, logistics is a way of thinking about planning and synchronising related activities. Figure 3.4 also shows how logistics management crosses conventional functions.

3.3 Reverse logistics

Reverse logistics may be defined as:[6]

> The process of planning, implementing and controlling the efficient, cost-effective flow of raw materials, in process inventory, finished goods and related information from the point of consumption to the point of origin for the purpose of recapturing value or proper disposal.

Previously, the two principal drivers of interest in reverse logistics have been the increased importance attached to environmental aspects of waste management and disposal (including perceived reputational benefits) and recognition of the potential return that can be obtained from the reuse of products or parts or the recycling of materials. However, with the legislative pressures such as the Waste Electrical and Electronic Equipment (WEEE) Directive together with EU council directive on landfill of waste[7] (EU Council Directive 99/31/EC) and amendments to the Packaging Directives are mandating certain actions and raising costs. As a consequence reverse logistics is becoming an industry in its own right.

Figure 3.5 shows that the main reverse logistics activities include collection of returnable items, their inspection and separation and the application of a range of disposition options, including repair, reconditioning, upgrading, remanufacture, demanufacture (parts reclamation) and recycling. Disposition logic also includes channel or routing logic – that is, the returned items and components can be sent back to the customer, routed to a warehouse or production or sold in secondary markets.

Increasingly, focus is on designing out waste, via lean processes and six sigma methodologies and designing in recyclable technologies while an advanced reverse logistic infrastructure is also being developed. The emergence of Smart Materials, that aid disassembly when returned to manufacturers or salvagers.

Figure 3.5 Reverse logistics network

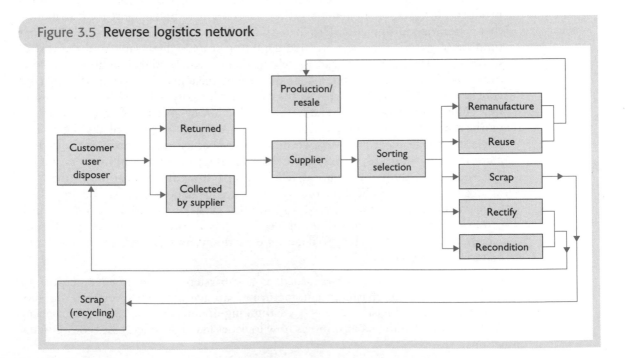

In line with the principle of the polluter pays, the automotive world is working towards total recyclability. The Think City is an all electric vehicle, 95 per cent of which is recyclable. Mercedes have already produced a 100 per cent recyclable concept vehicle. Software providers are also encompassing reverse logistics management modules within their solutions.

3.4 Supply chains

3.4.1 Definitions

There are many definitions of the term 'supply chain', of which the following is typical:[8]

> A supply chain is that network of organisations that are involved, through upstream and downstream linkages, in the different processes and activities that produce value in the form of products and services in the hands of the ultimate customer or consumer.

The above definition emphasises the following key characteristics of supply chains:

- *Supply chains are 'networks'* – traditionally, supply chains were loosely linked associations of discrete businesses. The network concept implies some coordination of 'cow to customer' processes and relationships. An alternative definition is that a supply chain is:

  > A network of connected and interdependent organisations mutually and cooperatively working together to control, manage and improve the flow of materials and information from suppliers to end users.[9]

  Networks are further considered in section 4.3.

- *Supply chain linkages are upstream and downstream* – *upstream* means 'against the current' and relates to the relationships between an enterprise and its suppliers and suppliers' suppliers. *Downstream* is 'with the current' and relates to the relationship between an enterprise and its customers. There can also be *upstream–downstream*, as is the case with organisations that have returnable containers, pallets, drums and so on or trade-in products.

- *Linkages* – the coordination of supply chain processes and relationships. A supply chain is only as strong as its weakest link.

- *Processes* – in the context of a business, a process is defined by Cooper *et al.*[10] as:

  > A specific ordering of work activities across a time and place with a beginning and an end and clearly identified inputs and outputs, a structure of action.

From a purchasing standpoint, the processes that comprise the supply chain are shown in Figure 3.6. From a supplier's standpoint the processes are shown in Figure 3.7.

Figure 3.6 Supplier chain processes from a purchasing perspective

Search	Acquire	Use	Maintain	Dispose

Figure 3.7 Supply chain processes from a supplier's perspective

Research	Design	Manufacture or provide	Sell	Service

- *Value* is defined by Porter[11] as 'what buyers are willing to pay'. Superior value stems from offering lower prices for equivalent benefits or providing unique benefits that more than offset a higher price.
- *The ultimate customer* – a customer is simply the recipient of the goods or services that result from all the processes and activities of the supply chain. A function or subsystem can be the customer of the preceding or succeeding link in a supply chain.

Customers may be either internal or external. The definition refers to the 'ultimate customer or consumer' so that the supply chain may extend beyond the customer from whom the direct order for goods or services emanates.

3.4.2 Types of supply chains

Supply chains can be classified in numerous ways. An organisation such as a food retailer will have many types of supply chains reflecting differences in products, services, production and distribution methods, customer–supplier relationships and information flows. Supply chains may be roughly classified according to four customer–supplier characteristics and also in relation to virtuality, scope, service, complexity, products, purpose and value.

Customer–supplier characteristics

These may give rise to:

- *concentrated chains* found in businesses such as the automotive industry that have:
  - few customers but many suppliers
  - customers with demanding requirements
  - EDI systems or a requirement for JIT deliveries.
- *batch manufacture chains* that have:
  - many customers and many suppliers
  - complicated relationship webs – an undertaking with which an enterprise is in contact may, at different times, be a customer, supplier, competitor or ally.
- *retail and distribution chains* that have:
  - many customers but relatively few suppliers
  - customised methods, such as vendor-managed inventory (VMI) of facilitating dealings with suppliers.
- *service chains* that implement the mission statements of organisations such as hospitals, libraries and banks concerned with the delivery of services, books, information and financial services or restaurants and cinemas delivering food and entertainment, for example – essentially service chains are not different from manufacturing chains as every service involves people, something physical (an asset or part of something performed), an action and a time element.

Other characteristics

- *Virtuality* – virtual is the opposite of real. Thus, a 'virtual' enterprise is the counterpart of a real, tangible business. As Christopher[12] states, 'a virtual supply chain is, in effect, a series of relationships between partners that is based upon the value-added exchanges of information'. In a virtual supply chain, information replaces the need for inventories. A mail-order business may have no inventory and simply call for supplies from the manufacturer when orders are received from customers.

- *Scope* – supply chains may be local, regional and international in scope. Some suppliers of gas, such as BP, for example, have the ability to put together delivery chains to bring gas supplies from Trinidad to Spain, from Siberia to China and from North Africa to Southern Europe.

- *Complexity* – Mentzer *et al.*[13] identify three degrees of supply chain complexity: 'direct', 'extended' and 'ultimate'. A *direct* supply chain, as shown in Figure 3.8, comprises a company or supplier and a customer involved in the upstream and/or downstream flow of products, services, finances and information.

Figure 3.8 Direct supply chain

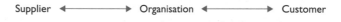

An *extended* supply chain, as shown in Figure 3.9, includes suppliers of the immediate supplier and customers of the immediate customer.

Figure 3.9 Extended supply chain

An *ultimate* supply chain, as shown in Figure 3.10, includes all the organisations involved in all the upstream and downstream flows of products, services, finances and information from the ultimate supplier to the ultimate customer.

Figure 3.10 Ultimate supply chain

- *Purpose* – a distinction can be made between *efficient* and *responsive* supply chains. *Efficient* supply chains are primarily concerned with reducing the cost of operations, as in lean supply chains. These work best when forecast accuracy is high and product variety low. *Responsive* supply chains are primarily concerned with minimising the delivery cycle time, as in agile supply chains. These work best when forecast accuracy is low and product variety high.

- *Products* – supply chains vary widely according to the end product. Examples are build-to-forecast and build-to-order supply chains and ones for innovative and functional products (see section 4.3.2).

- *Value chains* – these are dealt with later in the present chapter.

3.5 Supply chain management (SCM)

There is no universally agreed definition of SCM but one is given in section 3.7 below. Mentzer *et al.*[14] state that the many published definitions can be classified into three categories – a management philosophy, implementation of a management philosophy and a set of management processes.

SCM as a management philosophy

Mentzer *et al.* suggest that, as a management philosophy, SCM has the following three characteristics:

- a systems approach to viewing the supply chain as a whole and managing the total flow of goods inventory from the supplier to the ultimate consumers

- a strategic orientation towards cooperative efforts to synchronise and converge intra-firm and interfirm operational and strategic capabilities into a unified whole

- a customer focus to create unique and individualised sources of customer value, leading to customer satisfaction.

SCM as a set of activities to implement a management philosophy

The seven activities listed below as essential to the implementation of a management philosophy are:

- integrated behaviour
- mutually shared information
- mutually shared risks and rewards
- cooperation
- the same goal and same focus on serving customers
- integration of processes
- partners to build and maintain long-term relationships.

These activities are implied in the following list of SCM objectives:

- the integration of both internal and external competencies
- the building of alliances, relationships and trust throughout the supply system
- the reduction of costs and improvement of profit margins
- the maximisation of return on assets (net income after expenses/interests)

Figure 3.11 **Supply chain management: integrating and managing business processes across the supply chain**

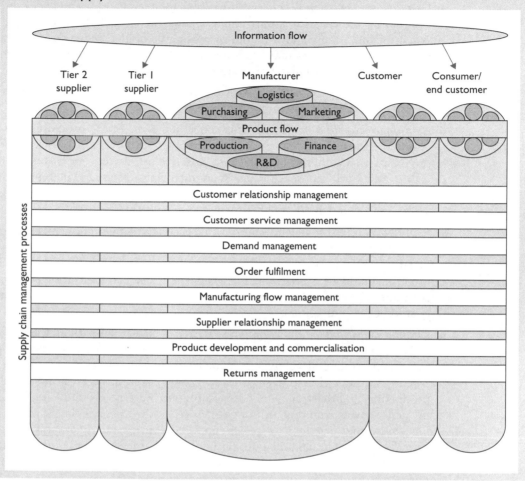

- the facilitation of innovation and the synchronisation of supply chain processes
- the optimisation of the delivery of products, services, information and finance both upstream and downstream and across internal and external boundaries.

SCM as a set of management processes

As shown by Figure 3.11, Lambert *et al.*[15] list eight SCM processes originally postulated by the International Centre for Competitive Excellence.

Each of these eight processes is briefly described below

- *Customer relationship management (CRM)* is concerned with learning about customers' needs and behaviour and the integration of sales, marketing and service strategies. CRM software, as Kalakota[16] states, 'helps organisations to manage their customer relationships better by tracking down customer interactions of all types'.
- *Customer service management (CSM)* is concerned with providing internal and external customers with high-quality goods and services, at the lowest cost, with the

shortest waiting times and maximum responsiveness and flexibility to their needs. This is clearly aligned with efficient customer response (ECR).

■ *Demand management* is concerned with balancing the requirements of internal and external customers with supply chain capabilities. It includes forecasting demand, synchronising supply and demand, increasing flexibility, reducing the variability of demand by means of standardisation and the control of inventory, for example. This is closely aligned with materials requirements planning (MRP) and JIT.

■ *Order fulfilment* is concerned with the fulfilment of customers' orders efficiently, effectively and at the minimum total cost.

■ *Manufacturing flow management* is concerned with all the processes and activities required to transform inputs and a variety of resources into finished goods and services. Order fulfillment is therefore closely aligned with operations management (OM) and such approaches as manufacturing resources planning (MRP II), manufacturing execution systems (MES) and quick response manufacturing (QRM). These approaches are described in most texts on OM.

■ *Supplier relationship management (SRM)* is concerned with how an enterprise interacts with its suppliers and, therefore, is the mirror image of CRM. Relationships may be either short-term or long-term and vary in intensity from 'arm's length' to high involvement. SRM is becoming increasingly critical as organisations concentrate on core competencies and rely on suppliers to maintain critical advantage or a superior position over competitors.

■ *Product development and commercialisation* is concerned with all the processes and activities involved in the development and marketing of new or existing products. In general, product development involves four main phases. First, idea generation, second, concept development, third, product and process design and, fourth, production and delivery. Marketing can contribute to product development (PD) in such ways as trial tests in limited markets or with customer panels to ascertain likely customer reactions to specific product features. SCM is involved because PD extends across internal and external boundaries. Internally, PD involves teamwork between marketing, design, purchasing, production, quality engineering and transportation. Externally, the uncertainties of supply and demand, shorter lifecycles, faster rates of technological change and the increased use of manufacturing, distribution and logistics partners has resulted in increasingly complicated supply chain networks. Some advanced companies have begun to transfer design responsibility upstream to the supplier base. Thus, Exostar, founded by BAE Systems, Lockhead Martin, Raytheon and Boeing, is designed to improve collaboration across the aerospace industry. Exostar, covering more than 37,000 suppliers worldwide, offers services that will allow trading partners and suppliers to collaborate on design, products and programmes that aim to provide customers with better products in a shorter timeframe.

■ *Returns management* is concerned with the activities indicated in section 3.3 relating to reverse logistics. Alternative terms such as 'green logistics', 'end of chain management' and 'post-consumer logistics' emphasise the importance of environmental factors, both in product design and SCM. Returns management has extended the supply chain to beyond the end consumer. It also extends relationships beyond customers and suppliers to include cooperation with agencies such as local authority and private waste collection, recycling and disposal.

3.5.1 SCM enablers

Research by Marien[17] identified four key enablers, all of which must be fully leveraged if SCM is to be successful. Marien also observed that these four enablers become barriers to effective SCM if they are not in place. Each of the four enablers also has its own set of attributes. The four enablers and their relative rankings by Marien's respondents are:

- organisational infrastrucuture   3.44 (4 = highest importance)
- technology   2.14
- strategic alliances   2.07
- human resource management   2.05

Organisational infrastructure

How business units and functional areas are organised, how change management programmes are led and coordinated with the existing organisational structure – these constitute organisational infrastructure. Important attributes of organisational infrastructure include:

- having a coherent business strategy that aligns business units towards the same goal
- having a formal process – flow methodologies to enable SCM improvements
- having the right process metrics to guide the performance of operating units towards the strategic organisational SCM objectives.

It is of interest that respondents ranked organisational infrastructure considerably ahead of technology.

Technology

The word 'technology' (not just IT but also the 'physical' materials management technologies for material design operations and materials handling) here also is a factor in the selection of business allies and how intercompany relationships are built and managed. Important attributes of technology include:

- having operations, marketing and logistics data coordinated within the company
- having data readily available to managers and the coordination of operations, marketing and logistics data between supply chain members.

Strategic alliances

This factor covers how external companies (customers, suppliers and logistics-service providers) are selected as business allies and how intercompany relationships are built and managed. Important attributes of strategic alliances include:

- having expectations clearly stated, understood and agreed to upfront
- collaboration on supply chain design and product and service strategies
- having top management of partnering companies interface on a regular basis
- having compatible IT systems.

Human resource management

This area involves managing how job descriptions are designed, positions filled, people are recognised and compensated and career paths directed. Important aspects of human resource management include:

- sourcing, hiring and selecting skilled people at all management levels
- finding change agents to manage SCM implementation
- having compensation and incentive programmes in place for SCM performance
- finding internal process facilitators knowledgeable about SCM.

3.5.2 Software as an SCM enabler

Four essential supply chain requirements are connectivity, integration, visibility and responsiveness.

Connectivity is the ability to exchange information with external supply chain partners in a timely, responsible and usable format that facilitates interorganisational collaboration.

Integration is the process of combining or coordinating separate functions, processors or producers and enabling them to interact in a seamless manner.

Visibility is the ability to access or view pertinent data or information as it relates to logistics and the supply chain.

Responsiveness is the ability to react quickly to customers' needs or specifications by delivering a product of the right quality, at the right time, in the right place, at the lowest possible cost. System availability is 24/7.

Initially, software providers specialised in either management planning or execution applications, as shown in Figure 3.12.

The current emphasis is on the creation of software that integrates each of the software types shown in Figure 3.12 and deals with the supply chain as a continuous process rather than as individual stages. Thus, enterprise resource management (ERP) may be defined as:

> A software solution that addresses the enterprise's needs, taking the process view of an organisation to meet the organisational goals by tightly integrating all functions of an enterprise.

The core ERP subsystems are sales and marketing master scheduling, materials requirements planning (MRP), capacity requirements planning (CRP), bills of materials, purchasing, shopfloor control, accounts payable and receivable and logistics.

Leading ERP vendors have either purchased or partnered with advanced planning and scheduling (APS) vendors and have developed Internet versions of their supply chain offerings. Internet supply chains cause the walls between internal and external supply chains to break down. Enterprise application integration (EAI) enables providers

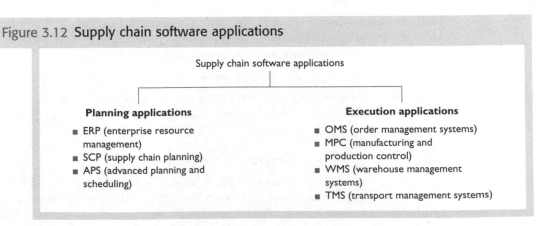

Figure 3.12 Supply chain software applications

Supply chain software applications

Planning applications
- ERP (enterprise resource management)
- SCP (supply chain planning)
- APS (advanced planning and scheduling)

Execution applications
- OMS (order management systems)
- MPC (manufacturing and production control)
- WMS (warehouse management systems)
- TMS (transport management systems)

to convert their entire suites of enterprise applications into e-business applications and provide a framework that ties businesses electronically to their customers, suppliers, electronic trading communities and business partners. Such suites offer several advantages, including that:

- an integrated suite presents a single view to the user from screen to screen and information is stored in a single database and the rekeying of information from one system into another is eliminated
- a single database provides a tighter integration of business processes
- maintenance is cheaper and upgrades easier when there is only one system to upgrade and one supplier to deal with
- for the above reasons, connectivity, integration, visibility and responsiveness are essential attributes of supply chain software.

3.6 Supply chain vulnerability

Supply chains are vulnerable due to both external and internal risks.

External risks are those attributed to environmental, economic, political and social causes, such as storms, earthquakes, terrorism, strikes, wars, embargoes and computer viruses.

Internal risks are those attributable to interactions between organisations in the supply chain. A Cranfield University report[18] identifies five categories of supply chain risk:

- *Lack of ownership* due to the blurring of boundaries between buying and supplying organisations arising from factors such as outsourcing and the creation of complicated networks of business relationships with confused lines of responsibilities.
- *Chaos risks* due to mistrust and distorted information throughout the supply chain. An example is the so-called 'bullwhip' effect, in which fluctuations in orders increase as they move upstream from retailers to manufacturers to suppliers.
- *Decision risks* due to chaos that makes it impossible to make the right decision for every player in the supply chain.
- *JIT relationship risks* due to the fact that an enterprise has little capacity or stock in reserve to cater for disruptions in the supply chain due to late deliveries, such as transport breakdowns.
- *Inertia risks* due to a general lack of responsiveness by customers or suppliers to changing environmental conditions and market signals with consequential inability to react to competition moves or market opportunities.

To the above may be added:

- *supplier base reduction*, especially single sourcing in which an enterprise is dependent on one supplier
- *globalisation* in which advantages of sourcing abroad may be offset by extended lead times, transport difficulties and political events
- *acquisitions, mergers and similar alliances* that may reduce supply chain availability.

The Cranfield report observes that 'supply chain risk management starts with the identification and assessment of likely risks and their possible impact on operations'.

To assess risk exposure, the company must identify not only direct risks to its operations, such as the loss of critical raw materials or process capability, but also the potential causes of those risks at every significant link along the supply chain.

The report also lists ten ways in which to manage supply chain risk. The first three of these measures run counter to current supply chain trends:

- *diversification* – multiple sourcing
- *stockpiling* – use of inventory as a buffer against all eventualities
- *redundancy* – maintaining excess production, storage, handling and transport capacity
- *insurance* – against losses caused by supply chain disruption
- *supplier selection* – more careful assessment of supplier capability and risks of dealing with particular suppliers
- *supplier development* – working closely with suppliers, sharing information and collaboration initiatives
- *contractual obligation* – imposing legal obligations with stiff penalties for non-delivery
- *collaborative initiatives* – spreading risk among grouped companies on an ad hoc basis or as part of a trade association
- *rationalisation of the product range* – companies, particularly distributors, may wish to exclude products with supply problems from their product ranges
- *localised sourcing* – reduction of risks arising from congested transport networks or intermodal transport transfer by shortening transport distances.

3.7 SCM and logistics

Some writers regard SCM and logistics as practically synonymous. Others, however, distinguish between them. Cooper[19] regards logistics as concerned with material and material flows and SCM as the integration of all business processes across the supply chain.

The relationship between SCM and logistics is well summarised by the UK Institute of Logistics and Transport:[20]

> The management of logistics makes possible the optimised flow and positioning of goods, materials, information and all resources of an enterprise.
>
> The supply chain is the flow of materials through procurement, manufacture, distribution, sales and disposal, together with the associated transport and storage.

The application of logistics is essential to the efficient management of the supply chain.

3.8 Value chains

Supply chains and value chains are synonymous. A value chain is:

> a linear map of the way in which value is added by means of a process from raw materials to finished delivered product (including service after delivery).

Important value chain models have been developed by Porter and Hines.

3.8.1 Porter's value chain model

Porter states that the activities of a business can be classified into five primary and four support activities, each of which will potentially contribute to competitive advantage. The activities, shown in Figure 3.13, comprise the value chain.

The five *primary* activities are as follows.

- *Inbound logistics* – all activities linked to receiving, handling and storing inputs into the production system, including warehousing, transport and stock control.

- *Operations* – all activities involved in the transformation of inputs to outputs as the final product(s). In a manufacturing enterprise, these would include production, assembly, quality control and packaging. In a service industry, these include all activities involved in providing the service, such as advice, correspondence and preparation of documents by a legal firm.

- *Outbound logistics* – activities involved in moving the output from operations to the end user, including finished goods warehousing, order processing, order picking and packing, shipping, transport, maintenance of a dealer or distribution network.

- *Marketing and sales* – activities involved in informing potential customers about the product, persuading them to buy and enabling them to do so, including advertising, promotion, market research and dealer/distributor support.

- *Service* – activities involved in the provision of services to buyers offered as part of the purchase agreement, including installation, spare parts delivery, maintenance and repair, technical assistance, buyers' enquiries and complaints.

Figure 3.13 Porter's supply chain

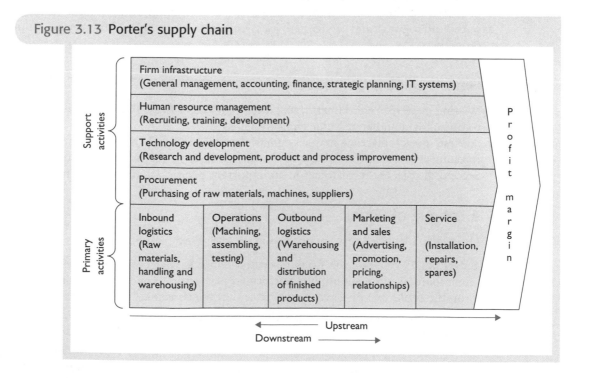

The four *support* activities for the above primary activities are the following:

- *Firm infrastructure* or general administration – including activities, costs and assets relating to general management safety and security, management information systems and the formation of strategic alliances.
- *Human resource management* – all the activities involved in recruiting, hiring, training, developing and compensating the people in an organisation.
- *Technology development* – activities relating to product design and improvement of production processes and resource utilisation, including research and development, process design improvement, computer software, computer-aided design and engineering and development of computerised support systems.
- *Procurement* – all activities involved in acquiring resource inputs to the primary activities, including the purchase of fuel, energy, raw materials, components, sub-assemblies, merchandise and consumable items from external vendors.

The word 'margin' on the right side of the Figure 3.13 indicates that the enterprise obtains a profit margin that is more than the cost of each of the individual activities or subsystems that comprise the value chain. Viewed differently, the end customer is readier to pay more for a product or service than the total cost of all the value chain activities or subsystems.

Linkages are the means by which the interdependent parts of the value chain – both internal and external – are joined together. Such linkages take place when one element affects the costs or effectiveness of another element in the value chain. Thus, intranets and the Internet are useful linkages as they may reduce the cost of supply chain administration. Linkages require coordination. Ensuring that products are delivered on time, for example, requires the coordination of operations (production), outbound logistics and service activities. Linkages are considered further in section 4.3, on networks.

3.8.2 Hines's value chain model

Writing in 1993, Peter Hines[21] recognised that Porter made two valuable contributions to our understanding of value chain systems.

First, Porter places a major emphasis on the materials management value-adding mechanism, raising the subject to a strategic level in the minds of senior executives. Second, he places the customer in an important position in the supply chain.

3.8.3 A critique of Porter

Hines also identified three major problems with Porter's model:

1 Neither Porter nor the firms discussed concede that consumer satisfaction – not company profit – should be their primary objective. The focus of Porter's model is on the profit margin of each enterprise, not the consumer's satisfaction.

2 Although Porter acknowledges the importance of integration, his model shows a rather divided network, both within the company and between the different organisations in the supply chain.

3 Hines believes that the wrong functions are highlighted as being important in Porter's primary and support activities.

Hines suggests that the above three criticisms result from the fact that Porter's model is based solely on American cases 'without reference to more innovative Japanese enterprises'. Porter's conclusions may therefore 'prove inappropriate for companies facing the challenges of the 21st century with the prospect of an array of more developed competitors. Indeed in some cases close adherence to Porter's methodology may prevent firms from further continual development'.

3.8.4 Alternative models

To correct the above problems, Hines offers two models:

- a *micro* integrated materials value pipeline
- a *macro* ten forces partnership model.

The micro integrated materials value pipeline is shown in Figure 3.14.

The main contrasts between the Porter and Hines models are summarised in Table 3.2. The following are the important features of Hines's model.

- The value chain points in the opposite direction to that in Porter's model, emphasising differences in both objectives and processes.
- Demand is determined by collective customer-defined price levels.
- Primary functions in each of the separate firms in the value chain must be integrated and 'traditional arm's length external barriers and internal divisions broken down'. The emphasis is on collaboration rather than competition.
- Key primary functions and secondary activities differ, as shown in Table 3.2. The significance of each of the secondary activities identified by Hines is, briefly, as follows:
  - Activity-based costing (ABC) enables the exact cost of products and the benefits of activities such as *kaizen* and value analysis to be ascertained. By allocating costs

Figure 3.14 Hines's micro integrated materials value pipeline

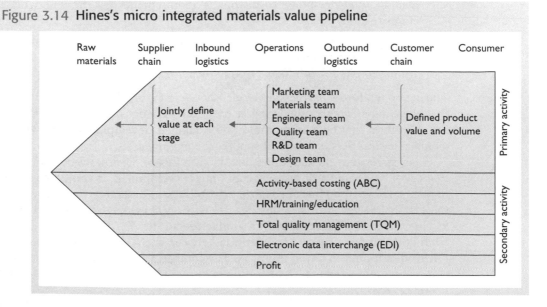

Table 3.2 Porter's and Hines's models contrasted

	Porter	Hines
Principal objective	Profitability	Consumer satisfaction
Processes	Push system	Pull system
Structure and direction	Series of chains linking firms pointing from raw materials source to customer	One large flow pointing from consumer to raw material source
Primary activities	Inbound logistics, operations, outbound logistics, marketing and sales service	Teams concerned with marketing, materials, engineering, quality, R&D and design
Secondary (support) activities	Firm infrastructure, HRM, technology development, procurement	Activity-based costing (ABC), HRM/training/education, TQM, EDI, profit

to activities rather than functions, we can identify the true costs involved in delivering the product. A simpler method of value chain analysis is to call the price charged to the customer at the end of the supply chain 100 per cent and, by working backwards, ascertain the cost of each supply activity. ABC is considered further in section 16.8. It enables the most serious non-value-adding problems to be identified first and addressed promptly.

– Human resources management (HRM) – especially employee training and education – facilitates effectiveness, efficiency and proactive thinking.

– Total quality management (TQM) provides a culture for all network members.

– Electronic data interchange (EDI) together with intranets, extranets and so on, all facilitate quick response to customers' requirements and draw network members closer together.

– Profit should be roughly equalised between network members and result from reducing total production and consumption costs to below what consumers are willing to pay for products meeting their specifications.

The macro ten forces partnership model shown in Figure 3.15 widens the analysis from that of a company with a single source to the whole range of supply pipelines and identifies the forces that encourage rapid and sustained development. The whole network includes several tiers or layers of supplying companies.

Hines states that the ten forces identified in Figure 3.15 describe a variety of forces that encourage rapid and sustained continual development. It should be noted that the model as shown by Hines in Figure 3.15 relates to assembly-type production. Thus, the first of the ten forces is the creative tension developed between competing final assemblers or original equipment manufacturers (OEMs). This creative tension results from both cooperation and competition between them. The cooperation derives from OEMs developing common suppliers. The competition is rivalry in attempting to meet consumers' requirements. Cooperation is fostered by supplier associations, referred to in section 8.8.

Figure 3.15 Hines's macro ten force partnership model

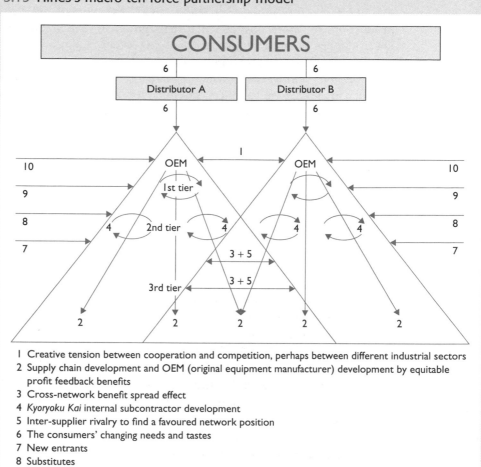

1 Creative tension between cooperation and competition, perhaps between different industrial sectors
2 Supply chain development and OEM (original equipment manufacturer) development by equitable profit feedback benefits
3 Cross-network benefit spread effect
4 *Kyoryoku Kai* internal subcontractor development
5 Inter-supplier rivalry to find a favoured network position
6 The consumers' changing needs and tastes
7 New entrants
8 Substitutes
9 Stable long-term cheap finance
10 Government agencies creating a developmental environment

3.9 Value chain analysis

Value chain analysis is concerned with a detailed examination of each subsystem in a supply chain and every activity within these subsystems with a view to delivering maximum value at the least possible total cost, thereby enhancing value and synergy throughout the entire chain.

Porter[22] states that there are two ways in which an enterprise can obtain a sustained competitive advantage: first, cost and, second, differentiation.

3.9.1 Cost

Cost analysis with regard to value chains is performed by assigning costs to the value chain activities. The approach of activity-based costing (ABC) is, as stated above, of particular relevance in this context.

Porter identifies ten major cost drivers that determine the value or cost of activities:

- *Economies or diseconomies of scale* – fixed costs spread over a large volume of production are more cost-effective than producing small quantities of an item. Diseconomies of scale in procurement can occur if large requirements meet an inelastic supply, forcing up input prices.
- *Learning and spillovers* – learning can reduce costs and can spill over from one industry to another via suppliers, ex-employees and reports of representatives.
- *Capacity utilisation* – changes in the level of capacity utilisation will involve costs of expanding or contracting.
- *Linkages between activities* – the cost or value of an activity is frequently affected by how other activities are performed. Linkages with suppliers centre on the suppliers' product design characteristics, such as service and quality. The way in which a supplier performs activities within the value chain can raise or lower the purchaser's costs.
- *Interrelationships* – sharing a value activity with another business unit can reduce costs. Certain raw materials can be procured more cheaply by combining units' requirements.
- *Degree of vertical integration* – every value activity employs or can employ purchased inputs and thus poses integration choices. The cost of an outbound logistics activity may vary depending on whether or not the enterprise owns its own vehicles.
- *Timing of market entry* – an enterprise may gain an advantage from being the first to take a particular action.
- *Firm's policy of cost or differentiation* – the cost of a value activity is always affected by policy choices a firm makes independently of other cost drivers. Policy choices reflect a firm's strategy and often deliberate trade-offs between cost and differentiation.
- *Geographic location* – location relative to suppliers is an important factor in inbound logistical cost.
- *Institutional factors* – government regulations, taxation, unionisation, tariffs and levies constitute major cost drivers.

An enterprise that controls the above drivers better than its rivals will secure a competitive advantage over them.

A cost advantage can also be gained by reconfiguring the value chain so that it is significantly different from those of competitors. Such reconfigured chains can derive from differing production processes, automation, direct instead of indirect sales, new raw materials or distribution channels and shifting the location of facilities relative to suppliers and customers.

3.9.2 Differentiation

Porter[23] states that a firm differentiates itself from its competitors when it provides something unique that is valuable to buyers beyond simply offering a new price. A differentiation advantage can be obtained either by enhancing the sources of uniqueness or reconfiguring the value chain.

The drivers of uniqueness are often similar to the cost drivers listed above and include:

- *policy choices* – about what activities to perform and how to perform them, such as what product features to include, services to provide, technology to employ or quality of outputs

- *linkages between activities* – such as delivery time, which is often influenced not only by outbound logistics but also by the speed of order processing
- *timing* – being the first to adopt a product image may pre-empt others doing so
- *location* – convenience of use for customers and other such factors
- *interrelationships* – sharing technologies or sales effort, for example
- *learning and spillovers* – learning how to perform an activity better; Porter observes that only proprietary learning leads to sustainable differentiation
- *integration* – providing a service in-house instead of leaving it to suppliers may mean that the organisation is the only one to offer the service or provide the service in a unique way
- *scale* – large-scale operations can allow an activity to be performed in a unique way not possible at a smaller volume
- *institutional factors* – good union relationships may avoid losses in production time due to strikes and so on.

Reconfiguring a value chain to create uniqueness can involve devising a new distribution chain or selling approach, forward integration to eliminate channels of distribution, backward integration to enhance quality and the adoption of new production technologies.

3.9.3 The main steps in value chain analysis

Porter[24] provides lists of the main steps in strategic cost analysis and differentiation analysis. For *strategic cost analysis* these steps are:

1 identify the appropriate value chain and assign costs and assets to it
2 diagnose the cost drivers of each value activity and how they interact
3 identify competitors' value chains and determine the relative costs to competitors and the sources of cost difference
4 develop a strategy to lower your relative cost position by controlling cost drivers or reconfiguring the value chain and/or downstream value
5 ensure that cost reduction efforts do not erode differentiation or make a conscious choice to do so
6 test the cost reduction strategy for sustainability.

Poirier[25] reports the following range of expenditures as percentages of the sales dollar for a large sample of USA manufacturing organisations:

- purchasing   55–65 per cent
- transport   3.5–7 per cent
- labour   2.5–6 per cent
- inventory   3–9 per cent
- system and administration 1.5–3 per cent
- facilities   0.7–2 per cent

Poirier observes that, although costs could be reduced in almost every category, most paled in comparison to purchasing. Dramatic results were recorded as organisations focused some of their best talent on this, the most costly segment.

3.10 Supply chain optimisation

Supply chain optimisation is different from SCM. The latter concentrates on controlling the various elements in the supply chain. Optimisation is about removing the non-value-added steps that have infiltrated or been designed into the link of processes that constitutes a particular supply chain. Optimisation is concerned with the removal of supply chain inefficiencies and has been defined as:

> the management of complicated supply chains in their entirety with the objectives of synchronising all value-adding production and distribution activities and the elimination of such activities that do not add value.

3.10.1 The objectives of supply chain optimisation

The above definition emphasises the importance of:

- synchronising all value-adding production and distributing activities
- eliminating activities that do not add value.

Other objectives include the following:

- *Providing the highest possible levels of customer service* – research shows a strong relationship between customer satisfaction and customer loyalty. Customer service levels should aim to create delighted customers by exceeding customers' expectations. Such expectations include responsiveness and value.

- *Achieving cost-effectiveness* – cost-effectiveness is also referred to as value for money and may be expressed as a ratio:

$$\frac{\text{Value of benefit received}}{\text{Cost of the benefit}}$$

- *Achieving maximum productivity from resources expended or assets employed* – productivity is also a ratio, relating outputs to one or more inputs. An increase in output per unit of input is an increase in productivity. Thus, the total productivity of a supply chain is:

$$\frac{\text{Total output}}{\text{Total input}}$$

The challenge is to increase the value of output relative to the cost of input. Productivity also increases when the same output is achieved with less input.

- *Optimising enterprise profits* – Cudahy[26] points out that 'the logic and aim of enterprise profit optimisation (EPO) is the simultaneous optimisation of the supply and demand sides of a business both within an enterprise and throughout its trading network. Thus by simultaneously improving operational efficiency and achieving profitable growth, EPO can enhance revenue and thereby complement cost reduction and asset productivity as a means of enhancing profitability.'

  Cudahy states that the introduction of a pricing and revenue optimisation (PRO) system involves the following four basic steps:

  - *Step 1: Segmenting the market* – identifying from historical transaction data the selection of groups of people who will be most receptive to a product. Frequent segmentation methods include demographic variables, such as age, sex, race, income and occupation, and psychographic variables, such as lifestyle, activities, interests and opinions.

- *Step 2: Calculating customer demand* – use of pricing software to predict how a customer or micro segment will respond to products and prices based on current market and other conditions.

- *Step 3: Optimising prices* – this is concerned with deciding what prices to offer to a particular customer to maximise a particular profit objective, market share or other strategic goals. Based on an analysis of cost, demand, market position, price elasticity and competitive pressures, it recommends optimum – not lowest – prices to achieve these goals.

- *Step 4: Recalibrating prices* – this is the fine-tuning of prices to customer buying behaviour.

Cudahy observes that pricing and revenue optimisation are not about competing on price but extracting the maximum value from a company's products and capacity.

■ *Achieving maximum time compression* – time compression is an important aspect in achieving customer satisfaction, cost-effectiveness and productivity. Wilding[27] rightly observes that while cost and transfer price comparisons are open to a variety of interpretations, time is a common measure across all supply chain partners. Speeding up the flow of materials downstream and the flow of information upstream increases productivity, provides competitive advantage by virtue of rapidly responding to customers' requirements and eliminates non-value-adding process time. Beesley[28] claims that at least 95 per cent of process time is accounted for by non-value-adding activities. Time compression has applications for all aspects of the supply chain but is of particular importance as, unlike material, time wasted cannot be replaced. In general, non-value-adding activities relating to time can be categorised as:

- queueing time – materials waiting to be processed

- rework time – rectifying errors

- time wasted due to managerial decisions (or indecisions)

- cost of inventory in the supply chain.

Regarding inventory, Beesley claims 'as a general rule the volume of inventory held in a supply chain is proportional to the length of time expressed as the total time to customer'. If the supply chain is compressed work-in-progress, cycle and buffer stocks are reduced, with consequent lower overhead, capital and operating costs.

3.10.2 Factors in supply chain optimisation

The important factors in supply chain optimisation are described below.

Reduction of uncertainty

Davis[29] refers to 'three distinct sources of uncertainty that plague supply chains':

■ *suppliers* – failure to fulfil delivery promises

■ *manufacturing* – machine breakdowns, computer foul-ups that route materials to the wrong place and so on

■ *customers* – uncertainty regarding order quantities and the 'bullwhip' effect or increase in demand variability further up the supply chain, e-orders from distributors fluctuating more than retail rates, which are fairly uniform.

All of the above increase inventory. Inventory exists as a simple insurance against uncertainty of supply. Reduction of uncertainty – by means of reliable, accurate and valid forecasts, the study of demand trends and use of statistical methods – can optimise the supply chain by avoiding holding excess stock and, conversely, delay in responding to customers' demands due to stockouts.

Collaboration

Optimisation is normally most likely to be achieved by collaboration between cross-functional teams within the organisation and customers and suppliers external to it. Such collaboration may optimise product and process design and customers' and suppliers' satisfaction.

Benchmarking

Before we can optimise, we must know what performance is possible. Benchmarking has been defined by Naylor[30] as:

> the practice of recognising and examining the best industrial and commercial practices in industry or in the world and using this knowledge as the basis for improvement in all aspects of business.

Benchmarking is more than imitation. As Naylor states, 'it is through analysis of success and a spreading of learning throughout the organisation'.

Key performance indicators (KPIs)

KPIs express abstract supply chain objectives in financial or physical units for the purpose of comparison. Data relating to various functions, processes or activities is assembled, quantified and transformed into physical or financial information that can be used to compare results – often against benchmarks – and then measure relative performance. Thus, the performance of both suppliers and customer with regard to delivery of orders on time can be expressed as a percentage of the orders placed. KPIs, considered in detail in section 11.10.2, can provide not only objectives to achieve but also the motivation to achieve or better the required performance.

Leadership

The impetus for supply chain optimisation and world class SCM must either derive from or have the support of top management. This requires two-way communication between top management and the senior managers responsible either for the integrated supply chain or functions and processes within it. Important leadership characteristics are the ability to articulate the vision of an optimised supply chain to other team members, set and motivate the team to achieve goals, innovate and introduce change, nurture the competences of team members, foster a culture of continuous learning and improvement and display high levels of personal integrity.

Actions to improve supply chain performance

Davis[31] suggests a number of actions that can be used to improve supply chain performance and reduce vulnerability to demand uncertainty in both products and processes.

For products, these actions include the use of standard components and sub-assemblies, lower tolerances, fewer product offerings and the production of a generic product.

For processes, typical actions may be to reward suppliers' performance, subcontract, inbound freight handling, remove bottlenecks, introduce self-managed work teams and devise improved forecasting techniques.

The strategic, tactical and operational level decision-making processes should all be influenced by the search for supply chain optimisation. Strategies also lead to structures, as described in Chapter 4.

3.11 Supply chains and purchasing

Most of this book is concerned with purchasing as a major supply chain subsystem. Purchasing has been well described as the glue that holds the expanded supply chain together.

The supply chain concept has profoundly influenced traditional purchasing philosophies, practices and procedures in such ways as the following.

- Purchasing is increasingly ceasing to be a discrete function and becoming a group of activities within an integrated supply chain.
- Research by the USA *Purchasing* magazine showed that, in 2002:[32]
  - one in four purchasing professional respondents identified SCM as their principal job responsibility
  - virtually all the other respondents viewed SCM as an important component of their job
  - SCM is generally regarded as expanding purchasing's role.
- The head of purchasing may report to a materials, logistics or supply chain manager rather than to someone at a higher level. Figures 3.16 and 3.17 are based on a 1997 survey by the Bourton Group.[33] Figure 3.16 shows that responsibility for supply

Figure 3.16 **The people who run the supply chain in a sample of 344 companies**

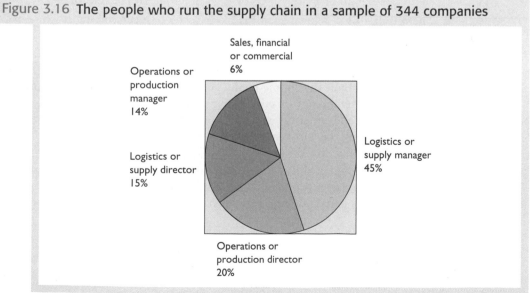

Figure 3.17 **The reporting levels of people with supply chain responsibility in a sample of 344 companies**

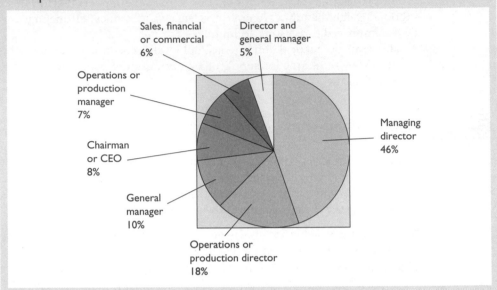

chain issues is headed by a dedicated director in about 15 per cent of responding companies and by a specific manager in another 45 per cent. In a further 20 per cent, responsibility lies with an operations or production director. Figure 3.17 indicates that the person running the supply chain reports to the managing director and chief executive officer in just under half of the responding companies. In the other half, ultimate responsibility is mainly with directors and general managers or with operations or production mangers or directors. Reporting responsibility for the supply chain appears to be below director level in about 16 per cent of cases.

■ The number of purchasing staff is likely to be reduced, owing to some former purchasing activities being made redundant by IT or taken over by other teams, such as supplier selection or inventory control.

■ Conversely there is a growing recognition that purchasing is more than a transactional activity in the supply chain. As world class operations require world class suppliers, the emphasis of purchasing will be less on price and more on supplier relationships and alliances and on contributing to the achievement of enterprise objectives along the entire supply chain.

■ Purchasing staff will have to acquire competence in other supply chain activities and general management skills, along with the capacity to think strategically rather than functionally and operationally. This gives further force to the observation of Lamming, that strategic purchasing requires a broad rather than a narrow knowledge.

Supply chains are essentially a series of suppliers and customers. Every customer in turn becomes a supplier to the next downstream activity or function until the finished product reaches the customer. As an upstream supplier-facing member, purchasing can undertake a number of strategic roles. Gadde-Lars and Hakansson[34] distinguish between rationalisation and development roles.

3.11.1 Rationalisation roles

These roles are 'all the numerous day-to-day activities performed to decrease costs successively' and are of three types.

- *Discovering what needs to be purchased and where*:
  - determining specifications for purchased goods and services in association with design, production, transportation and other supply chain functions
  - providing critical information to strategic managers on materials, prices, availability and supplier issues
  - selecting and rationalising the number of first-tier suppliers
  - advising on make-or-buy decisions, outsourcing, leasing and similar strategies
  - ensuring that suppliers meet performance expectations with regard to price, quality and delivery
  - evaluating the benefits and dangers of global sourcing
  - forging relationships and long-term partnerships with key suppliers
  - endeavouring to obtain maximum possible value from all suppliers by implementing value management, analysis and engineering.

- *Rationalisation of logistics*:
  - locating suppliers so that the least possible interruption is likely to occur to JIT and similar delivery arrangements
  - negotiating the best possible contracts and arrangements for transportation and distribution
  - undertaking responsibility for reverse logistics and the disposal of scrap and surplus by environmentally acceptable means
  - providing suppliers with accurate forecasts of requirements and facilitating such approaches as JIT and MRP.

- *Rationalisation of procurement routines, procedures and policies*:
  - involvement in the selection of appropriate supply chain packages and the reduction of purchasing costs via e-procurement
  - involvement in the design of all purchasing and supply chain structures
  - ensuring that staff receive appropriate training in general management, SCM and special aspects of purchasing
  - monitoring the ethical aspects of procurement
  - measuring all aspects of supply chain and purchasing performance.

3.11.2 Development roles

These involve coordinating the internal R&D activities of the purchaser with those of suppliers. Research by McGinnis and Vallopra[35] has shown that early supplier involvement in new product development contributes to competitive advantage in the areas of new products, time-to-market, achieving high quality, cost advantages, sales and profits. Supplier involvement is more likely in the design of manufactured than non-manufactured products, though it can apply to both. In general, enterprises that focus on upstream product specification and design activities where they can best use their resources will want to outsource downstream activities where they are not cost-effective or less competent than specialised suppliers, such as component manufacture, so that suppliers will have a greater roles to play in these areas. Important purchasing roles in supplier involvement in product development include participation in cross-functional product development teams, the identification of suppliers capable of contributing and supplier development and monitoring.

Case study

Wyldeburd Ltd

Wyldeburd Ltd (WL) is a small niche provider of products for garden birds including seeds, feeders and associated products. One of the best-selling products is sunflower seed hearts.

They are sold in 1kg, 3kg, 5kg and 10kg packs to 176 garden centres, 25 pet shops, two supermarket chains and direct to the public via the Internet.

The seeds are procured from China, packed in 50kg sacks delivered in minimum 11-tonne loads. The lead time from order to delivery to WL is quoted at 43 calendar days. WL use an agent to manage the freight forwarding to the WL packing and distribution plant. WL break the sacks down into the four different sized packs based upon the production forecast which is firmed up at the beginning of each month. Demand is variable, dependent upon the route to market and the season. Overall, it can vary from 5 to 20 tonnes per month.

The maximum storage capacity of the WL packing and distribution plant is 24 tonnes of finished products and 26 tonnes of the 50kg sacks.

Garden centres and pet shops order weekly, supermarkets forecast weekly but firm up at 6pm the day before delivery and products are on a sale or return basis. Customers ordering via the Internet before 3pm will have their products dispatched the same day. Delivery to local garden centres and pet shops is undertaken by WL's own transport and for distant outlets a national carrier is used. For supermarket deliveries, and returns, a different national carrier is used and for direct to public sales the Royal Mail parcel service is used.

The company has experienced a number of issues relating to its logistical activities. Namely:

- returned goods from pet shops and garden centres because of damaged packaging during transit or offloading
- large volume returns from supermarkets as a new season's products are substituted in the valuable gondola-end displays within the retailer
- shortages of 1kg and 3kg packs
- insufficient storage capacity within the packing and distribution plant.

Tasks

You have been appointed as a new logistics manager and have been given free rein to review the logistics operation.

1 What issues can you identify that are related to your function and what solutions could you suggest?

2 What issues do you anticipate having to discuss with other departments such as sales, production and procurement, and what facets of their responsibilities would you seek to persuade them to change?

Discussion questions

3.1 Why is logistics so important to the military?

3.2 Define logistics in a non-military environment and comment on how logistics impacts upon:
(a) a retail organisation selling clothing
(b) an international airline
(c) a construction company with projects in Europe and the Middle East.

3.3 A trade-off is where an increased cost in one area is more than offset by a cost reduction in another, so that the whole system benefits. Within the concept of logistics, where may the conflicts occur when the procurement department wants to purchase in bulk to obtain aggregated discounts and rebates? Consider in your answer the role of procurement, finance, warehousing and transport.

3.4 The environmental aspects of waste management and disposal have a very high profile in many countries. If you consider the next decade, what initiatives can be taken by procurement to stimulate more reverse logistics activities?

3.5 Map out a supply chain for a construction project, assuming the project is to take place on a brownfield site.

3.6 A manufacturing company has a strategic raw material supplied from the only source in the world. That source is located in a country that is subjected to the harshest environment for four months of each year. This is ice and snow that makes internal transport impossible during that time. How would you identify the risks created by this phenomena and what other related risks arise?

3.7 What, if any, are the differences between a supply chain and a 'pipeline'? If there are differences, are there problems that could occur with pipelines and not supply chains and vice versa?

3.8 From your experience, provide examples to support the following statement by Peter Drucker: 'The economy is changing structure. From being organised around a flow of things and the flow of money, it is becoming organised around the flow of information.'

3.9 Taking an example of a key purchase in your organisation, draw a process map of the supply chain, estimating what each process adds in cost and time.

3.10 The major retailers purchase vegetables from many parts of the world. This gives the consumer the maximum choice throughout the year. If you were asked to write a critical report on the effects of this strategy on the environment and cost, what would your main points be?

3.11 If you were asked to take a procurement initiative to incentivise suppliers to reduce your inventory, shorten supply cycles and reduce purchase costs, what factors would you include for:
(a) those things that could be improved within your organisation?
(b) those things that could be improved by the suppliers?

3.12 The biggest problem in managing a supply chain is the purchaser's inability to accurately forecast demand. This builds inefficiency into the whole system. Discuss.

Past examination questions

1 CoffeeCo is a medium-size chain of 20 coffee shops operating nationwide.

  Recently the company has experienced supply chain difficulties, resulting in late delivery of critical/bottleneck items from its suppliers (such as coffee and food supplies, in particular). This has resulted in disappointed customers and two of the outlets in one region have had to close during their busiest weekend trading period.

  One of CoffeeCo's food and coffee suppliers blames its distribution company for late deliveries. CoffeeCo knows that its much larger high street competitors have suppliers which always deliver on time. CoffeeCo has identified that many of its suppliers also service the large competitors.

  Strategically, CoffeeCo has been looking at what can be done to improve its supply chain.

Tasks

(a) Using the supply positioning model, describe **five** ways in which CoffeeCo might reduce the risk of 'critical' or 'bottleneck' failures in its supply chain.

(b) CoffeeCo is in direct competition with other high street coffee shops. Describe **two** ways in which CoffeeCo could try to increase its competitive advantage.

CIPS, *An Introduction to Purchasing Strategy*, November 2008

2 Multi-FixIt is an organisation which acts as a 'one-stop shop' supplier of fixing products to the building industry globally. Multi-FixIt now has more than 2,000 suppliers with a third-party spend in excess of $250m per annum. Its supplier base covers many categories, such as raw materials, manufacturing, distribution and storage contracts.

  The purchasing director of Multi-FixIt has committed to implementing a supplier development programme.

Tasks

(a) Construct the supply positioning model diagram.

(b) Choose **two** categories from your supply positioning model diagram and explain why these suppliers would be chosen by Multi-FixIt for a supplier development programme.

(c) Identify **four** key elements of Multi-FixIt's supplier development programme.

(d) Outline **three** advantages for Multi-FixIt of implementing supplier development programmes.

(e) Outline **two** disadvantages for Multi-FixIt of implementing supplier development programmes.

CIPS, *An Introduction to Purchasing Strategy*, May 2008

3 State **five** costs affecting purchasing that result from product diversity.

CIPS, *An Introduction to Purchasing Strategy*, May 2007

References

[1] NATO, *Logistics Handbook*, 1997, paras 103–4

[2] EU Council Directive 99/31/EC

[3] Knight Wendling, 'Logistics Report', 1988 (published for private consultation)

4 Crompton, H. K. and Jessop, D. A., *Dictionary of Purchasing and Supply*, Liverpool Business Publishing, 2001, p. 88

5 Council of Logistics Management Professionals USA, 12 February, 1998

6 Institute of Logistics and Transport, *Glossary of Inventory and Materials Management Definitions*, 1998, p. 10

7 Rogers, D. S. and Tibben-Lembke, R., *Going Backwards: Reverse Logistics Trends and Practices*, Reverse Logistics Executive Council, Pittsburgh, USA

8 As 7 above

9 Atken, J., quoted in Christopher, M., *Logistics and Supply Chain Management*, 2nd edn, 1998, Pearson Education, p. 19

10 Cooper, M. C., Lambert, D. M. and Pugh, J. D., 'Supply Chain Management – more than a new name for logistics', *International Journal of Logistics Management*, Vol. 8, No. 1, 1997, pp. 1–4

11 Porter, M. E., *Competitive Advantage*, Free Press, 1985, p. 3

12 Christopher, M., as 9 above, p. 266

13 Mentzer, J. T., De-Witt, W., Keebler, J. S., Soonhong, M., Nix, N. W., Smith, C. D. and Zacharia, Z. G., 'Defining supply chain management', *Journal of Business Logistics*, Vol. 22, No. 2, 2001

14 As 13 above

15 Adapted from Lambert, Douglas M., Cooper, Martha C. and Pagh, Janus D., 'Supply chain management: implementation, issues and research opportunities', *The International Journal of Logistics Management*, Vol. 9, No. 2, 1998, p. 2

16 Kalakota, R. and Robinson, M., *E-business 2.0 Roadmap for success*, 2nd edn, Addison-Wesley, 2001, p. 172

17 Marien, E. J., 'The four supply chain enablers', *Supply Chain Management Review*, Vol. 4, No. 1, March/April 2000

18 Cranfield University School of Management, 'Supply chain vulnerability', Final Report, 2002, pp. 35–7

19 As 10 above

20 Institute of Logistics and Transport Publicity Leaflet, *What is Logistics and what does a Career in Logistics Involve?* Undated

21 Hines, P., 'Integrated materials management: the value chain redefined', *International Journal of Logistics Management*, Vol. 4, No. 1, 1993, pp. 13–22

22 As 11 above, pp. 62–118

23 As 11 above, pp. 119–63

24 As 11 above, pp. 118 and 162–3

25 Poirier, C. C., *Advanced Supply Chain Management*, Berrett-Koehler Publishers, 1999, p. 15

26 Cudahy, G., 'The impact of pricing on supply chains' in Gattorna, J. L. (ed.) *Gower Handbook of Supply Chain Management*, 5th edn, 2003, Gower, pp. 62–75

27 Wilding, R., 'Supply chain optimisation: using the three "Ts" to enhance value and reduce costs', *IFAMM Global Briefing*, 2004, pp. 18–19

28 Beesley, A. T., 'Time compression: new source of competitiveness in the supply chain', *Logistics Focus*, June, 1995, pp. 24–5

29 Davis, T., 'Effective supply chain management', *Sloan Management Review*, summer, 1993, pp. 35–45

30 Naylor, J., *Introduction to Operations Management*, 2nd edn, Prentice Hall, 2002, p. 535

31 As 29 above

32 'Supply chain management – what is it?', *Purchasing*, 4 September, 2003, pp. 45–9

33 Bourton Group, 'Half delivered: a survey of strategies and tactics in managing the supply chain in manufacturing businesses', 1997, pp. 26–7

34 Gadde-Lars, Erik, and Hakansson, H., *Supply Network Strategies*, John Wiley, 2001, pp. 8–10

35 McGinnis, M. A. and Vallopra, R. H., 'Purchasing and supplier involvement' in *New Product Development and Production/Operations Process Development and Improvement Center for Advanced Purchasing Studies*, University of Alabama, 1998

Chapter 4

Structure and supply chains

Learning outcomes

With reference, where applicable, to supply and value chains, this chapter aims to provide an understanding of:

- specialisation, coordination and control as aspects of organisational structure
- some determinants of organisational structure
- factors in network configuration
- why and how traditional bureaucratic structures have been replaced with new approaches, including networks, lean and agile organisations
- supply chain mapping.

Key ideas

- Specialisation and outsourcing, coordination as integration and the essentials of 'control'.
- Age, technical systems, power and the environment as determinants of structure.
- The reasons for and characteristics of new type structures.
- Network structures: basic concepts, classifications, configurations and optimisation.
- Tiering: levels, reasons for tiering, responsibilities of first-tier suppliers and the consequences of tiering.
- Lean organisations and lean thinking, production, structures and the advantages and disadvantages of lean production.
- Agile organisations: the drivers, characteristics and enablers of agile manufacturing and the concepts of postponement and agility.
- Supply chain mapping: forms, purposes, methodology of supply chain mapping and value stream mapping tools.

Introduction

This chapter falls into two broad sections. The first provides a general introduction to organisational structures. The second is concerned with 'new type' structures, such as networks, lean and agile organisations and the implications for supply chains. Purchasing organisations are dealt with in Chapter 5.

4.1 Organisational structures

Mintzberg[1] has defined organisational structure as:

> The sum total of the ways in which the enterprise divides its labour into distinct tasks and achieves coordination among them.

4.1.1 Specialisation

Traditionally, specialisation was the division of organisational activities into functions, occupations, jobs and tasks. By means of vertical integration, enterprises also aimed at self-sufficiency – both in the supply of materials and the in-house manufacture of products.

Stemming from the work of Prahalad and Hamel,[2] however, the present emphasis of specialisation relates to *core competences*, or competitive advantage, that satisfy three criteria:

- potential access to a wide variety of markets
- significant contribution to the perceived benefit of the end product(s)
- ideally, a core competence should be difficult for a competitor to imitate.

Core competences arise from the integration of specialist technologies and the coordination of diverse production skills. They result in core products. Examples of enterprises and their core products are:

- Pilkingtons and glass products
- Black and Decker and small electric motors
- Honda and petrol engines.

Such core products can be used to launch a variety of end products. Honda engines have applications ranging from cars, motorcycles and lawnmowers to portable generators.

Concentration on core competences has led to the outsourcing of non-core activities. Six consequences of outsourcing include the:

- transfer of non-core manufacturing activities to specialist contract manufacturers that, by leveraging their fixed costs over multiple customers, can produce more for less
- transfer of non-core service activities, such as catering or training, to specialist providers
- removal from corporate balance sheets of manufacturing assets, such as tools and equipment
- reduced payroll by eliminating non-core employees
- ability to combine the power of several highly specialised contributions into a single, flexible, value-adding entity
- opportunity for purchasing to create better leverage of procured parts, products and services.

4.1.2 Coordination

Traditionally, coordination is an aspect of organisational theory related to ensuring that people and resources grouped into discrete functions worked together to accomplish organisational goals. The hierarchy of authority was itself a powerful coordinating influence.

Today, coordination is synonymous with *integration*. Essentially, integration is conflict resolution. On the assumption that separate organisational elements and interests will inevitably conflict over scarce resources, objectives, status and similar factors, there must be integrating mechanisms to ensure unity of effort. Where such integration is not achieved, the result will be waste, conflict and low productivity, or *sub-optimisation*. Integration can be both intra-organisational and inter-organisational.

Intra-organisational integration

Figure 4.1 indicates a continuum of intra-organisational mechanisms to enhance communication and integration between the parts of an organisation, or, in the present context, supply chain elements. A matrix organisational structure is shown in Figure 4.2.

Figure 4.1 A continuum of intra-organisational mechanisms

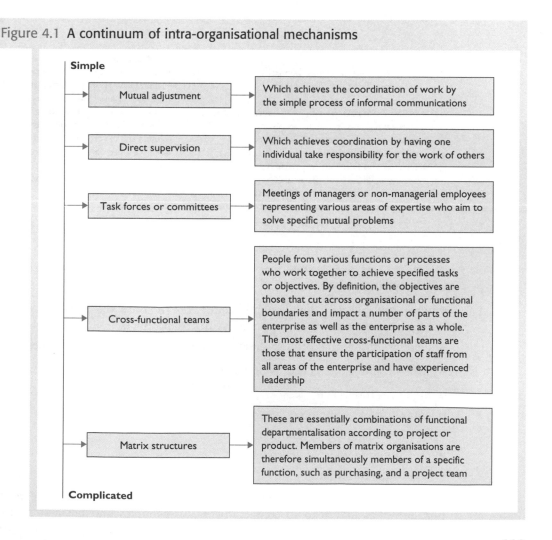

119

Figure 4.2 **A matrix organisational structure**

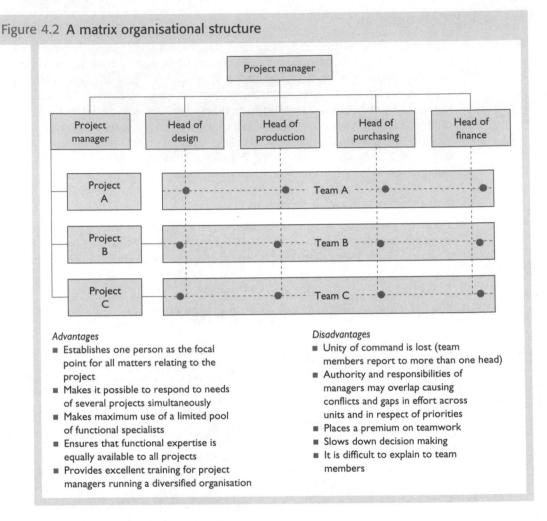

Advantages

- Establishes one person as the focal point for all matters relating to the project
- Makes it possible to respond to needs of several projects simultaneously
- Makes maximum use of a limited pool of functional specialists
- Ensures that functional expertise is equally available to all projects
- Provides excellent training for project managers running a diversified organisation

Disadvantages

- Unity of command is lost (team members report to more than one head)
- Authority and responsibilities of managers may overlap causing conflicts and gaps in effort across units and in respect of priorities
- Places a premium on teamwork
- Slows down decision making
- It is difficult to explain to team members

Grinnel and Apple[3] state that matrix structures should be considered only for the following situations:

- when complicated, low-volume production runs are the principal outputs of an organisation, such as aerospace construction products
- when a complicated product design calls for both innovation and timely completion.

Matrix structures are generally applicable when the following factors obtain:

- high uncertainty
- complicated technology
- medium/long project duration
- medium/long internal dependence
- high differentiation.

Most of the disadvantages of matrix structures derive from the dual or multiple relationships that may lead to conflicts between resources and business managers and confusion about where authority lies. More positively, the horizontal communication linkages of matrix organisations encourage integration and teamwork. Horizontal structures and cross-functional management structures are referred to in Chapter 5.

Integration also involves *formalisation*, or the extent to which work behaviour is constrained by rules, regulations, policies and procedures. Formalisation is greatest when the individual discretion given to employees is low. The extent to which an organisation is formalised indicates how top decision makers view their subordinates. Douglas McGregor[4] proposed two contrasting sets of managerial assumptions about the work attitudes and behaviour of their subordinates, which he termed Theory X and Theory Y.

Theory X assumes that the average worker is lazy, dislikes work, will do as little as possible, lacks ambition and seeks to avoid responsibility. Managers therefore maximise their control over worker behaviour.

Theory Y assumes that the work setting determines whether workers consider work to be a source of satisfaction or a chore. Where work is a source of satisfaction, close control of worker behaviour is unnecessary as employees will exercise self-control and be committed to organisational goals.

Inter-organisational structures

No business is an island. Every organisation has relationships as customers, suppliers or as collaborators in innovation with many other organisations. Mechanisms must therefore be developed to resolve possible interorganisational conflicts arising from factors such as loss of control and influence, increased uncertainty, consensus problems and standardisation issues.

By far the most important influence in both intra- and inter-organisational integration is Information Technology (IT). Prior to IT, it was important that organisational structures should, for reasons of coordination or integration, be in physical proximity. With IT, grouping tasks, functions or people in close physical proximity is unnecessary. With e-mail, video conferencing and to a lesser degree fax machines, it is possible to establish and integrate links within and across all organisational boundaries. Software applications such as MRP, MRPII, ERP, ECR and VMI are all approaches to the integration of resources and relationships.

4.1.3 Control

Control is a third aspect of organisational structure. A control system requires two essential elements:

- a power base
- a control mechanism, which may be of one of the following generic types.
  - *Centralisation* – decision making is either carried out by a centralised authority or requires the approval of the centralised authority before it is implemented.
  - *Formalisation* – as stated under the heading 'Intra-organisational integration' in section 4.1.2 above, this relates to regulations, policies, rules and procedures that provide guidelines, objectives or goals.
  - *Output control* – determining objectives or goals that provide the criteria for decision making.
  - *Cultural control* – the shared values and norms that guide decision making. It is often suggested that where culture is strong, strong structures are unnecessary.

Cultural control is often exercised via informal structures. Informal organisation covers not only the friendships and animosities of people who work together but also their shared traditions and values that guide their behaviour sometimes to achieve and sometimes to block organisational goals. In practice, the relationship of the informal to the formal organisation determines how effectively the latter will function. No manager can succeed without understanding the informal structures that operate within a particular work setting.

4.1.4 The determinants of structure

What is known as the contingent approach emphasises that there is no one ideal structure. Mintzberg[5] has identified four contingency or 'situational' factors, which are age and size, technical systems, power and the environment.

Age and size

Mintzberg states that the older and larger an organisation, the more standardised will be its behaviour, policies and procedures. Because of these factors, changes are more difficult to implement in older, larger organisations.

Technical systems

Mintzberg suggests that the more a technical system controls the workforce, the more standardised will be the operating system and bureaucratic the organisational structure. Conversely, information and computer technologies may transform a bureaucratic to a flexible structure and lead to changes in the nature of managerial work, job design and working practices.

Power

Power may be defined as the capacity of an individual or group to influence decisions or effect organisational outcomes. Five sources of power are identified by French and Raven[6] under the classifications shown in Figure 4.3.

- *Reward power* is based on individual or group perceptions that another individual or group has the ability to provide varying amounts and types of rewards.
- *Legitimate power* is based on the values held by an individual or the formation of particular values as a result of socialisation. It exists when an individual or group accepts that it is legitimate for another individual or group to influence their actions.

Figure 4.3 **The sources of power**

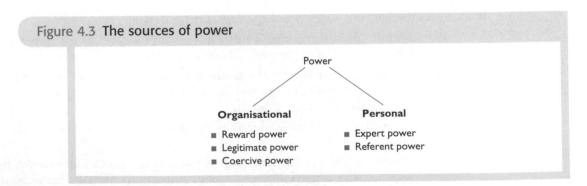

- *Coercive power* is based on individual or group perceptions that another individual or group has the ability to administer penalties.

- *Expert power* is based on individual or group perceptions that another person or group has greater knowledge or expertise than them and is thus worth following.

- *Referent power* is based on the desire of an individual or group to identify with or be like another person or group.

There are significant differences between organisational and personal power. Organisational power is conferred and dependent on the position of the individual or group in the organisational hierarchy. Personal power is inherent and dependent on the personal characteristics of the holder. Personal power is therefore less removable from the holder than organisational power.

Often the importance of purchasing in an organisation derives from the reputation of the head of purchasing or team leader for competence and the attractiveness of his or her personality to others. Political power, for example, has been described as a combination of respect and liking.

Other research[7] has shown that, in relation to departments or operations, those who are most powerful in an organisation control important resources, have to cope effectively with uncertainty and have scarce expertise. This research implies that the most powerful departments or operations are those concerned with uncertainty, such as marketing in highly competitive industries and purchasing where materials form a high proportion of the total cost, particularly where the prices of the materials are unstable and where there are extreme vagaries in supply. The factors determining buyer and supplier power in the marketplace as identified by Porter are set out in Figure 2.6 in Chapter 2.

The environment

The importance of environmental scanning to the formulation of strategies was discussed in Chapter 2. Environments are both general and specific. Both these aspects must be considered in relation to organisational structures and decision making.

The general environment comprises political, economic, social, technological, environmental and legal conditions (PESTEL) within which all organisations operate at a given time. The specific environment consists of the people, groups and organisations with whom a particular enterprise must interact. These include clients, customers, regulators, resource suppliers, trade unions and numerous others.

Both general and specific environments have specific significance for organisations that operate internationally.

Mintzberg[8] states that environments can range from:

- *stable to dynamic* – in stable environments, more mechanistic structures will apply; the more dynamic the environment, the more organic will be the structure

- *simple to complicated* – the more complicated the environment, the more decentralised the organisational structure, and vice versa

- *integrated to diverse* – the more diversified the organisation's markets, the greater the propensity for it to split into market-based units (these give favourable economies of scale)

- *munificent (liberal and friendly) to hostile* – an extremely hostile environment will drive an organisation to centralise its structure, at least temporarily.

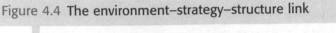

Figure 4.4 The environment–strategy–structure link

Strategy and structure

Mintzberg's analysis emphasises that different environments lead to different strategies. Different strategies require different structures. Thus, as Chandler[9] concluded after a study of almost 100 large American companies, changes in corporate strategy precede and lead to changes in organisational structure – that is, structure follows strategy. This environment–strategy–structure link is shown in Figure 4.4.

Later writers,[10] however, suggest that Chandler's strategy–structure relationship is too simplistic, that structure may constrain strategy and, once an organisation has been locked into a particular environment–strategy–structure relationship, it may have difficulty pursuing activities outside its normal scope of operations. Often an organisation cannot change strategy until it implements changes in structure.

4.1.5 McKinsey's 7S model

McKinsey, as quoted by Waterman,[11] also regarded Chandler's strategy–structure model as inadequate and identified seven interrelated factors that organisations wishing to become more customer-orientated need to address. These factors are shown in Figure 4.5.

Figure 4.5 shows that shared values are at the core of the organisation. While formal structure is important, the critical issue is not how activities are divided up but, rather, the ability to focus on those dimensions that are important to organisational development. From a purchasing standpoint, these seven dimensions are the following.

- *Shared values* – the importance of purchasing sharing in the corporate culture or 'ways in which things are done around here'. The recognition by the organisation and purchasing that purchasing is a contributor to the achievement of organisational objectives. Relating all purchasing activities to the ethical and environmental policies of the organisation is vital.

- *Structure* – the breaking down of functional barriers based on specialisation and the integration of purchasing into logistics and supply chain processes in a seamless manner.

- *Skills* – the development of staff knowledge and competences relative to purchasing and the sharing of such knowledge and competence with both internal and external suppliers.

- *Strategy* – in what ways can purchasing contribute to the achievement of marketing, alliance, growth, diversification, outsourcing and similar strategies?

- *Style* – the building of supplier goodwill and cooperation by creating good supplier relationships based on trust, courtesy, information sharing and adherence to ethical principles.

Figure 4.5 McKinsey's 7S model

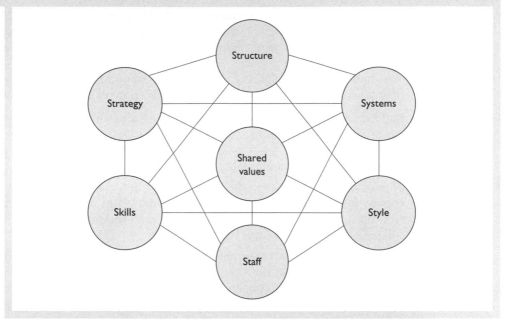

- *Staff* – securing the right mix of purchasing and support staff to ensure that procurement contributes to competitive advantages, training and rewarding staff.
- *Systems* – the development of procedures, information flows and the facilitation of e-procurement.

4.2 New type organisations

Traditional bureaucratic structures characterised by vertical 'silos', departmentalisation of functions, rigid hierarchies and 'red tape' are becoming dysfunctional because they are widely regarded as too rigid, slow and insufficiently innovative to meet the requirements of flexible, fast-moving and rapidly changing enterprises and their customers.

Quinn[12] lists five factors that have influenced the reform of traditional hierarchical organisations.

1 The pursuit of 'right-sizing' and 'horizontal' organisations, resulting in the reduction of management layers and flat structures.
2 Concurrent actions, including the re-engineering of business processes, followed by organisational redesign and the greater use of multifunctional teams.
3 The need for precision, speed and flexibility in the execution of programmes and strategies.
4 The development of powerful information systems and automated knowledge capture, with the resultant empowerment of employees in the management of business processes.
5 The focus on customer satisfaction and retention by means of enhanced organisational responsiveness.

In purchasing, a further factor is the transition from being a purely transactional activity to a key contributor to organisational competitiveness and performance in which the emphasis is on sourcing rather than buying. While many organisations still organise purchasing along traditional hierarchical lines, the above factors are increasingly leading to the adoption of purchasing and supply chain networks and the adoption of lean and agile philosophies.

Hastings[13] has identified seven characteristics of new type organisations, all of which have implications for purchasing and supply chain management.

1 *Radical decentralisation* – this, combined with a belief that 'small is beautiful', splits the organisation into many small, autonomous units, the smallest of which is the individual who, when 'empowered', is given considerable autonomy with consequent responsibility and accountability.

2 *Intense interdependence* – this emphasises interdependence and multidisciplinary approaches and is implemented by assembling teams and coalitions to pursue common objectives. Both individuals and the organisation itself realise that in order to compete they have to cooperate.

3 *Demanding expectations* – organisations and the individuals in them have a clear sense of the goals that they are expected to achieve. Individuals are demanding of others and expect their cooperation as a right.

4 *Transparent performance standards* – demanding performance standards and performance measures are set and communicated in a transparent fashion so that all are aware of how they are doing in relation to others. The emphasis is on improvement, not winners and losers.

5 *Distributed leadership* – leadership is not confined to senior management but is distributed among people in the company generally, who are required to display maturity and responsibility.

6 *Boundary busting* – to achieve adaptability and flexibility, physical, personal, hierarchical, functional, cultural, psychological and practical barriers to cooperation and communication are identified and systematically eliminated.

7 *Networking and reciprocity* – direct relationships and communication between individuals – irrespective of their roles, status, functions, culture or location – are encouraged and facilitated by the abandonment of conventional rigid organisation structures so that a pervasive culture of reciprocity and exchange mediates all relationships.

The movement from traditional bureaucratic/mechanistic to modern adaptive/organic structures is described in Table 4.5.

Examples of new type organic structures – emphasising empowerment, functional redundancy and the facilitation of communication between employee 'teams' and external 'parties' – are networks, which are lean and agile.

4.3 Networks

4.3.1 Network structures

A network structure is a series of strategic alliances that an organisation forms with suppliers, manufacturers and distributors to produce and market a product. Such structures enable an enterprise to bring resources together on a long-term basis, reduce costs and enhance quality without the high expenditure involved in investing in specialised resources, including research and design, and dedicated technology or the employment of an army of managers and operatives. It follows that:

■ a network, as Ford *et al.*[14] point out, is 'not a world of individual and isolated trans-actions. It is the result of complex interactions within and between companies in relationships over time', so, as Ford *et al.*[15] state elsewhere, 'the time dimension of a relationship requires managers to shift their emphasis away from each discrete pur-chase or sale towards tracking how things unfold in the relationship over time and changing these when appropriate'

■ network structures allow organisations to bring resources (especially expertise), together on a long-term basis to reduce costs, which is why enterprises in Europe and the USA are increasingly turning to global networking as a means of gaining access to low-cost overseas inputs

■ networks relate to all aspects of the supply chain, including marketing and distribu-tion, but this book is primarily concerned with networking with suppliers.

4.3.2 Network basics

The typical supply chain network is shown in Figure 4.6.

The nodes represent the business or 'actors', such as suppliers, producers, customers and service providers. The links between the nodes represent relationships. Relationships between actors are like bridges as they give one actor access to the resources and competences of another. Harland[16] points out that some researchers use the term 'net-work' to describe a network of actors, while others use it to discuss a network of processes or activities. The study of networks can therefore be related to networks of actors (organisations or individuals), activities (or processes) and resources. When

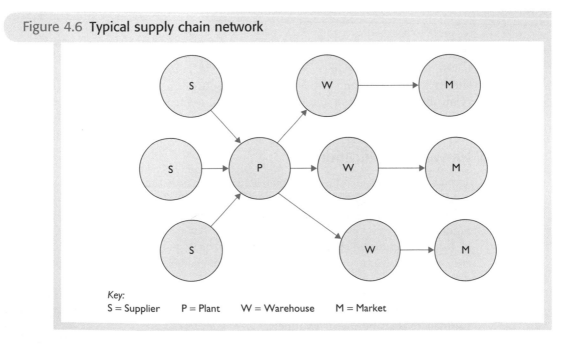

Figure 4.6 **Typical supply chain network**

Key:
S = Supplier   P = Plant   W = Warehouse   M = Market

Figure 4.7 Network model

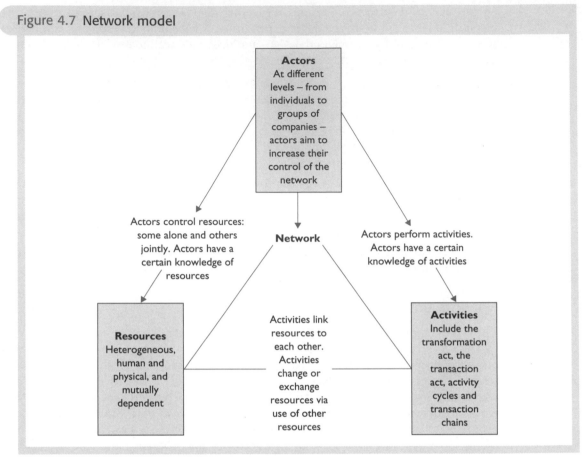

Source: Hakansson, H., *Industrial Technological Development*, Croom Helm, 1987

discussing networks, it is essential to specify whether or not networks of actors or networks of activities are being considered. The network model shown in Figure 4.7[17] shows the connections between actors, resources and activities and how, via their relationships, it is possible for actors to mobilise resources.

Further aspects of network structure are considered in section 4.4 below.

4.3.3 Network classifications

Typical of numerous classifications of networks are those of Snow *et al.*[18] Lamming *et al.*[19] Harland *et al.*[20] and Craven *et al.*[21]

Snow *et al.*[22] distinguish between internal, stable and dynamic structures – shown in Figure 4.8.

Internal network firms own most or all of the assets associated with the business and endeavour to capture entrepreneurial and market benefits without engaging in much outsourcing.

In *stable networks*, assets are owned by several firms but dedicated to a particular business. As shown, the suppliers nestle round a large core enterprise, either providing supplies or distributing its products.

Figure 4.8 Common network types

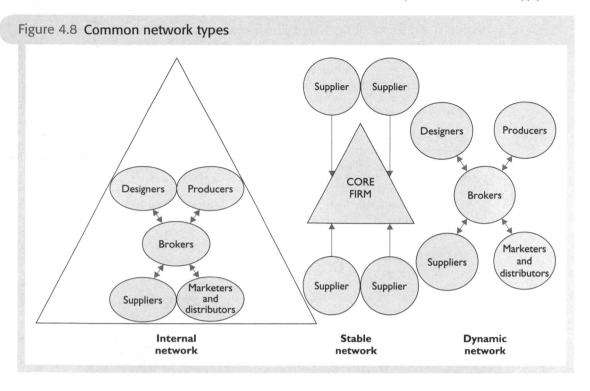

With *dynamic networks*, there is extensive outsourcing. The lead firm identifies and assembles assets owned wholly or largely by other enterprises on whose core skills it relies. Examples of such core skills cited by Snow *et al.* are manufacturing, such as Motorola, research and development, such as Reebok, or design and assembly, such as Dell Computing. In dynamic organisations, key managers create and assemble resources controlled by outside resources and can therefore be thought of as brokers. Some enterprises rely purely on brokering and are therefore virtual organisations. In virtual organisations an enterprise designs and markets a product but outsources manufacturing to specialist providers and possibly distributors. Some advantages and disadvantages of dynamic networks are shown in Table 4.1.

Lamming *et al.*,[23] building on earlier work by Fisher,[24] suggest two distinctive types of supply networks relating, respectively, to products that are 'innovative-unique' (such as drugs, communications technology and electronics) and 'functional' (such as canned soft drinks, brake cylinders and car window wipers). In each case, a distinction is made, as shown in Table 4.2, between products of higher or lower complexity, competitive priorities and sharing of resources and information.

Harland *et al.*[25] provides a taxonomy of supplier networks based on two dimensions, which are, first, whether the supply network operates under dynamic or stabilised (routinised) conditions and, second, whether the influence of the focal firm over other supply chain actors, such as customers and suppliers, is high or low.

The contributions of the above dimensions provide four types of supply networks, as shown in Table 4.3. The taxonomy outlined in the table aims to provide insight into ways of networking for managers to employ in dealing with different types of networks.

Table 4.1 Some advantages and disadvantages of dynamic networks

Advantages	Disadvantages
Networks allow organisations to specialise in what they do best and, thus, develop distinctive competences	Network structures have less control over operations. Even slight misunderstandings can result in product misspecifications
Networks can display the technical specialisation of functional structures, the market responsiveness of divisions and the balanced orientation of matrix structures	Network organisations are vulnerable to competition from their manufacturing contractors
Synergy – that is, the whole is greater than the sum of its parts – results from the cooperation of the network partners	If a network partner fails or goes out of business, the entire network can break down. It is difficult to guard innovations developed, designed and manufactured by network partners. Dynamic organisations lose their organic advantage when they become legalistic, secretive and too binding on the other partners

Table 4.2 Characteristics of supply networks for products (Lamming *et al.*, 2000)

Characteristics	Products	
	Innovative and unique	Functional
Higher complexity	*Competitive priority*: speed, flexibility, quality, supremacy *Sharing of resources and information*: large amounts of non-strategic information enabled by IT – problematic when involving sensitive information and knowledge	*Competitive priority*: cost reduction, quality, sustainability, service *Sharing of resources and information*: large amounts of non-strategic information enabled by IT – generally unproblematic, but may include cost breakdowns and strategic knowledge
Low complexity	*Competitive priority*: speed and flexibility, innovation, quality, supremacy *Sharing of resources and information*: problematic, exchange of sensitive information and knowledge – IT less critical	*Competitive priority*: cost (by high-volume production), service *Sharing of resources and information*: generally unproblematic – may include cost and strategic knowledge – IT less critical

Craven *et al.*[26] proposed two dimensions for the classification of network organisations: the volatility of environmental changes and the type of relationship between network members, whether it is collaborative or transactional.

Highly volatile situations require that enterprises should have:

- flexible internal structures capable of rapid adjustment to new environmental conditions
- flexible external relationships that allow for alteration or termination in a relatively short time period.

Network relationships may range from highly collaborative to largely transactional links. *Transactional linkages* imply discrete exchanges of values where a major issue is

Table 4.3 **A taxonomy of supply networks (Harland *et al.*, 2001)**

Network designation	Dynamic/stability factors	Factors in focal firm influence	Applicable networking activities
Type 1 dynamic/low degree of focal firm influence	Internal process characteristics: ■ high process variety, including large numbers of network configurations, low volumes or both ■ sometimes high levels of promotional activity External market conditions: ■ uncertain demand ■ many competitors ■ high frequency of new product launches	Low influence due to: ■ direct network value added by focal firm producing low volumes relative to other network players ■ focal firm has low profile in the network relating to its lack of drive to innovate	■ Human resources integration and knowledge capture within the network ■ Encouraging other network players to invest in innovation by motivating (incentives) and risk and benefit sharing ■ Demand management problems – buffer stocks ■ Coping with the network
Type 2 dynamic/ high degree of focal firm influence	As above	High influence due to: ■ direct value added by focal firm producing large volumes relative to other network players ■ reputation for innovative capability ■ focal firm provides access to rest of the network, either as a bottleneck or a conduit, which will influence the network	■ Human resources integration and knowledge capture to advance innovation ■ Motivation and risk and benefit sharing less critical to focal firm but still important for successful partnerships ■ Focal firm in a position to choose partners ■ Focal firm's decisions have implications for other actors ■ Demand management problems – buffer stocks managing the network

Type 3 routinised low degree of focal firm influence	Internal process characteristics:
	■ low variety
	■ high volumes
	■ promotional/activities not frequent enough to make network dynamic
	
	External market conditions:
	■ stable demand
	■ few competitors
	■ difficulty of switching
	■ low frequency of product launches
		Low influence due to Type 1 factors	■ Process rather than product innovation critical to improving operational processes. Enhance quality and minimise costs
			■ Critical activities are:
			  – equipment resource integration and information processing
			  – motivation and risk and benefit sharing
			■ Stock minimisation
			■ Coping with network

Type 4 routinised high degree of focal firm influence	As Type 3	High influence due to Type 2 factors Focal firm often in a position to gain control of the network	■ Focal firm in a position to choose with whom to work and make decisions on behalf of the supply network ■ Equipment resource integration and information processing ■ Stock minimisation ■ Managing network

Figure 4.9 **Classification of network organisations**

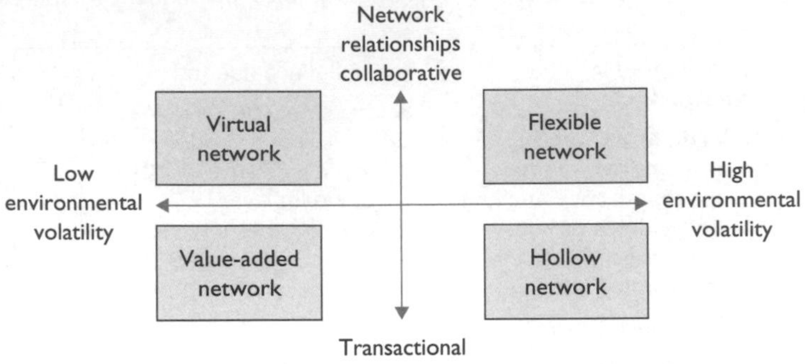

price, typified in the economics model of buyer–seller relationships. Transactional links are most likely to occur between parties that do not require collaboration.

Collaborative links may:

- involve various forms of inter-organisational cooperation and partnering, including the development of formal alliances and joint ventures
- considerate interactions between organisations to achieve common objectives
- continuing relationships between the parties that, when they are long-term ones, are likely to involve strategic alliances as a networking method.

Based on the two dimensions of volatility and relationships, Craven classifies networks as hollow, flexible, value-added and virtual, as shown in Figure 4.9.

As shown by Figure 4.9, virtual and value-added networks are appropriate to conditions of low environmental volatility. When environmental volatility is high, flexible and hollow networks are applicable. Conversely, value-added and hollow networks are appropriate to transactional relationships. When relationships are collaborative, virtual and flexible networks are applicable. The conditions under which a core organisation is most likely to employ each of the four networks are set out in Table 4.4.

4.3.4 Network configuration and optimisation

Configuration

Deciding the configuration of the network – the number, location, capacity and technology of suppliers, manufacturing plants, warehouses and distribution channels – is important for the following reasons:

- the strategic configuration of the supply chain influences tactical decisions relating to the aggregate quantities and material flows relating to the purchasing, processing and distribution of products
- the supply chain configuration involves the commitment of substantial capital resources, such as plant and machinery, for long time periods
- factors such as changes in consumer demand and technology and global sourcing lead to changes in network configurations. There is, however, evidence that, configurations, once determined, are difficult to change.

Table 4.4 Characteristics of alternative network forms, from Craven *et al.*, 1996

Characteristics	Flexible network	Hollow network	Virtual network	Value-added network
Environmental fluctuations	Short-term	Short-term	Long-term	Long-term
Network coordinator/ member relationships	Collaborative but flexible	Transactional	Collaborative (vertical and horizontal)	Transactional
End-user relationships	Transactional	Collaborative	Collaborative/ transactional	Transactional
Market structure	Diverse end-users' needs/wants	Highly segmented end-user focus	Complicated, segmented and dynamic	Diffused preferences difficult to segment
Technological complexity	Production/ distribution processes are complicated	Technology is centred on network's members	High level of technology involving an array of capabilities	Product innovation
Core competency of coordinating organisation	Market knowledge and process design leveraging with specialists	Marketing function/focus	Product innovation and production skills	Product design, production and marketing coordination
Network members' core competency	Specialists	Network members' capabilities matched to end-users' needs	Market access and specialised technological capabilities	Specialists in narrowly defined functions with major cost advantages

Arbulu and Tommelein[27] studied supply chain practices for pipe supports used in the construction of power plants. A pipe support is an assembly of components including springs, bearings and pipe shoes (pieces of pipe that transfer gravity loads to a structure underneath the pipe). Although relatively inexpensive, problems relating to the design and supply of pipe supports can compromise the success of the overall power plant project.

Arbulu and Tommelein identify the following five supply chain configurations for the supply of pipe supports:

- *Configuration 1*: Engineering firm designs the pipe supports. Supplier details, fabricates and supplies the supports. Contractor installs. (This is the common practice.)
- *Configuration 2*: Engineering firm routes pipes and performs pipe stress analysis. Supplier designs, details, fabricates and supplies the supports. Contractor installs.
- *Configuration 3*: Supplier fully designs pipe supports. Contractor installs.
- *Configuration 4*: Contractor takes responsibility for pipe support design and fabrication, though, usually, subcontracts the work and then installs.
- *Configuration 5*: Fabricator takes responsibility for pipe support design and fabrication. Contractor installs.

Optimisation

The optimisation of supply chain networks is concerned with decisions relating to what constitutes the ideal number of operating facilities and their locations, as well as the amount of supplies to purchase, the quantity of outputs to manufacturing and the flow of such outputs through the network to minimise total costs.

Network optimisation models (NOM) aim to facilitate optimal materials sourcing, processing, activity and material and product flows throughout the supply chain, taking into account forecasts of future demand. They are a measure of the performance of all the key supply chain operating characteristics and provide indications of risks and returns under a variety of operating environments. A large number of commercial off-the-shelf (COTS) supply chain optimisation software packages are available that focus on both strategic and tactical issues.

Within the FMCG (fast moving consumer goods) sector, companies such as Walmart, Tesco and Procter & Gamble utilise Collaborative Planning, Forecasting and Replenishment (CPFR[28]), which is a set of business processes that entities in a supply chain can use for collaboration on a number of retailer/manufacturer functions towards overall efficiency in the supply chain.

4.4 Factors in configurations

Network configurations are contingent and will vary widely among organisations. Lambert *et al.*[29] state that an explicit knowledge and understanding of how the network structure is configured is a key element of supply chain management and identify three primary elements: identification of the supply chain members, structural dimensions and the horizontal position of the focal enterprise.

■ *Identification of the supply chain members* – that is, all the organisations with which the focal company interacts directly or indirectly via its suppliers or customers from the point of origin to the point of consumption. These may be divided into primary and supporting network members. The former are those who actually perform operational or managerial activities in the processes leading to the production of a final product. The latter are organisations that provide resources, knowledge, utilities or assets for the primary members of the network, such as those that lease machinery to a contractor or banks that lend money to a retailer.

■ *The structural dimensions of the network* – these dimensions are the horizontal and vertical structures and the horizontal position of the focal company within the parameters of the supply chain. The *horizontal structure* is the number of tiers across the supply chain. Supply chains may be short with few tiers or long with many tiers. The *vertical structure* is the number of suppliers or customers represented within each tier. Thus, an enterprise can have a narrow or wide vertical structure with few or many suppliers or customers respectively.

■ *Horizontal positioning* – this refers to the positioning of the focal organisation in the supply chain. An enterprise may be located at or near the initial source of the supply, at or near to the ultimate customer or at some intermediate supply chain position.

4.4.1 Tiering

Tiering levels

Lamming[30] points out that the terms 'first' and 'second' tiers are 'used to indicate the degree of influence the supplier exerts in the supply chain, rather than some fixed position in the hierarchy', and offers the following definitions:

> First-tier suppliers are those that integrate for direct supply to the assembler or who have a significant technical influence on the assembly while supplying indirectly.

> Second-tier suppliers are those that supply components to first-tier firms for integration into systems or provide some support service, such as metal finishing, etc.

Tiering may extend further. Exceptionally, an enterprise may have six or more tiers. The Olympic Delivery Authority responsible for building the infrastructure for the 2012 games is seeking to influence an extended number of tiers and engage SMEs via an online tendering tool called CompeteFor (Figure 4.10).

CompeteFor is targeting around 20 per cent of the contracts in the London 2012 supply chain, not to mention those flowing from the five host London Boroughs and others.

Figure 4.10 ODA Supply chain

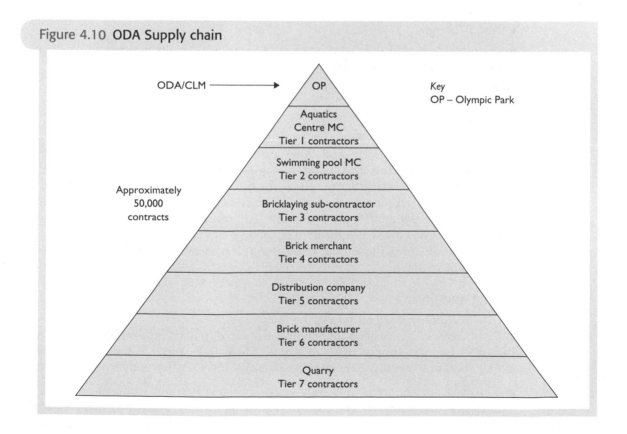

135

Reasons for tiering

Lamming shows that tiers may form for three reasons:

1 Because the assembler may require first-tier suppliers to integrate diverse technologies not possessed by one organisation.

2 Components required for systems will be very specialised and, thus, made by a small number of (large) firms, in large quantities (such as electronic parts), so it is sensible for first-tier suppliers to buy these from specialist makers.

3 The third level of subcontracted work covers simple, low value-added items required by first-tier and second-tier suppliers, such as presswork, fasteners.

Responsibilities for tiering

First-tier suppliers are direct suppliers, usually making high-cost, complicated assemblies. They are empowered to relay the assembler's standards to second-tier or indirect suppliers and are responsible for large numbers of second-tier suppliers.

The responsibilities of first-tier suppliers as identified by Lamming include:

■ research and development, especially relating to technologies that are being applied to the assembler's product for the first time

■ management of second-tier and lower-tier suppliers, including integration previously undertaken by the assembly

■ true JIT supply

■ customer-dedicated staff who work in association with the design and production departments of the assembler

■ warranties and customer claims.

Some consequences of tiering

The key word at all levels of tiering levels is *collaboration* as much of the competitive advantage required for lean production (described below) derives from the ability to deal with sub-contractors as collaborators or partners.

Where tiering is carried out for either the first or second reasons stated above, the relationship between the two suppliers becomes more akin to a strategic joint venture than a purchasing link. The product technology resides in both firms, so the first-tier supplier would find it just as difficult to replace the specialist second-tier supplier as vice versa. In this situation, the suppliers may even set up special companies to conduct business as joint ventures.

Tiering and linking

Tiering is closely related to linking.

Lambert *et al.*[31] identified four 'fundamentally different' process links that can be identified between supply chain members. These links provide indications of how closely focal firm executives integrate and manage links further away from the first tier.

■ *Managed process links* – the focal company integrates and manages process links with first-tier customers and suppliers, although it may be actively involved in the management of other process links beyond the first tier. These are critical processes in the supply chain shown in Figure 4.11 (the managed process links are shown by the thickest solid lines).

Figure 4.11 Types of intercompany business process links

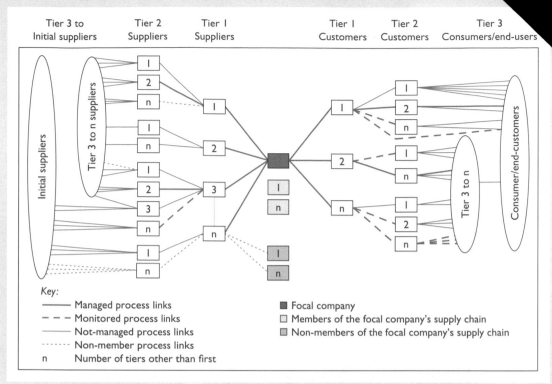

- *Monitored process links* – the focal company monitors or audits as frequently as necessary how the process links are integrated and managed between other member companies. These will be less critical but still important processes (in Figure 4.11 the monitored process links are indicated by the thick dashed lines).

- *Not-managed process links* – the focal company fully trusts other supply chain members to manage the process links appropriately or, because of limited resources, leaves it to them. These will be links that the focal company is not actively involved in or critical enough to use resources for monitoring. Thus, a manufacturer may have one or more suppliers of wooden pallets. Normally, the focal company will not choose to integrate and manage the links beyond the pallet manufacturer all the way back to the growing of the trees (in Figure 4.11 the not-managed process tasks are shown by the thin solid lines).

- *Non-member process links* – non-member process tasks are links between members of the focal company's supply chain and non-members of the supply chain. Such non-members links are not considered to be links of the company's supply chain structure, but they can, and often will, affect the performance of the focal company and its supply chain – a supplier to the focal company may also be a supplier to a competitor, for example. Such a supply chain structure may have implications for the supplier's allocation of manpower to the focal company's development process, availability of supplies in times of shortage or confidentiality of information (in Figure 4.11 non-member process links are shown by the thin dashed lines).

anisations

king

cept of lean thinking is the Japanese term *muda*, exemplified by the practices of
tor manufacturers described by Womack *et al.*[32] in their book *Machines That
World*. *Muda* means 'waste' or any human activity that absorbs resources but
alue. Examples of *muda* are spoiled production, unnecessary processing steps,
the purposeless movement or movements of employees and goods, time wasted in waiting
for materials, uneconomic or unnecessary inventories and goods and services that fail
to meet customers' requirements. Lean thinking is mean because it does more with less.

A report by research teams from the Universities of Bath and Warwick[33] on the 'people'
implications of lean organisations identified three phases of lean development and their
associated production and human resources approaches. These are shown in Table 4.5.

Table 4.5 **The three phases of lean development**

Phase	Concerned with	Approaches
1 Leanness as transition	Efforts made by the organisation to become lean	Delayering – flattening the organisation Downsizing – a reduction in the workforce Outsourcing – focusing on core activities and subcontracting non-core activities to outside providers
2 Leanness as an outcome	Assumed structural flexibility following a period of delayering, downsizing and outsourcing	Business process re-engineering (BPR) The fundamental rethinking and radical redesign of business processes to achieve dramatic improvements in critical contemporary measures of performance, such as cost, quality, service, speed Lean production characterised by: ■ elimination of waste in terms of both material and human resources ■ low inventories ■ zero defects – prevention rather than rectification of faults ■ integrated production chains ■ team working ■ involvement of all employees and suppliers in a continuous process to improve products and job design
3 Leanness as a process	Focuses attention on the attributes of those organisations that can respond to environmentally produced change	Total quality management (TQM). Management philosophy and company practices that aim to harness the human and material resources of the organisation in the most effective way to achieve the objectives of the organisation just-in-time (JIT). An inventory control philosophy whose goal is to maintain just enough material in just the right place at just the right time to make just the right amount of product

4.5.2 Lean production

Some aspects of lean production, such as the attempt to eliminate waste, the purchase of whole assemblies and tiering, have been referred to above. Other aspects of lean production, as identified by Womack *et al.*, include the following.

- Target costing – for example, a car assembler establishes a target price for the vehicle, then the assembler and suppliers work backwards to ascertain how the car can be made for the price, while allowing a reasonable profit for both the assembler and suppliers. This differs from the traditional approach in which:

$$\text{Sales price} = \text{Cost} + \text{Profit}$$

The lean production approach is:

$$\text{Profit} = \text{Sales price} - \text{Cost}$$

- The use of value engineering, value analysis and learning curves to reduce initial and subsequent cost of suppliers.
- The use of cross-functional teams of highly skilled workers and highly flexible automated machines.
- A just-in-time (JIT) pull system in which nothing is moved or produced until the previous process is completed.
- Zero defective parts. When a supplier fails to meet quality or reliability requirements, a cooperative effort is made to ascertain the cause. In the interim, part of the business is transferred to another supplier.
- Cooperation between the assembler and first-tier suppliers effected by supplier associations. They meet to share new findings on better ways to make parts. Some companies also have associations with their second-tier suppliers.
- After negotiations, the assembler and supplier agree on a cost-reduction curve over the four-year life of the product. Any supplier-derived cost savings beyond those agreed go to the supplier.
- Relationships between the assembler and suppliers are based on a 'basic contract' that expresses a long-term commitment to working together for mutual benefit. The contract also lays down rules relating to prices, quality assurance, ordering, delivery, proprietary rights and materials supply.

4.5.3 Lean production structures

Lean production, as Toni and Tonchia[34] point out, leads to a management by process organisation designed to link all the activities in order to achieve the unified objective of customer satisfaction in all its aspects.

The primary justification of management by process is to overcome functional rigidity (functional silos) where single functions of units often have different and contradictory performance objectives (such as manufacturing versus delivery punctuality).

In a manufacturing organisation, three processes can be considered fundamental:

- product development
- manufacturing or assembly (materials processing)
- logistics (material handling).

Features of process-orientated organisations are:

- they are end product-orientated and determined by the aggregation of competences and activities
- responsibility is linked to roles rather than levels
- they become horizontal, as with materials management and supply chains
- their aim is the integration of subtasks, with functional responsibilities coordinated by the process logic.

4.5.4 Advantages and disadvantages of lean production

Advantages include greater flexibility, reduced waste, quicker response to customers' demands, shorter throughput time, lower supervision costs, lower stock levels and improved quality as feedback is quicker.

Trade union objections to lean production include:

- increases in workers' responsibilities can lead to pressure and anxiety not present in traditional systems
- expansion of job requirements without comparable increases in pay
- the company is the main beneficiary of employee-generated improvements.

The two principal limitations of lean production, however, are its inability to deal with turbulence and change and that the pursuit of perfection may eliminate the scope for flexibility. Lean production depends on a stable business environment as then it can maximise its efficiencies of scale.

4.6 Agile organisations and production

Agile production is the latest stage of a development away from the mass production of the 1970s, through the decentralised production of the 1980s and on to the supply chain management and lean production of the 1990s.

4.6.1 Drivers of agility

The main drivers of agility include rapidly changing and unpredictable markets, the rapid rates of technological innovation, customers' requirements for customisation and choice, competitive priorities of responsiveness, shorter lifecycles, concern for the environment and international competitiveness. Goldman et al.[35] state that the four underlying components of agility are:

- delivering value to the customer
- being ready for change
- valuing human knowledge
- forming virtual partnerships.

4.6.2 Agile characteristics

Based on Goldman, Aitken et al.[36] have identified the core characteristics of agile manufacture shown in Table 4.6.

Table 4.6 Comparison of lean and agile production systems

Factor	Lean production	Agile production
Primary purposes	Meeting predictable demand efficiently at the lowest possible cost Elimination of waste from the supply chain	Rapid response to unpredictable demand to minimise stockouts, forced markdowns and obsolete inventory
Manufacturing focus	Maintenance of a high average utilisation unit	Deployment of excess buffer capability
Inventory strategy	High stock turnover and minimum inventory	Deployment of significant buffer stocks of parts to respond to demand
Lead time focus	Shortened lead time, providing it does not increase cost	Investing aggressively in resources that will reduce lead times
Approach to supplier selection	Selecting for cost and quality	Selecting primarily for speed, flexibility and quality
Supply linkages	Emphasis on long-term supply chain partnerships that are consolidated over time	Emphasis on virtual supply chains where partnerships are reconfigured according to new market opportunities
Performance measurement	Emphasis on world class measures based on such criteria as quality and productivity	Emphasis on customer-facing metrics, such as orders met on time, in full
Work organisation	Emphasis on work standardisation – doing it the same way every time	Emphasis on self-management and ability to respond immediately to new opportunities from all involved in work processes
Work planning and control	Emphasis on the protection of operation's core by a fixed period in the planning cycle to help balance resources, synchronise material movements and reduce waste	Emphasis on the need for immediate interpretation of customer demand and instantaneous response

4.6.3 Postponement

Postponement and decoupling are important concepts of agility. By making customised product changes as close as possible to the time of purchase by the end-customer it is possible to provide a wide variety of customised products without incurring high inventory, processing and transportation costs. Suppose the manufacture and assembly of a product requires 40 steps. By proceeding as far as step 30 and then putting the partly completed product into inventory, the final 10 steps have been postponed.

The above is an example of *manufacturing postponement*, the object of which is to maintain flexibility by keeping products in a neutral or uncommitted state for as long as possible. Examples of manufacturing postponement are found in vehicle manufacturers when colours and non-standard components or additions are deferred until the receipt of specific instructions from the customer. In house building, the basic shell may be constructed, but kitchen and bathroom fitting and decorating will not proceed until the requirements of the individual customer have been ascertained.

There is also *geographic*, or *logistics*, *postponement*, which is the exact opposite. The basic notion of geographic postponement according to Bowersox *et al.*[37] is 'to build and stock a full line inventory at one or two strategic locations'. Forward deployment of inventory is postponed until customers' orders are received. An example is the keeping of critical spares at a service centre to ensure their rapid availability to customers. Once an order for spares is received, it is transmitted electronically to the central service centre, from where the required items are rapidly transported to the customer and replacements manufactured. The outcome is highly reliable customer service with low inventory.

Van Hoek[38] has identified the following advantages of postponement:

- inventory can be held at a generic level so that there will be fewer stock variants and, therefore, less total inventory
- because inventory is generic, its flexibility is greater – that is, the same components or modules can be embodied on a variety of end products
- forecasting is easier at the generic level than for finished products
- the ability to customise products locally means that a higher level of variety may be offered at a lower cost.

4.6.4 Decoupling

The decoupling point is defined by Christopher[39] as 'the point to which real demand penetrates upstream in a supply chain'. Decoupling is closely associated with postponement and the type of customer demand. Figure 4.12 shows how the positioning of the decoupling point changes with different supply chain structures.

Figure 4.12 Family of supply chain structures

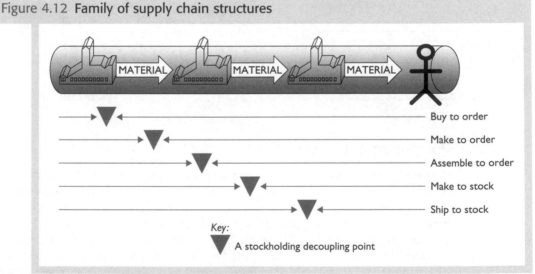

Key:
▼ A stockholding decoupling point

Buy to order
Make to order
Assemble to order
Make to stock
Ship to stock

Source: Hoekstra and Romme, 1992[40]

The organisations downstream from the decoupling point are organised for agility and the ability to cope with variability in demand volume and high levels of product variety. Upstream organisations work to a stable demand with relatively low variety and can therefore focus on lean, low-cost manufacture.

Christopher and Towill[41] point out that, in real-world supply chains, there are actually two decoupling points. The first relates to 'material' and is where strategic inventory is held in as generic a form as possible. Inventory should therefore lie as far downstream in the supply chain and as near to the final marketplace as possible. The second is the 'information' decoupling point. Ideally this should lie as far as possible upstream as, in effect, it is the furthest point to which information on real final demand penetrates. Reference to the concept of 'leagility' is made in section 4.6.6 below.

4.6.5 Enablers of agile manufacturing

Gunasekaran[42] identified seven enablers of agile manufacturing:

1 *Virtual enterprise* – each functional aspect of the manufacturing design, production and marketing of a product may be performed by many different organisations using an Internet-assisted manufacturing system.

2 *Physically distributed teams and manufacturing* – 'the physically distributed enterprise is a temporary alliance of partner enterprises located all over the world, each contributing their core competences to take advantage of a specific business opportunity or fend off a market threat'.

3 *Rapid partnership formation tools/metrics* – achievable by means of such tools as IT, including the Internet, EDI, quality function development (QFD) techniques and financial and non-financial metrics.

4 *Concurrent engineering* – provides a quick response to the need for shorter product development cycles and appropriate tools for this include functional analysis, computer-aided manufacturing (CAM), solid modelling, value engineering, failure mode and effect analysis (FMEA) and robust engineering.

5 *Integrated product/production/business information systems* – the diverse systems of participating organisations must be integrated, either by redesign or the adoption of strategies aimed at the sharing of information by means of advanced technologies, such as the Internet and EDI.

6 *Rapid prototyping tools* – 'prototyping refers to the design and generation of an early version of a product. Advanced computer technologies such as computer-aided design (CAD), computer-aided estimates (CAE) and computer engineering (CE) help to improve responsiveness to customer requirements by reducing product development times and non-value added activities at the design stage'.

7 *E-commerce* – this can improve responsiveness to customers' demands by directly collecting their requirements via an online communication system, such as the Internet, and reducing cycle and order fulfilment times.

4.6.6 Lean and agile production

Lean and agile production are sometimes regarded as synonymous, but there are significant differences. Aitken *et al.*[43] note that 'Webster's Dictionary makes the distinction clearly when it defines lean as "containing little fat" whereas agile is defined as "nimble"'. Some comparisons between lean and agile production systems are shown in Table 4.6.

Naylor *et al.*[44] distinguish between the two terms as follows:

Leanness means developing a value stream to eliminate all waste, including time, and to enable a level schedule.

Agility means using market knowledge and a virtual corporation to exploit profitable opportunities in a volatile marketplace.

Table 4.7 Comparison of lean and agile supply: the distinguishing attributes

Distinguishing attributes	Lean supply	Agile supply
Typical products	Commodities	Fashion goods
Marketplace demand	Predictable	Volatile
Product variety	Low	High
Product lifecycle	Long	Short
Customer drivers	Cost	Availability
Profit margin	Low	High
Dominant costs	Physical costs	Marketability costs
Stockout penalties	Long-term, contractual	Immediate and volatile
Purchasing policy	Buy goods	Assign capacity
Information enrichment	Highly desirable	Obligatory
Forecasting mechanism	Algorithm	Consultative

An alternative comparison of lean and agile supply is shown in Table 4.7.[45]

In general, lean production is best in situations where volumes are high, variety low and demand predictable. Conversely, agile production is suited to volatile demand and where products are customised. Thus, as Mason-Jones et al.[46] observe, 'fashion products, such as trendy clothing, have a short lifecycle and high demand uncertainty and therefore expose the supply chain to both stockouts and obsolescence risks. Commodities, e.g. tinned soups, have relatively long lifecycles and low demand uncertainty due to the fact that they tend to be well-established products with a predictable consumption pattern.'

Leanness and agility are complementary rather than competing terms and leanness should often be regarded as an enabler of agility. As indicated in section 4.6.4, the strategic use of a decoupling point may combine leanness and agility and thereby exploit the benefits of both approaches. Naylor et al.[47] have termed this combined approach 'leagility', which they define as:

> The combination of the lean and agile paradigms within a total supply chain strategy by positioning the decoupling point so as to best suit the need for responding to a volatile demand yet providing level scheduling upstream from the marketplace.

4.7 Supply and value chain mapping

A map is a visual representation of some actuality. Maps also enable us to comprehend and communicate information. Maps assist comprehension as a picture is 'worth a thousand words'. Maps also communicate specific and general information. Architects'

Table 4.8 Distinguishing strategic supply chain and process mapping

Characteristics	Supply chain mapping	Process mapping
Orientation	*External*: focuses on how goods, information and money flow upstream and downstream and through a firm	*Internal* (typically): focuses on a single operation or system with an enterprise
Level of detail	*Low to moderate*: emphasises high-level measures, such as volume, cost or lead time. Gives an overall perspective on how processes work together between enterprises. May exclude non-critical entities	*High*: breaks down a process into activities and steps. Every step includes information to characterise the system being mapped
Purpose	*Strategic*: mapping aims to create a supply chain conforming to a strategy or ensure that the current chain fulfils that strategy adequately	*Tactical*: process map originates from the recognition of a problem area and the need to improve operating efficiency. Goal is to make changes in current operations. Efforts normally limited to one process or function at a time

plans and road maps communicate specific and general information respectively. A supply network diagram is a form of supply chain mapping.

4.7.1 Forms of mapping

As supply and value chain mapping is undertaken for a specific purpose – normally for supply chain redesign or modification or the elimination or reduction of waste – the number of options for mapping to meet the needs of users is large. Gardner and Cooper[48] distinguish between strategic supply chain mapping and process mapping regarding three characteristics: orientation, level of detail and purpose. These distinctions are set out in Table 4.8.

4.7.2 The purpose of supply chain mapping

Gardner and Cooper[49] state that a well-executed strategic supply chain map can:

... enhance the strategic planning process, case distribution of key information, facilitate supply chain redesign or modification, clarify channel dynamics, provide a common perspective, enhance communications, enable monitoring of supply chain strategy and provide a basis for supply chain analysis ... Thus a map can be quite helpful in understanding a firm's supply chain, for evaluating the current supply chain and for contemplating realignment of a supply chain.

4.7.3 The methodology of mapping

A supply chain map may be linked to or built directly from a database or built by hand. Gardner and Cooper state that 'the complexity of mapping is influenced by three supply chain map attributes: geometry, perspective and implementation issues'.

Geometry is concerned with such aspects as:

- the number of sequential business units performing transactions leading to the final consumer
- direction – whether it is supplier-orientated or customer-orientated or both
- length – the number of tiers up and down
- aggregation (width) – the degree of specificity within a tier, which may be high (one box per tier), medium (types of firms at each level identified) or low (some firms are named at each level)
- spatial – is the map geographically representative?

Perspective is concerned with issues relating to:

- the focal point – whether the maps takes a firm-centred or industry-centred view
- scope – whether the breadth of product coverage included in the map is SBU-wide or by product category, product or component
- whether or not the map includes key processes beyond logistics
- whether or not the map includes a complete set of key business processes
- whether or not the map includes reverse logistics and other feedback loops.

Implementation issues:

- whether the density of information integrated into the visual map is high or low
- whether or not the map is linked to an existing corporate or supply chain database
- how the completed map shall be made available – paper, electronically or on the Web?

4.7.4 Value stream mapping tools

Hines and Rich[50] distinguish between traditional supply or value chains and value streams. The former include the complete activities of all the companies involved, while the latter refers only to the specific parts of the firms that actually add value to the product or service under consideration.

Hines and Rich identify seven mapping tools designed to reduce or eliminate seven forms of waste in a manufacturing organisation – overproduction, waiting, transportation, inappropriate processing, unnecessary inventory, unnecessary motion and defects. These take three forms, which are product (not identified by inspection and passed on to customers), service (not directly relating to products but to service, such as late delivery or incorrect documentation) and internal scrap (defects identified during inspection). The seven mapping tools are described in Table 4.9.

It is impractical in this book to give a detailed explanation of the implementation of the above tools[51] so we will confine ourselves to the following observations.

The process activity mapping tool provides an example of a typical mapping exercise directed at eliminating or reducing waste.

The first step is the preparation of a *process map* – a detailed flow chart that indicates every activity involved in making or doing something. It is critical to include all activities – not only those that are obvious.

Table 4.9 Hines and Rich's seven value stream mapping tools

Mapping tools	Purpose and application
Process activity mapping	Reducing waste by eliminating unnecessary activities, simplifying other activities or changing process sequences
Supply chain response matrix	Reducing lead times and inventory amounts
Production variety funnel	Targeting inventory reduction and changes in the processing of products in companies with varying activity patterns
Quality filter mapping	Identifying, for the purpose of improvement, the location of product and service defects, internal scrap, and other problems, inefficiencies and wasted effort
Demand amplification mapping	Identifying demand changes along the supply chain within varying time buckets to manage or reduce fluctuations in regular, exceptional and promotional demand
Decision point analysis	Particularly applicable for regular, unvarying production of multiple identical items, as in a chemical plant. Involves identifying the point at which products stop being made in accordance with actual demand and start to be made against forecasts alone. Identifying this point indicates whether processes are aligned with push or pull philosophies
Physical structure	Overviewing a particular supply chain from an industry perspective. This information may result in a redesign along the lines indicated for process activity mapping

Once the process map has been developed, a value chart can be constructed that attaches a cost or value to every activity. This cost is obtained after considering factors such as the machine or area used for the activity, distance moved, time taken and number of people employed.

Activities fall into four categories:

1 production or service time (value-added activity)

2 inspection time – performing quality control (non-value-added activity)

3 transfer time – movement of products or components (non-value-added activity)

4 idle time – storage time or time wasting during the production process (non-value-added activity).

The lead time for the process is therefore:

Production time + Non-Value-added time

While in theory inspection and transfer time are regarded as non-value-added activities, they cannot, in practice, be completely eliminated.

The final stage involves using the process map and value chart to identify where savings can be made or value added.

Case study

Granite Housing Association

Granite Housing Association (GHA), a charitable organisation, is a Registered Social Landlord (RSL). Its operations are part funded by the Government. GHA is based in the south-east of England and manages 30,000 properties. It was created from seven other RSLs with portfolios ranging from 1,800 to 14,600 properties. Five of the original RSLs had their own maintenance workforce while the other two used external contractors; 30 per cent of the in-house workforces are also tenants. Each workforce has remained on its own terms and conditions of employment and operates independently of each other.

Activities associated with the workforce fell into three main areas:

1 reactive maintenance

2 void management and refurbishment

3 programmed capital works.

Reactive maintenance requests are initiated by the tenant requesting repairs for damage to property, broken locks, leaking windows, etc.

Void Management is triggered when a tenant leaves. Typically, the property needs to be made secure, which may involve boarding windows and doors and/or installation of alarms. While the property is vacant prior to a new tenant arriving and dependent upon the condition of the premises they may need full or partial refurbishment which may include central heating upgrades, kitchen and bathroom replacements.

Programmed capital works includes the significant upgrading of a number of properties in a locality which may, for example, include replacement double-glazed windows.

Two years remain on the framework agreements for the supply only of plumbing materials and supply only of building supplies, and four years remain on framework contracts for the supply and fitting of alarms, the supply only of kitchen units and the supply only of glazing products.

The accountant, James Andrews, has undertaken an analysis of a new government scheme to encourage renewable forms of energy and has proposed that a major capital programme can be undertaken to install solar panels on properties with a south-facing roof. For 8,000 properties the scheme is financially viable; for a further 7,000 properties this further work would require additional investigation to determine economic viability. The programme will be beneficial both to the tenant and to Granite. However, the in-house workforce does not have the capacity to undertake this activity.

Tasks

You are the procurement manager for GSA and you have been asked to consider:

(a) initiating the procurement of an externally managed programme of installation of solar panels

(b) outsourcing the three categories of activities undertaken by the in-house workforce.

1 What would you need to consider in relation to both the above initiatives?

2 What contractual matters would need consideration in the relation to the outsourcing initiative and the existing frameworks?

Discussion questions

4.1 Why, in your opinion, are many local authorities and central government outsourcing services that have traditionally been seen as strategic, for example, revenues and benefits? Do you believe that it is inevitable that purchasing will be a function that is, increasingly, outsourced?

4.2 Control is one facet of organisational structure. There are a number of generic types, including cultural control. Informal structures operate in all organisations. Can you identify the informal structures within your organisation and identify the key players?

4.3 Contrast the strengths and weaknesses in a large multinational organisation of 'centralised purchasing' and 'devolved purchasing'. Assume that in the latter situation there is complete autonomy for each operating division to own the purchasing strategy, even if the same goods and services are purchased in a number of locations.

4.4 Why is communication the basis of all coordination?

4.5 Why is it important for a purchasing or supply chain professional to know whether they are employed by organisations concerned with innovative-unique or functional-type products?

4.6 The three key characteristics of networks have been identified as:
   (a) transactional – what is exchanged between network members
   (b) the nature of links – the strengths and qualitative nature of the network relationships, such as the degree to which members honour their network obligations or agree about the appropriate behaviour in their relationships
   (c) cultural characteristics – how members are linked and the roles played by individuals within the network.
   With reference to suppliers with whom you network, identify examples to illustrate each of the above characteristics.

4.7 What is a lean supply chain?

4.8 Taking Lamming's definition of a first tier supplier, what responsibilities do they have to fully support the buying organisation at all stages of product design through to ultimate disposal?

4.9 If you were conducting a supplier selection on an 'agile' producer, what are the key questions you would ask to satisfy yourself that they are an agile producer?

4.10 What, according to Gunasekaran, are the seven enablers of agile manufacturing?

4.11 What is the purpose of a supply chain map?

4.12 If you were to evaluate the structure of a supplier's procurement operation what would you want to check to convince yourself that they satisfy a rating of 'excellent'?

Past examination questions

1 Explain **two** benefits to a buyer of analysing supply markets.

CIPS *Analysing the Supply Market*, November 2008

2 Construct a diagram to illustrate the typical distribution of total purchasing expenditure in an organisation's supply base.

CIPS *An Introduction to Purchasing Strategy*, November 2007

3 (a) Describe an appropriate process that an organisation could use to reduce its supply base.
  (b) State **five** benefits of supply base rationalisation.

CIPS *An Introduction to Purchasing Strategy*, May 2007

4 **Goodvibes Plc**

Goodvibes Plc designs engineering solutions and equipment for the construction and civil engineering industry worldwide. It is particularly concerned about supply problems occurring in the concrete machinery division of the company. These problems are causing a serious loss of customer confidence.

The root of the problem lies with one of products made and sold by Goodvibes – a vibrator that is used to settle and compact newly poured concrete. These vibrators are made from a number of precision engineered components that have to withstand not only those stresses resulting from the function inherent in the task they perform, but also the frequent abuse received from the often untrained operatives using them.

One particular component, the outer casing of the vibrator, often fails because of the inadequacy of the heat treatment process used to harden it. This process is critical. Not only has the temperature to be within narrow tolerance limits, but the length of time the component is subjected to that temperature is also critical.

Comfrey is a long-established and normally very reliable company that supplies the casing and subcontracts the specialised, but low cost, heat treatment work. Aware of the problem, Comfrey has already tried to source the work elsewhere, but without success. Many companies throughout the world provide heat treatment services but apparently few have the capability of meeting Goodvibes' specific standards.

Tasks

(a) Construct a diagram of the supply positioning model and locate on it the supply position between Comfrey and its sub-contractor, the heat treatment company.
(b) State **four** general solutions to dealing with purchases located within the category identified in your answer to part (a).
(c) Explain the practical steps Goodvibes should take in an attempt to resolve its supply chain problem.

CIPS, *An Introduction to Purchasing Strategy*, May 2007

References

[1] Mintzberg, H., *The Structure of Organisations*, Prentice Hall, 1979, p. 2

[2] The main ideas about core competences were developed by Prahalad, C. K. and Hamel, G. in a series of articles in the *Harvard Business Review*, Vol. 88, 1990, and in their book *The Core Competence of the Corporation*, Harvard Business Press, 1990

[3] Grinnel, S. and Apple, H. P., 'When two bosses are better than one', *Machine Design*, 9 January, 1975, p. 86

[4] McGregor, D. M., *The Human Side of Enterprise*, McGraw-Hill, 1960

[5] As 1 above, Ch. 15

[6] French, P., Jr. and Raven, B., 'The basis of social power' in Cartwright, D. (ed.), *Studies in Social Power*, Michigan Institute for Social Research, 1959

[7] Hickson, D., *et al.*, 'A strategic contingencies theory of organisational power', *Administrative Science Quarterley*, No. 16, 1971, pp. 216–19

[8] As 1 above

[9] Chandler, A. D., *Strategy and Structure: Chapters in the History of the Industrial Enterprise*, MIT Press, 1962

[10] For a discussion of this point, see Banter, D. K. and Gogne, T. E., *Designing Effective Organisations*, Sage, 1995, Ch. 16

[11] Waterman, R., 'The seven elements of strategic fit', *Journal of Business Strategy*, No. 3, 1982, pp. 68–72

[12] Quinn, J. B., *Intelligent Enterprise*, Free Press, 1992

[13] Hastings, C., *The New Organisation*, McGraw-Hill, 1993, pp. 7–8

[14] Ford, D., Gadde, L-E., Hakansson, H. and Snehota, I., *Managing Business Relationships*, 2nd edn, John Wiley, 2003, p. 18

[15] As 14 above, p. 38

[16] Harland, C. M., 'Supply chain management: relationships, chains and networks', *British Journal of Management*, Vol. 7, March, 1996, Special Issue, pp. 63–80

[17] This diagram, attributed to Hakansson, H., *Industrial Technological Development: A Network Approach*, 1987, Croom Helm, is used by Harland in 16 above

[18] Snow, C. C., Miles, R. E. and Coleman, H. J., 'Managing 21st century network organisations', *Organisational Dynamics*, 20:3, winter, 1992, pp. 5, 20

[19] Lamming, R., Johnsen, T., Zheng, J. and Harland, C., 'An initial classification of supply networks', *International Journal of Operations and Production Management*, Vol. 20, No. 6, 2000

[20] Harland, C., Lamming, R. C., Zheng, J., and Johnsen, T. E., 'A taxonomy of supply networks', *Journal of Supply Management*, Vol. 37, No. 4, Fall, 2001, pp. 21–7

[21] Craven, D. W., Piercy, N. F. and Shipp, S. H., 'New organisational forms for competing in highly dynamic environments', *British Journal of Management*, Vol. 7, 1996, pp. 203–18

[22] As 18 above

[23] As 19 above

[24] Fisher, M. L., 'What is the right supply chain for your product?', *Harvard Business Review*, March/April, 1997, pp. 105–16

[25] As 20 above

[26] As 21 above

[27] Arbulu, R. J., and Tommelein, I. D., 'Alternative supply chain configurations for engineered or catalogued made-to-order components: case study on pipe supports used in power plants', *Proceedings IGLC*, 10 August, 2002, Granada, Brazil

[28] CPFR is a registered trademark of the Voluntary Interdustry Commerce Solutions Association

[29] Lambert, D. H., Cooper, M. C. and Pagh, J. D., 'Supply chain management implementation issues and research opportunities', *International Journal of Logistics Management*, Vol. 9, No. 2, 1998, pp. 1–9

[30] Lamming, R., *Beyond Partnerships: Strategies for Innovation and Supply*, Prentice Hall, 1998, p. 17, and 1993 edn, pp. 186–90

[31] As 29 above

[32] Womack, J. P., Jones, D. T. and Roos, D., *The Machine that Changed the World*, Maxwell Macmillan, 1990

[33] See 'People management: applications of leaner ways of working', Chartered Institute of Personnel and Development, Working Party Paper No. 13. The authors are indebted to the CIPD for permission to use this table

[34] Toni, A. D. and Tonchia, S., 'Lean organisation, management by process and performance measurement', *International Journal of Operations and Production Management*, Vol. 16, No. 2, 1996, pp. 221–36

[35] Goldman, S. L., Nagel, R. N. and Preiss, K., *Agile Competitors and Virtual Organisations: Strategies for Enriching the Customer*, Van Nostrand Reinhold, 1995

[36] Aitken, J., Christopher, M. and Towill, D., 'Understanding, implementing and exploiting applications', *Supply Chain Management*, Vol. 5, No. 1, 2002, pp. 206–13

[37] Bowersox, D. J., Class, D. J. and Cooper, M. B., *Supply Chain Logistics Management*, International edition, 2002, McGraw-Hill, pp. 16–19

[38] Van Hoek, R., 'Reconfiguring the supply chain to implement postponed manufacturing', *International Journal of Logistics Management*, Vol. 9, No. 1, 1998, pp. 1223–47

[39] Christopher, M., 'Managing the global supply chain in an uncertain world', India Infoline Business School at: www.Indiainfoline.com/bisc/gscm.html, pp. 1–5

[40] Hoekstra, S. and Romme, J., *Integral Logistics Structures: Developing Customer-orientated Goods Flow*, McGraw-Hill, 1992, quoted in Naim, M., Naylor, J. and Barlow, J., 'Developing lean and agile supply chains in the UK housebuilding industry', Proceedings IGLC-7, 26–28 July 1999, University of California, pp. 159–68

[41] Christopher, M. and Towill, D. R., 'Supply chain migration from lean and functional to agile and customised', *Supply Chain Management*, Vol. 5, No. 4, 2000, pp. 206–13

[42] Gunasekaran, A., 'Agile manufacturing: enablers and implementation framework', *International Journal of Production Research*, Vol. 36, No. 5, 2000, pp. 1223–47

[43] As 36 above

[44] Naylor, J. B., Naim, M. M. and Berry, D., 'Leagility: interfacing the lean and agile manufacturing paradigm in the total supply chain', *International Journal of Production Economics*, Vol. 62, 1999, pp. 107–18

[45] Taken from Mason-Jones, R., Naylor, J. B. and Towill, D. R., 'Engineering the leagile supply chain', *International Journal of Agile Management Systems*, 2000

[46] Mason-Jones, R., Naylor, J. B. and Towill, D. R., 'Lean, agile or leagile? Matching your supply chain to the marketplace', *International Journal of Production Research*, Vol. 38, No. 17, 2000, pp. 4061–70

[47] Naylor, J. B., Naim, M. M. and Berry, D., 'Leagility: integrating the lean and agile manufacturing paradigm in the total supply chain', *International Journal of Production Economics*, Vol. 62, 1999, pp. 107–18

[48] Gardner, J. T. and Cooper, M. C., 'Strategic supply chain mapping approaches', *Journal of Business Logistics*, Vol. 24, No. 2, 2003, pp. 37–64

[49] As 48 above

[50] Hines, P. and Rich, N., 'The seven value stream mapping tools', *International Journal of Operations and Production Management*, Vol. 17, No. 1, 1997, pp. 37–64

[51] Interested readers are referred to Hines, P., Lamming, R., Jones, D., Cousins, P. and Rich, N., *Value Stream Mapping*, Part One, Pearson, 2000, pp. 13–92

Chapter 5

Purchasing structure and design

Learning outcomes

This chapter aims to provide an understanding of:

- the influence of environmental factors on purchasing structures
- purchasing as a functional department capable of adapting to changing demands
- horizontal organisations, processes and teams
- teams in purchasing and supply – key considerations
- cross-functional teams – their strengths and weaknesses
- cross-organisational teams
- divisional purchasing structures
- centralised purchasing
- decentralised purchasing
- purchasing in multi-plant organisations
- evolving purchasing structures
- organisational change, its inevitability and impact on purchasing.

Key ideas

- Mechanistic and organic structures.
- Downsizing, e-commerce, global sourcing, partnering and outsourcing as factors influencing purchasing organisation.
- The advantages and disadvantages of functional purchasing.
- Silo mindsets.
- The principles of horizontal organisation.
- The concept of core processes.
- The nature, purpose, structure, advantages and disadvantages of cross-functional teams.
- The basis of divisionalisation.
- Economies of scale and control as aspects of centralised purchasing.
- The advantages and disadvantages of decentralised purchasing.
- Purchasing structures in multi-plant organisations.
- The evolving nature of purchasing structures.
- The driving forces for organisational change.
- Structural, cultural and individual perspectives on organisational change.
- Implementing change.

Introduction

Contingency theory states that there is no best way to organise. The organisational structures and control systems adopted for a particular enterprise and for functions or groups of activities within the enterprise depend on or are contingent on the external environment in which the enterprise operates. Burns and Stalker[1] identified two basic structures derived from the ways in which the activities of an enterprise can respond to the environment. In a *mechanistic structure*, authority is centralised at the summit of the managerial hierarchy and vertical authority is used to control human and material resources. Mechanistic structures operate most effectively in stable environments. In an *organic structure*, authority is decentralised, employees are empowered to respond effectively to the unexpected and departments are encouraged to share information and other resources and take a cross-functional perspective. Organic structures operate most effectively in conditions of uncertainty and turbulence.

Van Weele and Rozenmeiger[2] observe that organisational development in terms of purchasing is more similar to a hiking trip, with many obstacles and obstructions on the way, than to a consciously chosen, rational and smoothly-running process. Our experiences show that knowledge and a good eye for the political, often unspoken, social processes, is essential for purchasing managers if they want to succeed in implementing effective organisational designs for purchasing.

After a brief discussion of some business environmental factors that influence both organisation and purchasing structures, this chapter will consider functional, centralised, decentralised and hybrid purchasing structures, some alternative structures, purchasing in multi-plant enterprises and, finally, some aspects of purchasing interfaces with other functions and the implementation of structural change.

5.1 Business environmental factors and purchasing structures

Five such factors are acquisitions, e-commerce, global sourcing, partnering and outsourcing.

5.1.1 Acquisitions

An acquisition is a transaction in which one firm buys controlling or 100 per cent interest in another firm with the intent of more effectively using a core competence by making the acquired firm a subsidiary business within its portfolio. It is inevitable that a purchasing strategy will be impacted by an acquisition. There will be two purchasing organisations but the synergy between the nature of purchases may be close, or not. If the synergy is close a major consideration will be to create a unified purchasing structure, however that may be organised. It may be totally centralised, centre-led, totally decentralised or some other structure. Strategic attention would be given to ensuring that most competitive purchases are made consistent with appropriate levels of staffing and service to all SBUs.

5.1.2 E-commerce

This facilitates communication between suppliers and customers and makes possible the streamlining of purchasing (and other) operational and management processes. By means of e-commerce and e-procurement, paper-based systems, bureaucratic authorisation processes and multilayered decision structures are superseded by source data capture, integrated transaction processing, electronic data interchange (EDI), real-time systems, online decision support and document management and expert systems. E-commerce also supports networking and reduces non-value-adding activities. E-commerce also impacts payment processes and requires fewer accounting staff.

5.1.3 Global sourcing

Procter & Gamble have some 90,000 suppliers of which 400 qualify as key partners and get about a quarter of Procter & Gamble's spend. There is a 1,700 strong global purchases group. The basic organisational structure is:

- Global purchases has strategic sourcing groups located in six regional centres (Cincinnati; Geneva, Switzerland; Frankfurt, Germany; Guangzhou, China; Singapore and Caracas, Venezuela). The staff uses software from SAP as the backbone of its spend-management efforts. It also uses Combinenet and Upside software.

- There is one purchasing leader for each category of spend who speaks for and represents all of P&G's business units for that category or industry. Among the spend categories are: chemicals; packaging; logistics; shared services such as MRO, IT, consulting and facilities management; and marketing.

- Additionally, many of those category leaders represent the global purchases organisation on business-unit leadership teams, providing a single point of contact for the business-unit presidents. 'That matrix allows us to stay in touch with our businesses and leverage scale and knowledge across the company', said vice-President Richard A. Hughes.

- Buyers are also part of the company's global business services organisation, leading supplier management and spend for outside services, such as consulting and professional services, facilities management, employee services and IT support.

- Of the 90,000 suppliers, 15,000 are in the marketing arena, a core competency for P&G as it is for many consumer-products companies. Those 15,000 include advertising agencies and other marketing-services-related suppliers around the world.

- About 600 other suppliers provide the finished products to P&G, like the Mr Clean Magic Eraser and Swiffer product lines. They actually make the final products in their own plants under the guidance of purchasing and operation staff in P&G's external supplies and global devices organisation.

5.1.4 Partnering

The context of this is strategic alliances, often between actual or potential competitors in order to achieve a number of strategic objectives. There have been many examples including AT&T and NEC of Japan, Motorola and Toshiba, and the Dutch electronics company Philips and Matsushita. There is no guarantee that such alliances will survive in the long term. Purchasing can be a strategic consideration to ensure that:

- intellectual property rights are protected
- contracts negotiated for the alliance can be recast if the alliance ends
- respective business cultures are respected.

5.1.5 Outsourcing

Outsourcing takes place for many reasons including, gaining access to technology and state-of-the-art knowledge, downsizing, off-shoring, off-loading non-core business activities and the need for immediate improvement in business performance. Outsourcing will have an impact on the purchasing function due to contracts being novated (transferred) to the outsourced partner and less direct contract management. Great care must be given to creating an effective 'client-side' contract management function to ensure that the contract obligations are met.

5.2 Purchasing as a functional department

When companies grow, two things happen. First, the range of tasks that must be performed expands. For example, it suddenly becomes apparent that the services of a professional purchasing manager or a marketing expert are needed to take control of specialised tasks. Second, no one person can successfully perform more than one organisational task without being overloaded. The answer for most companies is a functional structure as shown in Figure 5.1

The advantages of a functional structure so far as purchasing is concerned, include:

- the purchasing staff can learn from each other and skills can be transferred, making all of them more knowledgeable and productive
- they can be easily monitored to ensure they are performing tasks effectively and are achieving other objectives, such as cost reduction
- the manager has direct control over the purchasing activities and can report on his function's total effectiveness
- the role of purchasing is very clear to suppliers and other in-house functions
- it prevents disparate purchasing decisions being made across the business.

The possible disadvantages of a functional structure so far as purchasing is concerned, include:

- *communication problems between functions* – a classic problem is a design department not giving purchasing sufficient time to undertake supply market research effectively
- *strategic planning* – each functional area concentrates on its own strategy and fails to grasp how integration is essential
- *hidden talent* – the company fails to recognise talent that is capable of being developed into greater roles across the company.

Figure 5.1 Functional structure

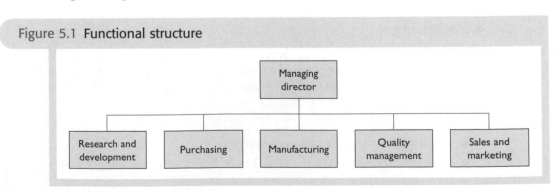

Carr, Kaynak and Muthusamy[3] have studied the coordination capability between operations and other functional areas within the firm. They conclude that when functional areas coordinate and cooperate they complete tasks or activities for the benefit of the entire organisation rather than to further their own interests. Coordination is dictated by the organisation with respect to which tasks or activities need to be performed and when they need to be completed. Cooperation relies on the willingness of the members of the organisation to work together voluntarily to complete their tasks or activities. They argue that cross-functional teams use information on quality data to build quality into the product rather than 'inspecting' quality into the finished product and removing defective products. Based upon the study, the operations, marketing, purchasing and engineering functional areas appear to have a tendency to work together and these working relationships have significant benefits. Some organisations have been shown to develop the coordination capability. The literature suggests the need for:

- the organisation culture to recognise participation and shared vision
- reward systems aligned with coordination and cooperation
- mutual trust between functions
- cross-functional training
- minimal turnover of staff in order to retain relationships and knowledge.

5.3 Horizontal organisations and processes

Horizontal organisations are not completely flat, but they have fewer layers than their vertical counterparts. Neither is necessarily incompatible with vertical structures. Ostroff and Smith[4] point out that each company must seek its own unique balance between the vertical and horizontal features needed to deliver performance. These writers also provide the following working list of ten principles 'at the heart of' horizontal organisations.

5.3.1 Horizontal organisations' principles and characteristics

- Organise around the process not the task.
- Flatten hierarchy by minimising the subdivision of workflows and non-value-adding activities.
- Assign ownership of processes and process performance.
- Link performance objectives and evaluation to customer satisfaction.
- Make teams, not individuals, the principal building blocks of the organisations' performance and design.
- Combine managerial and non-managerial activities as often as possible.
- Treat multiple competences as the rule, not the exception.
- Inform and train people on a 'just-in-time to perform' basis, not on a 'need to know' basis.
- Maximise supplier and customer contact.
- Reward individual skill development and team performance, not just skilled performance.

Table 5.1 Differences between vertical and horizontal organisations

Aspect	Vertical/functional organisation	Horizontal/process organisation
Performance objective	Profitability, shareholder value, financial results	Customer satisfaction
Focus of effort	Functional specific improvement	Company-wide processes linked to customer satisfaction
Business structure	Linking together business units, functions, departments and tasks	Linking together work flows
Basis of organisation	Individuals, positions and tasks	Teams
Management and non-managerial activities	Separate	Combined so far as possible – emphasis on empowerment
Expertise	Emphasise task specialisation in the service of functional excellence	Emphasise the importance of multiple competences
Information	Used for decision making and managerial control	Provided directly to users on a just-in-time basis
Supplier/customer contact	Often at arm's length	Encouraged as a means of ascertaining customers' needs, encouraging improvement and participation
Rewards	Individual performance, promotion	Wider roles within the team and core processes

In essence, the main differences between vertical and horizontal organisations can be summarised as in Table 5.1.

Essentially, horizontal organisations are concerned with core processes and teams, both of which have implications for purchasing structures.

5.3.2 Core processes

Kaplan and Murdoch[5] define a core process as: 'A set of interrelated activities, decisions and informational material flows which together determine the competitive success of the company.'

Core processes have the following important characteristics:

- An enterprise will generally have no more than three or four core processes that are critical to the achievement of its strategic objectives, core competences and core products. Such processes are not unrelated to Porter's primary activities, shown in Figure 3.13.
- Each core process is comprised of a number of key activities.
- Kaplan and Murdoch state that, as shown in Figure 5.2, with core processes 'work flows, decision-making organisation and information systems are redesigned in a parallel, integrated fashion rather than sequentially or independently. Core processes therefore cut across the functional, geographic and even company boundaries that

Figure 5.2 **The characteristics of core processes**

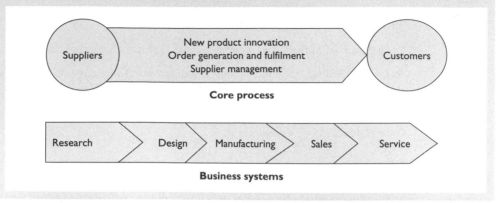

apply in a typical value chain or business framework which views a company as a sequence of functional activities each pursuing its own frequently conflicting objectives.'

■ Core processes may extend beyond organisational boundaries. This is clearly the case when new product innovation involves suppliers and, possibly, suppliers' suppliers.

In most organisations, purchasing is a support rather than a primary activity, such as supply management, logistics or materials management. A possible exception is retailing where 'buying' is a critical factor and satisfies the criteria for a core competence set out in section 4.1.1. Whether purchasing is a core process or an activity within such a process determines reporting levels, the content of the purchasing task and the positioning of purchasing in an organisational structure.

5.4 Teams

Teams are groups of people working together to achieve a common objective, such as customer satisfaction. The growing consensus is that teams are the best way to:

■ integrate tasks
■ integrate information
■ maximise competence
■ manage performance
■ manage resources
■ promote employee satisfaction and reduce stress
■ implement quality management and improvement.

The team concept also has implications for purchasing structures. If the person in control of purchasing or an area of purchasing is regarded as a team *leader*, it is arguable that the job content is different from that of a team *manager*. Although leadership – in the sense of directing the work of others – is one of the four functions frequently ascribed to management (the other three being planning, organising and controlling), it is widely agreed that the important qualities that distinguish leaders from managers are vision, innovation and adaptability. It is the possession of these qualities that transforms purchasing managers into purchasing strategists.

5.5 Cross-functional purchasing

5.5.1 Definition

The Institute of Supply Management (USA)[6] states that cross-functional teams are:

> groups of individuals from various organisational functions who are brought together to achieve clear, worthwhile, and compelling goals that could not be reached without a team. Teaming leverages organisational resources while utilising the expertise of team members. Purchasers typically participate in teams dealing with sourcing, commodities, quality, and new product/service development.

5.5.2 Reasons for the formation of cross-functional teams

The involvement of purchasing in multi-skilled teams drawn from several functions is attributable to at least six factors:

- the involvement of purchasing in strategic procurement decisions
- the concept of the 'supply chain', which emphasises the need to deal with work flow in an integrated way by means of materials management and logistics approaches
- teams may make better use of the vastly increased information availability and ability to communicate effectively provided by IT and ICT
- the development of such approaches as ERP, MRP and JIT, together with single and partnership sourcing and outsourcing
- the recognition that, because of such developments as global purchasing, more complicated price and cost analyses, the need to integrate purchasing processes with those of manufacturing and the enhanced importance of quality, purchasing often needs expert advice and support in decision making
- the recognition, based on research findings, that 'teams out-perform individuals acting alone or in large organisation groupings, especially when performance requires multi-skills judgements and experience.'[7]

5.5.3 The purpose and structure of cross-functional teams

Cross-functional teams may be formed for a wide variety of purposes covering the whole supply chain spectrum. Aspects of purchasing for which cross-functional teams have special relevance include sourcing, global sourcing, outsourcing, new product development, value management and analysis, quality management, capital equipment buying and staff development and training.

Cross-functional teams may be either short-term or long-term in duration. Short-term cross-functional teams are essentially task forces formed for a particular purpose and are disbanded when that purpose has been accomplished. Long-term teams are permanent or semi-permanent. With a project such as nuclear submarine design, development, build and commission, for example, the total cycle to decommissioning could exceed 20 years.

Short-term cross-functional teams will probably adopt a matrix-type structure, as shown in Figure 4.2. In such a team, staff will be seconded from various functions, either on a part-time or full-time basis, for the duration of the team's existence.

Long-term cross-functional teams will serve full time in a project team as members of a self-contained unit headed by a project manager.

5.5.4 The advantages of cross-functional teams

Parker[8] has listed six important competitive advantages that accrue to organisations that successfully implement cross-functional teams:

1 *speed* – reduction in the time it takes to get things done, especially the product development process
2 *complexity* – improvement in the organisation's ability to solve complicated problems
3 *customer focus* – focusing the organisation's resources on satisfying the customers' needs
4 *creativity* – by bringing together people with a variety of experiences and backgrounds, cross-functional teams increase the creative capacity of the organisation
5 *organisational learning* – members of cross-functional teams are more easily able to develop new technical/job skills, learn more about other disciplines and how to work with people who have different team player styles and cultural backgrounds
6 *a single point of contact* – the promotion of more effective cross-functional teamwork by identifying one place to go for information and decisions about a project or customer.

Another advantage is an increased understanding between functions of each other's problems. Production and quality assurance may develop an enhanced appreciation of the difficulties of dealing with suppliers and purchasing an awareness of the problems faced by production and design.

Purchasing staff can make high quality contributions to cross-functional teams by effectively dealing with such things as supply chain risk, preparing tailor made contracts, exposing product and services cost drivers, applying high level negotiation skills and conducting financial due diligence.

5.6 Some problems of cross-functional teams

A number of problems have been reported in relation to cross-functional teams. Sobek *et al.*[9] point out that:

> cross-functional coordination has improved, but at the cost of depth of knowledge within functions, because people are spending less time within their own functions. Organisational learning across products has also dropped as people rapidly rotate through positions. Standardisation across products has suffered because product teams have become autonomous. In organisations that combine functional and project-based structures, engineers are often torn between the orders of their functional bosses on the one hand and the demands of project leaders on the other.

Other problems of cross-functional teams include:

- the need for a substantial investment in the training and retraining of team leaders in interpersonal skills and of team members in adopting a cross-functional, rather than a silo, orientation
- cross-functional teams require members to attend numerous meetings

■ because of their expertise, some members are required to participate in several teams concurrently with a resultant competition for priorities.

Finally, it should not be forgotten that the basic reason for cross-functional teams is to break down functional silos. This does not mean the abdication of functional responsibilities. Those responsible for product design must retain that responsibility even when working in a product team. While cross-functional sourcing may share responsibility for decision making, purchasing is not absolved from the duty of ensuring that the team has full information on potential suppliers and products and services that provide maximum value for money spent.

5.7 Cross-organisational teams

These are a development on cross-functional teams, involving the inclusion of suppliers or customers in teams. As with functions, such involvement can give organisations a greater understanding of common problems. Trent and Monczka[10] state that, on average, teams that include qualified suppliers as members demonstrate greater overall performance. They also list four further benefits that can result from supplier participation:

■ greater satisfaction concerning the quality of information exchange between the team and its key suppliers
■ a greater reliance on suppliers to support directly the teams' goals and objectives
■ greater supply base management effectiveness and
■ greater supplier contribution in a number of critical areas; one significant development is that of the 'Guest Engineer', in which a member of the supplier's staff is permanently located in the works of the purchaser.

Such inter-firm cooperation is of special importance in relation to product innovation and development (see Chapter 8).

5.8 Divisional purchasing structures

As shown in Table 5.2, the focus of divisionalisation can be on the product or service, geography or customer.

Divisionalisation is usually the pattern for large, highly diversified organisations that, often, operate in several countries or continents, as with Volvo's 3P purchasing organisation, shown in Figure 5.3. The 3P organisation covers Mack, Renault and Volvo brands, involving 5 billion euros in spend across multiple categories of purchase.

Table 5.2 **The basis of divisional structures**

Type	Focus	Examples
Product or service	Product or service provided	ICI Paints Division; Rentokil Pest Control
Geographical	Location of activity	UK Division; European Division
Customer	Customer or client	UK government contracts

Figure 5.3 Volvo's 3P purchasing organisation

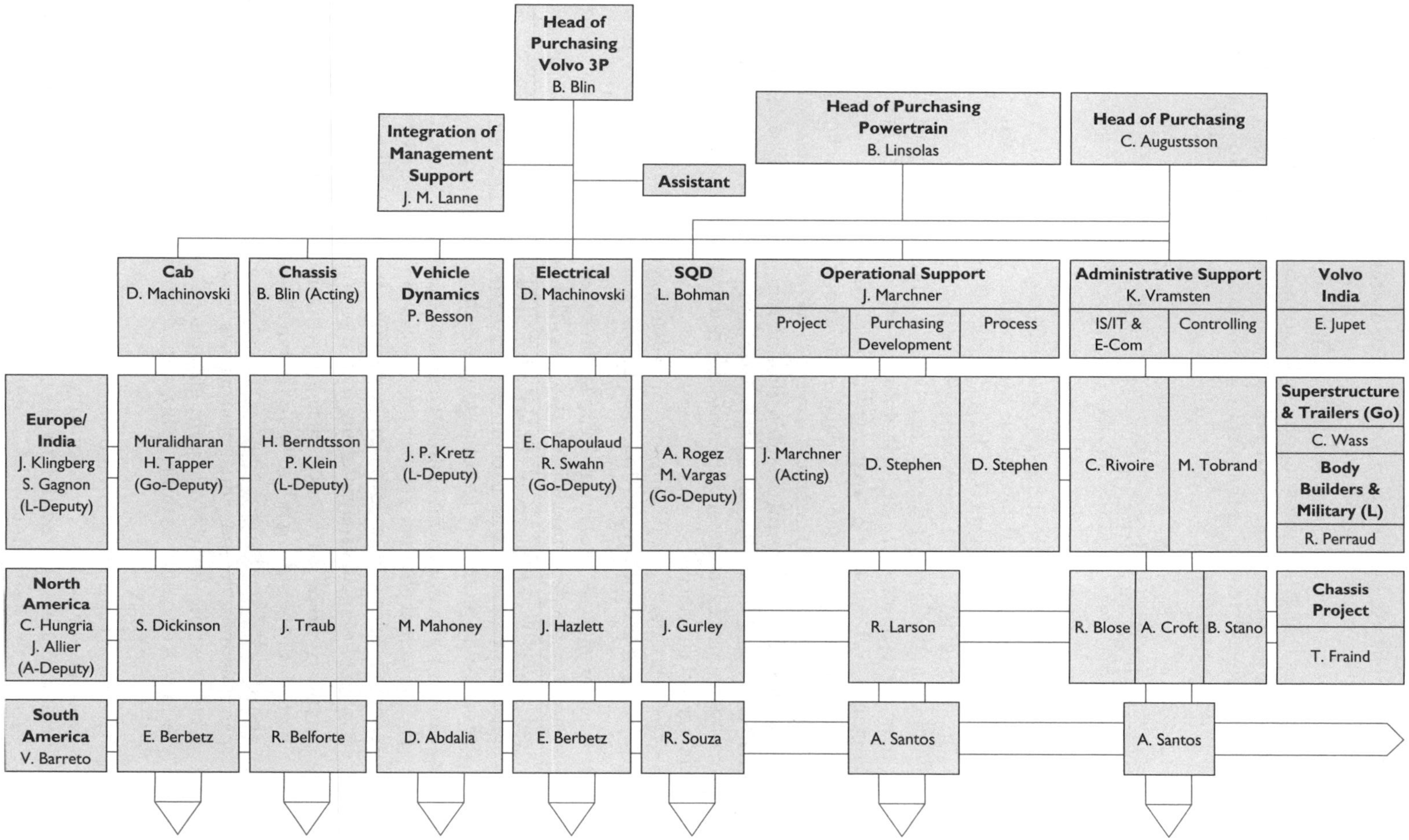

Head of Purchasing Volvo 3P — B. Blin
Head of Purchasing Powertrain — B. Linsolas
Head of Purchasing — C. Augustsson

Integration of Management Support — J. M. Lanne
Assistant

	Cab — D. Machinovski	Chassis — B. Blin (Acting)	Vehicle Dynamics — P. Besson	Electrical — D. Machinovski	SQD — L. Bohman	Operational Support — J. Marchner (Project / Purchasing Development / Process)	Administrative Support — K. Vramsten (IS/IT & E-Com / Controlling)
Europe/India — J. Klingberg, S. Gagnon (L-Deputy)	Muralidharan, H. Tapper (Go-Deputy)	H. Berndtsson, P. Klein (L-Deputy)	J. P. Kretz (L-Deputy)	E. Chapoulaud, R. Swahn (Go-Deputy)	A. Rogez, M. Vargas (Go-Deputy)	J. Marchner (Acting) / D. Stephen / D. Stephen	C. Rivoire / M. Tobrand
North America — C. Hungria, J. Allier (A-Deputy)	S. Dickinson	J. Traub	M. Mahoney	J. Hazlett	J. Gurley	R. Larson	R. Blose, A. Croft, B. Stano
South America — V. Barreto	E. Berbetz	R. Belforte	D. Abdalia	E. Berbetz	R. Souza	A. Santos	A. Santos

Volvo India — E. Jupet

Superstructure & Trailers (Go) — C. Wass
Body Builders & Military (L) — R. Perraud

Chassis Project — T. Fraind
A. Santos
A. Santos
A. Santos

Once established, each division is organised in a functional form with its own hierarchies and is self-contained and autonomous in terms of day-to-day operations. Most writers agree that divisionalised organisations exhibit superior profitability to centralised ones as it makes visible the contribution of each division to the profitability of the enterprise. The mere act of creating a division will not, however, of itself increase performance. What ultimately counts is the way in which resources are allocated and decisions made within the structure.

5.9 Centralised purchasing

The term, centralised purchasing, usually implies that all key strategies, policies and decisions are taken at a company headquarters level, although it sometimes means at a regional or divisional level. It is an emotive issue with many 'outlying' operating companies or centres resenting decisions forced upon them.

In July 2001, the Department of Health published a report by OXERA, 'A Fundamental Review of the Generic Drugs Market'. The report observed at [8] that in the primary-care sector, the NHS does not procure centrally, but rather 'fragments' its buying power by using a large number of pharmacists as its contractors. These pharmacists negotiate with their suppliers individually, and, together, do not have the same buyer power as the NHS would have if it were to negotiate as a whole. At [8.2] the report considers that rather than instituting a major change to centralised purchasing, the NHS could focus this option (of centralised purchasing of drugs in shortage) on the main weaknesses in the current system – price volatility and uncoordinated supply in the face of shortage.

The report goes on to consider the advantages of centralised purchasing through tendering of generic drugs as outlined below:

■ There would still be an incentive to negotiate low prices from suppliers for Category D, since it is the department itself that does the purchasing. Under the current system, this incentive is lost. Category D (of the drug tariff) is an element of the reimbursement system designed to secure that patients are supplied even when drugs are in shortage by protecting pharmacies in the short term from price increases.

■ The centralised agency would have greater buyer power and different incentives than the individual pharmacists over the suppliers that have Category D products in stock, which should result in lower prices than at present. Despite this, if only one supplier has supplies of an essential drug, then it would still be able to charge high prices.

■ Suppliers would have fewer incentives to hoard Category D products, since they would only be able to sell them to the purchasing agency. For the reasons mentioned above, they would not be able to extract the same high prices from the agency as they can now from the individual pharmacists. In addition, by selling to the agency, they would 'expose' themselves to the government (i.e. they would not be able engage in speculative trading without being noticed by the department, as occurs under the current system).

■ The purchasing agency would be better placed to ration products that are in serious shortage, for example, by supplying only a limited amount of the drug to each region (and providing information to the public on where they can obtain the product). At present, the distribution of Category D drugs over regions may be random since it depends on which pharmacists are quickest to find the drug.

5.9.1 Economies of scale

Centralised purchasing enables an organisation to leverage its purchasing power to the best effect as:

- forecasts can be prepared of the total quantities of items likely to be required by the whole organisation for a specified period
- such consolidation of quantities can form the basis for negotiating quantity discounts, rebates or learning curve reductions
- suppliers dealing with a centralised purchasing department have an incentive to compete for 'preferred supplier status' or the whole or a substantial proportion of the undertaking's requirements
- suppliers may be able to reduce prices by spreading overheads over longer production runs
- the supplier base may be reduced by the award of 'preferred supplier status' to one or two providers
- centralisation permits the employment of purchasing professionals in a way that is not possible with diversified purchasing and who can become expert in the procurement of special classes of materials or products following market trends and the development of reliable and economic supply sources or of import and export procedures where there is substantial global sourcing.

5.9.2 Coordination of activity

- Centralised purchasing tends to have a greater strategic focus than divisionalised purchasing due to proximity to major organisational decision makers.
- Uniform policies can be adopted, such as single sourcing.
- Competitive or 'maverick' buying between functions is eliminated.

5.10 Decentralised purchasing

A SIGMA[11] report set out the key arguments in support of decentralised procurement as:

- reduced incentives for corruption via large-scale protectionism or favouritism
- a closer matching of goods and services delivered to the detailed requirements of end users
- reduced scope for mistakes affecting large volume purchases that result in unnecessary over-spending
- less bureaucracy because of shorter time frames and fewer forms for both purchasers and suppliers
- greater possibilities for SMEs to compete successfully for contracts
- opportunities for local purchasers to obtain lower prices for locally manufactured goods
- more scope for employees to take individual responsibility and develop a 'service' mentality.

Some of the advantages and disadvantages of decentralised purchasing are shown in Table 5.3.

Table 5.3 Advantages and disadvantages of decentralised purchasing

Advantages	Disadvantages
Closer to users and better understanding of local needs	Reduced leverage that exists with consolidation of purchases
Response time to divisional or plant needs may be rapid and of higher quality	Focus on local rather than corporate and operational rather than strategic considerations
Possibly closer relationships with suppliers	Purchasing will tend to report to a lower organisational level
Local suppliers and consequent lower transportation costs	Limited expertise in requirements and few opportunities for cross-functional collaboration
Where plants are profit centres the view is expressed that if purchasing costs are a high percentage of total costs then each profit centre should make its own decisions regarding purchasing and suppliers	Possibly lack of standardisation Restricted career opportunities for local purchasing staff Cost of purchasing relatively high
Geographical, cultural, political, environmental, social, language and currency appropriateness	

5.11 Purchasing in multi-plant organisations

Decentralisation implies that an organisation's activities are spread over a number of plants or locations. The issue of centralisation or decentralisation, therefore, arises.

An investigation by Lyles and Payne[12] of 74 UK companies indicated three 'models' of procurement:

1 coordinated devolved procurement
2 centralised procurement
3 consultative centralised procurement.

These models are shown in Figure 5.4.

In the above investigation, Lyles and Payne report the following findings.

■ Most organisations that now have a centralised or consultative structure have evolved from a devolved model, such as that shown in Figure 5.4.

■ In 2000, the most common procurement model in the companies researched was one of centralised control and devolved authorisation. Of the respondents, 93 per cent considered that the control over the purchasing of products and services in their organisation was centralised – only 5 per cent describing such control as devolved. Conversely, 84 per cent of respondents stated that the authorisation of expenditure was devolved, 14 per cent that it was centralised. It can be deduced that about 9 per cent of the sample had both centralised control and authorisation of expenditure.

Purchasing will tend to be completely centralised where the items required at each plant are largely homogeneous. An example would be a confectionery company with a large number of plants each using large quantities of flour, sugar and other common ingredients.

Figure 5.4 Models of procurement for multi-plant organisations

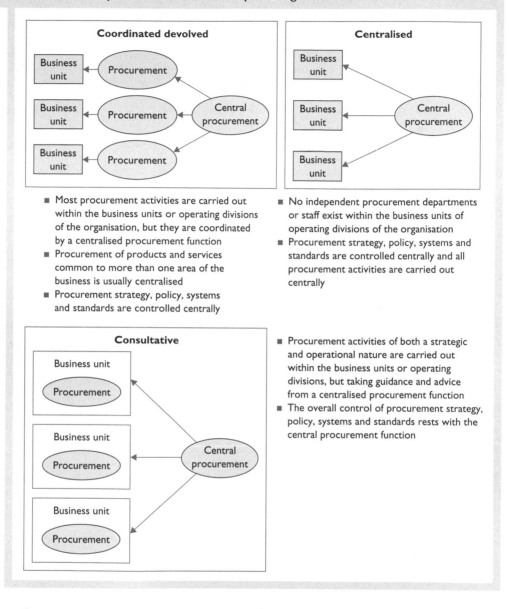

Coordinated devolved

- Most procurement activities are carried out within the business units or operating divisions of the organisation, but they are coordinated by a centralised procurement function
- Procurement of products and services common to more than one area of the business is usually centralised
- Procurement strategy, policy, systems and standards are controlled centrally

Centralised

- No independent procurement departments or staff exist within the business units of operating divisions of the organisation
- Procurement strategy, policy, systems and standards are controlled centrally and all procurement activities are carried out centrally

Consultative

- Procurement activities of both a strategic and operational nature are carried out within the business units or operating divisions, but taking guidance and advice from a centralised procurement function
- The overall control of procurement strategy, policy, systems and standards rests with the central procurement function

In this case, orders would be placed centrally and deliveries made against contract as required by the local plants.

Purchasing may be coordinated and devolved where the group is a conglomerate consisting of a number of plants, each producing dissimilar products. In this case, purchasing is done at plant level as the materials and components used are specific to that location. Reasons for organising purchasing in this way include that:

- as the efficiency of purchasing influences profitability, the manager of each plant should have control over the expenditure incurred for materials for that plant
- centralised purchasing proliferates paperwork and leads to delays

- some plants are so large that the economies of scale referred to earlier are already present and there is an optimum after which *diseconomies* of scale set in.

One relevant objection to complete decentralisation is that the competition between plants may lead to a loss of group purpose.

As Lyles and Payne show, in most group undertakings there is a compromise – some purchasing activities being undertaken centrally and others at plant level. It is, therefore, necessary to determine:

- what activities shall be undertaken centrally
- what activities shall be centralised
- how coordination between central and plant-level purchasing shall be achieved.

In each case, the options chosen will depend on the undertaking, but the following arrangements are typical.

5.11.1 Centralised activities

- Determination of major purchasing strategies and policies, such as vertical integration, outsourcing, single and partnership sourcing, countertrade, reciprocal sourcing.
- Purchase of leverage, strategic and bottleneck products (see Figure 2.12).
- Purchase of capital equipment and systems.
- Negotiation of bulk contracts for homogeneous supplies used by a number of plants.
- Purchasing research into market conditions, vulnerability and similar matters.
- Rationalisation of the share of orders to be received by specific suppliers. This will apply particularly when the purchasing organisation controls a large proportion of the available orders or, for social reasons, needs to spread its purchasing power fairly among a number of dependent suppliers.
- Control of group inventory.
- Staff training and development.

5.11.2 Decentralised activities

- Small-value orders and maintenance, repair and operating (MRO) items.
- Items used only by that plant.
- Emergency purchases – where local initiative may avoid an interruption of production, for example.
- Local buying to save transport costs.
- Local purchasing undertaken for social reasons – that is, a plant is part of the community in which it is situated and can, by exercising its purchasing power, contribute to the prosperity of the locality.
- Staff purchases.

5.11.3 Procurement councils

Procurement councils as Cavinato[13] points out are a variant of decentralisation. The councils are comprised of purchasing staff whom, although located at different plants, have similar requirements for products and services. The council members meet and coordinate a single source or quantity as though they were one group, thus removing the disadvantages of reduced leverage resulting from the non-consolidation of purchases, adversity of suppliers and lack of standardisation. In practice, procurement councils may disband due to the absence of leadership or top management support.

5.12 Evolving purchasing structures

Cavinato[14] suggests that, increasingly, organisations are moving away from defined departments and issues such as centralisation and decentralisation, to whom purchasing should report, and the title of the most senior purchasing officer are of less consequence now than in the past: 'Suppliers are accessing the firm through links other than just the purchasing department. The firm is increasingly gaining entry into customer operations through channels other than sales and marketing.'

Apart from traditional centralised and decentralised purchasing, Cavinato identifies five other models of purchasing organisation that have evolved and have significant implications both for purchasing and logistics.

5.12.1 The centralised coordinator model

This is when decentralised purchasing reports to a plant or divisional general managers with a centralised coordinating purchasing group at corporate headquarters. The central group takes a macro view of purchasing and logistics issues concerning the entire organisation and provides services and information to the individual plants or divisions.

Cavinato claims that this model has the advantage of scope and authority in dealing with suppliers without the full overhead cost often associated with fully centralised groups.

5.12.2 The area planner concept model

In this model, a central procurement group handles issues of vendor sourcing, selection and performance monitoring while users handle the processing of requisitions and day-to-day orders for inbound supplies.

The area planner approach thus removes procurement from the transaction cycle.

5.12.3 The supply manager concept model

Here, one person has responsibility for the flow of a product or a few products from the supplier input, through production to delivery to the ultimate customer. Performance is based on a contribution margin computed from selling price less costs accumulated up to the packing end of the production line.

A major problem with this arrangement is the difficulty of recruiting people with the wide range of skills required for each product.

5.12.4 Commodity teams

Like the supply manager concept model, this is a supply chain rather than primarily purchasing model. Logistics pipelines seek to enhance collaboration between purchasers and suppliers. An example is the collaborative forecasting and replenishment (CFAR) initiative developed between Walmart and Procter & Gamble. Teams from both companies forecast sales of Procter & Gamble products at Walmart stores and jointly plan replenishments. Continuous replenishment programs (CRP) are driven by withdrawals of products from retailers' warehouses rather than by point-of-sale (POS) data at retail stores and vendor-managed inventory (VMI), where inventories at the wholesaler or retailer are monitored and replenished by the manufacturer or wholesaler, are variations on the pipeline model. With pipeline models, the supplier is undertaking many of the processes traditionally performed by purchasers.

5.12.5 The market segmentation model

This model is associated with Cannon.[15] The 'market' in this model comprises all the orders/contracts that the organisation wishes to place. Each item purchased can be categorised according to four variables:

1 rapidity of technological change associated with the item
2 total volume of spend
3 number of orders placed annually
4 number of suppliers.

Cannon suggests that, on the basis of such segmentation, interaction between purchasing and its internal customers can be related to the following three scenarios.

1 Where the total value of spend is low, the internal customer should do the buying and the purchasing function should provide training in areas such as vendor appraisal, the legal significance of contract terms and conditions, tender/quotation evaluation, negotiation, contracts administration and dispute resolution. This arrangement has the advantages of eliminating requisitions, enhanced speed and reduced costs.

2 Where the total value of spend is high and there is also a high rate of technological change, internal customers/users should collaborate when procuring the organisation's requirements. In this scenario, purchasing will again provide training in the areas listed above. Service agreements will, additionally, demarcate areas of buying responsibility and the possibility of using targeted added-value approaches should be investigated by both parties.

3 When the total value of spend is high but the rate of technological change is low, purchasing should be the responsibility of a professional department, which offers its internal customers added value, service and expertise.

All the above five models have important structural and organisational implications for purchasing. Often they will change the responsibilities and reduce the size of the purchasing function and expedite the change from vertical to horizontal structures. In extreme cases, purchasing may become a virtual activity.

5.13 Organisational change

5.13.1 Types of change

Daft[16] has identified five basic types of change that affect organisations and apply to purchasing and other functions:

1 *technology* – such as IT and e-procurement

2 *product or service* – purchasing, for example, was traditionally mainly a transactional process, concerned with obtaining items for production or other internal use, but is increasingly involved with strategic issues

3 *administrative* – the movement from discrete purchasing 'departments' to cross-functional procedures, such as the scanning, screening and selection of suppliers by cross-functional teams, for example

4 *people* – such as the need for trained purchasing professionals

5 *business relationships* – which arise from acquisitions, mergers, joint ventures and partnership alliances.

5.13.2 Forces for change

Forces for change may be both external and internal.

External forces are those outside the organisation that create pressure to devise and implement new strategies to meet the challenges of competition or technology.

Internal forces are those within the organisation that may be the result of changing environmental conditions, such as declining competitive advantage, rising production costs or outdated facilities. Such factors may create internal pressure for new corporate strategies.

5.13.3 Perspectives on organisational change

Changes due to the above causes can be considered from three perspectives – structural, cultural and individual.

Structural change

If structure follows strategy, then changes in strategy arising from any of the above five drivers will be followed by structural changes. This can be exemplified by technological drivers, such as IT, and administrative or business drivers resulting in the decision to outsource.

IT, with its capability to communicate and share information, has caused traditional hierarchies to be replaced with horizontal structures. The need to physically locate people and units together to ensure coordination and supervision or to choose between centralised or decentralised structures is also increasingly invalidated by IT, with a consequent focus on projects and processes rather than standard procedures and tasks. IT can be substituted for layers of management and a number of managerial tasks. Lucas and Baroudi[17] give examples of how IT can create virtual organisations that do not exist in physical form. Mail-order companies, for example, employ individuals working from home using a special phone connected to an 0800 number to take orders from customers who have their catalogues. Manufacturers can use parts suppliers to substitute for their inventory. The supplier, linked electronically with the manufacturer, can use overnight delivery to ensure that the parts are delivered just-in-time for production. The manufacturer, thus, has a virtual parts inventory that is owned by the supplier until it arrives for production.

Outsourcing may lead to the complete disappearance of a function from an organisational structure.

Cultural change

Organisational culture is a 'pattern of belief and expectations shared by organisational members'[18] or 'the way things are done around here'.[19]

Culture is an important aspect of change as culture might either block or facilitate it and also because changes in organisational strategies usually require changes in organisational structure. Thus, a change from transactional to partnership purchasing will require a cultural reorientation on the part of the staff involved so that its suppliers are no longer regarded as adversaries to be kept at arm's length, but, instead, as allies. Developments such as total quality management (TQM) require the acceptance by all employees of a culture of continuous improvement in which people at all organisational levels accept responsibility for identifying quality problems early on. TQM also requires a culture of 'learning together', with guidance and support for the learning process being provided by management. With TQM it is also a management responsibility to develop a culture in which every employee is encouraged and empowered to take ownership of outputs, customer problems and improvement actions. Such changes in cultural outlook will usually require a significant investment in education and training and the use of an internal or external change agent responsible for ensuring that the planned change is properly implemented.

Individual change

People usually respond to change with hostility and apprehension due to numerous factors, including insecurity, lack of information regarding proposed changes, the break-up of work groups, perceived threats to expertise, status or earnings, inconvenience of new working conditions and changes in management and supervisory personnel.

Preparing for change

An evaluation by management of structural, cultural and individual issues is the essential first step in the implementation of change at both organisational and functional levels.

5.13.4 The implementation of change

Kurt Lewin[20] a behavioural scientist, argues that the process of implementing change involves three basic steps:

1 *unfreezing* – enabling people or organisations to be willing to change

2 *changing* – selection of techniques to implement change

3 *refreezing* – reinforcing and supporting the change so that it becomes a relatively permanent part of organisational processes.

Lewin's view of the change process is shown in Figure 5.5.

Numerous writers have produced step-by-step guides for the implementation of change and the following extension of Lewin's approach by Kotter and Schlesinger[21] is typical. This model suggests an eight-step process for the successful implementation of change – the first four steps being directed at the defrosting of a hardened status quo (or culture), steps five and seven introduce new practices and the last step corresponds to Lewin's 'refreezing', which helps to make them stick. The eight steps are:

Figure 5.5 **Lewin's view of the change process**

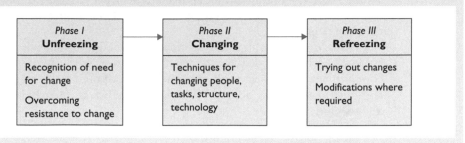

1 *establishing a sense of urgency* – recognising the need for the enterprise or a function within the enterprise to change if it is to achieve and retain competitive advantage or cope with crises and opportunities

2 *creating the guiding coalition* – creating and empowering a group to lead change and encouraging the group to work as a team

3 *developing a vision and a strategy* – 'vision' in this context means having a clear sense of what the future requires and the strategies required to turn the vision into reality

4 *communicating the change vision* – using every available communication media to create an awareness of the visions and strategies to employees and others affected and secure their cooperation and involvement

5 *empowering broad-based action* – removing obstacles, changing structures or systems and encouraging new approaches

6 *generating short-term wins* – strategies usually involve some shorter-term goals as the achievement of these goals provides encouragement to sustain people in their efforts to attain longer-term objectives

7 *consolidating gains and producing more change* – reinvigorating the process with new projects, themes and change agents

8 *anchoring new approaches in the culture* – stabilising change at the new level and reinforcing it by means of such supporting mechanisms as policies, structure or norms.

Collins[22] criticises what he terms 'n-step' models of change implementation on three grounds:

■ they assume that organisations act in a rational predictable way, while the reality is that they consist of a diverse range of people with diverse ideas and opinions about the right course of action

■ n-step models assume that change management can be reduced to a number of discrete, sequential steps and that change has an identifiable beginning and end, while the reality is that it is uncertain, unpredictable and contingent and 'we cannot expect the processes and final outcomes of change to map out clearly before us'

■ n-step models fail to recognise that the creative and critical skills required by managers to successfully engender change cannot be captured in 'a few rules or simple recipes for success'.

Collins, therefore, concludes that, rather than offer simplistic n-step accounts, writers should recognise that their models need to incorporate some of the complexities of real life. N-step models are dishonest and paint an inaccurate and oversimplified picture of the change process.

Probably the best approach is to recognise the importance in all change situations of communicating the need for change, consultation with all affected by the change and commitment to the successful implementation of change by all involved. In any event, learning organisations do not suddenly adopt strategic change but, rather, are perpetually seeking it.

Case study

Crank Ltd

Crank have been in business since the 1920s and have three locations in the UK. Their head office and main manufacturing site is in Leicester. This site makes complex tubular assemblies for defence organisations, oil and gas and transportation. There is a site at Southampton making tubular shafts for golf clubs, and a site in Glasgow manufacturing aerospace duct assemblies up to 8 inches in diameter.

The procurement organisation is currently decentralised. At Leicester there is a purchasing manager, whereas at Southampton and Glasgow, each site has a chief buyer in charge of small procurement teams. There is a new chief executive of Crank who fervently believes he needs a new approach for the group in the way procurement is structured. Over the past month he has, quietly, been obtaining some salient facts. The more important of these are:

- each site operates as a 'profit centre' and the site director has to deliver a targeted return on capital employed.
- there are no group purchase contracts
- five major purchases account for 61 per cent of total group expenditure – they are all raw material including different specifications of tubing
- there are more than 40 suppliers for the five major purchases
- no formal tendering has taken place, on any site, for more than two years
- capital equipment is purchased by the group chief engineer
- the company has embraced modern logistics practices including JIT and OTIF (On Time In Full)
- there is no savings plan for purchasing
- the purchasing teams do not liaise.

The chief executive intends to consider an alternative purchasing structure that can deliver benefits for the group and each operational site. Based upon your knowledge and the salient facts above what advice could you give him?

Tasks

1 What alternative structures could be considered?
2 What are the potential obstacles to change?
3 What business benefits could accrue from a changed purchasing structure?

Discussion questions

5.1 If you worked for a national construction company which had five operating divisions in Wales, England and Scotland, each with their own divisional managing director, what organisational structure would you recommend for procurement? You should take into account the need for each project to deliver a profit.

5.2 Your managing director has stated that he no longer feels the need for a purchasing department. Her logic is that if each manager runs their own budget they will ensure the best price will be obtained. What are your views?

5.3 Your purchasing manager wants to control everything to the last degree, including the fact that no supplier has a meeting on your site unless purchasing is present. Is this a sustainable policy?

5.4 In what way can the adoption of a partnering strategy with key suppliers impact on the design of purchasing structures?

5.5 In which type of structure would you prefer to work: (1) vertical or (2) horizontal? What does your choice probably reveal about you?

5.6 Environmental management is a strategic imperative. What impact is this having on organisational structures, including purchasing?

5.7 'Project teams are a waste of resources when a task can be handled effectively through the existing structures' (Charles Handy, *Understanding Organisations*, 4th edn, Penguin, 1993, p. 269). Discuss this statement with special reference to cross-functional teams.

5.8 In many local authorities the responsibility for purchasing is with service heads. Taking IT as an example, what are the strengths and weaknesses of such an approach?

5.9 You have been asked to conduct research among your strategic suppliers asking them what they think about your purchasing structure. Write a one-page letter setting out your specific questions that you would like answered.

5.10 Consider the applicability of each of the five evolving purchasing structures described in section 5.12 to your organisation.

5.11 Outsourcing is not an uncommon approach to dealing with services. Do you consider that purchasing is a good candidate for outsourcing? What are your perceived advantages in such an organisational approach?

5.12 Your company has recently been purchased by a USA food manufacturer. Within one week of the purchase the new parent company has said that it intends to close the UK purchasing function and relocate it to Texas. You are the purchasing manager and have been offered a senior post in Texas. What dilemma and opportunity does this present and what would you do to deal with the fears and aspirations of your staff?

Past examination questions

1 The following questions relate to strategy and how this may influence the purchasing function:
   (a) Explain the **three** levels of strategy commonly present in organisations.
   (b) Describe how purchasing could support an organisation in the pursuit of a strategy of product-differentiation or service-differentiation.
   (c) Explain the purpose of a mission statement

   CIPS, *The Business Environment for Purchasing and Supply*, November 2009

2 Explain **two** advantages of a centralised procurement department compared to a decentralised procurement department.

   CIPS, *The Business Environment for Purchasing and Supply*, November 2009

3 Suggest **five** questions to be considered when reviewing purchasing expenditures within a spending category.

   CIPS, *An Introduction to Purchasing Strategy*, November 2008

4 Discuss which individuals might be expected to have legal capacity to enter into a contract on behalf of an organisation.

   CIPS, *Preparing and Managing Contracts*, May 2010

References

[1] Burns, T. and Stalker, G. H., *The Management of Innovation*, Tavistock, 1968

[2] Van Weele, A. J. and Rozenmeiger, F. A., *Revolution in Purchasing: Building Competitive Power through Pro-active Purchasing*. Philips Electronics – Eindhoven University of Technology, 1996

[3] Carr, A. S., Kaynak, H. and Muthusamy, S., 'The cross-functional coordination between operations, marketing, purchasing and engineering and the impact on performance', *International Journal Manufacturing Technology and Management*, Vol. 13, No. 1, 2008, pp. 55–77

[4] Ofstroff, F. and Smith, D., 'Redesigning the corporation: the horizontal organisation', *McKinsey Quarterly*, No. 1, 1992, pp. 148–67

[5] Kaplan, R. B. and Murdoch, L., 'Rethinking the corporation: core process redesign', *McKinsey Quarterly*, No. 2, 1991, pp. 27–43

[6] Institute of Supply Managementusa (USA), *Glossary of Key Supply Management Terms*, see ISM website: www.ism.ws

[7] Torrington, D. and Hall, L., *Personnel Management*, Prentice Hall, 1991, p. 208

[8] Parker, G. M., 'How to succeed as a cross-functional team', Proceedings of 79th Annual International Purchasing Conference of the National Association of Purchasing Managers, 1 May, 1994

[9] Sobek, I. I., Durward, K., Liker, J. K. and Ward, A. C., 'Another look at how Toyota integrates product development', *Harvard Business Review*, Vol. 76.4, July/August, 1998, p. 36

[10] Trent, R. J. and Monczka, R. M., 'Effective cross-functional sourcing teams: critical success factors', *International Journal of Purchasing and Materials Management*, Fall, 1994, pp. 3–13

[11] CCNM/SIGMA/PUMA, '*Centralised and Decentralised Public Procurement*', 2000, 108, p. 5

[12] Lyles, J. and Payne, R., 'Strategic purchasing review report', prepared for *Market Research Focus 2000*, p. 7. The authors are grateful to Market Research Focus Ltd for permission to quote from the report

13 Cavinato, J. L., 'Evolving procurement organisations: logistics implications', *Journal of Business Logistics*, Vol. 1, No. 1, 1992, pp. 27–44

14 As 13 above

15 Cannon, S., 'Purchasing's segmented market', *Purchasing and Supply Chain Management*, Nov. 1994, pp. 35–9

16 Daft, R. L., *Organisation Theory and Design*, West Publishing, 1983, quoted in Thomason, J. L., *Strategic Management*, Chapman & Hall, 1990, p. 590

17 Lucas, H. C. and Baroudi, J., 'The role of information technology in organisation design', *Journal of Management Information Systems*, Vol. 10, No. 4, Spring, 1994, pp. 9–23

18 Hellriegel, D., Slocum, J. W. and Woodman, R. W., *Organisational Behaviour*, West Publishing, 1986, p. 340

19 Handy, C., *Understanding Organisations*, 4th edn, Penguin, 1993

20 Lewin, K., *Field Theory in Social Science*, Harper & Row, 1951

21 Kotter, J. P. and Schlesinger, L. A., 'Choosing strategies for change', *Harvard Business Review*, March–April, 1979, pp. 107–9

22 Collins, D., *Organisational Change*, Routledge, 1998. The authors are indebted to Harty, C., 'Do n-step guides for change work?' CIPS Knowledge in Action series, for the information contained in this section

Chapter 6

Purchasing procedures and supporting tools

Learning outcomes

With reference to purchasing and supply management, this chapter aims to provide an understanding of:

- traditional purchasing procedures and their inefficiencies
- the need to transform purchasing procedures to encourage radical thinking
- e-commerce, e-business, e-SCM and e-procurement
- e-procurement tools and the opportunity for enhancing systems and procedures
- the positive contribution of purchasing and supplier manuals
- legal considerations when contracting.

Key ideas

- Phases of the purchasing cycle.
- E-commerce, e-business, e-SCM and e-procurement.
- Electronic data interchange (EDI).
- E-hubs, exchanges and marketplaces.
- E-catalogues and reverse auctions.
- E-payment.
- Processing of small-value orders.
- Purchasing and supplier manuals.
- Contract essentials, 'the battle of the forms' and the general structure of contracts.

Introduction

A *procedure* is a system of sequential steps or techniques for getting a task or job done. Procedures are also the formal arrangements by means of which policies linking strategies are implemented. A cluster of reliable procedures, each comprised of a number of operations that, together, provide information enabling staff to execute and managers to control those operations, is called a system.

6.1 The sequence and impact of purchasing procedures

It is essential that there are purchasing procedures to set out how purchasing departments make their contribution at key phases of the purchasing cycle and explain how stakeholders and others interface with the procedures. There are, potentially, serious implications when purchasing procedures are not complied with.

6.1.1 Identification of need and specification development

A purchasing procedure will set out:

- how purchasing will engage in each facet of the process
- the need to deal effectively with intellectual property rights
- the methodology for engaging with the supply market
- how to avoid creating a monopoly supply scenario
- the need for forecasts of usage to be as accurate as possible
- how potential suppliers will be pre-qualified through the use of pre-qualification questionnaires.

6.1.2 Notification of authority to purchase

The purchasing procedure will set out:

- how to raise an appropriate requisition or other means to authorise the purchase
- budget approval and appropriate finance code
- issue of bills of material when these apply
- the management of emergency needs to purchase and to permit a standard procedure to be bypassed according to defined rules.

6.1.3 Requests for quotations (RFQs) and invitations to tender (ITTs)

The purchasing procedure will set out:

- how the value of the purchase will impact on the methodology to be adopted, for example, high value contracts must have a minimum number of quotations/tenders
- the content required when RFQs or ITTs are submitted
- the methodology to be applied to the evaluation of RFQs or ITTs to avoid biased decisions being made
- how and in what circumstances negotiations shall be permitted
- the time lines for decision making
- how authority to purchase shall be signed off at this stage
- how to evaluate risk appropriate to the purchase.

6.1.4 Creating a legally binding contract

The purchasing procedure will set out:

- how purchase orders are to be raised and issued
- the methodology for dealing with order acknowledgements and the implications of accepting the supplier's sales acknowledgement
- what actions to take when a supplier fails to enter into a contract
- how to create and maintain a master contract file.

6.1.5 The contract management phase

The purchasing procedure will set out:

- who is accountable for contract management actions
- the requirement for prompt supply of management information
- the involvement of purchasing when disputes arise
- acceptance procedures for goods and services
- payment processes
- contract close-out procedure
- feedback of supplier's performance into a vendor rating system.

In summary, purchasing procedures are essential but the danger is that they can become mechanistic and stifle business initiatives. Reactive purchasing is not the way forward.

6.2 Analysing a procurement process

A report on a procurement process[1] highlights flaws in a procurement process. It is important to note that it is a public sector procurement, hence a need to comply with Public Supply Contract Regulations. The following extracts show aspects of a process that are worthy of consideration in a wide range of circumstances.

- there would appear to be little documentation at the early stage of the procurement process regarding the proposed strategy
- at the time of the decision to proceed with the Minna-type procurement, a technical specification had not yet been worked up
- of the 12 completed PQQs received, only 8 were subject to a full assessment against the selection criteria
- it would appear that SFPA was not justified in specifying preferred manufacturers or types and certainly not to the extent it did
- no formal tender evaluation appears to have taken place at that time
- justification is therefore required that the final bid stage in the Minna-type procurement process did not give rise to a distortion of competition as between the three tenderers; unfortunately, such justification would not appear to exist
- no minutes of the site visits are on file.

6.3 E-commerce, e-business, e-SCM and e-procurement

6.3.1 E-commerce

In March 2002 the United States General Accounting Office (GAO)[2] produced a report that sought to clarify e-commerce (in an international context) and e-business. The report observes that there has been:

> a general acceptance of transaction-based definitions many of which require an online commitment to sell a good or service for an activity to be categorised as electronic commerce. In a transaction-based definition, electronic commerce is restricted to buying and selling, as distinct from conducting e-business – includes all aspects of online business activity – purchasing, selling, tracking inventory, managing production, handling logistics, and supply communications and support services.

6.3.2 E-business

In July 2001, the Department for International Development published its 'e-Business Strategy' report'. They had eight key programmes that had a combined capital expenditure budget of £22.8 million. They were:

- EDRM: Electronic Document and Record Management
- PRISM: system for recording, analysing and disseminating project management performance information
- MIS Rewrite: redesign of the management information system and the other systems it feeds into
- CMIS and e-Tendering: system to manage the contracting and tendering process electronically
- InSight and Knowledge Management: development of intranet and DFID knowledge management processes
- HR and Payroll System: system to allow electronic recruitment, training, scheduling and integrated payroll
- Satellite links: use of satellite links to ensure access to internal systems for all overseas staff
- Assist 2000: new desktop PC and software upgrade to MS Office 2000 for all DFID staff.

This is a good representation of a public sector body implementing an e-Business strategy. Such implementation must be tailored to the organisation, sector and trading circumstances. In a Canada Transportation Act review there was a very useful analysis of the barriers to e-Business adoption. This analysis can be summarised as follows:

- cost can prevent any firm from adopting Internet technology more extensively
- many marine and rail industry participants already have electronic data transfer and legacy information systems in place, reducing the commercial benefits of adopting more accessible Internet-based systems
- much of the uncertainty about potential benefits arises from inadequate customer readiness
- lack of action by all participants in the supply chain

- interoperability between logistics providers
- insufficient interoperability also arises from shipper demands for specific formats and methods of communication
- inadequate technical skills and training
- security and protecting commercially sensitive information is also a concern
- organisational culture and traditional practices in both carrier and partner firms are key factors to overcome.

6.3.3 E-SCM

E-supply chain management (e-SCM) is concerned with streamlining and optimising the whole supply chain by means of internal applications, with the aim of ensuring maximum sales growth at the lowest possible cost. This includes setting up an internal online purchasing system, joining an industrywide electronic marketplace and implementing e-SCM across the entire value chain.

The concepts of supply chain management and supply chain optimisation were discussed in sections 3.5 and 3.10. Unsurprisingly, the Internet provides present and future benefits to both the management and optimisation of supply chains. Purchasers and suppliers can derive the following benefits from e-SCM.

Purchase benefits include:

- the ability to purchase, both directly and indirectly, materials at a lower cost, primarily due to price transparency and competition, so, while large purchasers can exert powerful leverage to obtain more substantial price reductions and discounts, small purchasers using such systems can obtain more favourable prices as many suppliers are competing for the business of purchasers via the medium of e-marketplace and trading exchanges
- achievements of greater efficiency when purchasing goods and services and ultimately lowering the overall cost of transactions, as business-to-business marketplaces often offer smaller purchasers opportunities to discover lower prices for things that would be prohibitively expensive to discover by human effort alone
- purchasers being able to form strong ties with suppliers, in forecasting, scheduling and planning production data and sharing product data designs to develop supplier collaboration.

Supplier benefits

Supplier benefits tend to fall into two classes, depending on whether the e-SCM program emphasises collaboration or commercial opportunities. The latter includes the enhancement of forecasting ability, resulting in the capacity to meet and exceed customers' demands, achieve the right combination of products and services at the right time and align their production schedules, manufacturing capacity and inventory to customers' buying patterns.

When the emphasis is on collaboration, suppliers can benefit from participating in large, active online marketplaces. If frequented by a critical mass of buyers, such marketplaces can provide a cost-effective way to reach new customers and increase sales.

'A Survey and Implementation of e-Commerce in Supply Chain Management' by Hui-Chun Lee (KSI-Chicago) resulted in the production of the following figure which is an example of an integration model of e-SCM.

Figure 6.1 An example of an end-to-end integrated model of e-SCM

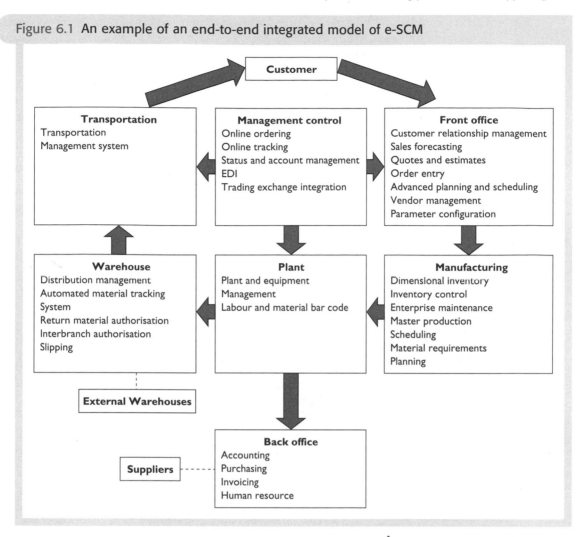

6.3.4 E-procurement — Chartered Institute of Procurement & Supply.

The CIPS definition of e-procurement is:

> E-procurement is using the Internet to operate the transactional aspects of requisitioning, authorising ordering, receiving and payment processes for the required services or products.

The CIPS statement also points out that e-procurement is typically the focus of local business administrators (one of the key goals of e-procurement is to devolve buying to local users) and covers the following areas of the buying process:

- requisition against agreed contract
- authorisation
- order
- receipt
- payment.

The key enabler of all the above is the ability of systems to communicate across organisational boundaries. While the technology for e-commerce provides the basic means, the main benefits derive from the resultant changes in business procedures, processes and perspectives. E-commerce is made possible by the open standard of extensible mark-up language (XML) – a structured computer programming language that allows for the easy identification of data types in multiple formats and can be understood across all standard Internet technologies. Adoption of XML will help organisations to integrate applications seamlessly and exchange information with trading partners.

6.4 The evolution of e-procurement models

Kalakota and Robinson[3] have identified seven basic types of e-procurement trading models. These, together with their key differences, are shown in Table 6.1.

Table 6.1 Comparison of various e-procurement models (Kalakota and Robinson[4])

Trading model	Characteristics
EDI networks	■ Handful of trading partners and customers ■ Simple transactional capabilities ■ Batch processing ■ Reactive and costly value-added network (VAN) charges
Business-to-employees (B2E) requisition applications	■ Make buying fast and hassle-free for a company's employees ■ Automated approvals routing and standardisation of requisition procedures ■ Provide supplier management tools for the professional buyer
Corporate procurement portals	■ Provide improved control over the procurement process and let a company's business rules be implemented with more consistency ■ Custom, negotiated prices posted in a multi-supplier catalogue ■ Spending analysis and multi-supplier catalogue management
First-generation trading exchanges: community, catalogue and storefronts	■ Industry content, job postings, and news ■ Storefronts: new sales channel for distributors and manufacturers ■ Product content and catalogue aggregation services
Second-generation trading exchanges: transaction-orientated trading exchanges	■ Automated requisition process and purchase order transactions ■ Supplier, price and product/service availability discovery ■ Catalogue and credit management
Third-generation trading exchanges: collaborative supply chains	■ Enable partners to closely synchronise operations and enable real-time fulfilment ■ Process transparency, resulting in restructuring of demand and the supply chain ■ Substitute information for inventory
Industry consortia: buyer and supplier led	■ The next step in the evolution of corporate procurement portals

6.5 Electronic data interchange (EDI)

6.5.1 Definition

secure

Electronic data interchange (EDI) may be defined as follows:

> The technique based on agreed standards, which facilitates business transactions in standardised electronic form in an automated manner directly from a computer application in one organisation to an application in another.

A *transaction* in EDI-speak is a term used to describe the electronic transmission of a single document. Each transaction set is usually referred to by a name and number, which are defined by the ASC X12 or EDIFACT standards referred to below. Thus, a purchase order in X12 is number 850. Each line of a transaction is termed a *segment* and piece of information in the line an *element*. In a purchase order, for example, the segment is the name and address of the purchaser or supplier. The segment is broken down into such data elements as organisation name, address line 1, address line 2, address line 3, postcode and country.

6.5.2 Standards

Data elements and codes are described in a directory relating to the message standard used. By the use of trade, national and international standards, organisations can trade electronically. Early message standards were developed by communities of organisations relating to an industry, such as automotive, construction and electronic enterprises, which had an interest in trading together. Thus, automotive manufacturers, including Ford, General Motors, Saab, Renault, Fiat, Austin Rover and Citroën and suppliers Lucas, Perkins, Bosch, GKN, SKF and BCS, set up ODETTE (Organisation for Data Exchange by Tele-Transmission in Europe). ODETTE sets the standards for e-business, engineering data exchange and logistics management that link the 4000 plus businesses in the European motor industry and their global partners.

Although there are still many EDI standards, only two – namely ASC X12 and EDIFACT – are widely used and recognised. ASC X12 standards were created in 1979 by the Accredited Standards Committee of the American National Standards Institute. These standards define the data formats and encoding rules for business transactions, including order placement and transportation. EDIFACT (EDI for Administration, Commerce and Transport) was developed by the United Nations in 1985 for the purpose of providing EDI standards that would support world trade. This international standard has been ratified as ISO 9735. UN/EDIFACT directories are published twice yearly by the United Nations.

6.5.3 How EDI works

How EDI is implemented is shown by Figure 6.2. The sequence is as follows:

1 Company A creates a purchase order using its internal business software.

2 EDI software translates the order.

3 Company A sends the 850 purchase order to company B over a third-party value-added network (VAN) or encrypted in EDIFACT format over the Internet.

4 Company B receives the 850 purchase order document and will translate it from EDI to its proprietary format and, typically, company B will send an acknowledgement to company A.

Figure 6.2 **EDI implementation**

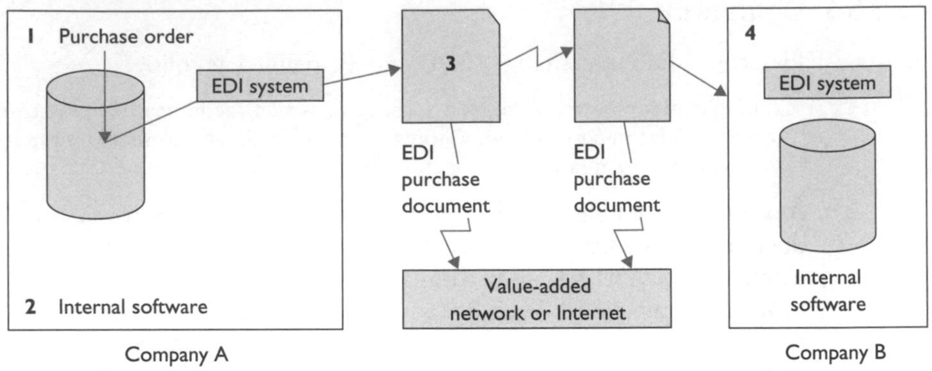

6.5.4 The advantages of EDI

■ Replacing the paper documents – purchase orders, acknowledgements, invoices and so on – used by buyers and sellers in commercial transactions with standard electronic messages conveyed between computers, often without the need for human intervention.

EDI at the supermarket

One of the best examples of EDI is EPOS (electronic point-of-sale) at the supermarket. When a product is purchased, the checkout operator scans a barcode on its label, which automatically registers the price on the cash till.

That same signal also triggers a computer process that reorders the item from the manufacturer, sets off a production cycle, and arranges invoicing, payment and transportation of the new order. EDI effectively puts the product back on the shelf with no paperwork and a minimum of human involvement.

■ Reduction in lead times as buyers and suppliers work together in a real-time environment. Armstrong and Jackson[5] provide a real-life example of pre-EDI and post-EDI lead times. The latter shows a reduction of eight days for acknowledging the order and five days to deliver it. The total time was therefore reduced from 19 to 11 days.

   – Day 1: Order prepared and authorised electronically, then posted to EDI service.
   – Day 2: Order taken from EDI service by recipient and put straight into order processing system. An acknowledgement is created automatically and sent to the EDI service.
   – Day 3: Manufacturing process begins (seven days). The acknowledgement is received by the originator and processed automatically.
   – Day 9: Manufacturing is completed.
   – Day 11: Delivery complete.

■ Reduction in the cost of inventory and release of working capital.

- Promotion of such strategies as JIT as a consequence of the previous two points.
- Better customer service.
- Facilitation of global purchasing using international standards, such as EDIFACT, which is compatible with most equipment in most countries. In 1970, SITPRO (Simplifying International Trade Procedures Board) was established in the UK and whose primary objectives are to reduce the costs of trading particularly to business, and to help the UK meet the challenges of globalisation. SITPRO works with the British Standards Institution (BSI) in connection with EDI standards.
- Facilitation of invoice payments by the computer-to-computer transfer of money, which eliminates the need for the preparation and posting of cheques.
- The integration of functions, particularly marketing, purchasing, production and finance.
- EDI tends to promote long-term buyer–supplier relationships and increase mutual trust.

6.5.5 Some potential problems in implementing EDI

Killen and Kamauff[6] point out that before adopting EDI an organisation should:

- ensure that exchanging information electronically supports the overall organisational strategy
- consider the cost and ramifications of EDI's standard tools and techniques, including implementation, software maintenance, manpower and participant training and how to promote systems and applications integration
- consider the organisational and process changes involved.

In relation to the second point, Norman[7] states that the more the data is processed and reprocessed, the more room there is to save time and money. Potential EDI users should therefore calculate the cost per transaction. If it is cheaper to fax or manually perform the task, the buyer probably lacks the volume to invest in EDI. Monczka and Carter[8] propose the following indicators of a reasonable opportunity for the application of EDI in the purchasing environment:

- a high volume of paperwork transaction documents
- numerous suppliers
- a long internal administration lead time associated with the purchasing cycle
- a desire for personnel reductions, new hire avoidance or both
- a need to increase the professionalism of purchasing personnel.

6.5.6 EDI limitations

Historically, the two principal limitations of EDI relate to cost and flexibility.

Cost

EDI was, and still is, an expensive option, given that, until recently, organisations sent all EDI transactions over a VAN (value-added network) that had set-up and running costs often on a per thousand characters transmitted basis. The scope of EDI was also intentionally limited to ensure controlled activity within a closed door environment. The heavy overheads associated with EDI infrastructure were prohibitive for many small-sized to medium-sized enterprises.

Table 6.2 Comparison of EDI and extranets

Characteristics	EDI	Extranets 外联网
Infrastructure	Customised software	Packaged solutions that leverage and extend existing Internet technology and intranet investment
Transmission costs	Extensive VANS or leased lines, slow dial-up connections	Inexpensive and fast Internet connections
Access	Proprietary software	Web browsers support EDI protocols as well as many other open standards
Scale	Restricted to only the largest vendors who can support EDI infrastructure	Support real-time buying and selling, allowing for tighter and more proactive planning

Internet and extranet approaches can, however, enable a small business to link into secure EDI networks at minimal cost. The Internet pricing model of flat monthly rates has forced most of the VAN networks to lower their pricing structures. A new market shift is also underway in which organisations are moving from proprietary technology to extranet solutions. A comparison of EDI and extranet technologies is shown in Table 6.2.

Small businesses using the Internet can compete on a level playing field with large competitors, expand globally and improve their trading partner relationships.

Inflexibility

EDI is a cumbersome, static and inflexible method of transmitting data, most suited to straightforward business transactions, such as the placement of purchase orders for known requirements. It is not suitable for transactions requiring tight coupling and coordination, such as the consideration of several possible purchase alternatives or supply chain optimisation. Unlike human beings, computers are poor at interpreting unstructured data and cannot derive useful information from Web documents that are not predefined and permanent. The standard document language used to create web pages is hypertext mark-up language (HTML). While HTML is able to display data and focuses on how data look, it cannot describe data. While HTML can state what items a supplier can offer, it cannot describe them. Traditional EDI approaches do not, therefore, provide the flexibility required in a dynamic Internet environment.

6.5.7 EDI and XML

XML (referred to in section 6.3.4 above) is an attempt to meet the problems of cost and inflexibility and the provision of a whole new way of communicating across the Internet and beyond.

The major difference between EDI and XML is that the former is designed to meet business needs and is a *process*. XML is a *language* and its success in any business will always depend on how it is being used by a given application.

As a language, XML provides a basic syntax that can be used to share information between many kinds of computer, different applications and different organisations.

XML can also describe – as distinct from display – data. It can, for example, enable a purchaser to understand in detail what a supplier has to offer. It also ensures that a purchase order accurately describes what the purchaser requires. It therefore provides a direct route between purchaser and supplier; irrespective of the size of either, that was unavailable with EDI.

XML/EDI is an attempt to provide a standard framework for the exchange of different types of data, such as a purchase order, invoice or healthcare claim, so that the information, whether in a transaction, exchanged in an application program interface (API) database portal catalogue or a work flow document or message, can be searched, decoded, processed and displayed consistently and correctly by first implementing EDI questionnaires and extending our vocabulary via online repositories to include our business language, rules and objectives. Thus, by combining XML and EDI, we create a new, powerful approach that is different from XML and EDI.

In addition to EDI and the Internet, there are other ways of transmitting data electronically between two or more organisations. For small businesses, encrypted e-mails are very cost-effective. Orders can be collected securely online and put into existing in-house systems that automatically e-mail suppliers when stock values reach lower limits. Technology is also changing. Although until recently PCs were the Internet access device of choice, preferred substitutes, such as mobile phones and personal digital assistants (PDAs), are outselling PCs several times over.

The National Computing Centre[9] points out that, 'the latest business buzz word is Business Process Integration' (BPI), which is all about the processes that cross the buying and selling organisations – that is, there is greater benefit from automating the interactions than in the transactional aspects of ordering and invoicing.

Business process integration is important because of:

- an increasing business imperative to increase process efficiency
- a focus on making core processes more flexible and efficient
- increasing traceability within a process
- an increasing requirement to understand how data is passed and by what applications
- improved recoverability
- reduced elapsed process delivery time.

6.6 E-hubs, exchanges, portals and marketplaces

Some writers believe that a distinction can be made between these terms.

6.6.1 Hubs

In the context of internal technologies, a hub is a device that connects several networks together. As used in e-businesses, a hub generally means a central repository or private exchange, such as the star network shown in Figure 6.3.

In the network shown in Figure 6.3, the *server* is a control computer that holds databases and programs for many PC workstations or terminals, which are called *clients*. The clients of the information hub may be internal customers or external organisations, such as suppliers.

Figure 6.3 A star network

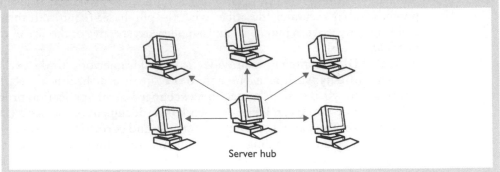

Server hub

6.6.2 Exchange

An exchange is a business-to-business (B2B) website where purchasers and suppliers meet to transact business. A distinction may be made between private and public exchanges.

Private exchanges can be either one-to-one (1T1) or one-to-many connections (1TM). The former are direct connections, while the latter connect all the actors through the central Internet hub. Private exchanges are normally specified by a single operation and available by invitation only to the organisation's suppliers and trading partners. Such private exchanges are frequently used for collaborative business procedures, such as real-time supply chain management and logistics.

Public exchanges – often referred to as *portals* – extend outside the boundaries of the company and involve many-to-many (MTM) interactions. Public exchanges may be run either by a consortium of big players within a specific industry (consortium portals) or by an independent entity starting up its business as an intermediary (independent portals).

Independent portals, such as ChemConnect and Verticainet, have some advantages relative to consortia and private e-markets. They can act more rapidly as they do not need to mediate among multiple owners as consortium portals do. Because they have comparatively few proprietary interests, they are also seen to be neutral, unlike the consortia and private e-markets. With all public exchanges, organisations pay a fee to become a member and possibly an additional transaction fee.

Both private and public exchanges can be either buy-side or sell-side, although this distinction is more usual with private exchanges. A *buy-side exchange* is built to interact with suppliers. Conversely a *sell-side exchange* is built to interact with customers. These are shown in Figure 6.4.[10]

6.6.3 Marketplace

Like an exchange, a marketplace is a website that enables purchasers to select from many suppliers. With e-marketplaces, the buyer is in control as open marketplaces enable purchasers to evaluate all potential suppliers for a particular product or service and make informed decisions regarding what and where to buy.

E-marketplaces are particularly applicable where:

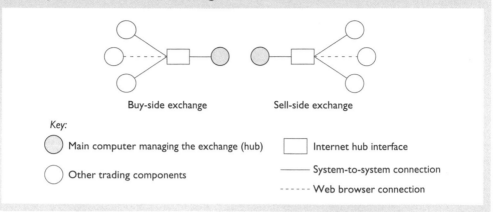

Figure 6.4 **Buy-side and sell-side exchanges**

- markets are large and the search costs to find suppliers are high because of the large number of potential suppliers
- product specifications and information are subject to rapid change
- buyers have difficulty in comparing similar products from different vendors because of an excess of features and characteristics that may not be clearly indicated
- internal costs of such processes as locating, appraising and evaluating the performance of suppliers are high.

In summary, it may be said that e-marketplaces offer greater functionality than exchanges, which, in turn, offer more functionality than hubs.

Figure 6.5 shows how hubs, exchanges and marketplaces interrelate in context with existing electronic communications, such as EDI, e-mail and fax.

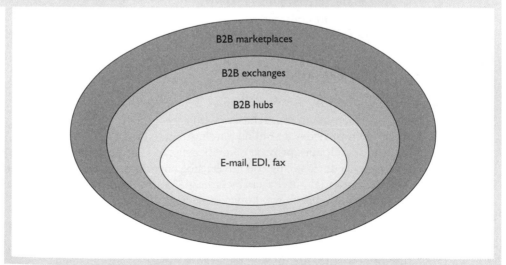

Figure 6.5 **Hubs, exchanges and marketplaces in context**

6.7 E-catalogues

The Belgian Federal Public Service set up an e-Catalogue platform, implementing one of the modules of the large e-Procurement project. The Belgian e-Catalogue Platform is an autonomous, open, secure, inter-operable, and re-configurable platform where public officers and companies can perform multiple tasks relating to their electronic purchase process. The electronic catalogues' format is based on the VBL 2.0 standard.

6.7.1 Definition

At their simplest, B2B marketplaces are just online catalogues. An e-catalogue may be defined as:

> A web page that provides information on products and services offered and sold by a vendor and supports online ordering and payment capabilities.

6.7.2 Advantages of e-catalogues

E-catalogues benefit both purchasers and suppliers in that they:

- facilitate real-time, two-way communication between buyers and sellers
- allow for the development of closer purchaser–supplier relationships due to improved vendor services and by informing purchasers about products of which they might otherwise be unaware
- enable suppliers to respond quickly to market conditions and requirements by adjusting prices and repackaging
- virtually eliminate the time lag between the generation of a requisition by a catalogue user and the issue of the purchase order as:
  - authorisation, where required, can be done online and notified and confirmed by e-mail
  - where users are authorised to generate their own purchases (subject to value and item constraints), the order can be automatically generated without the intervention of the purchasing department
- maverick or 'off-contract' purchasing is reduced because it is simpler and quicker to purchase from contracted suppliers than to go outside the official system.

6.7.3 Types of e-catalogue

Sell-side catalogues

These provide potential purchasers with access to the online catalogues of a particular supplier who provides an online purchasing facility.

Sell-side catalogues provide many benefits to suppliers, including ease of keeping the contents up to date, savings on advertising costs and the costs of processing a sale. The benefits to potential purchasers include 24/7 access to information and ease of ordering.

Sell-side catalogues have, however, several disadvantages, including:

- purchasers having insufficient time to surf all the available supplier websites
- buyers perhaps becoming overly dependent on particular suppliers as training in the use of new software may be required if suppliers are changed

Figure 6.6 Buy-side catalogue operation

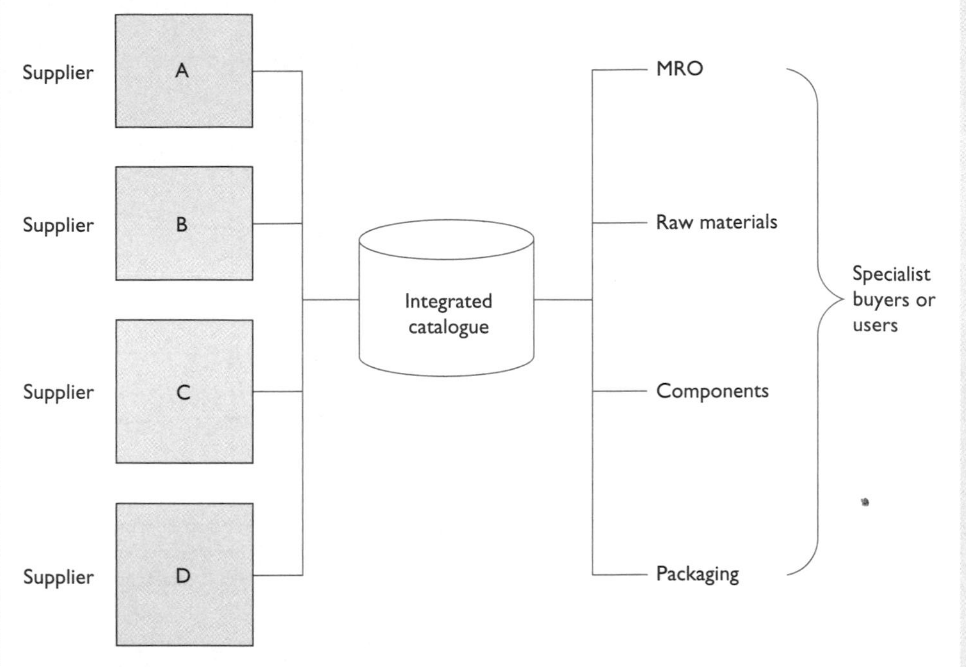

- where the price of a product differs from one purchaser to another, the use of personalised, restricted, prenegotiated catalogues or encrypted catalogues may be necessary.

Buy-side catalogues

These are catalogues created by purchasing organisations. Normally, such catalogues are confined to goods covered by prenegotiated prices, specifications and terms and run by a program that is integrated into the purchasing organisation's intranet. An example of the operation of buy-side catalogues is shown in Figure 6.6.

The benefits to purchasers include:

- reduced communication costs
- increased security
- many catalogues can be accessed via the same intranet application.

The compilation and updating of buy-side catalogues does, however, require a large investment in clerical resources that will be uneconomical for all but the largest organisations. Suppliers wishing to be included in the catalogue will also be required to provide their content in a standard format. For suppliers dealing with a large number of purchasers, the workload in terms of providing information in the form required by each online catalogue will be unsustainable.

Third-party catalogues

The disadvantages of sell-side and buy-side catalogues can be minimised by outsourcing the process to an electronic marketplace or buying consortium. This can be done by

Figure 6.7 **Third-party catalogues**

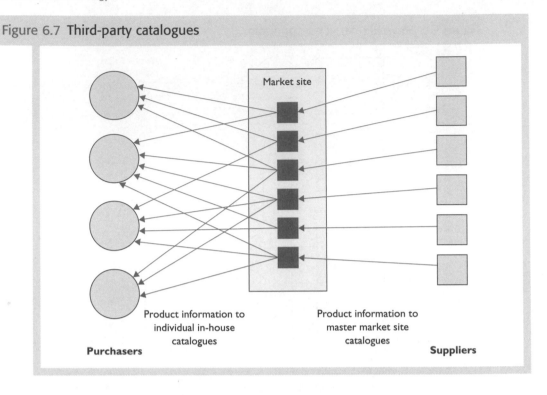

Product information to individual in-house catalogues

Product information to master market site catalogues

Purchasers

Market site

Suppliers

linking the in-house e-procurement catalogue to a master catalogue administered by the marketplace, as shown in Figure 6.7.[11]

- Standard information for inclusion in the 'market site' or 'master catalogue' is provided by the suppliers. This information is then made available to the in-house catalogues of individual purchasing organisations.

- Product information from suppliers can either reside in the in-house catalogue or be hosted in the master catalogue.

- The responsibility of managing and updating product and other information rests with the suppliers.

Advantages of this system include that:

- suppliers have a good incentive to provide information in the specified standard format as the master catalogue will be available to a large number of purchasing organisations

- the in-house procurement catalogues draw product and other information from the master catalogue and purchasers or users can pass electronic orders to suppliers via the market site

- product information can be divided into two parts – public and encrypted and public information will include a basic product description and specification, often accompanied by an illustration or diagram, while encrypted information will provide details of prices, discounts and similar matters applicable to specific purchasers that cannot be accessed by unauthorised users.

6.8 E-auctions

One step up from e-catalogue is e-auctions. An e-auction may be defined as:[12]

> An electronic market, which can exist in both business-to-business and business-to-consumer contexts. Sellers offer goods or services to buyers through a website with a structured process for price setting and fulfilment.

Web auctions may follow English, Dutch, sealed-bid and reverse-bid processes.

■ *English bid process* – in this process, bids are successively replaced by higher bids to obtain the highest price for a given item.

■ *Dutch bid process* – the English process is unsuitable for selling thousands of items to a number of different buyers. This can, however, be easily and quickly done in a 'Dutch auction', developed in the seventeenth century in Amsterdam for the sale of flowers. In a Dutch auction, the auctioneer starts at a high price and then descends by steps until a bid is received. The successful bidder then decides whether to buy the whole or a portion of the items on offer at that price. The auctioneer increases the offer price for any items remaining in the current lot and then again descends by steps and continues in this manner until either all the items comprising the lot are sold or a reserve price is reached.

■ *Sealed-bid process* – this is broadly similar to tendering. A potential purchaser issues a request for bids to be submitted by a prescribed date and time according to a sealed format. At the specified date and time, the purchaser's representatives will evaluate and compare the bids according to a rating grid. The winning bid is the one that achieves the maximum score. Should several bids obtain the same score, the bid offering the best price is the winner.

■ *Reverse-bid processes* – see section 6.9.

Intergraf[13] have observed that among the several e-commerce business forms, e-auctions are a very special one. Reverse auctions (in which supplier companies compete for a job providing increasingly lower prices) are particularly interesting, but can be dangerous for competing companies if transparency, clarity and honesty aren't assured.

The Code of Conduct published by Intergraf in 2005 includes:

> The **promoter** and the **participant buyer** are bounded to guarantee the honesty, transparency and equity of the conditions in which the e-auction is done, namely regarding the relations with the participant supplier and the following topics:
>
> ■ Supply to all the participant suppliers the same information, according to the same divulgation criteria
>
> ■ Supply to each participant supplier all the information necessary to present the bid, namely:
> - specify all the technical, packaging and service aspects relevant to each product or service of the buyer's proposal, as well as all the details that can contribute to define the price. The promoter/buyer must, as a consequence, provide each participant supplier a sample of the product or products taken to auction, at least 10 days before the auction takes place. If this sample is not available, an equivalent or similar product must be provided
> - specify whether mixed proposals – which have different products and/or services – are accepted
> - specify the duration of the electronic auction
> - specify the conditions of the contract, namely the ones regarding payment conditions, currency to be used in the business, delivery places, minimum and maximum amount per delivery place, deadline accorded after the issuing of the order, etc.

- Supply all the participant suppliers with a complete list of participant suppliers in the e-auction, at least 24 hours before it starts
- Clear identification of the participant suppliers' pre-selection and selection criteria and of the relative importance of each of these criteria; reasons for not being selected must be communicated to the non-selected.

6.9 Reverse auctions

6.9.1 What is a reverse auction?

In a reverse auction, buying organisations post the item(s) they wish to buy and price they are willing to pay while suppliers compete to offer the best price for the item(s) over a prescribed time period.

For example, a buying organisation is interested in purchasing 1000 castings to a published specification at the lowest possible price. It therefore creates a reverse auction, stating the dimensions, quality, performance and delivery requirements and, often, bid decrements. Suppliers enter the marketplace and bid on the auction. Winners are declared according to the agreed auction rules. Thus, e-auctions may be structured using the lowest price or most economically advantageous tender (MEAT) options.

At the conclusion of the auction, both purchaser and supplier are bound by the sale. If a reserve price is set but not met, the buying organisation decides the winning bid. Suppliers can bid more than once in the prescribed time. Apart from the names of the suppliers and reverse sealed bid auctions, all the bids are available for everyone to see. Most online auction sites use automatic bidding against agents or a 'proxy bidder' that automatically place bids on the suppliers' behalf.

Example 6.1

Reverse auction 1

Bids are solicited for 100 product Xs. The opening bid is £25 per product, with bid decrements of £5:

- supplier A bids £25 each for 100 items
- supplier B bids £20 each for 50 items
- supplier C bids £15 each for 50 items.

The result of the auction is that:

- supplier A is unsuccessful
- supplier B sells 50 items for £20
- supplier C sells 50 items for £15.

There are several variations on the bidding process. In what is known as the reverse English manual system, the buying organisation specifies the opening bid and the supplier bids higher. At the conclusion of the auction, the purchaser selects the winners manually. Each winning bidder sells at the bid price made. The criteria for the winning bid may not be disclosed.

Example 6.2

Reverse auction 2

Bids are solicited for 100 product Xs. The opening bid is £25:

- supplier A bids £18 per item for 100 items
- supplier B bids £20 per item for 100 items
- supplier C bids £20 per item for 100 items.

The result of the auction is that:

- supplier A is unsuccessful
- supplier C sells 100 items for £20, because of closer geographical proximity to the purchaser than supplier B.

6.9.2 When to use reverse auctions

Most reverse auctions are used for spot buying and eliminate the time-consuming offline process of selecting suppliers, requesting quotations and comparing quotes received. Marketplaces with many suppliers can offer purchasers a compiled list of suppliers. Purchasing organisations conducting reverse auctions on their own sites must invite prospective suppliers in advance if they wish such suppliers to participate. Reverse auctions are particularly useful in the following circumstances:

- when there is uncertainty as to the size of the market and the willingness of sellers to supply a product
- when purchasing large quantities of an item for which clear specifications are possible
- when selling surplus assets
- for some services, such as car rentals, freight services, travel.

The consensus used to be that the lowest-price reverse auction process should be used only when there is little concern about production specifications or the selected suppliers. Reverse auctions were not considered appropriate for complicated products or projects requiring collaboration or considerable negotiation. *Buy IT*[14] however, states that software providers are now expanding their offerings to ensure that online auction tools become an integral part of the broader procurement strategy process, including the creation and management of optimal long-term value partnerships. As the goods or services became more difficult to specify and the relationships between purchasers and suppliers became more integrated, online auctions became less about driving cost out of the supply chain and more of a tool for collaboration.

6.9.3 The reverse auction process

Figure 6.8 indicates the principal steps involved.

Figure 6.8 The reverse auction process

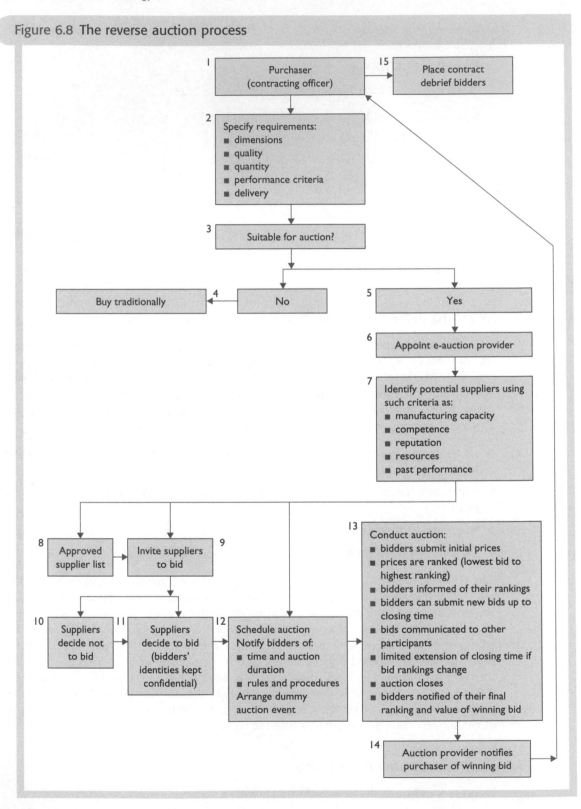

Figure 6.9 Online reverse auction

6.9.4 Reverse auction guidelines

A useful summary of online auction 'dos and don'ts', which, if followed, all help to ensure a successful auction, is shown in Figure 6.9.[15]

6.9.5 Advantages of reverse auctions

Reverse auctions provide benefits for both buyers and sellers. The benefits for buyers include:

- savings over and above those obtained from normal negotiations as a result of competition – on average, the auction process drives down supplier process by 11 per cent, with savings ranging from 4 to 40 per cent[16]
- reductions in acquisition lead times
- access to a wider range of suppliers
- a global supply base can be achieved relatively quickly
- sources of market information are enhanced
- more efficient administration of requests for quotations (RFQs) and proposals
- auctions conducted on the Internet generally provide total anonymity so time is not wasted on seeing suppliers' representatives.

The benefits for suppliers include:

- an opportunity to enter previously closed markets, which is particularly important for smaller companies
- reduced negotiation timescales
- provision of a good source of market pricing information
- clear indications of what must be done to win the business.

6.9.6 Disadvantages of reverse auctions

Some objections to reverse auction include that they:

- are based on a win–lose approach – the seller is trying to get the most money while the buyer is after the best deal and the goal is to screw your opponent to win either a good deal or a profitable deal at the other person's expense, so the logical progression is always towards cheating and, therefore, such a system cannot be sustained without burdensome watchdogs and regulators
- can cause an adverse shift in buyer–seller relationships as the supplier may feel exploited and become less trustful of buyers
- can have long-term adverse effects on the economic performance of both suppliers and purchasers as:
  - some suppliers may not be able to sustain sharp price reductions in the long term
  - suppliers that cannot compete at the lower price levels may be removed, or ask to be removed, from the purchaser's approved supplier list so those purchasers eventually have reduced supplier bases
  - in order to ensure that the exact goods and services required are obtained, considerable time may be needed to complete detailed specification sheets.

6.10 E-payment

E-payment may be by a standalone method, as with a purchasing card, or incorporated into software, as with the UK Ministry of Defence's purchase to payment (P2P) system. This last system enables:

Figure 6.10 Solutions landscape for electronic invoicing and payments

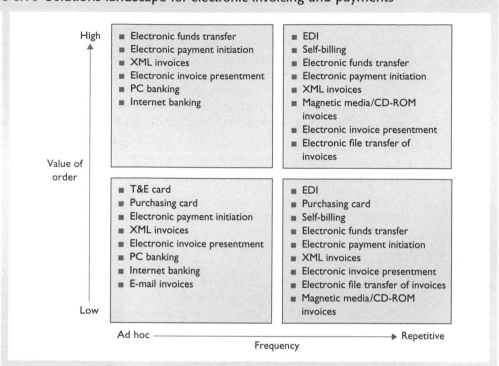

Source: CIPS[17]

- an electronic order for goods and services to be sent to a trading partner

- an electronic receipt to be held and linked to the order for goods and services

- an electronic invoice to be sent to the MOD

- the order, receipt and invoice to be matched online, generating an electronic message authorising the processing of payment that is sent to the trading partner.

Figure 6.10 provides a useful map of e-payment and invoicing applications and the vendors that provide them, placing the different options according to whether the value of the purchase to which the payment relates is high or low and also the frequency of payments.

Security and auditing are important aspects of e-payments. Security risks include unauthorised access by hackers, illegal acquisition of PINs and data theft. Approaches to security concerns include:

- *encrypted technologies* – the art of encoding information in such a way that only the holder of a secret password can decode and read it

- *certification authorisations* – organisations that clarify and provide proof that a signature is valid.

In any e-payments system, it is vital that each invoice and payment is traceable throughout the system. The audit trail should track every line of data right back to the file where it originated.

6.11 Low-value purchases

There can be a disproportionate amount of time spent by purchasing departments processing small value purchases where the administrative expenditure cannot be counterbalanced by any savings. The potential scale of these small value purchases can be illustrated by reference to the Acquisitions Branch of Public Works & Government Services Canada who in 2002 issued 33,000 contracts and 11,000 amendments worth more than $10bn in goods, services and construction. Of those contracts 62 per cent were below $25,000.

Low-cost procedures for the efficient handling of low-value purchases include the following.

6.11.1 Delegated order placement to users

This is the placement of own orders by users within specified limits and with approved suppliers over the Internet.

6.11.2 Purchasing cards

These are similar to credit cards and involve a provider such as Barclays Bank Plc and usually an issuing bank. When used for low-value purchases, they enable any user, such as a foreman on a building site, to make purchases and provide payments to suppliers. Richardson[18] has listed the following benefits of using purchasing cards:

■ compliance levels can improve where more orders are going through preferred suppliers, which can lead to better volume discounts

■ average transaction and order processing costs can drop dramatically

■ implementation costs are 10 to 100 times less than for an ERP or e-procurement system

■ suppliers are paid faster, enabling them to invest in their business and improve their services to clients

■ greater and improved documentation of data on accounts, suppliers and taxes

■ less purchasing employee time spent on order paperwork and chasing, allowing more time for strategic and tactical work.

Clearly the issue and use of purchasing cards has to be carefully controlled. The cardholder should be held responsible for protecting the purchasing card and for all purchases made using a particular purchasing card number.

Neither the physical purchasing card nor its account number should be shared with or transferred to any other person to use. A purchasing card internal review should be held periodically to ensure compliance with controls, appropriateness of purchases, that cards are actually in the possession of the authorised holders and that there is general adherence to specific purchase procedures.

6.11.3 Other methods of dealing with low-value purchases

Other methods of dealing with low-value purchases are listed below.

■ *Telephone orders* – requirements are telephoned to the supplier who is provided with an order number. The agreed price is recorded on the order form, but this is not sent to the supplier. The goods are invoiced by the supplier against the order form.

■ *Petty cash purchases* – items are obtained directly from local suppliers on presentation of an authorised requisition form and paid for at once from petty cash. The main problem is that of controlling the numbers and sizes of such purchases. This can be done by providing potential users with a petty cash imprest, out of which such payments are made.

■ *Standing orders* – all orders for a range of items, such as electrical fittings, fasteners, are placed with one supplier for a period of, say, 12 months. A special discount is often negotiated and quantities may or may not be specified. Required items are called off by users who transmit releases directly from the supplier via a fax, telephone or computer interface. The amount due is summarised by the supplier, either electronically or tabulated as a single invoice, and segregated by users' cost centres for easier coding by the accounts function.

■ *Self-billing* – this uses EDI. When the former Rover Group, which traded electronically, received goods from a supplier, it checked that the goods were ordered and then simply paid. The supplier did not need to raise an invoice. Self-billing enables both customer and supplier to make saving.

■ *Blank cheque orders* – a system devised in the USA. A cheque form with a specified liability is attached to the order form. On forwarding the goods, the supplier fills in the cheque, which he or she deposits in his or her own bank. The cheque can only be deposited, not cashed, until authorised by the purchaser. The need for invoicing and forwarding of payment is thus avoided.

■ *Stockless buying* – this is virtually the same as blanket ordering, but the supplier agrees to maintain stocks of specified items.

6.12 Purchasing manuals

6.12.1 What is a purchasing manual?

Essentially, a purchasing manual is a medium for communicating information regarding purchasing policies, procedures, instructions and regulations.

■ *Policies* may be general or consequential. *General policies* state, in broad terms, the objectives and responsibilities of the purchasing function. *Consequential policies* state, in expanded form, how general policies are applied in specific activities and situations, such as the selection of suppliers.

■ *Procedures* prescribe the sequence of activities by which policies are implemented, such as the receipt of bought-out goods.

■ *Instructions* give detailed knowledge or guidance to those responsible for carrying out the policies or procedures, such as suppliers with who call-off contracts have been negotiated.

■ *Regulations* are detailed rules regarding the conduct of purchasing and ancillary staff in the various situations arising in the course of their duties, such as concerning the receipt of gifts from suppliers.

When drafting a purchasing manual, it is useful to keep these distinctions clearly in mind.

6.12.2 Advantages of purchasing manuals

Advantages claimed for purchasing manuals include the following:

- writing it down helps with precision and clarity
- the preparation of the manual provides an opportunity for consultation between purchasing and other departments to look critically at existing policies and procedures and, where necessary, change them
- procedures are prescribed in terms of activities undertaken or controlled by purchasing, thus promoting consistency and reducing the need for detailed supervision of routine tasks
- a manual is a useful aid in training and guiding staff
- a manual can help the annual audit
- a manual coordinates policies and procedures and helps to ensure uniformity and continuity of purchasing principles and practice, as well as providing a point of reference against which such principles and practice can be evaluated
- a manual may help to enhance the status of purchasing by showing that top management attaches importance to the procurement function
- computerisation, which needs detailed and well-documented systems, has given further impetus to the preparation of purchasing manuals.

6.12.3 Disadvantages of purchasing manuals

Some disadvantages of manuals are that they:

- are costly to prepare
- tend to foster red tape and bureaucracy and stifle initiative
- must be continually updated to show changes in procedures and policy.

6.12.4 Format

Although hard copy manuals are still produced, the most suitable format is that of an operational database used to process the information needed to perform operational tasks. This can be available internally via an intranet or externally on the Internet. As the manual is freely accessible, it encourages transparency and can easily be updated.

Contents

A purchasing manual may consist of three main sections, dealing respectively with organisation, policy and procedures.

- *Organisation*
  - Charts showing the place of purchasing within the undertaking and how it is organised, both centrally and locally.
  - Possibly job descriptions for all posts within the purchasing function, including, where applicable, limitations of remits.
  - Teams relating to purchasing and supply chain activities.
  - Administrative information for staff, such as absences, hours of work, travelling expenses and similar matters.

- *Policy*
  - Statements of policy, setting out the objectives, responsibilities and authority of the purchasing function.
  - Statements, which can be expanded, of general principles relating to price, quality and delivery.
  - Terms and conditions of purchase.
  - Ethical relationships with suppliers, especially regarding gifts, and entertainment.
  - Environmental policies.
  - Supplier appraisal and selection.
  - Employee purchases.
  - Reports to management.
- *Procedures*
  - Descriptions, accompanied by flow charts, of procedures relating to requisitioning, ordering, expediting, receiving, inspecting, storing and payment of goods with special reference to procurement.
  - Procedures relating to the rejection and return of goods.
  - Procedures regarding the disposal of scrap and obsolete or surplus items.

6.13 Supplier manuals

Supplier manuals provide information for the providers of goods and services. Such manuals may relate to a specific aspect of supplier relationships, such as quality or delivery requirements and ethical or environmental issues, or be a comprehensive publication covering all aspects of supply.

6.13.1 The purpose of supplier manuals

Supplier manuals may achieve the following:

- Set out the parameters within which the purchaser is prepared to trade with the supplier. Most supplier manuals contain a statement that:

  variation from the requirements/standards prescribed in this manual will only be permitted with the specific written agreement of the supply manager.

- Provide the legal basis for trading, such as:

  compliance with the requirements of this manual is a requirement of the conditions of purchase that form part of the XYZ trading terms and conditions and that suppliers accept when agreeing to supply goods or services to XYZ. Failure to comply is a breach of contract.

- Provide essential information required by the supplier relating to the purchaser's requirements regarding such issues as packaging, transportation, deliveries, delivery locations, environmental and ethical polices and e-procurement.

6.13.2 The content of supplier manuals

Robert Bosch GmbH[19] have a 'Supplier Logistics Manual' that sets out the logistics requirements of the Bosch Group. In the preamble it states that 'competition in national and international markets has been significantly tougher in recent years. The increased individuality of our customers places high requirements on our business, and as a result also on the logistics functions, in terms of quality and flexibility. The quality of logistics is becoming more and more decisive to the competitiveness of our business, and is an increasingly important factor in our strategic success.'

The content includes:

1 information logistics
2 packaging logistics
3 dispute logistics
4 logistics quality
5 outlook
6 abbreviations
7 attachments.

6.14 Legal aspects of purchasing

Although purchasing procedures may have changed from manual to electronic methods, all commercial transactions must conform to the requirements of a valid contract.

6.14.1 The essentials of a contract

A valid contract is a promise or agreement that the law will enforce. To be legally enforceable, a contract must satisfy the following essentials.

- *Intention* – both parties must intend to enter into a legal relationship.
- *Agreement* – in a dispute, the court must be satisfied that the contracting parties had reached a firm agreement and were not still negotiating. Agreement will usually be shown by the unconditional acceptance of an offer. It is important to determine by whom the offer is made, whether the offer is valid and if it has been accepted.
- *Consideration* – English law of contract is concerned with *bargains*, not mere promises. Thus, if A promises to give something to B, B will have no remedy if A breaks his promise. If, however, B has undertaken to do something in return so that A's promise is dependent on B's, the mutual exchange of promises turns the arrangement into a contract. The consideration must also exist and have some ascertainable value, however slight, otherwise there is no contract.
- *Form* – certain exceptional types of agreement are only valid if made in a particular way, such as in writing. Thus, conveyances of lands and leases for over three years must be by deed. The absence of written evidence, while not affecting the validity of a contract, may make it unenforceable in the courts. This evidence may be from correspondence or any other documentation made at the time the contract was made or subsequently. Such written evidence must clearly identify the parties against whom the evidence is to be used or by authorised agent.

■ *Definite terms* – there will be no contract if it is not possible to determine what has been agreed between the parties. Where essential terms have yet to be decided, the parties are still in the stage of negotiation. An agreement to agree in future is not a contract.

■ *Legality* – some agreements, such as contracts to defraud the Inland Revenue, or immoral contracts, such as agreements to fix prices or regulate supplies, while not illegal are void under the Competition Acts, unless the parties can prove to the Restrictive Practices Court that their agreement is beneficial and in the public interest.

6.14.2 The 'battle of the forms'

One of the essential elements of a valid contract (that is, a contract that can be enforced) is an unconditional acceptance by the offeror (that is, the party to whom the offer is made) of an offer made by the other party, known as the offeree. If the acceptance seeks to vary the terms of the offer in any way, there is a counter-offer and the original offer lapses.

Thus, in the case of *Hyde* v *Wrench* (1840), Wrench (W) offered to sell his farm to Hyde (H) for £1000. H replied, offering £950, which W refused and, without informing H of his intention, sold the farm elsewhere. H later wrote, accepting the original price of £1000 and, on finding the farm sold, sued W for breach of contract. The contract held that the counter-offer of £950 rejected the original offer, which could only be revived by W.

Quotations, order forms and acknowledgements often contain, on their reverse side, or make reference to standard conditions of sale or purchase. The situation that can arise is shown in Figure 6.11.

The term 'battle of the forms' was coined by Lord Denning in the case of *Butler Machine Tool Co. Ltd* v *Ex-Cell-O Corporation (England) Ltd* (1979), which arose from differing sets of standard conditions. Butler, the sellers, made a quotation offering to sell a machine tool to Ex-Cell-O, the buyers, for £75,000. The offer was stated to be

Figure 6.11 In the event of a dispute between A and B, which conditions prevail?

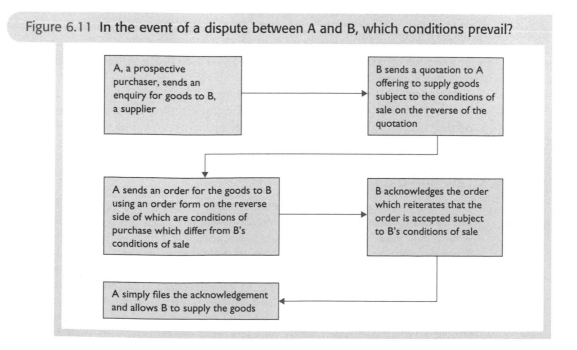

subject to terms and conditions that 'shall prevail over any terms and conditions in the Buyer's order'. These included a price variation clause for the goods to be charged at the price ruling on the date of delivery. The buyers ordered the machine, their order being subject to terms and conditions materially different from those of the sellers' and containing no price variation clause. At the foot of the buyers' order was a tear-off acknowledgement of receipt of the order stating, 'We accept your order on the Terms and Conditions stated hereon'. The acknowledgement was completed by the sellers and returned to the buyers with a letter stating that the buyers' order was being entered in accordance with the sellers' quotation.

On delivery, the sellers claimed a price increase of £2892, which the buyers refused to pay. The sellers brought an action, claiming that the variation clause entitled them to increase their price. Although the buyers contended that the contract had been concluded on their terms and was therefore a fixed-price contract, the judge found for the sellers on the grounds that the contract had been concluded on the basis that the sellers' terms were to prevail as variation was stipulated in the opening offer and this applied to subsequent negotiations.

This verdict was, however, reversed on appeal on the grounds that the sellers, by completing and returning the buyers' terms, could not therefore claim to increase the price under the price variation clause contained in their offer. The sellers' letter referring to the quotation was irrelevant as it referred only to the price and identity of the machine and did not incorporate the sellers' terms into the contract.

This case is important as it emphasises that whether or not the buyers' or sellers' terms and conditions apply depends on the facts of the case. As Lord Denning stated:

> In most cases when there is a battle of forms there is a contract as soon as the last of the forms is sent and received without any objections being taken to it . . . The difficulty is to decide which form or part of which form is a term or condition of the contract. In some cases the battle is won by the man who fires the last shot. He is the man who puts forward the latest terms and conditions and, if they are not objected to by the other party, he may be taken to have agreed to them. In some cases the battle is won by the man who gets his blow in first . . . There are yet other cases where the battle depends on the shots fired by both sides . . . The terms and conditions of both parties are to be construed together.

Thus, in the situation shown in Figure 6.11, it would be the sellers' terms and conditions that would prevail.

It is advisable for buyers to include a clause in their conditions of purchase stating that liability will only be accepted for orders placed subject to the terms and conditions stated on their order forms, which the sellers accept by signing and returning an acknowledgment form referring to those conditions within a stipulated time – say 14 days.

6.14.3 Law and the buyer

Commercial or mercantile law includes agency agreements, contracts for the sale of goods and services, insurance, negotiable instruments and carriage by land, sea and air. Clearly all such legislation, together with that relating to electronic trading and European procurement, is applicable to purchasing. There are at least three good reasons for all purchasing professionals to have a working knowledge of commercial law. First, the principle of *ignorantia juris non excusat* (ignorance of the law does not excuse) means that a company (which, in law, is a legal person) and its servants, such as purchasing specialists, are presumed to know the law. Second, all purchasing staff should have an awareness of the possible legal consequences of their actions. Third, 'a little knowledge is a dangerous thing' and a knowledge of the law should indicate when it is advisable for buyers to seek professional advice.

6.14.4 The general structure of a contract

- *The agreement* – this names the parties to the contract. In a standard contract, it is only necessary to change the names and any other relevant details. If the parties sign on the front page, this saves leafing through the whole, but there should be a statement that the parties have read and understood all the terms and conditions appertaining to the contract.

- *The terms and conditions* – these are comprised of the following points:
  - *Definitions* – these are inserted to avoid ambiguity and avoid the repetition of long sentences. When, in the text, a capital letter is used for a word, it indicates that the word has been defined in the 'definitions' section.
  - *General terms* – these are the general agreements clause, changes, alterations and variations clause, 'notice' clause – stating how and by what method any notice relating to the contract is to be sent – and a clause stating that the headings and definitions are for information only.
  - *The commercial provisions* – these set out the rights and obligations of the supplier and, in a separate clause, the rights and obligations of the purchaser. Another separate clause will specify payment terms.
  - *Secondary commercial provisions* – these deal with such matters as conditions, warranties, confidentiality, intellectual property, indemnity and termination.
  - *Boilerplate clauses* – these are standard clauses that appear in almost all contracts, such as the following:
    - *severability* – the right of a court to remove a term or condition that is invalid, void or unenforceable without prejudice to the rest of the contract
    - *waiver* – a statement that failure to enforce a 'right' at a given time will not prevent the exercise of that right later
    - *force majeure* – applicable where a 'major force', such as an act of God, war, riots, floods, tempests and so on, prevents or delays the performance of the contract
    - *law and jurisdiction* – the law that governs the contract – *The Principles of International Contracts*, produced by the International Institute for the Unifications of Private Law (UNIDROIT) in 1994 aim to:

      . . . establish a balanced set of rules designed for use throughout the world, irrespective of the legal traditions and the economic and political conditions of the countries in which they are to be applied.

These principles have no legal force and depend for their acceptance on their perceived authority. When, however, the parties agree, they can become legally binding.

6.14.5 The interpretation of contracts

It is usual for purchasing staff to know something of the general principles of interpretation and the rules of evidence, including how the courts will construe the words used, resolve ambiguities, take account of trade usages, vary written terms and 'fill in the gaps' with regard to issues not covered in the contract.

Case study

Orwell Financial Services (OFS)

OFS are a long-established Financial Services organisation, selling a wide range of products, including insurance, mortgages and wealth advice. Their headquarters are in Newcastle-Upon-Tyne. The organisation works in classic silos, the largest being IT, Facilities Management, Marketing, Print & Stationery, Distribution and HQ Services. Purchasing has, traditionally, held a reactive, transactional role and various attempts have been made to make it a strategic and policy-based function. A surprise visit by the Financial Services Authority, during which they discussed 'risk' with the OFS chief executive, has led to the unhealthy conclusion that there are no purchasing procedures in place. Each 'silo' works to practices they have found acceptable to them.

The chief executive called a meeting with the nominal buying manager of OFS and the head of internal audit. The latter stated that there has never been a formal audit of purchasing procedures and practices. The buying manager stated that all attempts to introduce companywide practices were always rebuffed by the respective 'heads' of the silos. The chief executive asked the buying manager if she had any evidence of 'bad practice' that warranted a detailed scrutiny. The buying manager recognised this as a major opportunity to obtain the authority to put purchasing on the map at OFS. Co-incidentally, she had been tracking certain events over the past month and used six examples to highlight current practices to the chief executive and head of internal audit.

1 A major piece of IT equipment had been returned to the original supplier for testing, upgrading and reinstallation. No paperwork was in place for the equipment's removal from site and no purchase order had been raised. The insurance position was not clear.

2 In facilities management, purchase orders were raised after invoices had been received to enable invoices to be cleared.

3 Marketing did place purchase orders but regularly exceeded their transaction expenditure limit of £10,000. They also filed suppliers' acknowledgements unread and unchallenged.

4 Invoices for services on site and charged by the hour were paid without timesheet evidence.

5 In print and stationery, requisitions were sometimes accepted without any authorising signature.

6 There were isolated examples where invoices for purchases authorised by the head of security had been paid twice.

You have been asked, in your role as buying manager, to attend the next board meeting. You have been given 10 minutes to talk on the subject of 'Control of Purchases through effective procedures'.

Tasks

1 How would you explain the corporate benefits of effective purchasing procedures?

2 How will introducing such procedures reduce risk?

3 Would you recommend internal audit conduct a complete review of purchasing and if so, why?

Discussion questions

6.1 (a) Prepare a flow chart of a traditional, paper-based purchasing system from the receipt of a requisition to the payment of the supplier.
   (b) Estimate the time taken and the cost of each stage in the above process.
   (c) Prepare a flow chart showing how the same activities would be done under e-procurement.
   (d) Estimate the savings in time and cost using e-procurement.

6.2 Why, in many organisations, is e-procurement limited to MRO (maintenance, repair and operating) items?

6.3 E-procurement can rarely be a total success because it depersonalises the process. The absence of personal contact can lead to misunderstandings and weaken relationships. Would you agree with this? Why do you hold your views?

6.4 What are the classic problems of introducing EDI?

6.5 Why is Business Process Integration of strategic importance to an organisation?

6.6 Do you purchase using an e-catalogue? If you do, what are your views on:
   (a) how it is kept up to date?
   (b) how the range of products compares with what is available in the market?
   (c) its advantages over a buyer conducting their own market search?

6.7 Reverse auctions are an increasing facet of procurement. At the end of the process prices are agreed without any face-to-face negotiation. Comment on this in regard to the following:
   (a) It is impossible to understand the cost drivers.
   (b) The purchase was made on price alone.
   (c) The supplier with the lowest price must cut his quality to make a profit.

6.8 What is the content of your organisation's purchasing manual? When was it last reviewed and revised?

6.9 You will have standard conditions of contract for purchasing goods and services. What do they say about:
   (a) termination of the contract?
   (b) the recovery of damages?
   (c) price reviews?
   (d) dispute resolution?

6.10 XML offers its users many advantages, including:
   (a) simplicity
   (b) extensibility
   (c) interoperability
   (d) openness.
   Give one example of how XML provides each of the above advantages.

6.11 In what ways do you predict the use of e-procurement will next develop? When you respond please consider:
   (a) the international dimension of procurement
   (b) the fact that supply chains are becoming extended through many tiers

(c) the need for effective contract management

(d) the potential for fraud with electronic systems.

6.12 Will procurement ever take the lead in forming contracts and have the knowledge to handle complex contracts?

Past examination questions

1 The introduction of computer systems into organisations has changed the way purchasing activities are conducted. The following questions relate to computer systems in purchasing.
   (a) Explain **two** advantages of electronic data interchange (EDI) in the 'tender' process.
   (b) EDI can help organisations in reducing costs of routine purchases. Describe **two** of these cost reduction areas.
   (c) Explain **two** ways in which a computer system can be used to support a vendor rating system.

   CIPS, *The Business Environment for Purchasing and Supply*, May 2009

2 Identify **five** stages of a typical purchasing cycle.

   CIPS, *An Introduction to Purchasing Strategy*, May 2010

3 Identify **five** pieces of information that should be contained in a Request for Quotation (RFQ).

   CIPS, *Preparing and Managing Contracts*, November 2007

4 Construct and label an appropriate diagram to allow an organisation to assess and manage risk and impact.

   CIPS, *An Introduction to Purchasing Strategy*, May 2009

References

[1] Report on the Minna Type Vessel Procurement Process, dated 22 May, 2006, from the Scottish Fisheries Protection Agency (SFPA)

[2] International Electronic Commerce. Definitions and Policy Implications, GAO-02-404

[3] Kalakota, R. and Robinson, M., *E-business 2.0*, 2nd edn, Addison Wesley, 2001, p. 310

[4] As 3 above

[5] Armstrong, V. and Jackson, D., 'Electronic data interchange: a guide to purchasing and supply', CIPS, 1991, pp. 15–16

[6] Killen, K. H. and Kamauff, J. W., *Managing Purchasing*, Irwin, 1995, p. 60

[7] Norman, G., 'Is it time for EDI?', Logistics Supplement, *Journal of Purchasing and Supply Management*, June, 1994, p. 20

[8] Monczka, R. M. and Carter, J. R., 'Implementation of electronic data interchange', *Journal of Purchasing and Supply Management*, Summer, 1998, pp. 2–9

[9] National Computing Centre, 'The impact of e-purchasing on supply chain management', *My IT Adviser*, 17 September, 2002

[10] Adapted from Ronchi, Stefano, *The Internet and the Customer Supplier Relationship*, Ashgate, 2003, p. 48

[11] We are indebted to the ACTIVE Secretariat, 20 Eastbourne Terrace, London W2 6LE, for permission to use this figure, taken from 'The e-Business Study', 2000, p. 20

[12] Epicor 2000, *The Strategy*, p. 91

[13] International confederation for printing and allied industries, 'E-Auctions – Code of Conduct', March 2005

[14] *Buy IT*, 'Online auctioning: e-procurement guidelines', issued by Buy IT Best Practice Network, October, 2001, pp. 13–14

[15] The authors are grateful to David Eaton and the *Buy IT* e-procurement Best Practice Network for permission to use this figure, taken from 'Buy IT Online Auctions', 2001, p. 5

[16] Lascelles, D., *Managing the Supply Chain*, Business Intelligence, 2001, p. 44

[17] We are grateful to CIPS for permission to reproduce this figure, taken from 'The CIPS e-procurement guidelines: e-invoicing and e-payment'

[18] Richardson, T., 'Guide to purchasing cards', Supplement, *Purchasing and Supply Management*, 2003, p. 7

[19] Bosch.Logistics@de.bosch.com

Part 2

Strategy, tactics and operations 1: purchasing factors

Chapter 7

Supplier relationships

Learning outcomes

This chapter aims to provide an understanding of:

- planning relationship purchasing
- the strategic nature of buyer–seller relationships
- models of supplier relationships
- skills and knowledge requirements
- the benefits of long-term relationships
- the termination of supplier relationships.

Key ideas

- Effective planning to create positive relationships.
- Contrast between transactional and relationship purchasing.
- Relationship formation.
- Classification and analysis of supplier relationships.
- Contract governance principles.
- The practical usefulness of supplier relationship models.
- Evaluating the mutuality of benefits from the relationship.
- Factors to consider when terminating relationships.

Introduction

This chapter is concerned with providing an understanding of purchasing–supplier relationships from the perspectives of both theory and practice. A critical scrutiny of the history of such relationships will demonstrate the opportunities for buyer and seller when genuine long-term relationships can be established. For this to be achieved it will require an investment of resources, changes in attitudes and the abandonment of adversarial business practice.

217

7.1 Relationship purchasing and purchasing relationships

A relationship is defined, inter alia, as a 'connection or association'.[1] Relationships apply when individuals, organisations and groups within and external to an enterprise interact. Apart from the field of industrial sociology, concerned with the study of group interaction within a workplace environment, the application of the study of business relationships began with the concept of relationship marketing.

Supplier Relationship Management (SRM)[2] is an approach between two parties to work towards the integration of their organisations, where that integration will bring greater value for money for the customer and enhanced margin for the supplier and will assist in meeting the strategic objectives of both. It is not an agreement to sole source, or outsource to a supplier, rather to integrate aspects of the two organisations for mutual benefit. These benefits must be real and tangible, not just relationship indicators.

The most successful relationships are those where customers and suppliers develop trust and an understanding of their respective requirements and interests, accompanied by a desire for both learning from and providing assistance to each other. Where such conditions exist, the ultimate outcome should be the creation of established and dependable purchasing–supplier relationships. Such relationships are the basis of networks and provide competitive advantages for both parties.

7.2 The contrast between transactional and relationship purchasing, taking account of contractual requirements

Table 7.1[3] has been adapted to include a consideration of contractual requirements to emphasise that, regardless of the relationship, the supplier is agreeing to meet certain contractual obligations.

7.3 Collaborative business relationships

The British Standards Institution[4] have published BS 11000–1:2010 'Collaborative business relationships – Part 1: A framework specification.'[5] It is relevant to note that BS 11000–2 was in preparation when this book went to print. PAS 11000:2006 is superseded and is withdrawn.

The aim of the British Standard is to provide a strategic framework to establish and improve collaborative relationships in organisations of all sizes. Collaboration is an admirable business objective but proven to be difficult to attain, as evidenced by high-profile contractual disputes. BSI point out that 'Collaborative approaches have been shown to deliver a wide range of benefits, which enhance competitiveness and performance (for example, but not limited to, better cost management, improved time, improved resource and risk management and delivering incremental business value and innovation'.

BSI then explained that collaborative relationships in the context of BS 11000 can be multi-dimensional, 'They can be individual one-to-one relationships but more frequently they are networked relationships which might involve multiple parties, including external collaborators/partners or alliance partners, suppliers, various internal divisions and often customers, working together. These are often described as business networks, supply chains, clusters, ecosystems or extended enterprises. It might

Table 7.1 The main differences and contractual requirements of transaction and relationship purchasing

Transactional	Relationship	Contractual requirement
Focus on discrete purchasing actions and one-off contracts	Focus on supplier retention providing KPIs are satisfied	One-off as opposed to long-term contract with commitments to offtake
Short-term orientation	Long-term orientation	Supplier commitment to continuous improvement and investment in research
Arms length	Closeness	Creation of joint partnering board, Open Book and sharing of long-term business plans
Sample buyer–seller relationship	Integrated relationship with involvement of stakeholders	Dedication to bringing about teamwork, effective contract review meetings and effective evaluation of issues
Emphasis on price, quality and delivery. No innovation	Sophisticated requirement for innovation, continuous improvement, opportunity for gainshare and visibility of research	Create requirement for demonstrable innovation with defined benefits for both parties
Moderate (or modest) supplier contact	High level of contact, including at senior level in both organisations. Consistent review of performance	Creation of operational and partnering boards, good frequency of review meetings
Little sharing of information; opaqueness	Significant sharing of information	Provision of management information, Open Book on costs and profit, transparency of business plans
Intellectual property not a key consideration	Intellectual property is a key consideration offering additional benefits through exploitation in market as a whole	IP ownership is joint when buyer sharing cost or acting as a BETA site. Licence agreed on agreed financial basis

also be applicable to consortia and joint ventures, even where the individual organisations might not be implementing the standard overall'.

The British Standard specifies an eight-stage framework that reflects the overall life cycle of a collaborative relationship. The eight key stages are shown in Table 7.2.

Table 7.2 Eight key stages of the collaborative relationship framework

STAGE 1	AWARENESS	This addresses the overall strategic corporate policy and processes which lead towards incorporating collaborative working as a recognised approach where it can identify added value. Within what BSI refers to as Clause 3, there are subsets of Stage 1 including, for example, appointing a Senior Executive Responsible (SER).
STAGE 2	KNOWLEDGE	This focuses on the development of knowledge against a specifically identified opportunity to create a business case and benefits analysis. BSI explain that this should include issues which would influence the overall strategy relating to competencies, training and development, knowledge management, risk management, value analysis and initial exit strategy conditions.

Table 7.2 Continued

STAGE 3	INTERNAL ASSESSMENT	This is intended to ensure that organisations undertake a structured assessment of their capability and maturity to successfully engage in a collaborative initiative. Acknowledging internal strengths and weaknesses ensures that the collaboration is not established with a bias towards the performance of the external parties.
STAGE 4	PARTNER SELECTION	This addresses the need to undertake a structured approach to the identification, evaluation and selection of appropriate partners. It assesses not only the performance aspects of each collaborative partner but also the way in which the two organisations can work together with a more integrated approach for mutual benefit.
STAGE 5	WORKING TOGETHER	This focuses on ensuring that the partners establish the appropriate operational structure, governance, roles and responsibilities to effectively achieve desired business objectives. In this, the organisations establish and agree a formal foundation for working together, including contractual frameworks or agreement of roles and responsibilities.
STAGE 6	VALUE CREATION	This is specifically focused on the need to establish approaches that seek to build value out of the joint relationship.
STAGE 7	STAYING TOGETHER	This addresses the need to ensure effective measurement and monitoring of the relationship to maintain its optimum performance.
STAGE 8	EXIT STRATEGY	This addresses the need to develop and maintain an effective strategy for disengagement where appropriate.

The standard includes at Table C.1 the competencies and behaviours, reproduced below:

Context	Core competency skills	Organisational enablers
Business skills required in the management of collaborative programmes	*Key competencies specific to the role of developing and managing collaborative programmes*	*Key cultural aspects that enable collaborative working and underpin operational practices*
■ Leadership ■ Business planning ■ Communications skills ■ Team management ■ Negotiation skills ■ Conflict resolution ■ Commercial and financial management ■ Change management ■ Project and programme management ■ Contract management ■ Risk management	■ Leadership through influence ■ Coaching and mentoring ■ Stakeholder management ■ Cultural awareness ■ Creating strategic alignment ■ Value proposition development ■ Collaborative negotiation ■ Partner selection ■ Governance development ■ Measurement and matrix setting ■ Collaborative working ■ Joint business planning ■ Organisational alignment	■ Leadership commitment ■ Joint governance structures ■ Shared goals/objectives ■ Cultural alignment ■ Joint business planning ■ Defined and appropriate measurement ■ Strategic alignment ■ Collaborative ethos ■ Clearly defined roles and responsibilities ■ Supportive processes and infrastructure ■ Clearly defined issue resolution mechanisms ■ Risk and reward sharing ■ Clear autonomy and accountability

Context	Core competency skills	Organisational enablers
Business skills required in the management of collaborative programmes	*Key competencies specific to the role of developing and managing collaborative programmes*	*Key cultural aspects that enable collaborative working and underpin operational practices*
■ Knowledge management ■ Business process development	■ Relationship management ■ Transition management ■ Problem solving and decision making	■ Adequate resources ■ Effective stakeholder communications ■ Competency skills development ■ Delegation of authority ■ Aligned incentive programmes

Critical behaviours

- Information sharing, constructive questioning, open and honest feedback
- Listen effectively, respecting opinions of others
- Communicate effectively, consistently, openly, honestly and in a responsive manner
- Recognise the objectives of all parties and seek ways to help maximise their achievement
- Negotiate without taking advantage
- Appreciate and respect differences in cultures; be proactive to resolve potential difficulties and overcome barriers
- Learn from and share experience and setbacks
- Understand and support others in the achievement of their own goals
- Establish joint needs and outcomes and deliver against objectives; act in the best interests of the joint effort
- Balance risk and reward when considering innovative thinking and future possibilities
- Consider the possible future implications of current issues
- Address short-term imperatives without losing sight of long-term objectives; learn from experience and to embrace changes
- Constructive and flexible attitude to change; facilitate creativity in others by encouraging challenge and new ideas
- Accommodate needs of all stakeholders in order to deliver shared goals
- Demonstrate respect and consideration for all partners and consider the impact of actions upon others
- Aim to create mutual understanding but hold people to account for unacceptable behaviour

7.3.1 Summary of BS 11000

This British Standard represents a valiant attempt to capture the salient points of creating and maintaining collaborative business relationships. In the authors' opinion it does not completely grasp the nettle of how to overcome traditional adversarial behaviour of buyer–seller relationship. Procurement lies at the heart of many processes to find suppliers who can become a partner. Overall, this is not a mechanistic approach. It requires the exercise of expert skills, particularly negotiation. It requires a meeting of the minds at executive level who are prepared to share long-term sensitive business plans.

7.4 Relationship formation

Holmlund and Strandvik[6] classify interactions between two or more enterprises as taking place on five different aggregation levels – actions, episodes, sequences, relationships and partner base. These are hierarchical levels, ranging from a single exchange to the portfolio of relationships of one particular enterprise.

- *Actions* – 'individual initiatives by the focal enterprise', such as a telephone call or plant visit, which may relate to products, information, money or social contacts.

- *Episodes* – groups of interrelated actions, such as a negotiation encompassing a number of actions.
- *Sequences* – larger and more extensive entities of interactions. This level may be defined in terms of a contract, product, campaign or project. Holmlund and Strandvik[7] also point out that:

> a sequence, in enterprises, can also be related to the presence of a significant human action in either of the organisations. A sequence may then end when a particular person is replaced by another in either firm. Even if the relationship continues, the quality of the relationship may change due to the influence of one single person . . . The completion of a sequence constitutes a vulnerable period of time during which the parties make important evaluations. The evaluation may cause a potential termination of the relationship, since a sequence represents a time-framed commitment, which is defined by the particular sequence.

- *Relationships* – comprise all the sequences, which, in turn, comprise all related episodes and actions in one particular relationship between two firms.
- *Partner base* – the relationship portfolio of a particular enterprise, that is all the relationships that a particular enterprise has at a particular point of time.

The formation of long-term personal relationships usually develops by going through the same stages. Thus, a meeting (action level) may develop into a friendship (episode level), courtship (sequential level) and marriage (relationship level). Each level is normally of a longer and more permanent duration than the preceding one. The model of supplier integration shown in Table 7.3 follows this pattern.

Jarvelin,[8] however, argues that, for practical purposes, the quality of relationships can be studied at two levels: episodes and relationships.

Table 7.3 Stages of supplier integrations

One-night stand	Regular date	Going steady	Living together	Marriage
				Cobusiness integration
				Core competences totally aligned, such that rationalisation will release added value
			Strategic alliances	
			Single sourcing and joint investment strategies; interdependence becomes the driving force	
		Performance partnerships		
	Preferred suppliers	Benchmarking still applied to assess value but now joint definition of improvement plans and priorities, joint supplier and purchaser fusion teams with specific improvement objectives, some job rotation		
Competitive leverage	Proven track record in quality, delivery and cost, hence smaller supplier base, less frequent bidding			
Bids, tenders and tactical negotiation on an ongoing basis				

Low ◄──► High

Degree of strategic alignment and integration of core competences

Source: Johnson, S., Tinsley Bridge Ltd, 'Managing change through teamwork', ISCAN, Sheffield, 1997, pp. 7–17

7.5 Models of supplier relationships

There are several classifications, of which the following, by Cox and Bensaou are typical.

7.5.1 The Cox model

Cox[9] presents a stepladder of external and internal relationships, as shown in Figure 7.1.

Figure 7.1 **A stepladder of external and internal contractual relationships**

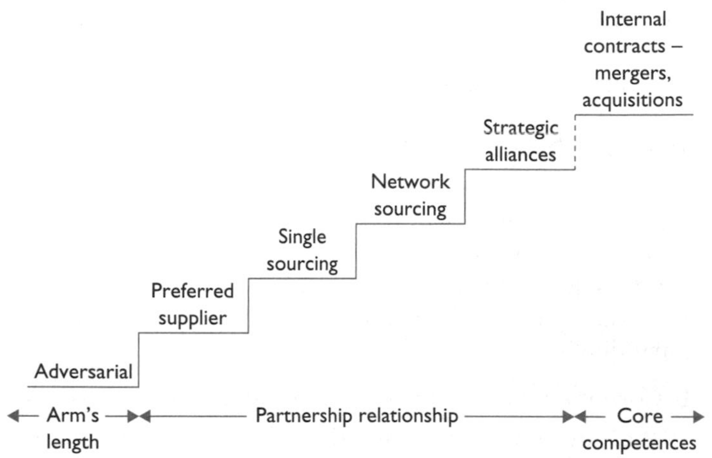

Source: Adapted from Cox, 1996[9]

Cox gives two reasons for the omission from the ladder of 'partnership sourcing', referred to later in this book:

■ the concept of partnership sourcing is generic and refers to a complicated range of collaborative relationships, such as from preferred supplier to strategic alliance

■ the term partnership sourcing is used to refer to all forms of non-adversarial collaborative relationships.

The Cox model draws heavily on concepts associated with transaction cost and resource-based theories of the firm.

Transaction cost theory (TCT)

Transaction cost theory (TCT), associated with Coase[10] and Williamson,[11] refers to the idea of the cost of providing for some good or service if it was purchased in the marketplace rather than from within the firm. Three key concepts are those of transaction costs, asset specificity and asymmetrical information distribution.

Transaction costs comprise:

■ search and bargain costs

■ bargaining and decision costs

■ policing and enforcement costs.

Asset specificity is the relative lack of transferability of assets intended for use in a given transaction to other uses. Williamson identifies six main types of asset specificity:

- site
- physical asset
- human asset
- brand names
- dedicated assets
- temporal.

Asymmetrical information distribution means that the parties to a transaction have uneven access to relevant information. One consequence is that, within contractual relationships, either party may engage in post-contractual opportunism if the chance of switching to more advantageous partnerships arises.

Resource-based theory (RBT)

Resource-based theory emphasises that each firm is characterised by its own unique collection of resources of core competences. Thus, Kay[12] argues that the source of competitive advantage is the creation and exploitation of distinctive capabilities that are difficult to build and maintain, codify and make into recipes, copy and emulate and can't simply be bought off the shelf. Kay identifies three basic types of distinctive capability.

1 *Corporate architecture* – the capacity of the organisation to:
   - create and store organisational knowledge and routines
   - promote more effective cooperation between network members
   - achieve a transparent and easy flow of information
   - adapt rapidly and flexibly.

2 *Innovation* – the capacity to lower costs, improve products or introduce new products ahead of competitors. The successful exploitation of new ideas incorporating new technologies, designs and best practice is difficult and uncertain. Often, innovation can only be achieved by cooperating and collaborating with partners.

3 *Reputation* – the capacity to instil confidence in an organisation's credibility, reliability, responsibility, trustworthiness and, possibly, accountability. Organisations can only achieve a positive reputation over time, but, once achieved, their ability to provide quality assurance may enable them to obtain a premium price for products.

From the insights provided by TCT and RBT, Cox derives the following propositions.

- *Arm's length relationships* are associated with low asset specificity and low supplier competences that can easily be bought off the shelf as there are many potential suppliers.
- *Internal contracts* – in-house provision – are associated with high asset specificity and core competences:

    The more competences approximate to core competences of high asset specificity, then the greater the likelihood that external relationships may lead to merger or acquisition or, failing that, result in very close, single-sourced negotiated contracts in which both parties have some clear ownership rights in the goods and services produced.[13]

■ *Partnership relationships* (as shown in Figure 7.1) apply to assets of medium specificity and ascend in steps according to the distance of the complementary competences
provided by external suppliers from the core competences of a particular firm:

> The nearer they [complementary competences] are to the core competences of the firm, the
> more the firm will have to consider vertical integration through merger and acquisition.
> The further away from the core competences of the firm the less there is a need for medium
> asset-specific skills to be vertically integrated.[14]

Cox's classification of contractual relationships

The five steps in the ladder of contractual relationships shown in Figure 7.1 each
represent a higher level of asset specificity and strategic importance to the firm of the
specific goods and services. Each step also represents relative degrees of power between
the relationship's participants and in the relative ownership of the goods and services
emanating from the relationships. Strategic supplier alliances are the final stage before
a firm considers a complementary supplier to be so important that vertical integration
through merger and acquisition is undertaken.

■ *Adversarial leverage* – up to the mid-1980s, approaching the marketplace on an
adversarial basis was the norm. Thus, Porter,[15] writing in 1980, advocates that purchasers should multi-source, negotiate short-term contracts, maintain secrecy regarding costs, sales and product design and make (or receive) no improvement suggestions
to (or from) suppliers.

■ *Preferred suppliers* – providers of complementary goods and services of medium
asset specificity or strategic importance who have been placed by the purchaser on a
restricted list of potential suppliers after a process of vendor rating and accreditation.

■ *Single sourcing* – purchasing from a single supplier of medium asset specificity
complementary goods or services of relatively high strategic importance. As Cox
observes, the aim of single sourcing is to reduce transaction costs and economise, but
without the costs associated with vertical integration.

■ *Network sourcing and partnerships* – networks have been considered earlier in
section 4.3. According to Cox, network sourcing 'is the idea that it is possible to
create a virtual company at all levels of the supply chain by engineering multiple
tiered partnerships at each stage, but without moving to vertical integration'. With
network sourcing:

- the prime contracting firm acts as the driver for the reduction of transaction costs
  within the whole supply and value chain
- cost reduction is achieved by a partnership between the prime contractor and
  a first-tier supplier who controls an important medium asset for the prime
  contractor and also forms similar partnerships with second-tier suppliers (see
  section 4.4.1)
- each tiering level of the supply chain is effectively a joint venture in which firms
  at each stage will inform and educate their respective partners by sharing best
  practice and 'fit for purpose' techniques
- such network sourcing relationships will only be possible in mature industries
  'where asset specificity has constantly been reduced and multiple and serial
  subcontracting thereby facilitated. In such supply chain relationships issues of
  ownership, control and power become increasingly difficult to allocate.'

■ *Strategic supplier alliances* – classically referred to as joint ventures, these are defined by Cox as 'negotiated single-sourced relationships with the supplier of a complementary product or service'. Such relationships form a completely new and independent legal entity, distinct from the firms comprising the alliance. As both parties have some degree of proprietorship (not necessarily 50/50) in the outcome of the relationship, the basis of such relationships is power equivalence and a high degree of complementarity.

7.5.2 The Bensaou model

The Bensaou model is based on a study of eleven Japanese and three US automobile manufacturers. Bensaou[16] suggests a framework for managing a portfolio of investments for the purpose of enabling senior managers to answer two questions.

Q1 Which governance structure or relational design should a firm choose under different external contingencies?

This is a strategic decision because it affects how a firm defines its boundaries and core activities.

Q2 What is the appropriate way to manage each different type of relationship?

This is an organisational question.

Bensaou suggests four buyer relationship profiles:

■ market exchange
■ captive buyer
■ captive supplier
■ strategic partnerships.

For each profile, Bensaou identifies distinguishing product, market and supplier characteristics.

Finally, he suggests that the four profiles can be arranged in a matrix to indicate whether the buyer's and the supplier's tangible or intangible investments in the relationship are high or low. Tangible investments, in this context, are buildings, tooling and equipment. Intangible investments are people, time and effort spent in learning supplier–purchaser business practices and procedures and information sharing.

The Bensaou matrix, as adapted, is shown in Figure 7.2.

Bensaou also identified three management variables for each profile, which are:

■ information-sharing practices
■ characteristics of 'boundary-spanner' jobs
■ the social climate within the relationship.

The management practices that high performers in each cell use to match the coordination, information and knowledge exchange requirements presented by the external context shown in Figure 7.5 are subsequently shown in Figure 7.3.

Bensaou concluded the following:

■ Many large firms in manufacturing are moving away from traditional vertical integration and towards the external contracting of key activities.

Figure 7.2 Supplier's specific investment

High

Captive buyer

Product characteristics:
- technically complicated
- based on mature, well-understood technology
- little innovation and improvement to the product

Market characteristics:
- stable demand with limited market growth
- concentrated market with few established players
- buyers maintain an internal manufacturing capability

Supplier characteristics:
- large supply houses
- supplier proprietary technology
- few strongly established suppliers
- strong bargaining power
- car manufacturers heavily depend on these suppliers, their technology and skills

Strategic partnership

Product characteristics:
- high level of customisation required
- close to buyer's core competency
- tight mutual adjustments needed in key processes
- technically complicated part or integrated subsystem
- based on new technology
- innovation leaps on technology, product or service
- frequent design changes
- strong engineering expertise required
- large capital investment required

Market characteristics:
- strong demand and high growth market
- very competitive and concentrated market
- frequent changes in competitors due to instability or lack of dominant design
- buyer maintains in-house design and testing capability

Partner characteristics:
- large multiproduct supply houses
- strong supplier proprietary technology
- active in research and innovation (R&D costs)
- strong recognised skills and capabilities in design, engineering and manufacturing

Market exchange

Product characteristics:
- highly standardised products
- mature technology
- little innovation and rare design changes
- technically simple product or well-structured complicated manufacturing process
- little or no customisation to buyer's final product
- low engineering effort and expertise required
- small capital investments required

Market characteristics:
- stable or declining demand
- highly competitive market
- many capable suppliers
- same players over time

Supplier characteristics:
- small 'mom and pop' shops
- no proprietary technology
- low switching costs
- low bargaining power
- strong economic reliance on automotive business

Captive supplier

Product characteristics:
- technically complicated products
- based on new technology (developed by suppliers)
- important and frequent innovations and new functionalities in the product category
- significant engineering effort and expertise required
- heavy capital investments required

Market characteristics:
- high growth market segment
- fierce competition
- few qualified players
- unstable market with shifts between suppliers

Supplier characteristics:
- strong supplier proprietary technology
- suppliers with strong financial capabilities and good R&D skills
- low supplier bargaining power
- heavy supplier dependency on the buyer and economic reliance on the automotive sector in general

Low

Relationship investment   Low   High

Figure 7.3 Management profile for each contextual profile

Captive buyer	Strategic partnerships
Information-sharing mechanisms: ■ 'broadband' and important exchange of detailed information on a continuous basis ■ frequent and regular mutual visits **Boundary-spanner tasks' characteristics:** ■ structured tasks, highly predictable ■ large amount of time spent by buyer's purchasing agents and engineers with supplier **Climate and process characteristics:** ■ tense climate, lack of mutual trust ■ no early supplier involvement in design ■ strong effort by buyer towards cooperation ■ supplier does not necessarily have a good reputation	**Information-sharing mechanisms:** ■ 'broadband' frequent and 'rich media' exchange ■ regular mutual visits and practice of guest engineers **Boundary-spanner tasks' characteristics:** ■ highly ill defined, ill structured ■ non-routine, frequent, unexpected events ■ large amount of time spent with supplier's staff, mostly on coordinating issues **Climate and process characteristics:** ■ high mutual trust and commitment to relationship ■ strong sense of buyer fairness ■ early supplier involvement in design ■ extensive joint action and cooperation ■ supplier has excellent reputation
Market exchange	**Captive supplier**
Exchange-sharing mechanisms: ■ 'narrowband' and limited information exchange, heavy at time of contract negotiation ■ operational coordination and monitoring along structured routines **Boundary-spanner tasks' characteristics:** ■ limited time spent directly with suppliers' staff ■ highly routine and structured tasks with little interdependence with supplier's staff **Climate and process characteristics:** ■ positive social climate ■ no systematic joint effort and cooperation ■ no early supplier involvement in design ■ supplier fairly treated by the buyer ■ supplier has a good reputation and track record	**Information-sharing mechanisms:** ■ little exchange of information ■ few mutual visits, mostly from supplier to buyer **Boundary-spanner tasks' characteristics:** ■ limited time allocated by buyer's staff to the supplier ■ mostly complicated, coordinating tasks **Climate and process characteristics:** ■ high mutual trust, but limited direct joint action and cooperation ■ greater burden put on the supplier

■ As interfirm relationships increase, firms cannot manage with one design for all relationships and so need to manage a portfolio of relationships.

■ There are two kinds of successful relationship: high requirement–low capabilities and low requirements–high capabilities. There are also two paths to failure: underdesigned and overdesigned relationships. *Overdesign* takes place when firms invest in building trust as a result of frequent visits and cross-company teams when the market and product context call for simple, impersonal control and information exchange. Such overdesign is both costly and risky, especially in terms of the intangible investments in people, information or knowledge.

■ Building or redesigning relationships according to the Bensaou model therefore involves the following three analytical steps:

1 the strategic selection of relational types to match the external conditions relating to the product, the technology and the market (see Figure 7.5)

2 the identification of an appropriate management profile for each type of relational design

3 matching the design of the relationship, which could be overdesigned or under-designed, to the desired management profile.

7.6 Practical considerations of supplier relationship management

Day[17] argues that supplier relationship management is becoming a strategic battle-ground within organisations and procurement isn't the only function jostling for supremacy. He goes on to say that a number of areas can be improved through diligent supplier relationship management. They include:

- the ability to model costs more accurately
- utilisation of cross-organisation teams
- reduction in the impact of price fluctuations on cost structures
- early supplier involvement in product and service development
- transfer of knowledge through the supply chain
- planning and design synergy
- use of metrics to drive change for both organisations
- improved risk management and continuity of supply
- access to, and speed of, innovation.

Birmingham[18] advances the view that the ability to manage supplier relationships in a consistent, formalised programme is a growing practice among corporations of all sizes, across all industries. Figure 7.4 shows a model intended to assist companies in assessing their supplier relationship management efforts.

The Bayer Group have introduced SUPREME[19] an approach to supplier relationship management which has, as its goal, to concentrate procurement volume on the best suppliers through a global and standardised approach. Profitability and performance are primary objectives at Bayer. Material costs represent a substantial portion of the total cost of a Bayer product. Managing these costs is critical to Bayer's success. Working with our suppliers, we will identify optimisation potentials through a structured evaluation of quantitative and qualitative criteria, and together we will implement improvements.

SUPREME comprises:

- supplier selection
- supplier evaluation
- supplier optimisation.

Supplier selection – each supplier will go through a six-step process including:

1 demand analysis
2 market analysis
3 supplier pre-selection
4 supplier qualification
5 request for quotation
6 negotiation.

Supplier evaluation is shown in Figure 7.5.

Figure 7.4 Model for assessing supplier relationship management efforts

	Spend visibility	Supplier segmentation	Collaboration	Performance	Risk management
Leveraging SRM	Spend visibility drives category strategy and P2P efforts. Insight into total cost of ownership. Aligns with enterprise strategy	Drives behviour of sourcing organisation	Continuous improvements efforts reaping benefits in areas outside of traditional sourcing arena. Advanced relationship	Recognition programme in place, 360 evaluations, continuous improvement	Monitor the supply chain risk status and contingency plans
Utilising SRM	Spend visibility contributes to the SRM strategy consistently and aligns with the strategic sourcing goals	Supports rationalisation and RF × efforts	Lifecycle management across contracts, relationship, technology and innovation	Publish scorecards and metrics. Conduct performance reviews with suppliers on a timely basis	Contingency plans in place. Detailed risk management plan with anticipated scenarios
Implemented SRM	Understand supply base with relation to spend and use this knowledge in segmentation process. Contributes to strategic sourcing plan	Supplier segmented and expectations communicated to the suppliers. Internal stakeholders aligned with segmentation	Business culture aligned, two-way interaction between stakeholders. Satisfaction surveys and 360s in place for data gathering	Distribute surveys, evaluate results, develop and implement remediation plans	Weigh factors applied to risks. Develop contingency plans
Need identified	Data gathering and spend analysis being completed, possible vendor master scrub if needed	Defined 'status' (e.g. preferred, key, strategic.) with explicit criteria for each tier. Potentially using a tiering tool	External stakeholders identified satisfaction surveys and 360s in development for data gathering	Develop key performance indicators, decide on frequency of evaluation. Obtain stakeholder buy in	Identify risks from financial, technology, security, exclusivity, and contract perspective as applicable
Limited/ none	No visibility into supplier data, vendor master not cleansed; spend analysis not completed	No formal segmentation in place. Internally and externally supplier 'status' is unknown	Stakeholders/ executive sponsors not identified. Reactive participation and little strategic interaction with only internal stakeholders	Reactive approach to performance, little or no visibility into metrics. Tracked on an ad-hoc basis	No action plan in place for any risk management; not aware of all potential risks

Figure 7.5 Supplier evaluation – identify areas of improvement

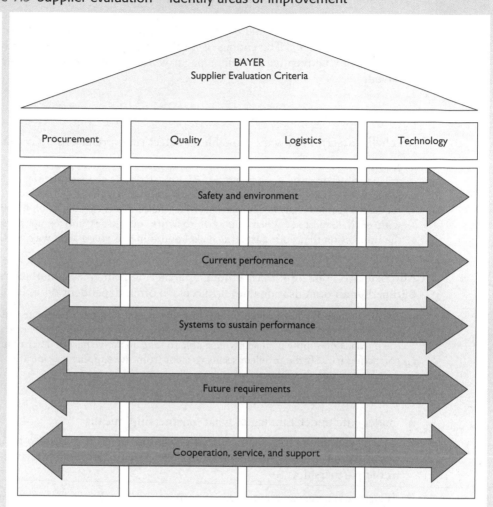

Supplier optimisation consists of five steps, namely:

1 Analysis of evaluation results – supplier ratings are analysed and recommendations for improvements are made.

2 Definition of the material group/supplier strategy market, demand, supplier information and future development is defined for each supplier.

3 Developments of improvement actions – detailed steps for overcoming deficits in performance are defined.

4 Communication and implementation – the supplier receives the evaluation results and if necessary, improvement actions are implemented.

5 Action controlling – all improvement actions are entered into a centralised database. Progress is followed and regular reports are sent to management.

7.7 The termination of relationships

No relationship can or should be expected to last forever as organisations operate in a dynamic environment. The ending of a relationship does not necessarily mean failure and there may be positive as well as negative outcomes for one or both of the parties involved.

7.7.1 Reasons for termination

Mitchell[20] describes how it is possible to detect that a relationship is changing:

> A primary tip-off that the nature of the relationship is changing can be seen in requests that are made by you or by the supplier. Are multiple requests necessary before action is taken? Are requests necessary for items or service that used to be offered without asking? Perhaps the request is granted, but the requester feels like he or she is cashing in on his or her last favour with each request . . . When you start to work out issues and compromises and you get the impression that your partner is nickel and dimeing you all the way you know that your alliance is coming to an end.

Mitchell also points out that, although partnering principles and objectives can be well outlined at an organisational level, success is often dependent on individuals:

> All individuals for both organisations must be committed and resistance can begin on either side of the fence. If the problems have roots in the purchasing and supply organisation, at least the purchasing supply manager will be able to take an active part in determining the cause and correcting it . . . If the problem seems to stem from the supplier organisation, the outcome is a bit more unpredictable.

In practice, most partnership break-ups derive from:

- inadequate understanding of what 'partnership' means
- rapidly changing circumstances that cause one or both parties to revise their priorities and concentrate on achieving their own organisational objectives at the expense of the partnership.

Such circumstances, as identified by Southey[21] in the UK and Campbell and Pollard[22] in the USA, include:

- *changes in business direction(s)* – an existing partnership may no longer have value if either the purchasing or supplier organisation has shifted its strategic direction
- *product obsolescence* – the product or service provided by the supplier is becoming obsolete without any replacement options
- *the supplier is unable to meet service levels* – certain objectives basic to the partnership can no longer be met
- *short-term attitude* – either partner may consider that the long-term benefits of the partnership have not been realised sufficiently quickly or have been insufficient to warrant a continued commitment to a particular supplier/purchaser
- *economic factors* – a supplier has become 'at risk' financially, with the danger of potential liquidation
- *external economics* – a recession may force suppliers to cut back on product development, training and other resources, such as product engineers, and, consequently, they will be unable to meet the 'continuous improvement' objectives of the partnership

- *mergers and acquisitions* – such ventures can create new business models for either the purchaser or supplier
- *corporate divestiture* – may create a situation where, because parts of the business have been sold, the organisation can no longer provide a product or service
- *instability and inconsistency* – acquisitions or disposals of companies or rapid changes in key personnel or organisational philosophy often adversely affect years of previous relationship building based on trust and stability.

In the last analysis, however, successful partnerships can only be built if trust and cooperation exist between purchaser and supplier.

7.7.2 The process of termination

It is a truism that good contract management is not reactive but aims to anticipate and respond to future contingencies. Every well-written contract should anticipate the possibility of terminating the relationship.

Some writers, however, criticise the inadequacies of legal contracts for governing partnerships, especially in the face of uncertainty and dependence. Sitkin and Roth,[23] for example, describe legalistic remedies as weak, impersonal substitutes for trust. Contractual provisions may also lack flexibility, which might enable terminations to be made more amicably and easily than following the 'letter of the law'. Ouchi,[24] however, points out that formal control mechanisms are more effective in obtaining compliance with specifiable objectives than in obtaining commitment to a general value orientation.

Timing, relationship aspects, legal considerations and succession issues are important aspects of termination.

7.7.3 Timing

Mitchell[25] states that, whenever possible, the timing of the termination should be synchronised with the expiration of the agreement currently in force. Giving too much advance warning to a supplier can lead to deterioration in service. Conversely, termination may not come as a surprise to a supplier that has received regular negative feedback on performance. Decisions may also have to be made on whether the termination should be immediate or gradual. Such decisions may be governed by terms and conditions relating to termination in the current agreement.

7.7.4 Relationship aspects

Terminations may be amicable or hostile. Campbell and Pollard[26] refer to the three Ps that can aid in minimising possible hostility encountered in the termination process:

- positive attitude
- pleasant tone
- professional treatment

A positive attitude recognises that both organisations will survive apart and that recriminations will help neither. Further, both organisations may need each other in the future. A pleasant tone can be more effective than harsh words. Professional justification for the termination is essential. Termination is not a personal issue. The purchasing executive's job is to obtain the best possible value in order that his or her organisation can remain ahead of the competition.

7.7.5 Legal considerations

Among such factors are:

- *the financial consequences of terminating the agreement* – in some cases, it may be possible to negotiate a settlement, in others the contract will be specific regarding payments to be made in the event of fault or non-fault termination.
- *confidentiality agreements* – where such agreements are part of the contract terms, they must be honoured for the prescribed time.
- *intellectual property issues* – drawings, designs prepared during the agreement, computer software and so on.
- *capital property issues* – especially in relation to materials or capital equipment located at the supplier's site.
- *security issues* – it is necessary to change passwords or security codes shared with the other party to the agreement.
- *obtaining clear signed records of any settlement*
- *employee rights* – if they were transferred under the Transfer of Undertakings (Protection of Employment) (TUPE) Regulations.

7.7.6 Succession issues

Before deciding to terminate, it will be necessary to ensure that steps have been taken to ensure a continuity of supplies. This will entail:

- discussion with internal customers regarding groups, systems and projects that will be affected by the change of supplier
- reflecting on the lessons learned from the terminated relationship
- conducting market analysis to determine other supplier options
- preparing specifications (possibly revised)
- selection of a new supplier – an important factor will be the potential supplier's reputation for trustworthiness
- negotiation of a relationship agreement.

Finally, as Campbell and Pollard[27] observe:

> As a result of thinking through the options and creating a professional plan for separation, supply managers can disprove the old maxim that 'marriages are made in heaven, but the divorce is the very devil'.

7.8 Further aspects of relationships

These include collaboration in innovation and design, the supply base, supplier appraisal, outsourcing, make-or-buy decisions, partnerships and supplier performance and they are dealt with in appropriate sections elsewhere in this book.

Case study

Maybury Security Ltd

Maybury Security Ltd (MSL) was awarded a ten-year contract to provide an IT system used in the detection and prevention of computer related offences used by specialist divisions of police forces. To the public and the media the contract was described as being won by 'Cyberia' a consortium of internationally respected security organisations who would be working with the police in a partnership to counter 'cyber crime'. The consortium was actually MSL acting as the prime contractor with a number of sub-contractors covering facilities management, building construction, software development, data centre management and systems integration.

Twelve months into the contract it has become clear that the relationships between all the parties are failing. MSL has deliberately kept the police representative and the sub-contractors apart from each other, despite their requests to involve each other in resolving technical issues. No payments had been made by the police for six months, using the reason that contractual performance is not being achieved.

Following a crisis meeting with the police, MSL's Managing Director, Geoff Maybury, agreed to remove the current project manager and the police agreed to provide a new senior responsible officer (SRO) who would manage the contract to eliminate any personality issues that may be at the root of the relationship problems.

The police issues were:

- milestones were late or inadequately completed
- costs of contract changes were excessive
- Maybury responses to contract changes always sought relaxations on previously agreed service levels.

Maybury Security Ltd complaints included:

- the police moving the contract 'goal posts' by changing the acceptance criteria
- decision making was excessively long and impacted on deliverables
- the number and volume of contract changes required large amounts of rework for which the police refused to pay.

The sub-contractors' complaints included:

- MSL were not communicating the police requirements adequately
- MSL were late in paying invoices (often 60 days late)
- too short notice giving approval for work done and for any changes in requirements.

You have been appointed as the new SRO and have with MSLs agreement invited the new MSL project manager together with her equivalent from each of the sub-contractors to a meeting to discuss a way forward.

Tasks

As the new senior responsible officer for the police, in considering a resolution to the problem:

1 what do you believe the police could do differently?
2 what other actions do you consider could help resolve the issues?
3 how would these other actions affect contractual matters?
4 how would you improve relationship management?

Discussion questions

7.1 Selecting your top five strategic suppliers, how would you describe the relationship?

7.2 'The most successful relationships are those where customers and suppliers develop trust and an understanding of their requirements and interests, accompanied by a concern for both learning from and providing assistance to each other.'
  (a) Define the words 'trust' and 'understanding'.
  (b) Can there be trust without understanding?
  (c) What are the characteristics of a 'learning organisation'?

7.3 Provide an example from your own experience of the progression of a supplier relationship from episodal to relationships.

7.4 To what extent do you consider 'adversarial leverage' to be still prevalent? Can you provide an example of adversarial leverage from your own experience?

7.5 What is the eight-stage framework set out in PAS 11000? How would you evaluate whether your own organisation is positioned to collaborate?

7.6 If you were seeking to establish the profile of a potential collaborative partner, how would you conclude whether they were a dynamic culture?

7.7 In your opinion does competitive tendering help or hinder buyer–seller relationships? Why?

7.8 Is the 'old fashioned' type of contract suitable for a partnering relationship? How would you take account of:
  (a) including 'damages' for non-performance in the contract?
  (b) including a clause for termination at the buyer's convenience?
  (c) including a clause requiring continuous improvement in manufacture/service delivery?

7.9 How would you 'sell' the concept of a single source of supply, with a long-term contract, for a strategically vital manufactured item to your company?

7.10 Can you name three international supply sources that create a captive buyer situation?

7.11 Who should be accountable for supplier relationship management? Is it better handled by purchasing or the department who are dependent on the supply of goods/services?

7.12 Giving due consideration to the Bayer model, how effective is your approach to supplier performance evaluation or 'vendor rating' as it is sometimes called?

Past examination questions

1 Explain **five** reasons why having a good relationship with a supplier would usually assist the process of contract management.
CIPS, Preparing and Managing Contracts, May 2009

2 Draw a flow chart showing the methods of resolving disputes with suppliers in order of ease of resolution and time taken.
CIPS, Preparing and Managing Contracts, May 2007

3 Identify **five** characteristics that the 'right supplier' will possess.
CIPS, Selecting the right supplier, November 2007

4 Palfrey Products Plc is a supplier of many different types of foodstuffs. Its main customers are major supermarket chains and small retailers. Palfrey has a wide range of suppliers, both in its own country and in other countries.

A new purchasing manager has recently been appointed, and problems and disputes with many suppliers have become apparent. These are generally due to late delivery problems and quality issues. This has resulted in bad publicity for Palfrey and its suppliers.

One such dispute has been with Zenon, a supplier of a range of important raw materials. Zenon is one of a small number of suppliers in a restricted supply market. The purchasing manager needs to find suitable ways of satisfactorily resolving these disputes and has been considering this difficult matter.

Tasks

(a) Explain **two** problems which might arise from using litigation to resolve the dispute with Zenon.

(b) Describe **two** benefits for Palfrey of using negotiation to resolve the dispute with Zenon.

(c) If negotiations were not successful and litigation were considered undesirable, explain how Palfrey might attempt to resolve disputes with suppliers in future.

References

1 *The Concise Oxford Dictionary*, Oxford University Press

2 Office of Government Commerce. Category Management Toolkit

3 The authors gratefully acknowledge permission to quote from the CIPS booklet 'How to manage supplier relationships', written by Dr Kenneth Lysons

4 BSI Group Headquarters, 389 Chriswick High Road, London W4 4AL

5 ISBN 978 0 580 69562 9

6 Holmlund, M. and Strandvik, T., 'Perception configuration in business relationships', *Management Decision*, Vol. 37 (9), 1999, pp. 686–96

7 As 3 above

8 Jarvelin, A. M., 'Evaluation of relationship quality in business relationships', academic disseration, University of Tampare, Finland, 2001, p. 38

9 Cox, A., 'Regional competence and strategic procurement management', *European Journal of Purchasing and Supply Management*, Vol. 2, No. 1, 1996, pp. 57–70

10 Coase, R. H., 'The nature of the firm', *Economica*, No. 4, 1937, pp. 386–405

11 Williamson, O. E., 'Transaction cost economics: the governing of contractual relations', *Journal of Law and Economics*, Vol. 22, 1979, pp. 232–61

12 Kay, J., *Foundations of Corporate Success: How Business Strategies Add Value*, Oxford University Press, 1995

13 As 8 above, p. 64

14 As 8 above, p. 63

15 Porter, M., *Competitive Strategy*, Free Press, 1980, pp. 106–7

16 Bensaou, M., 'Portfolio of buyer–supplier relationships', *Sloan Management Review*, Summer, 1999, pp. 35–44

17 Day, Alan., 'A winning position: supplier relationship management is becoming a strategic battleground.' *CPO Agenda* 10 April 2007. Available from www.stateofflux.co.uk

18 Birmingham, P. A., 'Supplier Relationship Management Maturity Model' – 93rd Annual International Supply Management Conference, May, 2008

19 Bayer Group, Contact SUPREME office. BBS – Procurement and Logistics Global Community Support, e-mail: supreme@bayer-ag.de

20 Mitchell, L. K., 'Breaking up is hard to do – how to end a supplier relationship', ISM resource article at: www.ism.ws/ResourceArticles/2000/cpoomitchell.cfm

21 Southey, P., 'Pitfalls to partnering in the UK', PSERG Second International Annual Conference 1993, in Burnett, K. (ed.) *Readings in Partnership Sourcing*, CIPS, 1995

22 Campbell, P. and Pollard, W. M., 'Ending a supplier relationship', *Inside Supply Management*, September, 2002, pp. 33–8

23 Sitkin, S. B. and Roth, N. L., 'Explaining the limited effectiveness of legalistic "remedies" for trust/distrust', *Organisation Science*, Vol. 4 (3), 1993, pp. 367–92

24 Ouchi, W. G., 'A conceptual framework for the design of organisational control mechanisms', *Management Science*, Vol. 25 (9), 1979, pp. 833–48

25 As 19 above

26 As 21 above

27 As 21 above

Chapter 8

Purchasing: product innovation, supplier involvement and development

Learning outcomes

With reference, where applicable, to purchasing and supply management, this chapter aims to provide an understanding of:

- product and process innovation
- new product development
- supplier development
- supplier associations
- concurrent engineering
- the innovative nature of purchasing.

Key ideas

- Innovation and *kaizen*.
- Drivers of innovation.
- The stages of new product development.
- Environmental factors in design.
- Purchasing contributions to new product development.
- Early buyer involvement (EBI).
- Early supplier involvement (ESI).
- Results and process-orientated supplier development.
- The steps involved in supplier development.
- The aims and objectives of *Kyoryoku Kai*.
- Perceived benefits and disadvantages of supplier associations.

8.1 Innovation and *kaizen*

8.1.1 Innovation

Innovation is the process of turning ideas and knowledge into products and services that create a consumer demand within the marketplace.[1]

- *Product innovation* is the process of transforming technical ideas or market needs and opportunities into a new product (or service) that is launched on to the market.
- *Process innovation* is the introduction or development of new methods or technology by means of which products or services can be manufactured or delivered more effectively or efficiently. An example of process innovation is the introduction of robots and other forms of automated equipment.
- *Breakthrough innovation* is completely new or revolutionary products, such as new scientific discoveries in pharmaceuticals. Commonplace products, such as the radio, television and aircraft were once breakthrough innovations.
- *Incremental innovations* are gradual improvements in a product or service.

Treasy[2] points out that every innovation carries two risks:

1 a technology risk – 'Will it work'?

2 a marketplace risk – 'Will people buy it'?

The technology risk arises when we seek to achieve breakthrough innovations. The marketplace risk can arise because the cost of the resultant product to potential customers is too high or because the market is not ready for the innovation.

8.1.2 Kaizen

Kaizen is a Japanese term and means continuous improvement. The concept of *kaizen* is the basis of total quality management (TQM) and is strongly associated with Japanese lean production.

Although analogous to incremental innovation, *kaizen* is, as shown by Table 8.1, generally different from innovation.

Both innovation and *kaizen*, however, share the common objective of enabling an organisation to achieve a sustainable advantage.

8.1.3 Drivers of innovation

In addition to achieving sustainable advantage, these drivers include:

- the need to meet the challenges of global and domestic competition
- the challenges of rapid and complicated technological advances
- the enhancement of the value of the enterprise derived from a reputation for innovation and new product development.

8.1.4 Important aspects of innovation

- Recognition of an unmet need in the market.
- Time or the need to bring an innovatory product or service to the market ahead of competitors.

Table 8.1 Differences between innovation and kaizen

Characteristics	Innovation	Kaizen
Focus	Large, short-term, radical changes in products	Small, frequent, gradual improvements over a long time
Expertise	Leading-edge breakthrough	Conventional know-how
Sources	Scientific or technological discovery or invention	Design, production and marketing
Capital requirements	Substantial investment in equipment and technology	Relatively modest investment
Progress	Dramatic breakthroughs	Small incremental steps
Results	Spontaneous	Continuous
Risks	High	Low
Involvement	Corporate activity	Individual or small team
Recognition	Results	Effort

There is strong evidence that speed to market creates enhanced market share and a reputation for market leadership:

> By introducing 6 all new vehicles within a l4-month period, Toyota captured a 43 per cent share of the auto sales in Japan . . .

A 1987 study showed that the Japanese could then, on average, create a new car about l8 months faster than either their US or Western-European competitors, at a cost of about half a billion dollars in lost profits to the lagging firms.[3] Time-based strategies embody the value-added dimensions of time-responsiveness and customisation. For engineered products, time-to-market can be reduced by advanced computer-aided engineering and concurrent engineering.

Computer-aided engineering (CAE) eliminates entirely some of the traditional steps in the new product development process and allows others to be performed simultaneously. Mileham *et al.*[4] state that, where used properly, appropriate software can reduce cycle times, costs and risks by 90 per cent.

8.1.5 Concurrent engineering

Definition

> Concurrent engineering is a systematic approach to the integrated, concurrent design of products and their related processes, including manufacture and support.[5]

Typically, concurrent engineering involves the formation of cross-functional teams, which allows engineers and managers of different disciplines to work together simultaneously in developing product and process design. This approach is intended to cause the developers from the outset, to consider all elements of the product lifecycle from Concept through disposal, including quality, cost, schedule, and user requirements.

Australia's National Institute for Manufacturing Management[6] has published *A Guide to Introducing Concurrent Engineering in Your Organisation*. They pose a question for companies to ascertain whether concurrent engineering is for them:

'Does my company face any of the following problems in product development?

- increasing competitive pressure to develop new products
- product launch delays
- higher costs in processing and developing products than is acceptable
- a predominantly internally focused product development process
- little or no direct knowledge of customer requirements
- no or low involvement by marketing in the early stages of product development
- shift in responsibility for product development from one function to another as the project progresses and transfer points often characterised by conflict
- poor transfer of learning from one product development project to the next.'

The guide, unwittingly perhaps, relegates the function of purchasing to a non-contributor in the early and crucial stages of concurrent engineering, as shown in Figure 8.1. The logic for early buyer involvement (EBI) is covered later in this chapter (page 247). The guide shows the potential benefits of concurrent engineering by reference to achievements from companies from various industries. These are shown in Table 8.2.

A proactive purchasing function can positively influence the concurrent engineering process by:

- promoting the logic for the early involvement of suppliers in the design process to ensure the true cost and maintainability of materials and components
- becoming a key member of the concurrent engineering team, through an effective challenge to specifications
- the effective management of the procurement of samples for test and production prototypes
- ensuring that emerging contractual detail includes supplier's obligations for replacing faulty materials and components
- providing training to the concurrent engineering teams on all facets of cost drivers impacting on through life costs

Figure 8.1 The functions of purchasing in concurrent engineering

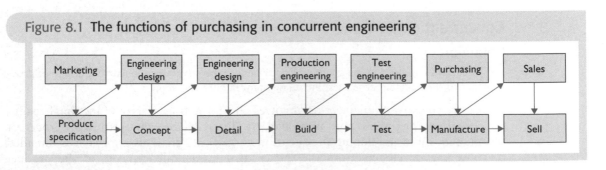

Table 8.2 Benefits obtained from concurrent engineering

Benefits and metrics	Results
Decreased lead time	
Development time	30–70%
Time to market	20–90%
Improved quality	
Engineering changes	65–90% fewer
Scrap and rework	Up to 75% less
Overall quality	200–600% higher
Reduced cost	
Productivity	20–110% higher
Return on assets	20–120% higher
Manufacturing costs	Up to 40% lower

- assisting in networking with other organisations who have successfully implemented concurrent engineering
- ensuring that a rigorous risk assessment process is in place for all facets of supplier engagement
- assisting in overcoming cross-functional team barriers by the application of negotiation skills.

8.2 Environmentally sensitive design

8.2.1 Factors in environmentally sensitive design

Pressures exerted by environmental groups and relevant legislation, such as the UK Clean Air Act 1956, the Radioactive Substances Act 1993 and the Environmental Protection Act 1990; require designers to devise socially responsible products. In the design of such products, special consideration must be given to:

- increasing their efficiency and economy in the use of materials, energy and other resources
- minimising pollution from chosen materials
- reducing any long-term harm to the environment caused by using the product
- ensuring that the planned life of the product is the most appropriate in environmental terms and that the product functions efficiently for its full life
- ensuring that full account is taken of the end-disposal of the product
- specifying packaging that can be recycled easily
- minimising nuisances, such as noise or odour
- analysing and minimising safety hazards.

Attention given to the above factors at the design stage can simplify production, enhance the manufacturer's reputation and prevent investment in products and processes that environmental legislation may make obsolete.

Figure 8.2 Product lifecycle

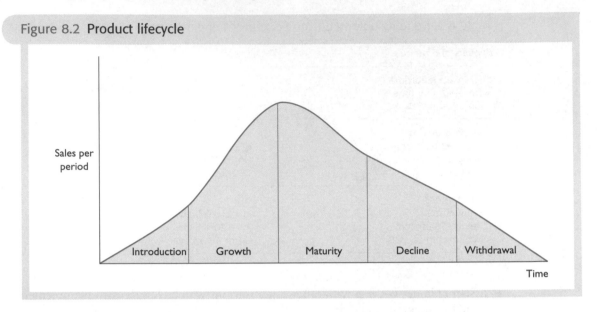

8.2.2 Approaches to environmentally sensitive design

Four important approaches are lifecycle analysis (LCA), design for disassembly (DFD), the use of environmentally preferred materials and guidance by the International Organisation for Standardisation (ISO).

8.2.3 Lifecycle analysis

This is based on the concept that all products have a lifecycle. The product lifecycle, or Gopertz curve, is shown in Figure 8.2.

8.2.4 Design for disassembly (DFD)

This has two aspects:

- *Recyclability* – this saves both energy and resources. Recycling aluminium, for example, requires 95 per cent less energy than producing aluminium from bauxite ore. Making paper from recycled stock requires 64 per cent less energy than using wood pulp. About 70 per cent of all metal discarded is used only once before it is discarded.
- *Repairability* – the aim is to prolong the life of products by ensuring that they can be repaired easily at low cost.

8.2.5 Use of environmentally preferred materials

Industrial ecology aims to manage human activity on a sustainable basis by:

- minimising energy and materials usage
- ensuring acceptable quality of life for human beings
- conserving energy and natural resources, such as minerals and forests.

Industrial ecology advocates the application of the following principles when selecting materials for product design:

- choose abundant, non-toxic materials whenever possible
- choose materials familiar to nature – for example, cellulose, rather than synthetic materials, such as chlorinated aromatics
- minimise the number of materials used in a production process
- use, where possible, recyclable materials
- where appropriate, use recycled materials.

8.2.6 Green procurement

There is a tremendous challenge facing all organisations to be innovative in their approach to green procurement. The challenge presents an opportunity for purchasing to make on impact on strategy and policy direction. On the 5 March, 2007 the UK government launched its Sustainable Procurement Action Plan. It presented a package of actions to deliver the step change needed to ensure that supply chains and public services will be increasingly low carbon, low waste and water efficient, respect bio-diversity and deliver wider sustainable development goals. The Financial Secretary to the Treasury said, 'Over the next decade procurement will become more central still in achieving value for money for the taxpayer and delivering the public services people need and expect.'

Policy on green procurement

The Public Works and Government Services (PWGSE) Canada[7] introduced a Policy on Green Procurement which became effective on 1 April, 2006. The context concerned achieving value for money. It requires the integration of environmental performance considerations into the procurement process including planning, acquisition, use and disposal. In this context, value for money includes the consideration of many factors such as cost, performance, availability, quality and environmental performance. Green procurement also requires an understanding of the environmental aspects and potential impacts and costs, associated with the lifecycle assessment of goods and services being acquired. In addition, the supporting administrative processes and procurement methods can also offer opportunities to reduce the environmental impacts of government operations.

Definitions

Environmentally preferable goods and services are those that have a lesser or reduced impact on the environment over the lifecycle of the good or service, when compared with competing goods or services serving the same purpose. Environmental performance considerations include, among other things: the reduction of greenhouse gas emissions and air contaminants; improved energy and water efficiency; reduced waste and support reuse and recycling; the use of renewable resources; reduced hazardous waste; and reduced toxic and hazardous substances.

Expected results

The government of Canada expects that the application of this policy will:

- benefit the environment by contributing to environmental objectives, such as:
  - reducing greenhouse gas emissions and air contaminants
  - improving energy and water efficiency

- reducing ozone depleting substances
- reducing waste and supporting reuse and recycling
- reducing hazardous waste
- reducing toxic and hazardous chemicals and substances.

■ lever the purchasing power of the federal government to achieve economies of scale in the acquisition of environmentally preferable goods and services, thereby reducing the cost for government and strengthening greener markets and industries

■ result in more environmentally responsible planning, acquisition, use and disposal practices in the federal government

■ support a healthier working environment for employees and for citizens in general through the purchase of environmentally preferable goods and services.

8.2.7 Guidance from the International Organisation for Standardisation (ISO)

The main ISO environmental standards are BS EN 14001, 14004, 14010, 14011, 14012, 14040 and 14050. ISO Guide 64 relates to the inclusion of environmental aspects in production standards.

8.3 Purchasing and new product development

8.3.1 Purchasing orientation and involvement

Dowlatshahi[8] has drawn attention to the differences in orientation that may arise between purchasing and design and these are set out in Table 8.3.

Dowlatshahi states that the reconciliation of these differing views is possible only in a concurrent engineering environment, which he defines as:

> The consideration and inclusion of product design attributes such as manufacturability, procurability, reliability, maintainability, schedularability, marketability and the like in the early stages of product design.

Wynstra et al.[9] state that purchasing participation in product development can range from ad hoc limited involvement to formal and extensive participation in the development team. A typology of six possible configurations of purchasing participation in product development is presented by Lakemond et al.[10]

A Engineers contact purchasing specialists external to the project team on an ad hoc basis.

B Purchasing specialists are integrated into the project team on a part-time basis and work closely with an engineer regarding specific parts/materials/technologies.

C Purchasing specialists are integrated into the project team on a full-time basis (dedicated) and work closely with engineers regarding specific parts/materials/technologies.

D A purchasing coordinator is added to the project team and takes care of coordinating purchasers external to the project team.

Table 8.3 **Differences in orientation between purchasing and design**

Purchasing orientation	Design orientation
■ Minimum acceptable margin of quality, safety and performance	■ Wide margins of quality, safety and performance
■ Use of adequate materials	■ Use of ideal materials
■ Lowest ultimate cost	■ Limited concern for cost
■ High regard for availability	■ Limited regard for availability
■ Practical and economical parameters, specification, features and tolerances	■ Close or near-perfect parameters, specifications, features and tolerances
■ General view of product	■ Conceptual abstraction of product quality
■ Cost elimination of materials	■ Selection of materials
■ Concern for JIT delivery and supplier relationship	■ Concern for overall product design

E   A purchasing coordinator is added to the project team in combination with purchasing specialists integrated into the project team on a part-time basis.

F   A purchasing coordinator is added to the project team in combination with purchasing specialists integrated into the project team on a full-time basis.

8.3.2 Early buyer involvement (EBI)

There is no consistency of views about when purchasing specialists should get involved in a new development project. Neither is there any such consistency when they get involved in other types of significant purchases. In the author's experience some of the determining influences will be:

1 legal advisors who claim to have the necessary purchasing skills

2 the project manager's perception of the impact and influence of purchasing specialists

3 the mistaken belief that purchasing will 'slow down' the decision making

4 the extent and nature of the supply chain

5 the complexity of negotiations, in particular around the cost drivers

6 demonstrable achievements of purchasing on other projects.

8.3.3 Some areas of purchasing involvement in product development

Wynstra *et al.*[11] have identified four areas of purchasing involvement in product development, each of which has a different time horizon and each involves different activities. These are shown in Table 8.4.

Table 8.4 **Areas of purchasing involvement in product development**

Area of involvement	Associated activities
Development management The higher the level of availability and stability and the lower the level of dependence, the greater the possibilities to 'buy' the technology and leave the development to suppliers	Determining which technologies to keep/develop in-house and which to outsource Policy formulation for supplier involvement Policy formulation for purchasing-related activities of internal departments Internal and external communication of policies
Supplier interface management Proactive, continuous research with the aim of identifying suppliers or technologies that may be relevant for the development of new products	Monitoring supplier markets for technological developments Pre-selecting suppliers for product development collaboration Motivating suppliers to build up/maintain specific knowledge or develop certain products Exploiting the technological capabilities of suppliers Evaluating suppliers' development performance
Project management Involves two sub-areas – product planning and project execution	Product planning activities are primarily carried out during or before initial development and include: ■ determining specific develop-or-buy solutions ■ selecting suppliers for involvement in the development project ■ determining the extent of supplier involvement Project execution involves activities during the project and includes: ■ coordinating development activities between suppliers and manufacturers ■ coordinating development activities between different first-tier suppliers ■ coordinating development activities between first-tier and second-tier suppliers ■ ordering and chasing prototypes

Product management
Directly contributing to the specifications of the new product
	Activities can be divided into two categories:
	■ extending activities – those aimed at increasing the number of alternatives, including:
	  – providing information on new products and technologies already available or in course of development
	  – suggesting alternative suppliers, products and technologies that can yield higher-quality results
	■ restrictive activities – those aimed at limiting the number of alternative specifications:
	  – evaluating product designs in terms of part availability, manufacturability, lead time, quality and costs
	  – promoting standardisation and simplification

8.4 Early supplier involvement (ESI)

ESI has been defined as:[12]

> A practice that brings together one or more selected suppliers with a buyer's product design team early in the product development process. The objective is to utilise the supplier's expertise and experience in developing a product specification that is designed for effective and efficient product roll-out.

ESI aims to secure access to the competences and technologies of selected suppliers in situations that preclude the option of vertical integration due to resource limitations and managerial constraints.

8.4.1 Development responsibility and risk

Wynstra and Ten Pierick[13] identified two important variables relating to the management of supplier involvement: the degree of responsibility for product development contracted out to the supplier and development risk.

Development responsibility

This is the level of responsibility delegated to the supplier in the development of a building block or component. Calvi *et al.*[14] state that this responsibility or 'supplier autonomy' is a function of the supplier's know-how and the importance of intellectual property rights owned.

The degree of supplier responsibility to be contracted out is determined by the manufacturer after answering such questions as the following:

- Considering the organisation's core technological competences, into how much detail should it go when developing specifications?
- Are there suppliers that have relevant product or production knowledge in relation to the component that is greater than that of the manufacturer?
- Are there suppliers that can do the development work more efficiently than the manufacturer?
- To what extent does the manufacturer need the development capacity (person hours) of suppliers to meet the project targets?

Development risk

Calvi *et al.* identify six combinative categories of risk that can be ascertained by asking the following questions.

- What is the link between the building block or component and the performance of the final product?
- What is the level of newness and differentiation brought by the building block or component?
- What is the position of the building block or component on the critical path – that is, what is the reliability of the supplier's capacity in meeting delivery schedules?
- How new are the production technologies involved?
- What is the weight of the building blocks' cost in the final product?
- How many different technologies are used in this building block? The presence of different technologies may produce difficulties in co-ordination among different suppliers.

Deciding the level of responsibility to assign to suppliers is a strategic decision because it involves an evaluation of the purchaser's and supplier's competences. It also involves an outsourcing or make-or-buy decision by a cross-functional team.

On the basis of the two variables of degree of assigned responsibility and development risk, Wynstra and Ten Pierick developed the supplier involvement portfolio shown in Figure 8.3.

The normal approach to 'filling' the portfolio is to:

1 ■ decide the degree of supplier responsibility for the development
   ■ decide the degree of development risk

Figure 8.3 Wynstra and Ten Pierick's supplier involvement portfolio

	Low	High
High	Arm's length development	Strategic development
Low	Routine development	Critical development

2 position the supplier component in the portfolio

3 reflect on the distribution of the various supplier/component combinations across the portfolio and, if necessary, reposition.

8.5 Advantages and problems of ESI

8.5.1 The advantages of ESI

The advantages of ESI in product development may be briefly summarised as:

- reduced concept-to-customer development time
- improved product specifications
- enhanced quality
- lower development costs
- access to new technologies ahead of competitors
- joint problem-solving
- interchange of knowledge and information
- improved manufacturability of products.

8.5.2 The disadvantages and problems of ESI

The disadvantages and problems of ESI have been summarised by Mikkola et al.[15] and Handfield et al.[16]

The major risks of collaborative product development listed by Mikkola et al. include 'leakage of information, loss of control or ownership, longer development lead time, conflicts due to different aims and objectives and collaborators becoming competitors'.

Handfield et al. point out that ESI raises such considerations as 'tier structure, degree of responsibility for design, specific responsibilities on the requirements selling process, when to involve suppliers in the process, intercompany communication, intellectual property agreements, supplier membership on the project team and alignment of objectives with regard to outcomes'.

Petersen et al.[17] highlight four factors as being of particular importance to the integration of suppliers into new product development.

- *Customer knowledge of the supplier* – such knowledge facilitates the integration of the supplier's staff into new product development teams and helps to achieve an alignment between the buying company's needs and the supplier's capabilities, from both technical and cultural standpoints.

- *Technology and cost information sharing* – technology sharing can often lead to better supplier solutions, which may also result in lower costs. Petersen and his colleagues report that several organisations in their sample employed 'target pricing methods', which involved joint buyer–seller teams exploring alternative solutions to meeting a target cost. Such efforts might require suppliers to 'open their books' and reveal their methods of cost allocation. Such transparency is only likely to take place when a high level of trust exists between the purchasers and suppliers.

- *Supplier involvement in decision making* – suppliers are often asked to collocate a design engineer on the purchasing company's design team. This collocation may be on a full-time or part-time basis. In Petersen's research, the extent of the supplier's participation was the factor most strongly associated with the achievement of project goals.

- *Technology uncertainty* – such uncertainty can derive from new-to-the-world technologies, new applications of existing technologies and technologies outside the company's field of expertise. In general, the greater the technological uncertainty or the complexity of the product, the greater the need for ESI in new product development. The degree of collaboration will also be higher for customised products and where the rate of technological change is fast.

Dowlatshahi[18] makes the point that the investment in research and development required by purchasers and suppliers respectively should be clearly delineated. A supplier's specific suggestions with regard to a new product should be viewed as equivalent to the R&D invested by the purchaser. Realistically, only suppliers with long-term contracts can be expected to make a significant investment in R&D.

8.6 Supplier development

8.6.1 Definition

Supplier development has been defined as:

> Any activity that a buyer undertakes to improve a supplier's performance and/or capabilities to meet the buyer's short-term or long-term supply needs.[19]

Supplier development programmes can be either results-orientated or process-orientated.

- *Results-orientated programmes* focus on solving specific problems for suppliers and normally involve step-by-step changes relating to supplier's costs, quality and delivery. Hartley and Jones[20] identify three characteristics of results-orientated supplier development:
  - the process is standardised and buyer-driven
  - the changes made are primarily technical
  - the process is of short duration and requires limited follow-up.

With this approach, the supplier improves while the buyer's supplier development team is on site and the achieved level of performance can be maintained after the team has left. The results approach is basically an attempt to transfer an organisation's in-house capabilities across boundaries.

■ *Process-orientated programmes* focus on increasing the supplier's ability to make production improvements without hands-on assistance from the buyer. This requires the supplier to learn the problem-solving techniques required for continuous improvements. Such learning is complicated, may require the 'unlearning' of old practices and the encoding of new knowledge in organisational routines.

Kaizen, referred to in section 8.1.2, is an important aspect of supplier development.

8.6.2 The steps of supplier development

The actual process may differ according to the organisation and, as stated above, whether the development is primarily results-orientated or process-orientated. There are nine steps in a typical supplier development programme. These are briefly explained as follows:

1 *Identify critical products* – this is done using a portfolio approach, such as that of Kraljic (see section 2.13.11). These will be mainly strategic and bottleneck products.

2 *Identify critical suppliers* – this involves consideration of such questions as the following.

   ■ What is the capability of the suppliers? Sako[21] identifies three levels of capability:
     – *maintenance capability* – the ability to maintain a particular level of performance consistently
     – *improvement capability* – that which affects the pace of performance improvements
     – *evolutionary capability* – the capacity for capability building, which is different from dynamic capabilities in that the emphasis is less on 'adapting, integrating and reconfiguring internal resources in response to changing environments and more on the sustained accumulation of the other two capabilities'.

   ■ Are the present suppliers capable of meeting future needs?

   ■ Are the present suppliers worth developing or is it time to source new ones?

3 *Appraise supplier performance* – supplier performance appraisal is considered in Chapter 11.

4 *Determine the gap between present and desired supplier performance* – gap analysis involves identifying the differences between the current and a desired business situation. It is important to recognise that gaps may be considered from a supply-side as well as a demand-side perspective.

Typical demand-side gaps

Supplier output demands	Supplier service demands
Supplier cost/price structure	Supplier prices desired
Supplier quality achieved ← Gap →	Quality required
Existing supplier flexibility	Desired supplier flexibility
Too low value	Too high cost

Typical supply-side gaps

Purchaser information supplied	Supplier service demands
Level of profitability obtained from the contract ← Gap →	Level of profitability required from the contract

There may also be combined gaps, such as the level of collaboration or where the level of purchaser–supplier relationships satisfies neither party.

5 *Form cross-functional supplier development team* – this team will be responsible for appraising present and potential suppliers, identifying gaps and negotiating with suppliers to try to devise mutually acceptable resolution of problems.

6 *Meet with supplier's top management team* – meeting with the top management team of the supplier provides an insight into the extent to which a collaborative relationship with the purchaser is required. It also provides an opportunity for both sides to know each other as individuals, discuss areas of cooperation not previously identified, exchange views frankly and build trust. Negotiated improvements can also be minuted and thereby provide an agreed record of decisions made.

7 *Agree how the perceived gaps can be bridged* – approaches may include:

- seconding purchaser's staff to the supplier
- seconding supplier's staff to the purchaser
- purchaser on site audits at the supplier's premises
- third-party assessment, as is required for ISO 9000 registration
- loan of machinery and IT hardware
- granting access to IT systems, such as CAD
- negotiating improved transportation contracts
- joint value analysis exercises
- improved costing approaches
- using the purchaser's leverage to obtain materials and other items for the supplier at cheaper cost
- the offer of incentives
- the formation of a supplier association (see section 8.7).

8 *Set deadlines for achieving improvements* – these should be reasonable, agreed by both parties and strictly enforced. The supplier should understand that failure to effect improvements by the agreed date may lead to loss of business. The emphasis, however, should be on constructive help rather than punitive measures.

9 *Monitor improvements* – even after achievement of the required standards, the performance of suppliers should be carefully monitored. Handfield *et al.*[22] state that the pitfalls of supplier development fall into three categories: supplier-specific, buyer-specific and buyer–supplier interface. Supplier-specific pitfalls stem chiefly from the supplier's lack of commitment or lack of technical or human resources. Buyer-specific factors derive from a reluctance to commit to supplier development fully when the purchaser sees no obvious potential benefits in so doing, such as a supplier being considered of insufficient importance to justify the investment. The principal buyer–supplier interface pitfalls are due to lack of mutual trust, poor alignment of organisational cultures and insufficient inducements to the supplier. As Handfield and his co-authors state:

> Initiating supplier performance improvement is not an easy task . . . Our findings suggest that such an accomplishment takes time and is only achieved by patient relationship managers who are tenacious enough to pay follow-up visits to suppliers and continually enforce a strong programme of supplier evaluation and performance feedback.

8.7 Supplier associations (SA)

8.7.1 What is a supplier association?

The supplier association (SA), or *Kyoryoku Kai*, has been a feature of Japanese manufacturing since the 1950s. Assisted by *Kyoryoku Kai*, large Japanese manufacturers such as Toyota have been able to both coordinate and develop their sub-contractors in such ways as the dissemination of best practice, provision of technical assistance and, in some instances, training. Supplier associations also help to develop a climate of trust between the parties involved.

Hines and Rich[23] define a supplier association (SA) as:

> A mutually benefiting group of a company's most important suppliers brought together on a regular basis in order to achieve strategic and operational alignment through the development of awareness, education and implementation programmes designed to achieve both radical and incremental improvements.

The above writers report that, in 1998, about 50 customer companies in the UK and Europe were using the SA approach with a total of approximately 600 suppliers. Originally associated with the automotive sector, SA has now been adopted by a range of industries, including office equipment, distribution, telecommunications, steel, general engineering, aerospace and medical equipment.

8.7.2 The aims and objectives of *Kyoryoku Kai*

These have been summarised by Hines[24] as being to:

- improve the abilities and skills of suppliers, particularly in terms of JIT, TQM, statistical process control (SPC), value analysis, value engineering (VA/VE), management flexibility and cost reduction
- produce a uniform supply system using the same types of techniques
- facilitate the flow of information and strategy formulation to and from and within supplier networks
- increase trust between buyer and supplier, allowing for closer business relationships
- keep suppliers and customers in touch with market developments and, hence, aid the translation of 'the voice of customers'
- enhance the reputation of the customer as something suppliers should try to do (and increase) business with
- help smaller suppliers lacking specialist trainers
- increase length of business relationships
- allow development benefits to be shared
- provide an example to sub-contractors of how to coordinate and develop their own suppliers.

Gullander[25] refers to two kinds of SAs that he designates steering groups and working groups.

A *steering group* is comprised of one or two representatives from each supplier and the customer. Representatives – normally the CEO or director of quality production or purchasing – are normally empowered to make important decisions on SA joint advisers. The steering group meets two to three times a year with some ten to fifteen members present and, most often, all member firms represented.

A *working group* focuses on a specific task, such as the introduction of a quality technique, and continues until the task has been completed. The group is comprised of representatives of member firms, but only those firms that believe in competence improvement in the selected area participate. Normally, there is one representative per firm. Gullander states that being excellent in a particular field is not a reason for non-participation. Such a firm might take the role of teacher or facilitator of the work in the working group. Several working groups with different foci may operate simultaneously.

8.7.3 Perceived benefits and disadvantages of SAs

In a study of eight Welsh SAs, Izushi and Morgan[26] reported that:

- a majority of the firms surveyed thought that their SA helped them to form good relationships with other suppliers and build mutual trust between the participants
- the majority also considered that their SA gave them a better understanding of the customer firm and built mutual trust, the understanding deriving from improved communication and 'stable orders' for goods from the customer, early announcement of the customer's development plans and a less than arm's length approach on the customer's part to problem-solving in scheduling and delivery
- a majority of the firms found their SA useful in assessing the competitive positions and learning general principles of best practice.

There were, however, a number of reservations. There was significant, if minority, support for the following statements:

- 'A supplier association is no more than a gesture to show loyalty to a customer firm.'
- 'A customer firm uses a supplier association to gain more control of its suppliers.'

In addition, SAs were criticised on the following grounds:

- they may become 'talking shops' about general techniques that the customer leaves to suppliers to implement themselves
- generalised presentations of techniques often pose difficulties in implementation because of suppliers' idiosyncrasies and problems
- the 'implement it yourself' approach may inhibit the development of mutual trust between customers and suppliers so that, for example, a customer asks suppliers to introduce techniques but refuses to disclose the results of implementation in its own organisation
- there may be difficulty in keeping momentum going between meetings.

Izushi and Morgan suggest that such shortcomings might be overcome by:

- customer leadership in putting techniques into action and disclosing to customers how it implements them at its site
- making the best use of expertise possessed by member suppliers
- use of measurable goals and regular checking of achievements
- selection of member suppliers who are conducive to collaboration and focus on particular products or processes

■ provision of training for the staff of supplier development teams to enable them to communicate with suppliers as partners.

8.7.4 Further aspects of design, including 'robust design'

QFD and FMEA are discussed in sections 9.9.6 and 9.9.7, respectively, value management, engineering and analysis in section 9.11.

Case study

The Veroxide Group (VG) manufactures a range of pharmaceutical products, namely prescription drugs and human vaccines. VG has its headquarters in Berne, Switzerland, a research and development unit in Stockholm, Sweden, and manufacturing sites in Leeds, UK, Pretoria, South Africa and Berne. In the past year, R&D spending rose 3.9 per cent, equivalent to 17.3 per cent of core business sales. There are several potential new products in the pipeline but 'Zentonex' is widely anticipated to receive regulatory approval in six months' time.

VG has located its production buying operation in Leeds, but it may be noted that the R&D unit has its own buying function. There is little contact between the two buying functions, largely because the R&D director insists that he is the custodian of his budget. When a drug goes into mass production, much larger quantities of feedstock are required.

When 'Zentonex' enters production, one of the stock items needed is 'Onolun' – a special chemical. To meet the forecasted production scheme, two tonnes of it will be required every three months. This chemical has been supplied to VG by Gardners Ltd, which produces it in its Birmingham, UK, manufacturing plant. Gardners has been a regular supplier to the R&D unit for five years and has impeccable delivery and quality performance. Gardners has three competitors located in Brazil, Canada and France. VG plans to make 'Zentonox' in its Pretoria location.

Anne Fortescue, the VG buying director, commissioned a report on Gardners' ability to manufacture and supply 'Onolun'. The salient extracts from the report are:

Buying is done by an untrained buyer who takes instructions from the plant director. Buying is an unsophisticated operation and would require three key suppliers to provide stock for 'Onolun'. These suppliers can manufacture in the quantities required and to the quality standards. The quality management is excellent and we have complete confidence in this aspect.

It became evident that Gardners will need to invest £500k in new plant and equipment. The company has not planned this expenditure and would need to extend its bank overdraft to fund the purchase. The lead time for purchasing, installing and commissioning the new facility would be 18 weeks. The chief engineer would be accountable for the project, including procurement.

The feedback is that shelf-life is restricted (seven weeks) and so the supply chain and inventory management will be critical. The person accountable for this is the Stores Manager. This causes us serious concern and is identified as a major risk.

If VG signs a contract with Gardners it will have to make a commitment to supplier development. This is our key recommendation.

Task

If you were Anne Fortescue, what would you identify as being the key features of a supplier development programme in the above circumstances?

Discussion questions

8.1 Give two examples each of:
   (a) product innovation
   (b) process innovation
   (c) incremental innovation.

8.2 When a company is involved with breakthrough innovation, such as a new drug, what is the role for procurement?

8.3 What is 'concurrent engineering'? What specific roles can procurement play to ensure the success of new product development?

8.4 If you were asked to ensure that your suppliers are using environmentally preferred materials, how would you find out if they were doing so? If you went to audit their processes, what six practices would you expect to find?

8.5 A multi-functional team is being created to develop a new waste recycling process. The basis of the new process is the use of advanced engineering and electronics. Your director has asked you if you could contribute to the supply chain risk management and developing new contracts with suppliers. The director wants to know what would be the major benefits of involving procurement at this very early stage. What are they?

8.6 'A problem with early supplier involvement, is that you cannot trust them with highly sensitive product information. It will, inevitably, leak to your competitors.' Do you agree?

8.7 'Supplier development is a structured approach to creating additional, competent, sources of supply. In consequence, no buyer should ever be in a position where they are a captive buyer and unable to negotiate.' Do you agree?

8.8 Long-standing barriers between design, production and purchasing can be difficult to overcome. Suggest how such barriers might be broken down and what benefits might accrue from replacing conflict with collaboration.

8.9 How should purchasing and/or other managers weigh the relative strengths and weaknesses of potential suppliers in areas such as technological knowledge, manufacturing capabilities, length of relationship with the supplier, degree of trust and alignment of technology?

8.10 You have been asked to make a presentation on behalf of procurement to the board of directors of a key supplier. They have a reputation of being old-fashioned, unresponsive to design queries and lacking in customer care. It has got to the point where your engineering director wants you to find an alternative supplier. What points would you make to the board of directors at your supplier?

8.11 Consider Wynstra's six possible configurations of purchasing participation described in section 8.3.1. Which of the configurations most nearly describes purchasing participation in your own organisation?

8.12 Discuss the viewpoints that, in supplier involvement or development:
   (a) 'the customer receives most of the benefits and the supplier receives few'
   (b) 'cooperative relationships are often cooperative in name and suppliers do more than their fair share of cooperating'.
   How might you seek to deal constructively with these objections?

Past examination questions

1 (a) Describe **two** advantages of implementing a supplier development programme.
  (b) Outline a technique that could be used to identify potential suppliers which might be included in a supplier development programme.
  CIPS, *An Introduction to Purchasing Strategy*, May 2010

2 Describe the **four** stages of a typical product lifecycle model.
  CIPS, *Analysing the Supply Market*, May 2009

References

1 London Development Agency, *Why Innovate?* www.lda.gov.uk

2 Treasy, M., 'Innovation as a last resort', *Harvard Business Review*, July–August, 2004, pp. 29–30

3 Mendez, E. G. and Pearson, J. N., 'Purchasing's role in product development', *International Journal of Purchasing and Materials Management*, 1 January, 1994, pp. 3–12

4 Mileham, A. R., Morgan, E. J. and Chatting, J., 'An attribute approach to concurrent engineering', Proceedings of the Institute of Mechanical Engineers, Vol. 218, Part B, 2004, pp. 995–1005

5 Winner, R. L., Pennel, J. P., Bertrams, H. E. and Slusarczuk, M. M., 'The role of concurrent engineering in weapon system acquisition', *IDA Report R-338*, AD-A203 615, 1988

6 Website – www.smartlink.net.au

7 Public Works and Government Services Canada 'Policy on Green Procurement', 1 April, 2006

8 Dowlatshahi, S., 'Purchasing's role in a concurrent engineering environment', *International Journal of Purchasing and Materials Management*, winter, 1992, pp. 21–5

9 Wynstra, F., Axelsson, B. and van Weele, A. J., 'Driving and enabling purchasing involvement in product development', *European Journal of Supply Management*, Vol. 6, No. 2, 2000, pp. 129–41

10 Lakemond, N., van Echtelt, F. and Wynstra, F., 'A configuration typology for involving purchasing specialists in product development', *Journal of Supply Management*, Vol. 37, No. 4, November, 2001, pp. 11–20

11 Wynstra, F., van Weele, A. and Axelsson, B., 'Purchasing involvement in product development', *European Journal of Purchasing*, Vol. 5, 1999, pp. 129–41

12 Institute of Supply Management, 'Glossary of key purchasing and supply terms', www.ism.ws

13 Wynstra, F. and Ten Pierick, E., 'Management of supplier involvement in new product development', *European Journal of Purchasing and Supply Management*, Vol. 6, 2000, pp. 49–57

14 Calvi, R., Le-Dain, M. A., Harbis, A. and Bonotta, H. V., 'How to manage early supplier involvement (ESI) into the new product development process (NPDP)', Proceedings of the 10th International Annual IPSERA Conference, 2001, pp. 158–62

15 Mikkola, J. H. and Joetti-Larsen, S. K., 'Early supply involvement: implications for new product development outsourcing and supplier-buyer interdependence', *Global Journal of Flexible Systems Management*, Vol. 4, 2003, pp. 31–41

16 Handfield, R. B., Raqatz, K., Petersen, K. J. and Monczka, R. M., 'Involving suppliers in new product development', *California Management Review*, Vol. 42, No. 1, Fall, 1999, pp. 59–82

17 Petersen, K. J., Handfield, R. B. and Ragatz, G. L., 'A model of supplier integration into new product development', *Journal of Production and Innovation Management*, Vol. 20, 2003, pp. 284–99

18 Dowlatshahi, S., 'Early supplier involvement: theory versus practice', *International Journal of Production Research*, Vol. 37, No. 18, 1999, pp. 4119–39

19 Handfield, R. B., Krause, D. R., Scannell, T. V. and Monczka, P. M., 'Avoid the pitfalls in supplier development', *Sloan Management Review*, winter, 2000, pp. 37–48

20 Hartley, J., and Jones, G., 'Process oriented supplier development', *International Journal of Purchasing and Materials Management*, Summer, 1997

21 Sako, M., 'Supplier development at Honda, Nissan and Toyota', *Comparative Case Studies of Organisational Capability Enhancement*, November, 2003

22 As 18 above

23 Hines, P. and Rich, N., 'Outsourcing competitive advantage', Proceedings of the Second Worldwide Research Symposium on Purchasing and Supply Chain Management, IPSERA, London, 1–3 April, 1998, pp. 268–94

24 Hines, P., *Creating World Class Suppliers*, Pitman, 1994, p. 143

25 Gullander, S., 'Supplier associations: a tool for regional development', paper presented at the conference SMES and Districts, Castellanza, Italy, 5–7 November, 1998

26 Izushi, H. and Morgan, K., 'Management of supplier associations: observations from Wales', *International Journal of Logistics Research and Application*, Vol. 1., 1998, pp. 75–91

Chapter 9

Specifying and managing product quality

9.1 What is quality?

9.1.1 Definitions

There are numerous definitions of quality. ISO 8402 (replaced in December 2000 by ISO 9000 and updated in September 2005) defined the fundamental terms relating to quality concepts, states that quality is:

> The composite of all the characteristics, including performance, of an item, product or service, that bears on its ability to satisfy stated or implied needs. In a contractual environment, needs are specified, whereas, in other environments, implied needs should be identified and defined. In many instances, needs can change with time; this implies periodic revision of requirements for quality. Needs are usually translated into characteristics with specified criteria. Quality is sometimes referred to as 'fitness for use', 'customer satisfaction', or 'conformance to the requirements'.

In this definition there is the implication of an ability to identify what quality aspects can be measured or controlled or constitute an acceptable quality level (AQL). Needs which are defined relate to the value of the product or service to the customer, including economic value as well as safety, reliability, maintainability and other relevant features.

Crosby[1] defines quality as 'conformity to requirements not goodness.' He also stresses that the definition of quality can never make any sense unless it is based on what the customer wants, that is, a product is a quality product only when it conforms to the customer's requirements.

Juran[2] defines quality as 'fitness for use'. This definition implies quality of design, quality of conformance, availability and adequate field services. There is, however, no universal definition of quality. Garvin, for example, has identified five approaches to defining quality[3] and eight dimensions of quality.[4] The five approaches are as follows:

- The *transcendent approach* – quality is absolute and universally recognisable. The concept is loosely related to a comparison of product attributes and characteristics.

- The *product-based approach* – quality is a precise and measurable variable. In this approach, differences in quality reflect differences in the quantity of some product characteristics.

- The *use-based approach* – quality is defined in terms of fitness for use or how well the product fulfils its intended functions.

- The *manufacturing-based approach* – quality is 'conformance to specifications' – that is, targets and tolerances determined by product designers.

- The *value-based approach* – quality is defined in terms of costs and prices. Here, a quality product is one that provides performance at an acceptable price or conformance at an acceptable cost.

These alternative definitions of quality often overlap and may conflict. Perspectives of quality may also change as a product moves from the design to the marketing stage. For these reasons, it is essential to consider each of the above perspectives when framing an overall quality philosophy.

Garvin's eight dimensions of quality are:

1 *performance* – the product's operating characteristics

2 *reliability* – the probability of a product surviving for a specified period of time under stated conditions of use

3 *serviceability* – the speed, accessibility and ease of repairing the item or having it repaired

4 *conformance* – measures the projected use available from the product over its intended operating cycle before it deteriorates

5 *durability* – measures the projected use available from the product over its intended operating cycle before it deteriorates

6 *features* – 'the bells and whistles' or secondary characteristics that supplement the product's basic functioning

7 *aesthetics* – personal judgements about how a product looks, feels, sounds, tastes or smells

8 *perceived quality* – closely identified with the reputation of the producer and, like aesthetics, it is a personal evaluation.

While the relative importance attached to any of the above characteristics will depend on the particular item, the most important factors in commercial or industrial purchasing decisions will probably be performance, reliability, conformance, availability and serviceability.

Other factors that determine 'the right quality' for a particular application include:

■ *price* – as the competitive selling price of the product in which the item is to be incorporated will determine the prices paid for bought-out items

■ *customer specifications* – or those laid down by statutory or similar organisations

■ *durability* – this influences the quality specifications for components as, if the expected life of the final product is only three years, for example, there is little point in incorporating a component with a life of five years where cheaper alternatives are available, though the reputation of the product must, however, be of paramount consideration.

Quality is therefore determined by balancing technical considerations, such as fitness for use, performance, safety and reliability, with economic factors, including price and availability. It is therefore the *optimum* quality for the application that should be sought, rather than the *highest* quality.

In drafting quality specifications, the aim should always be the minimum statement of optimum (not the highest) quality so as not to increase the cost unnecessarily, restrict processes of manufacture nor limit the use of possible alternatives.

9.1.2 Reliability

As shown above, reliability is an attribute of quality. It is, however, so important that the terms 'quality and reliability' are often used together. Reliability has been defined as:[5]

> A measure of the ability of a product to function successfully when required, for the period required, under specified conditions.

Reliability is usually expressed in terms of mathematical probability, ranging from 0 per cent (complete unreliability) to 100 per cent (or complete reliability).

Failure mode and effect analysis (FMEA), performed to evaluate the effect on the overall design of a failure in any one of the identifiable failure modes of the design components and to evaluate how critically the failure will affect the design of performance, is referred to in section 9.9.7 below.

9.2 Quality systems

9.2.1 What is a quality system?

A *quality system* is defined as:[6]

> The organisational structure, responsibilities, procedures, processes and resources for implementing quality management.

A quality system typically applies to, and interacts with, all activities pertinent to the quality of a product or service. As shown in Figure 9.1 it involves all phases, from the initial identification to final satisfaction of requirements and customer expectations.

All organisations have a quality management system. This may, however, be informal and insufficiently documented. The advantages of a properly documented system, such as that required by BS EN ISO 9001:2008, are that it:

- ensures all aspects of quality are controlled
- ensures consistent, efficient work practices
- indicates best practice
- provides objective evidence for determining and correcting the causes of poor quality
- increases customer confidence
- gives competitive advantage.

Figure 9.1 The quality loop

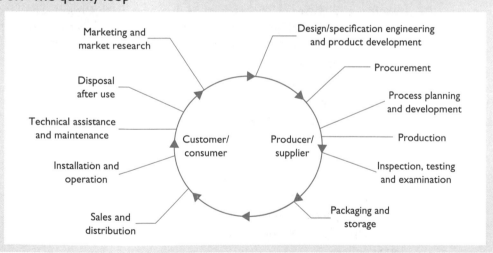

Source: British Standards Institution, reproduced with permission

9.3 The importance of TQM

9.3.1 Definitions

Total quality management (TQM) has been defined as:[7]

> A way of managing an organisation so that every job, every process, is carried out right, first time and every time.

This means that each stage of manufacture or service is 'total' – that is, 100 per cent correct before it proceeds. An alternative definition is:[8]

> An integrative management concept of continually improving the quality of delivered goods and services through the participation of all levels and functions of the organisation.

9.3.2 TQM principles

TQM is based on three important principles.

1 *A focus on product improvement from the customer's viewpoint* – the key ideas in this principle are product improvement and customer product improvement. Juran[9] emphasised the importance of achieving annual improvements in quality and reductions in quality-related costs. Any improvements that take an organisation to levels of quality performance that they have previously not achieved is termed a 'breakthrough'. Breakthroughs are focused on improving or eliminating chronic losses or, in Deming's[10] terminology, 'common causes of variation'. All breakthroughs follow a common sequence of discovery, organisation, diagnosis, corrective action and control. The term 'customer' in this context is associated with the concept of 'quality chains', which emphasises the linkages between suppliers and customers. Quality chains are both internal and external. Thus, internally, purchasing is a customer of design and supplier production. Staff within a function or activity, are also suppliers and customers. Like all chains, the quality chain is no stronger than its weakest link. Without strong supplier–customer links, both internally and externally, TQM is doomed to failure. Quality chains are one way in which to outmode the functional conflict and power tactics referred to elsewhere in this book. The first step in implementing an internal quality chain approach is for each activity to determine answers to the following questions relating to customers and suppliers.[11]

- **Customers**
  - Who are my internal customers?
  - What are their true requirements?
  - How do, or can, I find out what their requirements are?
  - How can I measure my ability to meet their requirements?
  - Do I have the necessary capability to meet their requirements? (If not, then what must change to improve the capability?)
  - Do I continually meet their requirements? (If not, then what prevents this from happening when the capability exists?)
  - How do I monitor changes in their requirements?

- **Suppliers**
  - Who are my internal suppliers?
  - What are my true requirements?
  - How do I communicate my requirements?
  - Do my suppliers have the capability to measure and meet the requirements?
  - How do I inform them of changes in the requirements?

The second step, based on answers to questions such as the above, is to determine the level of service that a function such as purchasing will provide. Cannon[12] has identified four factors affecting decisions about service types and levels:

- what the customer wants
- what the function can provide
- close collaboration to solve disagreements
- redefining both type and level of service at regular intervals.

It is also important to determine the technical expertise of purchasing as 'it is this expertise which enables the function to add value to the procurement activity beyond that which the internal customer can perform without the function's assistance'. The questions posed earlier in this section can also be reframed by substituting the word 'external' for 'internal' so that external quality chains can be considered from both supplier and customer angles, too. In the capacity of customers, purchasing organisations expect suppliers to compete in terms of quality, delivery and price. Zaire[13] states that the best approach to managing suppliers is based on JIT, which, from its inception, has the objective of obtaining and sustaining superior performance. The other important aspect of external customer supplier value chains refers to the management of customer processes as the purpose of TQM is customer enlightenment and long-term partnerships.

2 *A recognition that personnel at all levels share responsibility for product quality –* the Japanese concept of *kaizen,* or ongoing improvement, affects everyone in an organisation, at all levels. It is therefore based on team rather than individual performance. Thus, while top management provides leadership, continuous improvement is also understood and implemented at shop floor level. Some consequences of this principle include:

- provision of leadership from the top
- creation of a 'quality culture' dedicated to continuous improvement
- teamwork – that is, quality improvement teams and quality circles
- adequate resource allocation
- quality training of employees
- measurement and use of statistical concepts
- quality feedback
- employee recognition.

Zaire[14] states:

> Once a culture of common beliefs, principles, objectives and concerns has been established, people will manage their own tasks and will take voluntary responsibility to improve processes they own.

3 *Recognition of the importance of implementing a system to provide information to managers about quality processes that enable them to plan, control and evaluate performance.*

Most of this chapter is concerned with various aspects of quality implementation.

9.3.3 Factors that have contributed to the development of TQM

- *Global competition* for sales, profits, jobs and funds in both the private and public sectors, leading to the concept of 'world class manufacturing', with the emphasis on using manufacturing to gain a competitive edge by improving customer service.

■ *JIT* and other similar strategies based on the philosophy of zero defects – that is, it is cheaper to design and build quality into a product than attempt to ensure quality by means of inspection alone.

■ *Japanese quality procedures* such as *kaizen* (unending improvement) and *Poka-Yoke* (fool proofing), and a quality culture implemented in European manufacturing units, such as at Toyota and Nissan.

■ *Quality philosophies* associated with internationally respected experts.

9.3.4 The development of TQM

TQM originated in Japan as a result of a group of American management consultants and statisticians helping to rebuild Japanese industry after the Second World War. TQM transformed cheap and unreliable products labelled 'Made in Japan' into goods with an international reputation for high quality, innovation and reliability. These consultants were principally W. Edwards Deming, Joseph Juran and A. V. Feigenbaum. The DTI publication, *The Quality Gurus*, identifies 'three clear groups of quality gurus' (a 'guru' is an influential teacher) covering the period since the Second World War. Brief details of these gurus are set out in Table 9.1.

Table 9.1 The quality gurus

Name	Principal book	Important principles
The early Americans		
W. Edwards Deming	*Quality, Productivity and Competitive Position*, MIT Press, 1982	Deming's 14 points. Points 3, 4 and 9 are especially relevant to purchasing: 3: cease dependence on inspection to achieve quality, eliminate the need for inspection on a mass basis by building quality into the product in the first place 4: end the practice of awarding business on the basis of price tag and, instead, minimise the total cost by moving towards a single supplier for any one item for a long-term relationship of loyalty and trust 9: break down barriers between departments – people in research, design, sales and production must work as a team to foresee problems of production and use that may be encountered with the product or service
Joseph M. Juran	*Quality Control Handbook 1988*, McGraw-Hill, 1988	■ Quality is 'fitness for use', which can be broken down into quality of design, quality of conformance, availability and field service ■ Companies must reduce the cost of quality ■ Quality should be aimed at controlling sporadic problems or avoidable costs and unavoidable costs. The latter requires the introduction of a new culture intended to change attributes and increase companywide knowledge
Armand V. Feigenbaum	*Total Quality Control*, McGraw-Hill, 1983	'The underlying principle of the total quality view . . . is that . . . control must start with identification of customer quality requirements and end only when the product has been placed in the hands of a customer who remains satisfied. Total quality control guides the coordinated actions of people, machines and information to achieve this goal. The first principle is to recognise that quality is everybody's job'

Table 9.1 *Continued*

Name	Principal book	Important principles
The Japanese		
Kaoru Ishikawa	*What is Total Quality Control? The Japanese Way*, Prentice Hall, 1985	■ The first to introduce the concept of quality control circles ■ Originator of fishbone or Ishikawa diagrams, now used worldwide in continuous improvements to represent cause–effect analysis ■ Argues that 90–95 per cent of quality problems can be solved by simple statistical techniques
Genichi Taguchi	*Introduction to Quality Engineering*, Asian Productivity Association, 1986	■ Defines the quality of a product as the loss imparted by the product to society from the time the product is shipped. The loss may include customers' complaints, added warranty costs, damage to company reputation, loss of market lead, etc. ■ Uses statistical techniques additional to statistical process control (SPC) to enable engineers/designers to identify those variables that, if controlled, can affect product manufacture and performance
Shigeo Shingo	*Zero Quality Control: Source Inspection and the Poka-Yoke System*, Productivity Press, 1986	■ Development of just-in-time and, consequently, the Toyota production system ■ *Poka-Yoke*, or fool proofing, also known as the zero defects concept
The new Western wave		
Philip B. Crosby	*Quality is Free*, McGraw-Hill, 1983	Five absolutes of quality management: 1 'Quality conformity to requirements – not elegance' 2 'There is no such thing as a quality problem although there may be an engineering machine problem' 3 'It is always cheaper to do the job right first time' 4 'The only performance indicator is the cost of quality' 5 'The only performance standard is zero defects.' The 14-step quality improvement programme traits
Tom Peters	*A Passion for Excellence*, Profile Books, 1964	Twelve traits of quality revolution based on a study of the quality improvement programmes of successful American companies
Claus Moller	*A Complaint is a Gift* (with Janelle Barlow), Time Management International, 1996	■ Administrative rather than production processes offer more opportunity for productivity gain ■ Personal development of the individual will lead to increased competence in the three vital areas of productivity, relationships and quality

9.3.5 The benefits of TQM

TQM is a *philosophy* about quality that involves everyone in the organisation. It follows that the success of TQM depends on a genuine commitment to quality by every organisational member. Some benefits claimed for TQM include:

■ improved customer satisfaction

■ enhanced quality of goods and services

■ reduced waste and inventory with consequential reduced costs

- improved productivity
- reduced product development time
- increased flexibility in meeting market demands
- reduced work-in-progress
- improved customer service and delivery times
- better utilisation of human resources.

9.3.6 Criticisms of TQM

TQM is not without its critics. Some objections include:

- that overly zealous advocates of TQM may focus attention on quality even though other priorities may be important, such as changes in the market – exemplified by the manager who said:

  > Before we invested in TQM, we churned out poorly made products that customers didn't want. We now churn out well-made products that customers don't want.

- that it creates a cumbersome bureaucracy of councils, committees and documentation relating to quality
- that it delegates the determination of quality to quality experts because TQM is a complicated entity beyond the comprehension of the average employee
- that some workers and unions regard TQM as management-by-stress and a way of de-unionising workplaces.

9.4 Specifications

9.4.1 Specifications and purchasing

It is very important that purchasing staff are knowledgeable about specifications because:

- The supplier's ability to meet the specifications has a significant impact on the buying organisation's business performance and, in consequence, the purchasing process must be designed to select competent suppliers.
- The linkage between the specification compliance and contractual terms and conditions is vital, particularly the supplier's liabilities if the specification is not met.
- The design of pre-qualification questionnaires must include probing questions about the supplier's methodology for satisfying the specification requirements.
- The buyer must ensure that the contract is very clear on the methodology of evaluating and measuring compliance with the specification.
- The buyer should promote active discussions with the supplier to obtain continuous improvement to reduce the service or product cost and to continually challenge the specification.

9.4.2 Definitions

Specifications must be distinguished from standards and codes of practice. A *specification* has been defined as:

A statement of the attributes of a product or service.[15]

A statement of requirements.[16]

A statement of needs to be satisfied by the procurement of external resources.[17]

A *standard* is a specification intended for recurrent use.

Standards differ from specifications in that, while every standard is a specification, not every specification is a standard. The guiding principle of standardisation, considered later in this chapter, is the elimination of unnecessary variety.

Codes of practice are less specific than formal standards and provide guidance on the best accepted practice in relation to engineering and construction and for operations such as installation, maintenance and service provision.

9.4.3 The purpose of specifications

Both specifications and standards aim to:

- *indicate fitness for purpose or use* – as indicated in Table 9.1, fitness for purpose or use was the definition of quality given by Joseph Juran, who also stated that quality is linked to product satisfaction and dissatisfaction, with satisfaction relating to superior performance or features and dissatisfaction to deficiencies or defects in a product or service

- *communicate* the requirements of a user or purchaser to the supplier

- *compare* what is actually supplied with the requirements in terms of purpose, quality and performance stated in the specification

- *provide evidence*, in the event of a dispute, of what the purchaser required and what the supplier agreed to provide.

9.4.4 Types of specification

As shown in Figure 9.2, specifications can broadly be divided into two types.

Several of the elements listed in Figure 9.2 may, of course, be combined in one specification. Thus, a specification for a component (a thing) may also state how it shall be made (a process) and how it shall be tested (a procedure). The specification may also state what the component is intended to do (function) and what a product or service should achieve under given conditions (performance).

Figure 9.2 Types of specification

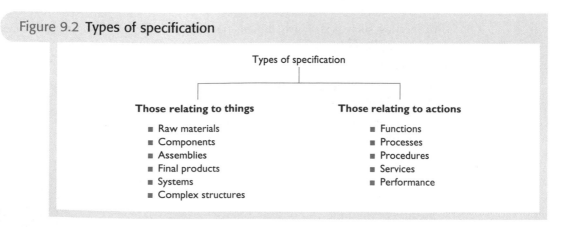

Types of specification

Those relating to things
- Raw materials
- Components
- Assemblies
- Final products
- Systems
- Complex structures

Those relating to actions
- Functions
- Processes
- Procedures
- Services
- Performance

9.4.5 Request for quotation (RFQ) or request for proposal (RFP)

The terms RFQ and RFP are interchangeable and are formal processes by which a potential purchaser communicates requirements to potential suppliers. The documents will include the details of the specification and other information to facilitate the preparation of quotations or proposals or for the potential suppliers to decide not to submit a quotation or proposal.

9.4.6 The contents of a specification

These will vary according to whether the specification is written from the standpoint of the user, designer, manufacturer or seller. The specification will also vary according to the material or item concerned. For a simple item, the specification may be a brief description, while in the case of a complicated assembly it will be a comprehensive document that perhaps runs to many pages. The following order of presentation for a specification relating to a product, process or service is adapted from BS 7373-3:2005:[18]

1 *identification* – title, designation, number, authority
2 *issue number* – publication history and state of issue, earlier related specifications
3 *contents list* – guide to layout
4 *foreword* – the reason for writing the specification
5 *introduction* – description of the content in general and technical aspects of objectives
6 *scope* – range of objectives/content
7 *definitions* – terms used with meanings special to the text
8 *requirements/guidance/methods/elements* – the main body of the specification
9 *index* – cross-references
10 *references* to national, European or international standards or other internal company specifications.

The requirements specified may relate to the following:

■ conditions in which the item or material is to be installed, used, manufactured or stored
■ characteristics, such as:
  – design, samples, drawings, models, preliminary tests or investigations
  – properties, such as strength, dimensions, weight, safety and so on, with tolerances where applicable
  – interchangeability – functional, dimensional
  – materials and their properties, including permissible variability and approved or excluded materials
  – requirements for a manufacturing process, such as heat treatment – this should be specified only when critical to design considerations
  – appearance, texture, finish, including colour, protection and so on
  – identification marks, operating symbols on controls, weight of items, safety indications and so on
  – method of marking

- performance:
  - performance under specified conditions
  - test methods and equipment for assessing performance, where, how and by whom they are to be carried out and reference to correlation with behaviour in operation
  - criteria for passing tests, including accuracy and interpretations of results
  - acceptance conditions
  - certification and/or reporting – that is, reports, test schedules or certificates required
- life
- reliability – under stipulated conditions and tests and control procedures required
- control of quality checking for compliance with specification:
  - method of checking compliance
  - production tests on raw materials, components, sub-assemblies and assemblies
  - assurance of compliance, such as by suppliers' certificates or independent manufacturer/supplier
  - instructions regarding reject material or items
  - instructions with regard to modification of process
  - applicability of quality control to sub-contractors and others
- packing and protection
  - specifications of packaging, including any special conditions in transit
  - condition in which the item is to be supplied, such as protected, lubricant free and so on
  - period of storage
  - marking of packaging
- information from the supplier to the user, such as instructions and advice on installation, operation and maintenance.

9.4.7 Some principles of specification writing

Purdy[19] has identified four principles that should be observed by all specification writers. These and other principles are as follows:

- *If something is not specified it is unlikely to be provided* – the corollary is that all requirements should be stated in the specification before awarding the contract. Suppliers will normally charge requirements subsequently added as 'extras'.
- *Every requirement increases the price* – all specifications should therefore be subjected to rigorous value analysis (considered later in this chapter).
- *The shorter the specification, the less time it takes to prepare it* – the expenditure in staff time devoted to the preparation of a specification can be high. This can be significantly lower when the length of a specification and the time taken in its preparation is reduced.
- *The specification is equally binding on both the purchaser and the vendor* – omissions, incorrect information or imprecision in a specification can be cited by the vendor in any dispute with the purchaser. A rule of evidence is that words are construed

against the party who wrote them. Where there is uncertainty about the meaning of a specification, the court will generally interpret it in the vendor's favour.

■ *Specifications, should, so far as possible, be presented in performance terms rather than as a detailed design* – this is particularly applicable to items about which the purchaser has little expert knowledge. According to section 14(3) of the Sale of Goods Act 1979 as amended by the Supply and Sale of Goods Act 1994, where the seller sells goods in the course of a business and the buyer expressly, or by implication, makes known to the seller any particular purpose for which the goods are being bought, there is an implied 'term' that the goods supplied under the contract are of satisfactory quality. For the purpose of the Supply and Sales of Goods Act 1994 (SSGA), goods are of satisfactory quality if 'they meet the standard that a reasonable person would regard as satisfactory, taking account of any description of the goods, the price (if relevant) and all other relevant circumstances'.

■ *Specifications, should, whenever possible be 'open', not closed* – closed specifications are referred to in section 9.5.3 below. Open specifications are written so that the stated requirements can be met by more than one supplier. By making the requirements sufficiently flexible to be met by several suppliers, competition is encouraged and prices reduced.

■ *Specifications must not conflict with national or international standards or health, safety or environmental laws and regulations* – national and international specifications should be incorporated into individual specifications and identified by their numbers and titles.

9.5 Alternatives to individual specifications

9.5.1 Existing specifications

It should only be necessary to write a specification for non-standard requirements. For most standard industrial and consumer products it is usually sufficient to use:

■ manufacturers' standards, as stated in catalogues or other promotional literature
■ national or international standards.

All products or services will require materials, components or other elements for which existing standards will be available. An essential first step for designers or specification writers is to ascertain what relevant standards already exist. Searching for such standards is facilitated by consulting reference publications, especially the British Standards Catalogue (available in most large libraries), or databases. Especially useful are the services provided by Technical Indexes Ltd (www.iberkshire.co.uk), which offer comprehensive, reliable, full-text databases of manufacturers' technical catalogues, national and international standards and legislative material, delivered online via the Internet on an annual subscription basis. Technical Indexes' Ltd information services cover more than 90 per cent of the world's most commonly used standards, including:

■ British Standards Online – a complete collection of over 35,000 British Standards
■ Worldwide standards on the Internet
■ UK and US defence standards
■ US Government Specifications Service.

9.5.2 Adapting existing specifications

This is often the most economical approach for construction projects or computer systems where architects or suppliers may be able to amend existing specifications to meet a new application.

9.5.3 Alternative methods of specifying

These include the use of brand or trade names and specifying by means of samples.

The use of a brand or trade names

England[20] lists the following circumstances in which descriptions by brand may be not only desirable but necessary, such as when:

- the manufacturing process is secret or covered by a patent
- the vendor's manufacturing process calls for a high degree of 'workmanship' or 'skill' that cannot be defined exactly in a specification
- only small quantities are bought so that the preparation of specifications by the buyer is impracticable
- testing by the buyer is impracticable
- the item is a component so effectively advertised as to create a preference or even a demand for its incorporation into the finished product on the part of the ultimate purchaser
- there is a strong preference for the branded item on the part of the design staff.

The main disadvantages of specifying branded items are as follows.

- The cost of a branded item may be higher than that of an unbranded substitute.
- The naming of a brand effectively results in what Haslam[21] refers to as a 'closed specification', which can take the form of naming a particular brand and the manufacturer or supplier not permitting the use of alternatives. Closed specifications are most applicable when the need for duplication of an existing product is important or it is desirable to maintain a low spares range. Such specifications inhibit competition but also cut out fringe suppliers that may be unable to meet the quality requirements.

Specification by sample

The sample can be provided either by the buyer or seller and is a useful method of specification in relation to products such as printing or materials such as cloth. When orders are placed and products specified by reference to a sample previously submitted by a supplier, it is important that the sample on which the contract is based should be:

- identified
- labelled
- the signed and labelled samples retained by both purchaser and supplier.

Under section 5 of the Supply of Goods and Services Act 1982 (SGSA) and section 15 of the Sale and Supply of Goods Act 1994 (SSGA) there is an implied 'term' (later defined as a 'condition') that where goods are sold by sample:

- the bulk must correspond to the sample in quality
- the buyer must have a reasonable opportunity to compare the bulk with the sample
- the goods must be free from any defect making 'their quality unsatisfactory' (not unmerchantable), which a reasonable examination of the sample would not reveal.

Specification by a user or performance specification

Here, the purchaser informs the supplier of the use to which the purchased item is to be put. This method is particularly applicable to the purchase of items about which the buyer has little technical knowledge.

Under section 14(3) of the SSGA and sections 4 and 5 of the SGSA as amended by the SSGA, where the seller sells goods in the course of a business and the buyer, expressly or by implication, makes known to the seller any particular purpose for which the goods are being bought, there is an implied 'term' that the goods supplied under the contract are of satisfactory quality. For the purpose of the SSGA, goods are satisfactory if 'they meet the standard that a reasonable person would regard as satisfactory, taking account of any description of the goods, the price (if relevant) and all the other relevant circumstances'. Under section 2B of the SSGA, the quality of the goods includes their state and condition and the following (among others) are, in appropriate cases, aspects of their quality:

- fitness for all purposes for which goods of the kind in question are commonly supplied
- appearance and finish
- freedom from minor defects
- safety
- durability.

Under section 2C of the SSGA, the 'term' does not extend to any matter making the quality of goods unsatisfactory:

- that is specifically drawn to the buyer's attention before the contract is made
- where the buyer examines the goods before the contract is made as that examination ought to reveal such matters
- in the case of a contract of sale by sample, matters that would have been apparent on reasonable examination of the sample.

Section 4 of the SSGA provides that, when the seller can prove that the deviation from the specification is only slight, it would be unreasonable for the buyer to reject the goods. The buyer may not treat the breach of contract as a condition entitling him to reject the goods, but only as a warranty giving a right to damages arising from the breach.

Section 4 also makes a distinction between commercial buyers and consumers. If the buyer is a consumer, the right to reject the goods on the grounds that the quality of the goods is unsatisfactory is not affected.

Section 3(2) states that the section applies unless a contrary intention appears in, or is to be implied from, the contract.

As Woodroffe[22] observes:

> This time buyers must look to their own terms and conditions, for a well-drafted clause will enable a buyer to terminate a contract for any breach of sections 13–15 (SSGA) whether slight or not.

9.5.4 Public sector buyers

Public sector buyers should note that EU Procurement Regulations has a principle of the equal treatment of all enquiries so as not to eliminate on the basis of the nationality of the supplier or the origin of the goods or services. This includes the banning of national technical specifications liable to discriminate against foreign tenderers.

9.6 Standardisation

Standards are documents that stipulate or recommend minimum levels of performance and quality of goods and services and optional conditions for operations in a given environment. Standards may be distinguished according to their subject matter, purpose and range of applications.

9.6.1 Subject matter

This may relate to an area of economic activity, such as engineering, and items used in that field, such as fasteners. Each item may be further subdivided into suitable subjects for standards. Thus, 'fasteners' may lead to standards for screw threads, bolts and nuts, washers and so on.

9.6.2 Purpose

Standards may relate to one or more aspects of product quality. These include:

- *dimensions* thus encouraging interchangeability and variety reduction – for example, BS EN ISO 6433:1995 is a British Standard that lays down technical drawing principles and conventions widely accepted in the UK and will be easily understood worldwide.

- *performance requirements* for a given purpose, such as PD 5500:2009, which covers the specification for unfired fusion welded pressure vessels necessary for a design to meet statutory requirements and those of manufacturers and users of safe performance.

- *environmental requirements* relating to such matters as pollution, waste disposal on land, noise and environmental nuisance – for example, environmental performance objectives and targets are covered by BS EN ISO 14001:2004.

In addition to the above, standards may also cover codes of practice, methods of testing and glossaries. Codes of practice, as stated earlier, give guidance on the best accepted practices in relation to engineering and construction techniques and for operations such as installation, maintenance and provision of services. Methods of testing are required for measuring the values of product characteristics and behaviour standards. Glossaries help to ensure unambiguous technical communication by providing standard definitions of the terms, conventions, units and symbols used in science and industry.

9.6.3 Range of application

This relates to the domain in which a particular standard is applicable. There are several kinds of standards and it is also the case that different standards and specifications can often be used in conjunction.

- *Individual standards* – these are laid down by the individual user.

- *Company standards* – these are prepared and agreed by various functions to guide design, purchasing, manufacturing and marketing operations. Ashton[23] has drawn attention to the importance of keeping registers or databases of bought-out parts and company standards that can be referred to by codes listed in a codes register as a means of variety reduction and obviating variations in tolerances, finishes, performance and quality.

- *Association or trade standards* – these are prepared by a group of related interests in a given industry, trade or profession, such as the Society of Motor Manufacturers and Traders.

- *National standards* – British Standard specifications of particular importance are BS 4778 Quality vocabulary, BS 6143 Guide to the economics of quality, BS 7850 Total quality management and BS EN ISO 9000:2005 Quality management systems.

- *International standards* – the two principal organisations producing worldwide standards are the International Electrotechnical Commission (IEC) and the International Organisation for Standardisation (ISO). The former, established in 1906, concentrates on standards relating to the electrical and electronic fields. The latter, founded in 1947, is concerned with non-electrical standards. Both organisations are located in Geneva. In Western Europe, progress is being made in the development of standards that will be acceptable as both European and international standards. This work is being done via the European Committee for Standardisation (CEN), formed by Western European standards organisations. The demarcation of European standardisation mirrors the international arrangement, with CEN covering non-electrical aspects and the European Committee for Electrotechnical Standardisation (CENELEC) and the European Telecommunications Standards Institute (ETSI) being responsible for the others.

9.6.4 BS EN ISO 9000

Although TQM preceded the ISO 9000 series as a method by which organisations could increase their reputation for quality and profitability, compliance with ISO standards and ISO certification is widely regarded as providing the framework and essential first step to TQM.

The British Standards Institution (BSI) was established in 1901 as the Engineering Standards Committee, but, after being granted a Royal Charter in 1929, changed to the present name in 1931.

The CEN (European Committee for Standardisation) and CENELEC (European Committee for Electrotechnical Standardisation) were created in the late 1960s – the former to 'promote technical harmonisation in Europe in conjunction with worldwide bodies and its partners in Europe'.

The ISO (International Organisation for Standardisation) was founded in 1946 as the existence of non-harmonised standards for similar technologies can constitute technical barriers to international trade. BS EN ISO 9000:2005, as the worldwide derivative of BSI's BS 5750 Quality Management System, launched in 1979, appeared in 1987. ISO standards, now adopted by over 140 countries, are revised every five years.

The current BS EN ISO 9000:2005 series, published in September 2005, provides the principles that are put into practice by the BSI system for the Registration of Firms' Assessed Capability. To be registered, an organisation is required to have a documented quality system that complies with the appropriate parts of BS EN ISO 9000 and a quality

Figure 9.3 The main documents relating to ISO 9000:2005 standards

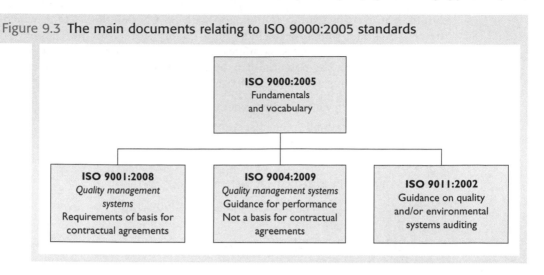

assessment schedule (QAS) that defines in precise terms the scope and special requirements relating to a specific group of products, processes or service. QASs are developed by the BSI in cooperation with a particular industry after consultation with purchasing and associated interests.

When an undertaking seeking registration has satisfactory documentation procedures, the BSI arranges for an assessment visit by a team of at least two experienced assessors, one of whom is normally from the BSI inspectorate. Afterwards, a report confirming any discrepancies raised and the outcome of the assessment is sent to the undertaking seeking registration. The initial assessment is followed by regular unannounced audit visits at the discretion of the BSI to ensure standards are maintained.

As shown by Figure 9.3, the main documents relating to the system are a vocabulary and separate standards.

Although the revised 9001:2008 and 9004:2009 are standalone standards, they constitute a 'consistent pair' aimed at facilitating a more user-friendly introduction of quality management systems into an organisation.

9.6.5 Purchasing and BS EN ISO 9000:2005

BS EN ISO 9000:2005 defines the standards for any requirements of a quality system under four main headings:

- management responsibility
- resource management
- product realisation
- measurement, analysis and improvement.

Purchasing is referred to under 'resource management' in clause 7.4. In this context, the word 'organisation' refers to the undertaking that is seeking conformity with the standard that is 'us'. The term 'supplier' refers to 'our' suppliers. An 'interested party' is a person or group having an interest in the performance or success of an organisation.

Clause 7.4 contains provisions relating to the purchasing process (7.4.1), purchasing information (7.4.2) and verification of purchased produce (7.4.3). These sections should, however, be read in conjunction with BS EN ISO 9004:2009, which specifies the activities that should be included in a quality system for purchasing. Subsection 7.4.2, for example, provides examples of ways in which an organisation can ensure that suppliers have the potential capability to provide required products 'effectively, efficiently and within schedule', such as:

- evaluation of relevant supplier experience
- performance of suppliers against competitors
- review of purchase product quality, price, delivery performance and response to problems
- audits of supplier management systems.

Cognisance should also be taken of the ISO 14000 series.

9.6.6 Purchasing and standardisation

Purchasing staff should be aware of the major trade, national and international standards applicable to their industry and the items bought. They should also appreciate the advantages that standardisation offers to the buyer:

- clear specifications and the removal of any uncertainty as to what is required on the part of both buyer and supplier
- standardisation helps to achieve reliability and reduce costs
- saving of time and money by eliminating the need to prepare company specifications and reducing the need for explanatory letters, telephone calls and so on
- the saving of design time may also reduce the time for production of the finished product
- accurate comparison of quotations as all prospective suppliers are quoting for the same thing
- less dependence on specialist suppliers and greater scope for negotiation
- reduction in error and conflict, thus increasing supplier goodwill
- facilitation of international sourcing by reference to ISO standards
- saving in inventory and cost as a result of variety reduction (see Chapter 10) – by coordinating the efforts of purchasing, design and production, a company reduced 30 different paints to 15, 120 different cutting fluids to 10, 50 different tools steel to 6, and 12 different aluminium casting alloys to 3. Standardisation and coding of items also discovered 36 different terms in use for a simple washer
- reduced investment in spares for capital equipment
- reduced cost of material handling when standardisation is used
- elimination of the need to purchase costly brand names
- irregular purchases of non-standard equipment supplies are revealed.

9.6.7 Directories of ISO 9000-certified companies or organisations and standards

There is no complete database of ISO-certified organisations, but reference may be made to the following:

- ISO 9000 Web Directory
- ISO Register
- QSU Online ISO 9000 Registered Company Directory
- Quality Digest – International ISO Database
- The International Quality Systems Directory

Further information on standards can be obtained from Rhodes and Fallon.[24] Useful websites are:

- British Standards Institution at: www.bsi-global.com/
- British Standards Online at: http://bsol.bsigroup.com/en/bsolhomepage
- BSI catalogue at: www.shop.bsi-global.com

9.6.8 Independent quality assurance and certification

Independent quality assurance and certification is of great benefit to the user, purchaser and manufacturer. The BSI, via its Kitemark, Safety Mark, Registered Firms and Registered Stockist Schemes, put into practice the principles of BS EN ISO 9000, setting out procedures by which a product's safety and a suppliers' quality management systems can be independently assessed.

About 30 third-party certification bodies are members of the Association of British Certification Bodies (ABCB). Some are set up by trade associations, such as the Manchester Chamber of Commerce Testing House for the Cotton Trade, Bradford Chamber of Commerce for the Wool Trade, the Shirley Institute, Manchester, and the London Textile Trading House. Certification bodies assessed by the National Accreditation Council for Certification Bodies (NACCB) are entitled to use the NACCB National Quality 'Tick'.

9.7 Variety reduction

Variety reduction can make substantial savings in inventory by standardising and rationalising the range of materials, parts and consumables kept in stock. Variety reduction can be proactive or reactive.

Proactive variety reduction can be achieved by using, so far as possible, standardised components and sub-assemblies to make end products that are dissimilar in appearance and performance so that a variety of final products use only a few basic components. Proactive approaches to variety reduction can also apply when considering capital purchases. By ensuring compatibility with existing machinery, the range of spares carried to insure against breakdowns can be substantially reduced.

Reactive variety reduction can be undertaken periodically by a special project team comprised of all interested parties who examine a range of stock items to determine:

- the intended use for each item of stock
- how many stock items serve the same purpose
- the extent to which items having the same purpose can be given a standard description
- what range of sizes is essential
- how frequently each item in the range is used
- what items can be eliminated

- to what extent sizes, dimensions, quality and other characteristics of an item can be standardised
- what items of stock are now obsolete and unlikely to be required in the future.

The advantages of variety reduction include:

- reduction of holding costs for stock
- release of money tied up in stock
- easier specifications when ordering
- narrower range of inventory
- a reduced supplier base.

9.8 Quality assurance and quality control

9.8.1 Quality assurance

Quality assurance is defined as:[25]

> All those planned and systematic activities implemented within the quality systems and demonstrated as needed to provide adequate confidence that an entity will fulfil requirements for quality.

Quality assurance is concerned with defect prevention. Therefore, it can involve a number of approaches, including:

- quality systems, including BS EN ISO 9000
- new design control, aimed at getting it right first time
- design of manufacturing processes aimed at eliminating defects at source
- incoming materials control – most organisations now require that their suppliers provide proof, such as BS EN ISO 9000 certification, that their processes are under statistical control
- supplier appraisal, to ensure that only suppliers able to meet quality requirements are approved – this is especially important with JIT purchasing.

9.8.2 Quality control

Quality control (QC) is defined as:[26]

> The operational techniques and activities that are used to fulfil requirements for quality. Quality control is concerned with defect detection and correction and relates to such activities as determining where, how and at what intervals inspection should take place, the collection and analysis of data relating to defects and determining what corrective action should be taken.

As defects are detected after they have been made, Schonberger[27] has referred to QC as 'the death certificate' approach.

9.9 Tests for quality control and reliability

It is impracticable in this book to attempt even an outline of quality assurance, control and liability techniques. So, in this section, brief mention is made of inspection, statistical

Figure 9.4 **The four main inspection activities**

Inspection activities			
Receiving inspection	**Classification inspection**	**Control inspection**	**Audit inspection**
Materials or components received from outside suppliers are inspected for conformance to specifications	Inspection to separate parts into categories according to specifications	Inspection of periodic sample of work-in-progress or an end product to detect and correct deviations	Ensuring that procedures and processes are being followed to ensure the validity and reliability of inspection operations

quality control and six sigma, quality loss function, robust design, quality function deployment (QFD) and failure mode and effects analysis (FMEA).

9.9.1 Inspection

Although inspection is a non-value-adding activity, some form of inspection, either at source or on delivery, is often unavoidable. The four main inspection activities are shown in Figure 9.4.

Important aspects of inspection are as follows:

■ *How much to inspect and how often* – only rarely is a 100 per cent inspection required, and the greater the frequency of inspections, the greater the cost. In general, operations with a high human input necessitate more inspection than mechanical operations, which tend to be more reliable. The usual basis of inspection is an agreed sample, such as 5 per cent. The size of the sample will be determined by which statistical quality control method is to be used. Often the checking of dimensions or measurements can be done automatically by the use of go/no-go gauges.

■ *Where to inspect* – most operations have numerous possible inspection points. Generally, inspection should take place:
   – when material is received from suppliers, although the tendency is for responsibility for quality to be placed with the supplier
   – before dispatch, as repairing or replacing products after delivery is more costly than at the factory and there is also damage to customer goodwill
   – before a costly operation
   – before parts are joined irreversibly to other parts
   – before a covering process, as painting or plating can often mask defects.

9.9.2 Statistical quality control

The basis of statistical quality control is sampling. A sample is a subset of a population or an entire set of objects or observations that have something in common. If a factory produces 1000 items of component X in one day, the population or 'universe' of component X for that day is 1000.

There are three main reasons for using sampling rather than 100 per cent inspection:

■ sampling saves time
■ sampling saves money
■ sampling provides a basis for control.

From the quality standpoint, sampling can take one of two forms:

■ *Acceptance sampling* tests the quality of a batch of products by taking a sample from each batch and testing to see whether the whole batch should be accepted or rejected. Acceptance sampling can be applied when bought-out items are received from suppliers or as a final inspection of goods produced before they are dispatched to customers.

■ *Process control* is a more proactive approach, aimed at ensuring that parts and components meet specifications during the production process, not after a batch has already been manufactured.

The concepts of the arithmetic mean and standard deviation (referred to in the next section) provide the basis for the book *Economic Control of Manufactured Products*, published in 1931 by Dr Walter Shewart of the Bell Telephone Company. This book is the foundation of modern statistical process control (SPC) and provides the basis for the philosophy of total quality management by means of sampling.

Shewart also developed the statistical process control chart to provide a visual indication of quality variations.

If, for example, the ideal length of a steel spindle is 6 cm and there is a tolerance of 0.005 cm, then components of 5.995 cm or 6.005 cm will be acceptable.

As sample batches of the spindle are taken, the average value of each batch is calculated and logged on the chart, as shown in Figure 9.5.

Figure 9.5 Statistical process control chart

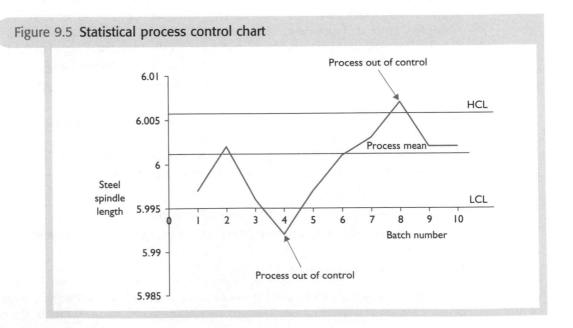

Figure 9.6 A normal distribution curve

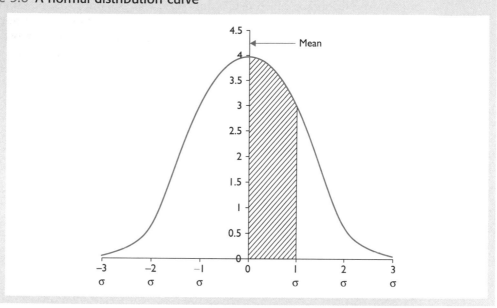

So long as the results are within the upper and lower limits, there is no need for action. However, if a value falls outside these limits – as with samples 4 and 8 – the reason(s) must be investigated and rectified. It is possible, for example, that the machine settings for these batches needed resetting or adjusting.

9.9.3 Six Sigma

The concept of the arithmetic mean, standard deviation and normal curve are the basis of Six Sigma. The business management strategy Six Sigma was originated at Motorola in the early 1980s and is an approach for improving customer satisfaction, by reducing and eliminating product defects. It aims to achieve virtually defect-free processes and products.

A normal distribution curve is shown in Figure 9.6.

The arithmetic mean (x) is obtained by dividing the sum of two or more quantities by the number of items. For example, the arithmetic mean of 5, 10 and 12 is 27/3 = 9.

The standard deviation measures the extent to which sample scores are spread around the mean or average. For example, suppose that the scores from a series of inspections are normally distributed with a mean of 80 and a standard deviation of 8. Then the scores that are within one standard deviation of the mean are between 80 − 8 = 72 and 80 + 8 = 88. One standard deviation from the mean in either direction accounts for somewhere around 68 per cent of all items in the distribution. Two standard deviations from the mean accounts for roughly 95 per cent and three standard deviations for 99 per cent of the distribution spread. The term 'Sigma' is a Greek alphabet letter 'σ', used to describe variability. In Six Sigma the common measurement is defects per million operations (DPMO). Six Sigma – or six standard deviations from the mean – therefore indicates a target of 3.4 defects per million opportunities (or 99.99966 accuracy), which is as close as anyone is likely to get to perfection.

Achieving a Six Sigma level of quality output means reducing process variation by means of a technique called define, measure, analyse, improve and control (DMAIC), which uses a variety of statistical tools, including process maps, Pareto charts, control charts, cause and effect diagrams and process capability ratio, most of which are beyond the scope of this book. Suffice to say that, as a result of the application of DMAIC, organisations identify and eliminate special cause variations from their processes until Six Sigma quality output is achieved.

9.9.4 Quality loss function (QLF)

This, together with the concept of robust design referred to in section 9.9.5, below, developed from work undertaken by Dr Genichi Taguchi while working for the Japanese telecommunications company NTT in the 1950s and 1960s.

Taguchi's approach is based on the economic implications of poor quality. He defines quality as:[28]

> The quality of a product is the minimum loss imparted by the product to society from the time the product is shipped.

The loss to society includes costs arising from the failure of the product to:

■ meet customers' expectations
■ achieve desired performance characteristics
■ meet safety and environmental standards.

QLF is based on the principle that 'quality should be measured by the deviation from a specific target value rather than by conformance to preset tolerance limits'. Thus, the greater the deviation from a given target, the greater will be customers' dissatisfaction and the larger the loss concept.

The QLF approach is shown in Figure 9.7. The aim is to keep the product as near to the target as possible.

Figure 9.7 Taguchi's loss function

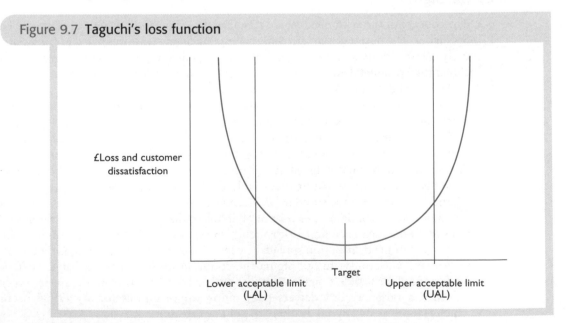

£Loss and customer dissatisfaction

Lower acceptable limit (LAL)

Target

Upper acceptable limit (UAL)

This loss function can be approximately calculated by using the formula:

$$L(x) = R(x - T)^2$$

Where:

L = the loss in monetary terms
x = any value of the quality characteristics
T = the target value
R = some constant

Example 9.1

Example of use of the loss function

Assume a quality characteristic has a specification of 0.500 ± 0.020. Further, assume that, on the basis of company records, it has been found that if the quality characteristic exceeds the target of 0.020 on either side, there is a probability that the product will fail during the warranty period and the cost of rectifying it will be £100.
Then:

$$£100 = R(0.020)^2$$

$$R = \frac{100}{(0.020)^2} = \frac{100}{0.0004} = 250,000$$

Therefore, the loss function is:

$$L(x) = £250,000(x - T)^2$$

Thus, if the deviation is only 0.005, the estimated loss will be:

$$L(0.005) = £250,000(0.005)^2 = £6.25$$

For a batch of 50 products, the cost would be 50 × 6.25 = £312.50

The loss function approach has been criticised on the grounds that the practicalities of determining the constant R with any degree of accuracy are formidable.

The Taguchi loss function can be applied to any non-conformance cost, such as complaint handling, inspection and testing, rework of defective parts, scrap and warranty repairs. All such costs arise from not doing the work right first time. By improving quality, such costs can be reduced. Thus, the cost of quality is a misnomer as quality can actually produce a profit.

9.9.5 Robust design

Some products are designed for use only within a narrow application range. Others will perform well in a much wider range of conditions. The latter have robust design. Think of a pair of bedroom slippers. These are clearly unsuitable for walking in mud or snow. Conversely, a pair of Wellington boots is exactly what is required. The Wellington boots are more robust than the slippers.

A product or service may be defined as 'robust' when it is insensitive to the effects of source of variability, even though the sources themselves have not been eliminated. The more designers can build robustness into a product, the better it should last, resulting in a higher level of customer satisfaction.

Similarly, environmental factors can have a negative effect on production processes. Furnaces used in the production of food, ceramics and steel products may not heat uniformly. One approach to the problem might be to develop a superior oven. Another is to design a system that moves the product during operation to achieve uniform heating.

Taguchi's approach involves determining the target specifications of limits for the product or design process and reducing variability due to manufacturing and environmental factors. As shown in Figure 9.8, Taguchi distinguishes between controllable and non-controllable factors, or 'noise'.

'Noise' factors are primarily responsible for causing the performance of a product to deviate from its target value. Hence, by means of analytical methods or carefully planned experiments, parameter design seeks to identify settings of the control factors that make the product more robust – that is, less sensitive to variations in the noise factors. Taguchi states that many designers consider only system and tolerance factors. He maintains, however, that without parameter design it is almost impossible to produce a high-quality product.

Taguchi's concepts of QLF and design have been criticised mainly on the grounds that the constant R in the QLF equation is difficult to determine with any degree of accuracy and that the large number of possible parameters in robust design make it

Figure 9.8 Taguchi's concept of controllable and non-controllable factors

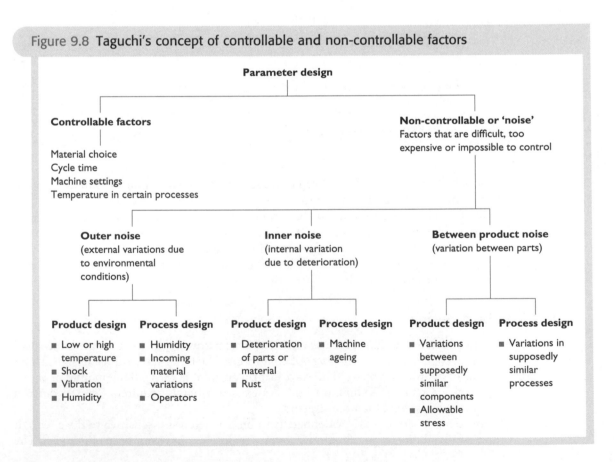

impossible to investigate all such combinations. Nevertheless, his methods are used by many world class organisations.

9.9.6 Quality function deployment (QFD)

QFD is a translation of the Japanese *Kanji* characters *Hin Shitsu Ki Ten Kai*, which can be broadly translated as meaning, 'how we do understand the quality that our customers expect and make it happen in a dynamic way?'

QFD has been defined as:

> A structured approach to defining customers' needs or requirements and translating them into specific plans to meet those needs.

The term used to describe stated or unstated customer requirements is the 'voice of the customer'.

Information on customers' requirements is obtained in a multiplicity of ways, including market research, direct discussion, focus groups, customer specifications, observation, warranty data and field reports.

QFD ensures that customers' requirements are met by means of a tool called the 'house of quality' – an outline of which is shown in Figure 9.9. Using this tool, producers are able to reconcile customers' needs with design and manufacturing constraints.

The house of quality or product planning is, however, only the first of a four-stage process – the other three sequential phases being product design, product planning and process control. These four phases are shown in Figure 9.10.

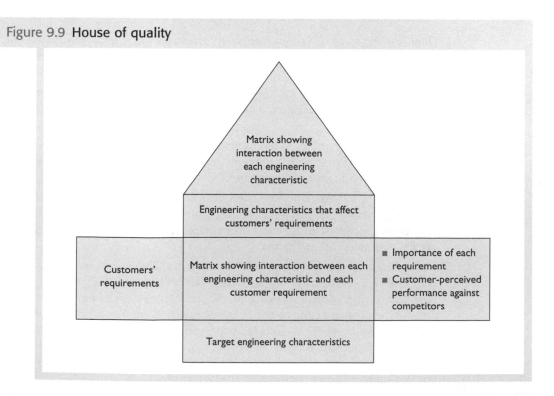

Figure 9.9 **House of quality**

Figure 9.10 **The four phases in QFD**

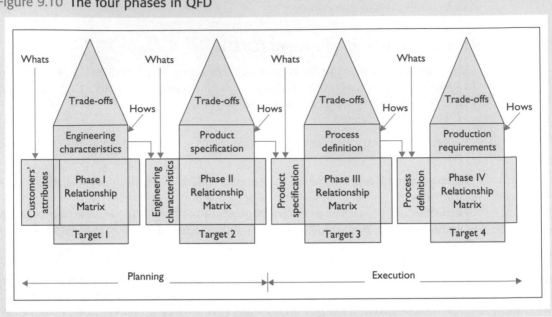

The QFD process involves the following steps:

1 Details of customers' requirements, or 'attributes', are obtained from sources such as those referred to earlier and listed under 'Customers' requirements' in the house of quality.

2 The relative importance assigned to each attribute is expressed on a scale of 1–5 or in percentage terms and entered under 'Importance of each requirement' in the house of quality.

3 For products that are intended to beat the competition, it is essential to know how they compare with those of competitors. A comparison of the rankings of each attribute will be made under 'Customer-perceived performance against competitors'.

4 Customers' attributes are translated into key engineering characteristics. Thus, for a car, the customers' attribute of 'fast start' would be translated into a 'specified' acceleration from 0 to 60 mph and entered into 'Engineering characteristics that affect customers' requirements'.

5 The strength of the relationship between customers' requirements and the technical requirements can be explored and expressed as 'very strong', 'strong' or 'weak' and entered into the 'Matrix showing interaction between each engineering characteristic and each customer requirement'. Blank rows or columns indicate no relationship or technical requirements as no customer requirement exists. It is also now possible to compare the performance of the product against customers' requirements and those of competitors and to set targets for improved design or performance. These are entered under 'Target engineering characteristics'.

6 The 'roof' of the house matrix encourages creativity by considering potential trade-offs between engineering and customer characteristics, such as performance and cost. This may lead to some changes in the target outcomes. While some organisations go no further than the first house of quality concerned with customers' requirements, others continue the process through the further stages of product specification, process definition and production requirements shown in Figure 9.10.

■ The *production specification house* is concerned with the detailed characteristics of subsystems and components and the determination of target values for such aspects as fit, function and appearance.

■ The *process definition house* is where components characteristics are related to key process operations. This stage represents the transition from planning to execution. If a product component parameter is critical and is created or affected during the process, it becomes a control point. This tells us what to monitor and inspect and becomes the basis for a quality control plan for the achievement of customer satisfaction.

■ The *production requirements house* relates the control points to specific requirements for quality control and includes the specification of control methods and what sample sizes are required to achieve the appropriate quality level.

Thus, as shown in Figure 9.10, the target technical levels of 'hows?' of one stage are used to generate the 'whats?' of the succeeding stage.

The main benefits of QFD are that:

■ the design of products and services is focused on customers' requirements and driven by objective customers' needs rather than by technology

■ it benchmarks the performance of an organisation's products against those of competitors

■ it reduces the overall length of the design code

■ it substantially reduces the number of post-release design changes by ensuring that focused effort is put into the planning stage or stages

■ it promotes teamwork and breaks down barriers between the marketing, design and production functions.

9.9.7 Failure mode and effects analysis (FMEA)

What is FMEA?

FMEA, which originated in the USA aerospace industry, is an important reliability engineering technique that has the following main objectives:

■ to identify all the ways in which failure can occur

■ to estimate the effect and seriousness of the failure

■ to recommend corrective design actions.

FMEA has been defined as:[29]

> A systematic approach that applies a tabular method to aid the thought process used by engineers to identify potential failure modes and their effects.

As a tool embedded within six sigma methodology, FMEA can help identify and eliminate concerns early in the development of a product or process. It is a systematic way to prospectively identify possible ways in which failure can occur.

Types of FMEA

It can take three forms:[30]

1 *Systems FMEA* is used to analyse systems and subsystems in the early concept and design stages. System function is the design or purpose(s) of the system and is derived from customers' wants. It can also include safety requirements, government regulations and constraints.
2 *Design FMEA* is used to analyse products before they are released to production.
3 *Process FMEA* is used to analyse products before they are released to the customer.

The preparation of an FMEA

The Ford Motor Company, which was the first of the UK motor manufacturers to request suppliers to use FMEA in its advance quality planning, recommends a team approach led by the responsible system, product or manufacturing/assembly engineer, who is expected to involve representatives from all affected activities. Team members may be drawn from design, manufacturing, assembly, quality, reliability, service, purchasing, testing, supplier and other subject experts as appropriate. The team leader is also responsible for keeping the FMEA updated.

For proprietary designs, the preparation and updating of FMEAs is the responsibility of the suppliers.

With a design FMEA, for example, the team is initially concerned with identifying how a part may fail to meet its intended function and the seriousness of the effect of a potential failure, which is rated on a ten-point scale, as shown in Table 9.2.

Starting with the failure modes with the highest severity ratings, the design FMEA team then ascertains the possible causes of failure, based on two assumptions:

■ that the part is manufactured/assembled within engineering specifications
■ that the part design may include a deficiency that may cause an unacceptable variation in the manufacturing or assembling process.

The team then proceeds to ascertain:

■ the probability of failures that could occur over the life of the part – see Table 9.3
■ design evaluation techniques that can be used to detect the identified failure causes – see Table 9.4
■ what design actions are recommended to reduce the severity, occurrence and detection ratings.

The completed design FMEA for a lighting switch subsystem is shown in Table 9.2. The technique is further described in BS EN ISO 9000.

Advantages of the FMEA approach

These include:

■ improved quality, reliability and safety of products and processes
■ increased customer satisfaction

Table 9.2 Severity rating table for design FMEA

Effect	Rating	Criteria
No effect	1	No effect
Very slight effect	2	Very slight effect on vehicle's performance. Customer not annoyed. Non-vital fault noticed sometimes
Slight effect	3	Slight effect on vehicle's performance. Customer slightly annoyed. Non-vital fault noticed most of the time
Minor effect	4	Minor effect on vehicle's performance. Fault does not require repair. Customer will notice minor effect on vehicle's or system's performance. Non-vital fault always noted
Moderate effect	5	Moderate effect on vehicle's performance. Customer experiences some dissatisfaction. Fault on non-vital part requires repair
Significant effect	6	Vehicle's performance degraded, but operable and safe. Customer experiences discomfort. Non-vital part inoperable
Major effect	7	Vehicle's performance severely affected, but drivable and safe. Customer dissatisfied. Subsystems inoperable
Extreme effect	8	Vehicle inoperable but safe. Customer very dissatisfied. System inoperable
Serious effect	9	Potentially hazardous effect. Able to stop vehicle without mishap – gradual failure. Compliance with government regulation in jeopardy
Hazardous effect	10	Hazardous effect. Safety related – sudden failure. Non-compliance with government regulation

Note: Severity rating corresponds to the seriousness of the effect(s) of a potential failure mode. Severity applies only to the effect of a failure mode.

Table 9.3 Probability of failure rating table

Probability of failure	Failure probability	Ranking
Very high: failure is almost inevitable	>1 in 2	10
	1 in 3	9
High: repeated failures	1 in 8	8
	1 in 20	7
Moderate: occasional failures	1 in 80	6
	1 in 400	5
	1 in 2000	4
Low: relatively few failures	1 in 15,000	3
	1 in 150,000	2
Remote: failure is unlikely	<1 in 1,500,000	1

Table 9.4 Design evaluation – detecting causes of failure

Detection	Likelihood of detection by design control	Ranking
Absolute uncertainty	Design control *cannot* detect potential cause/mechanical and subsequent failure mode	
Very remote	*Very remote* chance the design control will detect potential cause/mechanism and subsequent failure mode	
Remote	*Remote* chance the design control will detect potential cause/mechanism and subsequent failure mode	
Very low	*Very low* chance the design control will detect potential cause/mechanism and subsequent failure mode	
Low	*Low* chance the design control will detect potential cause/mechanism and subsequent failure mode	
Moderate	*Moderate* chance the design control will detect potential cause/mechanism and subsequent failure mode	
Moderately high	*Moderately high* chance the design control will detect potential cause/mechanism and subsequent failure mode	
High	*High* chance the design control will detect potential cause/mechanism and subsequent failure mode	
Very high	*Very high* chance the design control will detect potential cause/mechanism and subsequent failure mode	
Almost certain	Design control *will* detect potential cause/mechanism and subsequent failure mode	

- early identification, rectification and elimination of potential causes of failure
- ranking of product or process deficiencies
- documentation and tracking of actions to reduce failure risk
- minimisation of late product or process changes and associated cost
- it is a catalyst for teamwork and the cross-functional exchange of ideas and knowledge.

Some disadvantages of the FMEA approach

The disadvantages include:

- the required detail makes the process time consuming
- the process relies on recruiting the appropriate participants
- FMEA assumes the causes of problems are all single event in nature
- requires open and trusting behaviour, not defensiveness of vested interests
- requires follow-up sessions otherwise the process will not be effective
- it is difficult to examine human error and this facet is sometimes not scrutinised.

9.10 The cost of quality

9.10.1 Definitions

The cost of quality may be defined as the costs of conformance plus the costs of non-conformance or the cost of doing things wrong.

The cost of conformance (COC) is defined by BS 6143 – 1:1992 as:

> The cost of operating the process as specified in a 100 per cent effective manner. This does not imply that it is efficient or even a necessary process but rather that the process when operated with the specified procedures cannot be achieved at a lower cost.

The cost of non-conformance (CONC) is defined as:

> The cost of inefficiency with the specified process, i.e. over resourcing or excess cost of people, materials and equipment arising from unsatisfactory inputs, errors made, rejected outputs and various other sources of waste. These are regarded as non-essential process costs.

BS 6143 – 1:1992 points out that:

> Quality costs alone do not provide sufficient information for management to put them into perspective with other operating costs or to identify critical areas in need of attention.

To establish the significance of quality costs, it is necessary to use ratios showing the relationships between total quality costs and the costs of prevention, appraisal and failure. Typical ratios include:

Prevention costs: Total quality cost

and

Cost of supplier appraisal: Prevention costs

The main costs of quality are set out in Table 9.5.

9.11 Value management, engineering and analysis

The terms value management (VM), value engineering (VE) and value analysis (VA) are often regarded as synonymous. Each term may, however, be distinguished from the others.

9.11.1 Value management (VM)

VM is defined by BS EN 12973:2000 as:

> A style of management, particularly dedicated to mobilise people, develop skills and promote synergies and innovation with the aim of maximising the overall performance of an organisation.

As indicated by this definition, VM is a style of management aimed at instilling a culture of best value throughout an organisation. 'Best value' implies that a product or service will meet customers' needs and expectations at a competitive price. VM applies at both the corporate and operational levels of an organisation. At the corporate level it emphasises the importance of a value-orientated culture aimed at achieving value for customers and stakeholders. At the operational level it seeks to implement a value culture by the use of appropriate methods and tools.

The Society of American Value Engineers (SAVE), formed in 1959, became the prototype for similar institutions in other countries. In the UK, the Institute of Value

---

Table 9.5 The costs of quality

Cost of conformance

Prevention costs	*Appraisal costs*
Costs of any action taken to investigate, prevent or reduce defects and failures, including:	Cost of assessing the quality achieved:
■ quality engineering (or quality management, department or planning)	■ laboratory acceptance testing
■ quality control/engineering, including design/specification review and reliability engineering	■ inspection tests, including goods inward
■ process control/engineering	■ product quality audits
■ design and development of quality measurement and control equipment	■ set-up for inspection and test
■ quality planning by other functions	■ inspection and test material
■ calibration and maintenance of production equipment used to evaluate quality	■ product quality audit
■ maintenance and calibration of test and inspection equipment	■ review of test and inspection data
■ supplier assurance, including supplier surveys, audits and ratings, identifying new sources of supply, design evaluation and testing of alternative products, purchase order review before placement	■ field (on-site) performance testing
■ quality training	■ internal testing and release
■ administration, audit and improvement	■ evaluation of field stock and spare parts
	■ data processing inspection and test reports

Costs of non-conformance

Internal failure	*External failure*
Costs arising within the manufacturing organisation before transfer of ownerships to the customer:	After transfer of ownership to the customer:
■ scrap	■ complaints
■ rework and repair	■ product or customer service, product liability
■ troubleshooting or defect/failure analysis	■ products rejected and returned, recall reject
■ reinspect, retest	■ returned materials for repair
■ scrap and rework, fault of vendor, downtime	■ warranty costs and costs associated with replacement
■ modification permits and concessions	
■ downgrading – losses for quality reasons resulting from a lower selling price	

Management was formed in 1966, while, in 1991, the European Committee for Standardisation (CEN) sponsored the Federation of National Associations to produce BS EN 12973: Value Management, published in 2000.

9.11.2 Value engineering (VE)

Value engineering is an organised effort directed at analysing the functions of systems, equipment, facilities, services and supplies for the purpose of achieving the essential functions at the lowest lifecycle cost consistent with required performance, reliability, quality and safety.

Value engineering emphasises the importance of applying this discipline as early as possible in the design process. VE follows a structured thought process to evaluate options, namely the:

- gathering of relevant information
- consideration of what is being achieved now, if it is an existing product or service?
- measurement of all facets of performance, e.g. mean time between failures (MTBF)
- consideration of how alternative designs and performance will be measured?
- analysis of functions
- consideration of what must be done as opposed to 'nice to haves'
- consideration of the actual cost?
- generation of ideas through structured open challenge
- consideration of alternatives?
- evaluation and ranking of ideas for further action
- ideas which appear to offer the greatest potential
- development and expansion of these ideas
- consideration of the impacts and cost?
- consideration of the performance?
- presentation of ideas and agreement of action plan.

The US Department of Defense (DOD) has applied VE to many purchases, including:

- equipment and logistics support
- parts obsolescence
- software architecture development
- publications, manuals, procedures and reports
- tooling
- training
- construction.

There is an increasing use of value engineering change proposals (VECPs) which are used to incentivise the contractor to propose contract modifications which reduce cost without reducing product or process performance. Brian Farrington Ltd[31] has used VECPs in outsourcing contracts for the provision of back-office services, property and construction. These contracts include a 'Gainshare' provision whereby the contractor retains an agreed percentage of the savings achieved.

9.11.3 Value analysis

Value analysis (VA) was developed by the General Electric Company in the USA at the end of the Second World War. One of the pioneers of this approach to cost reduction was Lawrence D. Miles, whose book *Techniques of Value Analysis and Engineering* (McGraw-Hill, 1972) is still the classic on the subject.

The term 'value engineering' (VE) was adopted by the US Navy Bureau of Ships for a programme of cost reduction at the design stage, the aim of which was to achieve economies without affecting the needed performance, reliability, quality and maintainability. Miles has described value analysis as:

A philosophy implemented by the use of a specific set of techniques, a body of knowledge, and a group of learned skills. It is an organised, creative approach which has for its purpose the efficient identification of unnecessary cost, i.e. cost which provides neither quality nor use, nor life, nor appearance, nor customer features.

VA results in the orderly utilisation of alternative materials, newer processes and the abilities of specialist suppliers. It focuses engineering, manufacturing and purchasing attention on one objective: equivalent performance at lower cost. Having this focus, it provides step-by-step procedures for accomplishing its objective efficiently and with assurance. An organised and creative approach, it uses a functional and economic design process that aims to increase the value of a VA subject.[32]

The key words for an understanding of VA are 'function' and 'value'. The function of anything is that which it is designed to do, and should normally be capable of being expressed in two words – a verb and noun. Thus, the function of a pen is to 'make marks'. 'Value' is variously defined. The most important distinction is between use value – that is, that which enables an item to fulfil its stated function – and esteem value – factors that increase the desirability of an item. The function of a gold-plated pencil and a ballpoint pen, costing £70.00 and 50p respectively, is, in both cases, to 'make marks'. The difference of £69.50 between the price of the former over the latter represents esteem value.

9.11.4 Implementing VA

The necessary implementation of VA depends on choosing the right people and the right projects.

The right people

VA may be carried out by the following:

- a team of representatives from such departments as cost accounting, design, marketing, manufacturing, purchasing, quality control research and work study
- a specialist VA engineer, where the company's turnover warrants such an appointment, who will often have the responsibility of coordinating a VA team, so such a person should have:
  - experience of design and manufacturing related to the product(s)
  - understanding of a wide range of materials, their potentials and limitations
  - a clear concept of the meaning and importance of 'value'
  - creative imagination and a flair for innovation
  - knowledge of specialist manufacturers and the assistance that they can provide
  - the capacity to work with others and a knowledge of how to motivate, control and coordinate.

Just-in-time approaches emphasise the importance of consultation with suppliers and their co-option to VA teams.

The right project

In selecting possible projects, the VA team or engineer should consider the following:

- what project shows the greatest potential for savings – the greater the total cost, the larger the potential savings, so, for example, consider two hypothetical projects, A and B:

	A	B
Present cost each	10p	100p
Possible savings (10%)	1p	10p
Annual usage	100,000	1000
Projected annual savings	£1000	£100

Component A offers the greatest potential return for the application of VA.

- what products have a high total cost in relation to the functions performed – that is, whether or not it is possible to substitute a cheaper alternative
- what suggestions for projects emanate from design, production staff and suppliers
- are there any drawings or designs that have been unchanged in the last five years?
- manufacturing equipment installed more than, say, five years ago that may now be obsolete
- any inspection and test requirements that have not been changed in the last five years
- single-source orders where the original order was placed more than, say, two years ago that may offer possibilities for savings.

Here are some typical areas warranting VA investigation:

- Product performance – what does it do?
- Product reliability – reducing or eliminating product failure or breakdown.
- Product maintenance – reducing costs of routine maintenance, such as cleaning, lubrication and so on and emergency repairs and replacement.
- Product adaptability – adding an extra function or expanding the original use.
- Product packaging – improving the saleability of or protection given to the product.
- Product safety – eliminating possible hazards, such as sharp edges, inflammability.
- Product styling – specifying lighter, stronger or more flexible materials or simplifying instructions.
- Product distribution – making it easier to distribute by, for example, reducing its weight or finding better transportation options.
- Product security – making the product less liable to theft or vandalism by using better locks, imprinting the customer's name on easily moveable equipment and so on.

9.11.5 Value analysis procedure

The job plan for a VA project involves the following six stages:

1 *Project selection* – see the list above.

2 *Information stage*
  - Obtain all essential information relating to the item under consideration – cost of materials and components, machining and assembly times, methods and costs, quality requirements, inspection procedures and so on.
  - Define the functions of the product, especially in relation to the cost of providing them.

3 *Speculation or creative stage* – have a brainstorming session in which as many alternative ideas as possible are put forward for achieving the desired function, reducing costs or improving the product. Some questions that may promote suggestions at this stage include the following.

- What *additional* or *alternative* uses can we suggest for the item?
- How can the item be *adapted* – what other ideas does the item suggest?
- Can the item be *modified*, especially with regard to changes in form, shape, material, colour, motion, sound or odour?
- Can the item be *augmented* – made stronger, taller, longer, thicker or otherwise developed to provide an extra value and so on?
- Can the item be *reduced* – made stronger, smaller, more condensed, lighter or unnecessary features omitted?
- Can the item be *substituted* – would other materials, components, ingredients, processes, manufacturing methods, packaging and so on improve it?
- Can we *rearrange* the item – change its layout or design, alter the sequence of operations, interchange components?
- Can the item or aspects of the item be *reversed* – reversing its roles or functions or positions, turning it upside-down or front to back?
- What aspects of the product can be *combined* – its functions, purposes, units, other parts and so on?

4 *Investigation stage* – select the best ideas produced at the speculation stage and evaluate their feasibility. When VA is organised on a team basis, each specialist will approach the project from his or her own standpoint and report back.

5 *Proposal stage* – recommendations will be presented to that level of management able to authorise the suggested changes. The proposals will state:

- what changes or modifications are being suggested
- statements relating to the cost of making the suggested changes, the projected savings, the period(s) over which the savings are likely to accrue.

6 *Implementation stage* – when approved by the responsible executive, the agreed recommendations will be progressed through the normal production, purchasing or other procedures.

9.11.6 VA checklists

The following checklist, which every material, component or operation must pass, was prepared by the General Electric Company:

- Does its use contribute value?
- Is its cost proportionate to its usefulness?
- Does it need all its features?
- Is there anything better for the intended use?
- Can a usable part be made by a lower-cost method?
- Can a standard product be found that will be usable?
- Is it made on the proper tooling, considering the quantities used?

Figure 9.11 **Miller's checklist**

Question	Brief description of suggestion	Estimated savings of suggestion
1 What standard item do you have that can be satisfactorily substituted for this part? 2 What design changes do you suggest that will lower the cost of this item? 3 What part of this item can be more economically produced (considering tooling and so on) by casting, forging, extruding, machining or any other process? 4 What material can you suggest as a substitute? 5 What changes in tolerances would result in lower manufacturing costs? 6 What finish requirements can be eliminated or relaxed? 7 What test or qualification requirements appear unnecessary? 8 What suggestions do you have to save weight, simplify the part or reduce its cost? 9 What specifications, tests or quality requirements are too stringent?		
Will you attend a meeting to discuss your ideas if requested? Do you have a formal value analysis programme? If not, would you like help in setting one up? Company: Address: Signature: Title: Date:		

- Are the specified tolerances and finishes really necessary?
- Do materials, reasonable labour, overheads and profit total its cost?
- Can another dependable supplier provide it for less?
- Is anyone buying it for less?

As stated earlier, whenever appropriate, suppliers should be invited to participate in a VA exercise. Miller[33] has prepared the checklist given in Figure 9.11. It can accompany requests for quotations or be used in supplier discussions relating to the design of a new product.

9.11.7 VA and functional analysis (FA)

As stated in section 9.11.3, the function of anything is 'that which it is designed to do'. Value can be defined as:

$$\frac{\text{Performance capability}}{\text{Cost}} \quad \text{or} \quad \frac{\text{Function}}{\text{Cost}}$$

Figure 9.12 **Using the components of a ballpoint pen as an example of cost function analysis**

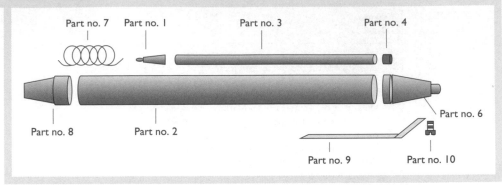

Functional analysis (FA) involves identifying the primary and secondary functions of an item and decomposing them into the sub-functions at an ever increasing level of detail. The application of FA particularly at the information and creative stages can indicate ways of reducing cost either by eliminating or modifying output functions. Conversely, a designer may seek to enhance value by adding new functions to an output. The latter can only be achieved when the target profit exceeds the cost of providing the additional functions. An extension of function analysis is cost function analysis, which identifies the cost of alternative ways of providing a given function.

9.11.8 Cost function analysis

This involves the following steps, which we shall illustrate by reference to a ballpoint pen, the existing components of which are shown in Figure 9.12.

Step 1: Identify the primary and secondary functions of the item

Primary functions are those that the output must achieve. Thus, the primary function of a ballpoint pen is 'to make a mark'.

Secondary functions are support functions. These may be a necessary part of the function but do not themselves perform the primary function. Thus, to 'make a mark', secondary functions such as 'put colour' and 'hold pen' are required.

As stated earlier, the function should be capable of being expressed by two words – a verb and a noun – and, wherever possible, should have measureable parameters, such as 'prevent rust', 'reduce noise'.

Step 2: Arrange the functions in a tree model

Define the primary functions first and decompose them to lower-level functions. Thus, for the ballpoint pen, the resultant tree might be like that shown in Figure 9.13.

Step 3: Undertake a cost function analysis

A cost function analysis involves breaking down each function into components or general areas and allocating a target or estimated cost to each. A component or area

Figure 9.13 Tree model of pen's function

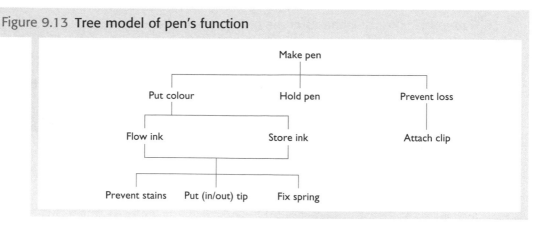

Table 9.6 A cost function analysis of the parts of a ballpoint pen

Part numbers	Names of parts	Functions		Cost (£)
		Transitive verb	*Noun*	
1	Tip	Flow	Ink	0.50
2	Barrel	Hold	Pen	0.70
3	Cartridge	Store	Ink	0.23
4	Top	Store	Ink	0.15
5	Ink	Put	Colour	0.10
6	Cap	Pull in/out	Tip	0.01
7	Spring	Pull in/out	Tip	0.09
8	Stopper	Fix	Spring	0.10
9	Clip	Prevent	Loss	0.10
10	Screw	Attach	Clip	0.02
				2.00

may contribute more than one function. It is important to know how much each component or area contributes to each function. Thus, the initial design for the ballpoint pen could include details of the parts and costs set out in a matrix, as shown in Table 9.6.

From such a matrix, it is possible to account for the total cost of each part by adding them together horizontally and the cost of each function by totalling them vertically. The total cost of each function is usually expressed as a percentage of the total cost of the activity. It is at this stage that the VA team will use its judgement to decide whether the cost of each function is high, reasonable or low – that is, whether or not it represents good value.

It should be noted that, of itself, cost function analysis does not provide savings or solutions. The purpose of such analysis is to:

■ provide the VA team with an in-depth understanding of the VA project by identifying the purpose of each element of cost

Figure 9.14 **The components of the ballpoint pen after redesigning**

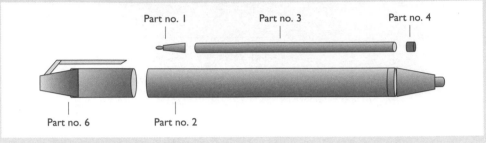

Table 9.7 **Revised cost function analysis of the parts of the redesigned ballpoint pen**

Part numbers	Names of parts	Functions		Cost (£)
		Transitive verb	*Noun*	
1	Tip	Flow	Ink	0.40
2	Barrel	Hold	Pen	0.80
3	Cartridge	Store	Ink	0.23
4	Top	Store	Ink	0.15
5	Ink	Put	Colour	0.10
6	Cap	Pull in/out	Tip	0.01
				1.69

■ indicate what functions provide poor value or where, because of the high cost of a function relative to the total cost of the activity, there is a potential for reducing cost or increasing value.

Assume that, as a result of the cost function analysis, the ballpoint pen is redesigned, using the components shown in Figure 9.14. Also, assume that, by negotiating with suppliers and dealing with new suppliers, the price for Part no. 1 has been reduced, but the cost of Part no. 2 has slightly increased as it now incorporates former Part no. 6. The new cost function matrix is as shown in Table 9.7.

■ The above approach is particularly useful when the aim is to produce an item to a target cost. The aim in the above example might have been to produce a ballpoint pen at a target cost of below £1.75 (the component prices given in the example are for example only and bear no relation to reality).

■ In general, the more components required to make an item, the greater the complexity. The greater the complexity, the greater the cost. Product(s) should therefore be designed with as few components as possible.

■ Wherever possible, standard components should be used. Non-standard components increase costs and reduce flexibility. Standard components can be obtained from many suppliers, with short lead times at low cost and in smaller quantities.

9.11.9 Two simple examples of VA

Example 9.2

Example of VA

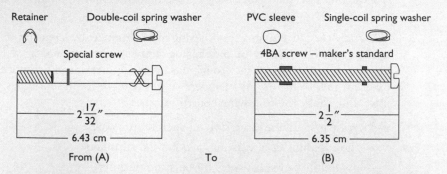

The function of the connecting screw shown in A is to secure parts and carry electrical current, the retainer holding the two items loosely together as a subassembly when the screw is released from a third point.

In B, a maker's standard screw is now in use, the retainer being replaced by a small PVC sleeve. A single-coil spring washer takes the place of the double-coil one. Total saving = 76 per cent.

Example 9.3

Another example of VA

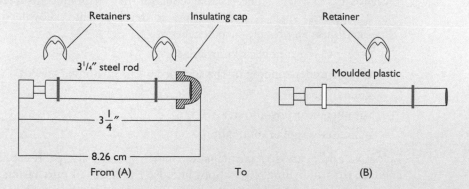

A push rod moving a contact operates against springs under digital pressure. It had been a machined steel rod with two retainers (for the springs) and an insulating cap because, on occasions, direct digital contact would be made (A).

It was decided to mould the rod in plastic, complete with a flange to replace one retainer. The insulating cap is no longer necessary because the rod itself is now an insulator. The cost of the new mould was recovered in less than four months and a total saving made of 60 per cent.

9.11.10 Value and purchasing

Two quotations from Miles,[34] himself a purchasing agent, indicate the close relationship between VE, VA, VM and purchasing:

> Close and extensive relationships must exist between purchasing and value analysis.
>
> Effective value analysis greatly improves the grade and degree of purchasing work and efficient execution of certain purchasing activities greatly improve the degree and amount of value analysis accomplishments.

VA and VE can enhance purchasing performance by creating a value culture that permeates every aspect of purchasing activity. Purchasing, as a boundary-spanning activity, has the opportunity to increase value as a result of its internal interactions and external involvements. As members of a VA team, representatives of purchasing can, inter alia, make the following contributions:

- Provide essential information on such matters as:
  - the capabilities of existing or potential suppliers
  - availability of substitutes for existing outputs
  - quality issues
  - prices and costs of suggested alternatives
  - delivery times
  - legal, economic, ethical and environmental issues
  - make-or-buy decisions.
- Provide a purchasing perspective to contrast with the perspectives of design and production representatives on the value project team.
- Establish buyer–supplier relationships. Purchasing can work closely with suppliers to reduce costs, improve quality and shorten lead times. It can also be a link between the value team and suppliers so that the latter can also be a source of innovation and creativity. Hartley[35] suggests that collaborative arrangements between purchasers and suppliers, such as partnerships, co-development, co-ownership and supplier associations can provide such benefits as:
  - access to the supplier's knowledge
  - greater understanding by the supplier of the customer's needs
  - greater trust
  - suppliers learning about VA
  - increased supplier motivation.

By active and aggressive participation in VA, purchasing professionals will not only enhance their individual reputations but also the status of purchasing throughout their organisation and, often, with suppliers.

Case study

Winstanley Airlines is an international airline with headquarters at London's Heathrow Airport, flying into 110 airports around the world. It operates short- and long-haul flights, operating a range of 777, 747, 737 and Airbus aircraft. Some of the aircraft are over five years old and 45 have had major internal refits of aircraft seating and in-flight catering equipment, including ovens for cooking a variety of hot foods for passengers, cabin crew and flight crew. This case study will concentrate on a quality problem with the ovens.

The contract for the ovens was awarded, after a tendering and an e-auction process. The successful bidder was Ozland Flight Equipment (OFE), situated in Perth, Australia. At the prequalification stage, OFE demonstrated that it had quality accreditation and supplied Quantas, Air New Zealand and South African Airways with complete in-flight catering equipment. References were taken up and very positive feedback was received.

It is nine months since the last of the 45 aircraft was refitted. The first aircraft was refitted 14 months ago. There has been a series of incidents in the past six weeks. This has affected 14 aircraft and, in all instances, the ovens have failed in flight. This equipment is not safety critical and would not lead to the mandatory grounding of an aircraft. There has been a flood of complaints received by the catering department of Winstanley Airlines and the chief executive officer. Specifically, air crew have threatened a strike, first-class and business-class passengers are irate and other passengers have registered complaints. The airline has issued vouchers to a total value of £85,000 to passengers as a goodwill gesture.

You are the buyer now responsible for resolving the quality issue with OFE. Your quality manager has produced a report in which it is alleged that the oven wiring system is faulty, causing cut-outs. He has attributed the problem to the actual wiring, which is stamped 'OKRC KOREA'. The ovens were supplied and installed by OFE. Winstanley Airlines has no spare ovens and has removed 10 of the OFE ovens and rewired them, at a cost of £3000 each, including wiring and labour. You have contacted OFE by e-mail and its response is not encouraging:

> Thank you for drawing this matter to our attention. We confirm that at the time of installation and acceptance the wiring was in working condition. If Winstanley Airlines rewires our ovens it will invalidate the product warranty. If you return the alleged faulty ovens to our Perth factory, we will conduct, at your cost, a full quality inspection. After that time, we will forward our report. At this stage we do not wish to predict an outcome. We can make available, on a conference call, our Manufacturing Manager, obviously by arrangement.

Task

It is vital that this matter is resolved at the earliest opportunity and you should prepare an ideal action plan to fully resolve the quality problem. Your plan should include consideration of the fact that your aircraft are continually in various parts of the world. What elements would you take into account? What would be your ideal solution?

Discussion questions

9.1 Can you identify the role of procurement in managing quality throughout the complete cycle of events from specification through to end-of-life of a product?

9.2 What is the difference between an output specification and a prescriptive specification? Which one would you believe a supplier would prefer and why?

9.3 Take two similar products, such as two washing machines or two vacuum cleaners and compare them to Garvin's eight dimensions of quality. On the basis of your comparison, recommend which of the two you consider gives the best value for money.

9.4 An important aspect of *kaizen* is the creation of a quality culture. One definition of 'culture' is:

'The system of shared values, beliefs and habits within an organisation, that interacts with the formal structure to produce behavioural norms.'

(a) How would you go about creating a quality culture?
(b) How might a quality culture sometimes clash with marketing and production cultures?

9.5 With what 'quality guru' do you associate the following?
(a) quality loss function
(b) *poka-yoke*
(c) 'It is always cheaper to do the job right first time.'
(d) 'Quality is fitness for purpose.'
(e) robust design.

9.6 Are there different quality considerations when you purchase a service as opposed to a manufactured good?

9.7 What are Purdy's four principles that should be observed by all specification writers?

9.8 BS 7373: 3:2005 suggests ten headings for a specification. How many can you recall?

9.9 Standards have roughly five areas of application. What are they?

9.10 If you are purchasing an off-the-shelf software product, how do you know what quality standard has been applied in its production?

9.11 When buyers negotiate a price they are certain to reduce the quality! Do you agree?

9.12 An international airline may purchase meals from suppliers in many different countries. The suppliers will purchase the ingredients from many suppliers. How is it possible to manage quality in such a complex business?

9.13 A manufacturer of high-performance, high-quality automotives has recently had new vehicles catching fire when being driven. The manufacturer has decided to call in all 250 cars that have been sold. What are the implications if:
(a) the fault is due to a manufacturing problem in their own factory?
(b) the fault is due to a part supplied by a strategic supplier?

9.14 How would you define FMEA? What are the main objectives of FMEA?

9.15 What is a definition of value management? What contribution does procurement make to the overall performance of an organisation?

9.16 The US DoD has applied value engineering to a wide range of purchases. How would you approach applying value engineering to the following facets:
(a) learning and development?
(b) construction work?
(c) facilities management?
(d) hire of vehicles?

9.17 If a company providing your organisation with a range of back-office services did not have ISO 9001:2008 registration, what arguments would you use to persuade them to do so?

9.18 Quality of services and products is an essential contractual requirement. What do your terms and conditions of contract say about quality?

9.19 If you were asked to head a quality inspection of a strategic supplier how would you approach each of the following:
   (a) those who should be part of the inspection team?
   (b) the role of procurement?
   (c) the evidence that you would require to prove compliance with all the specification requirements?
   (d) the benefits of 'spot' inspections?

9.20 What exactly does the term 'cost of quality' mean? Can you give ten examples of the cost of quality?

Past examination questions

1 The design department of Mouse-It, a light engineering company, has developed a new mousetrap for a growing number of households that are reluctant to kill or injure mice for ethical reasons.

   The new mousetrap consists of a tube, both to locate the bait (mice prefer chocolate to cheese), and also to contain the mouse and prevent its escape until it is relocated by the householder. The unique selling point of this development is that it saves the householder from either walking or driving a long distance to release the mouse as it is well known that mice will return to their territory.

   Highly sophisticated devices incorporated by the design team not only restrain the mouse but also disorientate it to such an extent that it will happily establish new territory very close to the release site. These devices are very expensive and the marketing department reports that, however revolutionary and innovative the product might be, there is simply no market for it.

Tasks

   (a) Outline **three** reasons for early involvement of the purchasing function in the development of the new mousetrap.
   (b) If it is decided that a value analysis exercise is to be conducted on the new mousetrap, state **four** business functions that should be represented.
   (c) Explain how the purchasing department may help reduce the cost to make the product in order to make it more marketable.

   CIPS, *An Introduction to Purchasing Strategy*, May 2007

2 Explain **five** consequences of defective quality in the supply chain.

   CIPS, *An Introduction to Purchasing Strategy*, November 2009

3 Identify **five** functions or departments that are typically involved in a team which seeks to improve product quality.

   CIPS, *An Introduction to Purchasing Strategy*, May 2010

4 Identify **five** principles of total quality management.

   CIPS, *The Business Environment for Purchasing and Supply*, May 2008

References

[1] Crosby, P. B., *Quality is Free*, Mentor Books, 1980, p. 15

[2] Juran, J. M., *Quality Control Handbook*, 3rd edn, McGraw-Hill, 1974, section 2, p. 27

[3] Garvin, D. A., 'What does product quality really mean?', *Sloan Management Review*, Fall, 1984, pp. 25–38

[4] Garvin, D. A., 'Competing in eight dimensions of quality', *Harvard Business Review*, November/December, No. 6, 1987, p. 101

[5] Logothetis, N., *Managing Total Quality*, Prentice Hall, 1991, pp. 216–17

[6] As 3 above

[7] DTI, *Total Quality Management and Effective Leadership*, 1991, p. 8

[8] Evans, J. R., *Applied Production and Operations Management*, 4th edn, 1993, p. 837

[9] See Table 9.1

[10] See Table 9.1

[11] As 3 above, p. 10

[12] Cannon, S., 'Supplying the service to the internal customer', *Purchasing and Supply Management*, April, 1995, pp. 32–5

[13] Zaire, M., *Total Quality Management for Engineers*, Woodhead Publishing, 1991, p. 193

[14] As 13 above, p. 216

[15] BSI, *British Standards Specification* (BS) 7373

[16] Purdy, D. C., *A Guide to Writing Successful Engineering Specifications*, McGraw-Hill, 1991

[17] The Office of Government Commerce, 'Specification writing', *CUP Guidance Note 30*, CUP, 1991

[18] British Standards Institute, 21 December, 2005, ISBN 0580474372

[19] As 16 above

[20] England, W. B., *Modern Procurement*, 5th edn, Richard D. Irwin, 1970, p. 306

[21] Haslam, J. M., 'Writing engineering specifications', E. and F. N. Spon, 1988, p. 31

[22] Woodroffe, G., 'So farewell then market overt', *Purchasing and Supply Management*, February, 1995, pp. 16–17

[23] Ashton, T. C., 'National and International Standards', in Lock, D. (ed.) *Gower Handbook of Quality Management*, 2nd edn, 1994, pp. 144–5

[24] Rhodes, J. and Fallon, E., *Information on Standards: A Guide to Sources*, British Library, London, 1988

[25] BS EN ISO 8402 1995, section 3.5, pp. 25–6

[26] BS EN ISO 8402 1995, section 3.4, p. 25

[27] Schonberger, R. J., *Building a Chain of Customers*, Free Press, 1992

[28] Taguchi, G., *Introduction to Quality Engineering*, Asian Productivity Organisation, 1986, p. 1

[29] Ford Motor Co. Ltd, *Failure Mode and Effects Analysis Handbook*, 1992, p. 22

[30] As 28 above, pp. 24–5

[31] See website www.Brian Farrington.com

[32] BSI 'PD6663:2000 Guidelines to BS EN 12973 Value Management', BSI, 2000, p. 26

[33] Miller, J., 'The evolution of value analysis', NAPM, *Insights*, 1 December, 1993, pp. 13–14. Original source of this checklist was George Fridholm Associates

[34] Miles, D., *Techniques of Value and Value Engineering*, 3rd edn, McGraw-Hill, 1989, p. 243

[35] Hartley, J. L., 'Collaborative value analysis: experiences from the automotive industry', *Journal of Supply Management*, Fall, 2000, pp. 27–36

Chapter 10

Matching supply with demand

Learning outcomes

With reference to purchasing and supply management, this chapter aims to provide an understanding of:

- inventory and inventory management
- the impact of inventory on working capital
- the tools of inventory management
- dependent and independent demand
- 'push', 'pull' and hybrid demand systems
- inventory control
- engagement of the supplier in inventory decisions.

Key ideas

- Inventory classifications.
- ABC analysis.
- Barcoding and RFID technology.
- Acquisition, holding and stockout costs.
- Safety stocks.
- Approaches to forecasting.
- Economic order quantities (EOQs) and periodic systems.
- Just-in-time (JIT) systems and their objectives.
- JIT II.
- MRP, MRP II, ERP, DRP and VMI systems.

10.1 Inventory, logistics and supply chain management

The Institute of Logistics and Transport[1] defines inventory as:

A term used to describe:

- all the goods and materials held by an organisation for sale or use
- a list of items held in stock.

An alternative definition is:[2]

> Materials in a supply chain or in a segment of a supply chain, expressed in quantities, locations and/or values (synonym stock).

As shown in Figure 3.2, inventory and its management are related both to materials management (MM) and physical distribution management (PDM). MM and PDM together constitute logistics management, or the process of managing both the movement and storage of goods and materials from their source to the point of ultimate consumption. As logistics is an aspect of the wider subject of supply chain management (SCM), it follows that inventory is a key business consideration in the attempt to achieve supply chain optimisation. As indicated in section 3.5, control of inventory is also an important element in demand management, which constitutes one of the eight supply chain processes identified by the International Centre for Competitive Excellence. In this chapter, inventory and demand management are considered primarily from the standpoints of materials management and production.

10.2 Reasons for keeping inventory

Notwithstanding such developments as just-in-time (JIT), discussed later in this chapter, computer-based production methods and the aims of lean production, a number of reasons may be deduced for all organisations keeping some inventory. These include wanting to:

- reduce the risk of supplier failure or uncertainty – safety and buffer stocks are held to provide some protection against such contingencies as strikes, transport breakdowns due to floods or other adverse weather conditions, crop failures, wars and similar factors

- protect against lead time uncertainties, such as where supplier's replenishment and lead times are not known with certainty – in such cases an investment in safety stocks is necessary if customer service is to be maintained at acceptable levels

- meet unexpected demands, or, demands for customisation of products as with agile production

- smooth seasonal or cyclical demand

- take advantage of lots or purchase quantities in excess of what is required for immediate consumption to take advantage of price and quantity discounts

- hedge against anticipated shortage and price increases, especially in times of high inflation or as a deliberate policy of speculation

- ensure rapid replenishment of items in constant demand, such as maintenance supplies and office stationery.

10.3 Inventory classifications

The term 'supplies' has been defined as:[3]

> All the materials, goods and services used in the enterprise regardless of whether they are purchased outside, transferred from another branch of the company or manufactured in-house.

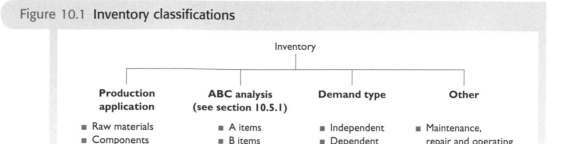

Figure 10.1 **Inventory classifications**

The classification of supplies for inventory purposes will vary according to the particular organisation/business. In a manufacturing enterprise, for example, inventory might be classified as:

- raw materials – steel, timber, cloth and so on in an unprocessed state awaiting conversion into a product
- components and sub-assemblies – ball bearings, gearboxes, and so on that are to be incorporated into an end product
- consumables – all supplies in an undertaking classified as indirect and that do not form part of a saleable product and that may be subclassified into production (such as detergents), maintenance (such as lubricating oil), office (such as stationery), welfare (such as first-aid supplies) and so on – all of which are often referred to as maintenance, repair and operating (MRO) items
- finished goods – products manufactured for resale that are ready for dispatch.

Following supply chain usage, inventory may also be classified into:

- primary inventory – raw materials, components and sub-assemblies, work-in-progress (WIP) and finished goods
- support inventories – MRO consumables of various categories.

A third classification is shown in Figure 10.1.

10.4 Scope and aims of inventory management

10.4.1 The scope of inventory management

Inventory management covers a wide variety of activities. These activities will vary from organisation to organisation. The scope of inventory management will also be influenced according to whether it is primarily concerned with MM or PDM or centralised or decentralised. There is clearly a significant difference in the complexity of managing inventory based at a single location and that where inventory is located at possibly hundreds of distribution centres. Globalisation is another factor that increases the complexity of inventory management. Irrespective of such considerations, however, inventory management is likely to be comprised of such activities as:

- demand management – ensuring that required operational and maintenance supplies are available in the right quantities and at the right time
- forecasting future demand requirements
- managing items with difficult supply and demand patterns related to seasonal demand, changes in end use applications or meeting demands for the customisation of products
- reviewing safety stock levels and controlling minimum and maximum amounts of inventory in terms of both quantity and value
- implementing lean inventory policies, such as JIT contracts to minimise investment in inventory
- liaising with purchasing to ensure that supplies are replenished in accordance with corporate and procurement policies
- developing cost-effective systems and procedures relating to the ordering, procurement and budgeting of supplies
- controlling the receipt, inspection (where necessary), recording, location and issue of supplies to users
- ensuring the safety and security of supplies and the avoidance of loss as a result of deterioration, theft, waste and obsolescence
- coordination of inventory to ensure that supplies can be rapidly located
- variety reduction and standardisation of inventory
- preparation and interpretation of reports on stock levels, stock usage and surplus stock
- liaison with auditors regarding all aspects of inventory
- appropriate disposal of scrap, surplus and obsolete items.

10.4.2 The aims of inventory management

The four main aims of inventory management are to:

- provide both internal and external customers with the required service levels in terms of quantity and order rate fill
- ascertain present and future requirements for all types of inventory to avoid overstocking while avoiding 'bottlenecks' in production
- keep costs to a minimum by variety reduction, economical lot sizes and analysis of costs incurred in obtaining and carrying inventories
- provide upstream and downstream inventory visibility in the supply chain.

10.5 Some tools of inventory management

ABC analysis, barcoding, radio frequency identification (RFID) and inventory software are four important tools of inventory management.

10.5.1 ABC analysis

A household will buy many different items in the course of a year. The weekly shopping will include a number of basic food items, such as bread, milk, vegetables and so on. These basic food items may account for the bulk of the annual expenditure in shops. Because these items are so important in the household budget, it is worth taking care to choose a shop that gives good value. Information about the prices charged elsewhere can be obtained from advertisements and visits to other retail outlets. In ABC analysis these items are known as Class A items. They merit close day-to-day control because of their budgetary importance.

Other items, such as replacement rubber washers for water taps, may be needed occasionally. A packet of washers costs between 30 and 50 pence. Spending hours comparing the prices of these at different suppliers does not make economic sense. The possible saving is, at most, a few pence and a year or more may elapse before another packet is needed. Items like these that account for only a small proportion of spending, are known as Class C items.

Class B is the set of items that is intermediate between Class A and Class C. They should be regularly reviewed but are not as closely controlled as Class A items.

The Italian statistician Vilfredo Pareto (1848–1923) discovered a common statistical effect. About 20 per cent of the population own 80 per cent of the nation's wealth. About 20 per cent of employees cause 80 per cent of problems. About 20 per cent of items account for 80 per cent of a firm's expenditure. The two terms 'Pareto analysis' and 'ABC analysis' are used interchangeably.

Table 10.1 summarises the main points of ABC analysis. In the table, the term 'usage' means the value in money terms of the stock items consumed.

Table 10.1 ABC analysis

	Percentage of items	Percentage value of annual usage	
Class A items	About 20%	About 80%	Close day-to-day control
Class B items	About 30%	About 15%	Regular review
Class C items	About 50%	About 5%	Infrequent review

The following example illustrates how items may be divided into classes A, B or C.

Example 10.1

ABC analysis

A purchasing department surveyed the ten most commonly used components last year.

Item number	101	102	103	104	105	106	107	108	109	110
Unit cost (pence)	5	11	15	8	7	16	20	4	9	12
Annual demand	48,000	2,000	300	800	4,800	1,200	18,000	300	5,000	500

▶

Step 1

Calculate the annual usage in £s and the usage of each item as a percentage of the total cost.

Item number	Unit cost (pence)	Annual demand	Usage (£) $\dfrac{Demand \times Cost}{100}$	Usage as % of total $= \dfrac{Usage \times 100}{Total}$
101	5	48,000	2400	32.5%
102	11	2,000	220	3.0%
103	15	300	45	0.6%
104	8	800	64	0.9%
105	7	4,800	336	4.5%
106	16	1,200	192	2.6%
107	20	18,000	3600	48.8%
108	4	300	12	0.2%
109	9	5,000	450	6.1%
110	12	500	60	0.8%
Total usage			7379	

Step 2

Sort the items by usage as a percentage of the total. Calculate the cumulative percentage and classify the items (see Table 10.2).

Table 10.2 **Calculations for step 2**

Item number	Cumulative % of items(*)	Unit cost (pence)	Annual demand	Usage (£)	% of total	Cumulative % of total	Classification
107	10	20	18,000	3600	48.8	48.8	A
101	20	5	48,000	2400	32.5	81.3	A
109	30	9	5,000	450	6.1	87.4	B
105	40	7	4,800	336	4.5	91.9	B
102	50	11	2,000	220	3.0	94.9	B
106	60	16	1,200	192	2.6	97.5	B
104	70	8	800	64	0.9	98.4	C
110	80	12	500	60	0.8	99.2	C
103	90	15	300	45	0.6	99.8	C
108	100	4	300	12	0.2	100.0	C

* Column 2 – There are 10 items, so each item accounts for 10/100 = 10% of usage

Step 3

Report your findings (see Table 10.3).

Table 10.3 **Results of calculations for step 3**

Items	Item number	Percentage of items	Percentage usage	Action
A	107, 101	20	81.3	Close control
B	109, 105, 102, 106	40	16.2	Regular review
C	104, 110, 103, 108	40	2.5	Infrequent review

Step 4

Illustrate your report with a diagram if required. The diagram is a percentage ogive and is called a Pareto diagram. This is done by plotting the cumulative percentage usage against the cumulative percentage of items. The data needed has been extracted to create Table 10.4.

Table 10.4 **Data for Pareto diagram for step 4**

Item number	107	101	109	105	102	106	104	110	103	108
Cumulative % items	10	20	30	40	50	60	70	80	90	100
Cumulative % usage	48.8	81.3	87.4	91.9	94.9	97.5	98.4	99.2	99.8	100
Classification	A	A	B	B	B	B	C	C	C	C

In practice, there may be hundreds of items in inventory and use. Computer software can easily determine the percentage of annual usage for each item and sort the items into A, B or C categories.

10.5.2 Barcoding

Invented in the 1950s, barcodes accelerate the flow of products and information throughout business. The most familiar example of the use of barcodes is electronic point of sale (EPOS), which is when retail sales are recorded by scanning product barcodes at checkout tills. An EPOS system verifies, checks and charges transactions, provides instant sales reports, monitors and changes prices and sends intra-store and inter-store messages and data.

Some production applications for barcoding include:

- counting raw materials and finished goods inventories
- automatic sorting of cartons and bins on conveyor belts and palletisers
- lot tracking
- production reporting
- automatic warehouse applications, including receiving, put away, picking and shipping
- identification of production bottlenecks
- package tracking
- access control
- tool cribs and spare parts issue.

Barcoding provides the following benefits:

- *Faster data entry* – barcode scanners can record data five to seven times as fast as a skilled typist.
- *Greater accuracy* – keyboard data entry creates an average of one error in 300 keystrokes, but barcode entry has an error rate of about 1 in 3 million.
- *Reduced labour costs* – as a result of time saved and increased productivity.

- *Elimination of costly overstocking or understocking* and the increased efficiency of JIT inventory systems.

- *Better decision making* – barcode systems can easily capture information that would be difficult to collect in other ways, which helps managers to make fully informed decisions.

- *Faster access to information.*

- *The ability to automate warehousing.*

- *Greater responsiveness to customers and suppliers.*

10.5.3 Radio frequency identification (RFID)

An RFID tag contains a silicon chip that carries an identification number and an antenna able to transmit the number to a reading device. This means improved inventory management and replenishment practices, which, in turn, results in a reduction of interrupted production or lost sales due to items being out of stock.

The reduction in the cost of silicon chips to a point where they can be used to track high-volume, low-cost stores and individual items rather than an aggregate SKU (stock keeping unit) is revolutionary in its implications for inventory control and intelligence.

The following advantages and limitations of RFID technology are listed by GS1 UK.[4]

Advantages

- *Line of sight* – tags can be read without being visible to the scanner. They can be read as long as they pass through the field emitted by the reader. This reduces manual handling and, therefore, cost.

- *Range* – tags can be read over a very long range – many hundreds of metres in the case of specialised tags. RFID devices used in mass logistics applications need a range of at least 1 metre and up to 4 or 5 metres.

- *Bulk read* – many tags can be read in a short space of time – a typical read rate is hundreds of tags per second.

- *Selectivity* – data can be inserted into the tags so that they are only read if the value requested from the reader is the same as the value embedded within the tag. This allows the reader to read only pallets or only outer cases.

- *Durability* – barcodes can be ripped, soiled and performance is impaired if they become wet. These are not issues that affect RFID tags.

- *Read/write* – data incorporated within the tags can be updated to accommodate simple changes in status – such as 'paid for' or 'not paid for' retail electronic article surveillance tags – or more complicated information, such as a car's warranty and service history.

Limitations

- *Cost* – RFID tags will always be more expensive than barcodes. The cost is offset by the extra business benefits that RFID technology can provide. It is envisaged that the cost of tags will drop dramatically as production volumes are increased.

- *Moisture* – depending on the frequency used, radio waves may be absorbed by moisture in the product or the environment.

- *Metal* – radio waves are distorted by metal. This means that tags might be unable to be read if there is metal within packaging or the environment (warehouse automation).
- *Electrical interference* – electronic noise, such as fluorescent lights or electric motors, may produce interference with radio frequency communications.
- *Accuracy* – it can be difficult to identify and read specific tags separately from all the others that are within the range of the reader. For example, when attempting to read a tag identifying a pallet, the reader may also read the tags on all the cases on the pallet as well.
- *Overcompensation* – additional data stored within the tag will provide functionality. However, this will increase both the cost of the tag and the time required to read it.
- *Security* – the ability to write information into tags is one of the main benefits of RFID technology. The mechanism required, however, needs to be secure to ensure that rogue parties are unable to write false information into the tag.

10.5.4 Software

Numerous software programs are available, providing complete inventory and stock management systems. Such software can provide such facilities as maintaining supplier and customer databases, create picking lists and receipts, provide instantaneous stock balances and automatic reordering, barcode reading, support grouping of inventory items, remove barriers between suppliers and customers, enhance profitability and implement such approaches as JIT, MRO, ERP, DRP and VMI, described later in this chapter.

10.6 The economics of inventory

The economics of inventory management and stock control are determined by an analysis of the costs incurred in obtaining and carrying inventories under the following headings.

10.6.1 Acquisition costs

Many of the costs incurred in placing an order are incurred irrespective of the order size, so, for example, the cost of an order will be the same irrespective of whether 1 or 1000 tonnes are ordered. Ordering costs include:

- preliminary costs – preparing the requisition, vendor selection, administering the procurement process
- placement costs – order preparation, stationery, postage
- post-placement costs – progressing, receipt of goods, materials, handling, inspection, certification and payment of invoices.

In practice, it is difficult to obtain more than an approximate idea of ordering costs as these vary according to:

- the complexity of the order and the seniority of staff involved
- whether order preparation is manual or computerised
- whether or not repeat orders cost less than initial orders.

Sometimes the total cost of a purchasing department or function over a given period is divided by the number of orders placed in that time. This gives a completely false figure as the average cost per order reduces as the number of orders placed increases, which may be indicative of inefficiency rather than the converse.

10.6.2 Holding costs

There are two types of holding costs:

- *cost proportional to the value of the inventory* such as:
  - financial costs, such as interest on capital tied up in inventory, which may be bank rate or, more realistically, the target return on capital required by the enterprise
  - cost of insurance
  - losses in value due to deterioration, obsolescence and pilfering.
- *cost proportional to the physical characteristics of inventory* such as:
  - storage costs – storage space, stores' space charges, light, heat and power
  - labour costs, relating to handling and inspection
  - clerical costs, relating to stores' records and documentation.

10.6.3 Cost of stockouts

The costs of stockouts – the costs of being out of inventory – include:

- loss of production output
- costs of idle time and of fixed overheads spread over a reduced level of output
- costs of any action taken to deal with the stockout, such as buying from another stockist at an enhanced price, switching production, obtaining substitute materials
- loss of customer goodwill due to the inability to supply or late delivery.

Often the costs of stockouts are hidden in overhead costs. Where the costs of individual stockouts are computed, these should be expressed in annual figures to ensure compatibility with acquisition and holding costs. Costs of stockouts are difficult to estimate or incorporate into inventory models.

10.7 Inventory performance measures

A number of key performance indicators (KPIs) have been devised to measure the extent to which an undertaking has the right quantity of inventory in the right place at the right time. Some of the most useful performance indicators are the following.

- *Lead times* – the length of time taken to obtain or supply a requirement from the time a need is ascertained to the time the need is satisfied.
- *Service levels* – the actual service level attained in a given period, which can be ascertained from the formula:

$$\frac{\text{Number of times the item is provided on demand}}{\text{Number of times the item has been demanded}}$$

Service levels are closely related to safety stocks, as shown later.

- *Rate of stock turn* – this indicates the number of times that a stock item has been sold and replaced in a given period and is calculated by the formula:

$$\frac{\text{Sales or issues}}{\text{Average inventory (at selling price)}}$$

What is considered a good stock turn varies by product and industry. Turnover of supermarket breakfast foods is 20–25 times that of pet foods. For car showrooms, a stock turn of six means that, on average, the stock of a particular car changes every two months.

- *Stockouts in a given period* – this can be expressed as a percentage of the total stock population during a given period.

- *Stock cover* – this is the opposite of stock turn and indicates the number of days the current stock of a stock keeping unit (SKU) will last if sales or usage continues at the anticipated rate. As an historic figure, it can be calculated by dividing the rate of stock turn into the yearly number of working days or 365 to give the average days' cover. For a simple SKU it can be calculated as:

$$\text{Days' stock coverage} = \frac{\text{Current quantity in stock}}{\text{Anticipated future daily rate of usage or sales}}$$

The ratio can be used to evaluate the effect of longer lead times or the danger of imminent stockouts.

10.8 Safety stocks and service levels

Safety stock is needed to cover shortages due to the agreed lead time being exceeded or the actual demand being greater than that anticipated.

Figure 10.2 shows that the service levels and safety stock are related. Thus, by increasing the investment on inventory, service levels can be increased.

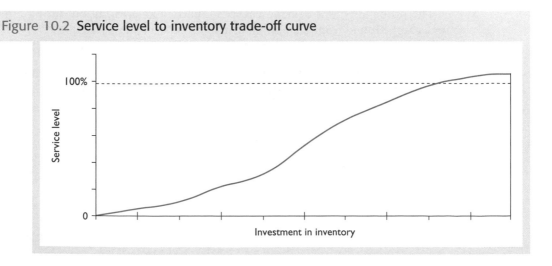

Figure 10.2 **Service level to inventory trade-off curve**

Figure 10.3 **The normal distribution curve**

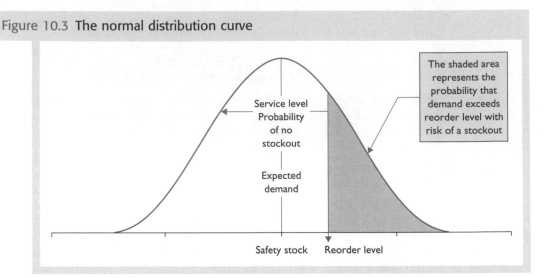

For single items, an extra investment in inventory (higher levels of safety stock) will always increase customer service levels. Conversely, higher service levels imply larger quantities of safety stocks and an increased investment in inventory.

It is not possible to achieve 100 per cent service levels for the total inventory. High levels of safety stocks for all items would be uneconomical and the costs would be prohibitive.

JIT implies a low level of or zero inventory. This is achieved by removing uncertainty regarding supply. Safety stock is a cost-adding factor and so should, as far as possible, be eliminated.

If the uncertainty regarding supply cannot be eliminated, safety stocks are required.

In practice, the items that have high stockout costs can be identified by ABC analysis and, for such items, an acceptable risk of stockout should be determined.

Statistical theory provides methods for ensuring that the chances of a stockout do not exceed an acceptable risk level.

The probability that demand exceeds a particular distribution during a given lead time can be found from the normal distribution (see Figure 10.3).

Tables of this distribution, such as Table 10.5, are found in statistics textbooks.

■ For each SKU, find the data on which the order was placed and the date of delivery. From stores' records, calculate the demand between these dates.

■ Find the mean or arithmetic average demand during the lead time:

$$\text{Mean(x)} = \frac{\text{Sum of the demands}}{\text{Number of lead times}} = \frac{\Sigma x}{n}$$

■ Calculate the standard deviation (s or σ) of demand from the formulae:

$$\sigma = \sqrt{\frac{\Sigma(x - \bar{x})^2}{n-1}} \quad \text{or} \quad \sigma = \sqrt{\frac{\Sigma x^2 - \dfrac{(\Sigma x)^2}{n}}{n-1}}$$

Table 10.5 Probabilities table

Reorder levels in standard deviations above the mean	Service level %	Probability of a stockout %
1.00	84.13	15.87
1.05	85.31	14.69
1.10	86.43	13.57
1.15	87.49	12.51
1.20	88.49	11.51
1.25	89.44	10.56
1.30	90.32	9.68
1.35	91.15	8.85
1.40	91.92	8.08
1.45	92.65	7.35
1.50	93.32	6.68
1.55	93.94	6.06
1.60	94.52	5.48
1.65	95.05	4.95
1.70	95.54	4.46
1.75	95.99	4.01
1.80	96.41	3.59
1.85	96.78	3.22
1.90	97.13	2.87
1.95	97.44	2.56
2.00	97.72	2.28
2.05	97.98	2.02
2.10	98.21	1.79
2.15	98.42	1.58
2.20	98.61	1.39
2.25	98.78	1.22
2.30	98.93	1.07
2.35	99.06	0.94
2.40	99.18	0.82
2.45	99.29	0.71
2.50	99.38	0.62
2.55	99.46	0.54
2.60	99.53	0.47
2.65	99.60	0.40
2.70	99.65	0.35
2.75	99.70	0.30
2.80	99.74	0.26
2.85	99.78	0.22
2.90	99.81	0.19
2.95	99.84	0.16
3.00	99.87	0.13

or by using the statistical functions on your calculator or spreadsheet. In simple terms, calculating the standard deviation involves the following steps:

1 Determine the mean (average (x)) of the set of numbers:

$$1, 2, 3, 4, 5 = \frac{15}{5} = x = 3$$

2 Determine the difference between each number and the mean:

$$(1) = -2, (2) = -1, (3) = 0, (4) = +1, (5) = +2$$

3 Square each difference:

$$+4 \quad +1 \quad 0 \quad +1 \quad +4 \quad = \quad 10$$

4 Calculate the square root of $10/(n-1) = \sqrt{(10/4)} = \sqrt{2.5}$

$$\text{Standard deviation } (\sigma) = 1.58$$

The reorder level required and stockout probability can then be found from Table 10.5.

Example 10.2

Calculating the required reorder level

The average (mean) demand is 10. A 99 per cent service level is required – that is, the probability of stockout is 1 per cent or less. Assume an average reorder level of 140.

Table 10.5 shows that, for a service level of 99.1 per cent, the reorder level should be 2.35 standard deviations above the mean.

Thus, the reorder level is $140 + (2.35 \times 10) = 163.5$ or 164.

10.9 The right quantity

In manufacturing or assembly-type organisations, the most important factors that determine the right quantity are as follows:

- The demand for the final product into which the bought-out materials and components are incorporated.
- The inventory policy of the undertaking.
- Whether job, batch, assembly or process production methods are applicable.
- Whether demand for the item is independent or dependent (see section 10.10 below).
- The service level – that is, the incidence of availability required. The service level required for an item may be set at 100 per cent for items where a stockout would result in great expense due to production delays or, as with some hospital supplies, where lack of supplies may endanger life. For less crucial supplies, the service level might be fixed at a lower level, such as 95 per cent. The actual service level attained in a given period can be computed by the formula:

$$\frac{\text{Number of times the item is provided on demand in period}}{\text{Number of times an item has been demanded in period}}$$

- Market conditions, such as financial, political and other considerations that determine whether or not requirements shall be purchased on a 'hand-to-mouth' or 'forward' basis.
- Factors determining economic order quantities (see section 10.13.2 below). In individual undertakings, the quantity of an item to be purchased over a period may be ordered or notified to purchasing in several ways, as shown in Table 10.6.

Table 10.6 Purchasing and quantities

Type of purchase	Indicators of quantities
Materials or components required for a specific order or application, such as steel sections not normally stocked	■ Material specifications or bill of material for the job or contract
Standard items kept in stock for regular production, whether job, batch or continuous flow	■ Materials budgets derived from production budgets based on sales/output target for a specified period ■ One-off material specifications or bills of materials showing quantities of each item needed to make one unit of finished product. These are then multiplied by the number of products to be manufactured ■ Material requisitions raised by storekeeping or stock control ■ Computerised reports provided at specified intervals – daily, weekly – relating to part usage, stocks on hand, on order and committed. With some programs, reordering can be carried out automatically
Consumable materials used in production, plant, maintenance or office administration, such as oil, paint, stationery and packing materials	■ Requisitions from stores or stock control or computerised inventory reports as above. These may be ordered directly by users against previously negotiated contracts or purchasing consortia arrangements
Spares – these may be kept to maintain production machinery or bought-out components for resale to customers who have bought the product in which the component is incorporated	■ Requisitions from sales department ■ Computerised inventory reports as above

10.10 The nature of demand

When forecasting the future requirements for supplies, we have to distinguish between independent demand and dependent demand.

The main points of difference are set out in Table 10.7.

Table 10.7 The main differences between independent and dependent demand

Independent demand	Dependent demand
Independent demand items are finished goods or other end items	Dependent demand items are typically sub-assemblies or components used during the production of a finished or end product
Demand for independent items cannot be precisely forecast	Demand is derived from the number of units to be produced – for example, demand for 1000 cars will give rise to a derived demand for 5000 car wheels

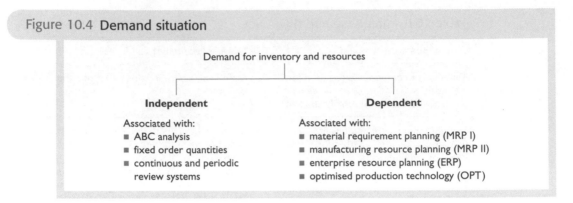

Figure 10.4 **Demand situation**

As shown in Figure 10.4, the distinction between dependent and independent demand is fundamental to inventory management.

10.11 Forecasting demand

10.11.1 What is forecasting?

Forecasting, which may be defined as the prediction of future outcomes, is the basis of all planning and decision making. We listen to the weather forecasts, for example, before planning a picnic. Similarly, the decision to enlarge a factory will be based on a forecast of increased demand for the product manufactured.

Forecasts, however, are rarely spot on, simply because they are always based on assumptions that may be wrong or affected by unforeseen events, such as war, economic and social factors and even the weather. All forecasts, therefore, are subject to uncertainty. This uncertainty will be enhanced as the time horizon of the forecast increases.

10.11.2 Forecasting issues

Forecasting involves asking six basic questions.

1 *What is the purpose of the forecast?* The answer to this question determines the accuracy required and expenditure on the resources necessary to obtain the required information.

2 *What is the time horizon?* All forecasts must have a time limit. Forecasts may be classified as being for the long, medium or short term.

 – Long-term forecasts – with time horizons exceeding two years – usually apply to strategic planning and carry the greatest uncertainty.

 – Medium-term forecasts – with time horizons of between three months and two years – apply to both strategic and tactical planning and carry less uncertainty than long-term forecasts.

 – Short-term forecasts – with time horizons of less than three months – apply to tactical planning and are likely to achieve a high level of accuracy.

The above times are, however, arbitrary and depend on circumstances. Thus, long, medium and short term may equally be one year, between three months and one year and three months respectively.

Figure 10.5 Forecasting techniques

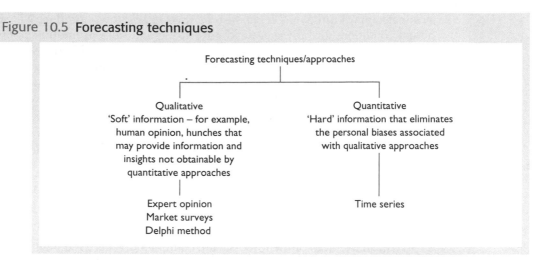

3 *What forecasting technique(s) is/are most appropriate?* See Figure 10.5.

4 *On what data must the forecast be based and how shall it be analysed?* This depends on the purpose of the forecast, the accuracy required and the resources available for forecasting.

5 *In what form shall the completed forecast be presented?* This will normally be in some form of report stating the purpose of the forecast, what assumptions have been made, the forecasting techniques used and the forecasts or conclusions reached.

6 *How accurate is the forecast?* All forecasts should be monitored to ascertain the degree of accuracy achieved. Where actual events are substantially different from those predicted, the forecast, assumptions, techniques and validity of the data must be examined and, where necessary, the original forecast revised.

10.11.3 Forecasting techniques

As shown in Figure 10.5, forecasting techniques or approaches fall into two broad categories.

10.11.4 Qualitative approaches

■ *Expert systems* – gathering judgements or opinions from people with special knowledge or experience. Such people may be executives, external consultants or sales or production personnel who have first-hand experience of what customers require or operating problems encountered. The value of their opinions, however, depends on the knowledge and experience of those giving them. Experts are sometimes wrong.

■ *Test marketing* – this is frequently used as a forecasting technique in connection with new products to ascertain the percentage of customers likely to adopt the product. It may also be used to work out why sales are declining or what aspects of competing products appeal to buyers. It can also be used to see how a product will sell under actual conditions and the success of advertising and sales promotion campaigns. It has been estimated that only about a third of products tested in this way are finally put into production. An extension of test marketing is the market survey, which uses published data and survey techniques to find out what the total market is for all products serving a similar purpose, such as family cars, and the percentage of the market likely to be achieved by an individual manufacturer.

- *Delphi method* – named after the ancient Greek religious site where the gods were believed to communicate answers to humans' questions about the future, this technique involves the following four steps.

1 Estimates or forecasts are solicited from knowledgeable people within a company or industry about the matter under consideration. The names of the people approached are not known to each other.

2 Statistical averages of the forecasts are computed. If there is a high level of agreement about the forecasts, the procedure ends there.

3 If, as often happens, there is considerable divergence between the forecasts, the group averages are presented to the individuals who made the original forecasts, asking them why their forecasts differ from the average or group consensus and asking for new estimates.

4 Steps 2 and 3 are repeated until agreement is reached.

The Delphi method is particularly useful where there is a lack of historical information on which to base a more objective forecast and predict changes in technology.

10.11.5 Quantitative approaches

A *time series* is a set of observations measured at successive times over successive periods. Time series forecasting methods make the assumption that past patterns in data can be used to forecast future data points. Time series demand consists of the following five components:

1 *average* – the mean of the observations over time

2 *trend* – a gradual increase or decrease in the average over time – a trend pattern exists when there is a long-term pattern of growth (upwards trend) or decline (downwards trend) in sales

3 *seasonal influence* – a predictable short-term cycling behaviour due to the time of day, week, month or season, so, for example, sales of swimming costumes are greater in the summer than the winter

4 *cyclical movement* – unpredictable long-term cyclical behaviour due to business or product/service lifecycles. Sales of dishwashers, refrigerators and similar household appliances reflect a fairly constant cyclical pattern

5 *random error* – the remaining variation that cannot be explained by the other four components, such as when sales fluctuate in an erratic manner and reflect inconsistency.

The most frequently used methods of calculating time series are moving averages and exponentially weighted averages.

10.11.6 Moving averages

A *moving average* is an artificially constructed time series in which each annual (or monthly, daily and so on) figure is replaced by the average or mean of itself and values corresponding to a number of preceding and succeeding periods.

Example 10.3

Moving averages

The usage of a stock item for six successive periods was 90, 84, 100, 108, 116 and 127. If a five-period moving average is required, the first term will be:

$$\frac{90 + 84 + 100 + 108 + 116}{5} = 99.6$$

The average for the second term is:

$$\frac{84 + 100 + 108 + 116 + 127}{5} = 107$$

At each step, one term of the original series is dropped and another introduced. The averages, as calculated for each period, will then be plotted on a graph. There is no precise rule about the number of periods to use when calculating a moving average. The most suitable, obtained by trial and error, is that which best smooths out fluctuations. A useful guide is to assess the number of periods between consecutive peaks and troughs and use this.

10.11.7 Exponentially weighted average method (EWAM)

The moving average method has been largely discarded for inventory applications as it has a number of disadvantages:

■ it requires a large number of separate calculations
■ a true forecast cannot be made until the required number of time periods have elapsed
■ all data are equally weighted, but, in practice, the older the demand data, the less relevant it becomes in forecasting future requirements
■ the sensitivity of a moving average is inversely proportional to the number of data values included in the average.

These difficulties are overcome by using a series of weights with decreasing values that converge at infinity to produce a total sum of one. Such a series, known as an *exponential series*, takes the form:

$$a + a(1 - a) + a(1 - a)^2 + a(1 - a)^3 \ldots = 1$$

where a is a constant between 0 and 1.

In practice, the values of 0.1 and 0.2 are most frequently used. Where a small value such as 0.1 is chosen as the constant, the response, based on the average of a considerable number of past periods, will be slow and gradual. A high value – $a = 0.5$ – will result in 'nervous' estimates responding quickly to actual changes. With exponential smoothing, all that is necessary is to adjust the previous forecast by a fraction of the difference between the old forecast and the actual demand for the previous period, that is, the new average forecast is:

$$a \text{ (actual demand)} + (1 - a) \text{ (previous average forcecast)}$$

Example 10.4

Exponentially weighted average

The actual demand for a stock item during the month of January was 300 against a forecast of 280. Assuming a weighting of 0.2, what will be the average demand forecast for February?

Solution

$$0.2(300) + (1 - 0.2)(280) = 60 + 224$$

Forecast for February = 284. By subtracting the average computed for the previous month from that calculated for the current month, we obtain the trend of demand.

10.11.8 The bullwhip effect

All forecasting depends on the reliability of the information on which the forecast is based. The so-called 'bullwhip effect' is the uncertainty caused by information flowing upstream and downstream in the supply chain. In particular, forecasts of demand become less reliable as they move up the supply chain from users or retailers to wholesalers, to manufacturers, to suppliers. Conversely, the forecast demand variability, though present, lessens as the point of forecast moves downstream.

The most common drivers of demand distortion are:

■ unforecasted sales promotions, which have a ripple effect throughout the supply chain

■ sales incentive plans when extended to, say, three months often result in sales distortion

■ lack of customer confidence in the ability of suppliers to deliver orders on time, leading to over ordering

■ cancellation of orders, often resulting from previous over ordering

■ freight incentives, such as transportation discounts for volume orders, that may cause customers to accumulate orders and then order in bulk.

The results of the bullwhip effect are:

■ excessive inventory quantities

■ poor customer service

■ cash flow problems

■ stockouts

■ high material costs, overtime expenses and transport costs.

Example 10.5

Impact of supply disruption due to the bullwhip effect

Customer demand forecast is 40 units.

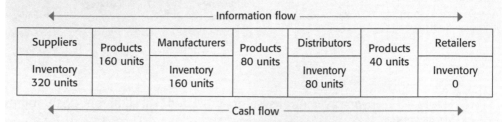

The distributor anticipates a shortage and decides to keep a buffer stock of twice the demand forecast.

To accommodate anticipated demand fluctuations, manufacturers also increase their inventories by twice that required.

The suppliers, at the head of the supply chain, receive the harshest impact of the bullwhip effect. The result is a general lack of coordination throughout the supply chain.

In a worst-case scenario, working capital reduces, costs increase, customer service is unsatisfactory, lead times lengthen, production needs to be rescheduled and sales are lost.

The fundamental approach to resolving the bullwhip problem is to ensure transparency and information sharing throughout the supply chain. Many of the problems can be avoided by relying less on forecasting and more on direct demand data. Supply chain systems that provide open communication and reliable demand data avoid situations in which small demand fluctuations become high variability swings at the production stage.

10.12 'Push' and 'pull' inventories

'Push' and 'pull' inventories derive from push and pull strategies.

A *push strategy* is when products are manufactured in anticipation of demand and production is based on long-term forecasts and, therefore, uncertain. Push-based supply chains are associated with high inventory levels and high manufacturing and transportation costs, due to the need to respond quickly to demand changes.

A *pull strategy* is when products are manufactured to specific orders rather than forecasts. Thus, demand is certain and inventory is low or non-existent. Because information about customer demand is quickly transmitted to the various supply chain participants, the bullwhip effect is avoided.

Push–pull strategies are those in which some (usually the first stages) of the supply chain are operated on a push basis and the remaining stages on a pull basis. The interface between the push-based and pull-based stages is known as the push–pull boundary and occurs at a place somewhere along the supply chain timeline. Postponement, which

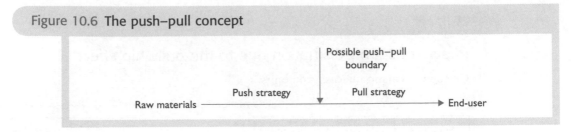

Figure 10.6 **The push–pull concept**

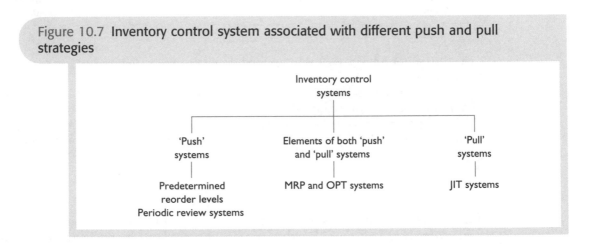

Figure 10.7 **Inventory control system associated with different push and pull strategies**

was mentioned earlier in section 4.6.3, aims to cater for customisation requirements by keeping products in a neutral or uncommitted state for as long as possible and this is a good example of a push–pull strategy. The concept of push–pull is shown in Figure 10.6.

The inventory control systems associated with each of the three above strategies are shown in Figure 10.7.

10.13 Independent demand

The nature of independent demand was discussed in section 10.10 above. Independent demand is related to 'push' systems as (see Figures 10.4 and 10.7) both are concerned with fixed order quantities and periodic review systems.

10.13.1 Fixed order quantities

With fixed order quantities, inventory is replenished with a predetermined quantity of stock every time the inventory falls to a specific order level. The reorder level is the quantity to be used during the lead replenishment time plus a reserve. This level can be calculated by using the formula:

$$\text{Maximum usage} \times \text{Maximum lead time}$$

Thus, if the lead time is 25 to 30 days and the maximum usage in the lead time is 200 units, then the reorder level will be:

$$200 \times 30 = 6000 \text{ units}$$

Reorder levels may be indicated by:

- simple manual methods, such as the two-bin system, which is that the stock of a particular item is kept in two bins and when the first bin is empty, a supply is reordered
- computerised systems, which trigger replacements when inventory has fallen to the specified reorder point – such systems usually use barcoding to record withdrawals from stock.

The fixed quantity is, however, usually based on an economic order quantity (EOQ).

10.13.2 Economic order quantity (EOQ)

The economic order quantity (EOQ) is the optimal ordering quantity for an item of stock that minimises cost.

To calculate the EOQ, a mathematical model of reality must be constructed. All mathematical models make assumptions that simplify reality. The model is only valid when the assumptions are true or nearly true, so, when an assumption is modified or deleted, a new model must be constructed.

The basic (or simple) EOQ model makes the following assumptions:

- demand is uniform – that is, certain, constant and continuous over time
- the lead time is constant and certain
- there is no limit on order size, due either to stores capacity or other constraints
- the cost of placing an order is independent of the size of the order – the delivery charge is also independent of the quantity ordered
- the cost of holding a unit of stock does not depend on the quantity in stock
- all prices are constant and certain – there are no bulk purchase discounts
- exactly the same quantity is ordered each time that a purchase is made.

The two basic types of inventory costs are:

1 acquisition (see section 10.6.1)
2 holding (see section 10.6.2).

There are several ways in which to calculate EOQs, but the basic formula is:

$$EOQ = \sqrt{\frac{2DS}{CI}}$$

where:

EOQ = economic order quantity
C = cost of the item
I = annual carrying cost interest rate
D = annual anticipated demand
S = order cost per order

Example 10.6

Worked example of the basic EOQ formula

Assume the following figures:

- annual demand = 1500 units
- unit cost per item = £10
- cost per order = £50
- carrying cost interest rate = 20 per cent.

Then:

$$EOQ = \sqrt{\frac{2 \times 1500 \times £50}{10 \times 0.20}} = \sqrt{\frac{150,000}{2}} = \sqrt{75,000} = 274$$

In practice, the EOQ would be increased to 300 items ordered five times yearly.

It should be recognised, however, that the EOQ may be misleading for the following reasons:

- annual demand is a forecast, so it is unlikely to be an exact figure
- order costs are assumed to be constant, but these may change due to use or the introduction of e-purchasing
- the interest rate is assumed to be constant, but, in practice, interest rates frequently change
- cost per item is likely to change in the course of a year, so we have to decide whether to use average cost, replacement cost, actual cost or anticipated future cost in the equation.

Many of the criticisms of EOQs derive from inaccurate data inputs, such as exaggerated carrying and order costs. Many ERP packages also have built-in programs that calculate EOQs automatically. Often, these built-in programs need modification to deal with changes in usages and products.

Sometimes EOQs are regarded as being in conflict with JIT approaches, but EOQs can be used to determine what items fit into the JIT model and what level of JIT is economically advantageous to the particular organisation.

While EOQs are not applicable to every inventory situation, they should be considered for repetitive purchasing situations and MRO items.

10.13.3 Periodic review system

As the name implies, in this system an item's inventory position is reviewed periodically rather than at a fixed order point. The periods or intervals at which stock levels are reviewed will depend on the importance of the stock item and the costs of holding that item. A variable quantity will be ordered at each review to bring the stock level back to maximum – hence, the system is sometimes called the 'topping-up' system.

Maximum stock can be determined by adding one review period to the lead time, multiplying the sum by the average rate of usage and adding any safety stock. This can be expressed as:

$$M = W(T + L) + S$$

where:

M = predetermined stock level
W = average rate of stock usage
T = review period
L = lead time
S = safety stock

Safety stock may be calculated in a similar manner to that indicated for the fixed order point system.

Example 10.7

Periodic review system

Assume that:

- average rate of usage is 120 items per day
- review period is 4 weeks – say, 20 days
- lead time is 25 to 30 days
- safety stock is 900 items

$$M = 120 \,(20 + 30) + 900 = 6900 \text{ items}$$

If, at the first review period, the stock was 4000 items, an order would be placed for 2900 items – that is, 6900 maximum stock minus actual stock at the review date.

10.13.4 Advantages and disadvantages of fixed order point and periodic review systems

Fixed order point

Advantages:

- on average, levels of stock are lower than with the periodic review system
- EOQs are applicable
- enhanced responsiveness to demand fluctuations
- replenishment orders are automatically generated at the appropriate time by comparing actual stock levels with reorder levels
- appropriate for widely differing inventory categories.

Disadvantages:

- the reordering system may become overloaded if many items of inventory reach their reorder levels simultaneously
- random reordering pattern, due to items coming up for replenishment at different times.

Periodic review

Advantages:

- greater chance of elimination of obsolete items due to periodic review of stock
- the purchasing load may be spread more evenly, with possible economies in placing of orders
- large quantity discounts may be negotiated when a range of stock items is ordered from the same supplier at the same time
- production economies, due to more efficient production planning and lower set-up costs, may result from orders always being in the same sequence.

Disadvantages:

- on average, larger stocks are required than with fixed order point systems as reorder quantities must provide for the period between reviews as well as between lead times
- reorder quantities are not based on EOQs
- if the usage rate changes shortly after a review period, a stockout may occur before the next review date
- difficulties in determining appropriate review period, unless demands are reasonably consistent.

10.13.5 Choice of systems

- A fixed order point system is more appropriate if a stock item is used regularly and does not conform to the conditions for periodic review systems.
- A periodic review system is most likely to be appropriate if orders are placed with and delivered from suppliers at regular intervals, such as daily, monthly, or a number of different items are ordered from and delivered by the same supplier at the same time.

10.14 Dependent demand

Dependent demand is associated with pull systems and push–pull systems, discussed in section 10.12 above, and relates to just-in-time (JIT), materials and requirements planning (MRP), distribution requirements planning (DRP), enterprise resource planning (ERP) and vendor-managed inventory (VMI).

10.15 Just-in-time (JIT)

10.15.1 What is JIT?

The following comprehensive definition of JIT is provided by the American Production and Inventory Control Society:[5]

A philosophy of manufacturing based on planned elimination of all waste and continuous improvement of productivity. It encompasses the successful execution of all manufacturing activities required to produce a final product from design engineering to delivery and including all stages of conversion from raw material onward. The primary elements include having only the required inventory when needed; to improve quality to zero defects; to reduce lead time by reducing set-up times, queue lengths and lot sizes; to incrementally revise the operations themselves; and to accomplish these things at minimum cost.

In short, JIT production is:

Making what the customer needs, when it is needed and in the quantity needed using the minimum resources of people, materials and machinery.

From the above definitions, it can be seen that JIT is more than delivering an item where and when required and at the right time. JIT is both a production scheduling and inventory control technique and an aspect of total quality management (TQM). As a production control technique, it is concerned with adding value and eliminating waste by ensuring that any resources needed for a production operation – whether raw material, finished product or anything in between – are produced and available precisely when needed. This emphasis on waste elimination means that JIT is an essential element in lean production, discussed in section 4.5.2. As a philosophy that aims at zero defects or never allowing defective units from the preceding process to flow into and disrupt a subsequent process, it is an aspect of TQM.

A useful distinction may be made between its two forms:

- *BIG-JIT* or lean production focusing on all sources of waste, as outlined in the first of the above definitions
- *Little-JIT* focusing more narrowly on scheduling goods, inventories and providing resources where needed.

It is with 'little-JIT' that the present section is primarily concerned.

10.15.2 The background of JIT

JIT is generally agreed to have been developed by Talichi Ohno, a vice-president of the Japanese Toyota motor company in the 1960s. It should be noted, however, that Henry Ford practised mass production with a JIT approach in 1921. By 1924, the production cycle of the Model T – from processing the core material to the final product – was only four days.

10.15.3 The objectives of JIT

These have been concisely summarised as:

- *zero defects* – all products will more than meet the quality expectations of the customer
- *zero set-up time* – no set-up time results in shorter production time, shorter production cycles and smaller inventories
- *zero inventories* – inventories, including work-in-progress, finished goods and sub-assemblies, will be reduced to zero – this is the opposite of the traditional manufacturing philosophy of maintaining buffer stocks as a precaution against unreliable suppliers or fluctuating demand
- *zero handling* – the elimination, so far as possible, of all non-value-adding activities
- *zero lead time* – in some markets, this is impossible, but the aim is to increase flexibility by using small batches of components or assemblies

■ *lot size of one* – this makes it possible to adapt quickly when demand is changing so if, for example, the lot size is 200 and demand is changing, either the supplier or customer ends up with a quantity of inventory that will either never or only very slowly reduce.

The requirements for successful JIT:

■ uniform master production schedules
■ 'pull' production systems
■ good customer-supplier relationships
■ short distance between customer and supplier
■ reliable delivery
■ consistent quality with zero defects
■ standardisation of components and methods
■ material flow system.

10.15.4 JIT and kanban systems

The *kanban* system is an essential aspect of JIT. In Japanese, the word *kanban* means 'ticket' or 'signal' and in JIT refers to an information system in which instructions relating to the type and quantity of items to be withdrawn from the preceding manufacturing process are conveyed by a card that is attached to a storage and transport container. The card identifies the part number and contained capacity. The two principal types of *kanban* are:

■ *production kanban, or P kanban* signals the need to produce more parts
■ *conveyance kanban, or C kanban* signals the need to deliver more parts to the next work centre.

The operation of a two-card *kanban* system within a work cell is shown in Figure 10.8. The rules for operating a two-card *kanban* system are therefore:

■ each container must have a *kanban* card
■ parts are only 'pulled' – that is, the user centre must go for them
■ no parts can be obtained without a conveyance *kanban*
■ all containers hold standard quantities and only standard quantities can be used
■ no extra production is permitted – production can only start with a production *kanban*.

It follows that the amount of work-in-progress inventory is equal to the number of *kanban* cards issued multiplied by the capacity of the container used. The *initial* number of *kanban* cards required is calculated by the formula:

$$\text{Number of K cards} = \frac{D \, (T_w + T_p)(1 + a)}{C}$$

Where:

D = average daily production rate, as indicated by the master production schedule
T_w = waiting time of *kanban* cards in decimal fractions of a day
T_p = the processing time per part in fractions of a day
C = the capacity of a standard container
a = a policy variable determined by the efficiency of the work centre using the part

Figure 10.8 A two-card *kanban* system – the flow within a cell

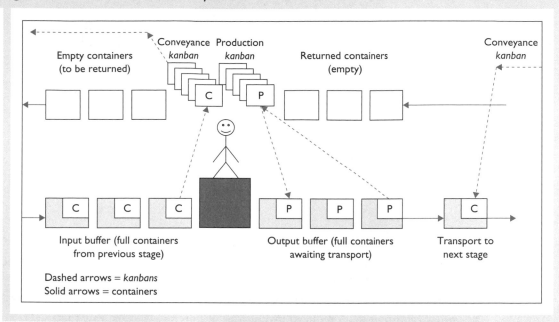

Dashed arrows = *kanbans*
Solid arrows = containers

Thus, if:

$$D = 100 \text{ parts/day}, T_w = 0.25, T_p = 0.15, C = 10 \text{ and } a = 1$$

then the number of *kanban* cards will be:

$$\frac{100 \ (0.25 + 0.15)(1 + 1)}{10} = 8$$

The dual card system described above is used by Toyota for car production. A more common approach is a one-card system, which signals requirements from the preceding work centre, as shown in Figure 10.9.

In Figure 10.9, a signal is sent back from the consuming work centre to the supplying work centre (or supplier). This is a signal:

■ to send some more (a transfer batch), via a buffer stock

■ to produce some more (a process batch), at the supplying work centre.

10.15.5 Benefits of JIT

The potential benefits of JIT to an organisation and its purchasing function in particular, have been summarised by Schonberger and Ansari[6] as follows:

■ *part costs* – low scrap costs, low inventory carrying costs

■ *quality* – fast detection and correction of unsatisfactory quality and, ultimately, higher quality of purchased parts

Figure 10.9 One-card system signaling requirements from previous work centre

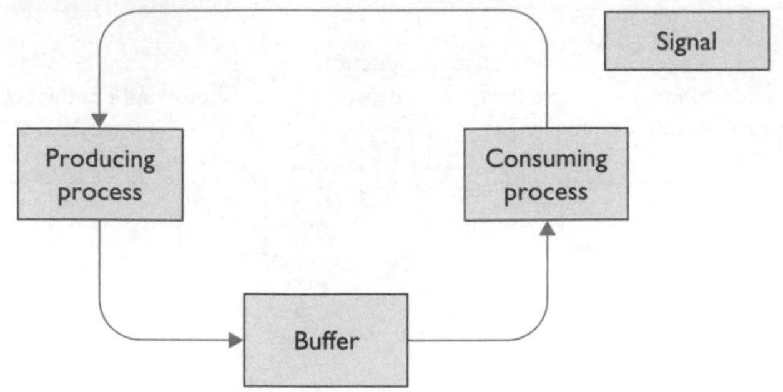

- *design* – fast response to engineering change requirements
- *administrative efficiency* – fewer suppliers, minimal expediting and order release work, simplified communications and receiving activities
- *productivity* – reduced rework, reduced inspection, reduced parts-related delays
- *capital requirements* – reduced inventories of purchased parts, raw materials, work-in-progress and finished goods.

10.15.6 Possible disadvantages of JIT

Some organisations have experienced problems with JIT for the following reasons:

- faulty forecasting of demand and inability of suppliers to move quickly to changes in demand
- JIT requires the provision of the necessary systems and methods of communication between purchasers and suppliers, ranging from vehicle telephones to EDI, so problems will arise if there is inadequate communication both internally – from production to purchasing – and externally – from purchasing to suppliers – and vice versa
- organisations with, ideally, no safety stocks are highly vulnerable to supply failures
- purely stockless buying is a fallacy – lack of low-cost C class items can halt a production line as easily as a failure in the delivery of high-priced A class items
- the advantages of buying in bulk at lower prices may outweigh the savings negotiated for JIT contracts as suppliers may increase their prices to cover costs of delivery, paperwork and storage required for JIT
- JIT is not generally suitable for bought-out items that have short lifecycles and are subject to rapid design changes
- JIT is more suitable for flow than batch production and may require a change from batch to flow methods, with consequent changes in the systems required to support the new methods
- even for manufacturers that mass-produce items, a substantial percentage of components are made by number, if not value, in batches, as well as a small number of high-value components, on dedicated flow lines

- apart from suppliers, JIT requires the total involvement of people from all disciplines and the breaking down of traditional barriers between functions within an organisation, which may involve a substantial investment in organisational development training
- Rhys *et al.*[7] have drawn attention to Japanese transport factors arising from some suppliers relocating at greater distances from purchasers (although these are normally still nearer to users than in Europe), road congestion and lighter vehicles – that is, for every one vehicle required in Europe, two or three are required in Japan, so JIT in Japan is now 'neither lean nor green'.

Further, Hayes and Pisano[8] suggest that the problems of implementing JIT derive from the fact that:

> most companies focus on the *mechanics* of JIT and TQM rather than on their *substance*, the skills and capabilities that enable a factory to excel and make it possible for improvement programmes to achieve their desired results. The consequence of this outlook is that managers have tended to view such programmes as solutions to specific problems rather than as stepping stones in an intended direction.

Hayes and Pisano also warn that, if an organisation lacks the skills, such as low set-up times and defect rates, that make JIT work, the adoption of the approach is likely to be costly. Adopting the system, will, however, provide strong incentives to develop such skills and induce an ethic of continuous improvement. Over time, a true JIT system may emerge.

10.15.7 JIT and purchasing

Apart from the general commitment to JIT mentioned above, two things essential to the successful implementation of JIT are that:

- all parts must arrive where they are needed, when they are needed and in the exact quantity needed
- all parts arriving must be usable.

Where these requirements are not achieved, JIT may easily become 'just-too-late'.

In achieving these requirements, purchasing has the responsibilities summarised below.

- *Liaison with the design function* – the emphasis should be on *performance* rather than *design* specifications. Looser specifications enable suppliers to be more cost-effective by being more innovative with regard to the quality and function aspects of supplies. In JIT purchasing, value analysis is an integral part of the system and should include suppliers.
- *Liaison with suppliers* to ensure that they understand thoroughly the importance of consistently maintaining lead times and a high level of quality.
- *Investigation of the potential of suppliers* within reasonable proximity of the purchaser to increase certainty of delivery and reduction of lead time.
- *Establishing strong, long-term relationships with suppliers* in a mutual effort to reduce costs and share savings. This will be achieved by the purchaser's efforts to meet the supplier's expectations regarding:
  - continuity of custom
  - a fair price and profit margin

- agreed adjustments to price when necessary
- accurate forecasts of demand
- firm and reasonably stable specifications
- minimising order changes
- smoothly timed order releases
- involvement in design specifications
- prompt payment.

■ *Establishment of an effective supplier certification programme* which ensures that quality specifications are met before components leave the supplier so that receiving inspections are eliminated.

■ *Evaluation of supplier performance* and the solving of difficulties as an exercise in cooperation.

10.15.8 JIT II

This is a registered trademark of the Bose Corporation and is a customer–supplier partnerships concept practised by a number of companies and their suppliers. In a JIT II relationship, a supplier's representative – referred to as an 'in-plant representative' – functions as a member of the customer's purchasing department while being paid by the supplier. The representative issues purchase orders to his/her own company on behalf of the customer. The representative is also involved in such activities as design, production planning and value analysis.

It is claimed that this arrangement provides benefits to both the customer and the supplier.

From the customer's perspective, benefits include that because:

■ the supplier's representatives are full-time employees of their customer's, they have ready access to information that can be used to reduce lead times and inventories and lead time reductions due to JIT II partnerships are generally greater than those achieved with conventional JIT

■ communications are improved because the representatives have a real-time awareness of the supplier's needs

■ transportation costs are lower as a result of organisations partnering transportation companies to deliver incoming items

■ the supplier is involved in concurrent design and value analysis so that it works with the customer from the inception of the design

■ material costs are reduced by large orders with consequent discounts and lower transportation costs

■ administrative costs are lower as there is a reduction in paperwork and the customer's purchasing staff are released for other duties.

From the supplier's perspective, benefits include that:

■ once a JIT II partnership has been agreed, an 'evergreen' contract is awarded, which has no end date and no requoting or tendering is required, and the resultant security enables the supplier to direct financial resources to managing the customer's account rather than seeking or renegotiating business.

JIT II is clearly not without risks and not always appropriate. There are various factors to be considered:

- the volume of business must be sufficient to assign a representative exclusively to one customer and, unless this is achieved, the JIT II approach may not be effective, so it is only an option for a customer able to place a very substantial volume of business with one supplier

- a supplier may be reluctant to share costs or processes with a customer and, conversely, a customer may be reluctant to divulge information about new designs or processes to a supplier

- a customer may be reluctant to award a long-term contract because of the fear that the supplier's performance might deteriorate.

Pragman[9] states that the JIT II concept has expanded from merely purchasing materials to include logistics, engineering and services. It does, however, demand a strategic alliance between partners based on trust.

10.16 Materials and requirements planning (MRP)

MRP, developed in the 1960s, is a technique that assists in the detailed planning of production and has the following characteristics:

- it is geared specifically to assembly operations
- it is a dependent demand technique
- it is a computer-based information system.

The aim is to make available either purchased or company manufacturing assemblies just before they are required by the next stage of production or for delivery. MRP enables items/batches to be tracked throughout the entire manufacturing process and assists purchasing and control departments to move the right supplies at the right time to manufacturing or distribution points.

10.16.1 MRP and JIT

MRP has many similarities to JIT. Some comparisons are shown in Table 10.8.

JIT and MRP should not, however, be thought of as opposing systems. In many organisations, the two systems are successfully combined. For example, it is important that a strong MRP II (see section 10.17) planning environment will facilitate JIT execution. Ideally the two systems are not alternative but complementary.

10.16.2 MRP terminology

MRP has its own terminology, as follows:

- a *bill of materials*, or BOM, contains information on all the materials, components and sub-assemblies required to produce each end item

- an *end item*, or master scheduled item, is the final product sold to the customer and the inventory for end items, from the accounting standpoint, will either be work-in-progress or finished goods

Table 10.8 Comparison of MRP and JIT

Operating system characteristics	MRP	JIT
System	'Push' system	'Pull' system
Focus	Bottlenecks	'Quality'
Rates of output	Variable production plan	Level schedule
Work authorisation	Master production schedule	*Kanban*
Inventory status	Inventory no problem, but the less the better	Reducing inventory to zero
Administrative personnel	Increased	Fewer
Forms of control	Management reports	Shop floor, visual
Capacity adjustment	Capital requirements planning (deferred)	Visual, immediate (demand surge)
Scheduling	MRP says 'which job next'	*Kanban* says 'make it now'

- a *parent* is an item manufactured from one or more component items
- a *component* is one item that goes through one or more operations to be transformed into a parent
- an *intermediate item* is one that has at least one parent and one component – classified as work-in-progress
- a *sub-assembly*, as it is 'put together', rather than other means of transformation, is a special case of intermediate item
- a *purchased item* is one that has no components because it comes from a supplier but has one or more parents, so, for accounting purposes, inventory or purchased items, is regarded as raw materials
- *part commodity* is the extent to which a component (part) has one or more parents – a concept related to standardisation – so a standard ball bearing may have numerous parents
- *usage quantity*, which is the number of units of a component required to make one unit of its parent
- a *bucket* is a time period to which MRP relates, for example, one week.

10.16.3 The essential elements of an MRP system

These are shown in Figure 10.10.

10.16.4 MRP inputs and outputs

The process starts at the top level with a master production schedule (MPS). The information in the MPS comes from a number of sources, including orders actually received and forecasts of demand, usually produced using the forecasting techniques described earlier. Two key MPS activities are the determination of planning horizons for the end product and the size of time buckets.

Figure 10.10 Essential elements of an MRP system

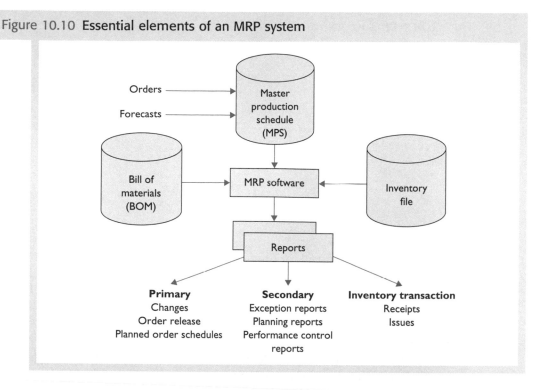

- *The master production schedule(s) (MPS)* uses the inputs from marketing and sales to forecast demand for quantities of the final product over a planned time horizon subdivided into periods known as time buckets (see Figure 10.11). These buckets are not necessarily of equal duration. Without the MPS(s), MRP cannot generate requirements for any item.
- *The bill of materials file (BOM)* also known as the product structure, this lists all the items that comprise each assembly and sub-assembly that make up the final product or end item. Each BOM is given a level code according to the following logic:
  - Level 0: the final product or end item not used as a component of any other product
  - Level 1: direct component of a level 0 item
  - Level 2: direct component of a level 1 item
  - Level n: direct component of a level $(n-1)$ item.

Figure 10.11 Master production schedule

Week	1	2	3	4	5	6	
Product X	30		14		10	8	Time horizon
Product Y		38	13	30	13	13	Time buckets

Figure 10.12 **Product structure for X**

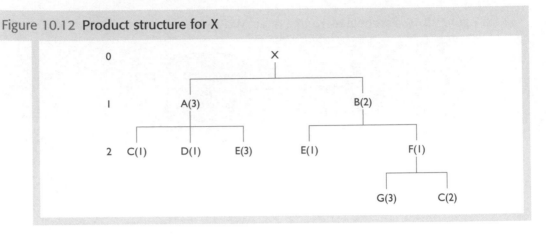

Assume the demand for product X is 30 units. Each unit of X requires three units of A and two of B. Each A requires one C, one D and three Es. Each B requires one E and one F. Each F requires three Gs and two Cs. Thus, the demand for A, B, C, D, E, F and G is completely dependent on the demand for X. From the above information, we can construct a BOM or product structure for the related inventory requirements, as in Figure 10.12.

- *The inventory file* is the record of individual items of inventory and their status. The file is kept current by the online posting of inventory events, such as the receipt and issue of items of inventory or their return to store.

- *The MRP package* uses the information provided by the MPS, BOM and inventory files to:

  - explode or cascade the end product into its various assemblies, sub-assemblies or components at various levels, so the number of units of each item needed to produce 30 units of product X would be:

Part A = 3 × no. of Xs   3 × 30   = 90
Part B = 2 × no. of Xs   2 × 30   = 60
Part C = 1 × no. of As + 2 × no. of Fs (1 × 90) + (2 × 60) = 210
Part D = 1 × no. of As   1 × 90   = 90
Part E = 3 × no. of As + 1 × no. of Bs (3 × 90) + (1 × 60) = 330
Part F = 1 × no. of Bs   1 × 60   = 60
Part G = 3 × no. of Fs   3 × 60   = 180

So, to produce 30 units of X, we shall need 90 units of A, 60 units of B, 210 units of C, 90 units of D, 330 units of E, 60 units of F and 180 units of G

  - offset for lead time – lead times for each item must be fed into the system, then, subtracting them from the date of the net requirement so as to position the planned order release date in advance of the timing of the net requirement it covers is called *offsetting the lead time*

  - net out on-hand and on-order balances using the equation:

$$\underset{}{\text{Net}} \atop \text{requirements} = \underbrace{\underset{}{\text{Gross}} \atop \text{requirements}}_{\text{Total requirements}} - \underbrace{\underset{}{\text{Inventory}} \atop \text{on hand} + \underset{}{\text{Units}} \atop \text{on order}}_{\text{Available inventory}}$$

In an MRP system, net requirement quantities are always related to some date or period – that is, they are time phased (as shown by Figure 10.11). The primary outputs of the MRP system are:

- order release instructions for the placement of planned – that is, future – production or purchasing orders
- rescheduling instructions notifying the need to advance or postpone open orders to adjust inventory coverage to net requirements
- expediting instructions that relate to overdue orders
- cancellation or suspension instructions relating to open orders.

MRP systems also have the capacity to produce much secondary data, such as reports relating to exceptions or deviations from normal planning and performance.

10.16.5 Applications of MRP

While having elements in common to all inventory situations, MRP is most applicable where:

- the demand for items is dependent
- the demand is discontinuous – 'lumpy' and non-uniform
- in job, batch and assembly or flow production, or where all three manufacturing methods are used.

10.17 Manufacturing resource planning (MRP II)

10.17.1 Definition

MRP II may be defined as:

> The extension of computerised MRP to link together such functions as production planning and control, engineering, purchasing, marketing, financial/cost accounting and human resource management into an integrated decision support system.

In MRP II, the production process is still driven by a master production schedule, but additional inputs are received from production control, purchasing and engineering. The computerised system also collects data to support financial or cost accounting, marketing and human resource management.

10.17.2 The advantages of MRP II

An overview of MRP II is provided by Figure 10.13.

- It coordinates the efforts of production, engineering, purchasing, marketing and human resources to achieving a common strategy or business plan.
- Managers are able to analyse the 'What if . . . ?' implications of their decisions, such as what if the sales forecasts of marketing cannot be met by the available production capacity? What would be the financial implications of outsourcing?

Figure 10.13 An overview of an MRP II system

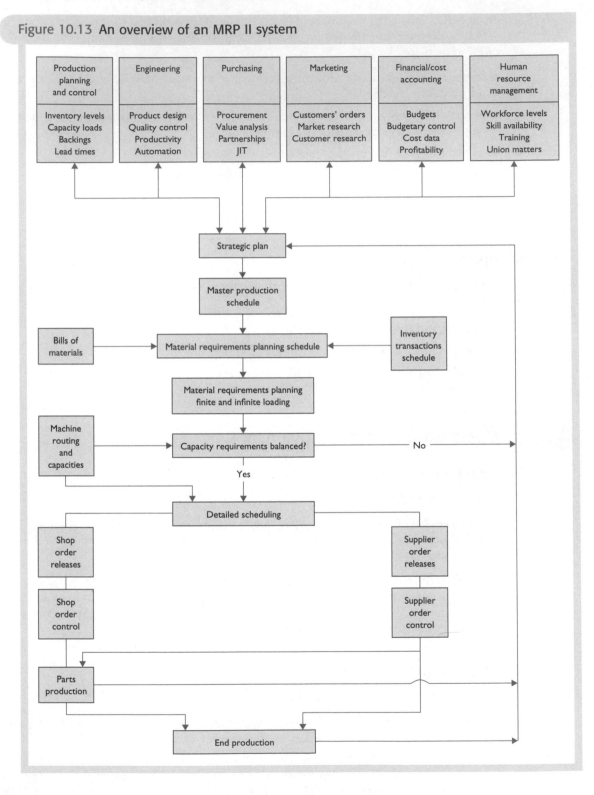

- Better utilisation of marketing, finance and human resources in addition to physical plant and equipment.

- Changes can be easily factored into the system as they arise, such as rush orders.

- Cost of resources used or considered for use can be converted into money values, thus facilitating budgeting and budgetary control.

- Coordination of production with purchasing, marketing and human resources in such ways as timing of supplies deliveries, using sales forecasts to determine master budgets and planning recruitment or run-down of personnel.

10.18 Enterprise resource planning (ERP)

10.18.1 What is ERP?

ERP is the latest and possibly the most significant development of MRP and MRP II. While MRP allowed manufacturers to track supplies, work-in-progress and the output of finished goods to meet sales orders, ERP is applicable to all organisations and allows managers from all functions or departments to have a consolidated view of what is or is not taking place throughout the enterprise. Most ERP systems are designed around a number of modules, each of which can be standalone or combined with others.

- *Finance* – this module tracks financial information, such as accounts receivable and payable, payroll and other financial and management accounting information throughout the enterprise.

- *Logistics* – this module is often broken down further into submodules covering inventory and warehouse management and transportation.

- *Manufacturing* – this module tracks the flow of orders or products, including MRP and the progress and coordination of manufacturing.

- *Supplier management* – this module tracks the purchasing process, from requisitioning to the payment of suppliers, and monitors delivery of supplies and supplier performance.

- *Human resources* – this module covers many human resource management activities, including planning, training and job allocation.

ERP can be defined as:

> A business management system that, supported by multimodule application software, integrates all the departments or functions of an enterprise.

Initially, ERP systems were enterprise-centric. The development of the Internet and e-business has, however, made the sharing of accurate real-time information across the whole supply chain essential to business success. Gartner – the consultancy that coined the term ERP – now uses ERP II to refer to systems that facilitate collaborative commerce, or c-commerce, in which a key requirement is the sharing of information outside the enterprise. Some differences between ERP and ERP II are shown in Table 10.9.

Table 10.9 Differences between ERP and ERP II

Factor	ERP	ERP II
Role	Concerned with optimising within an enterprise	Concerned with optimising across the whole supply chain by collaborating with business partners
Domain	Focused on manufacturing and distribution	Crosses all sectors and segments of business, including service industries, government and asset-based industries, such as mining
Function	General applications	Designed to meet the needs of specific industries, thereby providing steep functionality for users
Process	Internally focused	Externally focused, especially on connecting trading partners, irrespective of location
Architecture	Monolithic and closed	Web-based and open to integrating and interoperating with other systems. Built around modules or components that allow users to choose the functionality they require
Data	Information on ERP systems is generated and consumed within the enterprise	Information available across the whole supply chain to authorised participants

10.18.2 The advantages of ERP

These can be summarised as:

- *faster inventory turnover* – manufacturers and distributors may increase inventory turns tenfold and reduce inventory costs by 10 to 40 per cent
- *improved customer service* – in many cases, an ERP system can increase fill rates to 80 or 90 per cent by providing the right product in the right place at the right time, thus increasing customer satisfaction
- *better inventory accuracy, fewer audits* – an ERP system can increase inventory accuracy to more than 90 per cent while reducing the need for physical inventory audits
- *reduced set-up times* – ERP can reduce set-up time by 25 to 80 per cent by grouping similar production jobs together, ensuring coordination of people, tools and machinery, together with the efficient use of equipment and minimising downtime by virtue of efficient maintenance
- *higher-quality work* – ERP software, with a strong manufacturing component, pro-actively pinpoints quality issues, providing the information required to increase production efficiency and reduce or eliminate rework
- *timely revenue collection and improved cash flow* – ERP gives manufacturers the power to proactively examine accounts receivable before problems occur instead of just reacting, which improves cash flow.

10.18.3 The disadvantages of ERP

- *ERP implementation is difficult* – this is because implementation involves a fundamental change from a functional to a process approach to business
- *ERP systems are expensive* – this is especially so when the customisation of standard modules to accommodate different business processes is involved – it has been estimated that some 50 per cent of ERP implementations fail to deliver the anticipated benefits and the cost is often prohibitive for small enterprises
- *cost of training employees to use ERP systems can be high*
- *there may be a number of unintended consequences* such as employee stress and a resistance to change and sharing information that was closely guarded by departments or functions
- *ERP systems tend to focus on operational decisions* and have relatively weak analytical capabilities (this topic is briefly dealt with below).

10.19 Supply chain management systems

While ERP systems can provide a great deal of planning capability, the various material, capacity and demand constraints are all considered separately in relative isolation from each other. Further, ERP systems have many tasks to fulfil. Analytical supply chain management systems, however, can consider all relevant factors simultaneously and perform real-time adjustments in the relevant constraints. Thus, while getting decisions or information from an overloaded ERP system can take hours, a separate SCM system may provide the required answers in minutes. SCM systems such as Technologies and Manugistics usually span all the supply chain stages and have the analytical capabilities to produce planning solutions and strategic-level conditions. Analytical systems do, however, rely on legacy systems or ERP systems to provide the information on which the analysis is based. Because of this, there is currently a rapid convergence of ERP and SCM software.

10.20 Distribution requirements planning (DRP)

10.20.1 What is DRP?

Distribution requirements planning (DRP) is an inventory control and scheduling technique that applies MRP principles to distribution inventories. It may also be regarded as a method of handling stock replenishment in a multi-echelon environment. An 'echelon' is defined by *Chamber's Dictionary* as 'A stepwise arrangement of troops, ships, planes, etc.' Applied to distribution, the term 'multi-echelon' means that, instead of independent control of the same item at different distribution points using EOQ formulae, the dependent demand at a higher echelon (such as a central warehouse) is derived from the requirements of lower echelons (such as regional warehouses). DRP is useful for both manufacturing organisations, such as car manufacturers that sell their cars via several distribution points, such as regional and local distributors, and purely merchandising organisations, such as supermarkets (see Figure 10.14).

All levels in a DRP multi-echelon structure are dependent, except for the level that serves the customer, which are the retailers in Figure 10.14.

Figure 10.14 A supermarket multi-echelon distribution system

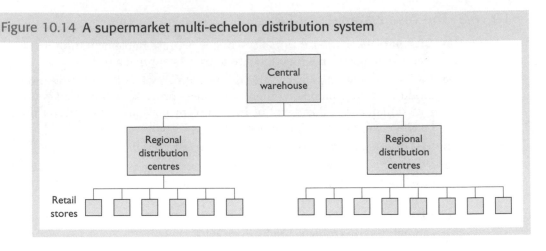

Table 10.10 Comparison of MRP and DRP

MRP	DRP
■ The bill of materials applies time-phased logic to components and sub-assemblies to products in the MOM (management of materials) network	■ The bill of distribution (the network) uses time-phased order point logic to determine network replenishment requirements
■ An 'explosion' process from a master production schedule to the detailed scheduling of component replenishments	■ An 'implosion' process from the lowest levels of the network to the central distribution centre
■ Goods in course of manufacture	■ Finished goods

10.20.2 DRP and MRP

DRP has been described as the mirror image of MRP. Some of the contrasts between the two approaches are set out in Table 10.10.

MRP and DRP approaches have, however, many common aspects:

■ as planning systems, neither uses a fixed or periodic review approach
■ both are computerised systems
■ just as MRP has been expanded into MRP II, so DRP has been expanded into DRP II
■ DRP utilises record formats and processing logic consistent with MRP.

The last point is the most important of all as it provides the basis for integrating the database throughout the whole supply chain, from purchasing through to distribution. Thus, both MRP and DRP contribute to a logistics system, as shown in Figure 10.15.

Thus as Vollman et al.[10] observe:

Distribution requirements planning serves a central role in coordinating the flow of goods inside the factory with the system modules that place the goods in the hands of the customers. It provides the basis for integrating the manufacturing planning and control (MRP) system from the firm to the field.

Figure 10.15 Distribution requirements planning and logistics

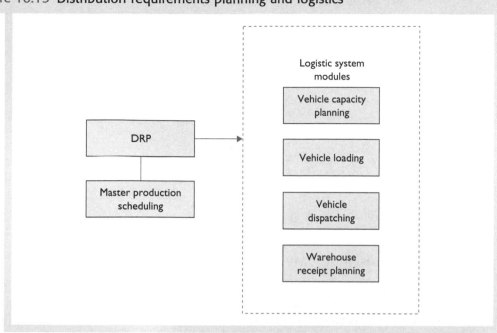

Source: Adapted from Vollman, T. E., Berry, W. L. and Whybark, C. D., *Manufacturing Control Systems*, 2nd edition, Irwin, 1988, p. 788

10.21 Vendor-managed inventory (VMI)

Vendor-managed inventory (VMI) is a JIT technique in which inventory replacement decisions are centralised with upstream manufacturers or distributors. Acronyms for VMI include:

- continuous replenishment programs (CRP)
- supplier-assisted inventory management (SAIM)
- supplier-assisted inventory replenishment (SAIR)
- efficient consumer response (ECR).

VMI may also be considered to be an extension of distribution requirements planning (DRP).

10.21.1 The aim of VMI

This is to enable manufacturers or distributors to eliminate the need for customers to reorder, reduce or exclude inventory and obviate stockouts. With VMI, customers no longer 'pull' inventory from suppliers. Rather, inventory is automatically 'pushed' to customers as suppliers check customers' inventories and respond to previously agreed stock levels. VMI is particularly applicable to retail distribution. VMI can also relieve the customer of much of the expense of ordering and stocking low-value MRO items.

Figure 10.16 **A simple VMI model**

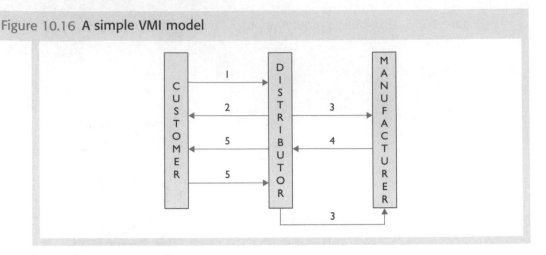

10.21.2 Implementing VMI

A simple model of VMI is shown in Figure 10.16.

This model is based on the assumption that the customer has entered into a collaborative or partnership agreement with a distributor, under which the latter agrees to stock a specified range of items and meet specified service levels. In return, the customer undertakes to buy the specified items solely from the distributor and no longer keeps the items in stock. There must, therefore, be a high level of trust between the customer and the distributor.

The various steps in Figure 10.16 may be explained as follows:

Step 1 The customer sends information on items sold to the distributor. This information may be collected by barcoding and scanning technology and transmitted to the distributor by EDI or the Internet.

Step 2 The distributor processes the information and forwards an acknowledgement to the customer, giving details of the quantities and descriptions of the products to be delivered, delivery date and destination, and releases the goods.

Step 3 The distributor collects details of all the customer's orders, which are consolidated and sent daily to the manufacturers via EDI or the Internet.

Step 4 The manufacturer replenishes the distributor's stock.

Step 5 The distributor invoices the customer, who remits payment. Very large customers may transmit their requirements directly to the manufacturer, from whom they receive direct deliveries.

Normally, VMI implementation involves four stages:

1 *Preparation* – in addition to initial negotiations between a customer and the supplier and setting up project teams with clearly defined roles and responsibilities, this stage involves collaborative planning, forecasting and replenishment (CPFR), the aim of which is to minimise inventories and focus on value-added process activities. By focusing on the flow of supply to consumers without the complication of inventory, the project's participants can often discover previously undetected hidden bottlenecks in the flow that can be eliminated.

2 *Pre-implementation* – this is an extension of CPFR involving the determination of forecast quantities, safety stocks, lead time, service levels and key performance indicators and ownership issues.

3 *Implementation*

4 *Refinement* – improvements that may be made in the light of experience, including the resolution of technical difficulties encountered subsequent to implementation.

10.21.3 Advantages of VMI

VMI is advantageous to both suppliers and customers. For suppliers, the advantages include:

- *demand smoothing* – VMI information improves forecasts of customers' requirements, thereby enabling manufacturers to plan production to meet customer demand
- *long-term customer relationships* due to the high cost to the customer of switching to an alternative supplier
- *enhanced operational flexibility* enabling production times and quantities to be adjusted to suit the supplier.

For customers, the advantages include:

- *reduced administrative costs* due to the elimination of the need to monitor inventory levels, paper to computer entries and reduced reordering costs
- *enhanced working capital* due to reduced inventory levels and obsolescence and enhanced stock turn with improved cash flow
- *reduced lead times* with enhanced sales and a reduction of list sales due to stockouts.

10.21.4 Disadvantages of VMI

These also apply to both suppliers and customers. Disadvantages for suppliers include:

- *transfers of customer costs to the supplier* – these include those relating to administration and the cost of carrying increased inventory to meet customer demand
- *reduced working capital* due to the enhanced inventory and administration costs stated above.

Disadvantages for customers include:

- *increased risk* resulting from dependence on the manufacturer or distributor
- *disclosure of potentially sensitive information to the supplier* – the possession of such information will put the supplier in a strong position when a contract is renegotiated
- *customers may be better positioned than suppliers to make replenishment decisions* – Chopra and Meindl[11] point out that:

> One drawback to VMI arises because retailers often sell products from competing manufacturers that are substitutes in the customer's mind. For example, a customer may substitute detergent manufactured by Proctor & Gamble with detergent manufactured by Lever Brothers. If the retailer has a VMI agreement with both manufacturers, each will ignore the impact of substitution when making its inventory decisions. As a result, inventories at the retailer will be higher than optimal.

10.22 Purchasing and inventory

Inventories matter for business, financial and reputational reasons. The development of systems such as MRP, MRP II, ERP and VMI has meant that purchasing as a supply chain activity has possibly less involvement, especially with dependent demand items. In many organisations, an inventory management function will be responsible for many of the activities outlined in this chapter. It is important, however, that purchasing professionals should have a sound grasp of inventory management, for at least the following four reasons.

1 Inventory in many undertakings – for example, the construction industry – is an important asset. In some small companies, inventory may be the most important asset.

2 Inefficient inventory management will increase costs and reduce profitability. Too much working capital tied up in inventory can cause problems of cash flow, result in expensive borrowing and prevent desirable expenditure in other directions. There are also the ever-present risks of theft, deterioration and obsolescence. Conversely, holding inventory can, in a time of rising prices, be a source of windfall profits.

3 Holding inventory can enhance flexibility and provide competitive advantage, due to the ability to respond rapidly to customers' requirements, as with agile production. What inventory policy to pursue is therefore an important strategic decision.

4 Efficient and effective inventory management can only be achieved with the cooperation of efficient and effective suppliers. The selection of such suppliers and negotiation of all aspects of contracts relating to inventory are activities in which purchasing professionals should expect to play a leading role. The importance of sourcing is discussed in the next chapter.

Case study

You have applied for the position of head of procurement and inventory management at Refined Bus Ltd. They have a large manufacturing site in Doncaster, England. On the same site there is a Service Support Centre (SSC) who supply parts to any company operating buses manufactured in the past by Refined Bus Ltd.

You are to be interviewed, tomorrow, by Refined Bus's managing director who has sent you some outline information. The annual procurement expenditure is £325 million and ten strategic suppliers account for 80 per cent of the expenditure. They supply products such as, aluminium sheets, glass, seating, tubular fabrications, doors, carpeting and electronics. Inventory carried for production is currently £96 million. The SSC annual sales are £30 million and they have £26 million of inventory and have a client demand satisfaction rate of 67.3 per cent. Refined Bus are supplying parts for vehicles that were manufactured more than 20 years ago.

The managing director, in his letter, advises you that if you are the successful candidate he will demand dramatic improvements in procurement (who do not practice JIT or partnering) and inventory where the working capital is not used effectively. You will be asked at the interview to explain the approaches you would follow to deliver significant business benefits.

Task

1 What specific techniques will you explain to the managing director as being relevant in this situation?

2 What, in your view, should the annual stockturn be for (a) production and (b) SSC?

3 Should procurement have accountability for inventory management? If you are asked to explain your reasons for procurement having such accountability what would be your reasons?

Discussion questions

10.1 Can you explain the role of procurement in managing inventory in a business? Having explained the role, can you differentiate between this role in:

1 a fashion retailer?

2 engineering inventory in an international airline?

3 the stock of stationery in a government department?

10.2 Calculate the rate of stock turn using the following information:

Turnover at *selling* price = £125,000
Mark-up = 25%
Opening stock at *selling* price = £160,000
Closing stock at *selling* price = £70,000

10.3 Calculate the rate of stock turn using the following information:

Turnover at *cost* price = £100,000
Opening stock at *cost* price = £48,000
Closing stock at *cost* price = £56,000

10.4 How may the cost of ordering MRO items be reduced?

10.5 The Bluebird Transport company manufactures a range of travel homes. The production Director has suggested that any inventory valued at less than £5 an item be made available on open access on the shop floor. No requisitions will be used in future. What is the procurement issues attached to this suggestion?

10.6 What information does an operations manager require to make effective use of dependent demand inventory models?

10.7 The Horsk Shipping company have reviewed the inventory held at their strategic warehouses in Cape Town, Southampton and New York. They have found that the cost of carrying slow moving stock, e.g., engine, parts, steel-plate and furnishings, is 30 per cent of the value. What percentage would you predict might be allocated to each of the following constituents?

(a) cost of money, that is, interest on capital tied up in stock
(b) rates
(c) warehouse expenses
(d) physical handling
(e) clerical and stores control
(f) obsolescence
(g) deterioration and pilferage.

10.8   You have been asked to suggest four ways in which inventory costs might be reduced. What would you suggest?

10.9   The major disadvantages of bar-coding are uniformity and cost. Discuss this statement.

10.10   As RFID systems make use of the electromagnetic system, they are relatively easy to jam using energy at the right frequency. What might the implication be for:
(a) customers at a supermarket checkout?
(b) hospitals or military applications of RFID?

10.11   If a company categorises its inventory into three classes according to their usage value, calculate the usage values of the following items and classify them along Pareto lines into A, B and C items.

Item no.	Annual quantity used	Unit value
1	75	£80.00
2	150,000	£0.90
3	500	£3.00
4	18,000	£0.20
5	3,000	£0.30
6	20,000	£0.10
7	10,000	£0.04

10.12   What term would you use to describe the effect of information delays up and down the supply chain? What might be the consequence for inventory and profitability of such information delays?

10.13   There are six basic questions associated with forecasting, what are they?

10.14   What are the advantages of Enterprise Resource Planning (ERP)?

10.15   What arguments would you advance to persuade a supplier to hold their stock in your stores and to only charge after the stock has been used?

10.16   If it were to be suggested that your organisation should outsource the stores function what advantages and disadvantages could you identify?

Past examination questions

1 Identify **five** potential problems with using the economic order quantity (EOQ) method.
CIPS, *Managing Inventory*, May 2010

2 Identify **five** activities which would typically take place within a store or warehouse facility following the receipt of goods.
CIPS, *Managing Inventory*, May 2010

3 Materials requirements planning (MRP) and manufacturing resource planning (MRPII) are techniques often adopted by manufacturing organisations to control inventory and plan production. The following questions relate to these techniques:
(a) Describe the purpose of the **three** files required by an MRP system and explain how these files work together.

(b) For an MRP system to work effectively, identify **five** conditions that need to be met.

(c) Describe **two** differences between the MRP and the MRPII systems.

CIPS, *Managing Inventory*, November 2009

4 In the terms of utilising a model to calculate a quantity of items to order, a common formula used is as follows:

$$E = \sqrt{\left(\frac{2AB}{CD}\right)}$$

Identify what A, B, C, D and E represent.

CIPS, *Managing Inventory*, November 2009

5 A manufacturer of stereo systems is considering a stock replenishment system to manage its production to meet customer demand.

The demand is 500 per week.
The ordering cost is £100 per order.
The cost of storage is 20%.
The unit price is £25.
The supply lead time is two weeks.
The safety stock is 750.

(a) Explain how a 're-order point' system works.

(b) State **one** reason why a 're-order point' system might fail.

(c) Explain **four** principles of the economic order quantity (EOQ) formula.

(d) Suggest **five** reasons why an EOQ may not be accurate.

CIPS, *Managing Inventory*, May 2009

References

[1] Institute of Logistics and Transport, *Glossary of Inventory and Materials Management Definitions*, 1998

[2] Institute of Logistics and Transport, *How to Manage Inventory Effectively*, Added Value Publication Ltd, 2003, p. 94

[3] Compton, H. K. and Jessop, D., *Dictionary of Purchasing and Supply Management*, Pitman, 1989, p. 135

[4] See GS1 UK's website at: www.e-centre.org.uk

[5] The Association for Operation Management (APICS), Chicago, Illinois. Founded in 1957 as the American Production and Inventory Control Society

[6] Schonberger, R. J. and Ansari, A., 'Just-in-time purchasing can improve quality', *Journal of Purchasing and Materials Management*, Spring, 1984

[7] Rhys, D. G., McNash, K. and Nieuwenhuis, P., 'Japan hits the limits of Just-in-Time EIU', *Japanese Motor Business*, December, 1992, pp. 81–9

[8] Hayes, R. H. and Pisano, G. P., 'Beyond world class: the new manufacturing strategy', *Harvard Business Review*, January–February, 1994, p. 75

[9] Pragman, C. H., 'JIT II: a purchasing concept for reducing lead times in time-based competition', *Business Horizons*, July–August, 1996, pp. 54–8

[10] Vollman, T. E., Berry, W. L. and Whybark, C. D., *Manufacturing Control Systems*, 2nd edn, Irwin, 1988, p. 788

[11] Chopra, S. and Meindl, P., *Supply Chain Management*, Prentice Hall, 2001, p. 247

Chapter 11

Sourcing and the management of suppliers

Learning outcomes

This chapter aims to provide an understanding of:

- tactical and strategic sourcing
- the sourcing process
- the location, appraisal and assessment of suppliers
- supplier performance and evaluation
- policy issues in sourcing
- sourcing decision making
- factors in deciding where to buy
- outsourcing
- partnering
- sustainability.

Key ideas

- Sourcing information.
- Analysis of market conditions.
- The main aspects of supplier appraisal.
- The purpose, scope and methods of evaluating supplier performance.
- The supplier base.
- Make-or-buy decisions.
- Outsourcing.
- Subcontracting.
- Partnering.
- Reciprocity.
- Intra-company trading, local suppliers and small or large suppliers.
- Purchasing consortia.
- Factors in deciding where to buy.
- Buying centres, teams and networks.
- Straight rebuy, modified rebuy and new buy purchasing situations.

11.1 What is sourcing?

Definition: Sourcing is the process of identifying, selecting and developing suppliers.

Ideally, the process will be driven by procurement, which will involve key decision makers in the organisation such as operational and finance staff. When category management is in place, sourcing is one of their accountabilities. A key differentiator for all organisations is the extent to which they have tactical and strategic sourcing in place.

11.1.1 Tactical sourcing

Tactical and operational sourcing is concerned with low-level procurement decisions that may relate to low-risk, non-critical items and services. Tactical sourcing is also concerned with short-term adaptive decisions as to how and from where specific requirements are to be met. For example, there may be a strategic sourcing strategy to obtain contract staff from one source who have a five-year call-off contract. In a short-term emergency, caused by flooding, it could be necessary to use other suppliers to obtain the immediate skills that are required.

11.1.2 Strategic sourcing

A sourcing strategy is a process, not an isolated decision.[1] It continuously

- balances internal and external activities, services and know-how
- aligns business strategy, business processes and 'product' requirements
- balances the results that must be achieved and the future options available.

The OGC[2] explains that the strategic sourcing process is an iterative cycle, in which a number of distinct stages of maturity can be identified. The level of maturity ranges from development of short-term tactical plans to long-term sourcing strategies. Figure 11.1 shows the stages in the maturity profile.

Figure 11.1 Stages in the sourcing strategy maturity cycle

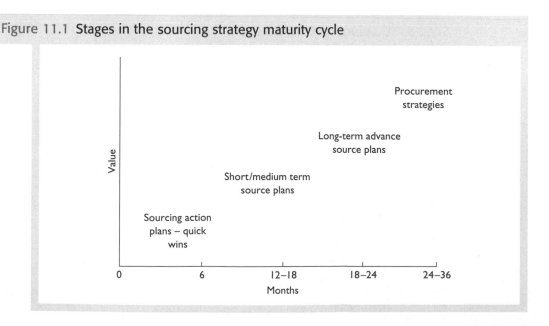

Strategic sourcing is concerned with top-level, longer-term decisions relating to high-profit, high supply risk strategic items and low-profit, high supply risk bottleneck products and services. It is also concerned with the formulation of long-term purchasing policies, the supplier base, partnership sourcing, reciprocal and intra-company trading, globalisation and countertrade, and the purchase of capital equipment and ethical issues.

The status and importance purchasing now has required a transition from thinking of it as a purely tactical activity to seeing it as a strategic activity. In transactional sourcing, purchasing is viewed as a function concerned with the placement of orders. In strategic sourcing, purchasing is viewed as a knowledge-based activity concerned with the total cost of ownership rather than the price paid per item with optional mix of relationships to provide competitive advantage.

11.2 The sourcing process

Strategic sourcing is a complicated process involving a number of interrelated tasks. Not surprisingly, a number of models of the strategic process have been devised. A typical model is that of Novack and Simco,[3] who present the following 11-stage sourcing process.

Stage 1   *Identify or re-evaluate needs*

In some instances, needs must be re-evaluated because they have changed.

Stage 2   *Define or evaluate users' requirements*

Stage 3   *Decide to make or buy*

Stage 4   *Identify type of purchase*

The three types of purchases – from least amount of time and complexity to most amount of time and complexity – are:

1 straight rebuy or routine purchase

2 a modified rebuy, which requires a change to an existing supplier or input

3 a new buy, which results from a new user need.

Stage 5   *Conduct market analysis*

A source of supply can operate in a purely competitive market (many suppliers), an oligopolistic market (a few large suppliers) or a monopolistic market (one supplier) – see section 12.3.

Stage 6   *Identify possible suppliers*

This may include suppliers that the purchaser has not previously used.

Stage 7   *Prescreen possible suppliers*

This process will reduce the number of suppliers to those that can meet the purchaser's demands.

Stage 8   *Evaluate the remaining supply base*

This activity is often accomplished by means of competitive bidding.

Stage 9   *Choose supplier*

The choice of supplier determines the relationships that will exist between the purchasing and supplier organisations and how the relationship will be structured and implemented. It will also determine how relationships with non-selected suppliers will be maintained.

Stage 10 *Deliver product/perform service*

The completion of this activity also begins the generation of performance data to be used for the next activity.

Stage 11 *Post purchase/make performance evaluation*

The supplier's performance must be evaluated to determine how well the purchaser's needs have been met. This will provide data for future sourcing.

11.3 Sourcing information

Sourcing information can be divided into the areas shown in Figure 11.2.

Figure 11.2 **Areas of sourcing information**

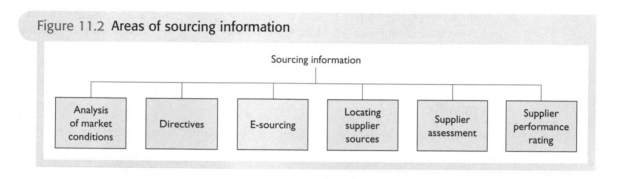

11.4 Analysis of market conditions

11.4.1 What is a market?

The term 'market' can mean:

- a place where goods and services are bought and sold – for example, the European Union is a market created by agreement between the participating countries to reduce barriers to the internal movement of labour and capital
- large groups of buyers and sellers of wide classes of goods, such as the consumer goods market, the equipment market and so on
- demand and supply of a single class of community, such as the steel market, the cotton market
- the general economic conditions relating to the supply of goods and services applying at a particular time – of special importance to purchasing is the distinction between a buyer's and a seller's market.

11.4.2 Why is the analysis of market conditions important to sourcing?

Strategic purchasing involves using business intelligence to analyse the purchasing environment and make appropriate decisions and recommendations. Only on the basis of intelligence can strengths, weaknesses, opportunities and threats that impact supplies be evaluated. Business intelligence also provides information on how the organisation – and purchasing as an activity within the business – is performing relative to competitors. Analysis of market conditions as an aspect of business intelligence is useful for the following reasons:

■ it helps in forecasting the long-term demand for the product, of which bought-out materials, components and assemblies are part, so it also has an interest in market research

■ it assists in forecasting the price trends of bought-out items and how material costs are likely to affect production costs and selling prices, so, for example, the need for cheaper prices may influence sourcing decisions

■ it indicates what alternative goods and supply sources are available – it might be more economical to source items from abroad

■ it gives guidance on the security of supply sources, which is particularly important with sensitive commodities sourced abroad

■ information relating to pay trends, commodity prices, political factors and the like can assist in deciding whether to adopt a strategy of forward buying and stockpiling or hand-to-mouth buying and minimum stocks.

11.4.3 What sources of information relating to market conditions are available?

Information relating to market conditions may be obtained from the following sources:

■ *primary data* – field research that can use one or more approaches, such as observation, analysis of internal records, such as sales trends and order book levels, visits to suppliers, questionnaires

■ *secondary data* – statistics and reports issued by external information, many of which are on databases

■ *international sources* – a useful survey of information sources is provided by globalEDGE™ created by the Center for International Business Education and Research for Michigan State University, which is a knowledge portal that connects business professionals worldwide to a wealth of information, insights and learning resources on global business activities, while a further useful site is Business Information on the Internet, provided by the Federation of International Trade Associations based in Reston, Virginia and New York.

■ *UK government sources* – full details of publications can be obtained from The Stationery Office. The most important sources include:
  – *Abstracts of Statistics*, published annually and monthly
  – *Economic Trends*
  – *Census of Production*
  – *Department of Employment Gazette*
  – *Department for Business, Enterprise & Regulations Reform reports/publications*
  – *Bank of England Reports*

■ *US government sources*
  – STAT-USA – The Department of Commerce's site for economic and business data: retail sales, wholesale trade, business conditions, CPI, gross domestic product, etc. Includes the full and up-to-date National Trade Databank. The office ceased

operations on 30 September 2010, but they have created a STAT-USA/Internet Transition web page with links to the data sources.

- The NTDB (National Trade Data Bank) – provides access to Country Commercial Guides, Market Research reports, Best Market reports. The NTDB also provides US import and export statistics, as well as over 75 other reports and programmes. This service was provided by STAT-USA, please see comments above.
- Foreign trade statistics – Census Bureau.
- Business Gateway at FirstGov – easy access to government services for US businesses. Includes e-services, buying and selling to the government, statistics, laws and regulations, international trade services, publications.
- Export.gov – online trade resources with links to many federally produced market research products.
- Small Business Administration – links to a multitude of federal, state and local government websites useful to the small businessperson – start-up help, financing, business opportunities and more.
- US Business Advisor – over 100,000 business, trade and labour web pages from government sites.
- EDGAR – filings for all US public companies are available from US Securities and Exchange Commission. Included are annual (10K), quarterly (10Q) reports, annual reports to shareholders and other material for a comprehensive overview of the financial condition of companies.

■ *non-government sources* – these include:
- Economist Intelligence Unit
- Chambers of Commerce
- professional associations – of particular importance to procurement staff is *Supply Management*, the journal of the Chartered Institute of Purchasing and Supply (CIPS), and both the CIPS and the USA Institute of Supply Management have online databases.

■ *the press in the UK* – such as *The Economist*, *Financial Times* and the 'quality' daily and Sunday newspapers

■ *economic forecasts* – such as the Confederation of British Industries' (CBI) 'Economic Situation Report' and Oxford Economic Forecasting's range of publications, including *UK Economic Prospects*, *World Economic Prospects*, *UK Industrial Prospects* and *European Economic Prospects*.

11.5 Directives

A 'directive' is a general instruction. Typical directives relating to sourcing include those issued by the EU, central and local government offices and companies.

11.5.1 EU directives

Background

Most organisations that receive public funding are likely to be affected by European procurement legislation. Such organisations include central government departments, local authorities, NHS Trusts and universities. The legislation covers most contracts for supplies (that is, goods), work and services. European directives take precedence over national law, irrespective of when the domestic law was enacted. The political aim is to create a single market for public procurement so that European companies may, in principle, have access to contracts without any kind of discrimination.

Breach of the EU public procurement rules may have significant legal consequences. Under the Remedies Directive and implementing regulations, for example, the High Courts of England and Wales, Northern Ireland and the Court of Session in Scotland have the power to review the award of a contract and apply a number of remedies, including:

- declaring the contract void
- varying the contract
- awarding damages to the injured party.

Details of current EU directives are available from regional EU information offices on the Internet. Directive 2004/18/EC has been implemented into UK law via the Public Contracts Regulations 2006 which came into effect on 31 January, 2006. The directive simplifies and consolidates three pre-existing directives for public works, supplies and services into a single text. Provisions have been added to take account of modern procurement methods and developments in best practice. These include explicit provisions regarding framework agreements, central purchasing bodies, e-auctions and dynamic purchasing systems. A procedure called the Competitive Dialogue has also been introduced.

11.5.2 Central and local government purchasing directives and guidance

In the UK, current public procurement policy is based largely on the white papers 'Setting new standards: a strategy for government procurement', Cm 2840, 1995, and 'Modernising government', Cm 4310, March, 1999 (a 'white paper' is a statement of government policy or an explanation of proposed legislation).

The UK Office of Government Commerce (OGC) publishes guidelines on a range of procurement issues, such as strategic supplier management, e-procurement and contract innovation. A number of guidance notes issued when the Central Unit in Procurement (now superseded) formed part of the Treasury, covering topics such as post-tender negotiation and quality assurances, are still available. Guidelines on procurement and reports on the effectiveness of government initiatives aimed at improving central and local government procurement are also issued by the Audit Commission and the National Audit Office. Typical of the latter is the handbook *Getting Value for Money from Procurement* and the report 'Improving procurement progress' by the Office of Government Commerce in *Improving Department's Capability to Procure Cost-effectively* (2004). In addition to EU directives, regulations and guidance for local authorities may be given in 'statutory instruments', which are laws written by a government minister exercising legislative powers delegated to him or her by an Act of Parliament. There are a number of HM Government reports including:

- 'Transforming Government Procurement', HM Treasury (ISBN 978-1-84532-240-3)
- 'Addressing the environmental impacts of Government Procurement', National Audit Office (ISBN 978-010-295-475-3)
- 'Local Government Sustainable Procurement Strategy', I & DEA, November 2007 (ISBN 074-389-286-6).

11.5.3 Company directives

Company directives may be issued by the top management of an organisation, instructing that, for reasons of strategy or in pursuance of agreements, particular supplies must be obtained from a specific source. An example would be directives relating to intra-company or reciprocal trading.

11.6 E-sourcing

E-procurement, along with e-marketplaces, e-catalogues and e-auctions, was discussed in Chapter 6. E-sourcing is defined by the CIPS[4] as:

> using the Internet to make decisions and form strategies regarding how and where services or products are obtained.

Although both e-procurement and e-sourcing are integral to the purchasing cycle, the two terms are usually distinguished. E-procurement is usually concerned with non-core goods and services. These can, however, cover far more than routine MRO items or office supplies. As Waller[5] has stated:

> For telecommunications companies, network switches are indirect goods. For oil refineries, large condensers, costing millions of dollars are indirect goods. For companies that operate petrol stations, forecourts signs and fascias are indirect goods.

E-sourcing allows research, design and purchasing personnel to find parts, components and sub-assemblies for prototypes and subsequent production models. As ePedas[6] has explained:

> The difference between e-sourcing and e-procurement is that, in e-sourcing, decisions are made on the basis of functionality and characteristics, not purely on the basis of product and price. The e-sourced products form part of the finished products. Therefore e-sourcing is to determine which direct goods to buy.

The difference between e-procurement and e-sourcing is succinctly put in the following:

> E-procurement may be seen as the focus of local business administrators with one of the key goals being to devolve the buying process to local users, covering the requisition against contract, authorisation, order, receipt and payment.

> E-sourcing covers those parts of the buying process which are not wholly at the discretion of the specialist buyers, which includes knowledge (such as competence analysis, and spend analysis), specification, request for quotation/e-tender/e-auction and contract evaluation/negotiation.

11.7 Locating suppliers

Suppliers can be located by checking a wide range of sources. This process has been made faster and easier by the World Wide Web. There are many sources for locating suppliers, including:

■ a comprehensible searchable list of more than 1.7 million UK businesses, broken down into over 2500 distinct classifications, at the Yell.com site from *Yellow Pages*: www.yell.com

- some of the searchable databases intended to promote exports, such as the UK Trade and Investments database of suppliers: www.uktradeinvest.gov.uk
- major overseas reference resources, such as the Thomas Global Register Europe at: www.tgreurope.com, which gives access to a searchable directory of over 210,000 industrial manufacturers, and a related website at: www.thomasnet.com, which covers 650,000 US and Canadian suppliers
- the Purchasing Research Service at: www.touchbriefings.com, which provides sector-by-sector supplier listings and news items.

Specialised sites include:

- the Applegate Directory at: www.applegate.co.uk, which covers suppliers in the electronics, engineering and plastics sectors
- the Used Equipment Network at: www.buyused.com, which offers secondhand plant and machinery – from aircraft to X-ray machines – covering more than 75,000 items from more than 10,000 dealers.

In addition to the above it can be quick and helpful to contact:

- Foreign Embassies and High Commissions
- Trade Associations
- other buyers through networking.

Databases can provide up-to-date information and may be space-saving substitutes for large reference collections. Access to such databases may be free and unrestricted or subscriber only.

Other useful ways in which to locate suppliers include:

- *salespeople* – the usefulness of salespeople is dependent on their knowledge of the product they are seeking to promote – they are often able to provide useful service information regarding suppliers, such as details of items other than those manufactured by their own undertaking
- *exhibitions* – these provide an opportunity to compare competing products, meet representatives of suppliers and attend presentations by exhibitors, and exhibition catalogues and other literature usually provide details of the main suppliers in a particular field, so should be retained for reference purposes
- *trade journals* – these provide buyers not only with information regarding new products, substitute materials and so on, but also trade gossip, which keeps buyers informed about changes in the policies of suppliers and their personnel.

11.8 Supplier assessment

11.8.1 When to assess suppliers

Supplier assessment will arise when a prospective supplier applies to be placed on the buyer's approved list, responds to the buyer's request to pre-qualify for a forthcoming tender process or where the buyer decides to conduct soft market testing and due diligence. The purpose of all these is to assure the buying organisation that the prospective supplier can, reliably, meet the technical, financial and commercial requirements.

Supplier assessment can be a time-consuming and costly activity, for the following reasons:

- designing an effective questionnaire
- designing the evaluation scoring and weightings model
- creating an evaluation team that represents a cross-section of interests
- analysing and reporting on the submissions
- making reference site visits
- taking up references.

The situations when assessment is essential include:

- one-off purchases where the buyer has no strategic source of supply
- where potential suppliers do not hold BS EN ISO 9000:2008
- purchase of outsourcing services
- purchase of construction, capital equipment and ICT systems
- locating competent SMEs and Third Sector suppliers
- when making purchasing consortia agreements
- when re-tendering Framework Agreements
- when engaged in global sourcing
- when 'local content' purchases are required as part of, for example, an off-shore defence contract
- major sub-contractors are to be appointed
- when long-term product support is required
- when a current strategic supplier is encountering adverse trading conditions.

11.8.2 What should be assessed?

Supplier appraisal is situational. What to appraise is related to the requirements of the particular purchaser. All appraisals should, however, evaluate potential suppliers from ten perspectives:

- finance
- insurance
- productive capacity and facilities/service support capability
- quality
- health and safety
- environmental management
- existing contracts held and performance
- organisational structure and key personnel – resources
- sub-contracting – proposed actions
- procurement capability and supply chain management.

This information is gathered, typically, by issuing a Pre-Qualification Questionnaire.

11.8.3 Finance

A robust financial appraisal should reduce, but will not eliminate, the risk of awarding a contract to a supplier whose financial viability is in doubt. It does, however, provide information enabling considered decisions to be made. It may, for example, lead to a decision to require an 'on-demand' performance bond. There are some checks that must be considered:

- the last three years' turnover, split between UK and off-shore business
- the profitability and the relationship between gross and net profit over the last three years
- any losses in any period being examined and reasons for such losses, for example, write-offs against poor contract performance
- the value of capital assets and return on capital assets
- the scale of borrowings and the ratio of debts to assets
- the possibility of takeover or merger affecting ability to supply
- the scale of pension fund deficits.

Such enquiries are advisable for small-sized and medium-sized enterprises (SMEs) in relation to one-off or annual contracts in excess of, say, £15,000 bearing in mind that their finances may not be entirely robust. In the UK, an appraisal can be undertaken internally by accounting staff who can study the supplier's annual report and accounts for the past three or four years.

In the USA, 'FORM 10K' is an annual report submitted by US companies to the Securities and Exchange Commission, pursuant to Section 13 or 15(d) of the Securities Exchange Act of 1934. There is also the 'FORM 10Q', a quarterly report. The information contained in these documents exceeds, greatly, that typically found in UK companies' annual reports. There is vital company and market intelligence of value to procurement decisions. Examples of information contained are details of companies' major markets, products, business risks, outstanding legal writs and their nature, divisional financial results, investments and competition. These reports can be obtained free of charge from the companies themselves and many are available on the Internet.

Credit reports may also be obtained from bankers or credit references and credit reports provided by such agencies as Dun and Bradstreet. Important information provided by Dun and Bradstreet's supplier evaluation reports include:

- *sales* – gives a picture of the firm's financial size in terms of sales/revenue volume
- *financial profile* – evaluates how the enterprise is doing financially compared with its industry and, to understand the profitability and solvency of a supplier, five key financial ratios are calculated that provide industry benchmarks against a peer group of suppliers
- *supplier risk score* – an evaluation of the risk involved in dealing with a supplier that presents an at-a-glance 1–9 rating based on financial and public records and operational information, with 1 being the lowest and 9 the highest risk (this predictive score helps purchasing to understand the general financial status of a supplier and benchmark it against others).

In addition, the Office of Government Commerce (OGC)[7] recommends that basic checks should be made on a UK company's title and its registered number at Companies

Table 11.1 Important balance sheet and income ratios when appraising potential suppliers

Ratio source	Name of ratio	Calculation of ratio	Purpose of ratio
Balance sheet ratios measure the liquidity and solvency (ability to pay bills) and gearing (the extent to which the business is dependent on creditors' funding)	Liquidity ratios – current ratio	$$\frac{\text{Total current assets}}{\text{Total current liabilities}}$$	Can the business pay its current debts with a margin of safety for possible losses in current assets? A generally acceptable ratio is 2:1. The minimum acceptable ratio is 1:1
	Quick ratio (the 'acid' test)	$$\frac{\text{Quick assets}}{\text{Current liabilities – Bank overdraft}}$$	Answers question 'if all sales revenue should disappear, could the enterprise meet its current obligations with the readily convertible quick funds on hand?' Ratio of 1:1 is minimum acceptable
	Working capital	Total current assets – Total current liabilities	More of a measure of cashflow than a ratio. The result must be a positive number
	Gearing ratio	$$\frac{\text{Fixed interest capital}}{\text{Fixed interest – Equity capital}}$$	Too high a gearing ratio is potentially unstable as it indicates undue dependence on external sources for long-term financing
Income statement Profit and loss account These ratios measure profitability	Gross profit margin ratio	$$\frac{\text{Gross profit}}{\text{Net sales}}$$	Gross profit = Net sales – Cost of goods sold. Measures the percentage of sales value left after deducting cost of manufacturing to pay the overhead costs of the enterprise. Can be compared to ratios of other businesses
	Net profit margin ratio	$$\frac{\text{Net profit before tax}}{\text{Net sales}}$$	Indicates percentage of sales revenue left after subtracting cost of goods sold and all expenses except tax

House to see whether the company is dormant or trading and whether it is owned by another company or supported by a venture capital organisation.

Balance sheet and profit and loss ratio analysis (see Table 11.1) should also be used. The OGC indicates a number of warning signs, including:

- falling cash levels
- falling profit margins
- increasing overdraft with static turnover
- increasing employment with static turnover
- increasing pension liabilities
- late filing of accounts
- changing auditors and bankers
- adverse press reports.

In the case of substantial contracts, the purchasing organisation should question whether or not the supplier is likely to become overly dependent on the buying company.

11.8.4 Insurance

Typically, a buyer will establish:

1 the types of insurance the prospective supplier holds and
2 the cover value of each insurance (establishing if the cover value is 'per claim' or 'in the aggregate').

The types of insurance include:

■ Public liability insurance covers any award of damages given to a member of the public because of an injury or damage to their property.

■ Employer's liability insurance enables businesses to meet the costs of damages and legal fees for employees who are injured or made ill at work through the fault of the employer.

■ Product liability insurance covers the fact that products must be fit for purpose. The supplier is legally responsible for any damage or injury that a product he supplies may cause.

■ Professional indemnity insurance protects a business against claims for loss or damage by a client or a third party if the company/consultant have made mistakes or are found to have been negligent in some or all of the services that have been provided.

11.8.5 Productive capacity and facilities/services support capability

'Capacity' has been defined as:[8]

> The limiting capability of a productive unit to produce items within a stated time period normally expressed in terms of output units per unit of time.

Capacity is an elusive concept because it must be related to the extent that a facility is used – that is, it may be the policy to utilise production capacity five days weekly, one shift daily or produce a maximum of 2000 units monthly. Plant capacity can normally be increased by working overtime or adding new facilities.

In appraising supplier capacity, attention should be given to the following considerations:

■ the maximum productive capacity in a specified working period

■ the extent to which capacity is currently over-committed or under-committed – for example, a full order book may raise doubts about the supplier's capacity to take on further work or else you have to wonder if a substantial amount of capacity is underutilised

■ how existing capacity might be expanded to meet future increased demand

■ the percentage of available capacity utilised by existing major customers

■ what percentage of capacity would be utilised if the potential supplier were awarded the business of the purchaser – this can also be assessed in terms of annual turnover, but, in any case, care should be taken to avoid making the supplier overly dependent on one or two customers

■ what systems are used for capacity planning?

An appraisal of production facilities depends on the purpose of it. Appraisal of machinery, for example, depends on what is to be produced. In general, attention should be given to answering the following kinds of questions.

■ Has the supplier the full range of machinery needed to make the required product?

■ How would any shortage of machinery be overcome?

- Are machines modern and well maintained? (Machine breakdowns will affect delivery.)
- Is the plant layout satisfactory?
- Is there evidence of good housekeeping?
- Has the supplier adopted such approaches as computer-aided design (CAD), computer-aided manufacture (CAM) or flexible manufacturing systems (FMS)?

11.8.6 Quality

For suppliers not included on the BSI's Register of Firms of Assessed Quality, appraisal may require satisfactory answers to such questions as the following:

- Has the supplier met the criteria for other BSI schemes, such as the Kitemark, Safety Mark and scheme for registered stockists?
- Has the supplier met the quality approval criteria of other organisations, such as the Ford Quality Awards, the Ministry of Defence, British Gas or others?
- To what extent does the supplier know about and implement the concept of total quality management?
- What procedures are in place for the inspection and testing of purchased materials?
- What relevant test and inspection process does the supplier use?
- What statistical controls are applied regarding quality?
- Does quality control cover an evaluation of quality?
- Can the supplier guarantee that the purchaser can safely eliminate the need for all incoming inspection? (This is especially important for JIT deliveries).

11.8.7 Health and Safety

It is necessary to establish:

- their Health and Safety policy
- their Health and Safety auditing arrangements
- details of Health and Safety Executive or Local Authority investigations/prosecutions
- first aid and welfare provision
- name and title of director responsible for Health and Safety
- how the company communicates its Health and Safety policy and procedures to employees.

11.8.8 Environmental management

ISO 14001 provides guidelines on environmental policies and, where applicable, suppliers should be expected to have an environmental policy and procedures for the implementation of such a policy. A large number of EU directives have also been issued relating to air, water, chemicals, packaging and waste.

Apart from those questions with reference to ISO 14001 and EU directives, other suitable questions to ask include the following.

- Has responsibility for environmental management been allocated to a particular person?
- Are materials obtained, so far as possible, from sustainable sources – such as timber?

- What is the lifecycle cost of the suppliers' product?
- What facilities does the supplier have for waste minimisation, disposal and recycling?
- What energy savings, if any, do the supplier's products provide?
- What arrangements are in place for the control of dangerous substances and nuisance?

11.8.9 Existing contracts held and performance

This subject matter directly relates to section 11.8.5 above. It is impractical to obtain details of all existing contracts held and their performance. The buyer should, however, probe:

- the six largest value contracts held and the pull on capacity/resources
- names of clients (noting that confidentiality may prevent disclosure)
- the extent of the supplier's bid pipeline
- whether contracts have been terminated for non-performance
- whether damages have been paid for non-performance.

11.8.10 Organisational structure and key personnel

It is advisable to establish:

- the structure of the company providing the goods or services
- the wider corporate structure and reporting accountabilities
- where purchasing/supply chain fits into the structure
- who are the key personnel that will be associated with the contract?
- if the supplier is a multinational who does the CEO (UK) report to?

11.8.11 Sub-contracting – proposed actions

The nature and extent of sub-contracting can have a great impact on contract performance; hence it is advisable to ascertain:

- Will sub-contracting take place?
- What is the extent of sub-contracting – value and specific goods/services?
- How are sub-contractors appointed?
- What are the specific contract terms and conditions used?
- Will key clauses be flowed down to sub-contractors, e.g. right of audit?

11.8.12 Purchasing capability and supply chain management

It is very surprising that these facets are rarely the subject of PQQs; they should be! As a minimum, the following questions should be answered:

- Is there a well-established purchasing function?
- Who is the head of the function and who do they report to?
- How is the function organised, e.g. category management?
- How will they manage costs throughout the project?
- Who is accountable for supply chain performance?
- What are the perceived purchasing risks?
- How will these risks be mitigated?

11.8.13 Obtaining information for supplier appraisal

This may be done by means of a suitable questionnaire, supplemented where appropriate by a visit to the potential suppliers.

11.8.14 Appraisal questionnaires

The topics in sections 11.8.3 to 11.8.13 above can easily be adapted to use in a questionnaire. Some general principles relating to questionnaires should be remembered:

- Keep the appraisal questionnaire as short as is reasonably possible.
- Ask only what is necessary and obtain only information that will be used.
- Divide the various sections of the questionnaire into 'fields', each relating to a particular area of investigation, as in sections 11.8.3 to 11.8.13 above.
- Consider whether or not it is likely that the respondent will know the answers to the questions and the difficulties they are likely to have providing the information.
- Consider whether or not respondents will understand the wording of questions – are you using technical or cultural-specific words or abbreviations, for example.
- Ask only one question at a time.
- Start with factual and then go on to opinion-based questions.
- Ensure that the questionnaire is signed, dated and the title of the respondent is indicated.

11.8.15 Supplier visits

Supplier visits should always be undertaken by a cross-functional team that includes a senior member of purchasing and specialists on quality and production engineering. Each member of the team is able to evaluate the supplier from a specialist viewpoint so this ensures shared responsibility for the decision to approve or reject a supplier. The purposes of a supplier visit include:

- the confirmation of information provided by the supplier in a structured questionnaire
- an in-depth discussion of the products and services offered by a potential supplier and ways in which the supplier can contribute to the requirements of the visiting organisation.

Prior to the visit, a checklist of matters to be reviewed should be prepared. This ensures that no important questions are overlooked, provides a permanent record of the visit and reasons for the decisions reached can be recorded. On supplier visits, important sources of information are observation and informal conversations. Particular attention should be given to the following areas.

- *Personal attitudes* – an observant visitor can sense the attitudes of the supplier's employees towards their work. This provides an indication of the likely quality of their output and service dependability. The state of morale will be evident from:
  - an atmosphere of harmony or dissatisfaction among the production workers
  - the degree of interest in customer service on the part of supervisory staff
  - the degree of energy displayed and the interest in getting things done
  - the use of manpower – whether economical, with everyone usually busy, or extravagant and costly, with excess people doing little or nothing.

- *Adequacy and care of production equipment* – close observation of the equipment in a plant will indicate whether it is:
  - modern or antiquated
  - accurately maintained or obviously worn
  - well cared for by operators or dirty and neglected
  - of proper size or type to produce the buyer's requirements
  - of sufficient capacity to produce the quantities desired.

  The presence or absence of ingenious self-developed mechanical devices for performing unusual operations will be indicative of the plant's manufacturing and engineering expertise.

- *Technological know-how of supervisory personnel* – conversations with foremen, shop superintendents and others will indicate their technical knowledge and ability to control and improve the operations of processes under their supervision.

- *Means of controlling quality* – observation of the inspection methods will indicate their adequacy to ensure the specified quality of the product. Attention should be given to:
  - whether or not the materials are chemically analysed and physically checked
  - frequency of inspection during the production cycle
  - employment of such techniques as statistical quality control
  - availability of statistical quality control.

- *Housekeeping* – a plant that is orderly and clean in its general appearance indicates careful planning and control by management. Such a plant inspires confidence that its products will be made with the same care and pride as to their quality. The dangers of breakdown, fire or other disasters will also be minimised, with a consequent increased assurance of continuity of supply.

- *Competence of technical staff* – conversations with design, research or laboratory staff indicate their knowledge of the latest materials, tools and processes relating to their products and anticipated developments in their industry.

- *Competence of management* – all the above areas are, in essence, a reflection of management and, therefore, indicate its quality. Particularly in the case of a new supplier, an accurate appraisal of executive personnel is of paramount importance.

11.9 Supplier approval

Supplier approval is the recognition, following a process of appraisal, that a particular supplier is able to meet the standards and requirements of the particular buyer. The approval may be for a one-off transaction or mean that the supplier is put on a list of approved suppliers.

There are three important aspects of approved supplier lists:

1 the current emphasis is on having a small supplier base and so additions to an approved list must be carefully controlled

2 when an application to be placed on an approved list emanated from the supplier, this should have been considered fairly and, as far as possible with the minimum of bureaucracy

3 directives such as those of the EU have reservations about whether or not approved lists invalidate the EU principles of transparency, equality of treatment, proportionality and mutual recognition.

Approval should be decided by a cross-functional team that may give various levels of approval, such as A for unconditional, B for conditional subject to the potential supplier meeting prescribed conditions or C for unsuitable for approval.

Approved suppliers may also be graded into such categories as:[9]

1 *partnership* – a one-to-one relationship with a supplier in which a corporate single-source agreement will be in place

2 *preferred* – there is an agreed number of suppliers for one product or service with a corporate agreement

3 *approved suppliers* – suppliers have been assessed as satisfactory suppliers for one or more products or services

4 *confirmed suppliers* – those that have been specifically requested by a user, such as design or production, and accepted by purchasing – the acceptance process being:

   (a) no preferred, partnership or approved supplier is on the purchasing database for an identical requirement

   (b) there will be no continuing demand on the supplier

5 *one-off supplier* – suppliers in this category are accepted on the following conditions:

   (a) no preferred, partnership or approved supplier is on the purchasing database for identical goods or services

   (b) purchasing card payment is not appropriate or possible

   (c) supplier will be closed after the transaction is complete.

In general, approval in the first instance should be for one year. Suppliers that consistently meet or exceed the prescribed standards over a period of, say, three years may be upgraded from 'approved' to 'preferred'. Conversely, suppliers that fail to meet performance standards should be removed from the database of approved suppliers.

11.10 Evaluating supplier performance

11.10.1 Why evaluate supplier performance?

There are various reasons for the evaluation of purchasing performance being important.

■ Evaluation can significantly improve supplier performance. Emptoris[10] states that, properly done, supplier performance management can provide answers to questions such as the following:

   – Who are the highest-quality suppliers?

   – How can relationships with the best suppliers be enhanced?

   – How can supplier performance be incorporated into total cost analysis?

   – How can buyers ensure that suppliers live up to what was promised?

   – How can feedback be shared based on experience with a supplier?

   – How can underperforming suppliers' problems be tracked and fixed?

■ Evaluation assists decision making regarding when a supplier is retained or removed from an approved list.

■ Evaluation assists in deciding with which suppliers a specific purchase order should be placed.

- Evaluation provides suppliers with an incentive for continuous improvement and prevents performance 'slippage'.
- Evaluation can assist in decisions regarding how to distribute the spend for an item among several suppliers to better manage risk.

11.10.2 What to evaluate?

Traditionally, the key performance indicators (KPIs) for the evaluation of supplier performance have been price, quality and delivery. While these are still basic to supplier evaluation, such developments as JIT, lean manufacturing, integrated supply chains and e-procurement have made the fuller evaluation of supplier relationships an important consideration. Such relationships, as Kozak and Cohen[11] point out, include such qualitative factors as intercompany communication and high levels of trust, which are not easy to assess other than subjectively. Apart from subjectivity, qualitative evaluations are often subject to 'halo effects' – the tendency to bias in favour of a particular supplier due to irrelevant considerations, such as the friendly approach of its sales representatives. There is, however, an element of subjectivity in all evaluation systems.

The number of KPIs that may be used is almost limitless. A USA survey by Simpson et al.[12] reported 142 evaluation items, which they arranged under 19 categories of criteria, the first 10 of which are shown in Table 11.2.

The researchers conclude that, on the basis of these criteria, suppliers should concentrate on quality issues first – especially the ability to meet customers' order requirements – followed by continuous improvement and innovation efforts. Importantly, while not completely ignoring pricing issues, suppliers may want to place less emphasis on price when attempting to secure and retain customers.

11.10.3 Quantitative approaches to supplier evaluation

The aim of quantitative ratings is to provide a sounder basis for evaluation than subjective ratings. There are a number of considerations, including:

- determining what can be quantified – there are the obvious candidates, including, deliveries on time, quality defects (perhaps graded according to severity and impact

Table 11.2 Supplier evaluation factors considered by relative frequency of mention and importance (Simpson et al.[13]) – first ten factors only

Evaluation criteria	Number of items by category	Percentage mentioning	Relative importance rating
Quality and process control	566	24.9	1
Continuous improvement	210	9.2	2
Facility environment	188	8.2	2
Customer relationship	187	8.2	2
Delivery	185	8.1	2
Inventory and warehousing	158	7.0	2
Ordering	132	5.8	2
Financial conditions	126	5.5	2
Certifications	81	3.6	3
Price	81	3.6	3

on the buyer's business), response times for resolving queries, fault correction times (I.T. software support), resolution of disputes and timely delivery of IT consumables

- the cost and ability to collect the relevant data on which ratings are based, recognising that there are now software programmes to facilitate this – depending on the nature of the buyer's business the ratings can be provided at specified intervals
- ratings are no more accurate than the assumptions on which they are based
- a recognition that the supplier's performance can be adversely affected by the buyer's or third-party actions.

11.10.4 Service levels

Service levels are performance requirements, referred to as 'service level agreements' that are usually provided in contracts for outsourcing back-office services and inter-departmental service provision in the same organisation. In external contracts it is usual for 'penalties' to be applied when the prescribed levels are not achieved.

The structure of service level agreements varies a lot. A simple structure would include:

- agreement overview
- goals and objectives
- stakeholders
- periodic review
- service agreement
  - service scope
  - customer requirements
  - service provider requirements
  - service assumptions
- service management
  - service availability
  - service requests.

11.10.5 The seven Cs of effective supplier evaluation

Many of the aspects of supplier appraisal are neatly summarised by Carter[14] as the 'seven Cs of supplier evaluation':

1 *Competency* of the supplier to undertake the tasks required
2 *Capacity* of the supplier to meet the purchaser's total needs
3 *Commitment* of the supplier to the customer in terms of quality, cost driving and service
4 *Control systems* in relation to inventory, costs, budgets, people and information
5 *Cash resources and financial stability* ensuring that the selected supplier is financially sound and is able to continue in business into the foreseeable future
6 *Cost* commensurate with quality and service
7 *Consistency* the ability of the supplier to deliver consistently and, where possible, improve levels of quality and service.

11.10.6 Evaluation of supplier performance – a case study

Fredriksson and Gadde[15] have published a 'Competitive Paper' which reviews the literature on supplier evaluation, presents a case study illustrating the evaluation of the

Table 11.3 Volvo evaluation model

Dimensions, criteria and scopes	Frequency (time horizon)	Method (quant = quantitative qual = qualitative)	People involved (department)
Module quality performance			
■ Function, geometry, looks and noise module features at and after the line	1 time/minute	Formal, quant. and qual.	Assembly operators (Assembly) QA engineers (Assembly) SQA engineers (Logistics)
■ Quality processes and structures	When quality	Semi-formal, quant.	SQA engineer (Logistics)
– inside module supplier	defects occur	and qual.	Assembly managers (Assembly)
– on its supply side	1–2 times/2 years	Formal	SQA engineer (Logistics)
– in interaction with Volvo	(future oriented)		Purchasing engineer (Purchasing)
Delivery precision performance			
■ Module carrier on time at loading dock	1–2 times/hour	Formal, quant.	Delivery controller (Logistics)
■ Modules in right box in carrier at line	1 time/minute	Formal, quant.	Assembly operator (Assembly)
■ No. of restrictions in Volvo's plans	On occurrence	Formal, quant.	Delivery controller (Logistics)
■ Logistics processes and structure	When delivery	Semi-formal, quant.	Delivery controller (Logistics)
– inside module supplier	deviations occur	and qual.	
– on its supply side	1–2 times/2 years	Formal, quant. and	Delivery controller (Logistics)
– in interaction with Volvo	(future oriented)	qual.	Logistics engineer (Purchasing)
Cost performance			
■ Module price			
■ Processes and structures	>1 time/year	Formal, quant.	Purchaser (Purchasing)
– inside module supplier and its suppliers	(future oriented)		
– in interaction with Volvo			Supplier park manager (Purchasing)
– contribution to supplier park			
■ Logistics costs	Varying, but about	Formal, quant. and	Logistics engineer (Logistics)
– processes and structures in relation to the total logistics system	1–2 times/year (future oriented)	qual.	
Overall performance			
■ Quality ■ Management	>1 time/2–4 years	Semi-formal,	Purchaser (Purchasing)
■ Delivery ■ Supply	(future oriented)	quantitative	Purchasing engineer
■ Cost management			(Purchasing)
■ Environment			

performance of a car manufacturer's suppliers and a discussion on the findings and implications of the case study.

Table 11.3 shows the Volvo perspective when evaluating a module supplier and its performance. It shows the use of a number of different evaluation dimensions, criteria, scope, time horizons and methods. Consequently, people with different expertise in several departments are involved in the evaluation of the supplier's performance.

11.11 Policy issues in sourcing

There are numerous aspects of sourcing policy and strategy, but ten of the main ones considered in this chapter are shown in Figure 11.3.

Figure 11.3 **Aspects of sourcing policy and strategy**

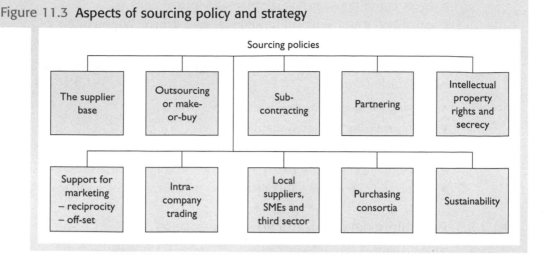

11.12 The supplier base

11.12.1 What is the supplier base?

The supplier base relates to the number, range, location and characteristics of the vendors that supply the purchaser.

Supplier bases may be described as broad, lean, narrow, single-sourced, local, national, international, diversified or specialised. They can relate to a 'family' or related products and suppliers or the totality of vendors with whom a purchaser does business.

Factors influencing the supply base of an enterprise include:

■ the range of purchases including goods and services
■ the core competencies of the buying organisation
■ investment requirements in product/service long-term capacity
■ supply chain risks
■ inventory investment
■ ability to respond to emergencies and changing market conditions
■ short-term purchasing actions or long-term partnering
■ miscellaneous factors such as the social responsibilities to local industry or support of SMEs and third sector.

11.12.2 Supplier base optimisation

Supplier base optimisation or rationalisation is concerned with determining a strategy that will identify the optimum number of suppliers required to fulfil the requirements to supply all purchasing categories.

In many organisations there are too many suppliers who are awarded business in an ad hoc manner. The need for rationalisation includes:

■ focusing purchases on a limited number of competent and cost effective suppliers
■ requirement to control cost and procurement processes
■ generate confidence for suppliers to make long-term investments

- encourage innovation and continuous improvement
- enhance the availability of meaningful management information
- optimise risks in the supply chain.

There are a number of approaches that can be adopted to achieve supplier base optimisation, including:

- electing for a single or dual source of supply
- an approved or preferred supplier list
- outsourcing a range of services thereby eliminating individual suppliers to the services
- redesign of products to reduce reliance on those owning previous IPRs
- aggregating purchases with other buyers to make quantity feasible to larger suppliers.

11.12.3 Possible risks of a reduced supplier base

These include:

- complacency resulting in repetitive actions cutting out innovation
- reduced competition in the supply market
- exit of marginal supplier reducing available capacity
- threats to supply arising from typical force majeure events
- lack of knowledge of supply market developments and market intelligence
- inflexibility in contractual obligations.

11.13 Outsourcing

11.13.1 What is outsourcing?

Verikatesan[16] observes that: 'Today manufacturing focus means learning how *not* to make things – how *not* to make the parts that divert a company from cultivating its skills, parts that its suppliers can make more efficiently.'
Outsourcing may be defined as:

a management strategy by which major non-core functions are transferred to specialist, efficient, external providers.

Central to outsourcing are:

- make-or-buy decisions
- partnerships between purchasers and suppliers – as outsourcing relationships are often unequal, it is sometimes suggested that such arrangements should be termed 'co-sourcing'.

11.13.2 What to outsource?

There is a thriving outsourcing market, both in manufacturing and the provision of services. The activities most easily outsourced are those that are:

- resource intensive – especially those with high labour or capital costs
- available from niche market suppliers with proven technology and skills

- relatively discrete with few interfaces and dependencies on complex supply chains
- subject to long-term, fluctuating work patterns
- requiring relatively little client-side management
- where very clear contractual accountabilities can be established.

11.14 Outsourcing manufacturing

11.14.1 Types of make-or-buy decisions

This is concerned with make-or-buy decisions. Probert[17] identifies three levels of make-or-buy decisions.

Strategic make-or-buy decisions

Strategic make-or-buy decisions (see Figure 11.4) determine the shape and capability of the organisation's manufacturing operation by influencing:

- what products to make
- what investment to make in machines and labour to make the products
- ability to develop new products and processes as the knowledge and skills gained by manufacturing in-house may be critical for future applications
- the selection of suppliers as they may need to be involved in design and production processes.

Conversely, inappropriate allocation of work to suppliers may damage an enterprise by developing a new competitor or damaging product quality or performance, profit potential, risk and flexibility.

Strategic decisions also provide the framework for shorter-term tactical and component decisions.

Figure 11.4 Decision processes for make or buy

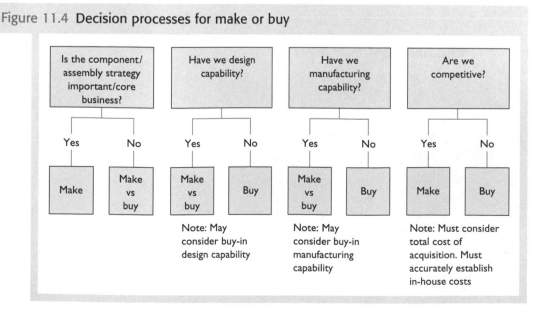

Tactical make-or-buy decisions

These deal with the issue of a temporary imbalance of manufacturing capacity:

- changes in demand may make it impossible to make everything in-house, even though this is the preferred option
- conversely, a fall in demand may cause the enterprise to bring in-house work that was previously bought-out, if this can be done without damaging supplier relationships and without defaulting on a contract.

In such situations, managers require criteria for choosing between the available options. Such criteria may be quantitative, qualitative or both.

Component make-or-buy decisions

Component make-or-buy decisions are made, ideally, at the design stage and relate to whether a particular component of the product should be made in-house or bought-in.

11.14.2 Cost factors in make-or-buy decisions

Accurate make-or-buy decisions often require the application of marginal costing and break-even analysis.

Marginal costing

Marginal costing is defined as:[18]

> a (costing) principle whereby variable costs are charged to cost units and the fixed costs attributable to the relevant period are written off in full against the contribution for that period.

The term 'contribution' in the above definition is the difference between the selling (or purchase price) and the variable cost per unit.

The marginal cost approach is shown by Examples 11.1 and 11.2.

Example 11.1

Marginal costing

	£
Direct materials	60
Direct pay	30
Direct expenses	10
Prime cost	100
Works overhead (100 per cent on direct pay)	30
Works cost	130
Office overhead (20 per cent on works cost)	26
	156
Selling overheads £14 per item	14
Cost of sales	170
Net profit	30
Normal selling price	200

Assume that:

1 works overheads are 60 per cent fixed and 40 per cent variable
2 office overheads are constant
3 selling expenses are 50 per cent fixed and 50 per cent variable.

Then, the *marginal* cost will be:

	£	
Direct materials	60	
Direct pay	30	
Direct expenses	10	
	100	
Works overhead	12	(40 per cent of £30)
Selling overheads £14 per item	13	(50 per cent of £26)
	125	

Any price over £125 represents a *contribution* to fixed overheads. If fixed overheads totalled £75,000, a selling price of £200 would represent a contribution of £75 per item to fixed overheads and it would be necessary to sell 1000 items before the undertaking would *break even*. If, however, the selling price were reduced to £150, it would be necessary to sell 3000 units before reaching the *break-even point* as the contribution per item would be only £25.

In make-or-buy decisions, it is necessary to compare the vendor's price with the marginal cost of making, plus the loss of contributions of work displaced.

Example 11.2

Marginal costing

A company manufactures assembly JMA 423, the normal annual usage of which is 10,000 units. The current costs are:

	£
Materials	90
Labour	40
Variable overheads	10
Fixed overheads	20
	160

The component could be purchased for £156 but the capacity used for its production would then be idle. Only 30 per cent of the fixed costs is recoverable if the component is bought.

Assuming that there are no other relevant factors, should component JMA 423 be made or bought?

Solution

A superficial comparison suggests that the item should be bought rather than made. The correct comparison, however, is between the marginal cost of making and the buying price.

	Make	Buy	Difference
Variable costs (£90 + £40 + £10) = £140	£140	£156	£16
Variable costs × volume	£1,400,000	£1,560,000	£160,000
Fixed costs			
(30 per cent of £20 × 10,000 units)	£60,000	£60,000	£0
	£1,460,000	£1,620,000	£160,000

The above figures indicate that it is more profitable to make than buy. This is because the fixed costs of £60,000 would be likely to continue and, as the capacity would be unused, the fixed overheads would not be absorbed into production. Consequently, by buying instead of making, profits would be reduced by £160,000.

Opportunity cost

As shown by Example 11.3, this is the potential benefit that is forgone because one course of action has been chosen over another – that is, if the production facilities used in making had been applied to some alternative purpose.

Example 11.3

Opportunity cost

An undertaking manufactures 100,000 of item X at a total cost of £120,000 and a marginal cost of £100,000. Item X could be bought-out for £1.50 each. The decision whether to make it in-house or buy-out depends on the cost of forgoing the opportunity to make something else. If the production capacity could be used to make an item with a contribution of £0.75 each, then the position would be:

Making	Buying but production capacity not used	Buying less opportunity cost
£100,000	£150,000	£150,000
		–£75,000
		£75,000

In this case, it would be more profitable to buy the item.

Break-even

The break-even point is:

the level of activity in units or value at which the total revenues equal the total costs.

Estimated production quotas and actual usage may differ. See Example 11.4.

Learning curves

Learning curves are dealt with in section 16.11. Suffice to say here, therefore, that when components are bought from a specialist manufacturer, there may be little opportunity for learning. When the items are new, however, the costs of both making and buying may have to be adjusted to take account of a learning factor. In comparing made in-house

Example 11.4

Break-even analysis

Using the data in Example 11.2, at what volume will the company be indifferent between buying and making component JMA 423?

Solution

This is found by the formula:

$$\frac{F}{(P - V)}$$

where:

F = fixed costs
P = purchase price
V = variable cost per unit

In this case:

$$\frac{£60,000}{(£156 - £140)} = \frac{£60,000}{£16} = 3750 \text{ units}$$

If only 3750 units are required, there will be no effect on profits from making or buying. If fewer than 3750 units are required, buying is the more profitable alternative. If more than 3750 units are required, making is the better alternative.

and bought-out prices, therefore, learning is a factor that must be considered, where applicable.

11.14.3 Other considerations in make-or-buy decisions

Apart from those mentioned above, a number of other quantitative and qualitative factors must be considered in deciding whether to make or buy.

Quantitative factors in favour of *making* include:

- chance to use up idle capacity and resources
- potential lead time reduction
- possibility of scrap utilisation
- greater purchasing power with larger orders of a particular material
- large overhead recovery base
- exchange rate risks
- cost of work is known in advance.

Quantitative factors in favour of *buying* include:

- quantities required are too small for economic production
- avoidance of costs of specialist machinery or labour
- reduction in inventory.

Qualitative factors in favour of *making* include:

- ability to manage resources
- commercial and contractual advantages
- worries are eliminated regarding such matters as the stability and continuing viability of suppliers or possible repercussions of changes in supplier ownership
- maintaining secrecy.

Qualitative factors in favour of *buying* include:

- spread of financial risk between purchaser and vendor
- ability to control quality when purchased from outside
- availability of vendor's specialist expertise, machinery and/or patents
- buying, in effect, augments the manufacturing capacity of the purchaser.

11.14.4 Making the make-or-buy decision

From the above, it is clear that, irrespective of whether it relates to the strategic, tactical or component levels, many quantitative and qualitative factors have to be considered when arriving at a make-or-buy decision. The approach shown in Figure 11.4 earlier is a simple procedure for answering the question 'Shall we make or buy?'

11.15 Outsourcing services

11.15.1 Categorisation of services

Most outsourcing relates to services. The range of services that can be outsourced is almost limitless and those listed below represent just a few of the possibilities:

- car park management
- cleaning
- building repairs and maintenance
- catering
- security
- transport management
- waste disposal
- reception
- library
- medical/welfare
- travel administration
- pest control
- training centre management
- computers and IT
- research and development
- estate management
- staff recruitment
- internal audit
- legal services
- payroll
- quality assurance and control
- records management
- asset repair
- telemarketing
- translation services
- customs brokerage
- vehicle maintenance
- procurement.

As service undertakings tend to be less capital-intensive than manufacturing companies, there is usually a large supplier base, especially for less specialised services, such as catering and building repairs. The drafting of service contracts and service-level agreements that may extend over several years does, however, tend to be complicated and involve considerable negotiation.

11.15.2 Outsourcing purchasing

Organisations may consider outsourcing purchasing in the following circumstances:

■ Where purchasing is a peripheral rather than a core activity. The characteristics of peripheral work, as identified by Atkinson and Meager,[19] are that it has:
- low or generalised skill requirements
- internally focused responsibilities
- well-defined or limited tasks
- jobs that are easily separated from other work
- no supply restrictions.

These are also the characteristics of low-level operational purchasing. Beauchamp[20] also identified the following items as suitable for outsourcing consideration:
- purchase orders, one-off and repeat needs
- locally and nationally procured needs (international sourcing and procurement may be rather specialised for outsourcing)
- low-value or low-value/large order acquisitions
- brand name requirements
- call-offs against internally approved agreements
- set-up of commodity-based or service-based contracts
- obtaining goods for batch or volume manufacturing
- stocking and providing for private-sector or public-sector needs
- computerised purchasing or software-based manufacturing procurement
- all administration and paperwork associated with purchasing needs
- supply of stores staff at varying levels of skill
- multidimensional and multidepartmental sourcing.

■ Where the supply base is small and based on proven cooperation and there are no supply restrictions, the following may be outsourced:
- well-defined or limited tasks
- jobs that are easily separated from other work
- jobs that have no supply restrictions.

The above characteristics also apply to low-level operational purchasing.

■ Where there is a small supplier base providing non-strategic, non-critical, low-cost/low-risk items. In such cases, purchasing may be outsourced to:
- specialist purchasing and suppliers organisations
- buying consortia.

Such organisations provide the advantage of:
- bulk purchasing, giving them a strong negotiating position over a wide range of products.

11.16 Drivers of outsourcing

Beulen *et al.*[21] suggest that there are five main drivers for outsourcing:

1 *Quality* – actual capacity is temporarily insufficient to comply with demand. The quality motive can be subdivided into three aspects: increased quality demands, shortage of qualified personnel, outsourcing as a transition period.

2 *Cost* – outsourcing is a possible solution to increasing costs and is compatible with a cost leadership strategy. By controlling and decreasing costs, a company can increase its competitive position.

3 *Finance* – a company has a limited investment budget. The funds must be used for investments in core business activities, which are long-term decisions.

4 *Core business* – a core business is a primary activity that enables an organisation to generate revenues. To concentrate on core business activities is a strategic decision. All subsequent activities are mainly supportive and should be outsourced.

5 *Cooperation* – cooperation between companies can lead to conflict. In order to avoid such conflict, those activities that are produced by both organisations should be subject to total outsourcing.

A further factor is that of human resource management. The internal culture and attitude of employees may result in strong trade union and internal opposition to the introduction of necessary changes in work processes and restructuring. Such changes may also require the acquisition of new employee skills. Outsourcing may avoid conflicts and provide expertise and experience within a matter of days to fill gaps for which recruitment and training would take some time.

Monczka[22] observes that, historically, outsourcing decisions have been limited to decisions about a particular outsource instead of the more holistic approach of asking 'Looking at the entire supply chain, who would be doing what?'

11.17 Types of outsourcing

In relation to IT, Lacity and Hirscheim[23] provide taxonomy of outsourcing options categorised as body shop, project management and total outsourcing.

- *Body shop outsourcing* is a situation where management uses outsourcing as a means of meeting short-term requirements, such as a shortage of in-house skills to meet a temporary demand.
- *Project management outsourcing* is employed for all or part of a particular project, such as developing a new IT project, training in new skills, management consultancy.
- *Total outsourcing* is where the outsourcing supplier is given full responsibility for a selected area, such as catering, security.

11.18 Benefits of outsourcing

There is a range of benefits from outsourcing. These benefits depend on the nature of the outsourcing and may include:

- obtaining immediate investment which is recovered over the long term
- accessing an ICT infrastructure that is 'state-of-the-art'
- reduced costs in excess of 10 per cent on service costs
- reduced staffing levels achieved through efficiency and use of systems
- freeing senior management time to concentrate on core business
- higher levels of service performance generating greater customer satisfaction
- agreed supplier commits to achieve higher performance levels
- accessing proven technical and commercial world-class practice.

11.19 Problems of outsourcing

Outsourcing is not, however, without its problems. It can be up to two years before an organisation begins to benefit from any savings and in some cases the whole process is cost neutral. Some problems associated with outsourcing are shown in Figure 11.5.

Figure 11.5 Problems with outsourcing

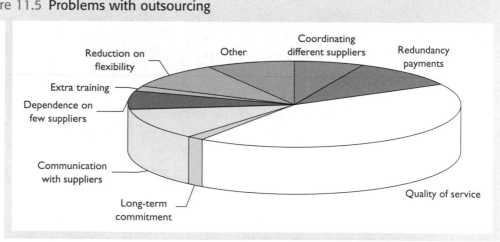

Source: Taken from Carrington, 1994[24]

Perkins[25] reports that an informal survey of his clients showed that:

By the end of the first year, more than 50 per cent of the companies that have outsourced major IT functions are unhappy with their outsources . . . By the end of the second year 70 per cent are unhappy.

Other surveys relating to aspects of outsourcing have shown that between 30 and 50 per cent of executives are disappointed with the results of outsourcing. Problems reported include:

- overdependence on suppliers
- cost escalation
- lack of supplier flexibility
- lack of management skills to control suppliers

■ unrealistic expectations of outsourcing providers due to over-promising at the negotiations stage.

Reilly and Tamkin[26] mention that a principal objection to outsourcing is the possible loss of competitive advantage, particularly in the loss of skills and expertise of staff, insufficient internal investment and the passing of knowledge and expertise to the supplier, which may be able to seize the initiative.

Lacity and Hirscheim[27] also point out that outsourcing does not seem to work well in the following areas:

■ where a specific or unique knowledge of the business is required
■ where all services are customised
■ where the employee culture is too fragmented or hostile for the organisation to come back together.

Problems reported in relation to outsourced suppliers include:

■ high staff turnover
■ poor project management skills
■ lack of commitment to the client or industry
■ shallow expertise
■ insufficient documentation
■ lack of control over larger suppliers
■ poor staff training
■ complacency over time
■ divergent interests of the customer and provider
■ cultural mismatches between customer and provider organisations.

11.20 Handling an outsourcing project

The practice will differ between the public and private sectors. In the former case there is the probability that the value of the project, typically a ten-year period, will exceed the threshold for advertising under EU Procurement Regulations. Outsourcing and the creation of a Public–Private Partnership (PPP) can take, in the public sector, up to 18 months from start to finish. The cost of such an exercise must not be under-estimated. Costs in excess of £500K are not unusual when outsourcing back-office services. Establishing a PPP will probably use the competitive dialogue process or in exceptional cases, the negotiated process.

The following steps will need to be considered, some taking place simultaneously.

1 Set up a project steering group to:
   ■ decide the scope of services to be outsourced
   ■ consider soft market testing
   ■ determine the strategic reasons for outsourcing
   ■ record the desired outcomes including cost reduction
   ■ evaluate potential risks

- commence an effective staff consultation and communication protocol
- determine what external support will be required, e.g. procurement and legal.

2 Issue a comprehensive pre-qualification questionnaire (PQQ) for completion by interested parties.

3 Commence preparation of:

- service specifications
- cost model and affordability envelope
- invitation to tender documentation (may be referred to in the public sector as 'invitation to participate in a competitive dialogue')
- the terms and conditions of contract and outline of schedules to the contract.

4 Evaluate responses to the PQQ:

- using pre-determined evaluation criteria and weightings
- having respondents make a presentation on key facets
- creating a short-list of potential suppliers.

5 Continue with essential actions, including:

- identifying contracts for novation
- prepare licence to occupy building or lease agreement
- risk register and mitigation strategies
- maintain the project plan.

6 Issue invitation to tender.

7 Evaluate responses to the tender

- use pre-determined evaluation criteria and weightings
- seek clarification on all matters of uncertainty.

8 Short-list the preferred supplier and appoint reserve bidder in case the negotiations break down.

9 Engage in post-tender negotiations (or clarification and fine tuning using the competitive dialogue) and finalise contract terms and schedules. This may include:

- finalising staff transfer arrangements including pensions
- applying damages for contractual non-performance
- confirming investment
- finalising the mobilisation and transformation phases
- novation of contracts
- partnering and operational boards terms of reference
- provision of performance bond or parent company guarantee
- transfer of assets
- rights of termination.

10 Make recommendations to award contract or not to proceed if the deal is wrong.

11 Award contract.

12 Commence contract management activity.

13 Conduct lessons learned from the project.

11.21 Sub-contracting

11.21.1 What is sub-contracting?

Sub-contracting may be distinguished from outsourcing in that the latter involves the total restructuring of an enterprise around core competences and outside relationships. Whatever the degree of outsourcing, enterprises must retain certain core capabilities. Outsourcing is a strategic long-term decision. Sub-contracting is a tactical, short-term approach.

> If you want the most beautiful lawn in the neighbourhood and you hire someone to take responsibility for every aspect of lawn care, including cutting the grass, weed control, watering and fertilising, it's strategic sourcing. But hiring someone to only cut your lawn is sub-contracting.[28]

11.21.2 Reasons for sub-contracting

The buyer encounters problems that call for sub-contracting in two main areas:

■ where the buyer's organisation is the employer or client entrusting work to a main contractor who, in turn, sub-contracts part of the work, which is the case with most construction contracts

■ where the buyer's organisation is the main contractor and sub-contracts work for such reasons as:
- overloading of machinery or labour
- to ensure completion of work on time
- lack of specialist machinery or specialist know-how
- to avoid acquiring long-term capacity when future demand is uncertain
- subcontracting is cheaper than manufacturing internally.

11.21.3 Organisation for sub-contracting

■ When sub-contracting is a regular and significant part of the activity of an undertaking, it may be desirable to set up a special sub-contracting section within or external to the purchasing department.

■ Arrangements must be made for adequate liaison between all departments connected with sub-contracting – design, production control, construction and site staff, inspection, finance and so on.

■ Friction over who should negotiate with the selected suppliers sometimes develops between purchasing and design or technical departments. This can be avoided by a proper demarcation of authority and responsibility, purchasing having a power of commercial veto, design and technical departments a technical veto.

11.21.4 Selection of sub-contractors

It may be necessary to check whether or not external approval of the selected sub-contractor is necessary, as in government contracts or where a specific sub-contractor has been specified by the client. Some construction contracts may provide that sub-contractors must not be selected on the basis of Dutch auctions.

11.21.5 Liaison with sub-contractors

Matters to be considered include the following:

- planning, to ensure that the sub-contractor can complete by the required date – techniques such as programme, evaluation and review techniques (PERT) are of assistance in this review
- ensuring that the sub-contractor is supplied with the most recent versions of all necessary documentation, including drawings, standards and planning instructions
- arranging with the sub-contractor for the supply, by the main contractor, of materials, tooling, specialist equipment and so on and the basis on which this shall be charged
- control of equipment and materials in the possession of sub-contractors
- arrangements for accountability at stocktaking of free issued materials in the possession of the sub-contractor
- arrangements for visits to the premises of the sub-contractor by progress and inspection staff employed by the main contractor
- arrangements for transportation, especially where items produced by the sub-contractor require special protection, such as components with a highly finished surface
- payment for any ancillary work to be performed by the sub-contractor, such as the painting on of part numbers.

11.21.6 Legal factors

These will depend on the circumstances of the specific contract. All major contracts for sub-contracting should be vetted by the legal department of the main contractor. Where the buyer's undertaking is the client entrusting work to a main contractor, it is useful to remember the following generic principles.

Unless the contract has been placed on the basis – express or implied – that the work will be wholly performed by the main contractor, the client will have no authority to prevent the sub-contracting of part of the work (this will not apply to contracts for personal service). If, therefore, the client wishes to specify particular sub-contractors or to limit the right of the main contractor to sub-contract, these matters must be negotiated when the order is placed. With construction and defence contracts, tenderers are often required to state what parts of the work will be sub-contracted. In particular, it is useful to include clauses stating that it is the duty of the main contractor to use best endeavours in the selection of sub-contractors and that responsibility for the performance of these sub-contractors shall lie with the main contractor exclusively.

11.22 Partnering

11.22.1 Partnering and outsourcing

Humbert and Passarelli[29] point out that, at its highest level, outsourcing can take the form of an alliance akin to a partnership (but not a strict legal partnership) or joint venture. Not all outsourcing agreements, however, are partnerships. Humbert and Passarelli state that 'the terms "partnering" or "strategic alliance" should not be used to describe an outsourcing agreement unless the contract is structured to reflect a true relationship of strategic alliance'. The characteristics of such an alliance include close working relationships built on trust, communication and mutual dependency 'where both parties have a vested interest in reducing costs and achieving a favourable business outcome'. Where these conditions obtain, the provider's 'reward' is based on results or attaining objectives rather than being compensated.

When comparing partnering and outsourcing, it is therefore important to distinguish between:

- *different levels of outsourcing* at the lower levels it will be purely transactional – only at the higher, strategic levels is outsourcing likely to merge into partnering
- *customer–supplier relationships and partnering* in the former, the emphasis is primarily on cost minimisation, while with the latter the emphasis is additionally on value enhancement and the achievement of joint venture objectives
- *the contractual differences between outsourcing and partnering* with the former, the contract relates to clearly specified inputs and these are cost-based over a defined period of time, for which the supplier receives an agreed reward, whereas, as the CIPS[30] points out, because partnerships are based on trust, in theory no form of contractual documentation should be necessary, but it is still desirable that the parties should agree to a set of general guidelines to regulate the partnership, such as the 12 key areas identified by Partnering Sourcing Ltd:[31]

  - general statement of principle
  - scope – what the partnership encompasses
  - costs
  - customer service levels
  - business forecasts
  - technological development strategies
  - continuous improvement policy
  - annual performance objectives
  - mutual assistance to resolve any problems that may arise
  - open book cost structures
  - minimising material costs
  - joint decisions on capital investment projects.

  (two important omissions from the above list are those relating to intellectual property rights and ownership of patents).

11.22.2 What is partnering?

The need for a broad approach to the concept of partnering is also recognised by Partnership Sourcing Ltd which defines partnering as:

> A commitment to both customers and suppliers, regardless of size, to a long-term relationship based on clear, mutually agreed objectives to strive for world class capability.

There may, however, be degrees of partnership. Lambert *et al.*,[32] for example, distinguish between:

- *type I partnerships* involving organisations that recognise each other as partners and, on a limited basis, coordinate activities and planning – such partnerships generally have a short-term focus and involve only a few areas within each organisation
- *type II partnerships* involving organisations that have progressed beyond coordination to integration of activities – such partnerships have a longer-term view of the partnership and involve multiple areas within both firms
- *type III partnerships* involving organisations sharing a significant level of operational and strategic integration – in particular, each partner can make changes to the other's systems without getting approval and such partnerships are of long-term duration with no end in sight, each party viewing the other as an extension of its own firm.

As Knemeyer *et al.*[33] state:

> The three types of partnership reflect increased strength, long-term orientation and level of involvement between parties . . . No particular type of partnership is better or worse than any other. The key is to try to obtain the type of relationship that is most appropriate given the business situation.

Partnering marks a shift from traditional pressures exerted by larger customers on small-sized and medium-sized suppliers in which the latter were regarded as subordinates. Partnering aims to transform short-term adversarial customer–supplier relationships focused on the use of purchasing power to secure lower prices and improved delivery into long-term cooperation based on mutual trust in which quality, innovation and shared values complement price competitiveness.

Some comparisons between traditional and partnering relationships are shown in Table 11.4.

Table 11.4 Comparison of traditional and partnering supplier relationships

Traditional	Partnership
Emphasises competitiveness and self-interest on the part of both purchaser and supplier	Emphasises cooperation and a community of interest between purchaser and supplier
Emphasis on 'unit price' with lowest price usually the most important buyer consideration	Emphasis on total acquisition costs (TAC), including indirect and hidden costs, such as production hold-ups and loss of customer goodwill due to late delivery of materials and components. Lowest price is never the sole buyer consideration
Emphasis is on short-term business relationships	Emphasis on long-term business relationships with involvement of supplier at the earliest possible stage to discuss how the buyer's requirements can be met
Emphasis on quality checks, with inspection of incoming supplies	Emphasis on quality assurance based on total quality management and zero defects
Emphasis on multiple sourcing	Emphasis on single sourcing, although it is not, of necessity, confined to single sourcing. It will, however, reduce the supplier base
Emphasis on uncertainty regarding supplier performance and integrity	Emphasis on mutual trust between purchaser and supplier

11.22.3 The drivers of partnership sourcing

Some of the main drivers for partnerships have been summarised by Southey[34] as:

- drive for lowest acquisition cost:
    - not only price, but all 'cost in use' elements, such as the benefits or exposure derived from actual product quality, delivery performance and the administration burden
- reduction in supplier base:
    - need to reduce the supplier base to a number that can be managed effectively
- shortening of product lifecycles:
    - need for faster response times
    - need for suppliers to be right first time
    - need for supplier involvement from day 1
- concentration on core business:
    - where most value can be added
    - where distinctive competences exist
    - avoiding unnecessary capital expenditure
- competitive pressures towards 'lean' supply:
    - competition creating fewer, more technologically sophisticated suppliers that have to collaborate more closely with their customers
    - earlier involvement of predetermined suppliers for development of each individual component
    - pressure on inventory, forcing closer matching customer–supplier output levels and systems
    - need to optimise all linkages in the supply chain network (both internal and external)
- adoption of 'best practices', creating dependence:
    - reduced system slack from TQM, JIT and EDI, creating greater dependence on suppliers
    - more dependency requiring forging of stronger supplier relationships
    - more dependency requiring closer integration of people, plans and systems, both internally and externally.

Southey states that customers enter into partnership sourcing arrangements because of their business-driven need to maximise competitive advantage. They see the benefits of partnering as being that it provides:

- a win–win scenario
- supply chain security
- close working relationships (arms around *vs* arm's length)
- a route to joint technological development
- the ability to extend total continuous improvement (TCI) culture to critical suppliers
- improved profit contribution (or reduced profit exposure).

11.22.4 What types of relationships are suitable for partnering?

Partnership Sourcing Ltd[35] has identified seven types of relationships that may be suitable for partnership:

- *high spend* – 'the vital few'
- *high risk* – items and services that are vital irrespective of their monetary value
- *high hassle* – vital supplies that are technically complicated to arrange and take a lot of time, effort and resources to manage
- *new services* – new products or services that may involve possible partners
- *technically complicated* – involving technically advanced or innovative supplies where the cost of switching would be prohibitive
- *fast-changing* – areas where knowing future technology or trends or legislation is critical
- *restricted markets* – markets that have few reliable or competent suppliers where closer links with existing or new suppliers might improve supply security.

11.22.5 Advantages of partnering

These are set out in Table 11.5 and Example 11.5.

Example 11.5

Benefits of partnering

A survey conducted by Partnership Sourcing Ltd in 1995 reported the following benefits (percentages are of those undertakings responding to the survey):

reduced cost	75.5 per cent
reduced inventory	72.9 per cent
increased quality	70.3 per cent
enhanced security of supply	69.4 per cent
reduced product development times	58.4 per cent

Partnership Sourcing Ltd[36] mentions the following important issues:

- ascertain your most important supplies by spend and criticality or customers by turnover and profit
- whether the potential partner is much bigger or much smaller than the enterprise, initiating the partnership is relatively important – small undertakings are more responsive and flexible; larger ones may have better systems
- a potential partner may already have some experience of building partnership relationships and such a company is worth targeting
- that potential partners recognise that:
  - the business of the enterprise seeking to initiate the partnership is important to them
  - there is scope for improvement in the product or service received – in short, that partnering offers potential rewards.

Table 11.5 Advantages of partnering

To the purchaser	To the supplier
Purchasing advantage resulting from quality assurance, reduced supplier base, assured supplies due to long-term agreements, ability to plan long-term improvement, rather than negotiating for short-term advantage, delivery on time (JIT), improved quality	*Marketing advantage* resulting from stability due to long-term agreements, larger share of orders placed, ability to plan ahead and invest, ability to work with key customers on products and/or services, scope to increase sales without increasing procurement overheads
Lower costs resulting from cooperative cost-reduction programmes, such as EDI, supplier's participation in new designs, lower inventory due to better production availability, improved logistics, reduced handling, reduced number of outstanding orders	*Lower costs* resulting from cooperative cost-reduction programmes, participation in customer's design, lower inventory due to better customer planning, improved logistics, simplification or elimination of processes, payment on time
Strategic advantage resulting from access to supplier's technology, a supplier who invests, shared problem-solving and management	*Strategic advantage* resulting from access to customer's technology, a customer that recognises the need to invest, shared problem-solving and management

11.22.6 Implementing partnership sourcing

1 *Identify purchased items potentially suitable for partnership sourcing* such as:
   - high-spend items and suppliers – Pareto analysis may show that a small number of suppliers account for a high proportion of total spend
   - critical items where the cost of supplier failure would be high
   - complicated items involving technical and innovative supplies where the cost of switching sources would be prohibitive
   - 'new buy' items where supplier involvement in design and production methods is desirable from the outset.

2 *Sell the philosophy of partnership sourcing* to:
   - top management – demonstrating how partnership sourcing can improve quality, service and total costs throughout the organisation
   - other functions likely to be involved, such as accounting (will need to make prompt payments), design (will need to involve suppliers from the outset), production (will need to schedule supply requirements and changes)
   - stress the advantages in section 11.22.5 above.

3 *Define standards that potential suppliers will be required to meet*; these will include:
   - a commitment to TQM
   - ISO 9000 certification or equivalent
   - existing implementation of or willingness to implement appropriate techniques, such as JIT, EDI and so on
   - in-house design capability
   - ability to supply locally or worldwide as required
   - consistent performance standards regarding quality and delivery
   - willingness to innovate
   - willingness to change, flexibility in management and workforce attitudes

Partnership Sourcing Ltd[37] state:

> Remember that people are key. It is people who build trust and make relationships work. Are the people right? Is the chemistry right?
>
> Partnership is two-way: if one of your customers was evaluating your business on the same criteria that you are using on suppliers, would you qualify? If not, perhaps you should think again about your minimum entry standards.

4 *Select one or a few suppliers as potential suppliers* do not attempt to launch too many partnerships at once as a byproduct of partnering is that a customer will be giving more attention to fewer suppliers, focusing available time where it will most benefit some issues.

5 *Sell the idea of partnering to the selected suppliers* – stress the advantages in section 11.22.5 above.

6 *If a commitment to partnership sourcing is achieved, determine on the basis of joint consultation what both parties want from the partnership* and:

- decide common objectives, such as:
  - reduction in total costs
  - adoption of TQM
  - zero defects
  - on-time payment
  - JIT or on-time deliveries
  - joint research and development
  - implementation of EDI
  - reduction or elimination of stocks
- agree performance criteria for measuring progress towards objectives, such as:
  - failure in production or with end-users
  - service response time
  - on-time deliveries
  - stock value
  - lead time and stability
  - service levels
- agree administrative procedures:
  - set up a steering group to review progress and ensure development
  - set up problem-solving teams to tackle particular issues
  - arrange regular meetings at all levels with senior management steering the process
- formalise the partnership, which should be on the basis of:
  - a simple agreement
  - a simplified legal contract

7 *Review and audit the pilot project* by:

- reviewing against objectives
- quantifying the gains to the business as a whole
- reporting back to senior management on what has been achieved.

8 *Extend the existing partnership* by:

- extending existing agreements
- committing to longer agreements
- getting involved in joint strategic planning.

9 *Develop new partners for the future.*

11.22.7 Effective partnering

In the Crown publication, *Effective partnering*,[38] an overview for customers and suppliers, there is a useful checklist for an SRO to consider whether a partnering arrangement would be a good way of meeting the business need.

- What kind of relationship does the business need suggest? Would partnering be appropriate? If so, then why? Is our organisation ready to work with a provider on a partnering basis?

- Do we have the leadership, skills and capability to make it work? What is our track record in building partnering relationships (if any)?

- Could existing relationships, ours or those of other organisations, act as models or exemplars for what we are planning?

- Can we define success in building this relationship, and then set targets, milestones and measures that will enable us to assess how successful we have been in creating it?

- Assuming the relationship can be created successfully, will users and stakeholders 'sign up' to it and add momentum to its development?

- What kind of provider could manage the risks we envisage allocating them? Realistically, would a provider be willing to take them on and can we give them sufficient control so that they can manage them?

- How do we think the provider community would view a partnering approach to meet this requirement?

The advice continues that the unique features of partnering are integrated into the business case.

- Do we still think that partnering is the right way forward for this project? If so, does the business case for the project include the explicit requirement for a partnering arrangement, and justify the approach in terms of business need?

- Are partnering aspects genuinely integral to the business case, or do they appear to be 'bolted on'? Has successful partnering, or a good working relationship, been identified as a critical success factor? If not, why not?

- Does the business case take account of the additional investment (in relationship management etc.) that a partnering arrangement will require, compared to traditional procurement?

- Does the business case take account of any changes in approach or behaviour that your organisation will need to make in order for partnering to work?

- What are the views of the likely providers on partnering and the key features they see as critical to success?

- Are outline plans in place for how risks should be allocated between the partners?

Figure 11.6 **Essential features of partnering**

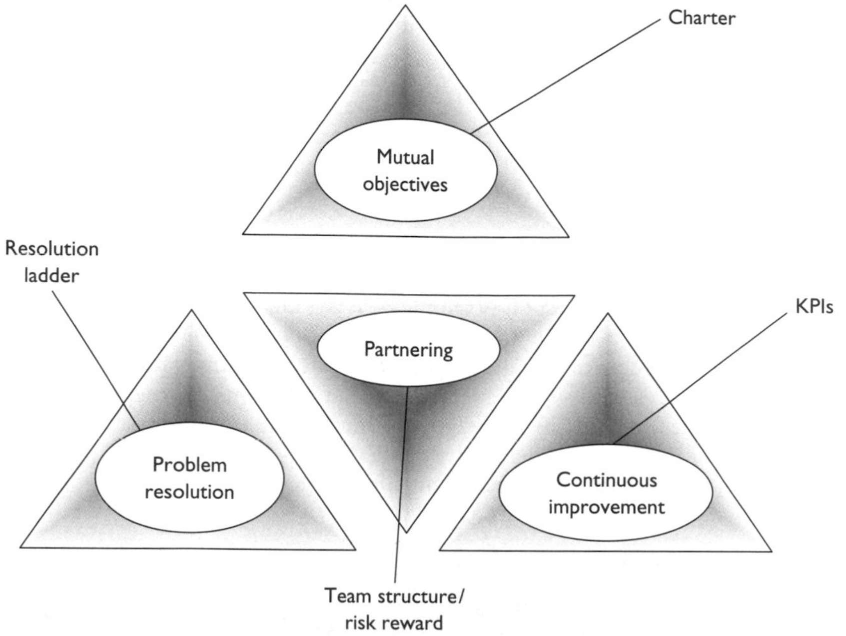

- Do risk plans take account of potential partners' likely attitudes to taking on risk? Is this based on actual discussion with the market, lessons from other projects, or assumption?
- Are management structures ready to open communication flows, both formal and informal, with the partner when the time comes?
- Does this project have the clear top-level commitment necessary to underpin a successful partnership-based approach?

The Centre for Construction Innovation[39] showed the essential features of partnering as illustrated in Figure 11.6.

11.22.8 Problems of partnership sourcing

- *Termination of relationships* – the aim should be to part amicably, preferably over a period of time according to an agreed separation plan.
- *Business shares* – the possibility of the customer being over dependent on the supplier. These issues need to be explored in joint consultation.
- *Confidentiality* – where prospective partners are also suppliers to competitors.
- *Complacency* – avoidance requires the regular review of competitiveness in regular meetings of a multifunctional buying team.
- *Attitudes* – traditionally adversarial buyers and salespeople will require retraining to adjust to the new philosophy and environment.
- *Contractual* – where, for reasons of falling sales, recession and so on, forecasts have to be modified.

■ *Legislative* – the CIPS[40] points out that it is less easy to establish partnership relationships in the public sector due to government and EU procurement directive rules. In general, partnership relationships in the public sector should not exceed three to five years, after which retendering should be required, although some partnering deals are 10 to 15 years in duration with an option to extend for a further period of time.

Other problems are that the sharing of information may create a competitor or potential competition and difficulties associated with sharing future profits and the possible foreclosure of other alliance opportunities.

Ramsay[41] rightly observes that:

> As a sourcing strategy, partnerships may be generally applicable to only a small number of very large companies. For the rest, although it may be useful with a minority of purchases and a very small selection of suppliers, it is a high-risk strategy that one might argue ought to be approached with extreme caution. In Kraljic's terms [see section 2.13.11] the act of moving the sourcing of a bought-out item from competitive pressure to a single-sourced partnership increases both supply risk and profit impact. Thus partnerships tend to push all affected purchases towards the strategic quadrant. Strategic purchases offer large rewards if managed successfully, but demand the allocation of large amounts of management attention and threaten heavy penalties if sourcing arrangements fail.

11.22.9 Why partnerships fail

Research by Ellram[42] covering 80 'pairs' of US buying firms and their chosen suppliers used 19 factors identified by previous studies as contributing to partnership failure. These factors, in the order of their ranking of importance by buyers, were:

1 poor communication
2 lack of top management support
3 lack of trust
4 lack of total quality commitment by supplier
5 poor up-front planning
6 lack of distinctive supplier value-added benefit
7 lack of strategic direction to the relationship
8 lack of shared goals
9 ineffective mechanism for cost revision
10 lack of benefit/risk sharing
11 agreement not supportive of a partnering philosophy
12 lack of partner firm's top management support
13 changes in the market
14 too many suppliers for customers to deal with effectively
15 corporate culture differences
16 top management differences
17 lack of central coordination of purchasing
18 low status of customer's purchasing function
19 distance barriers.

Table 11.6 Top factors contributing to partnerships that have not worked out or have been resolved

Factor	Buyer ranking	Supplier ranking
Poor communication	1	1
Lack of top management support	2	10
Lack of trust	3	4
Lack of total quality commitment by supplier	4	18
Poor up-front planning	5	5
Lack of strategic direction for the relationship	7	3
Lack of shared goals	8	2

As shown in Table 11.6, five of the top seven factors were common to both buying and supplying organisations.

There were also strong differences. Suppliers ranked central coordination of the buyer's purchasing function as 12 compared with a ranking of 17 by buyers. Similarly, the low status of the customer's purchasing function, lack of strategic direction and lack of shared goals were ranked significantly higher by suppliers than buyers.

The above findings broadly agree with earlier research, although Ellram's sample regarded corporate culture and top management differences as relatively unimportant.

11.23 Intellectual property rights and secrecy

11.23.1 Intellectual property rights

All sourcing policies must give due consideration to the range of intellectual property rights (IPRs) and their impact on procurement considerations. IPRs are a very specialised area of knowledge with potentially dire consequences if the buying organisation should infringe third party IPRs. Table 11.7 captures the type of IPRs and the salient points of each.

11.23.2 Secrecy

There are national security considerations on many products and services. When this is the case, the control of 'secret' matter must be applied from the outset of procurement. There are potential criminal charges that may ensue if the secrecy requirements are breached.

11.23.3 Procurement accountabilities

Procurement must take the lead in managing all facets of IPRs and secrecy. This may involve:

- getting confidentiality agreements signed when appropriate
- determining, with legal support, which facet of IPRs/secrecy apply

Table 11.7 Intellectual property rights – salient points

Patents	■ Must be applied for and, if granted, may last for 20 years (subject to renewal every four years) ■ Gives the patentee the right to prevent anyone else from making, using, selling or importing any goods or processes, which include the patented invention ■ A patentee may grant licenses
Copyright	■ Relates to the protection of works and exists automatically when the work to which it relates is created ■ The author (except where they are an employee) has the right to prevent anyone else from copying the work (copying includes photocopying and other forms of reproduction) ■ Generally expires 70 years after the death of the author
Registered designs	■ Aims to protect the appearance of articles made to the design and where those designs have a novel aesthetic element ■ Registration must be applied for and it provides protection for up to 25 years (renewable every 5 years) ■ The holder has the right to prevent anyone else making, using, or selling any goods which include the registered design ■ May grant licenses; royalties are usually payable
Design rights	■ Similar to copyrights in that they arise automatically ■ They protect the design of an article provided that it is not a feature which enables the article to fit with or match with or form an integral part of another article ■ The design must be recorded in a design document and must be original ■ The protection lasts for 15 years from the end of the year in which the design was first recorded (with additional complications)
Trade marks	■ These are visual symbols, such as brand names or logos, used to distinguish the goods or services to which they relate from those of other businesses ■ Protection of a registered trademark is maintained providing that the mark is in use and the registration is renewed by payment of renewal fees in the case of some old marks, after seven years, and in the case of newly registered marks, every ten years

■ drawing up contractual clauses to deal with the issues
■ negotiating license fees
■ arranging for Escrow
■ ensuring no 'reverse engineering' or 'copy action' occur.

11.24 Support for marketing

11.24.1 Reciprocity

What is reciprocity?

Reciprocity – often referred to as 'selling through the order book' – is a policy of giving preference to suppliers that are also customers of the buying organisation.

Reciprocity is influenced by two main factors:

■ *the economic climate* – pressures for reciprocity increase in times of recession when sales may attempt to put pressure on their suppliers to buy their products
■ *the type of product* – reciprocal dealing is greater when both supplier and buyer are producers of standard, highly competitive products – it does not arise where a purchaser has no alternative but to buy from a given supplier.

Reciprocity policies

The responsibility of purchasing professionals is to make procurement decisions on such considerations as price, quality, delivery and service, so reciprocity may be expressly excluded by specific purchasing policy statements, such as:

> In no circumstances will the XYZ Co. Ltd use a buying decision as a means of inappropriately enhancing a sales opportunity. Reciprocal trading practices are prohibited.

A more liberal approach is that reciprocity may offer advantages to both parties as:

- supplier and buyer may benefit from the exchange of orders
- supplier and buyer may obtain a greater understanding of mutual problems, thus increasing goodwill
- more direct communication between suppliers and buyers may eliminate or reduce the need for intermediaries and the cost of marketing or procurement operations.

11.24.2 Offset

There is a requirement in many contracts for the provision of offset. For example, a UK company seeking a transportation contract in the Far East will be required to purchase a fixed amount of the contract value for local suppliers. In the defence sector, more than 130 countries demand offsets in one form or the other. In India, defence purchases in terms of offset will mean maintenance, overhaul, up gradation, life extension, engineering, design, testing, defence related software or quality assurance services.

In all the above respects, purchasing can make a significant contribution to the marketing activities of an organisation.

11.25 Intra-company trading

Intra-company trading applies to large enterprises and conglomerates where the possibility arises of buying certain materials from a member of the group. This policy may be justified on the grounds that it ensures the utilisation and profitability of the supplying undertaking and the profitability of the group as whole. It may also be resorted to in times of recession to help supplying subsidiaries cover their fixed costs.

Policy statements should give general and specific guidance to the procurement function regarding the basis on which intra-company trading should be conducted. General guidance may be expressed in a policy statement such as the following:

> Company policy is to support internal suppliers to the fullest extent and to develop product and service quality to the same high standards as those available in the external market.

Specific guidance may direct buyers to:

- purchase specified items exclusively from group members regardless of price
- obtain quotations from group members that are evaluated against those from external suppliers with the order being placed with the most competitive source, whether internal or external.

Difficulties can arise where intra-company trading involves import or export considerations.

11.26 Local suppliers

What is 'local' must be determined bearing in mind such factors as ease of transport and communication. The advantages of using local rather than distant suppliers include the following:

- closer cooperation is facilitated between buyers and suppliers based on personal relationships
- social responsibility is shown by 'supporting local industries' and thus contributing to the prosperity of the area
- reduced transportation costs
- improved availability in emergency situations, such as the ease of road transport to collect urgently needed items, and the potential importance of localised confidence in the maintenance of lead times increases where a JIT system is adopted
- the development of subsidiary industries situated close to the main industry and catering for its needs is encouraged.

Within the public sector there are now strategic decisions and directions to use SMEs and third sector suppliers who offer local value for money, including expertise and a local presence.

11.27 Purchasing consortia

11.27.1 Definition and scope

Purchasing consortia may be defined as:

> A collaborative arrangement under which two or more organisations combine their requirements for a specified range of goods and services to gain price, design, supply availability and assurance benefits resulting from greater volumes of purchases.

In public purchasing, for example, several separate authorities may establish a central purchasing organisation to provide three basic supply services to its constituent members, namely delivery from stores, direct purchasing of non-stock items for users in constituent authorities and the negotiation of call-off or 'standing offer' contracts. Such an organisation is usually self-financed by virtue of the mark-up on the items supplied from store and volume rebates received from suppliers that the consortium negotiates.

Purchasing consortia exist in a wide range of industries and cover for-profit and non-profit organisations, including universities and libraries.

The Yorkshire Purchasing Organisation

A typical example of such a consortium is the Yorkshire Purchasing Organisation (YPO), serving schools and local authorities mainly in Yorkshire, Greater Manchester and Merseyside. YPO has an annual turnover of £400m.

Originally selling mainly to 12 constituent authorities, new autonomy, especially in education, means that the YPO is now selling to over 30,000 small customers whose orders have an average line value of under £10. Customers order by post or an EDI system devised by YPO using mail-order catalogues covering over 15,000 lines, ranging from alphabet pasta to xylophones. The consortium aims to meet a 97 per cent availability target.

11.27.2 Advantages of purchasing consortia

- The use of a consortium allows the constituent members to benefit from the economics of larger-scale purchasing than they could undertake individually.
- Members can utilise the relevant professional purchasing skills of the consortium staff who can develop wide-ranging product expertise.
- Saving of time in searching for and ordering standard items.
- Bulk purchasing enables the consortium to have strong buying leverage for a wide range of supplies.
- Costs are clearly identified.

11.27.3 Disadvantages of consortia

- A consortium cannot insist on the compliance of individual members, which may treat the consortium as only one of a number of suppliers. This may secure nominal price savings, but is unlikely to affect the administrative costs of appraising the consortium against alternative sources. It also weakens the strength of the consortium.
- When using a consortium, it may be more difficult to agree standard specifications than when dealing with one company.
- Significant areas of spend are not covered by what consortia can provide.
- Some forms of consortia may be prohibited under EU provisions. Thus, Article 85(1) of the EEC Treaty provides that:

  . . . all agreements, decisions and concerted practices (hereafter referred to as agreements) which have as their object or effect the prevention, restriction or distortion of competition within the common market are prohibited as incompatible with the common market . . . this applies, however, only if such agreements affect trade between Member States.

- In general, however, the Commission 'welcomes cooperation among small-sized and medium-sized enterprises where such cooperation enables them to work more efficiently and increase their productivity and competitiveness in a larger market'.[43]

11.28 Sustainability

A definition was put forward in 1987 by the World Commission on Environment and Development. It stated that: 'Sustainable development meets the needs of the present without compromising the ability of future generations to meet their own needs.'

The term sustainable procurement encompasses all issues where procurement is seen as having a role in delivering economic, social and environmental policy objectives. Procurement should consider sustainability at all stages of the procurement cycle but the specifications are vital. An idea of the scope is illustrated by the following categories:

- personal computers   (energy saving)
- laser printers   (energy saving)
- copying paper   (recycled content)
- wood products   (either recycled or from legally harvested trees)
- cars   (carbon emissions)

- lighting systems   (energy savings)
- paints and varnishes   (volatile organic compounds)
- soil products   (organic ingredients)
- textiles   (specific requirements for cotton fibres, wool fibres and synthetic polyamide and polyester)
- detergents   (biodegradability)
- glazing   (U-value)

11.29 Sourcing decisions

Sourcing decisions involve a consideration of:

- factors influencing organisational buying decisions
- buying centres or teams
- buying situations
- factors in deciding where to buy.

11.29.1 Factors in deciding where to buy

Webster and Wind[44] classify factors influencing industrial buying decisions into four main groups, as shown in Table 11.8.

11.29.2 Buying centres, teams and networks

A buying centre is essentially a cross-functional team, the characteristics of which were discussed in section 5.5. Essentially the buying centre is the buying decision-making unit of an organisation and is defined by Webster and Wind[45] as:

> all those individuals and groups who participate in the purchasing decision process and who share some common goals and the risks arising from the decision.

Table 11.8 Factors in industrial buying decisions

Environmental	Organisational	Interpersonal	Individual
These are normally outside the buyer's control and include: - level of demand - economic outlook - interest rates - technological change - political factors - government regulations - competitive development	Buying decisions are affected by the organisation's system of reward, authority, status and communication, including organisational: - objectives - policies - procedures - structures	Involving the interaction of several people of different status, authority, empathy and persuasiveness who comprise the buying centre	Buying decisions are related to how individual participants in the buying process form their preferences for products and suppliers, involving the person's age, professional identification, personality and attitude towards the risks involved in their buying behaviour

Normally a buying centre is a temporary, often informal, group that can change in composition according to the nature of the purchase decision.

Buying centres may also be more permanent groups responsible for the sourcing, selection, monitoring and evaluation of suppliers in relation to a specified range of items, such as food, drink, capital equipment and outsourced products and services. Such groups are often referred to as *procurement teams* and may also be responsible for framing purchasing policies and procedures. All teams should have a designated chairperson and clearly defined terms of reference and authority.

The composition of the buying centre or team can be analysed as follows:

- By individual participants or job holders, such as the managing director, chief purchasing officer, engineer or accountant.

- By organisational units, such as departments or even individual organisations, as when a group of hospitals decide to standardise equipment.

- The buying centre or team is comprised of all members of the organisation (varying from three to twelve) who play any of the following five roles in the purchasing decision process:

  - *users* who will use the product or service and often initiate the purchase and specify what is bought

  - *influencers* such as technical staff who may directly or indirectly influence the buying decision in such ways as defining specifications or providing information on which alternatives may be evaluated

  - *buyers* who have formal authority to select suppliers and arrange terms of purchase – they may also help to determine specifications, but their main role is to select vendors and negotiate within purchase constraints

  - *deciders* who have either formal or informal authority to select the ultimate suppliers (in routine purchasing of standard items, the deciders are often the buyers, but in more complicated purchasing, the deciders are often other officers of the organisation)

  - *gatekeepers* who control the flow of information to others, such as buyers, and may prevent salespeople from seeing users or deciders.

11.29.3 The buying network

The buying centre concept, developed in 1972, has proved remarkably durable and provided the basis for later models of organisational buying behaviour.[46] The Webster and Wind model, however, makes no reference to such aspects as the linkages between purchasing and corporate strategies and procurement decisions aimed at enhancing the competitive advantage of buying, such as the decision to source abroad.

Business practice has also changed since 1972 and process-driven management styles and philosophies such as partnering and the impact of IT have changed the way in which buyers and sellers interact.

Such considerations led Bristor and Ryan[47] to suggest that the concept of the buying centre as a group no longer captures the nature of buying behaviour and should be replaced by that of the buying network, which they define as:

> The set of individuals involved in a purchase process, over a specified time frame, and the set of one or more relations that link (or fail to link) each dyad [a dyad is a pair of units treated as one].

Networks have been discussed in section 4.3, but it is useful to mention here two dimensions of networks highlighted by Bristor and Ryan – structure and relationships. Structure relates to organisational aspects. Thus, the boundaries of a buying centre are those of the organisation. With buying networks, the issue arises as to whether or not it is appropriate to include buying network members from outside the organisation, such as customers or consultants. The nodes of buying centres can also represent roles rather than named individuals.

Relationship aspects of buying networks include communications and influence. IT not only makes information widely available to network members, but developments such as teleconferencing mean that they are no longer required to be in physical proximity.

11.30 Factors in deciding where to buy

Assuming that the decision is made that a product should be bought out rather than made in, many factors determine where the order is placed and by whom the decision is made. Such considerations include:

11.30.1 General considerations

- How shall the item be categorised – capital investment, manufacturing material or parts, operating, supply or MRO item?
- Where does the item fit into our purchasing portfolio – leverage, strategic, non-critical or bottleneck (see section 2.13.11)?
- What are our current and projected levels of business for the item?
- Is the item a one-off or a continuing requirement?
- Is the item unique to us or in general use?
- Is the item a straight rebuy, modified rebuy or new task?
- If it is a straight or modified rebuy, from what source was it obtained?
- Is/was the present/previous supplier satisfactory from the standpoints of price, quality and delivery?
- With regard to the value of the order to be placed, is the cost of searching for an alternative supply source justified?
- Which internal customers may wish to be consulted on the sourcing of the item?
- Within what timescale is the item required?

11.30.2 Strategic considerations

- What supply source will offer the greatest competitive advantage from the standpoints of:
  - price
  - differentiation of product
  - security of supplies and reliability of delivery
  - quality
  - added value in terms of specialisation, production facilities, packaging, transportation, after-sales services and so on?

- Is the source one with whom we would like to:
  - single source
  - share a proportion of our requirements for the required item
  - build up a long-term partnership relationship
  - discuss the possibilities of supplier development
  - outsource
  - subcontract?
- Does the supply source offer any possibilities for:
  - joint product development
  - reciprocity or countertrade?
- What would be our relationship profile with that supply source – market exchange, captive buyer, captive supplier or strategic partnership (see Figure 7.3)?
- What relationships does the supplier have with our competitors?
- Is it desirable that at least part of our requirements should be sourced locally for political, social responsibility or logistical reasons?
- What risk factors attach to the purchase? Is the product high profit impact/high supply risk, low profit impact/high supply risk, high profit impact/low supply risk, low profit impact/low supply risk?

11.30.3 Product factors

- Can the product or components and assemblies be outsourced?
- What critical factors influence the choice of suppliers? Chisnall[48] reports a research finding that seven critical factors were found to influence buyers in the British valve and pump industry in the choice of their suppliers of raw materials: delivery reliability, technical advice; test facilities, replacement guarantee, prompt quotation, ease of contact and willingness to supply range. These attributes helped to reduce the risk element to purchase decisions.
- What special tooling is required? Is such tooling the property of the existing supplier or the vendor?
- To what extent are learning curves applicable to the product? Are these allowed for in the present and future prices?
- Is the product 'special' or 'standardised'?
- In what lot sizes is the product manufactured?
- What is the estimated product lifecycle cost?

11.30.4 Supplier factors

Such factors are those normally covered by supplier appraisal and vendor-rating exercises.

11.30.5 Personal factors

Personal factors relate to psychological and behavioural aspects of those involved in making organisational buying decisions. All purchasing professionals should constantly keep in mind the exhortation of the Greek philosopher Diogenes: 'Know thyself.'

Knowledge of our strengths, weaknesses, prejudices, motivations and values will often prevent us from making purchasing or other decisions on irrational grounds or as a member of a team being pressurised by 'group-think' influences. Among the many personal factors that may influence decisions relating to where to buy and who to buy from are:

- cultural factors – the way in which we have been taught to do business
- the information available to us
- professionalism, including ethical values and training
- experience of suppliers and their products
- ability to apply lateral thinking to purchasing problems.

Purchasing professionals should also develop the capacity to understand the preferences of users for a particular product and the motivations of suppliers.

Case study

You are employed by the Gambell Financial Services Group (GFSG) as the category manager for IT procurement. You have just left a senior management team meeting, having presented a report on the status of IT procurement. The salient points were:

Annual expenditure (excluding one-off projects)	£30 million
Number of service providers	25
Locations to which IT services are provided	6
Amount of annual up-front payments	£18 million
Suppliers in default of contract obligations (last year)	4
Predicted increase in service charges (next year)	3.6% of annual expenditure

After you had presented these basic facts there was a heated discussion. It all began when you expressed the view that the IT support contracts that embrace all software maintenance, emergency call-out to IT problems, desktop replacement and laptop maintenance and replacement, should be outsourced on a long-term partnering basis (you recommended seven years with an option to extend for a further three years). The IT manager said that he did not agree and that the current arrangement should remain. He was convinced that the current suppliers were all specialists in their field and knew the software better than anyone else. Then the finance director joined in the discussion, stating that all he was interested in was cost! Not only did he not want a 3.6 per cent increase, he wanted a 10 per cent reduction in costs. He also wants the up-front payments stopped. The managing director who chaired the meeting has given you some actions (see Tasks below) and has asked that you report back to the senior management team in two weeks with an agreed position between you and the IT manager.

Tasks

1 What arguments can you assemble to support a long-term partnering strategy?
2 How would you contract to deliver the finance director's objective?
3 Assuming you lost the argument for partnering – what strategy would you deploy to make savings?
4 Do you anticipate intellectual property considerations having any part to play in your strategy?

Discussion questions

11.1 If you were involved in qualifying a strategic supplier for the manufacture of high-quality components for use in an aircraft engine what would be the six most important questions you want answering about the supplier's procurement department?

11.2 You purchase tyres for a range of cars, vans and lorries. For many years these have been sole sourced with a tyre manufacturer. You have been asked to challenge the procurement strategy. How would you find other possible sources of supply who would be invited to tender?

11.3 Situation analysis is concerned with taking stock of where an organisation or activity within an organisation has been recently, where it is now and where it is likely to end up using present policies, plans and procedures. As the executive in charge of the purchasing of management services, including temporary labour, facilities management, consultancy and security you are asked to effect economies without prejudicing the final product quality. How might an analysis of market conditions help you make constructive recommendations?

11.4 One of your major competitors has just appointed an administrator. They have severe cash flow problems and many of their contracts have been running at a loss. Your sales director has told you that your company has been offered two of their contracts, providing your organisation accept the work at the current contract prices and terms that the failed company had. He has asked for your opinion on a possible course of action, prior to the sales director talking to the two potential clients. The value of the work being offered is £10 million. This would represent 24 per cent of your current turnover. What would be your opinion and what would it be founded upon?

11.5 You are accountable for procuring all waste management services for a large Council. A trade fair is to be held shortly in Munich and you have asked to attend. Your request has been refused by the managing director who says that he is cutting down on 'jollies'. What can you say to persuade him that there are significant benefits in attending?

11.6 The cost of evaluating the performance of suppliers can be high.
  ■ What arguments would you use to justify the expenditure on evaluating performance?
  ■ What steps might you take to minimise such expenditure?
  ■ What are the benefits to suppliers in you evaluating their performance?

11.7 Trade unions are opposed to outsourcing of public services and yet there are demonstrable service improvements and quantifiable savings. In your opinion, is outsourcing a sound business strategy?

11.8 Suggest one way in which you might evaluate the performance of a supplier against each of the 'ten Cs' listed in section 11.10.5 of this chapter.

11.9 You will require management information (MI) to use in evaluating supplier's performance. What do you think about this MI being provided by suppliers rather than by your organisation?

11.10 It is common sense that if you aggregate purchases and shrink the supply base you should make dramatic savings. If this is true, then there is an inevitability that large companies will get the lions' share of work and small companies will lose out. What is an effective procurement strategy to deal with aggregation?

11.11 Supplier performance depends on the buying organisation meeting its contractual obligations. Your finance director has just told you that next month all suppliers will only be paid in 90 days rather than the 45 days currently agreed to. The finance director tells you that the decision to change payment terms is irrevocable. What actions would you now take, internally and externally?

11.12 You urgently need a sub-contractor to machine your free issue material. This is high-value, special steel. Your production director has asked you four questions:
1 What will the contract say about scrap management?
2 How will the issue and transportation of the free issue take place?
3 How will the capacity you require be guaranteed?
4 What happens if you cannot guarantee actual requirements other than on 24-hour notice?

11.13 Partnering often has a requirement for 'open book'. You are negotiating with a supplier who accepts the principle of open book but wants to know what you will use the information for. He has given you an example. He has planned a profit of 12.5 per cent. What happens if the open book shows that through his efficiencies he makes 16.9 per cent? What would you tell him about the specific and the wider principle?

11.14 What advantages do purchasing consortia offer?

11.15 You have had external consultants auditing energy costs. They say that you could save 45 per cent by switching suppliers. This would mean a saving of £2.45 million in the next three years. The consultants then say that they will reveal the source of lower energy costs when you agree to give the consultants 50 per cent of the savings. What would be your immediate actions?

11.16 Within the public sector there is the 'competitive dialogue'. Conduct some research and explain whether you think there are any principles that could be usefully applied in the private sector.

11.17 Your company requires 7000 hours of specialised design services associated with a military contract that your company has. You have invited tenders. One of the potential suppliers has offered a co-located design team who would work alongside your designers. The supplier's designers would use your IT systems and conform to your quality standards, working hours and practices. It is known by the procurement team that your designers are paid 16 per cent less than the co-located designers are paid. What are the arguments for and against the co-location?

11.18 What are the advantages of having category management specialists in a procurement department?

Past examination questions

1 (a) Describe an appropriate process that an organisation could use to reduce its supply base.
  (b) State **five** benefits of supply base rationalisation.

CIPS, *An Introduction to Purchasing Strategy*, May 2007

2 A large local government authority covers the following areas in its supplier appraisal policy:
  (a) financial information
  (b) technical ability
  (c) equal opportunities

(d) environmental sustainability

(e) health and safety.

Explain why each of these areas may be important to such an organisation.

CIPS, The Business Environment for Purchasing and Supply, May 2008

3 Describe **two** ways in which the use of a computer can help a business in the vendor rating process.

CIPS, The Business Environment for Purchasing and Supply, May 2008

4 Developments in information technology (IT) such as online auctions are becoming increasingly attractive to both buyers and sellers in businesses.

(a) Explain what is meant by an online auction.

(b) Identify **three** benefits for a purchaser of online auctions.

CIPS, The Business Environment for Purchasing and Supply, November 2007

References

1 Technology Partners International, Inc.: www.technologypartners.ca

2 Office of Government Commerce, 'Category Management Toolkit': contact website@cabinet-office.gsi.gov.uk for information

3 Novack, R. A. and Simco, S. W., *Journal of Business Logistics*, Vol. 12, Issue 1, 1991

4 CIPS Knowledge Works, *e-sourcing*: www.cips.org

5 Waller, A., quoted by Lascelles, D., in his *Managing the E-supply Chain*, Business Intelligence, 2001, p. 19

6 ePedas at: www.epedas.com.my/who.html

7 OGC, *Supplier Financial Appraisal Guidance*, October, 2001

8 Buffa, E. S. and Kakesh, K. S., *Modern Production Operations Management*, 5th edn, John Wiley, 1987, p. 548

9 These categories are used in the supplier management policy document of the University of Nottingham

10 Emptoris Supplier Performance Module at: www.emptoris.com/solutions/supplier_performance_management_module.asp

11 Kozak, R. A. and Cohen, D. H., 'Distributor–supplier partnering relationships: a case in trust', *Journal of Business Research*, Vol. 30, 1997, pp. 33–8

12 Simpson, P. M., Siguaw, J. A. and White, S. C., 'Measuring the performance of suppliers: an analysis of evaluation processes', *Journal of Supply Management*, February, 2002

13 As 12 above

14 Carter, R., 'The seven Cs of effective supplier evaluation', *Purchasing and Supply Chain Management*, April, 1995, pp. 44–5

15 Fredriksson, P. and Gadde, L. E., 'Evaluation of Supplier Performance – the case of Volvo Car Corporation and its module suppliers', Chalmers University of Technology Sweden, 2005

16 Verikatesan, R., 'Strategic sourcing: to make or not to make', *Harvard Business Review*, November–December, 1992, pp. 98–107

17 Probert, D. R., 'Make or buy: your route to improved manufacturing performance', DTI, 1995

18 ICMA, 'Management accounting', Official Terminology, ICMA, 1996

19 Atkinson, J. and Meager, N., 'New forms of work organisation', IMS Report 121, 1986

[20] Beauchamp, M., 'Outsourcing everything else? Why not purchasing?', *Purchasing and Supply Management*, July, 1994, pp. 16–19

[21] Beulen, E. J. J., Ribbers, P. M. A. and Roos, J., *Outsourcing van IT-clienstverlening:een-make or buy beslissing*, Kluwer, 1994. Quoted by Fill, C. and Visser, E., *The Outsourcing Dilemma: Management Decision 2000*, Vol. 38.1, MCB University Press, pp. 43–50

[22] Quoted in Duffy, R. J., 'The outsourcing decision', *Inside Supply Management*, April, 2000, p. 38

[23] Lacity, M. C. and Hirscheim, R., *Information Systems Outsourcing*, John Linley, 1995

[24] Carrington, L., 'Outside chances', *Personnel Today*, 8 February, 1994, p. 34, see Figure 11.5

[25] Perkins, B., *Computer World*, 22 November, 2003

[26] Reilly, P. and Tamkin, P., *Outsourcing: A Flexibility Option for the Future*, Institute of Employment Studies, 1996, pp. 32–3

[27] As 23 above

[28] The source of this quotation cannot be traced

[29] Humbert, X. P. and Passarelli, C. P. M., 'Outsourcing: avoiding the hazards and pitfalls', Paper presented at the NAPM International Conference, 4–7 May, 1997

[30] CIPS, 'Partnership Sourcing': www.cips.org

[31] Partnership Sourcing Ltd, *Making Partnerships Happen*: www.psicbi.com

[32] Lambert, D. M., Emmelhaing, M. A. and Gardner, J. T., 'Developing and implementing supply chain partnerships', *International Journal of Logistics Management*, Vol. 7, No. 2, 1996, pp. 1–17

[33] Knemeyer, A. M., Corsi, T. M. and Murphy, P. R., 'Logistics outsourcing relationships: customer perspectives', *Journal of Business Logistics*, Vol. 24, No. 1, 2003, pp. 77–101

[34] Southey, P., 'Pitfalls to partnering in the UK', PSERG Second International Conference, April, 2003, in Burnett, K. (ed.), 'Readings in partnership sourcing', CIPS (undated)

[35] PSL, *Creating Service Partnerships*, Partnership Sourcing Ltd, 1993, p. 7

[36] As 35 above

[37] As 35 above

[38] *Effective partnering*, Crown Copyright, 2003, an overview for customers and suppliers to check

[39] The Centre for Construction Innovation: an Enterprise Centre within the School of the Built Environment at the University of Salford

[40] As 30 above, pp. 5–6

[41] Ramsay, J., 'The case against purchasing partnerships', *International Journal of Purchasing and Materials Management*, Fall, 1996, pp. 13–24

[42] Ellram, L. M., 'Partnering pitfalls and success factors', *International Journal of Purchasing and Materials Management*, Spring, 1995, pp. 36–44

[43] *E.C. Journal*, 84–28.8, 1968

[44] Webster, F. E. and Wind, Y. J., *Organisational Buying Behaviour*, Prentice Hall, 1972, pp. 33–7

[45] As 44 above

[46] A useful summary of research in the 25 years prior to 1996 is provided by Johnston, W. J. and Lewin, J. E., 'Organisational buying behaviour: towards an integrative framework', *Journal of Business Research*, Vol. 35, No. 1, 1996

[47] Bristor, J. M. and Ryan, M. S., 'The buying centre is dead, long live the buying centre', *Advances in Consumable Research*, Vol. 4, 1987, pp. 255–8

[48] Chisnall, P. M., *Strategic Industrial Marketing*, 2nd edn, Prentice Hall, 1989, pp. 82–3

[49] Hegarty, E., *How to Succeed in Company Politics*, McGraw-Hill, 1976

Chapter 12

Managing purchase prices

Learning outcomes

With reference, where applicable, to purchasing and supply chain management, this chapter aims to provide an understanding of:

- price
- supplier pricing decisions
- the supplier's choice of pricing strategy
- price and cost analysis
- price variation
- price variation formulae
- competition legislation
- collusive tendering.

Key ideas

- The nature of supplier's pricing decisions.
- Competition legislation.
- Firm price agreements.
- Cost price agreements.
- Cost breakdown.
- Price analysis for the purposes of comparison and negotiation.
- Price adjustment formulae.
- Procedure for price adjustment.
- Techniques for obtaining best value for money spent.

12.1 What is price?

Price can be defined as:

> A component of an exchange or transaction that takes place between two parties and refers to what must be given up by the buyer in order to obtain something offered by the seller.

In effect, price has a different focus for the two parties. The buyer sees price as what is given up to obtain the benefits of goods or services. The seller sees price as generating income and, if correctly applied, in determining profit. While pricing is a key focus for companies examining profitability, pricing decisions are also vital for not-for-profit organisations, such as charities, educational institutions and third sector bodies.

12.2 The buyer's role in managing purchase prices

The whole task of managing purchase prices is both an emotional matter and a professional challenge. Traditional purchasing theory placed equal weighting on the need to obtain the right quality, right quantity, right delivery, right place and right price. It would, of course, be incorrect to assert that price should be the dominant factor in the sourcing decision. However, price can be seen as a function of the other 'right' characteristics. In other words, the seller will determine a price only when the other factors are known. In the final analysis, the purchasing department is accountable for the organisation's expenditure. There cannot be a more responsible task.

The 1970s was a period when pricing decisions were extensively researched and, uniquely, at PhD level.[1] Some of the observations and insights remain challenging. Leighton[2] asserted that, 'Price may be looked at in another way, that is, as the outcome of a power or bargaining relationship.' England and Leenders[3] put forward the view that, 'The determination of price to be paid is one of the major decisions to be made by a purchasing agent. Indeed, the ability to get a good price is sometimes held to be the prime test of a good buyer.' Winkler[4] expressed a somewhat extreme view: 'Inertia is a great weakness of British Buying and some suppliers enjoy enormous profit margins because their customers do not want to take the risk of upsetting the settled routine of things, or to investigate alternate sources of supply.' Ammer[5] stressed a rounded view of the role of procurement, 'In most cases the supplier does not have the last word on prices. Able buyers can exert tremendous leverage if they really understand how prices are set and don't hesitate to use their skills. In doing so, they are doing a service not only to their own company but also to the supplier and to the economy as a whole.'

The buyer's involvement in pricing decisions at the new buy, straight rebuy and modified rebuy phases of the procurement cycle is shown in Figures 12.1, 12.2 and 12.3.

12.2.1 The buyer's actions pre-tender

As with everything, purchasing actions are dependent upon what is being purchased and whether it has been purchased previously. The analysis that follows is generic in scope and some selectivity will be necessary when applying the logic to specific scenarios (see also Table 12.1).

Figure 12.1 New buy phase – purchase price management factors

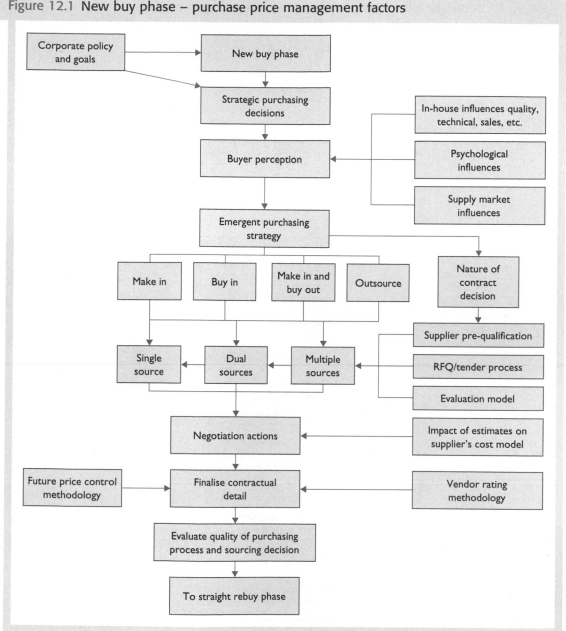

Cost estimating

Cost estimating is widely used to determine potential selling prices, recognising that some buyer's will have a propensity to negotiate and may have access to their in-house estimate to guide them. Tuns[6] points out that cost estimation is very critical and important in all types of manufacturing processes. Cost estimation is a critically important business function in all industries.

Figure 12.2 **Straight rebuy phase – purchase price management factors**

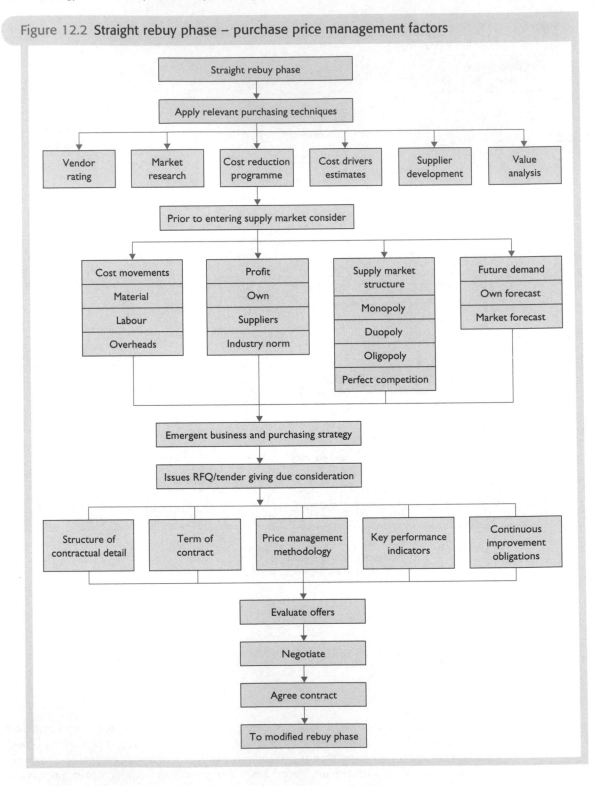

Figure 12.3 Modified rebuy phase – purchase price management factors

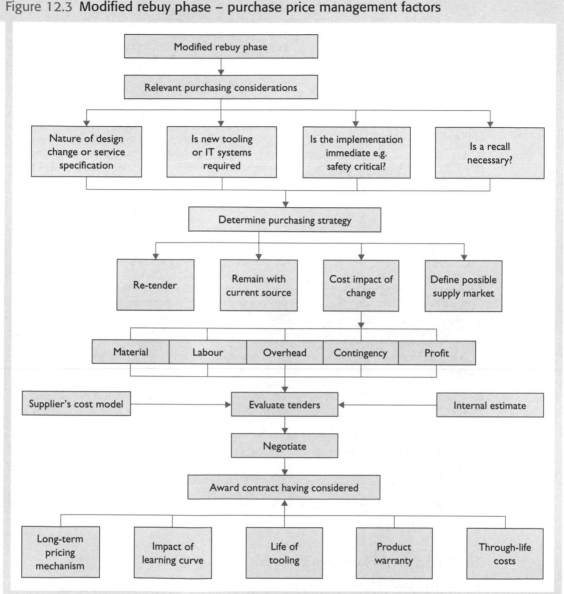

There are four kinds of cost estimation methodologies used throughout the forging industry:

- subjective estimation
- estimation by analogy (comparative estimation)
- parametric estimation (statistical estimation)
- bottom-up estimation (synthetic estimation).

Table 12.1 Pre-tender considerations

Soft market testing	This consists of making contact with existing suppliers in the marketplace and inviting their comments on relevant technical and commercial matters, including price. It may be possible to obtain a 'rough order of magnitude' price to assist with budgetary planning
Estimating – conventional	There is within some engineering, automotive and aerospace organisations an ability to calculate 'should costs' to assist the budgetary process and to give the buyer a target cost and negotiation leverage. Estimating is not a precise science, hence a need to be flexible when using estimates in price negotiations
Estimating – parametrics	This is an estimating technique that uses a statistical relationship between historical data and other variables (for example, square footage in construction, lines of code in software development) to calculate an estimate for activity parameters, such as scope, cost, budget and duration
Access to a benchmarking club	It is not uncommon for a number of local authorities to form a benchmarking club where they exchange price and service performance information
Contribute to a benchmarking service	There are many subscription-based price and performance services. For example, construction costs, telecommunications, pulp and paper, outsourced services and IT are readily available. It is vital, if using these services, to ensure that 'like-with-like' is being compared
Networking within the purchasing profession	Members of the purchasing profession are often reluctant to exchange price information. Ethical and confidentiality are influences but when organisations are non-competing there is less of an issue

The items that make up forging cost can be grouped as:

1 material cost
2 forging equipment cost
3 tooling cost
4 labour cost
5 overhead cost
6 billet heating cost
7 secondary operations cost (cleaning, heat treatment, inspection, etc.)
8 quality control cost
9 packaging and transportation cost.

These are elaborated upon in Figure 12.4.

Figure 12.4 Forging work breakdown structure (WBS)

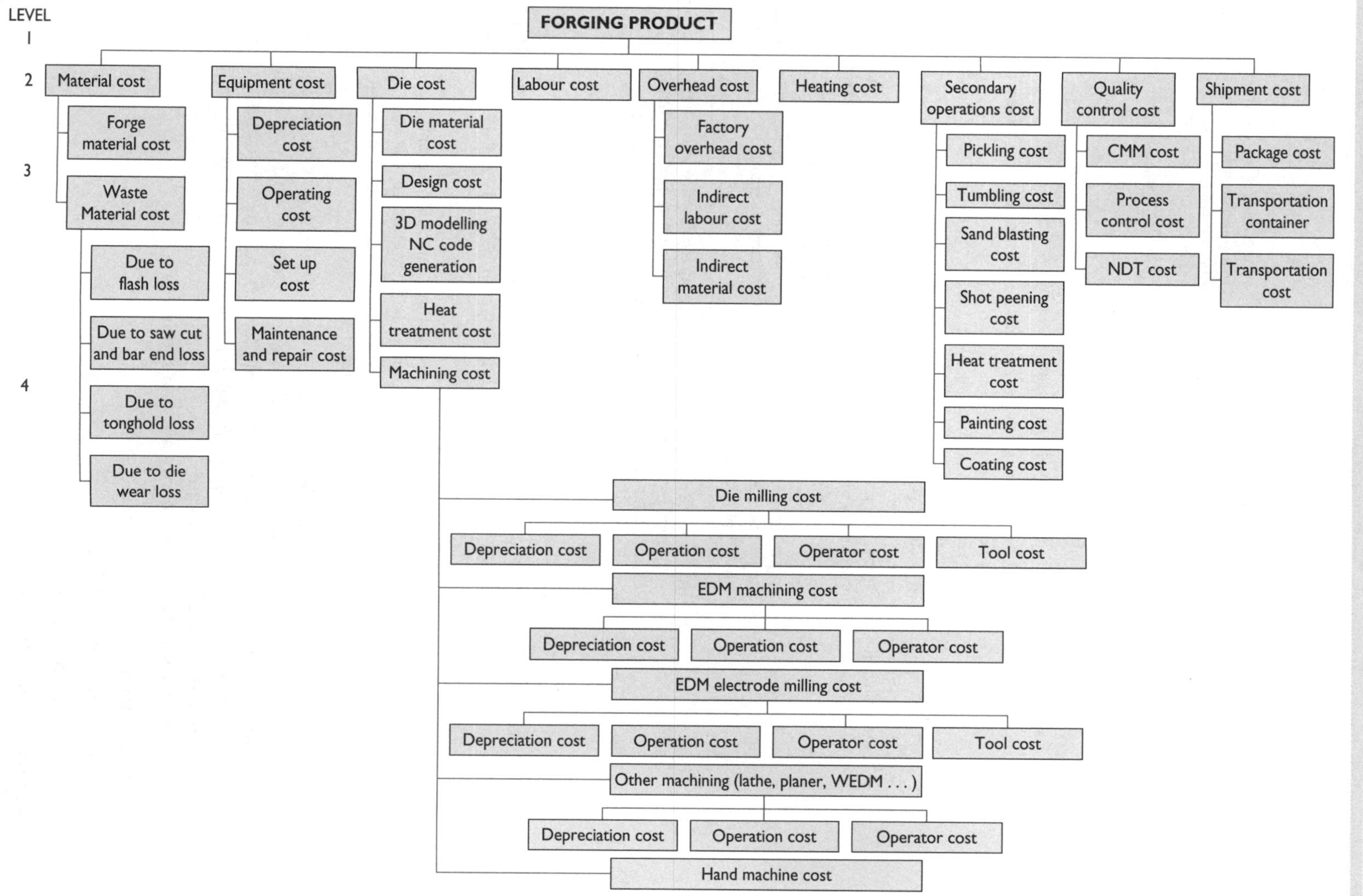

Table 12.2 Tender stage considerations

Lump sum prices	This is an unsophisticated approach to determining prices. The limit of information is a total lump sum price from each tenderer. If we assume that five tendered prices have been received: £111,865 £151,490 £154,076 £199,831 £245,641 there are many issues arising, including: 1 Why is there a 119 per cent difference between the lowest and highest prices? 2 Has the lowest priced bidder made a mistake or plans to cut the quality? 3 Is the lowest bidder desperate for work? 4 Is the highest bidder too busy and doesn't want the work?
Elemental cost breakdown	This is where the buyer asks each tenderer to breakdown the tendered price into its key elements, namely, labour, materials, overheads and profit. This methodology does give comparable data not available with a lump sum price
Detailed cost model	In this situation every facet of the tendered price is 'broken down' to give the buyer the classic 'open book' scenario. Refer to Figure 12.5 for an approach to obtaining detailed costs
Reverse auctions	At the tender stage the buyer has comparable price information and then subjects it to a reverse auction where one or more of the tendered prices will reduce, but not against cost disclosure

Parametric cost estimates

A parametric cost estimate is one that uses cost estimating relationships (CERs) and associated mathematical algorithms (or logic) to establish cost estimates. De Marco[7] observed that:

> Parametric tools can assist BPR. On one level, they can improve and streamline the BPR phases. On another level, parametric technology is 'best practice' for estimating. Parametric tools bring speed, accuracy and flexibility to estimating processes, processes that are often bogged down in bureaucracy and unnecessary detail.

A parametric hardware cost model provides estimates of system acquisition costs based upon quantitative parameters such as complexity, quantity, weight and size; and qualitative parameters such as environmental specification, type of packaging and level of integration; and schedule parameters such as months to first prototype, manufacturing rate and amount of new design.

Some uses of parametric hardware cost models are:

- estimates of cost to complete
- estimates of modifications
- should cost analysis
- most probable cost estimates
- evaluation of bids and proposals

Figure 12.5 **Designing a cost model**

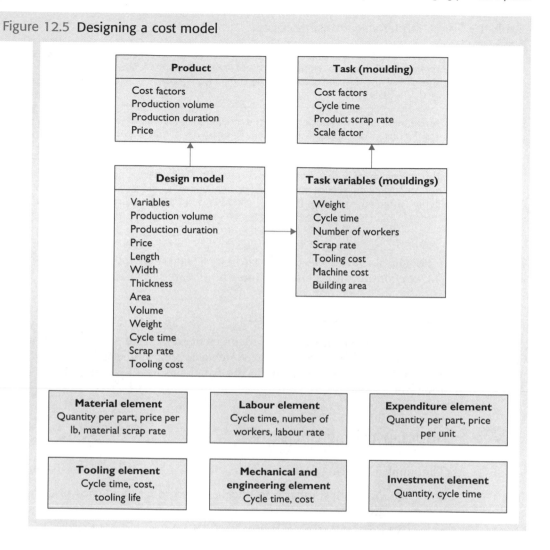

- vendor negotiations
- lifecycle cost estimates
- estimates of spare parts costs
- design to cost
- rough order of magnitude (ROM) cost estimates of new or advanced hardware systems.

At the tender stage there are a number of pricing considerations as outlined in Table 12.2.

There is a great deal of skill involved in designing a cost model, where proposed costs are very specific to the goods or service to be supplied. It is possible to purchase cost estimating software such as Deccapro.[8] Figure 12.5 is adapted from Deccan Systems schematic on using design and task variables to model costs.

When the priced tender has been received, the buyer has a key role in determining the credibility of the price. The key considerations are shown in Table 12.3.

Table 12.3 Post-tender stage considerations

Interrogate costs	When a detailed cost breakdown has been obtained, the buyer should lead the activity to interrogate all costs and overhead recovery and declared profit. This activity will require the support of technical and finance colleagues. The comparison between different tenderers' cost opinions can be very revealing
Clarification	Where there are discrepancies between tendered prices and between the in-house estimated price it is the buyer's task to seek clarification. This may reveal that the supplier cannot purchase materials competitively; labour costs are too high, long-term cost-in-use is too high and so on
Negotiation	The negotiation of price is a valid activity, providing the highest ethical standards apply. That means not conducting dutch auctions or revealing one tenderers' prices to another tenderer. Within the public sector, buyers must ensure they do not breach EU Regulations or Standing Orders

Pricing considerations continue to be relevant after the contract has been awarded. The key considerations effecting most buyers are shown in Table 12.4.

12.2.2 Procurement cost reduction

There is a continuing need for procurement to manage a cost reduction programme. There should be an agreed, and well-defined, programme for the procurement department and for each buyer. Table 12.5 sets out a range of possibilities for cost reduction attention.

12.3 Supplier pricing decisions

The supplier's pricing decision will be made in a number of scenarios, including:

- selling a range of standard products either through published price lists or 'ad hoc' pricing decisions
- one-off project requirement that has no directly comparable precedence
- launching a new product or service
- selling a product or service to meet an 'emergency' situation, e.g. a technical solution to the failure of a safety critical piece of equipment
- a strategic decision to stop selling a range of products at the end of their design life.

There will be many general considerations to take into account, including:

- the ability to achieve an appropriate profit
- the nature of demand and supply, and current market forces
- existing capacity to provide the goods/services
- available inventory
- the buyer's location and status, e.g. are they are a well-established customer or a 'one-off' buyer
- required levels of investment, if any
- demands made on key personnel

Table 12.4 Post-contract award stage considerations

Indexation	In many long-term contracts and projects the tendered price is subject to indexation, meaning the price could decrease and increase. Contracts may refer to VOP (variation of price), CPA (contract price adjustment) or PVF (price variation formula). They all mean the same. In each case there will be a published formula. This is further explained in section 12.8 in this chapter
Claims for extras	There are occasions in the life of a contract when the buying organisation will change the parameters, such as specification, delivery times and product support requirements. This will probably trigger a claim for extra payment. The detailed basis of the claim must be exposed and, when appropriate, negotiated to a level that is acceptable to the buying organisation
Contract change notices (CCN)	There is a provision in some contracts for a contract change notice (CCN) to be issued when a formal change to a contract is proposed. There will be a defined process to consider price and other impacts of the change, such as extending delivery date(s)
Cost in the event of termination	There is a possibility that a contract will be terminated prior to its defined end date. Termination is a regular source of disputes, many of which finish up in the courts. The contract should include a right for the buyer to terminate in the event of default and, in some cases, for 'convenience'. It is almost inevitable that some 'costs' will have been incurred by the supplier for which recompense will be required. There is an onus on the supplier to mitigate their losses
Continuous improvement obligations	A requirement for continuous improvement is not an unreasonable demand, particularly on long-term contracts for the supply of goods or services. It recognises that the supplier, with the buyer's support, should be able to reduce costs. The classic approach of value analysis and process improvements can help to reduce prices. In some service contracts there is a requirement to reduce annual costs by, say, 3 per cent. If a higher figure is obtained there can be a profit sharing arrangement
Apply benchmarking clause	Some contracts have an annual benchmarking requirement where, for example, prices are checked against a basket of comparable products. If the basket shows lower costs the supplier has the option of matching them, or the buyer can purchase the items elsewhere. This approach can, for example, be applied to IT supplies
Active cost reduction programme	In assertive purchasing departments there will be an active cost reduction programme and each buyer will be given a specific target. Achieving cost reduction will require varied initiatives. In a manufacturing environment, cost reduction is vital to maintaining market position and profitability. Engagement with the supply chain is essential if unnecessary cost is to be driven out
Resisting price increase requests	Price increases will erode competitiveness and profit in a manufacturing environment. In the public sector they will threaten the ability to provide the same level and quality of services. The skill of purchasing to resist price increase requests is an acid test of competence. The skill of evaluating the reasoning behind the proposed price increase is a professional requisite

Table 12.5 Possibilities for cost reduction attention

1 Challenge existing contracts for price competitiveness	■ Select long-term contracts ■ Benchmark in market ■ Establish the cost drivers
2 Challenge design/specification	■ Use concurrent engineering ■ Implement 'design for lean' ■ Use value analysis methodology
3 Look for overhead reduction	■ Electronic purchasing systems ■ Reduce levels of inventory ■ Build to order
4 Adopt standardisation	■ Reduce varieties ■ Use one supplier's range ■ Design out duplicate ranges
5 Challenge supply chain costs	■ Incoterms ■ Packaging ■ Mode of transport
6 Consider outsourcing	■ Select non-core services ■ Market test ■ Set sights high
7 Better use of working capital	■ Payment terms ■ No advance payments ■ Reduce inventory
8 Eradicate uncompetitive suppliers	■ Issue RFQs ■ Negotiation with new suppliers ■ Terminate ineffective contracts

- risk presented by the contractual terms and conditions
- any special environmental and health and safety requirements
- extent of sub-contracting and supply chain
- requirement for performance bonds/parent company guarantees
- product support requirements
- special insurances demanded
- intellectual property ownership
- urgency of requirement.

12.4 The supplier's choice of pricing strategy

A supplier has many options when deciding how to price goods or services. When a price is given to the buyer, it is difficult to know what approach has been taken, hence the need to probe tendered prices. Outlined below are some pricing strategies.

12.4.1 Skimming pricing

This involves charging a relatively high price for a period of time particularly where a new, innovative, or much improved product is launched on the market. The product may be protected by a patent as is often the case with pharmaceutical products. Of course, the protection will come to an end and competitors will then be attracted, hence dramatic reductions in price occur. For prestige goods and services, price skimming can be successful because the buyer is more concerned with prestige than price. First class air travel and designer-label clothing are examples where skimming prices occurs.

12.4.2 Penetration pricing

In this instance, the price charged for products and services is set artificially low in order to:

(a) gain entry into a customer who is held to be of long-term strategic importance and/or

(b) to gain market share.

It will be evident that such 'low' prices cannot be sustained in the longer term. When a buyer is faced with a tendered price that is, say, 40 per cent lower than the next ranked price there is the danger that the low price is linked to a perception of poor quality. So how does the supplier give such a low price? One way is to seek only to recover the net cost of materials and labour and to either not apply overhead recovery or to apply marginal overheads and not generate any profit.

12.4.3 Full cost pricing

The supplier, in this case, includes every cost that is believed to be attracted to the purchase. All material costs will be recovered, plus an allowance for scrap. All labour costs will be recovered at rates charged for each grade of labour, including management time. All overheads deemed to apply will be applied to labour and materials in a manner determined by Finance and may include corporate overheads imposed on the specific business operation. It is probable that a contingency provision will be included, as may be 'agent's fees', 'negotiation allowance', finance/cash/low risk provision and so on. It is believed that about 80 per cent of all supplier pricing decisions are made on the basis of full costs.

12.4.4 Buyer related pricing

A deliberate strategy is for the supplier to offer a price that, in some way, directly relates to the 'buyer's' competence. The supplier will form a view on competence by the manner in which the purchase is approached. The disclosure of a budget is not a sign of competence. Neither are the following comments:

'Please do the best you can.'

'We are not asking anyone else to quote.'

'No doubt your prices have increased since we last purchased.'

'Can you supply us immediately and sort out the price later?'

12.4.5 Promotional pricing

This is common in the retail field with BOGOF (Buy One Get One Free), buy two and get 50 per cent discount on the second product, and seasonal offers. They are not uncommon in industry when suppliers seek to dispose of slow moving inventory, dispose of products at the end of their life and in situations where the manufacturer is promoting a specific product for a limited period.

12.4.6 Prestige pricing

This is not dissimilar to skimming pricing and is used by suppliers who can capture part of a market and who want a 'prestige' service. The international airlines with first class travel at fares that can be six times 'economy' travel is one example, as are Savile Row suits, top-range motor vehicles and top-end wines.

The skill for buyers is to understand the basis of prices offered. This requires diligence in probing and understanding costs and, on occasions, the application of high level negotiation skills.

12.4.7 Diversionary pricing

Some have argued that this is a practice used by deceptive service firms, suggesting that it is somehow illegal. The fact is that it is a legitimate business practice where a low price is stated for one or more services (emphasised in promotion) to give an illusion that all prices are low. An example is an ice cream manufacturer who offers freezers at a very low purchase price but only on condition their products can be stored in them.

12.4.8 Target pricing

This is where the buyer provides a target price to suppliers. The context in which this is done should be understood before a supplier responds. The target price could be the outcome of a genuine cost estimate when the buying organisation has very good knowledge of the product or service. In this situation the target price has some credibility. However, the unethical buyer may 'make up' a target price and pressurise suppliers to meet it, even if they cannot make a profit.

12.5 Price and cost analysis

Price analysis is designed to show that the proposed price is reasonable when compared with current or recent prices for the same or similar goods or services, adjusted where necessary to reflect changes in market conditions, economic conditions, quantities, or/ and terms and conditions under contracts that resulted for adequate price competition achieved through a RFQ (request for quotation) or tendering process.

Cost analysis is the review and evaluation of the separate cost elements, overhead recovery and profit in the tendered price (including cost or pricing data or information other than cost or pricing data) and the application of professional judgement to determine how appropriate the proposed costs are to setting the purchase price, assuming reasonable economy and efficiency.

12.5.1 Considerations when requesting prices from suppliers

There are many considerations when requesting prices from suppliers, including:

- the value of the contract
- if detailed cost information is provided, who has the competence to evaluate it?
- do we have the ability to prepare the cost model template?
- what benchmarking information do we have?
- what layers of labour costs do we want, e.g. by labour grades and time?
- how do we want overheads (fixed, variable and corporate) to be shown?
- how will we evaluate profit returns, taking into account investment?
- how do we propose to evaluate costs associated with risk?
- recognition that a proposed price may not be related to cost
- dealing with discounts and/or rebates
- the use to which the data will be put, e.g. negotiation
- the need to respect the supplier's confidentiality.

12.5.2 Price analysis

When tendered prices are being compared there are various bases on which a comparison can be made. These include:

- a simple comparison of proposed prices once it is ascertained that 'all things are equal', including compliance with the specification and contract terms and conditions
- the use of parametric estimating methods where key metrics are available
- comparison with competitive published price lists
- the use of comparable market prices through third party consultants, e.g. energy pricing
- comparison with in-house generated 'should cost' estimates
- comparison with the output of value engineering/value analysis studies
- liaising with buyers in a wider procurement community, e.g. government buying operations in different departments.

12.5.3 Cost analysis

This is a far more demanding activity than price analysis because it requires the buying organisation to have the resources and expertise to analyse all costs, and to effectively challenge areas where it is believed the costs are inappropriate. The following facets of the price will need to be analysed, questioned and resolved:

- What constitutes material costs based ideally on a bill of materials and costed for base metals, materials, scrap allowance and bought-in sub-assemblies? Differences in these costs may be accounted for by good/bad procurement, efficiencies/inefficiencies in managing waste and so on.
- What constitutes labour costs, accounted for by the hourly cost of labour at various grades including operatives, supervision, management and any director involvement? There are significant differences between labour rates in, for example, UK, USA, India, Morocco, Vietnam and Israel.

Table 12.6 Extract from services cost model

Employee costs	ICT costs
Salaries	Hardware
Overtime	Software
Pensions	Depreciation
National Insurance	Support
Supplementary benefits	Internal recharging
Car allowance	Other (name)
Public transport	
Training	
Recruitment	
Temporary employees	
Other (name)	

- How are overheads being recovered? There are fixed and variable overheads to be considered and, depending on the suppliers' organisation structure, the possibility of corporate overheads used, for example, to recover corporate IT legal and financial services provision.
- It is probable that the supplier will apply a contingency factor, often a percentage of material, labour and overheads. The provision for contingency includes the potential of 'unexpected' factors arising such as labour disputes, unexpected surges in raw material prices, poor cost estimating and difficulties meeting the specification.
- The inclusion of costs to comply with the demands of the contract, such as:
  - provision for liquidated damages
  - provision of a performance bond or parent company guarantee
  - excessive inspection demands and testing procedures
  - attendance at contract review meetings.
- The declared profit that can be based on varied approaches, including:
  - the recovery of investment such as research and development
  - excessive profit return when skimming pricing used
  - demands made by 'corporate' to justify bidding for the contract
  - the need to generate financial reserves.

Tables 12.6 and 12.7 show examples of cost breakdowns, included to illustrate the depth of detail that can be pursued.

12.5.4 The buyer's control of purchase price

There should be a continuous review of the effectiveness of a buyer's control of purchase prices. This should include independent audits, taking into consideration, as a minimum:

- the award of contracts that are not subjected to tenders
- price increases allowed without scrutiny
- no scrutiny of cost drivers
- an absence of negotiation

Table 12.7 Elemental cost breakdown manufactured item

Element	% of total
Steel scrap	13.98
Pig iron	6.27
Other materials	7.55
Electricity	7.22
Coke	4.73
National Insurance	2.24
Oil	1.41
Gas	0.61
Labour	31.28
Depreciation	2.41
Repairs	12.41
Rates	0.68
Insurance	0.59
Carriage	2.05
Hire of equipment	1.52
Telephones	0.36
Commission	0.70
Bank interest	0.43
Other overheads	3.54

- an absence of benchmarking data
- contract terms extended without tendering
- contract 'extras' allowed without challenge
- poor contract change procedures
- no consideration of reverse auctions
- single tendering permitted
- no control over price variation formulae
- no control over purchase prices linked to currency movement.

12.6 Competition legislation

12.6.1 Introduction

On 18 March 2010, The National Audit Office published its report[9] 'Review of the UK's Competition Landscape'. At paragraph 2 it points out that the UK's competition regime is largely the result of the Competition Act 1998 and the Enterprise Act 2002. There is other legislation which impacts on the UK regime, such as the Communications Act 2003 and the underpinning EU framework.

12.6.2 UK anti-competition practices agencies

In the UK, the Secretary of State for the Department for Business, Innovation and Skills (DBIS) has overall responsibility for competition policy. The main UK competition bodies are the following:

■ *Office of Fair Trading (OFT)* – an independent body with statutory powers under the Competition and Enterprise Acts of 1998 and 2002 respectively. The DBIS is committed to work together with the OFT and share information. The OFT addresses anti-competition practices by means of a mix of enforcement and communication. It is to the OFT that complaints relating to competition should, in the first instance, be made.

■ *Competition Commission* – conducts in-depth inquiries into markets, mergers and the regulation of major industries at the request of the DBIS and OFT.

■ *Competition Appeal Tribunal (CAT)* – hears and decides appeals and other applications or claims involving competition.

■ *A number of regulators* – the Office of Communications, the Office of the Gas and Electricity Markets, the Water Services Regulation Authorities and the Office of Rail Regulation.

■ *European Commission (Directorate General for Competition)* – has powers to deal with restrictive agreements and anti-competition practices when trade between EU members is affected.

The UK competition regime is shown in Figure 12.6.[10]

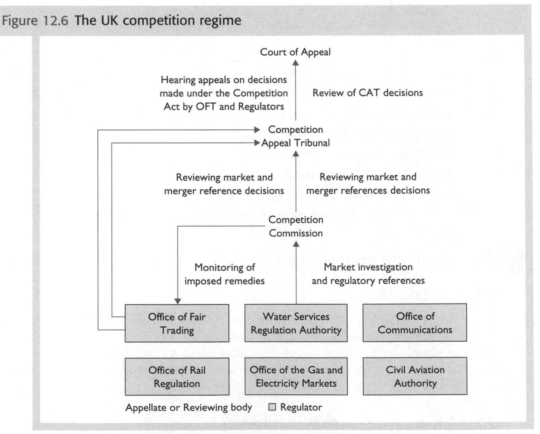

Figure 12.6 **The UK competition regime**

Notes: (1) The Civil Aviation Authority has powers to make a market reference of the Air Traffic Control Services market only. (2) The Secretary of State may also make a reference to the Competition Commission on grounds of public interest. (3) The diagram omits the Supreme Court of the UK and the European Court of Justice both of which are in the judicial structure which includes the Tribunal. It also omits the Northern Ireland Authority for Utility Regulation. (4) The Court of Appeal's jurisdiction only extends to England and Wales. The equivalent court in Scotland is the Court of Session, and in Northern Ireland, the Court Of Appeal of Northern Ireland.

12.6.3 *The Competition Act* 1998 and *The Enterprise Act* 2002

The Competition Act 1998 prohibited both anti-competition agreements and the abuse of a dominant position.

An 'agreement' is an undertaking or contract between companies or associated companies, whether in writing or otherwise. Examples of such agreements include:

- agreeing to fix purchasing or selling prices or other trading conditions
- agreeing to limit or control production, markets or technical developments of investment
- agreeing to share markets or supply sources
- agreeing to apply different trading conditions to equivalent transactions, thereby placing some parties at a competitive advantage.

An agreement is, however, considered to be unlikely to have an appreciable effect where the combined market share of the parties involved does not exceed 25 per cent. This said, agreements to fix prices, impose minimum resale prices or share markets may be regarded as having an appreciable effect even when the parties' combined market share is below 25 per cent.

Whether or not a company is in a 'dominant position' will be decided by the OFT according to the company's market share. In general, a company is unlikely to be regarded as dominant if it has a market share of less than 40 per cent, although a lower market share may be considered dominant if the market structure enables it to act independently of its competitors.

Ways in which a dominant company may abuse its position include:

- imposing unfair purchasing or selling prices
- limiting production, markets or technical development to the prejudice of customers
- applying different trading conditions to equivalent transactions and thereby placing certain parties at a competitive advantage
- attaching unrelated supplementary conditions to a contract.

12.7 Collusive tendering

When there is a competitive tendering process the buyer should bear in mind the potential for collusive tendering. When this occurs it eliminates competition among suppliers. A report[11] by the Office of Fair Trading commented that in the industry that is the subject of the Decision there are generally three types of arrangement that can result in a pre-selected supplier winning a contract.

- *Cover bidding* (also referred to as cover pricing) occurs when a supplier submits a price for a contract that is not intended to win the contract. Rather, it is a price that has been decided upon in connection with another supplier that wishes to win the contract.
- *Bid suppression* takes place when suppliers agree among themselves either to abstain from bidding or to withdraw bids.
- *Bid rotation* is a process whereby the pre-selected supplier submits the lowest bid on a systematic or rotating basis.

12.8 Price variation formulae

Traditionally, whenever, price variation formulae have been discussed, reference has been made to the formula developed by the British Electrotechnical and Allied Manufacturers Association (BEAMA). Variations in the cost of materials and labour are calculated in accordance with the following formula:

$$P_1 = P_0 \left(0.05 + 0.475 \left(\frac{M_1}{M_0} \right) + 0.475 \left(\frac{L_1}{L_0} \right) \right)$$

Where:

$P_1 =$ final contract price
$P_0 =$ contract price at date of tender
$M_1 =$ average of producer price index figures for materials and fuel purchased for basic electrical equipment as provided by the Office for National Statistics, commencing with the index last provided before the two-fifths point of the contract period and ending with the index last provided before the four-fifths point of the contract period
$M_0 =$ producer price index figure of materials and fuel purchased for basic electrical equipment last provided by the Office for National Statistics before the date of tender
$L_1 =$ average of the BEAMA labour cost index figures for electrical engineering published for the last two-thirds of the contract period
$L_0 =$ BEAMA labour cost index figure for electrical engineering published for the month in which the tender date falls.

It is essential that a professional buyer has a good working knowledge of the way in which price variation formulae are constructed and applied. The complexity will depend on the nature of the actual purchase.

The Indian Electrical and Electronics Manufacturers Association (IEEMA) have devised a PVF for a copper wound transformer. This is reproduced below.

The price quoted/confirmed is based on the input cost of raw materials/components and labour cost as on the date of quotation and the same is deemed to be related to prices of raw materials and all India average consumer price index number for industrial workers as specified in the price variation clause given below. In case of any variation in these prices and index numbers, the price payable shall be subject to adjustment, up or down in accordance with the following formula:

$$P = \left(13 + 23\frac{c}{c_0} + 27\frac{ES}{ES_0} + 9\frac{IS}{IS_0} + 5\frac{IM}{IM_0} + 11\frac{TB}{TB_0} + 12 \right)$$

Where:

$P =$ Price payable as adjusted in accordance with the above formula
$P_0 =$ Price quoted/confirmed
$C_0 =$ Average LME settlement price of copper wire bars
This price is as applicable for the month, *two* months prior to the date of tendering
$ES_0 =$ C&F price of CRGO Electrical Steel Sheets
This price is as applicable on the first working day of the month *one* month prior to the date of tendering.

IS_o = Wholesale price index number for iron and steel (base 1993–94 = 100)

This index number is as applicable for the week ending first Saturday of the month *three* months prior to the date of tendering.

IM_o = Price of insulation materials

This price is as applicable on the first working day of the month, *one* month prior to the date of tendering.

TB_o = Price of transformer oil base stock

This price is as applicable on the first working day of the month, *two* months prior to the date of tendering.

W_o = All India average consumer price index humber for industrial workers, as published by the Labour Bureau, Ministry of Labour, Government of India (base 1982 = 100)

C = Average LME settlement price of copper wire bars

This price is as applicable for the month, *two* months prior to the date of delivery.

ES = C&F price of CRGO electrical steel sheet

This price is as applicable on the first working day for the month, *one* month prior to the date of delivery.

IS = Wholesale price index number for iron and steel (base: 1993–94 = 100)

This index number is as applicable for the week ending first Saturday of the month, *three* months prior to the date of delivery.

IM = Price of insulating material

This price is as applicable on the first working day of the month, *one* month prior to the date of delivery.

TB = Price of transformer oil base stock

This price is as applicable on the first working day of the month, *two* months prior to the date of delivery.

W = All India average consumer price index number for industrial workers, as published by the Labour Bureau, Ministry of Labour, Government of India (base 1982 = 100)

This index number is as applicable on the first working day of the month, *three* months prior to the date of delivery.

Another price adjustment formula, this time one applied in the South African engineering sector is reproduced below.

In accordance with Clause 49(2), the value of each certificate issued in terms of Clause 52(1) shall be increased or decreased by the amount obtained by multiplying '*Ac*', defined in Clause 2 of this Schedule, by the Contract Price Adjustment Factor, rounded off to the fourth decimal place, determined according to the formula:

$$\text{CPAF} \equiv (1 - X)\left[\frac{aLt}{L_o} + \frac{bPt}{P_o} + \frac{cMt}{M_o} + \frac{dFt}{P_o} - 1 \right]$$

in which the symbols have the following meaning:

'*X*' is the proportion of '*Ac*' which is not subject to adjustment unless otherwise stated in the Appendix; this proportion shall be 0.15.

'*a*', '*b*', '*c*', and '*d*' are the co-efficients determined by the engineer and specified in the Appendix, and which are deemed, irrespective of the actual constituents of the work, to represent the proportionate value of labour, plant, materials (other than 'special

437

materials' specified, in terms of Clause 49(3), in the Appendix) and fuel respectively. The arithmetical sum of 'a', 'b', 'c' and 'd' shall be unity.

'L' is the 'Labour Index' and shall be the actual wage rate index for all workers in the civil engineering industry of the Central Statistical Service.

'P' is the 'Plant Index' and shall be the 'Civil Engineering Plant Index' as published in the Statistical News Release (PO 142.2) of the Central Statistical Service.

'M' is the 'Materials Index' and shall be the 'Price Index of Civil Engineering Materials', as published in the Statistical News Release (PO 142.20) of the Central Statistical Service.

'F' is the 'Fuel Index' and shall be the weighted average of the fuel indices for 'Diesel, before deduction of refund' and 'Diesel, after deduction of refund', as published in the Statistical News Release (PO 142.20) of the Central Statistical Service for the 'Coast' or 'Witwatersrand'. The weighting ratio and the use of the 'Coast' and 'Witwatersrand' indices shall be as specified by the engineer in the Appendix unless otherwise specified by the engineer in the Appendix, the weighting ratio shall be 1 to 1.

The suffix 'o' denotes the basic indices applicable to the base month, which shall be the month prior to the month in which the closing date for the tender falls.

The suffix 't' denotes the current indices applicable to the month in which the last day of the period falls to which the relevant payment certificate relates.

If any index relevant to any particular certificate is not known at the time when the certificate is prepared, the engineer shall estimate the value of such an index. Any correction which may be necessary when the correct indices become known shall be made by the engineer in subsequent payment certificates.

Case study

The East Shires Utility (ESU) company owns a number of companies engaged in the storage and distribution of water, including complicated pumping stations. There is a five-year engineering asset renewal and refurbishment programme, for which a budget of £450 million exists. Until six months ago, the Engineering Projects Division (EPD) handled the procurement process from start to finish. The situation changed when ESU appointed a new managing director. Within two weeks, he issued a mandatory instruction: 'All purchases will, in future, be handled by procurement.' The director of EPD did not welcome this change and made it very clear to ESU's procurement director that he did not agree with the instruction. Relationships are very strained between EPD and procurement.

There is a need to place a contract for the refurbishment of the Westhead Pumping Station. This is a medium-sized pumping station. The work will require labour, site management, the presence of construction plant and equipment, materials (such as electric motors, switchboards and turbine parts), scaffolding, painting, installation, testing, commissioning and provision of drawings. EPD and procurement have agreed to use the Westhead project as a model for all similar future projects.

EU procurement procedures were followed (the negotiated procedure) and three companies were selected to tender. Even before the process began, EPD made it known that it wanted the contract to be awarded to Tinnion Ltd, which has done pumping station work for ESU in the past. Internal records show that Tinnion has been a very effective contractor. EPD argued that experience of ESU plant is a vital factor and persuaded procurement to make 'experience of similar plant' a tender evaluation criterion, weighted at 20 per cent.

Yukon Construction was also shortlisted. It is owned by a French water utility, but is a registered UK business. It has satisfied all prequalification criteria and has relevant technical expertise.

The third shortlisted company is Normand Ltd – a large engineering project company. It has never done any work for ESU and has made it clear to procurement staff that Normand has been prevented from winning contracts by EPD which has, in effect, run a closed shop in the past.

Tenders have been received and all three potential suppliers have satisfied all technical requirements, so the price negotiations will decide who wins the contract.

The invitation to tender document requested a price breakdown in a specified form and the information that has been submitted is shown in the table below.

Price element	Normand £	Yukon £	Tinnion £
Site management	40,000	–	156,000
Labour	75,000	–	92,224
Construction plant and equipment	42,000	–	35,890
Materials	27,500	–	* (see below)
Subcontracted work	110,000	–	22,000
Subtotal	294,500	–	306,114
Overheads	29,450	–	61,222
Subtotal	323,950	–	367,336
Profit	32,395	–	45,917
Grand total	**£356,345**	**£280,000**	**£413,253**

* Materials at cost +5% handling fee +6.5% profit (estimated at £38,000)

The analysis and subsequent actions on a pricing decision are to be carried out by Evan Evans, a senior buyer with ESU. He first of all contacted Yukon to ask why it had not provided a price breakdown. It replied that it had not been a mandatory requirement in the invitation to tender document, which is correct. Its stance was that it would stand by its price and its policy was against breaking down costs or prices. Evans noted that 'under no circumstances will Yukon supply a price breakdown'.

Evans next contacted the director of EPD to ask for the budget figure for the work to be carried out at Westhead Pumping Station. The reply was £450,000. This assumed that the work would be completed within 24 weeks of the contract being awarded. All tenderers have agreed to that date. Evans asked how the £450,000 figure had been determined. The answer was experience and the director quickly pointed out some of the cost elements. Evans noted:

- crane hire
- helicopter
- design
- transport of equipment to site
- scaffolding
- painting
- site management
- site establishment
- inspection

■ on-site machining

■ divers

■ materials.

The discussion ended with the EPD director saying that procurement could not possibly evaluate these costs and it should be left to technical staff!

Task

1 If you were Evans, what action would you now take with the tenderers?

2 What lessons are there to be learned for procurement?

3 What type of pricing agreement would you put in place?

Discussion questions

12.1 How would you define price:
   (a) from the buyer's viewpoint?
   (b) from the supplier's viewpoint?

12.2 At the pre-tender phase of procurement, what are the possible advantages of:
   (a) engaging in soft market testing?
   (b) using parametric estimating?
   (c) networking within the purchasing profession?
   (d) contributing to a benchmarking service?

12.3 If a supplier provides a detailed cost breakdown, what roles can be played in evaluating it, by each of the following:
   (a) the buyer?
   (b) the accountant?
   (c) the technical specialist in the goods/service?
   (d) the estimator?

12.4 You have been asked to purchase a hot air balloon. Your sales director has obtained a single quotation from a well-known manufacturer. The price is quoted as £35,500 and the following information has been provided:

	£
Envelope	15000
Envelope scoop	1000
Padded covers × 4	500
Inflator fan	2500
Tether line	400
Shadow double burner	5500
Basket	4500
Fuel cylinders × 4	4500
Instruments	1000
Cushion floor	100
Other equipment	500
Artwork	AT COST

What specific actions would you consider taking in regard to:
(a) inviting other quotations?
(b) further investigating the cost breakdown?
(c) asking where the overhead recovery and profit is hidden?
(d) taking a negotiating stance to get the price reduced?

12.5 If you received a price increase request from a strategic supplier of goods, for which there is competition, and the request was for an increase of 4.5 per cent due to 'abnormal trading conditions, raw material increases, energy prices and overheads', what would you put in writing to the supplier?

12.6 What are the six most significant considerations that a supplier will take into account when making a price decision?

12.7 What considerations will the buyer take into account when requesting a price from suppliers?

12.8 You have been asked to draft a guidance procedure for inclusion in a Purchasing Manual. The topic is 'Conducting cost analysis on tendered prices'. What headings would you include and what, specifically, would you say about profit?

12.9 What are the salient facets of the UK competition regime?

12.10 Describe how a price variation formula is typically constructed and explain why they are used.

12.11 What types of pricing agreements would you recommend for the following situations?
(a) The provision of specialist consultancy services for a period of six months to support the purchase of a new IT system.
(b) The manufacture of a new component for incorporation in a new product that will be launched in six months time.
(c) The building of a new school where the contract requires the contractor to supply all the furnishings and equipment.
(d) The retention of a professional institute to provide three years training services where the content and quantity is currently unknown.
(e) A one-year contract for the supply of external catering services, including the provision of food.

12.12 'It is a myth to believe that any buyer controls prices. The initiative is always with the supplier.' Discuss.

Past examination questions

1 Purchasers often need to analyse purchasing costs and overall spend in order to consider purchasing strategies. This question relates to analysis and pricing methods.
(a) Describe, using a diagram, the process of 'ABC analysis' by which an organisation might analyse its purchasing expenditure.
(b) Explain **two** circumstances in which an organisation might consider a supplier rationalisation process worthwhile.
(c) (i) Describe **three** advantages of Fixed Price contracts.
    (ii) Describe **two** disadvantages of Fixed Price contracts.

CIPS, *An Introduction to Purchasing Strategy*, November 2009

2 Outline **two** different pricing policies that a firm may use to sell its products.

CIPS, *Analysing the Supply Market*, November 2008

3 Identify **five** elements of cost that would be included in the 'cost-plus' pricing method.

CIPS, *Analysing the Supply Market*, November 2007

References

1 Farrington, B., 'Industrial Purchasing Price Management', PhD, University of Brunel (Henley College), 1978

2 Leighton, D. S. R., *International Marketing*, McGraw Hill Co. Ltd

3 England and Leenders, M. R., *Purchasing & Materials Management*, RD Irwin

4 Winkler, J., *Winkler on Marketing Planning*, Wiley & Sons, 1973

5 Ammer, D. S., *Materials Management*, RD Irwin, 1968

6 Tuns, M., 'Computerised cost estimation for forging industry', a thesis submitted to the Graduate School of Natural and Applied Sciences of the Middle East Technical University, September 2003

7 DeMarco, A. A., CAPE (Computer Aided Parametric Estimating for Business Process Re-Engineering). PRICE Newsletter, October 1994

8 Deccan Systems Inc., Ohio, USA: www.deccansystems.com

9 National Audit Office, 'Review of the UK's Competition Landscape', published 18 March, 2010

10 As 9 above

11 Decision of the Office of Fair Trading, 'Collusive tendering in relation to contracts for flat-roofing services in the West Midlands', No. CA98/1/2004

Part 3

Strategy, tactics and operations 2: buying situations

Chapter 13

Contrasting approaches to supply

Learning outcomes

This chapter aims to provide an understanding of the purchase of:

- capital equipment and one-off purchases
- production materials, including raw materials, semi-finished goods and processed materials and component parts and assemblies
- commodities, including 'sensitive' commodities
- gas and electricity
- component parts and assemblies
- consumables
- construction supplies
- services.

Key ideas

- Categories of capital equipment.
- Characteristics of capital equipment and factors to be considered in its acquisition, financing and evaluation.
- Methods of buying raw materials, including forward buying and futures dealings.
- Commodity dealing.
- Gas and electricity supply chains.
- Energy markets, pricing, switching suppliers using online energy marketplaces.
- Use of energy consultants.
- Categories and characteristics of consumables.
- Construction supplies and Bills of quantities.

Introduction

The considerations that apply to purchasing products, and services, can be contrasted according to the nature of the product, the types of production and the principal uses to which a purchased item will be put. We can also distinguish between purchasing consumer, industrial and resale items and services.

- *Consumer products* used in this context are goods purchased by individuals and households for personal consumption.
- *Industrial products* are purchased by organisations for use in the manufacture of other products to make profits or achieve other objectives.
- *Resale products* are those purchased by organisations in order to resell them at a profit.
- *Services*.

This chapter is concerned with industrial products, consumables or maintenance and repair and operating (CMRO) supplies and services. Consumer products and retailing and wholesale purchasing will not be covered as they are beyond the scope of this book.

13.1 Industrial products

These may be subdivided into:

- capital equipment items
- production materials.

13.2 Capital investment items

13.2.1 Definitions

Capital equipment has been defined by Aljian[1] as:

> One of the subclasses of the fixed asset category and includes industrial and office machinery and tools, transportation equipment, furniture and fixtures and others. As such, these items are properly chargeable to a capital account rather than to expense.

Alternative terms include 'capital goods', 'capital assets' and 'capital expenditure', which can be defined as follows:

- *Capital goods*

    Capital in the form of fixed assets used to produce goods, such as plant, equipment, rolling stock.[2]

- *Capital assets*

    Assets used to generate revenues on cost savings by providing production, distribution or service capabilities for more than one year.[3]

- *Capital expenditure*

    An expenditure on acquisition of tangible productive assets which yield continuous service beyond the accounting period in which they are purchased.[4]

Of the above definitions, that for capital expenditure is the most useful as it emphasises the three most important characteristics of capital equipment, namely:

- *tangibility* – capital equipment can be physically touched or handled
- *productivity* – capital equipment is used to produce goods or services
- *durability* – capital equipment has a life longer than one year.

13.2.2 Categories of capital equipment

From the marketing standpoint, Marrian[5] has distinguished six types of industrial equipment.

1 *Buildings* – permanent constructions on a site to house or enclose equipment and personnel employed in industrial, institutional or commercial activities.

2 *Installation equipment (capital equipment, plant)* – essential plant, machinery or other major equipment used directly in producing the goods and services.

3 *Accessory equipment* – durable major equipment used to facilitate the production of goods and services or enhance the operations of organisations. Installation and accessory equipment often coincide, but there is a distinction. Aircraft purchased by an airline, for example, would be installation equipment; aircraft purchased by a manufacturing organisation to facilitate the movement of executive personnel would be accessory equipment.

4 *Operating equipment* – semi-durable minor equipment that is movable and used in, but not generally essential to, the production of goods and services, such as special footwear, goggles, brushes and brooms.

5 *Tools and instruments* – semi-durable or durable portable minor equipment and instruments required for producing, measuring, calculating and so on, associated with the production of goods and services, such as word processors, all tools, surgical instruments, timing devices, cash registers and other such items.

6 *Furnishings and fittings* – all goods and materials employed to fit buildings for their organisational purposes, such as carpets, floor coverings, draperies, furniture, shelving, counters, benches and so on, but not that equipment used specifically in production.

Some capital equipment can be placed in more than one classification. Thus, a computer system might be either installation or accessory equipment according to its primary application. The classifications are also useful headings for a 'register of capital equipment', in which all acquisitions, replacements and disposals are recorded. An alternative categorisation is given in section 13.5 below.

13.3 Capital expenditure

From the *accountancy* standpoint, expenditure on capital equipment results in the acquisition of fixed rather than current assets. One useful definition of capital expenditure other than those already quoted is:

> All expenditure that is expected to produce benefit to the firm over a period longer than the accounting period in which the expenditure was incurred.

13.3.1 Characteristics of capital expenditure

Expenditure on capital equipment differs from that on materials and components in many ways, including the following:

- the cost per item is usually greater
- the items bought are used up gradually to facilitate production rather than as a part of the end product
- capital expenditure is financed long-term capital or appropriations of profit rather than from working capital or charges against profit
- tax considerations, such as capital allowances and investment grants, have an important bearing on whether or not to purchase capital equipment and the timing of such purchases
- government financial assistance towards the cost of capital equipment may be available, such as where a manufacturing organisation is located in a development area
- the purchase of capital equipment is often postponable, at least in the short term
- the decision to buy capital equipment often results in consequential decisions relating to sales, output and labour – in the latter case, consultations with the appropriate unions may be necessary.

It is probable that the terms and conditions of purchase will have to be tailored to meet the circumstances arising from the acquisition of capital equipment.

All of these things mean that the purchase of capital equipment is usually more complicated than that of materials and components, a large proportion of which can be handled using repeat procedures.

13.4 Factors to be considered when buying capital equipment

Apart from the mode of purchase, finance and the return on the investment made, the following factors should be considered when buying capital equipment.

- *Purpose* – what is the prime purpose of the equipment?
- *Flexibility* – how versatile is the equipment? Can it be used for purposes other than those for which it is primarily being acquired?
- *Spares* – cost, lead times, initial purchase of essential spares, Escrow for drawings and length of time spares will be provided.
- *Standardisation* – is the equipment standardised with any already installed, thus reducing the cost of holding spares?
- *Compatibility with existing equipment.*
- *Life* – this usually refers to the period before the equipment will have to be written off due to depreciation or obsolescence. It is, however, not necessarily linked to the total lifespan of the item if it is intended that the asset will be disposed of before it is obsolete or unusable.
- *Reliability* – breakdowns mean greater costs, loss of goodwill due to delayed deliveries and possibly a high investment in spares.
- *Durability* – is the equipment sufficiently robust for its intended use?

- *Product quality* – defective output proportionately increases the cost per unit of output.

- *Cost of operation* – costs of fuel, power and maintenance. Will special labour or additional labour costs be incurred? Is consultation with the trade unions advisable?

- *Cost of installation* – does the price include the cost of installation, commissioning and training of operators?

- *Cost of maintenance* – can the equipment be maintained by your own staff or will special service support agreements with the vendor be necessary? What estimates of maintenance costs can be provided before purchase? How reliable are these?

- *Miscellaneous* – these include appearance, space requirements, quietness of operation (decibel level), safety and aspects of ergonomics affecting the performance of the operator.

- *Intellectual property rights* – who owns the design? Will the 'as built' drawings be provided?

13.4.1 Lifecycle costing

Lifecycle costing – terotechnology – is an important aspect of capital expenditure. Lifecycle costing is further considered in Chapter 16.

13.5 Controlling the acquisition of capital equipment

Acquisitions of capital equipment may be transformational or incremental. With *transformational acquisitions*, the new equipment may result in a fundamental change in the working of the whole organisation, as would be the case with the installation of a new computer system or the adoption of computer-integrated production. With *incremental acquisitions*, the new or replacement machinery will not fundamentally change the working of the organisation and the effects will generally be confined to the user, function or department. It follows, therefore, that the acquisition of certain items of capital equipment require considerably more deliberation regarding cost, suitability, lifespan and the consequences of acquisition than others. In order to determine the amount of deliberation that should be accorded to a request for permission to acquire capital items, it is useful to assign such requests to a particular category.

- *Category A* – strategic new equipment – that is, equipment not already in use that, if acquired, would replace or fundamentally change working methods throughout the company.

- *Category B* – operational new equipment – that is, equipment the use or application of which will be confined to a particular function, department, project or operation.

- *Category C* – replacement equipment – that is, equipment that replaces existing equipment that is obsolete or has depreciated to a point where repair or renovation would be uneconomical. The replacement of an obsolete machine will entail the acquisition of operational new equipment and is therefore Category B expenditure.

- *Category D* – vehicles and transportation – that is, new or replacement motorcars and lorries.

- *Category E* – administrative equipment – that is, office machinery, fixtures and fittings required to facilitate the provision of administrative support or office services.

- *Category F* – miscellaneous – that is, equipment not exceeding a prescribed value that cannot be assigned to any of categories A to E.

The amount of expenditure and therefore the level of management that will have to give approval of the expenditure will vary for each category.

- *Levels A and B* will usually require approval by the Board or Chief Executive. Both the Board and the Chief Executive will normally take specialist advice before making a decision.
- *Levels C, D and E* will, within prescribed limits and subject to budget approval, usually be at the discretion of senior managers.
- *Level D* will usually be on the basis that vehicles shall be disposed of and replaced at the end of a prescribed 'life', such as three years or on the attainment of a given mileage.

Such policies, when published in the form of a capital equipment guide circulated to all senior managers, provide clear guidelines on the procedures for obtaining approval of capital expenditure and such related matters as the disposal of redundant items.

13.6 New or used equipment

Various aspects of new and used equipment and their respective advantages and disadvantages are examined in Tables 13.1 and 13.2.

England[6] has suggested using the criteria set out in Tables 13.3 when deciding whether to buy new or used equipment.

Used equipment may be either rebuilt or reconditioned. With the former, the equipment will usually have been stripped down and built up again from the base. Worn and broken parts will have been replaced and worn surfaces reground and realigned to meet the original tolerances. The rebuilt machine will also have been thoroughly tested and will carry a limited warranty. Such machines will typically cost between 50 and 70 per cent of the cost of a new counterpart.

Reconditioned machines will not have been as thoroughly overhauled as rebuilt machines. They will, nevertheless, have been cleaned and had all broken or worn parts

Table 13.1 Factors to consider when buying new and used equipment

New equipment	Used equipment
■ Likely to incorporate the most up-to-date technology	■ Less likely to provide state of the art technology
■ Will provide maximum capital allowances	■ Capital allowances will be based on lower acquisition cost
■ Will probably provide lower maintenance costs, fewer problems and better warranties	■ Maintenance problems will only reveal themselves when the equipment is operating
■ Procurement will be more straightforward, requiring fewer tests and investigations	■ Manufacturers' warranties may not be available
■ Availability of spares may be better	■ Much used equipment is sold as seen. To avoid expensive mistakes, all potential purchases should be vetted by an expert
■ Should be environmentally more efficient	
■ Should incorporate the latest safety features	■ Difficulties in obtaining spares may be encountered

Table 13.2 Advantages and disadvantages of used equipment

Used equipment – advantages	Used equipment – disadvantages
■ Acquisition costs often significantly lower than for new equipment and may therefore offer a better return on investment and price–performance ratio	■ Equipment may be old, with a high risk of early obsolescence
■ Equipment may be thoroughly run in and the teething troubles associated with new equipment eliminated	■ Low cost of equipment may be offset by lower productivity, resulting in increased production costs
■ Used equipment may be available immediately, thus obviating the time required for the acquisition of new equipment	■ Warranties may not be given even when available
	■ Warranties are generally short and maintenance costs relatively high
■ Maintenance records should be available for inspection	■ Maintenance records require careful investigation. Who did the maintenance? Have any parts been replaced? Why were they replaced and when?

Table 13.3 Criteria to use to decide whether to buy new or used equipment

New equipment should be bought	Purchase of used equipment should be considered
■ When relative efficiency is great enough to be important	■ When price is important, either because the differential between new and used is vital or the buyer's funds are low
■ When the guarantee is better	■ For use with pilot or experimental plant
■ When better essential service is provided	■ For use with a special or temporary order over which the total cost can be amortised
■ When better credit terms are stated	■ When the machine will be idle for a substantial amount of time
■ When longer life is anticipated	■ For use by learners or apprentices
■ When less maintenance is required	■ For maintenance (not production) departments
■ When government finance is available	■ For better delivery time when time is essential
■ When it is desirable to strengthen vendor relationships	■ When a used machine can be easily modernised or is the latest model
■ When repair parts on used equipment may not be available	■ When labour costs are unduly high

replaced and been repainted to look like new. However, the guarantee or warranty may be less inclusive than for rebuilt equipment. Reconditioned items generally sell at between 40 and 50 per cent of the cost of new items.

13.6.1 Precautions to take when buying used equipment

Although protection is given by the Sale of Goods, Trades Description and Misrepresentation Acts, the purchaser of used equipment should work on the principle of *caveat emptor* – 'let the buyer beware'. Some questions that a prospective buyer of used equipment should ask include the following.

■ Is a history of the equipment available?

■ Is there any indication of age, such as a serial number?

■ How well has the equipment been maintained?

- Are spares readily available? Will they continue to be?
- How does the price asked for used equipment compare with the cost of buying new?
- Is the vendor well established? Has the vendor got a sound reputation?
- What special contractual terms and conditions, if any, apply to the purchase?
- Do any guarantees or warranties supercede the protection given under the Sale of Goods Act?
- What trials, test or approval period will the vendor allow?
- Will the vendor permit an inspection by an independent assessor?
- What will be the cost, where appropriate, of dismantling, transporting and re-erecting/ installing equipment?

13.7 Financing the acquisition of capital equipment

The acquisition of new or capital equipment may be financed by:

- outright purchase
- hire purchase
- leasing.

13.7.1 Outright purchase

The most obvious acquisition strategy for the purchase of equipment is for the buying organisation to pay the full price to the seller. The relative advantages and disadvantages of this strategy are shown in Table 13.4.

Table 13.4 Advantages and disadvantages of outright purchase of equipment

Advantages	Disadvantages
■ The total cost, particularly in comparison to rental, is low	■ Investment in fixed capital resources will reduce liquidity
■ Equipment may have a residual or second-hand value	■ Obsolescence or market changes may drastically reduce residual or second-hand market expectations
■ User has total control over the equipment (there may, however, be maintenance and software constraints)	■ Long-term commitment to maintenance and software may be necessary to protect the capital equipment investment
■ Capital allowances (normally 25 per cent annually on the reducing balance) may be set against tax	■ Equipment may rapidly become obsolete and the costs of upgrading by means of sale, trade-in or leasing may be expensive

The effect of a outright purchase is to increase fixed (equipment) and reduce current (cash) assets. The capital cost of acquisition and the revenue cost of maintenance may adversely affect the working capital of an enterprise and so must, in the long term, be expected to create a positive return on the investment.

13.7.2 Hire purchase

With a hire purchase (HP) agreement, when all the payments have been made, the business customer becomes the owner of the equipment. This ownership is transferred either automatically or on payment of an option to purchase fee.

For tax purposes, from the beginning of the agreement the business customer is treated as the owner of the equipment and can therefore claim capital allowance. This can be a significant tax incentive to invest in new plant and machinery.

HP agreements are different from ordinary credit agreements. With an HP agreement there are certain rules which apply including:

- you may not sell the goods until the money's paid off
- creditors may ask you to return the goods if you don't make regular payments.

The relative advantages and disadvantages of hire purchase of equipment are shown in Table 13.5.

Table 13.5 Advantages and disadvantages of hire purchase for equipment

Advantages	Disadvantages
■ Provides a compromise between straight purchase and leasing. Hire purchase agreements are easily negotiated and available	■ Financing arrangements impose more restrictions than when equipment is purchased outright
■ Subject to such factors as interest rates and the user's rate of return, hire purchase may be more financially effective than outright purchase or leasing	■ Interest rates and the user's rate of return may make hire purchase a less financially effective method than outright purchase or leasing
■ The most up-to-date technology may be hired and used to increase the company's productivity and efficiency	■ There will, in general, be no opportunity to upgrade
■ After all the payments have been made, the user becomes the owner of the equipment, either automatically or on payment of an option to purchase fee	■ The disadvantages of outright purchase as stated in Table 13.4
■ For tax purposes, the user is, from the start, regarded as the owner of the equipment and can claim capital allowance and VAT on the equipment	

13.7.3 Leasing

Leasing is a contract between the leasing company – the *lessor* – and the customer, the *lessee*.

- The leasing company buys and owns the asset that the lessee requires.
- The customer hires the asset from the leasing company and pays rental over a predetermined period for the use of the asset.

As shown in Figure 13.1, there are two types of leases: finance leases and operating leases. Leasing has both advantages and disadvantages, as listed in Table 13.6.

Other advantages of leasing include easier replacement decisions. Ownership of an asset sometimes has the psychological effect of locking the owner into the use of an asset that should be replaced by a more efficient item of equipment. Leasing is also a hedge against inflation. The use of the asset is obtained immediately. The payments are

Figure 13.1 Types of lease

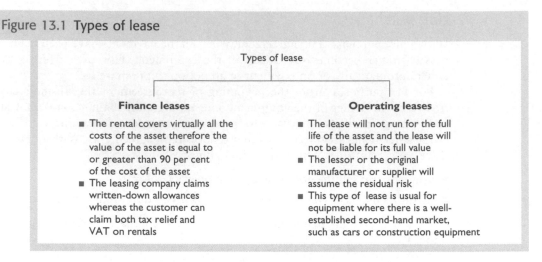

Types of lease

Finance leases

- The rental covers virtually all the costs of the asset therefore the value of the asset is equal to or greater than 90 per cent of the cost of the asset
- The leasing company claims written-down allowances whereas the customer can claim both tax relief and VAT on rentals

Operating leases

- The lease will not run for the full life of the asset and the lease will not be liable for its full value
- The lessor or the original manufacturer or supplier will assume the residual risk
- This type of lease is usual for equipment where there is a well-established second-hand market, such as cars or construction equipment

Table 13.6 Advantages and disadvantages of leasing equipment

Advantages	Disadvantages
■ Costs are known in advance and cannot be amended without agreement once the lease has been signed	■ Fixed obligation to pay rental may create an embarrassment in depressed conditions
■ Reduced need to tie up capital in fixed assets. Use of an asset can be obtained without capital outlay	■ Does not provide the prestige or flexibility of ownership
■ Leasing is concerned only with rentals and not with grants, allowances, depreciation or other calculations	■ Large organisations may be able to obtain capital or equal terms with lessors and, because of a steady flow of taxable profit, be able to obtain the use of capital allowances for themselves
■ Leasing provides a hedge against the risk of obsolescence	■ The flexibility to dispose of obsolete equipment before the end of the lease may be reduced

met out of future earnings and are made in real money terms with the real costs falling over the years.

13.7.4 Leasing or buying

In practice, the decision to lease or buy is complicated, depending on operating, legal and financial considerations.

- *Operating factors* relate to the advantages of a trial period before purchase, the immediate availability of cost-saving equipment, the period for which the assets are required and the hedges provided against obsolescence and inflation.
- *Legal factors* are important as the leasing agreements are one-sided in that most risks are transferred to the lessee. The lessee should therefore carefully examine the terms and conditions of the contract, especially with regard to such aspects as limitations on the use of the equipment and responsibilities for its insurance, maintenance and so on. Where possible, improved terms should be negotiated.

- *Financial factors* are usually crucial in deciding whether to lease or buy. These include:
  - the *opportunity cost* of capital – that is, what the purchase price of the equipment would earn if used for other purposes or invested elsewhere
  - the *discounted cost* of meeting the periodical rental payments over the period of the lease – note that 'flat' interest rates, calculated on the initial amount owing rather than on the average amount owed, can be misleading.

Example 13.1

How to work out whether it is best to lease or buy

(Taken from *The Lease–buy Decision*, BIM)

Cash price of asset £1000	Leased cost – 20 payments of £75 per quarter over 5 years £1500	Excess cost of leasing over purchase £500 or 50 per cent	Annual flat rate of interest 50%/5 = 10%

The true rate, however, is just over 20.4 per cent per annum, as can be seen from the following table.

Quarterly periods	Balance brought forward £	Repayment in advance £	Interest 20.4064% compound £	Balance carried forward £
1	1000.00	−75.00	43.95	968.95
2	968.95	−75.00	42.48	936.43
3	936.43	−75.00	40.94	902.37
4	902.37	−75.00	39.32	866.69
5	866.69	−75.00	37.62	829.31
6	829.31	−75.00	35.85	790.16
7	790.16	−75.00	33.98	749.14
8	749.14	−75.00	32.04	706.18
9	706.18	−75.00	29.99	661.17
10	661.17	−75.00	27.85	614.02
11	614.02	−75.00	25.62	564.64
12	564.64	−75.00	23.27	512.91
13	512.91	−75.00	20.81	458.72
14	458.72	−75.00	18.23	401.95
15	401.95	−75.00	15.54	342.49
16	342.49	−75.00	12.71	280.20
17	280.20	−75.00	9.75	214.95
18	214.95	−75.00	6.65	146.60
19	146.60	−75.00	3.40	75.00
20	75.00	−75.00	0.00	0.00
		−£1500.00	£500.00	

Ignoring tax, the lessee will be indifferent, on cost grounds, about whether to lease or buy if the opportunity cost of capital is about 20.4 per cent. If the cost of capital exceeds 20.4 per cent, however, then leasing will be cheaper in net present value (NPV) terms. If it is less, then leasing will be the most expensive proposition.

▶

Excluding such factors as the time value of money, capital allowances and maintenance and other ownership costs, the simple lease versus buy break-even point can be calculated by using the formula:

$$N = \frac{P}{L}$$

Where:

P = purchase cost of equipment
L = monthly leasing payment
N = the number of months needed to break even

Thus, if the equipment costs £5000 and the leasing payment is £200 monthly, the simple break-even point is 25 months. This indicates that, other considerations apart, owning is preferable to leasing if the equipment is going to be used for more than 25 months.

13.8 Selecting suppliers of capital equipment

The decision about which of several possible suppliers to accept, is normally undertaken by an evaluation panel consisting of procurement, technical and financial specialists because the acquisition of capital equipment is a high-risk, high-cost issue.

In general, the greater the technical nature and complexity of an item, the greater will be the influence of the technical staff as both users and deciders. This will apply to both the acquisition of new or used equipment and purchase or lease decisions and, although there tend to be differences between the criteria for purchasing and leasing, the most important considerations in both cases are technical and cost factors.

13.8.1 Technical factors relating to capital equipment

A matrix for the comparison and evaluation of quotations or tenders received from, say, three potential suppliers on the basis of technical factors is shown in Table 13.7. Points may be awarded to each factor or, alternatively, to a group of factors. The points awarded may be weighted according to the importance of the factor, as shown in Table 13.8.

The example given in Table 13.8 illustrates the difficulties of using a points system of evaluation. Using this system, the equipment supplied by B scores higher than that of A. If the evaluation teams however regarded A as having a greater suitability for use, then clearly the points allocation is flawed or the awarding of points is not based on a correct judgement.

13.8.2 Cost factors

References to the important financial factors relating to the acquisition of capital equipment are made in sections 13.7 and 13.9. Some additional cost aspects that apply to the acquisition of capital items are set out in Table 13.9.

Table 13.7 Capital equipment: technical factors evaluation sheet

Factor	Supplier			Points	Aggregate	Recommendations
	A	B	C			
General suitability for purpose						
Ease of installation						
Convenience of operation						
Ease of maintenance						
Power demand (kVA) ■ Normal running ■ Peak running						
Energy consumption ■ Power (kWh) ■ Fuel						
Other utility consumption ■ Steam ■ Water ■ Compressed air						
Equipment warranties						
Estimated life						
Life of items not subject to equipment warranties: estimates of normal operational wear						
Environmental considerations ■ Noise ■ Pollution ■ Effluent treatment						
Appraisal of ■ Electrical equipment ■ Instrumental and control equipment						
Standardisation with existing equipment						
Spare parts to be carried						
Interchangeability of spare parts						
Initial spares or tools to be supplied						
Services to be provided (if any) by supplier regarding: ■ Installation ■ Commissioning ■ operator training						
Supplier's after-sales service and spare parts availability						
Other relevant factors ■ Delivery time ■ Insurance ■ General reputation or previous experience of supplier						
Totals						

kVA – kilovolt ampere; kWh – kilowatt hour

Table 13.8 Weighting factors according to their importance for capital equipment

Factor	Assigned number of points	Points achieved A	Points achieved B
Overall suitability for purpose	500	400	300
General quality of technical design	400	300	400
Estimated life	400	300	400
Economy of performance and reliability	300	200	300
Economy of maintenance and after-sales service	300	250	200
Environment factors	300	200	300
General reputation of supplier	200	200	300
Estimated trade-in value at end of life or on disposal	200	20,0	300
Totals	**2600**	**2050**	**2500**

Table 13.9 Factors to be considered in quotations for capital equipment

Factor	Supplier A £	Supplier B £	Supplier C £	Notes
Ex-works cost of equipment				
Delivery and handling costs				
Cost of insurance				
Additional costs for essential spares				
Installation costs for essential spares				
Installation costs payable to supplier				
Cost of extra work specified by purchaser				
Customs or other duties/tariffs for imported equipment				
Price escalation charges computed by using accepted formulae				
Terms of payment				
Warranty/guarantee payments				
Servicing, if any by supplier				
Less discounts				
trade-ins				
other deductions				
Less capital allowances				
Final cost				

13.9 Evaluating capital investments

Although this is the province of the management accountant, buyers should have an awareness of the methods of appraising expenditure on capital items. Three highly simplified examples of these approaches – payback, average rate of return and two applications of discounted cash flow – are briefly considered below.

13.9.1 Payback

This is the time required for cash returns to equal the initial cash expenditure.

Example 13.2

The payback approach

An enterprise buys two machines, each costing £20,000. The net cash flows – after operating costs and expenses but not allowing for depreciation – are expected to be as shown below.

Year	Cash flow machine A (£)	Cash flow machine B (£)
1	5000	4500
2	5000	4500
3	5000	4500
4	5000	4500
5	5000	4500
6	–	4500
7	–	4500
	£25,000	£31,500

$$\text{Payback} = \frac{£20,000}{5000} = 4 \text{ years or } \frac{£20,000}{4500} = 4.4 \text{ years}$$

Example 13.2 shows the principle and fallacy of the payback approach. Machine A has the better payback figure as the initial cost is recovered in less time than for machine B. Machine B has an inferior payback, but the return extends over two further years.

The payback method, because of its simplicity, is probably the most popular method of investment appraisal. With this approach, the emphasis is on risk rather than profitability – that is, the risk with machine B is somewhat greater because it has a longer payback period.

13.9.2 Average rate of return (prior to tax)

This method aims to assess the average annual net profit after depreciation and other cash outlays as a percentage of the original cost. Three simple calculations are required:

1 *The annual rate of depreciation* – this is calculated by the 'straight line' method, namely:

$$\frac{\text{Cost} - \text{Residual value}}{\text{Estimated value}}$$

Assuming that machines A and B each had an estimated residual value of £1000, their annual depreciation rates would be:

$$\text{Machine A} = \frac{£20,000 - £1000}{5} = £3800$$

$$\text{Machine B} = \frac{£20,000 - £1000}{7} = £2714$$

2 *Deduct depreciation from the average annual profit*

$$\text{Machine A} = £5000 - £3800 = £1200$$
$$\text{Machine B} = £4500 - £2714 = £1786$$

3 *Express net annual profit after depreciation as a percentage of the initial cost*

$$\text{Machine A} = \frac{£1200 \times 100}{£20,000} = 6 \text{ per cent}$$

$$\text{Machine B} = \frac{£1786 \times 100}{£20,000} = 8.93 \text{ per cent}$$

An alternative formula is that of return on capital employed (ROCE):

$$\frac{\text{Average annual profit after depreciation}}{\text{Original capital invested}} \times 100 \text{ per cent}$$

This method shows that the investment in machine B is the most profitable and allows comparison with the returns anticipated from alternative investments.

13.9.3 Discounting

Discounting is the opposite process to compounding. *Compounding* shows the extent to which a sum of money invested now will grow over a period of years at a given rate of compound interest. Thus, £100 invested now at 10 per cent compound interest will be worth £110 in one year's time and £121 at the end of two years.

Discounting shows the value at the present time of a sum of money payable or receivable at some future time. This present value can be obtained by dividing the amount now held by that to which it would have grown at a given rate of compound interest. So:

$$\frac{£100}{£110} = 0.9091 \text{ or } \frac{£100}{£121} = 0.8264 \text{ or } \frac{1}{(1 + r)^n}$$

where r is the rate of interest and n the number of years we are discounting.

These present values are *discount factors* and state that £100 at the end of one year at 10 per cent is worth £0.9091 or £0.8264 at the end of two years. In practice, the discount factors would be obtained from present value tables, which give the following for £1 at 10 per cent and 12 per cent respectively:

Years	10%	12%
1	£0.9091	£0.8929
2	£0.8264	£0.7972
3	£0.7513	£0.7118
4	£0.6830	£0.6355
5	£0.6209	£0.5674
6	£0.5645	£0.5066
7	£0.5132	£0.4523

Net present value and yield methods illustrate two of a number of approaches based on discounted cash flow.

13.9.4 Net present value (NPV)

In this method, the minimum required return on the capital investment is determined. The present value of anticipated future cash flows is that discounted at this rate. If the sum of these discounted cash flows exceeds the initial expenditure, then the investment will be given a higher return than forecast. Using the figures given above and a minimum required rate of 10 per cent, the discounted cash flows for machines A and B would be:

Machine A

Year	Cash return	10% factor	Net present value
1	£5000	0.909	£4545
2	£5000	0.826	£4130
3	£5000	0.751	£3755
4	£5000	0.683	£3415
5	£5000	0.621	£3105
6	–	–	–
7	–	–	–
	£25,000	–	£18,950

Machine B

Year	Cash return	10% factor	Net present value
1	£4500	0.909	£4090
2	£4500	0.826	£3717
3	£4500	0.751	£3379
4	£4500	0.683	£3073
5	£4500	0.621	£2794
6	£4500	0.565	£2542
7	£4500	0.513	£2308
	£31,500		£21,903

Machine A has a total return that is less than the initial expenditure of £20,000 – that is, less than the 10 per cent required. In contrast, machine B will exceed the given figure. This approach is very useful in evaluating which of two alternative investment propositions to adopt.

13.10 The buyer and capital investment purchases

Purchasing capital equipment requires extensive liaison between procurement, technical specialists and finance to ensure that when a purchase is made the company/organisation is completely satisfied. So far as procurement is concerned the following considerations are paramount:

- It is likely to be a one-off procurement event for which there is no technical or commercial precedent.
- The specification must reflect the performance required, with sufficient allowance for the total capacity that may be required.

- The detail to be included in the contract must be established. Some facets of the contract include: the right to reject for failure to meet the specification; damages for late delivery; provision of drawings; provision of spare parts and their cost.
- The price and payment terms (including foreign currency considerations) must be thought out.
- The lifecycle cost of the equipment must be calculated.
- Supply market research should be conducted to identify potential suppliers.
- Disposal of displaced assets should follow a defined process.

13.11 Production materials

Risley[7] has classified materials and parts for use in manufacture under the following three headings:

- *Raw materials* – primarily from agriculture and the various extractive industries – minerals, ores, timber, petroleum and scrap – as well as dairy products, fruits and vegetables sold to a processor.
- *Semi-finished goods and processed materials* – to which some work has been applied or value added. Such items are finished only in part or may have been formed into shapes and specifications to make them readily usable by the buyer. These products lose their identity when incorporated into other products. Examples include: metal sections, rods, sheets, tubing, wires, castings, chemicals, cloth, leather, sugar and paper.
- *Component parts and assemblies* – completely finished products of one manufacturer that can be used as part of a more complicated product by another manufacturer. These do not lose their original identity when incorporated into other products. Examples include: bearings, controls, gauges, gears, wheels, transistors, radio and TV tubes, car engines and windscreens.

13.12 Raw materials

13.12.1 Characteristics of raw materials

Raw materials are:

- often 'sensitive' commodities
- frequently dealt with in recognised commodity markets
- safeguarded in many organisations by backward integration strategies.

13.12.2 Sensitive commodities

Sensitive commodities are raw materials – copper, cotton, lead, zinc, hides and rubber – the prices of which fluctuate daily. Here the buyer will aim to time purchases to fulfil requirements at the most competitive prices.

The main economic and political factors that influence market conditions are:

- interest rates, such as the minimum lending rate
- currency fluctuations, such as the strength of sterling
- inflation, such as the effect of increased material and labour costs

- government policies, such as import controls or stockpiling
- 'glut' or shortage supply factors, such as crop failure
- relationships between the exporting and importing country, such as oil as a political weapon.

13.12.3 Information regarding market conditions

The main sources of information regarding present and future market conditions for a commodity such as copper are as follows:

- *Government sources* – in the UK, the Department for Business, Innovation and Skills.
- *Documentary sources* – these may be 'general', such as the *Financial Times*, or specialised, such as *World Metal Statistics*, published by the World Bureau of Metal Statistics, or the *Metal Bulletin* and the *Mining Journal*.
- *Federations* – the British Non-ferrous Metals Federation or International Wrought Copper Council, Eurometaux – the European Association of Metals.
- *Exchanges* – these include independent research undertaken by brokers and dealers into metal resources and the short-term and long-term prospects for the commodity and daily prices of commodities dealt with by the exchange.
- *Analysts* – these include economists and statisticians employed by undertakings to advise on corporate planning and purchasing policies and external units, such as the Commodities Research Unit and the Commodity Research Bureau.

The task of the buyer is to evaluate information and recommendations from the above sources and put forward appropriate policies that fall broadly into two classes: hand-to-mouth and forward buying.

13.12.4 Hand-to-mouth buying

This is buying according to need rather than in the quantities that are most economical. Circumstances in which this policy might be adopted are where prices are falling or where a change in design is imminent and it is desirable to avoid large stocks.

13.12.5 Forward buying

This applies to all purchases made for the purpose of increasing stocks beyond the minimum quantities required to meet normal production needs based on average delivery times. Forward buying may be undertaken:

- to obtain the benefit of economic order quantities (EOQs)
- when savings made by buying in anticipation of a price increase will be greater than the interest lost on increased stocks or the cost of storage
- to prevent suspension of production, due to occurrences such as strikes, by stockpiling to avoid shortages
- to secure materials for future requirements when the opportunity arises, for example, some steel sections are only rolled at infrequent intervals.

Forward buying can apply to any material or equipment. A particular aspect of forward buying applicable to commodities is dealing in 'futures'.

13.13 Futures dealing

Futures dealing is an example of dealing in derivatives. *Derivatives* are financial contracts that have no intrinsic value but instead derive their value from something else. They hedge the risk of owning things that are subject to unexpected price fluctuations, such as foreign currencies and sensitive commodities. There are two main types of derivatives: futures and contracts for future delivery at a specified price and options that give one party the opportunity to buy from or sell to the other at a prearranged price.

A commodity such as copper may be bought direct from the producer or a commodity market. The latter provides the advantages of futures dealing. The London markets are divided into two main areas: metals and soft commodities. The six major primary non-ferrous metals dealt with on the London Metal Exchange (LME) are:

- primary high-grade aluminium
- 'A' grade copper
- high-grade zinc
- primary nickel
- standard lead
- tin.

The LME also offers contracts for secondary aluminium and silver. The soft commodities markets dealing in cocoa, sugar, vegetable oils, wool and rubber are the concern of the Futures and Options Exchange. The International Petroleum Exchange covers crude oil, gas, gasoline, naphtha and heavy fuel oil.

13.13.1 Functions of exchanges

Four functions of exchanges are to:

- enable customers, merchants and dealers to obtain supplies readily and at a competitive market price – on the LME, for example, contracts traded are for delivery on any market day within the period of three months ahead, except for silver, which can be dealt in up to seven months ahead
- smooth out price fluctuations due to changes in demand and supply
- provide insurance against price fluctuations by means of the procedure known as 'hedging' (see Example 13.3 below)
- provide appropriately located storage facilities to enable participants to make or take physical delivery of approved brands of commodities.

13.13.2 Differences between forward and futures dealing

- Futures are always traded on a recognised exchange.
- Futures contracts have standardised terms (see section 13.13.4 below).
- Futures exchanges use clearing houses to ensure that futures contracts are fulfilled. The London Clearing House (LCH), for example, is a professional, international clearing house owned by the six UK clearing banks. The responsibility for completing the execution of trade across the LME ring is transferred from the brokers to the LCH by what is called *novation*. The clearing house is, thus, the buyer and seller of last resort.

■ Futures trading requires margins and daily settlements. A *margin* is a cash deposit paid by a trader to a broker who, in effect, lends money to enable the futures contract to be purchased. Traders hope to sell their futures contracts for more than their purchase price, enabling them to repay the broker's loan, have their margins returned and take their profits. No broker may margin a contract for less than the exchange minimum. Each trading day, every futures contract is assessed for liquidity. If the margin drops below a certain level, the trader must deposit an additional, or 'maintenance, margin'. Futures positions are easily closed as the trader has the option of taking physical delivery.

13.13.3 The purpose of and conditions for futures dealing

The purpose of futures dealing is to reduce uncertainty arising from price fluctuations due to supply and demand changes. This benefits both producers and consumers as the producer can sell forward at a sure price and the consumer can buy forward and fix material costs in accordance with a predetermined price. Manufacturers of copper wire, for example, might be able to obtain an order based on the current price of copper. If they think the price of copper may rise before they can obtain their raw materials, they can immediately cover their copper requirements by buying on the LME at the current price for delivery three months ahead, thus avoiding any risk of an increase in price.

For futures dealing to be undertaken, five conditions *must* apply:

1 The commodity must be capable of being stored without deterioration for a reasonable period.

2 The commodity must be capable of being graded for the purpose of providing a basis for description in the contract.

3 The commodity must be capable of being traded in its raw or semi-raw state.

4 Producers and consumers must approve the concept of futures dealing in the commodity.

5 There must be a free market in the commodity, with many buyers and sellers, making it impossible for a few traders to control the market and, thus, prevent perfect competition.

13.13.4 Some terms used in futures contracts

■ *Arbitrage* – the (usually) simultaneous purchase of futures in one market against the sale of futures in a different market to profit from a difference in price.

■ *Backwardation* – the backwardation situation exists when forward prices are less than current 'spot' ones.

■ *Contango* – a contango situation exists when forward prices are greater than current 'spot' ones.

■ *Force majeure* – the clause that absolves the seller or buyer from the contract due to events beyond their control, such as unavoidable export delays in producing countries due to strikes at the supplier's plant. Note that there is now no *force majeure* clause in a London Metal Exchange contract. Customers affected by a *force majeure* declared by a producer or refiner can always turn to the LME as a source of supply. Equally, suppliers can deliver their metal to the LME if their customers declare *force majeure*.

- *Futures* – contracts for the purpose of selling commodities for delivery sometime in the future on an organised exchange and subject to all the terms and conditions included in the rules of that exchange.
- *Hedging* – the use of futures contracts to insure against losses due to the effect of price fluctuations on the value of stocks of a commodities either held or to be acquired. Essentially, this is done by establishing a position in the futures market opposite one's position in the physical commodity. The operations of hedging can be described by means of a simplified example, given in Example 13.3.

Example 13.3

Hedging

1 On 1 June, X (manufacturer) buys stocks of copper to the value of £1000, which X hopes to make into cable wire and sell on 1 August for £2000, of which £750 represents manufacturing costs and £250 profit.

2 The price of copper falls by 1 August to £750 so X sells at £1750 – that is, X makes no profit.

3 To insure against the situation in (2), X, on 1 June, sells futures contracts in copper for £1000.

4 In August, if the price remains stable X will buy at this price, thus making a profit of £250 on the futures contract, which will offset any loss in manufacturing. If the price rises to £1250, X will lose on the futures contract, but this will be offset by gains on manufacturing. While trading refers to actual physical copper trading, a futures transaction is really dealing in price differences and the contract would be discharged by paying over or receiving the balance due.

- *Options* – a buyer who expects the price of a commodity to rise may pay option money to a dealer for the right to buy it at a stated future date – a *call option* – or sell at a future date – a *put option*.
- *Spot price* – the price for immediate cash payment.
- *Spot month* – the first deliverable month for which a quotation is available in the futures market.
- *Options contracts* – relate to the sale or purchasing of commodities that will occur at a specified price on a specified future date, but only if the prospective buyer or seller wishes to exercise the option to buy or sell at the predetermined *strike* or *exercise price*. Options, as we saw above, can be either 'call' or 'put'. Buyers of call options are exposed to limited risk as the most they can lose is the amount of the premium or the sum of money paid when the option is purchased. They have, however, an unlimited profit potential. Conversely, writers of put options have unlimited risk but limited profit potential. Mathematically, however, the odds favour the put option writer.

13.13.5 Commodities at the right price

Buying commodities is the province of specialists who have access to current and relevant information. Such specialists use two approaches to determine the right price, namely *fundamental analysis* and *technical analysis*.

- *Fundamental analysis* relies heavily on an assessment, both statistically and in other ways, of supply and demand. Statistics in particular, indicate whether the trend of prices is up or down. In addition to trends, fundamentalists take into account production, consumption and stocks. Thus, an imbalance in production and consumption will affect prices. Prices will rise or fall according to whether less or more of a commodity is being produced than is consumed. Stock figures, according to the mood of the market, may be counted either way. In a *bull*, or rising, *market*, stocks tend to be held by producers or merchants, thus forcing consumers to bid higher for available stocks of the commodity. In a falling, or *bear market*, consumers hive off their stocks and buy less of the commodity than they are using, while producers reduce prices to a level at which they can turn unsold stock into cash. Additionally, fundamental analysis pays attention to news items that affect sensitive commodities, such as wars, weather, natural disasters, political developments, environmental legislation, labour unrest and macroeconomic statistics from major economies.

- *Technical analysis* claims to be quicker and more comprehensive than fundamental analysis as the market is efficient and the current market price clears the market or brings it into equilibrium. If this is so, it is unnecessary to do more than look at the record of prices to read the future of prices. Technical analysis, therefore, makes great use of chart formations, such as can be obtained from plotting prices on two different timescales, such as daily price movements and the one year rolling average – that is, every day, the latest day's price is added to the list of prices, the oldest year ago price is dropped and a new average for the past year is calculated. Chartists have developed a language of their own for interpreting their charts, such as 'base formation', 'break out', 'overprofit', 'oversold' and so on, to name a few. The results of charting are offered to commodity market makers, often at a considerable charge. The basic concept is that of using the past to predict the future. Chartists, however, are no more able to forecast the effects of news than those who rely on fundamental analysis. In practice, a combination of the two approaches is often used. It has been rightly observed that 'the whole point of having an idea of the "right price" is to spot when the market price is wrong'. Companies have been forced into liquidation by making long-term forecasts on the assumption that today's price is right when, in fact, it is wrong and vice versa.

13.14 Methods of commodity dealing

Dealing in commodities or derivatives is a highly complicated activity, involving the possibilities of heavy gains or losses. In 1995, Barings Bank 'went bust' when one of its employees, Nick Leeson, gambled that the Nikkei 225 index of 225 leading Japanese company shares would not move materially from its normal trading range. That assumption was shattered by the Kobe earthquake on 17 January 1995. Leeson, who attempted to conceal his gamble, lost the bank $14 billion. Warren Buffett[8] said:

> We view them [derivatives] as time bombs both for the parties that deal in them and the economic system . . . In our view derivatives are financial weapons of mass destruction, carrying dangers that, while now latent, are potentially lethal.

An organisation buying large quantities of a commodity will therefore employ a specialist buyer who has made a specialist study of that commodity and its markets. Often, commodity buying will be a separate department distinct from other purchasing operations. Where quantities or the undertaking are smaller, a broker may be retained to procure commodity requirements – in effect, subcontracting this aspect of purchasing.

Other approaches are designed to enable non-specialists to undertake commodity buying with a minimum of risk. These include the following.

13.14.1 Time budgeting or averaging

This is an application of hand-to-mouth buying in which supplies of the commodity are bought as required and no stocks are held. As supplies are always bought at the ruling price, losses are divided, but, of course, the prospect of windfall gains is obviated. This policy cannot be applied if it is necessary to carry inventory.

13.14.2 Budgeting or cost averaging

This approach is based on spending a fixed amount of money in each period – say, monthly. The quantity purchased therefore increases when the price falls and reduces when the price rises.

Example 13.4

The budgeting or cost averaging approach

Assume the monthly requirement for commodity X is 100 tonnes, the average price of which, from experience, is estimated at £100. We therefore budget to spend $£100 \times 100 = £10,000$ monthly. The price fluctuates as shown below.

Date	Cost per tonne	Amount spent	Tonnes purchased
January	£98	£10,000	102.04
February	£97	£10,000	103.09
March	£95	£10,000	105.26
April	£96	£10,000	104.16
May	£95	£10,000	105.26
June	£93	£10,000	107.52
July	£92	£10,000	108.69
August	£95	£10,000	105.26
September	£97	£10,000	103.09
October	£100	£10,000	100.00
November	£102	£10,000	98.03
December	£104	£10,000	96.15
		£120,000	1238.55

$$\text{Average cost per tonne, total cycle} = \frac{£120,000}{1238.55} = £96.89$$

Purchases over the total cycle exceed requirements by 38.55 tonnes. There is thus an average saving of £3.11 per tonne.

13.14.3 Volume timing of purchases

This approach is based on forward buying when prices are falling and hand-to-mouth buying when prices are rising. Its success depends on accurate forecasting of market trends.

Example 13.5

The volume timing approach

Assume that the price of a commodity with a constant monthly requirement of 100 tonnes is between £100 and £120 per tonne. The buyer is authorised to purchase up to three months' supply.

In January, market intelligence is that the current price of £100 is likely to rise over the next three months to £120. An order is therefore placed for 300 tonnes at £100 per tonne.

In early March, intelligence is that, over the next 3 months – April to June – the price of £120 will rise further to £135. A further 300 tonnes are ordered at £120 per tonne. In early June, it is forecast that prices will fall. For each of the months July, August, September and October, therefore, only one month's supply is bought, at £130, £125, £120 and £110 respectively. In September, the forecast is of a further rise to £125. Therefore, a forward order for three months' supply is placed at £110 per tonne.

The savings from forward buying on the upswing and hand-to-mouth buying on the downswing are shown in the table.

Date	Quantity purchased (tonnes)	Price paid per tonne £	Market price per tonne £	Actual cost £	Market cost £
January	100	100	100	10,000	10,000
February	100	100	110	10,000	11,000
March	100	100	120	10,000	12,000
April	100	120	125	12,000	12,500
May	100	120	130	12,000	13,000
June	100	120	135	12,000	13,500
July	100	130	130	13,000	13,000
August	100	125	125	12,500	12,500
September	100	120	120	12,000	12,000
October	100	110	110	11,000	11,000
November	100	110	120	11,000	12,000
December	100	110	125	11,000	12,500
	1200			136,500	145,000

$$\text{Average price paid per tonne over year} = \frac{£136,500}{1200} = £113.75$$

$$\text{Average market price per tonne} = \frac{£145,000}{1200} = £120.83$$

$$\text{Saving over total period} = \frac{\text{Average market price} - \text{Average price paid}}{\text{Average market price}}$$

$$= \frac{£120.83 - £113.75}{120.83} \times 100 = \frac{7.08}{120.83} \times 100$$

$$= 5.86\%$$

13.15 Purchasing non-domestic gas and electricity

The deregulation of energy supply started in the UK with the implementation of the Gas Act 1986. Then the Electricity Act 1989 brought chances and opportunities, risks and complexities for those responsible for purchasing non-domestic energy supplies. To exploit these opportunities and minimise the risks, purchasers of gas and electricity require a knowledge of energy regulation, the relevant supply chains and energy markets, pricing, the process of switching suppliers, the use of online retail energy marketplaces and energy consultants and management.

13.16 Energy regulation

The Office of Gas and Electricity Markets (Ofgem) is the regulator of Britain's gas and electricity. Ofgem was established in 1999 by the merger of the Office of Gas Supply (Ofgas) and Office of Electricity Regulation (Offer), set up under the Gas Act 1986 and the Electricity Act 1989 respectively. Under the Utilities Act 2000, Ofgem ceased to be an independent regulator and now reports to the Gas and Electricity Markets Authority (GEMA) and the Gas and Electricity Consumers Council. The Utilities Act also put Ofgem under the direct control of the Secretary of State for Trade and Industry (now DECC).

Ofgem also has enforcement powers under the Competition Act 1998 and the power to enforce consumer protection law under the Enterprise Act 2002. It can also name and shame companies that it believes are acting against the interests of gas and electricity consumers. In February 2008 Ofgem made a decision that National Grid had breached the Chapter II prohibition of the Competition Act 1998 and Article 82 of the EC Treaty. Ofgem fined National Grid £41.6million. National Grid appealed to the Competition Appeal Tribunal against the decision. CAT upheld Ofgem's decision but reduced the penalty to £30 million.

Any organisation seeking to supply gas and electricity to customers has to be licensed by Ofgem, which is one of its powers under the Gas and Electricity Acts. One area it does not licence is the offshore gas industry, which is regulated by the Department of Energy and Climate Change (DECC).

13.17 Energy supply chains in the UK

In March 2009 a report by the Electricity Networks Strategy Group (ENSG)[9] asked the three GB Transmission Licensees, National Grid Electricity Transmission (NGET), Scottish Hydro Electric Transmission Ltd (SHETL) and Scottish Power Transmission (SPT) to take forward a study to:

- develop electricity generation, and demand scenarios consistent with the EU target for 15 per cent of the UK's energy to be produced from renewable sources by 2020
- identify and evaluate a range of potential electricity transmission network solutions that would be required to accommodate these scenarios.

There are wide ranging conclusions in the report, including the potential for addition nuclear electricity generation.

In the UK gas is delivered to the seven reception points (called beach terminals) by gas producers operating offshore facilities from over 100 fields beneath the sea around the British Isles. In addition, a terminal at the Isle of Grain allows liquefied natural gas (LNG) to be delivered to the terminal by sea. The National Transmission System (NTS) is the high pressure part of National Grid's transmission system and it consists of more than 6600 kilometres of top quality welded steel pipeline operating at pressures of up to 85 bar. The gas is pushed through the system using 26 strategically placed compressor stations. From over 140 off-take points, the NTS supplies gas to 40 power stations, a small number of large industrial consumers and the twelve Local Distribution Zones (LDZs) that contain pipers operating at lower pressure which eventually supply the consumer.

13.18 Markets

Markets for gas and electricity are both wholesale and retail.

13.18.1 Wholesale markets

Wholesale markets are those in which electricity and gas are traded between parties before being sold to suppliers that, in turn, sell to consumers. In the present context, the parties to the wholesale market are gas producers, electricity generators, transmitters, distributors and suppliers.

The distributors or transmitters are monopolies regulated by price controls based on the RPI – X formula. Using this formula, the prices that transmitters or distributors can charge is limited to the increase in the retail price index less a proportion to drive up transmitter or distribution efficiency. Thus, if the RPI is 3 per cent and X is 2 per cent, prices cannot be increased by more than 1 per cent annually.

In 1999, Ofgem announced new (wholesale) trading arrangements for gas (NGTA) and electricity (NETA), which have been implemented. These arrangements are designed to produce prices that respond to competitive pressure and balance the supply for a utility. The aims are to be achieved by online trading on power exchanges – a balancing mechanism operated by the National Grid, a settlement process and associated derivatives markets. Like other exchanges, those for energy enable suppliers to place contracts with producers and generators either for several years ahead or on a daily basis for gas and at half-hour intervals for electricity. They can also reduce price volatility by means of the classic approaches of futures, hedging and options.

The process of balancing is best illustrated by reference to electricity supply. Approximately 24 hours before its physical delivery, suppliers begin to fine-tune their positions to cover any shortfall between their actual positions and that covered by their contracts on the forwards and futures market. Any shortages will be covered by short-term spot trading. Suppliers must declare their positions up to 35 hours before delivery. This is known as *gate closure*. From gate closure to the time of physical delivery, the operator (the National Grid) works to ensure that 'the lights stay on'. This is possible because the UK transmission systems are fully interconnected and the operator can use the bids made on the power exchanges to balance demand and supply.

13.18.2 Retail markets

Retail markets are those in which suppliers sell gas or electricity to consumers.

13.19 Pricing

13.19.1 Gas pricing

Gas was traditionally invoiced in therms, but now, like electricity, is charged in kilowatt hours (kWh). There are approximately 29.3 kilowatt hours to a therm.

The price paid for gas comprises:

- the supply price – that is, the price of the gas itself
- the price paid for transportation via Transco's distribution system.

Customers pay a total price to the supplier.

The price of gas can vary due to such factors as:

- the season – the price of gas is more in winter than summer
- the annual volume of gas used
- the location of the customer
- the duration of the contract
- whether the contract for the supply of gas is firm or interruptible – a firm supply is guaranteed unless there is an emergency whereas, due to weather or market conditions, interruptible customers may be required to interrupt their use of natural gas either by switching to an alternative fuel source or to curtail their use, but, in return, they enjoy lower rates than firm commercial customers.

13.19.2 Electricity pricing

A typical invoice for electricity will be broken down into the following elements.

- *Total kilowatts used* – this is known as the *energy charge*. The energy charge along with the profit, are the only negotiable elements. The most important aspect of the energy charge is the time at which the energy is used.
- *Transmission charge* – this is the amount paid to the National Grid (NG) in England and differs according to capacity and location. Such charges, for example, tend to be low in the north and high in the south of England. Suppliers pay three forms of transmission charges:
  - demand charges, based on demand during the three annual peak demand periods (triads), which differ depending on zones
  - energy consumption charges, based on the energy consumed between 1600 and 1900 hours throughout the year
  - charges for non-energy ancillary services, covering reserve generation and standby services to facilitate balancing.
- *Distribution charges* – these also vary according to the customer's regional location and the capacity held for the customer.
- *Meter charges* – these are discussed later.
- *Fossil fuel levy (FFL)* – a charge to reduce consumption of electricity produced by using fossil fuels, such as coal and oil, and increase usage of electricity produced by renewable energy sources, such as wind power and geothermal energy.

■ *The Climate Change Levy (CCL) is a tax on the use of energy in industry, commerce and the public sector. It was introduced in 2001. More information can be found on the Department of Energy and Climate Change website. The current CCL rates can be found on the HM Revenue and Customs website. A general guide to CCL is available at www.hmrc.gov.uk (click on the Environmental taxes' section of 'Excise and other').*

13.20 Procuring energy contracts

The procurement of energy contracts is a highly specialised task requiring considerable expertise. The traditional annual tender routine brings with it significant price risks. If the tender process coincides with high market prices the buyer could pay circa 50 per cent more than another buyer whose tender coincides with low prices. Gas and electricity markets are highly volatile and complex.

13.20.1 Price structure[10]

Electricity and gas prices (see Figure 13.2) are made up of the raw energy cost, transmission and distribution costs, data and meter service costs and supplier costs. Price elements are either fixed, such as regulated pass-through costs, or flexible, such as time-to-market decisions (when in the year to buy) or supplier negotiation.

Figure 13.2 Electricity and gas price structures

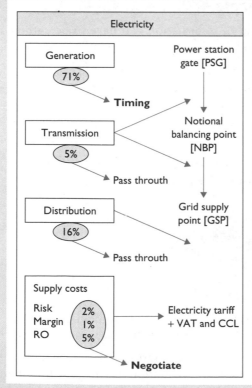
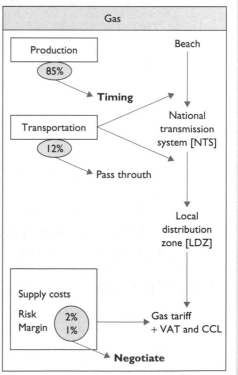

Electricity generated from fossil fuels, known as brown electricity, is subject to the Climate Change Levy (CCL). CCL was initially set at 0.43p/kwh, a rate which will increase in line with inflation from April 2007. Electricity generated from renewable sources, known as green electricity, is exempt from CCL but can incur a premium price. The premium can be negotiated with the supplier, with the cost neutral price being 0.43p/kwh which is equivalent to the CCL charge.

13.20.2 Market analysis[11]

In 2005, the UK energy market (including domestic, commercial and industrial customers) consumed 646 TWh of gas and 407 TWh of electricity. The public sector makes up approximately 6.5 per cent of the total market, i.e. around 50 TWh of gas and 21 TWh of electricity.

In terms of supply, the UK market has been through a process of national and international mergers. This has resulted in consolidating suppliers where ten suppliers now account for more than 90 per cent of the market. In the main, the dominant suppliers are the traditional energy companies which tend to be vertically integrated with production, generation and transportation functions. This market dominance and the low supply margins have acted as a barrier to entry for new entrants.

In terms of production (see Figure 13.3), nine companies produce 84 per cent of the UK's gas production and nine companies generate 75 per cent of the UK's electricity. In terms of gas production, the decline of North Sea gas and the switch to imported gas via pipeline or LNG will affect the production picture.

13.20.3 Organising to procure energy

Prior to tendering a great deal of information will have to be gathered and collated, including:

- full details of site(s) including activities, addresses and special characteristics
- electricity Meter Point Administration (MPA) number (a 21-digit reference introduced in 1998)
- all MPANs for gas and electricity
- meter serial number
- meter operator
- half-hourly data files for last twelve months
- working days
- shift patterns/hours of work
- details of any planned changes in usage
- agreed supply capacity.

13.20.4 Price risks

So what are the price risks involved?[12] There are four main aspects of risk energy contracts, which should be covered in a robust risk management strategy:

- *Volume risk* refers to the change in consumption either planned or unplanned which will affect budgets. Other volume considerations such as any minimum or maximum consumption clauses in contracts should also be taken into account in your risk

Figure 13.3 (a) UK electricity installed capacity 2005 and (b) UK gas production 2005

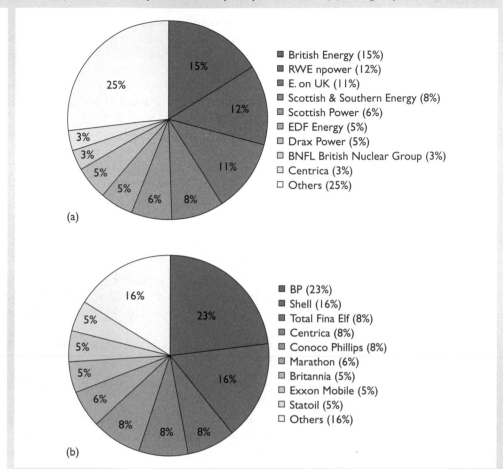

(a)

British Energy (15%)
RWE npower (12%)
E. on UK (11%)
Scottish & Southern Energy (8%)
Scottish Power (6%)
EDF Energy (5%)
Drax Power (5%)
BNFL British Nuclear Group (3%)
Centrica (3%)
Others (25%)

(b)

BP (23%)
Shell (16%)
Total Fina Elf (8%)
Centrica (8%)
Conoco Phillips (8%)
Marathon (6%)
Britannia (5%)
Exxon Mobile (5%)
Statoil (5%)
Others (16%)

strategy. These can attract high financial penalties and without proper control, they could have a significant impact on the overall costs.

- *Purchasing risk* refers to the level of authorisation and expertise of the person making the contract decision. In a stable market, no significant energy procurement expertise is required to choose the time to buy energy. However, in a volatile market, prices can be missed by a lack of necessary authorisation, and any price that is held open for a long period of time attracts a high price premium. Energy market analysis and expertise are therefore essential to ensure an understanding of the price drivers for the short-, medium- and long-term markets.

- *Operational risk* details contingency plans for dealing with problems which may prevent the purchase of energy such as ICT issues or key personnel being unavailable from both the supplier and purchaser side.

- *Value risk* essentially details the price risk and the measures being taken to minimise 100 per cent exposure to the markets. This can be achieved, for example by having stops and targets on time periods or choosing to build up the volume over time.

13.21 Energy consultants and management

Because of the complexity of energy management, companies may outsource both their energy buying and energy management. Consultants such as EnergyQuote undertake both to negotiate the best deals on behalf of clients and provide services beyond the procurement stage, too, such as energy audits, monitoring and bill checking. A register of approved energy consultants is kept by the Energy Institute, established in 2003. When consultants are used they should be remunerated with fixed fees, not shared savings agreements.

Buyers of gas and electricity can obtain much help from associations of purchasers that share information and expertise in exchange for a fee. Such associations include the Energy Information Centre, the government's Energy Efficiency Best Practice Programme and, for big companies, the Major Energy Users Council. Details of these organisations are available on the Internet.

13.22 Component parts and assemblies

A *component* is a structure that has parts and connections. The parts are also components and the *connections* are to other components. Essentially, components are proprietary, where the supplier owns the intellectual property, or the buyer's organisation owns the intellectual property.

When buying components there are many considerations, including:

Make *v* buy	There is, sometimes, the option of make or buy to which the buyer should be alert.
Pricing	The price of proprietary components can be negotiated and discounts/rebates applied in specific circumstances.
Tooling	Some components require tooling to be paid for. This may be a one-off charge or amortised over an agreed quantity.
Free issue	The buyer may consider supplying raw materials for conversion into components but will need to consider scrap arising.
Specification	The specification is vital for components, particularly when components have safety critical applications.
Quality	Agreement must be reached about how components will be checked for quality compliance, e.g. tested to destruction.
Quantity	There will be a relationship between price and quantity so it is an important decision to make how many to purchase.
Continuing supply	For proprietary components the buyer must make sure there is a continuing supply available otherwise there will be a resourcing cost.
Availability of drawings	If it is a proprietary item the buyer may consider requesting a copy of the drawings to facilitate supply if the supplier goes into administration or cannot meet an agreed lead time.
Inventory	The buyer may ask the supplier to supply on the basis of consignment stock or to guarantee supply from his own stock.

13.23 Consumables

13.23.1 Categories of consumables

These are categorised by Risley[13] into operating and maintenance, supply and overhaul items. Often the two categories are jointly referred to as maintenance, repair and operating (MRO) items.

- *Operating supplies* are defined by Risley as 'consumable items used in the operations of the business enterprise', such as stationery, office supplies, machine oil, fasteners, insecticides, fuel, small tools and packaging materials.
- *Maintenance, supply and overhaul items* are defined as 'items which are needed repeatedly or recurrently to maintain the operating efficiency of the business', such as electrical supplies, caretaking requirements, lubricants, paint, plumbing accessories and a wide range of repair parts or spares for plant and equipment.

13.23.2 Characteristics of consumables

Consumables and MRO items are, generally:

- low-cost, low-risk items – with the exception of 'critical' items, such as some spares
- Pareto category items
- revenue items, usually relating to one financial period in contrast to capital items relating to many financial periods
- 'called off' by the actual consumers against orders negotiated with approved suppliers by the purchasing function
- independent demand items suitable for fixed order and periodic stock control systems
- purchased by one of the simplified procedures for small orders
- linked to maintenance policies in the case of MRO items.

13.23.3 Maintenance and replacement policies

Breakdowns and repairs can never be totally avoided, but regular, systematic and thorough maintenance will reduce their number and consequential costs, such as lost production, idle time and hold-ups for other production items. Pareto analysis can provide a useful guide as to where maintenance attention should be placed – that is:

- *Class A* or critical items, which are essential parts of the machine or system, failure of which would result in total breakdown with high repair and other consequential costs
- *Class B* or major components, but where failure would not result in stoppage of the total system
- *Class C* or minor components, the failure of which would not, in the short term, affect the overall process or system.

There are five approaches to planned maintenance that are aimed at keeping equipment or facilities in good operating condition:

1 *Inspection* by visual means on a regular, planned basis.
2 *Breakdown (or corrective) maintenance* – actually waiting for the item to break down and then repairing it.

477

3 *Preventive maintenance* – combining inspection, repair and regular servicing, based on a detailed plan.

4 *Planned replacement* – setting fixed times or dates when components or machines will be replaced, irrespective of their condition.

5 *Breakdown replacement* – a positive policy, particularly appropriate for small items where maintenance costs would be disproportionately high or items that rapidly become obsolete.

13.23.4 Purchasing and consumables

Apart from negotiating the actual purchase of consumables and MRO items, the purchasing function can:

■ liaise with maintenance staff to ensure that information regarding the cost, availability and delivery times is available, especially for 'critical' items

■ advocate a policy of standardisation to avoid holding a variety of 'critical' spares

■ suggest alternatives, such as outsourcing of catering and cleaning, which can obviate the need to hold stocks of food and cleaning materials

■ minimise administrative and storage costs by the application of small order procedures and direct requisitioning by users against 'call-off' contracts, subject to approved safeguards

■ analyse proposed maintenance contracts offered by suppliers and advise whether or not these should be accepted.

13.24 Construction supplies and bills of quantities

13.24.1 Construction supplies

Construction supplies differ in a number of respects from supplies purchased for manufacturing and service organisations.

■ Construction supplies are purchased for use on a site that may be distant from the office that placed the orders or even in another country.

■ Many construction supplies have a high bulk relative to their value, such as bricks and steel. Because of the high cost of transport, it is desirable that construction supplies are procured as near as possible to the site where they will be used.

■ With many construction schemes, the purchasing department will probably be asked to negotiate agreements for electricity, gas and water supplies and, occasionally, for sewage or effluent disposal.

■ Specification of construction supplies will often be on the basis of:

– instructions given by the client to an architect or civil engineer

– architect's specifications.

These specifications are often stated in the bill of quantities.

■ In the interests of security, it is important that purchased supplies are delivered to site as close as possible to the time that they will be used.

- Because of the remoteness of the site from the contractor's office, procedures for recording of supplies received and issued will have to be agreed between the contractor's purchasing department and site engineer.

- Some construction supplies may be 'free issue' supplies or 'customer furnished equipment' (CFE) – that is, items provided by the client for use in connection with a construction project that is being undertaken on the client's behalf.

- Sub-contracting is an important aspect of purchasing for construction projects. Examples would be contracts for foundations, drainage, air-conditioning, lift installation, ventilation, structural steelwork and so on.

- Some construction supplies involve intra-company purchasing. Thus, a construction company may also own stone, sand and gravel quarries that supply other companies within the group.

- Supplies may be transferred from one site or construction contract to another. It is therefore important to know what supplies are available at each site.

- Some discretion must be allowed to the site engineer to arrange for the supply of materials and services, such as hiring plant for particular parts of the project. All such orders should be notified to the contractor's purchasing department to ensure that orders are placed and amounts due to suppliers are duly paid.

13.24.2 Bills of quantities

> Bills of quantities are documents prepared by quantity surveyors from drawings and specifications prepared by architects or engineers, setting out as priceable items the detailed requirements of the work and the quantities involved.

Bills of quantities are usually formidable documents running to many pages and incorporating schedules of conditions of the contract in addition to the specifications of labour and materials required for the particular construction project. A typical bill of quantities will have the following six sections.

- *Section 1: Preliminary items and general conditions* – this sets out the terms and conditions of the contract and responsibilities of the contractor, architect and other parties involved in the contract, altogether with provision for the settlement of disputes arising from the contract.

- *Section 2: Trade preambles* – this sets out the general requirements relating to such aspects of a construction contract as:
  - excavation and earthwork
  - concrete work
  - brickwork and blockwork
  - roofing
  - woodwork
  - structural steelwork
  - metalwork
  - plumbing installation
  - foul drainage above ground
  - holes/chases/covers/supports for services

- electrical and heating installations
- floor, wall and ceiling finishes
- glazing
- painting and decorating.

- *Section 3: Demolition and spot items* – Foundation work ⎫
- *Section 4: General alteration and refurbishment work* ⎪ These sections set
- *Section 5: Provisional sums and contingencies* ⎬ out the quantities
- *Section 6: Grand summary* ⎭ of work to be done

Typical extracts from Sections 2 and 4 relating to plumbing installations are shown in Figures 13.4 and 13.5.

The main aims of bills of quantities are to:

- enable tenderers to show against each item on the unpriced bill of quantities a price per unit covering labour, materials, overheads and profit and, when totalled in the 'grand summary', the items will provide the tender price for the contract
- enable the quantity surveyor, on receipt of the successful tender, to ensure that the contractor has made no serious errors that could cause complications at a later date
- avoid the inclusion by the tenderer of a large amount for contingencies
- assist in verifying the valuation of variations due to changes in design requested or agreed by the client after the contract has been placed.

13.25 Purchasing services

13.25.1 Purchasing and services

In any large organisation, expenditure on services is a major component of the total spend. Fearon and Bales[14] in a study of 116 large USA organisations reported that:

- over half of the purchase dollars (54 per cent) were spent on services
- only 27 per cent of the expenditure on services in their sample organisation was handled by purchasing staff
- of the total spend, the largest categories were utilities (9 per cent), insurance (82 per cent), sales/promotions (7.2 per cent), health benefit plans (6.1 per cent) and travel – air tickets (58 per cent), and in none of these areas was the purchasing department handling more than half the total expenditure
- two explanations for the low involvement of purchasing departments in the procurement of services are:
  - the users of services considered that they had greater expertise in the particular area of service buying than purchasing department staff
  - the purchase of services involves a closer personal relationship with suppliers than does the purchase of goods, yet Fearon and Bales suggest that 'if a logical purchasing process as normally used by purchasing professionals was employed substantial savings might be possible regardless of by whom the actual buying is done' and they also concluded that 'the opportunity to increase profits through more effective purchasing probably is greater in the buying of services than in the purchase of goods'.

Figure 13.4 Extract from a bill of quantities

Clause	SECTION 2 Plumbing installation Trade Preambles
R1	**General** Before pricing the specification, contractors tendering are requested to visit the site, peruse the drawings and make themselves fully conversant with the nature of the works for which they are tendering. **HOT AND COLD WATER** **GENERAL INFORMATION/REQUIREMENTS**

R2	**The installation**
	– Drawing references: See architect's layout
	– Cold water: Mains fed
	– Hot water – direct system(s): Unvented direct water storage cylinder
	  Heat source(s): Immersion heaters
	  Control: Thermostat on immersion heater
	– Other requirements: Remove existing pipework
	                                        Allow for general builder's work

R3	ELECTRICAL WORK in connection with the installation is not included, and will be carried out by the electrical contractor. Provide all information necessary for the completion of such work.
R4	SERVICE CONNECTIONS are covered elsewhere by a provisional sum.
R5	FUEL FOR TESTING: Costs incurred in the provision of fuel for testing and commissioning the installation are to be included in clause B40 section 1. **GENERAL TECHNICAL REQUIREMENTS**
R6	PIPELINE SIZES: Calculate sizes to suit the probable simultaneous demand for the building and to ensure: – a water velocity of not more than 1.3 m/s for hot water and 2.0 m/s for cold water – suitable discharge rates at draw-off points – a filling time for the cold water storage cistern of not more than 1 hour.
R7	INSTALLATION GENERALLY: – Install, test and commission the hot and cold water systems so that they comply with BS 6700, water supply bye-laws, and the requirements of this section to provide a system free from leaks and the audible effects of expansion, vibration and water hammer. – All installation work to be carried out by qualified operatives. – Store all equipment, components and accessories in original packaging in dry conditions. – Protect plastic pipework from prolonged exposure to sunlight. Wherever practicable retain protective wrappings until practical completion. – Securely fix equipment, components and accessories in specified/approved locations, parallel or perpendicular to the structure of the building unless specified otherwise, using fixing brackets/mountings etc. recommended for the purpose by the equipment manufacturer. – In locations where moisture is present or may occur, use corrosion-resistant fittings/fixtures and avoid contact between dissimilar metals by use of suitable washers, gaskets, etc. – All equipment, pipework, components, valves, etc., forming the installation to be fully accessible for maintenance, repair or replacement unless specified or shown otherwise.

Figure 13.5 **Extract from a bill of quantities**

		Plumbing Installations
		£ p

SECTION 4

Item	PLUMBING INSTALLATION	
	GENERAL	
A	Bring to site and remove from site on completion all plant required for the work in this section	Item
B	Maintain on site all plant required for the work in this section	... Item
	Installation as shown in the following sections to be carried out to the architect's drawings and specifications	
C	Soil and waste pipes	... Item
D	Hot and cold water supply including all fittings and rising mains	... Item
E	Dry riser installation	... Item
F	Sanitary fittings	... Item
G	Allow for carrying out all builder's work in connection with the plumbing installations as described including cutting and forming chases, cutting and forming holes, forming ducts through walls and floors, timber support battens, all dire stopping to walls and floors and everything necessary to complete the whole of the works to the reasonable satisfaction of the architect	Item
H	Allow for testing and commissioning to plumbing installations including obtaining any certificates to be handed to the architect	Item
J	Hand to the architect at practical completion of the works copies of the manufacturer's operation and maintenance instructions together with two sets of 'as fitted' drawings.	Item
	PLUMBING INSTALLATIONS CARRIED TO SUMMARY FOLIO NO. 4/63	
	£	

13.25.2 Differences in the purchasing of goods and services

Services can be defined as:[15]

> All those economic activities that are intangible and imply an interaction to be realised between service provider and consumer.

Characteristics of services are:

- *intangibility* – the result of a service transaction is not a transfer of ownership as with physical goods; a service is a process or act.
- *simultaneity* – the actualisation of a service implies the presence of a supplier as well as a customer, both of whom play an active part in the realisation of services.

Intangibility and simultaneity imply two further service characteristics:

- intangibility implies *perishability* – unlike tangible goods, services cannot be stored and used or resold at a future date.

■ simultaneity implies *heterogeneity* – or the large risk of a service being performed differently depending on such factors as the provider of the service, the particular customer, the physical setting or even the hour of the day.

These differences between services and goods are shown in Table 13.10.

Table 13.10 **Comparison of services and goods**

Services	Goods
■ An activity or process	■ A physical object
■ Intangible	■ Tangible
■ Service is produced and consumed simultaneously	■ Separation of production and consumption
■ Customers participate in production	■ Customer may or may not participate in production
■ Heterogenous	■ Homogenous
■ Perishable – cannot be stored for future use	■ Can be stored for future use or sale

From a purchasing perspective, there are other differences.

■ Boshoff[16] suggests that, because of their intangibility, services are riskier to purchase than physical products. This enhanced risk is due to:

– service buyers only knowing what they have bought after the buying decision

– the high level of human involvement and interaction, which makes the standardisation of a service not only difficult but, over time, almost impossible

– customers differing in the amount of information they seek before purchasing a service and satisfaction depending on factors such as prior experience and recommendations.

Boshoff suggests that service guarantees reduce the anxiety and uncertainty of potential service buyers.

■ Specifications for goods are generally more specific than service statements of work.

■ Cost analysis and negotiation are more difficult with services than for goods.

■ Services are likely to become a significant proportion of total spend as many non-core service competences are outsourced.

13.25.3 Segmentation of services

Services can be segmented or categorised in several ways.

■ The Kraljic matrix (see section 2.13.11) is equally applicable to services as it is to goods.

■ Hadfield[17] provides a matrix that categorises services according to their cost and strategic impact on a particular organisation. As applied to a bank, an example of this matrix is shown in Figure 13.6.

In Figure 13.6 the lower and upper quadrants respectively reflect lower and higher cost services. The left quadrants show services of the commodity type, of less importance to the bank's operations. The right quadrants hold services that are either essential or of strategic importance to the particular bank. Thus, security is of critical importance, dry cleaning is not.

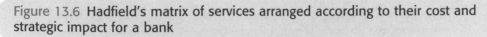

Figure 13.6 Hadfield's matrix of services arranged according to their cost and strategic impact for a bank

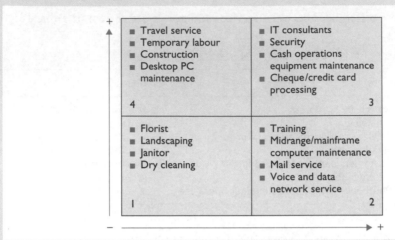

Figure 13.7 Lallatin's typology of services

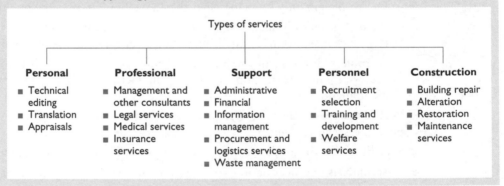

■ Lallatin[18] suggests simple groupings of five major types of service – personal, professional, support, personnel and construction – each of which has special characteristics from a purchasing standpoint. Typical examples of each type are shown in Figure 13.7.

Some services in Figure 13.7 can be categorised under more than one heading. Finance, for example, can be either 'support' or 'professional'.

Segmenting services as described above is essential for the analysis of what to spend and their importance.

From the standpoint of *spend*, such analysis shows:

■ *volume aggregation* – that is, the process of collecting and categorising purchasing spend to determine what services are being purchased throughout the entire organisation, who buys and from which suppliers

■ the percentage of spend relating to each category of service

■ areas of excessive service spending where control is required.

From the standpoint of importance, such analysis shows:

■ where a particular service falls on a Kraljic matrix or a cost/strategy matrix

■ whether a service should be provided internally or outsourced.

13.25.4 Processing the purchasing of services

This normally involves six steps.

■ *Step 1: Determine the appropriate process for procuring the service*

This involves consideration of:

– the nature and strategic importance of the service, with reference to the Kraljic matrix – Duffy and Flynn[19] advise:

> In general automate or routinise non-critical and leverage buys; identify a champion for each strategic service and form a team to eliminate bottlenecks

– where purchasing of services such as insurance, advertising, transport or energy is done by non-purchasing personnel, provide training in specialist purchasing techniques.

■ *Step 2: Prepare a statement of work*

A statement of work is defined as:[20]

> A statement outlining the specific services a contractor is expected to perform, generally indicating the type, level and quality of service as well as the time schedule required.

Much of the information relating to the content and principles of specification writing given in sections 9.4.6 and 9.4.7 applies equally to statements of work. Statements of work should clearly indicate:

– the services required

– where, when and to whom the services are to be provided

– under what conditions

– standards or levels of performance required

– period of initial provision and renewal intervals

– roles, if any, to be undertaken by the purchaser of the service(s), such as assistance with coordination, equipment, staff or research.

As with specifications, special attention should be given to language, such as the use of mandatory words 'shall', 'will' and 'must' and avoidance of ambiguous words or words with multiple meanings, such as 'adequate', 'necessary', 'as required'.

■ *Step 3: List the statement of work as the basis of a request for proposals (RFP) or quotations (RFQ)*

– Request that potential suppliers suggest their solution(s) for a given requirement.

– Provide scope for supplier innovation and suggestions.

– Such documents are useful for locating solutions or sources of supply.

■ *Step 4: Obtain quotations or tenders from potential suppliers*

Invitations may be advertised generally, thus giving all potential suppliers an equal opportunity to make proposals or quotations. Alternatively, RFPs or RFQs may be restricted to three or four selected suppliers. Reverse auctions are increasingly used as a means of obtaining the lowest price and allowing bidders to see those submitted by competitors. Reverse auctions need the requirements for a service to be clearly specified.

■ *Step 5: Evaluate quotations or tenders*

Evaluation should be by a cross-functional team. Individual evaluators should rank the offers received. The team should then discuss the individual rankings. The final decision should be on the basis of a consensus rather than a majority vote and should be recorded.

■ *Step 6: Notification and issue of contract*

Notify the successful and unsuccessful suppliers and issue the contract. Pohlig[21] states that it is critical – to make the contract enforceable – that the statement of work is either incorporated into the contract or included as an appendix.

13.25.5 Service level agreements (SLAs)

These are defined by Hiles[22] as:

An agreement between the provider of a service and its user which quantifies the minimum quality of service which meets business needs.

Normally an SLA is not a separate agreement covering service levels additional to the main contract terms and conditions. It is generally a part of the outsourcing agreement and should be regarded as a schedule (or part of a schedule) to the agreement.

The main advantages of SLAs are that:

■ the customers for and providers of specific services are clearly identified
■ attention is focused on what a particular service or services actually do, as distinct from what it is believed to do
■ customers are more aware of what services they receive and what additional services and levels of service a provider can offer
■ the real needs and levels of service required by the customer are identified and whether or not these can be modified, which could possibly reduce the cost
■ services and service levels adding value can be distinguished from those that do not
■ customers have a heightened awareness of what a service or level of service costs and can then evaluate the service or level on a cost–benefit basis
■ monitoring of services and service levels is facilitated
■ customer reporting of failure to meet service levels enables providers to eliminate the causes and effect improvements
■ understanding and trust is fostered between customers and providers.

Lysons[23] lists the principal reasons for SLAs failing as being the following:

■ lack of commitment by customers and service providers
■ an inadequate support structure, such as failure to implement the SLA concept by means of a project team, appointing an SLA manager and holding regular service level review meetings
■ additions to workloads – SLAs require an additional reporting system and, internally, transfer pricing, for example – so attention should be given to compensating for such extra work by relieving staff concerned of some existing duties

- they are too detailed
- they are not detailed enough
- inadequate staff training relating to the purpose, advantages and implementation of SLAs.

13.25.6 Reducing the cost of services

The Institute of Supply Management[24] has identified seven strategies that buying organisations can use to reduce the cost of purchased services. Some of these strategies have already been referred to in section 13.20 relating to the purchasing of gas and electricity:

- Take advantage of volume aggregation to negotiate quantity discounts.
- Commit to supplier development, thereby creating trust and cooperation, which can lead buyers and suppliers to work together to cut costs.
- Develop integrated sourcing strategies so that purchasing professionals can work with users of services to:
  - delay and control maverick spending
  - ensure adherence to agreed purchasing policies and procedures
  - ensure that advantage is taken of contracts negotiated with suppliers for the provision of services at reasonable rates
  - enforce financial controls, such as the verification of services, deliveries, prices and expense limits to prevent overcharging and cost overruns.
  - take advantage of discounts for prompt or early payment.
- Assign responsibility for service purchases to the right people who possess appropriate expertise, such as insurance and travel services.
- Consider consortium buying. This is especially beneficial to small organisations that have only a small requirement for a particular service.
- Outsource service purchases, such as advertising, insurance and so on, to a third party.
- Use reverse auctions.

Case study

The Universal Mining Company (UMC) is engaged in many countries, undergoing deep mining of precious metals. There is a decentralised engineering and procurement function located in each country of operation. One of the countries is in Southern Africa. A need has been identified for the design, preparation of detailed drawings, manufacture, supply, delivery to site, installation and commissioning of a vacuum ice pilot plant with a capacity of 350 tonnes per day. This will be a pilot plant, offering the design potential to increase the capacity to 700 tonnes per day.

The engineering function has been in discussions with UBV, a German company, for in excess of eight months. A decision has been made to invite a single tender from UBV. Procurement issued the tender, were engaged in its evaluation and, with the necessary approach, placed a contract four weeks ago. The agreed completion date is 14 months from the date of the contract. The internal audit department (a centralised unit) selected the UBV contract for audit and requested the relevant documents. The audit was conducted by Irene Philips.

Some key extracts from her report are as follows:

1 Only lump sum prices were obtained in the tender (see the details in the table).

Item	Description of work	Total price
1	Design and detailed drawings	Included
2	Manufacture and supply plant	£5,000,000
3	CIF and port charges (estimated)	£195,000
4	In-country delivery	£87,500
5	Site establishment charges	Included
6	Installation charges	Included
7	Commissioning charges	Included
8	Initial spares	£1,250,000
9	Special insurance charges	£100,000
Total		£6,632,500

Auditor's extract from the report: 'I regret to conclude that this is an unsatisfactory situation. There is inadequate detail and there is no guarantee that the tendered figure will be the final invoiced figure.'

2 Payment terms have been agreed at 30 per cent of contract value, with the contract (and this has already been paid but without a bank guarantee); 15 per cent of contract value 8 weeks after contract placement; 25 per cent of contract value prior to shipment; 10 per cent of contract value when plant on site; 15 per cent when installation completed; 5 per cent when the commissioning and the engineer's acceptance have been completed.

This is unacceptable practice in that payments should be made against milestones and retrospectively. There should be a retention for at least six months of 10 per cent of contract value.

3 The supplier's technical commentary includes the following (accepted and mentioned in our contract):

■ as this is a pilot plant, we are unable to offer a plant guarantee, but will use our reasonable endeavours to deal with plant failures

■ the initial list of spares is provided in good faith, but in the event that other parts are required, we will advise on the lead time

■ all parts supplied by our sub-contractors shall be repaired or replaced at their option

■ we reserve the right to collect data and operating experience and use it in future plant design – the resultant output will be our intellectual property.

No negotiations have taken place, no risk assessment has been undertaken and the impact of the above on our standard contract terms has not been assessed.

4 It is evident that many meetings have been held with UBV. All minutes of meetings on file were written and issued by UBV. One meeting's minutes included the following notes:

■ the tendered price was accepted and no technical problems were identified

■ UBV confirmed that the planned capacity of 350 tonnes per day would be an objective, but not a contractual obligation

- UBV confirmed that the extent of subcontracting is a commercial confidentiality and could not be released – this also applies to the names of sub-contractors (notes should be written and issued by UMC and the points above should have been challenged).

5 The first invoice carries the following comment on foreign currency: 'The above quoted exchange rate is indicative only as per today's rates and will be adjusted according to actual rates obtained on date of completion of transaction.' This is unacceptable financial practice and leaves currency risk entirely with UMC.

The report concludes, 'This is a disastrous contract, for which the relevant internal specialists should be disciplined. Despite a contract having been issued, urgent negotiations should be conducted with UBV to deal with the identified issues.'

Tasks

1 Based on the information provided, if you were representing procurement in any negotiations with UBV, how would you deal with the above issues?

2 Using only the points in this case study, produce a checklist that could be used for future capital asset procurements.

3 How would you deal with the future relationship with UBV?

Discussion questions

13.1 When procurement is involved in buying new capital equipment what specific commercial knowledge and skills can they apply to ensure the best value for money is obtained?

13.2 (a) Give an example of each of the following categories (i–iv) of capital equipment:
   (i) strategic new equipment
   (ii) replacement equipment
   (iii) vehicles and transportation
   (iv) administrative equipment, such as PCs.
   (b) How may acquisition policies and procedures differ in each case?
   (c) At what management level may decisions be taken for each category?

13.3 Draft a capital expenditure request form that can be used by senior managers seeking board approval for the acquisition of expensive capital equipment.

13.4 What criteria would you use to decide if new equipment should be purchased?

13.5 XYZ is considering whether to lease or buy a machine. The machine will cost £2000 and have a life of 3 years, at the end of which it will have no residual value. A loan for the purchase of the machine can be obtained for an annual interest rate of 7 per cent, payable at the end of each of the three years. The machine can also be leased from an equipment hire company in return for an annual payment of £762.50, payable at the end of each year.
   Ignoring taxation factors, which option will be the lowest-cost solution? What factors might you consider when making a decision?

13.6   Calculate the ROCE from the following figures.

Cost of machine	£160,000
Expected life	5 years
Estimated scrap value	£20,000
Estimated profits before depreciation	
Year 1	£40,000
Year 2	£80,000
Year 3	£60,000
Year 4	£30,000
Year 5	£10,000

Solution

Note: Average profit before depreciation £220,000/5 = £44,000

Total depreciation = £160,000 − £20,000 = £140,000

Average depreciation = £140,000/5 = £28,000

Average annual profit after depreciation = £44,000 − £28,000 = £16,000

$$\therefore \text{ROCE} = \frac{£16,000}{£160,000} \times 100\% = 10 \text{ per cent}$$

[Answer: 10 per cent]

13.7   What are the main economic and political factors that influence market conditions for sensitive commodities? Can you give examples using the 2011 tensions in the Middle East?

13.8   How would you explain hedging to the lay person?

13.9   Why is the price of gas so volatile? What role does the international market play?

13.10 What roles should the buyer play in a make or buy scenario?

13.11 In relation to futures markets, ascertain the meaning of the following terms:
(a) going long
(b) going short
(c) spot market price index.

13.12 What makes procurement for the construction sector quite different to buying parts for production assembly?

13.13 If you were asked to purchase a proprietary IT system what would be the major considerations?

13.14 If you were asked to purchase chemicals on a sample source contractual agreement with a supplier in Japan what risks could you identify?

Past examination questions

1 (a) Explain why it is important to analyse supply markets.
   (b) Describe, using examples, **six** domestic or international political influences that can effect organisations buying internationally.

CIPS, *Analysing the Supply Market*, November 2007

2 ElectrikCo

ElectrikCo is a major electrical components manufacturer. The company has recently made a strategic decision to investigate the outsourcing of the bulk of its non-core, high-volume production of sub-assembly components to a single, lower-cost supplier in another country.

Outsourcing would amount to 25 per cent of the total value of purchases by value. This five-year contract would be the largest single contract issued by ElectrikCo. These components are readily available in many different countries, and most suppliers have stock available for immediate delivery.

The decision to outsource was taken in response to mounting production costs in ElectrikCo's own country, and a desire by the senior management team to reduce the production cost base in order to increase profitability.

A multi-functional team has been assembled to visit potential production sites and short-listed suppliers in other countries. This team must report back to the Managing Director on issues which may impact on the success of the outsourcing project.

The production director of ElectrikCo is very concerned that the short-listed suppliers may not have the capability to produce the right products quickly enough, or to the very rigorous standards and specifications required.

Tasks

(a) Explain which quadrant of the supply positioning model is appropriate for the sub-assembly components.
(b) Describe **two** disadvantages for ElectrikCo of outsourcing the production of the sub-assembly components to a supplier in another country.
(c) Outline **four** areas ElecrikCo might investigate when visiting the potential suppliers in order to determine their suitability for the outsourcing contract.
(d) Comment on whether you believe the five-year term of the contract is appropriate, giving reasons for your answer.

CIPS, *An Introduction to Purchasing Strategy*, November 2010

3 Solid Gold Ltd

Solid Gold Ltd is a new company trying to establish itself in the marketplace for trading gold. The business operates by buying gold from individual customers via Solid Gold retail outlets. The aim is to acquire gold at below market value and re-possess it via melting plant into gold bullion which can be sold at a profit through commercial markets or back through its retail outlets.

During a month, Solid Gold has a stock of gold awaiting processing which has already been paid for, although there will often not be a customer for the gold until the gold is processed. The success of the business is therefore driven by buying enough gold at a price which allows for resale at a profit. The margin for error is relatively small and the company relies heavily upon its buyers and traders as well as keeping the cost of production as low as possible.

Earlier this year, Solid Gold researched the price variances of gold, Index numbers are used in this market, with the basis being US$. In a three-month period, the lowest price index was 1050 and the highest was 1210. Prices paid by commercial customers during the same time were 'the best they could get' which was between 1075 and 1100.

Solid Gold has also found that its retail sales are sometimes extremely good and sometimes extremely bad. From peak sales two years ago, monthly sales have now decreased to about half of the volume.

Tasks

(a) Explain **two** reasons why it is important for Solid Gold Ltd to analyse the supply market.

(b) Suggest **two** reasons why the price of gold appears to change quite significantly over a short period of time.

(c) Explain how 'cost plus pricing' could be used effectively by Solid Gold Ltd.

(d) Explain **two** reasons why Solid Gold Ltd may have experienced changes in the volume of sales of gold over the last few years.

CIPS, *Analysing the Supply Market*, May 2010

References

[1] Aljian, G. W., *Purchasing Handbook*, National Association of Purchasing Management, 1958, section 16.1

[2] Van Nostrand, *Dictionary of Business and Finance*, Van Nostrand, 1980

[3] Barfield, J. T., Raibon, C. A. and Kinney, M. R., *Cost Accounting*, West Publishing, 1994, p. 709

[4] Definition provided by the Inland Revenue

[5] Marrian, J., 'Marketing characteristics of industrial goods and buyers', in Wilson, A. (ed.) *The Marketing of Industrial Products*, Hutchinson, 1965, pp. 10–23

[6] England, W. B., *Modern Procurement Management*, Irwin, 1970, p. 743

[7] Risley, G., *Modern Industrial Marketing*, McGraw-Hill, 1972, pp. 24–5

[8] Buffett, W., 'Apocalypse is nigh: Buffett tells Berkshire Faithful', *Money Telegraph*, 4 April, 2005

[9] Electricity Network Strategy Group 'Our Electricity Transmission Network: A vision for 2020', March, 2009

[10] Regional Centres of Excellence 'How to be successful in energy procurement'. April, 2007

[11] As 10 above

[12] As 10 above

[13] As 7 above

[14] Fearon, M. E. and Bales, W. A., *Purchasing of Non-traditional Goods and Services*, Center for Advanced Purchasing Studies, USA, focus study executive summary, 1995

[15] Desmet, S., Van Looy, B. and Van Dierdonck, A., 'The nature of services' in Van Looy, B., Van Dierdonck, A. and Gemmel, P. (eds), *Service Management*, FT Management, 1998, p. 5

[16] Boshoff, C., 'Intention to buy a service: the influence of service guarantees: general information and price information advertising', *South African Journal of Business Management*, Vol. 34(1), 2003, pp. 39–43

[17] Hadfield, J. E., 'Purchasing services on the Internet', *Inside Supply Management*, May, 2002, p. 20

[18] Lallatin, C. S., 'How can I categorise my service purchases', *Purchasing Today*, November, 1997

[19] Duffy, R. J. and Flynn, A. E., 'Services purchases: not your typical grind', *Inside Supply Management*, Vol. 14, No. 9, p. 28

[20] ISM, 'Glossary of Key Supply Managment Terms': www.ism.ws

[21] Pohlig, H. M., 'Legal issues of contracting for services', *Inside Supply Management*, September, 2002, pp. 22–5

[22] Hiles, A., 'Service level agreements', *Payroll Manager's Review*, No. 7, July, 1989, pp. 70–1

[23] Lysons, C. K., 'How to prepare service level agreements', CIPS, 2001, p. 18

[24] ISM, 'Reducing the costs of purchased services': www.ism.ws

Chapter 14

Buying from overseas

Learning outcomes

This chapter aims to provide an understanding of:

- the terminology of international and global sourcing
- motives for buying overseas
- difficulties in buying overseas
- Incoterms 2010
- ocean shipping terminology
- distribution costs
- methods of payment in overseas trade
- countertrade
- factors in successful overseas buying.

Key ideas

- Motives and benefits of overseas buying.
- Information sources relating to buying overseas.
- Cultural, political, ethical, quality, exchange risk and legal factors in overseas buying.
- The format and meaning of Incoterms 2010.
- Complexities of Customs and Excise.
- Factors in freight costs.
- Freight agents.
- Open accounts, bills for collection and letters of credit.
- Purchasing and countertrade.
- The true cost of overseas buying.
- Factors in successful overseas buying.

14.1 Terminology

Birou and Fawcett[1] distinguish between international sourcing, multinational sourcing, foreign sourcing and strategic global sourcing. They define the first three terms as:

> Buying outside the firm's country of manufacture in such a way that does not coordinate requirements among worldwide business units of a single firm.

Strategic global sourcing is defined as:

> The coordination and integration of procurement requirements across worldwide business units, looking at common items, processes, technologies and suppliers.

Trent and Monczka[2] also differentiate between international and global sourcing. International purchasing is:

> A commercial transaction between a buyer and a seller located in different countries.

Global sourcing involves:

> Positively integrating and coordinating common items and materials, processes, designs, technologies and suppliers across worldwide purchasing, engineering and operating locations.

Among other important findings, Trent and Monczka conclude that firms engaging in global sourcing are likely to have competitors and be larger than those engaging in international purchasing and that 'one can easily conclude that international purchasing is best described as a functional activity while global sourcing represents a strategic direction and organisational process'.

These views are supported by Rexta and Miyamoto[3] who suggest that, in general, smaller firms are restricted in their capacity to search for and secure overseas suppliers by their lack of managerial knowledge and capital resources so that 'any supplier found among a small pool of qualified overseas suppliers is a potential candidate so long as it can meet their procurement requirements'. Moreover, the small quantities they are purchasing make the business of smaller firms less attractive to first-class overseas suppliers. In contrast, 'a depth of resource capacity allows large firms to aggressively pursue the full potential of international sourcing by capitalising on the world's best suppliers'.

Regarded from a strategic perspective, global sourcing is more complicated than international purchasing. There are, however, aspects where the two approaches converge and international purchasing is strategic as well as tactical. Smaller firms also engage in the development and early involvement of their overseas suppliers. Because of such convergence, Trent and Monczka use the generic term 'worldwide sourcing' to describe international purchasing and global sourcing. The phrase 'buying from overseas' used in this chapter, while also generic, is probably more closely equated with 'international purchasing'.

14.2 Motives for buying from overseas

There are many motives for buying from overseas, not all driven by the buying organisation's initiatives and self interests. Table 14.1 shows the drivers for buying from overseas, identifies and experienced by Brian Farrington Limited[4] – a specialist procurement and supply chain consultancy company.

Table 14.1 The drivers for buying from overseas

Business drivers	Reasoning*
Requirement for offsets	The business requirement where an offshore customer demands the procurement of local content. Offsets may include technology transfer, training and licensed production
OJEU advertisements	The public sector place OJEU advertisements and these sometimes attract overseas tenders. If such a tender is the 'best deal' then the contract will be placed overseas.
Pressure to reduce costs	There are good examples in IT and retail where advantage is taken of low cost economies, e.g. the outsourcing of call centres to India and the production of clothing in Sri Lanka
Manufacturing flexibility	Where there are restrictions on UK based manufacturing capacity, contracts can be placed overseas to guarantee additional capacity. An example is a transportation company contracting supplies from Poland
Access to specialist skills	The UK has deskilled in some fields, e.g. engineering design and, on occasions, will need to access relatively new skills, e.g. offshore wind farms and satellite technology
Market penetration	The desire to enter a new market can be greatly facilitated by procuring goods and services in the target market. Examples have been provided by having local supply of components that generate employment and overcome restrictive quotas
Domestic non-availability for raw materials	There are some essential raw materials that are not available in the UK, e.g. reserves of commodities such as copper, zinc and gold. This leaves no choice but to purchase overseas

* These are strategic reasons to purchase overseas; others will arise from time to time

14.3 Sources of information for overseas suppliers

A well-organised and structured research programme is required to identify potential overseas suppliers. Clearly, there is a risk to be managed if contracts are placed with suppliers who cannot maintain a high quality supply. There are many information sources including:

- UK Trade & Investment International Trade Team Database
- foreign embassies and high commissions
- import brokers
- trade journals
- directories, such as *Kompass*, *Thompson*, *Jaegar* and *Waldman*
- trade fairs and exhibitions
- the World Bank

- *The Official Journal of the European Communities*
- shipping and forwarding agents
- specialist enquiry agents, such as Dun & Bradstreet
- procurement consultants, such as Brian Farrington Ltd
- trading company websites
- professional and trade organisations
- the Internet.

14.4 Overcoming challenges when sourcing overseas

There are challenges when sourcing overseas because the professional degree of difficulty is a lot higher than purchasing in the home market. Some key considerations are shown in Table 14.2.

14.4.1 Cultural factors

Culture is the system of shared beliefs, values, behaviours and artefacts that the members of a particular society use to cope with their world and with one another. Culture differs with nationality and an understanding of such differences is essential when buying from or negotiating with overseas suppliers.

It is strongly advisable to research the culture of the country in which you will be negotiating. This investment of time will pay dividends and should ensure that positive relationships become the foundation for a business deal. The examples below will indicate the logic of research into a country's culture.

- *China*
  - will drag out negotiations to gain an advantage, therefore you should avoid revealing your deadlines
  - do not make exaggerated gestures or use dramatic facial expressions
  - be careful with colours – red is a lucky colour; white is the colour for funerals.
- *Finland*
  - they are direct and tend not to engage in small talk
  - can be heavy drinkers at lunch
  - folded arms signify arrogance.
- *Hong-Kong*
  - negotiations are often slow with excessive attention to detail
  - traditional greeting is a bow
  - do not give a clock as a present as it connotes death.
- *Italy*
  - tend to make excessive demands at the end of negotiations
  - authority is attributed to an individual not always to the title
  - hospitality is important, refusing an invitation to a meal will offend.

Table 14.2 **Key considerations when sourcing overseas**

Descriptor	Considerations
1 Buyer's experience	Requires the ability to research sources of supply, conduct vendor appraisal, negotiate and put in place a contract with acceptable risks
2 Currency fluctuations	Requires expert advice and support from finance/banking specialists to optimise the risk derived from currency fluctuation during the life of the contract
3 Supplier evaluation	There is a need to develop and apply a tailored supplier evaluation RFI document to probe logistics, product support, contract terms, supply chain, finances and quality management
4 Culture and language	Expert knowledge of cultural differences and how to deal with language barriers will be needed to prevent misunderstandings and breakdowns in communication
5 Political stability	From time to time there are serious political instabilities and uncertainties that impact on trade. Relatively recent examples have been in Thailand, Zimbabwe, Egypt, Libya and Cuba
6 Logistics support	The ability to move goods around the world is vital, as is the certainty of shipping, use of special containers and availability of emergency stocks are all hallmarks of a good supplier
7 Duty and Customs regulations	This is an ever changing scene and requires expert support either from in-house specialists or freight forwarders. Delays in customs can lead to contract failures
8 Contractual risk	The basis of legal jurisdiction, dispute resolution, currency, quality standards and inspection rights are classic areas requiring diligence
9 Contract management	Either the buying organisation or a third party will undertake contract management. Distance is an issue, as is the cost of the activity
10 International quality standards	The buyer will need to check the quality standards that apply to a specific purchase, recognising that some standards will exceed British Standards specifications

- *Malaysia*
  - there are three major ethnic groups, Malay, Chinese and Indian
  - very intrusive questions can be asked by a Malaysian
  - the left hand is considered unclean by Muslims and Hindus.
- *Russia*
  - compromise is seen as a sign of weakness
  - negotiation walk-outs are very commonplace
  - they will persist with points and play hardball.

Purchasing professionals buying overseas can benefit from studying the analysis of national cultures made by Hofstede,[5] Hampden-Turner and Trompenaars[6] and Lesem and Neubauer.[7]

14.4.2 Foreign exchange risks

This is the risk that a purchaser of an overseas product will be required to pay more (or less) than expected as a result of fluctuations in the exchange rates between the purchaser's currency and that of the supplier's currency in which payment may be made.

Assume that a UK company buys an item of capital equipment costing $100,000 at a 'spot' price of $2 to the pound, payable in six months' time meaning £50,000. If, at the time of payment, the pound has strengthened against the dollar, so that the exchange rate is $2.5 to the pound, the number of pounds required will be lower – in fact, £44,445. Conversely, if the pound has weakened against the dollar so that the exchange rate is $1.75 to the pound, the number of pounds required to buy $100,000 will be greater – in fact, £57,142. The risk of a rise in price due to an adverse exchange rate is termed *transaction exposure*.

Companies buying overseas can minimise foreign exchange risk in several ways, including the following:

- *Arranging to buy in the currency of the buyer* – this effectively transfers the risk of fluctuations in exchange rates to the supplier. This may not, however, be the best policy. Scott[8] suggests that, when negotiating international deals, purchasers should:
  - research exchange rates for one or two years previously to benchmark the range of fluctuations in the respective currencies
  - price goods in the currency of the supplier if it is anticipated that the purchaser's currency will strengthen further
  - price goods in the currency of the purchaser if it is anticipated that the purchaser's currency will weaken
  - when agreeing to price adjustment clauses, ensure that currency fluctuations are kept separate from cost increases.

- *Reduce the uncertainty by hedging with forward contracts* for a period of no longer than six months. If a purchaser knows that a supplier must be paid a fixed amount in foreign currency in, say, six months, the purchaser can arrange a six-month forward contract with the bank under which the bank will provide a fixed amount of the foreign currency at the end of that time.

- *Buy currency options* – such contracts give the purchaser the right (but not the obligation) to buy or sell foreign currency at a specified price within a specified time period. Under forward contracts, options allow the purchaser to benefit from favourable fluctuations in exchange rates.

- *Buy the overseas currency at the spot price on the day on which the overseas purchase is made* – this uses up capital, but interest may be earned on the currency held and the exchange rate is known from the outset.

- *Negotiate currency adjustment clauses* – these may include clauses specifying that:
  - payments may be in a currency other than that of the purchaser or supplier, such as sterling, dollars, Swiss francs

- 'this contract is subject to an exchange rate of X, plus or minus Y per cent; if the exchange rate exceeds these parameters then the contract price shall be renegotiated'
- 'the contract shall be subject to an exchange rate fluctuation equal to the average of the exchange rate at the time of signing the contract and that at the date of the delivery'.

Developments such as that of the single European currency may help to simplify currency prices and exchange rates in an international context.

14.4.3 Legal considerations

Contracting with an overseas supplier requires diligent attention to detail with the terms and conditions of contract. The detail will include:

- whose legal jurisdiction shall apply? For example, in the USA there is State Law and the Uniform Commercial Code (UCC)
- what are the arrangements for dispute resolution, arbitration or mediation?
- the different types of insurance required to cover off the risks of a transaction including Incoterms (see section 14.5)
- the scope of *force majeure* provisions, recognising the potential for *force majeure* across the whole supply chain, including shipment
- rights of inspection through in-house quality management or by a third party
- the certainty of price, taking into account currency movements, price change mechanism and impact of commodity price changes, e.g. copper, zinc and gold
- specifications, including units of measurement, national standards and terminology
- documentation, such as bills of lading, certificates of origin and customs entry forms
- redress of complaints – that is, the return to the supplier of goods rejected or damaged in transit – and, as the recovery of damages is awarded to the buyer by the courts or arbitration, it is useful to ascertain what assets, if any, the supplier has in the buyer's country so these can be restrained by the courts in payment of damages due
- avoidance of translation error when converting overseas contract into own language
- rights of cancellation and termination
- prevention of use of child labour, e.g. India
- rights of supplier to sub-contract or assign
- provision of performance bond/parent company guarantee.

The United Nations Convention on Contracts for the International Sale of Goods 1980 ('CISG') and the process by which it was created, by the United Nations Commission on International Trade Law (UNCITRAL) established a benchmark for the unification of commercial law in the post-war era. The CISG is an important document, since it establishes a comprehensive code of legal rules governing the formation of contracts for the international sale of goods, the obligations of the buyer and seller, remedies for breach of contract and other aspects of the contract. Readers may also wish to note that there is a 'United Nations Convention on the Use of Electronic Communication in International Contracts'.

The CISG has been adopted by 72 states but there has been non-ratification by the United Kingdom. In 2005 it was noted that companies doing business in Europe had to deal with 25 different jurisdictions. A number of reasons have been given for the UK lack of ratification, including the vagueness of some of the conventions' provision, such as Article 7 on statutory interpretation and good faith.

The Principles of European Contract Law (PECL) represent a groundbreaking project on the road to a common European Private Law. The principles were compiled by the Commission on European Contract Law ('Lendo-Commission') in the early 1980s and comprise three parts. Parts I and II dedicate themselves to the formation of contracts, validity, performance and remedies for non-performance. Part III focuses upon general contract law questions, prescription, set-off, plurality of debtors, illegality, unconscionability, conditions and capitalisation interest.

The International Chamber of Commerce (ICC) International Court of Arbitration is the world's leading institution for resolving international commercial and business disputes. In 2009, 817 cases were filed, involving 2095 parties from 128 countries. The following standard clause is recommended, subject to adjustment to fit national law and the special needs of the deal: 'All disputes arising out of or in connection with the present contract shall be finally settled under the Rules of Arbitration of the International Chamber of Commerce by one or more arbitrators appointed in accordance with the said Rules.'

14.5 Incoterms

14.5.1 What are Incoterms?

Incoterms refer to the set of international rules for the interpretation of the chief terms used in foreign trade contracts first published by the International Chamber of Trade in 1936 (now International Chamber of Commerce) and amended in 1953, 1967, 1976, 1980, 1990, 2000 and 2010.

The reason Incoterms are periodically revised is to ensure that they represent current practice. In the 1990 version, for example, the clause dealing with the seller's obligation to provide proof of delivery allowed paper documentation to be replaced by e-mail for that purpose for the first time.

Although the use of Incoterms is optional, they can materially reduce difficulties encountered by importers and exporters.

14.5.2 Format of Incoterms

The Incoterms®[9] rules explain a set of three-letter trade terms reflecting business-to-business practice in contracts for the sale of goods. The Incoterms rules describe mainly the tasks, costs and risks involved in the delivery of goods from sellers to buyers.

14.5.3 How to use the Incoterms® 2010 rules

(a) If you want the Incoterms® 2010 rules to apply to your contract, you should make this clear in the contract, through such words as 'the chosen Incoterms rule including the named place' followed by 'Incoterms® 2010'

(b) The chosen Incoterm rule needs to be appropriate to the goods, to the means of their transport, and above all to whether the parties intend to put additional obligations, for example such as the obligation to organise carriage or insurance on the seller or on the buyer

(c) The chosen Incoterms rule can work only if the parties name a place or port and will work best if the parties specify the place or port as precisely as possible. A good example of such precision would be: 'FCA 38 Cours Albertler, Paris, France', Incoterm® 2010.

14.5.4 Main features of the Incoterms® 2010 rules

The number of Incoterms rules has been reduced from 13 to 11. This has been achieved by substituting two new rules that may be used irrespective of the agreed mode of transport – DAT, Delivered at Terminal, and DAP, Delivered at Place – for the Incoterms 2000 rules DAF, DES, DEQ and DDU.

14.5.5 Classes of Incoterms

The 11 Incoterms® 2010 rules are presented in two distinct classes:

1 Rules for any mode of transport:

EXW	Ex Works
FCA	Free Carrier
CPT	Carriage Paid To
CIP	Carriage and Insurance Paid To
DAT	Delivered At Terminal
DAP	Delivered At Place
DDP	Delivered Duty Paid

2 Rules for Sea and Inland Waterway Transport:

FAS	Free Alongside Ship
FOB	Free On Board
CFR	Cost and Freight
CIF	Cost Insurance and Freight

In Table 14.3 there is a summary of the meaning of each Incoterm, salient points of carriage, risks and costs, noting that the summary is that of the author. For a full and complete description of all Incoterms® 2010 rules it will be necessary to purchase the ICC rules for the use of domestic and international trade terms.[10]

Table 14.3 Incoterms

Incoterm	Meaning	Carriage	Risks	Costs
EXW	Ex-works, means that the seller delivers when it places the goods at the disposal of the buyer at the seller's premises or at another named place (i.e., works, factory, warehouse, etc.)	The seller has no obligation to the buyer to make a contract of carriage	The seller bears all risks of loss of or damage to the goods until they have been delivered at the agreed point	Transfer from seller to buyer when goods are at the buyer's disposal noting that the buyer must pay, for example, any additional costs for failing to take delivery of the goods when they have been placed at its disposal
FCA	Free carrier, means that the seller delivers the goods to the carrier or another person nominated by the buyer at the seller's premises at an other named place	The seller has no obligation to the buyer to make a contract of carriage. However, if requested by the buyer or if it is commercial practice and the buyer does not give an instruction to the contrary in due time, the seller may contract for carriage on usual terms at the buyer's risk and expense	The seller bears all risks of loss of or damage to the goods until they have been delivered at the agreed point	The buyer must pay (a) all costs relating to the goods from the time they have been delivered at the agreed point and any additional costs incurred, for example, because the buyer fails to nominate a carrier or other person (see meaning)
CPT	Carriage Paid To, means that the seller delivers the goods to the carrier or another person nominated by the seller at an agreed place (if any such place is agreed between the parties) and that the seller must contract for and pay the costs of carriage necessary to bring the goods to the named place of destination	The seller must contract or procure a contract for the carriage of the goods from the agreed point of delivery, if any, at the place of delivery to the named place of destination or, if agreed, any point at that place	The buyer bears all risks of loss of or damage to the goods from the time they have been delivered to the contracted carrier	In summary the buyer must pay: (a) all costs relating to the goods from the time they have been delivered (b) all costs and charges relating to goods in transit (c) unloading costs (d) where applicable, all duties, taxes and other charges, as well as the costs of carrying out formalities
CIP	Carriage and Insurance Paid To, means that the seller delivers the goods to the carrier or another person nominated by the seller at an agreed place and the seller must contract for and pay the costs of carriage necessary to bring the goods to the named place of destination	The seller must contract or procure a contract for the carriage of the goods from the agreed point of delivery, if any, at the place of delivery to the named place of destination, or if agreed, any point at that place	This rule has two critical points, because risk passes and costs are transferred at different places. The buyer bears all risks of loss of or damage to the goods from the time they have been transferred as shown in column 1 (meaning) of this table	The buyer must pay all costs relating to the goods from the time they have been delivered, and all costs and charges relating to the goods while in transit, and unloading costs, and all duties, taxes and other charges as well as the costs of customs formalities and costs of any additional insurance procured at the buyer's request

DAT	Delivered At Terminal means that the seller delivers when the goods, once unloaded from the arriving means of transport, are placed at the disposal of the buyer at a named terminal at the named port or place of destination	The seller must contract at its own expense for the carriage of the goods to the named terminal at the agreed port or place of destination. The seller has no obligation to the buyer to make a contract of insurance	The buyer bears all risk of loss of or damage to the goods from the time they have been delivered as shown in column 1 (meaning) of this table	The buyer must pay all costs relating to the goods from the time they have been delivered, and any additional costs incurred by the seller if the buyer fails to fulfil its obligations and, where applicable, the costs of customs formalities as well as duties, taxes and other charges
DAP	Delivered At Place means that the seller delivers when the goods are placed at the disposal of the buyer at the arriving means of transport ready for unloading at the named place of destination	The seller must contract at its own expense for the carriage of the goods to the named place of destination or to the agreed point, if any, at the named place of destination. The seller has no obligation to the buyer to make a contract of insurance	The seller bears all risks involved in bringing the goods to the named place. The buyer bears all risks of loss of or damage to the goods from the time they have been delivered	The buyer must pay all costs relating to the goods from the time they have been delivered and, all costs of unloading necessary to take delivery of the goods from the arriving means of transport at the named place of destination and the costs of customs formalities, as well as all duties, taxes and other charges payable upon import of the goods
DDP	Delivered Duty Paid, means that the seller delivers the goods when the goods are placed at the disposal of the buyer, cleared for import on the arriving means of transport ready for unloading at the named place of destination	The seller must contract at its own expense for the carriage of the goods to the named place of destination or to the agreed point, if any, at the named place of destination. The seller has no obligation to the buyer to make a contract of insurance	The seller bears all risks of loss of or damage to the goods until they have been delivered. The risk then transfers to the buyer	The buyer must pay all costs relating to the goods from the time they have been delivered, all costs of unloading and any additional costs incurred if the buyer fails to fulfil its obligation to assist the seller at its request in obtaining any import licence or other official authorisation for the import of the goods
FAS	Free Alongside Ship means that the seller delivers when the goods are placed alongside the vessel (e.g. on a quay or a barge) nominated by the buyer at the named port of shipment	The seller has no obligation to the buyer to make a contract of carriage. If requested by the buyer or if it is commercial practice and the buyer does not give an instruction to the contrary in due time, the seller may contract for carriage on usual terms at the buyer's risk and expense	The risk of loss of or damage to the goods passes from the seller to the buyer when the goods are alongside the ship	The buyer must pay all costs relating to the goods from the time they have been delivered except, where applicable, the costs of customs formalities necessary for export as well as all duties, taxes and other charges payable upon export

Table 14.3 *Continued*

Incoterm	Meaning	Carriage	Risks	Costs
FOB	On Board means that the seller delivers the goods on board the vessel nominated by the buyer at the named port of shipment or procures the goods already so delivered	The seller has no obligation to the buyer to make a contract of carriage. However, if requested by the buyer or if it is commercial practice and the buyer does not give an instruction to the contrary in due time, the seller may contract for carriage on usual terms at the buyer's risk and expense	The buyer bears all risks of loss or of damage to the goods from the time they have been delivered. There are caveats on transfer of risk if the buyer fails to notify the nomination of a vessel or the vessel nominated fails to arrive on time to enable the seller to comply with delivery to the buyer	The buyer must pay all costs relating to the goods from the time they have been delivered and any additional costs incurred either because the buyer has failed to give appropriate notice or the vessel nominated by the buyer fails to arrive on time, is unable to take the goods or closes for cargo earlier than the time notified
CFR	Cost And Freight means that the seller delivers the goods on board the vessel or procures the goods already so delivered	The seller must contract or procure a contract for the carriage of the goods from the agreed point of delivery, if any, at the place of delivery to the named port of destination or, if agreed, any point at that port	The buyer bears all risks of loss or of damage to the goods from the time they have been delivered	The buyer must pay all costs relating to the goods from the time they have been delivered and all costs and charges relating to the goods while in transit, unloading costs including lighterage and wharfage charges, any additional costs incurred if it fails to give notice and where applicable all duties, taxes, and other charges and costs of carrying out customs formalities
CIF	Cost, Insurance and Freight means that the seller delivers the goods on board the vessel or procures the goods already so delivered	The seller must contract or procure a contract for the carriage of the goods from the agreed point of delivery, if any, at the place of delivery to the named port of destination or, if agreed, any point at that port	The buyer bears all risks of loss of or damage to the goods from the time they have been delivered. The buyer must, whenever it is entitled to determine the time for shipping the goods and/or the point of receiving the goods within the named port of destination, give the seller sufficient notice thereof	The buyer must pay all costs relating to the goods from the time they have been delivered, and all costs and charges relating to the goods while in transit until their arrival at the port of destination, and unloading costs including lighterage and wharfage charges and all duties, taxes and other charges plus costs of carrying out customs formalities

14.6 Ocean shipping terminology

It is useful for procurement to have a grasp of some of the salient ocean shipping terminology which includes:

Air Waybill	A bill of lading (see below) that covers both domestic and international flights transporting goods to a specified destination. This is a non-negotiable instrument of air transport that serves as a receipt for the shipper, indicating that the carrier has accepted the goods listed and obligates itself to carry the consignment to the airport of destination according to specified conditions.
All Risk	The broadest form of coverage available, providing protection against risks of physical loss or damage from any external cause. Does not cover loss or damage due to delay, inherent vice, preshipment condition, inadequate packaging, or loss of market.
Bill of Lading	The document issued on behalf of the carrier describing the kind and quantity of goods being shipped, the shipper, the consignee, the ports of loading and discharge and the carrying vessel. It serves as a document of title, a contract of carriage, and a receipt for goods.
Bulk Shipments	Shipments which are not packed, but are loaded directly into the vessel's holds. Examples of commodities that can be shipped in bulk are ores, coal, scrap, iron, grain, rice, vegetable oil, tallow, fuel oil, fertilisers, and similar commodities.
Carnet	A customs document permitting the holder to carry or send merchandise temporarily into certain foreign countries (for display, demonstration, or similar purposes) without paying duties or posting bonds.
Containerisation	Shipping systems based on large cargo-carrying containers ranging up to 48 feet long that can be easily interchanged between trucks, trains and ships without re-handling the contents.
Demurrage	A charge assessed by carriers to users who fail to unload and return equipment promptly.
Documentary Credit	A commercial letter of credit providing for payment by a bank to the name beneficiary, usually the seller of merchandise, against delivery of documents specified in the credit.
Duty	(a) *Ad valorem* duty means an assessed amount at a certain percentage rate on the monetary value of an import. (b) Specific duty: an assessment on the weight or quantity of an article without preference to its monetary value or market price. (c) Drawback: a recovery in whole or in part of duty paid on imported merchandise at the time of exportation, in the same or different form.

Free Trade Zone	A port designed by the government of a country for duty-free entry of any non-prohibited goods. Merchandise may be stored, displayed, used for manufacturing, etc., within the zone and re-exported without duties being paid. Duties are imposed on the merchandise (or items manufactured from the merchandise) only when the goods pass from the zone into an area of the country subject to the Customs Authority. Also called Foreign Trade Zone.
In Bond	A term applied to the status of merchandise admitted provisionally to a country without payment of duties – either for storage in a bonded warehouse or for trans-shipment to another point, where duties will eventually be imposed.
LCL	(Less-than-carload, also, Less-than-containerload) A shipment that occupies less space than is available in a railcar or cargo-carrying container.
Perils of the Sea	Fortuitous accidents or casualties, peculiar to transportation on a navigable water, such as stranding, sinking, collision of the vessel, striking a submerged object ort encountering heavy weather or other unusual forces of nature.
Reefer	A reference to refrigerated cargo-handling services utilising trucks, trailers, containers or railcars equipped with cooling units.
Shipping Conference	A group of ocean carriers that set identical rates for each member of the conference. Each conference operates only between specified origin and destination ports.
Valuation Clause	The clause in the Marine Policy that contains a fixed basis of valuation agreed upon by the assured and the Underwriter and which establishes the insured value of the merchandise. The clause determines the amount payable under any recoverable loss or General Average contribution.
War Risks	Those risks related to two (or more) belligerents engaging in hostilities, whether or not there has been a formal declaration of war. Such risks are excluded by the FC & S (Free of Capture and Seizure) warranty, but may be covered by a separate War Risk Policy, at an additional premium.
Wharfage	A charge assessed by a pier or dock owner for handling incoming or outgoing cargo.

14.7 Customs and excise

All goods, new or used, imported into the EU from outside the EU are subject to customs duty (import duty or import tax) and value added tax (VAT) according to their value and import tax classification. All goods imported into the UK from outside the EU must be declared to HM Revenue and Customs and, in most cases, this includes goods bought via the Internet. The importer is legally liable for import duty and VAT.

There is a UK Integrated Tariff, available online, as a subscription service. The Tariff is used to confirm commodity codes, find duty rates and compliance requirements for each type of 'good' commodity. The Tariff is split into three volumes: Volume 1 contains background and business-oriented information for importers and exporters about policy in specific areas. Volume 2 contains approximately 16,500 goods descriptions with their Commodity Codes and special measures which can be applied. Volume 3 is essential for importers and exporters. It contains a box-by-box guide for both manual and electronic C88 import and export declaration forms and a complete lot of Customs Procedure Codes (CPCs).

The rate of import duty varies according to the type of goods imported and the country of origin. Normally, import duty is based on a percentage of the value of the goods, plus the transport and insurance costs to the country of destination and may also include such costs as tools, dies, moulds, design work, royalties and licence fees. VAT, which varies across EU member states, is then added. The process is exemplified by the following illustration:

	£	£
Value of goods, say	100.00	
Shipping and insurance costs to the UK, say	15.00	
Total value for import duty	115.00	
Import duty payable at, say, 5 per cent	5.75	5.75
	120.75	
VAT on £120.75 at 20%	24.15	24.15
	144.90	29.90

From the above example, it can be seen that, in most cases, VAT will be the largest tax to pay on importation. The total tax payable is £29.90 on the original price of these goods.

In addition, a customs clearance fee will be charged by the courier, carrier, freight forwarder or import agent (including the Royal Mail or Parcel Force) for clearing the product through customs. There can be further charges for storage if the goods are held up in customs or due to late payment.

Further details of customs charges can be obtained from the websites of HM Revenue and Customs and the UK Department for Business, Innovation and Skills. Member states of the EU hold commodity codes in a database called the TARIC, or Tariff Intégré Communautaire. The UK Tariff is published once a year with ten monthly updates using data from the TARIC and is supplemented by UK specific data on VAT, licensing, restrictions and excise duties.

14.8 Transport systems, costs and considerations

14.8.1 Road transport

The road system has, of courses, developed enormously since the first asphalt road was laid in Babylon by 625 BC. China had, in 2007, a national highway system of 53,000 km. The road system and distribution now raises vital considerations of emissions, noise, safety, congestion, economy and weight of vehicles going across national boundaries.

There is very limited potential to achieve economies of scale, largely because of impositions by governments. Road transport does have advantages over other modes, including:

- market entry is relatively low cost
- capital costs of vehicles and distribution points are relatively low
- point-to-point delivery times can be effectively managed
- flexibility of route choice gives flexibility when bad weather or accidents occur
- market dominance for short-medium distance journeys
- road users do not bear the full operating costs, e.g. they do not pay for road building and maintenance, despite road taxes and tolls.

14.8.2 Rail transport

The characteristics of rail transport must take account of economic and territorial control. Many rail networks are monopolies or oligopolies. An example of the latter is North America where there are seven large rail freight carriers.

Key considerations of rail transportation include:

- there is effective use of space for the rail lines but distribution points (terminals) require vast space
- freight trains have severe gradient restrictions, e.g. approximately 10 metres per kilometre
- the design of freight wagons is quite flexible, such as hopper wagons for fertilisers and triple hopper wagons for coal
- the standard gauge of 1.435 metres is in wide use
- initial capital costs are very high with some rail companies investing close to 50 per cent of operating revenues in capital and maintenance costs
- the potential for more intermodal transport, for example, using COFC (containers on flat cars)
- emergence and development of high-speed rail networks
- the complexities of tracking shipments.

14.8.3 Pipelines

Under most circumstances, buyer's rarely have occasion to consider pipelines as a transportation mode. Pipelines do, however, play a key role in strategic considerations. Some considerations are:

- pipelines invariably are designed for a specific commodity, e.g. oil and gas
- they can be subjected to disruption through acts of terrorism
- they can be subjected to political intervention, e.g. Russia with natural gas
- terrain difficulties can be overcome, e.g. the trans-Alaskan pipeline
- operating costs are low.

14.8.4 Maritime

This facet of international supply chain is of great interest to purchasers. There has been very significant growth in freight traffic, occasioned by:

- it being a low-cost mode, strengthened by containerisation
- the growth in globalisation, e.g. retailers in the UK purchasing from the Far East

- movement of energy and mineral cargoes
- technology improvements in terminals.

There are two categories of freight – the first is bulk cargo (commodity cargo), classified as dry or liquid that is not packaged, such as iron ore (dry), gasoline (liquid). It often has a single client, origin and destination. Break-bulk cargo (general cargo) is the second category and is packaged in bags, boxes or drums.

Key considerations of maritime transportation include:

- bulk cargo approximates to some 65 per cent of all tonne miles shipped
- slow speeds averaging 15 knots
- severe delays in some ports
- significant capital outlay
- economies of scale, particularly with full container loads
- difficulties for the buyer to control transit times
- the operation of conference (formal agreements between companies engaged on particular trading routes).

14.8.5 Air transport

This is a vital aspect of international trade and transportation. It has a significant speed advantage, e.g. moving foodstuffs overnight and access to many geographic locations around the world. Some key considerations are:

- the threat to supply where there is severe weather, e.g. the Icelandic volcanic ash issue
- use of airspace and political interventions
- relatively high cost but fast speed and flexibility of routes
- high levels of investment and fixed costs
- possible impact of terrorism and security
- fluctuations in fuel prices which can be circa 30 per cent of operating costs.

14.8.6 Intermodalism

The need for an integrated supply chain management system played a large role in the evolution of intermodalism. Some key considerations are:

- containerisation facilitates a quick turnaround
- relatively low cost
- clients can use one bill of lading to get a through rate
- the TEU (Twenty-foot Equivalent Unit) can move 10 tons of cargo and a 40-foot box, circa 22 tons of cargo.

14.9 Freight agents

Large companies will often have staff specialising in import and freight procedures. Others will rely on the services of import or freight agents.

14.9.1 What is a freight agent or forwarder?

A freight agent or forwarder is a person or company, who, for a fee, undertakes to have goods carried and delivered to a destination. The services of freight agents are normally engaged when the carriage of goods involves successive carriers or the use of successive means of transport.

Traditionally, freight agents make contracts of carriage for their principals. Under the principles of the law of agency, a freight agent is under an obligation to the principal to conclude the contract on the agreed terms. Although in civil law freight agents are distinguished from carriers, the latter sometimes also act as freight agents.

14.9.2 The services of freight agents

In 1970, a report by the National Economic Development Office[11] defined the traditional functions of forwarders as involving:

- the preparation and handling of documentation, the main types of which are:
  - bills of lading
  - airway bills or equivalent
  - customs papers
  - certificates of origin
  - exchange control forms
  - insurance certificates
  - shipping notes
  - calling forward notes
  - collection orders
  - port rate forms
  - assistance in preparing invoices.
- planning and costing the route to give the desired combination of speed, economy and reliability, trading times against cost
- booking and coordinating transport and freight space, domestic, international and foreign
- arranging any ancillary services, such as warehousing, packing
- consolidating and paying charges payable to transport, such as operators, port authorities, customs and so on
- presenting goods for customs clearance, both for imports into the UK and abroad via overseas offices, and correspondence and so on for UK exports
- advising on special requirements, trade and financial, of foreign countries and providing necessary documents
- providing exporters with the necessary information to prepare quotations, particularly CIF or delivered to importers' premises
- advising importers of details and any changes in UK import procedures.

Other services offered by forwarders may include:

- consolidation or groupage – that is, the grouping of consignments from several consignors in a single load

- road haulage, such as the operation of a cargo collection and delivery service to and from sea or airports
- containers – some forwarders may operate container services or lease containers
- provision of warehousing, packing, insurance, financial and market research services
- coordination of the deliveries of multiple consignments.

14.9.3 Freight agents' fees

Freight agents or forwarders are paid a negotiated fee by the shipper or importer depending on the service or documents required. Fees are related to Incoterms in that they depend on the responsibilities undertaken by the different parties. They will be lower, for example, if the responsibilities end FOB at the departure port and increase as responsibilities extend DDP to the destination terminal.

14.9.4 Freight agents and the future

Willmott[12] points out that the development of logistics and supply chain management requires:

> the services of 'logistics practitioners' who can mesh themselves into the overall pattern, not just as suppliers of freight forwarding services but as links that might encompass several business functions.

Such functions are listed by Willmott as being:

- customerisation, or tailoring for individual markets or customers
- sourcing and delivery of raw materials
- allocation of materials and packaging
- manufacturing and capacity planning
- inventory determination and allocation to warehouses
- international movement by sea, road, rail and air
- domestic trunking and primary and multidrop distribution
- order fulfilment, including picking, packing and dispatch/delivery to customers
- e-commerce support of supply chain visibility
- reverse logistics, perhaps involving call centre management and collections for repair or servicing and so on.

Possible developments include:

- establishing 'one stop' entities by merging logistics and forwarding services, providing increased capabilities as suppliers of materials and components, enabling manufacturers to outsource non-core logistic and transport activities
- the secondment of the freight forwarder's staff to major customers to provide on-site freight expertise
- whole supply chains setting up in competition with each other rather than individual companies in that chain doing so, with the consequence that a freight forwarder may become a link in more than one chain.

14.10 Methods of payment

Overseas suppliers (exporters) may be unwilling to release goods until they have received payment. Conversely, buyers may be unwilling to pay before the goods have been delivered. SITPRO[13] (Simplifying International Trade) has produced the payments risk ladder shown in Figure 14.1, setting out some methods of payment and the risks of each to exporters and importers respectively.

Each of the four methods of payment shown in Figure 14.1 is briefly described below. SITPRO also advises that importers and exporters should consider their options carefully and hedge the risks with appropriate insurance and credit checks on overseas suppliers or customers.

14.10.1 Open account

This is similar to most home transactions. Goods are shipped and documents remitted to the buyer with an invoice for payment on previously agreed terms, such as 'net 30 days'.

14.10.2 Bills for collection

Under this system, the shipping documents – including the *bill of lading* (which is a receipt signed by a ship's master specifying the goods shipped on board and constituting a negotiable bill of title to such goods) are sent to the buyer's bank rather than direct to the buyer. These will be handed to the importer only when payment has been made (documents against payment) or against a promise to pay (documents against acceptance) and, until the documents are received, the title to the goods remains with the exporter. Documents against acceptance are usually accompanied by a *draft* or *bill of exchange* drawn on the buyer. Bills of exchange are the oldest method of payment for goods bought overseas. A bill of exchange (B/E) is defined as:[14]

> An unconditional order in writing, addressed by one person to another, signed by the person giving it, requiring the person to whom it is addressed to pay on demand, or at a fixed or determinable future date, a sum certain in money to or to the order of a specified person or to the bearer.

A cheque is a specialised form of B/E drawn on a bank to pay a specified sum to X on demand.

When a buyer (drawee) agrees to pay on a certain date – say, '30 days from acceptance' – the draft is said to have been accepted. It is against this acceptance that the goods are released to the buyer.

Figure 14.1 **The payments risk ladder for exporters and importers**

Exporter	Least secure →	Less secure →	More secure →	Most secure →
	Open account	Bills for collection	Documentary credits	Advance payment
Importer	← Most secure	← More secure	← Less secure	← Least secure

The *bills for collection* process is governed by the 'Uniform rules for collections' (Document 522, published by the International Chamber of Commerce). Over 90 per cent of the world's banks adhere to Document 522.

14.10.3 Letters of credit

With bills for collection, the bank acts only as an intermediary and enters into no payment undertaking. It is therefore a cheaper arrangement than a *letter of credit* (LOC), which is a legal instrument constituting a cash guarantee, obligating the bank to make a payment to a named beneficiary, such as an exporter, within a specified time against the presentation of documents such as the bill of lading, certificate of quality, insurance and origin, packing list and a commercial invoice. The risk of non-payment by the buyer is therefore transferred to the issuing bank. Letters of credit are governed by the ICC rules 'Uniform customs and practice for documentary credits' (Document UCP 500).

An LOC is opened by an importer (applicant) to ensure that the documentation requested proves that the seller has fulfilled the requirements of the underlying sales contract by making such requirements conditions of the LOC.

From the exporter's perspective, apart from cash in advance, an LOC is the most secure method of payment in international trade. The conditional nature of an LOC means that payment will not be made to the exporter unless all the credit terms have been precisely met.

LOCs may be conditional, standby or transactional:

- a *conditional LOC* may require some burden of proof by the owner that the contractor has not failed to perform before the bank will pay
- a *standby LOC* is normally used for open accounts (see section 14.10.1) and deals only with payment of documented sums within a specified period
- a *transactional LOC* applies to one specific transaction.

Most LOCs are irrevocable, which means that both parties must agree to any changes in terms.

While LOCs are a very secure method of payment, the security comes at a price. The security must therefore be weighed against the cost of higher bank charges.

14.10.4 Payment in advance

As shown in Figure 14.1, this is the least secure and most secure method of payment from the standpoint of buyers and sellers respectively. Often this method takes the form of a payment up front of, say, 50 per cent of the selling price, with the remainder payable on agreed credit terms.

14.10.5 What method of payment to use?

SITPRO[15] lists the following factors to bear in mind when deciding which method to choose:

- company policy
- cash flow considerations
- relationship with the overseas supplier

- the market conditions under which the overseas supplier operates
- the buyer's gut feeling.

The effectiveness and expeditiousness of all the processes involved in the exchange of documents and payments has been greatly facilitated by the various electronic means at our disposal.

14.11 Countertrade

14.11.1 What is countertrade?

Yasvas and Freed[16] define countertrade (CT) as:

> A generic term for parallel business transactions, linking sellers and buyers in reciprocal commitments that usually lie outside the realm of typical money-mediated trade.

Essentially, CT is a form of international reciprocal trading in which an order is placed by a purchaser with a supplier in another country (or vice versa) on condition that goods of an equal or specified value are sold or bought in the opposite direction.

CT often, but not necessarily, takes place in less well-developed, more centrally planned economies. The rising price of oil, higher interest rates and foreign debt have meant that many countries are unable to generate sufficient hard-core earnings by means of their exports to service their debts, but desperately need imports. As a result of economic, financial and political forces, CT has become an established feature of modern markets. Estimates vary but approximately 25 per cent of all world trade is accounted for by CT.

14.11.2 Forms of countertrade

Carter and Gagne[17] identify five distinct types of CT:

- *Barter or swaps* – a one-off, direct, simultaneous exchange of goods or services between trading partners without a cash transaction, such as an exchange of New Zealand lamb for Iranian crude oil. The term 'swap' is used when goods are exchanged to save transportation costs.

  Kreuze[18] instances the shipping of Russian oil to Greece rather than Cuba and the sending of Mexican oil to Cuba instead of Greece, thereby saving considerable transportation costs for both nations.

- *Counterpurchase* occurs when a company in country X sells to a foreign country Y on the understanding that a set percentage of the sale's proceeds will be spent on importing goods produced in country Y. Both trading partners agree to fulfil their obligations within a fixed time period and pay for the major part of their respective purchases in cash.

  In 1977, Volkswagen sold 10,000 cars to the then East Germany and agreed to purchase goods from a list compiled by the East Germans up to the value of the cars over the ensuing two years.

- *Buy-back or compensation* occurs when the exporter agrees to accept, as full or partial payment, products manufactured by the original exported product.

  Occidental Petroleum negotiated a deal with the former USSR under which they agreed to build several plants in the Soviet Union and receive partial payment in ammonia over a 20-year period.

The main differences between buy-back and counterpurchase are that, in buy-backs:

– the goods and services taken back are tied to the original goods exported, while this is not the case with counterpurchase

– buy-back deals usually stretch over a longer period of time than counterpurchase ones.

The Xerox Corporation sold plant and technology for the production of low-value photocopying machines to the People's Republic of China and contractually agreed to repurchase a large proportion of the machines produced in the Chinese plant.

■ *Switch trading* refers to the transfer of unused or unusable credit balances in one country to overcome an imbalance of money by a trading partner in another country. Country X sells goods of a certain value to country Y. Country Y credits country X with the value of the goods, which X can use to buy goods from Y. Country X, however, does not wish to buy goods from Y. X therefore sells the credits to a third-party trading house at a discount. The trading house then locates a country or company wishing to buy goods from Y. In return for a small profit, the trading house sells the credits to the country or company wishing to buy from Y.

■ *Offset* – this is similar to counterpurchase, except that the supplier can fulfil the undertaking to import goods or services of a certain percentage value by dealing with any company in the country to which the original goods were supplied.

This can be shown diagrammatically as in Figure 14.2.[19]

14.11.3 The advantages and disadvantages of countertrade

These have been identified by Forker,[20] as shown in Table 14.4.

Table 14.4 **Advantages and disadvantages of countertrade**

Advantages	Disadvantages
Acceptance of goods or services as payment can: ■ avoid exchange controls ■ promote trade with countries with inconvertible currencies ■ reduce risks associated with unstable currency values Overcoming the above financial obstacles enables countertrading enterprises to: ■ enter new or formerly closed markets ■ expand business and sales volume ■ reduce the impact of foreign protectionism on overseas business Countertrade has enabled participants to: ■ make fuller use of plant capacity ■ have longer production runs ■ reduce unit expenses due to greater sales volume ■ find valuable outlets for declining products	Countertrade negotiations tend to be longer and more complicated than conventional sales negotiations and must, sometimes, be conducted with powerful government procurement agencies Additional expenses, such as brokerage fees and other transaction costs, reduce the profitability of countertrade deals There may be difficulties with the quality, availability and disposal of goods taken as countertrade Countertrade may give rise to pricing problems associated with the assignment of values to products/commodities received in exchange Offset customers can, later, become competitors Commodity prices can vary widely during the lengthy periods of countertrade negotiation and delivery

Figure 14.2 Preferred items for export in countertrade transactions

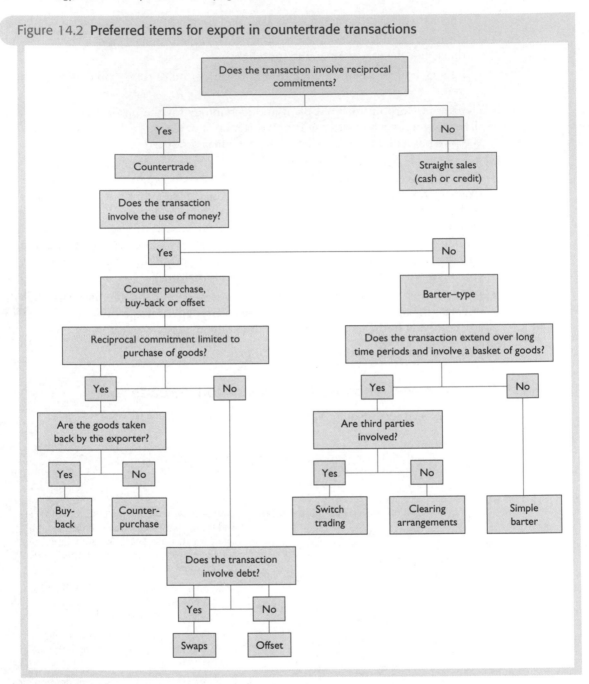

14.11.4 Problems of countertrade

The implementation of CT requires special expertise. The problems encountered will fall into one of the following categories: marketing, negotiation ability, attitudinal, managerial, pricing and procurement.

Examples of CT include:

- no control over quality of products traded and possible absence of specification detail
- pricing decisions and lack of knowledge on cost drivers
- lack of CT knowledge and relevant expertise
- difficult, complex and negotiations with multi-participants when there is no common agenda
- contractual relationships lacking clarity with jurisdictional issues
- difficulty reselling products
- added third-party costs
- unknown and unquantifiable risks.

14.12 The true cost of overseas buying

As indicated in earlier sections of this chapter, while the benefits of buying overseas can be substantial, there are also significant financial costs and risks. It is therefore important that such costs and risks should be evaluated before deciding to source abroad. Tables (such as Table 14.5) facilitate comparisons between the true costs of buying from abroad and from home-based suppliers. They also provide a list of some possible items for negotiation.

Many of the costs shown in Table 14.5 will also attract VAT. Costs will vary according to different weights, sizes and quantities. The effects of such variances are easily computed with the aid of a spreadsheet.

14.13 Buying capital equipment overseas

14.13.1 Reasons for buying overseas

Capital equipment can be sourced overseas for numerous reasons – lower prices, compatibility with existing equipment, the need for technology only available from overseas suppliers and to equip factories in or adjacent to the country in which the equipment is manufactured to name but a few.

14.13.2 Technical requirements of equipment bought overseas

Essentially these are the ones listed in section 13.4, although special attention will be given to lifecycle costs and the availability of spares – especially the speed at which they can be provided by air transport or other methods. Other important factors are international standardisation and, with some complex equipment, the provision of assistance with installation and post-purchase maintenance advice and services.

14.13.3 Cultural, contractual and currency factors

The cultural, political, ethical and foreign exchange factors referred to in this chapter apply equally to the purchase of capital equipment.

Table 14.5 Comparisons of costs of overseas and UK suppliers

Expense category	Costs: areas of expenditure	Overseas supplier	Home supplier
Basic price	Supplier's quoted price per item Packaging Sea/air freight Marine insurance Supplier's final price CIF/destination		
Handling/ transportation charges	Handling charges (port of entry) Storage Port costs Internal transport to buyer Freight forwarding fees Insurance		
Customs and associated charges	Customs duties Customs clearance fees		
International financing	Costs of documentation Currency conversion rates Exchange rate fluctuations Bank fees		
Inventory costs	Holding costs of higher inventory Levels at x per cent per annum		
Sourcing costs	Costs of visit to overseas supplier Estimated communication costs Costs of inspection by overseas agent Special fees, such as translation, legal		
Total actual or estimated costs			

Legal factors will also need special consideration, especially what legal system is applicable, and the provision for the international settlement of disputes by means of such agencies as the International Chamber of Commerce (ICC). Special clauses may need to be included in the contract, such as an undertaking by the supplier of the equipment to maintain stocks of spare parts for a prescribed minimum number of years.

Currency considerations which need to be taken into account are the same as those referred to in section 14.4.2. In some cases countertrade may be applicable, especially buy-back arrangements, whereby the country exporting capital equipment undertakes to buy back some of the products made in the buyer's country.

14.13.4 Import factors

These include the most suitable forms of transport and the way in which freight and import agents can provide assistance. All buyers of capital equipment from overseas should have a thorough understanding of Incoterms especially FOB, CIF and CFR.

Finally it is essential to make an evaluation, as shown in section 14.12, of the comparative costs of buying capital equipment from overseas and home sources, when these alternatives are available.

14.14 Factors in successful overseas buying

The Birou and Fawcett research referred to earlier in this chapter identified the factors listed in Table 14.6.

Other important considerations include ascertaining the total cost of ownership for all significant purchases, using overseas suppliers that practice TQM, providing overseas suppliers with accurate demand forecasts, a boundary-spanning philosophy for supply chain participants, as opposed to a narrow vision of business processes, and sensitivity to the interests and cultures of overseas suppliers. Most purchasing professionals can benefit from training in buying overseas, but hands-on experience is usually the best teacher of all.

Table 14.6 Factors influencing success in international sourcing (Birou and Fawcett, 1993)

Rank	Factor	Rating
1	Top management support	5.68
2	Developing communication skills	5.67
3	Establishing long-term relationships	5.65
4	Developing global sourcing skills	5.62
5	Understanding global opportunities	5.13
6	Knowledge of foreign business practices	5.09
7	Foreign supplier certification and qualifications	5.02
8	Planning for global sourcing	5.02
9	Obtaining expert assistance	4.79
10	Knowledge of exchange rates	4.53
11	Use of third-party logistics services	4.12

Note: all ratings are on a seven-point Likert scale, with seven for major challenge.

Case study

Chinn-Wagg Equipment Ltd (CWEL)

You are the new purchasing manager for Chinn-Wagg Equipment Ltd (CWEL). You have been in post for four months and are currently feel uneasy about goods procured overseas. You have reviewed three items purchased from Korea. There are no formal quotations and the items have been purchased through a UK agent. They have purchased on an ex-works basis (Incoterms). Matters got worse last week when you discovered that a casting, supplied by a UK company, is now three months overdue. You decided that you would conduct a 'spot check' and call unannounced on Green Ltd who are supplying the casting. They were embarrassed by having to disclose that they were purchasing the casting from a Chinese foundry and they, in turn, were sub-contracting the machining of the casting to a Chinese sub-contractor! You insisted on a full set of quality control plans. These were delivered to your office today – all in the Chinese language. You are still waiting for a definite delivery date. Meantime, your company is paying liquidated damages of 1 per cent a week on a contract for an off-shore oil development company. Their contract is worth £2m. The casting has a value of £150,000. There is no damages provision in the contract with Green Ltd.

You have had a brief meeting with the engineering director and quality manager of CWEL. You were pleasantly surprised when both said that in principle they have nothing against buying from overseas. You have agreed to produce a report at tomorrow's management meeting. It will address four matters:

1 proposed actions to obtain delivery of the casting

2 the future use of Incoterms

3 a procurement process for overseas buying

4 how to select 'candidates' for overseas buying.

Task

In respect of each facet of your report, list the bullet points you will need to address and be ready to discuss them at the management meeting.

Discussion questions

14.1 What are the potential risks when purchasing abroad, particularly in regard to financial and supply chain considerations?

14.2 Would you prefer to deal with a local agent of an overseas supplier or deal direct with them?

14.3 Define countertrade and identify the five distinct types of countertrade.

14.4 If you were selecting a freight agent to represent your interests, what would be the top six qualities you would be looking for?

14.5 What are the main differences between a Letter of credit and a Bill for collection?

14.6 If you purchased a piece of capital equipment from a supplier in Japan, how would you guarantee a continuing supply of spare parts to your engineering department?

14.7 Compare and contrast the movement of goods, internationally, by sea and air freight.

14.8 Customs provide no useful service, other than the collection of duties. Do you agree?

14.9 Name six Incoterms and explain their different applications.

14.10 What would be the dangers of signing a contract subject to a foreign jurisdiction?

14.11 How important are cultural differences when doing business overseas?

14.12 It is a fact that some countries make extensive use of child labour and sometimes have a disregard for health and safety. How would you seek to redress this when negotiating a contract?

Past examination questions

1 Describe **two** advantages of international trade.

CIPS, *Analysing the Supply Market*, May 2008

2 (a) Describe the overall aim of the Vienna Convention (UNCITRAL) in relation to international trade.
   (b) Describe **three** aspects of international trade where Incoterms help avoid misunderstandings.

CIPS, *Preparing and Managing Contracts*, November 2008

3 (a) Explain why it is important to analyse supply markets.
   (b) Describe, using examples, **six** domestic or international political influences that can effect organisations buying internationally.

CIPS, *Analysing the Supply Market*, November 2007

4 Perfect Produce Ltd (PP) is a new organisation looking to establish itself internationally. It has achieved steady growth over the last five years but currently only operates in countries that have a free market economy system in place. The managing director now wishes to consider where to target future expansion of the business and has been advised there may be an impact of operating in a country where a free market economy does not exist. This has led to the purchasing team providing some background information to help explain aspects of government policy and trade that can differ on an international basis. The managing director, wishes to gain a greater awareness over the mechanics of setting the prices for PP's products as well as considering desired production levels, in the absence of 'free markets'.

Tasks

   (a) Explain to PP's managing director the differences between a free-market economy, a mixed economy and a planned economy.
   (b) Explain to PP's managing director why and how a government intervenes in a mixed economy.

CIPS, *Analysing the Supply Market*, November 2007

References

1 Birou, L. H. and Fawcett, S. E., 'International purchasing benefits and requirements and challenges', *International Journal of Purchasing and Supply*, January, 1993, pp. 22–5

2 Trent, R. J. and Monczka, R. M., 'International purchasing and global sourcing: what are the differences?', *Journal of Supply Chain Management*, November, 2003

3 Rexta, N. and Miyamoto, T., 'International sourcing: an Australian perspective', ISM, *Resource* Article, Winter, 2000

4 Brian Farrington Limited: www.brianfarrington.com

5 Hofstede, G., *Cultures and Organisations*, McGraw-Hill, 1991

6 Hampden-Turner, C. and Trompenaars, F., *The Seven Cultures of Capitalism*, Piatkus, 1994

7 Lesem, R. and Neubauer, F., *European Management Systems*, McGraw-Hill, 1994

8 Scott, S., 'Strong dollar, weak contract', *Purchasing Today*, July, 1997, pp. 8–9

9 'Incoterms' is a registered trademark of the International Chamber of Commerce

10 Obtainable from ICC United Kingdom [the British affiliate of ICC] 12 Grosvenor Place, London, SW1X 7HH, ICC Publication No. 715E, ISBN 978-92-842-0080-1

11 National Economic Development Office, 'The freight forwarder', HMSO, 1970, pp. 1–3

12 Willmott, K., 'Understanding the freight business', in as 3 above, pp. 203–4

13 SITPRO (Simplifying International Trade) at: www.sitpro.org.uk/trade/paymentmethods.htm

14 Bills of Exchange Act 1882, section 3(1)

15 As 11 above – SITPRO is the UK's Trade Facilitation Agency, supported by the DTI

16 Yasvas, B. F. and Freed, R., 'An economic rationale for countertrade', *The International Trade Journal*, Vol. XV, No. 2, Summer, 2001, pp. 127–56

17 Carter, J. R. and Gagne, J., 'The dos and don'ts of countertrade', *Sloan Management Review*, Spring, 1988, pp. 31–7

18 Kreuze, J. G., 'International countertrade', *Internal Auditor*, Vol. 5, No. 2, April, 1997, pp. 42–7

19 Czinkota *et al.*, czinkota@georgetown.edu, 2005, p. 587

20 Forker, L. B., 'Purchasing's views on countertrade', *International Journal of Purchasing and Materials Management*, Spring, 1992, pp. 10–19

Part 4

Strategy, tactics and operations 3: negotiation, support tools and performance

Chapter 15

Negotiation

Learning outcomes

This chapter aims to provide an understanding of:

- approaches to negotiation
- the nature of negotiation
- the content of negotiation
- the negotiation process
- negotiation and relationships
- negotiation ethics.

Key ideas

- The distinction between adversarial or distributive and collaborative or integrative negotiations.
- Methods of influencing others.
- Substance and relationship negotiating roles.
- Time as a factor in negotiations.
- Planning as a key negotiation element.
- The stages of the negotiation process.
- Pre-negotiation, negotiation and post-negotiation considerations.
- Negotiating behaviour.
- Negotiation post-mortems.
- Positional and principled negotiation.
- Ethical aspects of negotiation.

Introduction

Negotiation has been described as:[1]

> Perhaps the finest opportunity for the buyer to improve his (or her) company's profits and obtain recognition.

There must be specific conditions that pertain before negotiation is used in an attempt to resolve differences between buyers and sellers. These will include any situation where:

- It is believed that a tender or quotation contains cost elements that are uncompetitive when compared with other bidders, or, where there is internal financial and technical expertise to show that bid costs are too high.

- A tender or quotation is unclear on major features, for example, the delivery date is unsupported by a detailed production plan showing key points of manufacture or where service implementation fails to identify milestones. This would require negotiation to probe these key points and to identify how the contract will include the delivery obligations required.

- There is reason to believe that the seller has a high probability of not fulfilling a critical feature of the contract, and where in consequence contractual safeguards are required. An example of this is a failure to mobilise resources on a project.

- IT product support is necessary and different levels, e.g. gold, silver and bronze, are available, and where the proposed cost in use is unclear or unacceptable. This will require negotiation to obtain definitive prices, service levels and understand the consequences of non-performance and to include these in the contract.

- There is good reason to believe that the tenderers are not pricing competitively. This could be through collusive practices, estimating deficiencies or a desire to price in such a way as to make excessive profit.

- The supply market is monopolistic thereby diminishing the normal forces of competition.

- The tenderers are reluctant to explain how they arrived at their price, particularly on high value contracts. If this situation is also accompanied by circumstances which make it probable that contract changes will be inevitable, negotiation is required to identify the price review mechanism which will operate in the contract.

- The purchase has a unique element, such as a once only purchase in a specialist area where the buyer has little expertise. This can occur in Information Technology purchasing where the seller will usually have expert knowledge.

- There is a contractual dispute that requires a detailed understanding of all the circumstances leading to the dispute.

- The buying company is contemplating a long-term contract such as outsourcing back office services for ten years and, hence, where the decision will involve long-term pricing considerations. In this case negotiation is necessary to ensure appropriate price control mechanisms such as indexation, continuous improvement, price benchmarking and possible incentivisation mechanisms.

- Technology refreshments are to be incorporated as an element of contract performance and where the recovery on investment needs to be specifically identified.

■ There is a price increase request from a seller which will have an adverse effect on operating costs, budgets and ability to compete in their markets.

■ Supply market research, identifies opportunities to obtain buying company competitive advantages previously denied them. Examples have been provided by outsourcing and offshoring.

■ It can be demonstrated that existing contracts are no longer competitive and/or where the technical solution is outdated.

This is not a comprehensive listing, although it identifies reasons why negotiation is frequently necessary. It must not become a predictable routine, such as asking for 5 per cent off the bid price. It must not involve disclosing one bidder's data to a competitor to gain a price reduction or some other contractual advantage. It must not involve the classic 'Dutch auction' in which bidders are continually played off against each other within short time spans.

The best negotiations are conducted under circumstances where there is mutual respect between buyer and seller and where both parties perceive that there are valid professional reasons for negotiations taking place.

Definitions

There are numerous definitions of negotiation. Three typical examples are given and commented on below.

> The process whereby two or more parties decide what each will give and take in an exchange between them.[2]

This definition of negotiation highlights:

■ its interpersonal nature

■ the interdependence of the parties

■ its allocation of resources.

A formal negotiation is:

> An occasion where one or more representatives of two or more parties interact in an explicit attempt to reach a jointly acceptable position on one or more divisive issues about which they would like to agree.[3]

This definition highlights that negotiation:

■ is restricted to occasions when two or more parties need to reach agreement

■ involves *representatives of the parties* – the buyer, sales executive and legal representatives, for example

■ is *explicit* – that is, the process genuinely and deliberately attempts to reach an agreement

■ involves *divisive issues* about which the parties would like to agree.

Third, negotiation is:

> Any form of verbal communication in which the participants seek to exploit their relative competitive advantages and needs to achieve explicit or implicit objectives within the overall purpose of seeking to resolve problems that are barriers to agreement.[4]

527

This definition stresses three elements of negotiation:

■ it involves communication – that is, the exchange of information

■ it takes place in a context in which the participants use their comparative competitive advantages and the perceived needs of the other party to influence the outcome of the negotiation process

■ each participant has implicit as well as explicit objectives that determine the negotiating strategies – a seller will explicitly wish to obtain the best price, for example, but, implicitly, will be seeking a contribution to fixed overheads and endeavouring to keep the plant and workforce employed.

Identifying aspects for negotiation

It is essential that quotations and tenders are professionally evaluated to identify those aspects which are unacceptable because of the seller's stance, and/or where there has been a non-compliant offer. The procurement specialist will be able to identify those aspects which can be accepted without further discussion and those areas where the attendant risk is unacceptable and where negotiation is a desirable business approach.

It is impossible to be prescriptive regarding everything that may be negotiable but it is possible to predict those aspects which would typically require negotiation effort:

■ obtain compliance with the specification

■ delivery milestones, completion dates and consequences of failure to meet them

■ financial safeguards, e.g. bank guarantees, performance bonds, and parent company guarantees

■ pricing of products and services, disclosure of data

■ long-term product support, e.g. releases of software and period of supportability

■ product guarantee conditions, e.g. repair/replace, then extension to guarantee?

■ compliance with statutory regulations, e.g. health and safety at work

■ pricing of non-recurring costs, e.g. tooling and software source code development

■ seller's requests for enhanced payment terms including advance payments

■ seller's exclusion clause proposals

■ insurance requirements, e.g. values and whether 'per claim' or 'in the aggregate'

■ termination clauses and consequences for both parties

■ price review mechanisms on long-term contracts, e.g. indexation

■ redetermination of prices for increased quantities

■ discount and/or rebate structures

■ use of licenses for computer software and payment, e.g. a site licence or user numbers

■ hourly rate composition and charges for weekends

■ *force majeure* – what is included

■ rights to intellectual property in design, copyright, etc.

■ use of sub-contractors and flow down of contract conditions

■ charges for commissioning, e.g. IT software

■ arbitration mediation and dispute resolution rights under contract

- jurisdiction
- mobilisation charges on major projects
- liquidated or unliquidated damages.

Note – these are broad headings only and would require a significant amount of planning to ensure that the detail is dealt with in ensuing negotiations.

15.1 Approaches to negotiation

Approaches to negotiation may be classified as adversarial or collaborative:

- *adversarial negotiation* – also termed *distributive* or *win–lose negotiation* – is an approach in which the focus is on 'positions' staked out by the participants, the assumption being that every time one party wins, the other loses, so, as a result, the other party is regarded as an adversary
- *collaborative negotiation* – also called *integrative* or *win–win negotiation* – is an approach in which the assumption is that, by means of creative problem-solving, one or both parties can gain without the other having to lose and, as the other party is regarded as a collaborator rather than an adversary, the participants may be more willing to share concerns, ideas and expectations than would otherwise be the case.

The characteristics of adversarial and collaborative negotiation are summarised in Table 15.1.

15.1.1 An evaluation of adversarial and collaborative strategies

Adversarial strategies may, on occasion, be appropriate in the following situations:

- where there is no ongoing relationship or the potential for one exists or it is desired – the deal is a one-off
- a quick, simple solution to a disagreement is required.

Collaborative strategies, while more time-consuming and difficult to achieve, have the following advantages:

- they are more stable and lead to long-term relationships and creative solutions to mutual problems
- they may also be the only way to obtain agreements when both parties to a negotiation have high aspirations and resist making concessions on these issues.

15.1.2 Transforming adversarial attitudes

Fisher and Ury[5] suggest five tactics designed to transform an adversarial into a collaborative approach. These approaches are discussed in section 15.10.

15.2 The content of negotiation

In any negotiation, two types of goals should receive consideration. These may be referred to as *substance goals* and *relationship goals*.

Table 15.1 Adversarial and collaborative negotiation contrasted

Adversarial negotiation	Collaborative negotiation
■ The emphasis is on competing to attain goals at the adversary's expenses	■ The emphasis is on ascertaining goals held in common with the other party
■ Strategy is based on secrecy, retention of information and low level of trust in the perceived adversary	■ Strategy is based on openness, sharing of information and high level of trust in the perceived partner
■ The desired outcomes of the negotiations are often misrepresented so that the adversary does not know what the opponent really requires the outcome of the negotiation to be. There is little concern for or empathy with the other party	■ The desired outcomes of the negotiation are made known so that there are no hidden agendas and issues are clearly understood. Each party is concerned for and has empathy with the other
■ Strategies are unpredictable, based on various negotiating ploys designed to outmanoeuvre or 'throw' the other	■ Strategies are predictable. Whilst flexible, such strategies are aimed at reaching an agreement acceptable to the other party
■ Parties use threats, bluffs and ultimatums with the aim of keeping the adversary on the defensive	■ Parties refrain from threats and so on, which are seen as counterproductive to the rational solution of perceived problems
■ There is an inflexible adherence to a fixed position that may be defended by both rational and irrational arguments. Primarily, the approach is destructive	■ The need for flexibility in the positions taken is assumed. The emphasis is on the use of imaginative, creative, logical ideas and approaches to a constructive resolution of differences
■ The approach is essentially hostile and aggressive – 'us against them.' This antagonism may be enhanced in team negotiations where members of the team may seek to outdo their colleagues in displaying macho attitudes	■ The approach is essentially friendly and non-aggressive, 'We are in this together'. This involves downplaying hostility and giving credit to constructive contributions made by either party to the negotiations
■ The unhealthy extreme of an adversarial approach is reached when it is assumed that movement towards one's own goal is facilitated by blocking measures that prevent the other party from attaining the goal	■ The healthy extreme of the partnership approach is reached when it is assumed that whatever is good for the other party to the negotiation is necessarily good for both
■ The key attitude is that of: 'We win, you lose'	■ The key attitude is, 'How can the respective goals of each party be achieved so that both win?'
■ If an impasse occurs, the negotiation may be broken off	■ If an impasse occurs, this is regarded as a further problem to be solved, possibly by the intervention of higher management or an internal or external mediator or arbitrator

15.2.1 Substance goals

Substance goals are concerned with the content issues of the negotiation. The possible content issues are legion and depend on the requirements relating to a situation. Most negotiations will be about high-value/usage items – that is, the 15–20 per cent of items that constitutes the major portion of inventory investment. Negotiation also applies to non-standard items, although a large user will seek, if possible, to negotiate preferential terms for standard supplies. Most negotiation topics affect price (and cost), either directly or indirectly. There are numerous ways in which content issues can be grouped,

Figure 15.1 **The price content of negotiation – some issues**

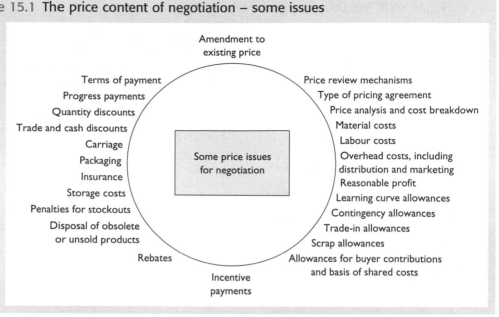

Figure 15.2 **The contractual content of negotiation – some issues**

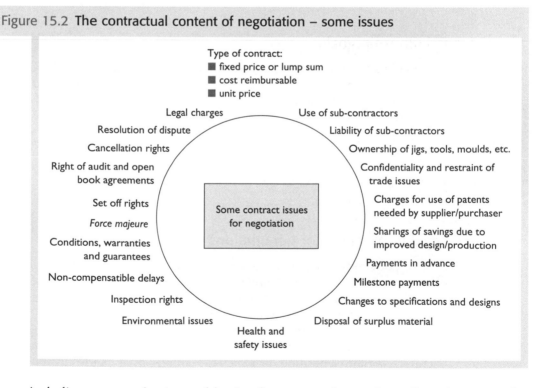

including overseas buying and buying for construction projects. Groupings may also relate to products, such as IT or commodities. Three typical groupings – shown in Figures 15.1, 15.2 and 15.3 respectively – relate to price, contractual and delivery issues in negotiation. The issues listed are in no way exhaustive and the lists often overlap.

Figure 15.3 The delivery content of negotiation – some issues

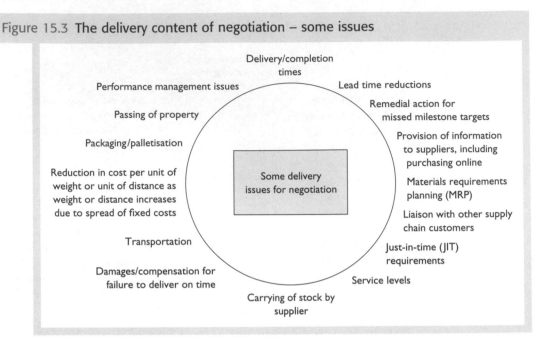

15.2.2 Relationship goals

Relationship goals are concerned with outcomes relating to how well those involved in the negotiations are able to work together once the process is completed and how well their respective organisations or 'constituencies' may work together. Some areas for relationship goals include:

- partnering sourcing
- preferred supplier status
- supplier involvement in design, development and value analysis
- sharing of technology.

15.2.3 Legal implications of negotiations

Some negotiations focus on a single issue, while others are complex with multi-issue discussions taking place. It is quite usual for legal specialists to become engaged in complex negotiations and buyers need to be aware of the legal implications of actions taken during and subsequent to negotiations.

If we assume that an offer has been made by the supplier, either through a quotation or tender, then any attempt to negotiate will amount, in law, to a counter-offer. This puts the seller into a position, by which the counter-offer can be accepted in full, or it can be rejected, or the seller may make a counter-offer. This is simply following the legal rules of formation of a contract through the rules of offer and acceptance.

The buyer must also be aware that the moment the seller's offer is challenged and any term(s) rejected this gives the seller the right to withdraw their bid. That is unlikely to happen except in extreme circumstances, but it could!

The Misrepresentation Act 1967 is relevant to negotiations. This states that where a person has entered into a contract after a misrepresentation has been made to him, and – (a) the misrepresentation has become a term of the contract; or (b) the contract has been performed; or both, then, if otherwise he would be entitled to rescind the contract without alleging fraud, he shall be so entitled, subject to the provisions of this Act, notwithstanding the matters mentioned in paragraphs (a) and (b) of Section 2 of the Act.

The inclusion of this reference is to emphasise the need to make contemporaneous notes of negotiations for future reference. Key words and phrases used in the negotiations should be noted and kept as part of the audit trail.

15.3 Factors in negotiation

Three important factors in negotiation are the negotiators, the negotiating situation and time.

15.3.1 The negotiators

In negotiations, buyers and sales people are individuals usually acting as representatives of their respective organisations. Their behaviour in negotiations will be influenced partly by their personalities and partly by their roles as representatives, influenced by their organisational culture.

Personality
This may be defined as:[6]

> The relatively enduring and stable patterns of behaving, thinking and feeling which characterise an individual.

It should be recognised, however, that there is no universal agreement about the meaning of personality because behavioural scientists define the term from different perspectives. In the present context, it can be loosely considered to mean 'how people affect others and how they understand and view themselves.' How people affect others depends primarily on:

- their external appearance – height, facial features, colour and physical aspects
- their behaviour – vulgar, aggressive, friendly, courteous and so on.

Studies have shown that personality variables, such as authoritarianism, anxiety, dogmatism, risk avoidance, self-esteem and suspiciousness, affect the degree of cooperation or competitiveness present in a negotiating situation. The implementation of negotiating strategies may be affected by personality factors and, equally, the mix of personality characteristics of the participants may determine the outcome of negotiations.

Transactional analysis, developed by Eric Berne in the 1950s, has considerable relevance to the understanding of negotiating behaviour. A 'transaction' is the unit of social interaction: 'If two or more people encounter each other . . . sooner or later one of them will speak, or give some other indication of acknowledging the presence of others.' This is called the *transactional stimulus*. Another person will then say or do something that is in some way related to the stimulus and that is called the *transactional response*.

Transactions tend to proceed in chains, so that each response is in turn a stimulus. Transactional analysis is based on the concept that people respond to each other in terms of three ego states – namely Parent, Adult and Child – or frames of mind, which lead to certain types of behaviour. It is impractical to fully describe transactional analysis in this book. Readers should refer to Eric Berne's book *Games People Play*[7] or the later account by T. Harris, *I'm OK – You're OK*.[8]

Negotiators as representatives

In negotiations, it is important for participants to know the extent of their authority to commit the organisations that they are representing as such authority prescribes their options and responsibility for the outcome of the negotiations.

The degree of authority may range from that of an emissary, commissioned to present, without variation, a position determined by his or her superiors to that of a free agent. The buyer must establish at the outset of negotiations that the person(s) who represent(s) the seller do have the authority to commit their organisation on technical, legal, financial issues and commercial. This authority is not necessarily related to job titles. It could be that a person with the title of Key Account Executive has no authority to negotiate all or any aspects of a deal. If it is established that the person has no authority the negotiation should not continue, otherwise the buyer will reveal his position, leaving nothing available in tactical terms, when, and if, the negotiations continue. There must be no embarrassment in asking if the negotiators have the appropriate authority.

There is evidence that the fewer constraints imposed on a negotiator, the greater will be the scope for his or her personal characteristics, such as knowledge, experience and personality to influence the negotiation process. Five sets of conditions prevent negotiators from responding spontaneously to their opposite number when:

- they have little latitude in determining either their positions or posture
- they are held responsible for their performance
- a negotiator has sole responsibility for the outcome of negotiations
- negotiators are responsible to a constituency that is present in the negotiations
- they are appointed rather than elected.

In the above situations, the behaviour of negotiators will be constrained by their obligations. The more complicated and open-ended the negotiations, the greater should be the status of the negotiators.

15.3.2 The negotiating situation

This relates to the strengths and weakness of the participants in the negotiation. The factors identified by Porter as affecting the relative strengths of supplier and buyer groups are outlined in Chapter 2 (see Figure 2.6). There are a number of factors that will impact upon the buyer's ability to negotiate, including:

- knowledge of the supply market and available competition
- technical and other data of the product or service being purchased
- intelligence on supplier's finances, organisation, production capability, etc.
- professional knowledge of buying and interface subjects

- perceived status of buying power
- use of appropriate negotiation skills, including comprehensive planning
- courage of convictions and persistence with demands
- ability to deal with long-term issues and to see the 'big picture'
- ability to handle time constraints imposed by others
- knowledge of past negotiations with seller, their behavioural pattern and concession pattern
- confidence in own ability to negotiate and to create an effective team.

In any negotiating situation, it is important to consider how to manage the process and influence the outcome. Having done so, there must be a concentration on the limited number of methods that can be used to influence others. There is a restricted choice (see Ashcroft, S. G., 'Commercial Negotiation Skills'[9]) although more than one is likely to arise in a specific negotiation. The ability is recognising which one, and why it is being deployed.

Adversarial – power and coercion

This is potentially the most dangerous form of negotiation and is likely to be destructive. Power is never one sided and therefore the person using power invites a like response. Unquestionably there may be short-term gains for one party but in the longer term it will not foster positive relationships between buyer and seller. Each side may have the upper hand when power is available to them but when market forces change, e.g. when demand exceeds supply the buyer who has used power may find supplies impossible to obtain. The large buyer who uses power to drive prices down to uneconomic levels may find the seller withdrawing from the market. The unsophisticated use of power can often be attributed to buyers with outsize egos who lack the finesse to act differently.

Attitude change involving emotion

Negotiations based purely on emotion require little investigative effort. The success of this approach is largely dependent upon the gullibility, inexperience and weakness of the seller. The experienced negotiator can readily counter such an approach on the basis of hard facts. The unprepared buyer will not be in a position to refute the detailed counter attack. Requests based on emotion are easily spotted because they will often be prefixed by anguished pleas such as 'surely you can . . .' and 'we will all be in trouble if you can't . . .' and 'my boss will make me redundant if you don't agree . . .'. There are occasions when emotion may have a place in the negotiation, but it is not the ideal approach.

There are a number of negotiators who adopt a two-person approach, the hard and soft negotiators to play on emotions. This is potentially a foolish tactic which can be spotted from afar by an experienced negotiator. When faced with this tactic the other party's confidence will be boosted on the basis that if this is the quality of the case it lacks substance. The negotiator who has a sound case should not need to resort to such shallow tactics.

Search for middle ground compromise

It is necessary, in all negotiations, to set targets for outcomes. Such targets may be derived from knowledge, pure emotion or brinkmanship. Once a target has been made known in a negotiation it must be persevered with until the judgement is that it cannot be achieved. At that point, the next demand must be tested at a level close to the original, otherwise the first lacks credibility. The buyer who persistently asks for 10 per cent off the price and will settle at 5 per cent is an amateur negotiator. If the negotiator offers in one move to 'split the difference' this should be viewed as a weakness and/or lack of planning.

The negotiator who hears expressions such as 'lets split the difference . . .' or 'meet me half way . . .' should be mindful of what is happening and should refuse such movements in the original position. Concessions may have to be made but it is their scale and timing which require careful thought in the heat of a negotiation.

Trading mutually advantageous concessions

The ability to trade concessions is the hallmark of a professional negotiator. The sales representative is trained to 'trade concessions, never give them away'. The buyer must carefully prepare what can be traded and must put a value on those factors. That value must be the value to the other party, not the cost to the buyer. The value to the other party may have an enhanced value. The buyer must get accustomed to making proposals for action in which demands are put on the table. The seller may offer one concession, say a slight reduction in price, providing the buyer agrees to enhanced payment terms and takes a greater quantity. At all times when concessions are being made or accepted a value must be placed upon them.

Logical persuasion

This tactic requires sophisticated purchase research because it depends entirely on detailed, factual knowledge. The buyer who seeks concessions on quotations and tenders through the use of logical persuasion will typically have available:

- comprehensive market knowledge
- a wide range of quotations/tenders
- economic analysis
- product knowledge
- raw material sources and prices
- product or service cost analysis
- supplier financial data
- supplier activity/capacity data.

A skilled negotiator with this extent of knowledge is a formidable opponent. Whatever is said by the other party, the facts opposing that view can be assembled and put forward in a non-emotive manner and a response sought. The remorseless tabling of demands, supported by accurate knowledge will have a positive, conditioning effect. It will also engender confidence and make the other party realise that the particular negotiation can be conducted in a spirit of factual exchange of information. This is the basis for sensible negotiations, leading to contractual agreements which have a high chance of being honoured.

Genuine business objectives

This method of negotiation demands integrity on both sides and accurate exchange of confidential information. It has as its base, a genuine desire to form long-term trading relationships. It is not the usual type of negotiation which ensues between buyer and seller where each party is 'keeping something up their sleeves'. This is usually evidenced at a late stage in negotiation when one party says, 'let's put all our cards on the table'. The obvious implication being that up to that point something was being withheld, hardly inspiring trust.

If this style of negotiation is to be pursued it does require an opening statement from the buyer which is quickly supported by action which demonstrates goodwill. When this is reciprocated by the seller the negotiations should then continue with a positive psychology. It is important however, not to put all your 'cards on the table' until the seller has demonstrated their reciprocal goodwill. The creation of trust is a challenge.

15.3.3 The impact of time on negotiations

Time is a vital consideration when planning negotiations. Procurement specialists must ensure there is an appropriate context to:

- Convince all those engaged in a procurement process that sufficient time must be provided to facilitate (if necessary) complex and prolonged negotiations.
- Prevent the other party engaging in procrastination and delaying tactics to put the buyer against a deadline and thereby preventing negotiation on difficult issues.
- Ensure that when negotiating overseas the buyer allows sufficient time to make return travel arrangements only when the objectives have been achieved.
- Ensure that the planned agenda is timed by topic, allowing sufficient time for active debate, review of positions and, for example, reworking cost models or redrafting contract clauses.
- Allow for respective decision making at executive level. It is not unusual for the outcome of negotiation to have to be approved at a senior level. In the public sector this could add at least a month to the procurement process.
- Prepare for the intervention of specialist advisers in a negotiation process, particularly lawyers, who are not noted for timely and speedy responses.

15.3.4 Influential factors

McCall and Norrington[10] have modelled the relationship between the behavioural predispositions of the negotiators and other factors influencing negotiation outcomes. This model is shown in Figure 15.4.

15.4 The negotiation process

Some negotiations concern a single issue and are relatively straightforward. A simple example is that of a product priced at, say, £9.70 each, when the buyer's objective is to purchase it at a price of, say, £8.30. All other aspects of the transaction may be agreed and it is the buyer's task to negotiate the lower price.

As shown by Figures 15.1, 15.2 and 15.3, other negotiations can be far more complicated and give rise to a multiplicity of issues relating to price, cost, contracts and delivery. Whether simple or complicated, however, the negotiation process will involve three phases: pre-negotiation, the actual negotiation and post negotiation.

Figure 15.4 Factors influencing negotiations and their outcomes

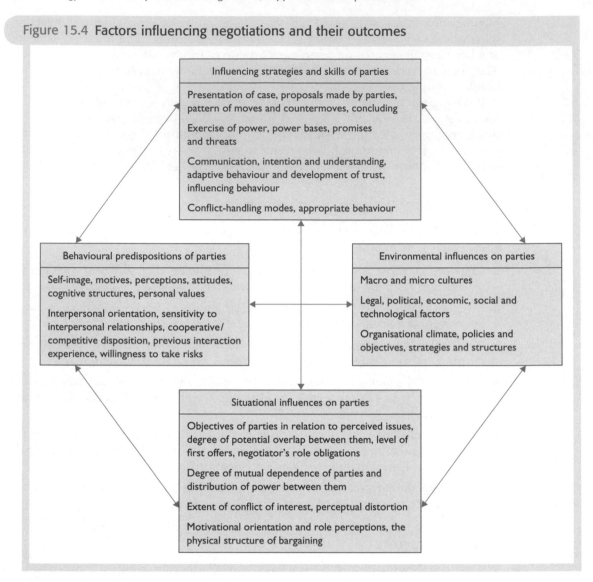

15.5 Pre-negotiation

'Cases are won in chambers' is the guiding principle in pre-negotiation – that is, legal victories are often the outcome of the preceding research and planning of strategy on the part of counsel. Buyers can learn much by studying the strategies and tactics of legal, diplomatic and industrial relations and applying them to the purchasing field. The skilled negotiator will pay equal attention to all phases of negotiation which impact on the outcome. The early stages of negotiation, will, of course, be very important. The matters to be considered at the pre-negotiation stage include:

- who is to negotiate
- the venue
- intelligence gathering

- negotiation objectives
- strategy and tactics
- rehearsal.

15.5.1 Negotiating agenda

It is inconceivable that serious negotiations could be conducted without an agenda. The agenda serves many purposes, including, it:

- instills discipline into the planning process
- establishes the content of the specific negotiation meeting
- establishes the order in which points will be raised
- assists in control of the meeting
- demonstrates a professional approach
- conditions the attitude and response of the other party
- demands attention to time management
- assists in the clarity of roles when in a team negotiation.

Agendas can be overt and circulated in advance. They can also be covert and used as an aide-mémoire. In the latter situation it has the advantage of not displaying the potential scope of the negotiation. Each party will have their different perceptions, intended structures and objectives for a negotiation. The process must seek to accommodate both; otherwise it runs the risk of being unproductive.

When planning the agenda, the following checklist is relevant:

- Identify the range of subjects to be dealt with.
- Consider the sequence in which subjects will be raised.
- Predict the other party's likely subjects.
- Decide the starting and finishing time (the latter may not be disclosed).
- Predict the possible time each subject will take.
- Plan for breakout sessions.
- Decide who will chair the negotiation (lead negotiator role).
- Decide the specific roles of team members.
- If flexibility is required, how will this be accommodated?
- Do not forget the need to make notes and summarise agreements.
- Permit time at the end for other subjects to be raised.
- Agree the next actions and who is accountable for them.

15.5.2 Who is to negotiate?

Negotiations can be between individual representatives or teams representing the buying and selling organisations respectively.

The *individual* approach

When negotiations are to be between two individuals, both should normally have sufficient status to settle unconditionally without having to refer back to a higher authority other than in exceptional circumstances. The other party's authority must be established. If it emerges that they have no negotiation authority the meeting should be terminated, unless key information can be obtained which will later help the buyer.

The majority of rebuy and modified rebuy negotiations are conducted on an interpersonal basis. The challenge for the individual undertaking negotiation is the ability to ask a question, note or document the response and prepare to ask the next question. This is a demanding task.

The *team* approach

For complex negotiations, where, for example, technical, legal, financial and other issues are involved or for new buy or capital purchases, a team approach is preferred. An individual buyer is rarely capable to act as sole negotiator in such situations.

In team negotiations it is important to:

- *allocate roles* – typical 'players' include:
  - the *spokesperson*, who actually presents the case and acts as captain of the team in terms of deciding how to respond to the situations arising in the course of the negotiation
  - the *recorder*, who takes notes of the negotiation
  - the *experts*, such as management accountants, engineers or other technical design or production staff, legal advisers, who provide back-up for the spokesperson – it is not essential for every member of the team to speak during negotiations in order to make a useful contribution to the negotiation
- *avoid disagreement* – there should be no outward disagreement between team members while negotiations are in progress, so any differences should be resolved in private sessions, but the desirability of devising a code of signals, enabling team members to communicate imperceptibly during negotiations, should be considered to avoid having to wait to make a decision.

There are drawbacks to team negotiation. These include:

- *the tendency for groupthink*, that is, for team members to hold illusions of group invulnerability, stereotyped perceptions of perceived opponents and unquestioning belief in group morality
- *the emphasis on win–win* (Cox, A.[11]) is, unless modified by the spokesperson, greater in team negotiations as team members may wish to demonstrate their 'toughness', inflexibility and ability to demolish rather than consider the merits of proposals made by the other side, so the importance of the role of spokesperson on each side in setting the 'tone' of the negotiations cannot be overemphasised.

15.5.3 The venue

Buyers, traditionally expect the seller to attend the buyer's premises. Both parties are comfortable with this arrangement and that may be advantageous. Two other potential locations of the negotiation are the seller's site or a neutral third-party location such as a conference centre. The buyer may learn more about the seller and his operation by visiting his site. It is a tactic worth considering, mindful of time constraints. A neutral location may be appropriate for longer, complex negotiations particularly where the ethos of partnering is being explored – neither party would be on 'home turf'.

15.5.4 Gathering intelligence

This normally involves:

- ascertaining the strengths and weaknesses of the respective negotiating positions
- assembling relevant data relating to costs, production, sales and so on
- preparing data that is to be presented at the negotiation in the form of graphs, charts, tables and so on so that it can be quickly assimilated.

Three important negotiation tools are:

1 price and cost analysis (see section 12.5)
2 situational analysis (see section 15.9)
3 value analysis (see section 9.11.3).

15.5.5 Determining objectives

The buyer's objectives must have been determined for the negotiation. They should also empathise with the likely objectives of other parties to the negotiation. Pena-Mora and Tamaki,[12] in a study of collaborative negotiations for large-scale infrastructure projects, draw attention to the different interests of owners/users, designers/engineers and contractors/suppliers. These differing interests are shown in Figure 15.5.

Figure 15.5 Varying interests of participants in negotiations relating to design and construction projects

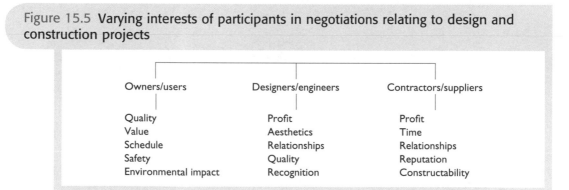

Source: Adapted from Pena-Mora and Tamaki[12]

Players in a negotiation process will have both cooperative and competitive characteristics. Sensitivity to the goals of other players by all participants will set the tone of negotiations and contribute to planned outcomes, including win-win. A model of bargaining applicable to negotiations relating to purchasing issues is shown in Figure 15.6. Thus, assuming that the negotiation relates to a pricing issue:

- axis A–B represents the range of positions that the negotiators could take
- IS_B represents the buyer's ideal settlement – the most favourable price that can, realistically, be achieved in negotiation – that is, £5
- IS_V represents the vendor's ideal settlement which is £13.

(*Note:* In most cases, IS will represent the starting position of each of the negotiators, subject, of course, to the fact that, if there is to be negotiation, the initial demands must not be too far apart to preclude bargaining.)

Figure 15.6 **A model of bargaining in a purchasing context**

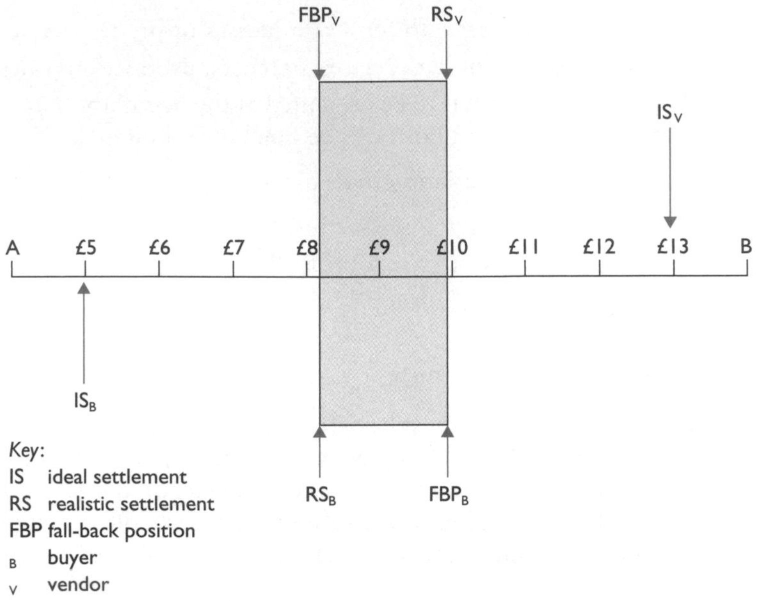

- RS_B is the buyer's realistic settlement – here, about £8 – or that point of settlement fully justified by bargaining power that would be reached with reasonable skill in negotiation and no adverse, unforeseen circumstances
- RS_V is the vendor's realistic settlement – around £10
- FBP_B is the buyer's fall-back position – around £10 – or the price beyond which they will not go; after this point, they break off negotiations or seek alternative means of meeting their requirements
- FBP_V is the vendor's fall-back position – around £8
- the shaded portion represents the area of settlement and this model is based on the convention that each side will normally be prepared to move from their original positions, so the negotiated price will typically be between £8 and £10, depending on the skills of the negotiators and assuming that the bargaining positions are approximately equal.

Before commencing negotiations, the buyer should have a clear mandate from his or her superiors to settle at any point not exceeding an agreed fall-back position. It is important to stress the importance of determining in advance what a *good* agreement is. Too often, negotiators consider that their goal is to arrive at *an* agreement or even *any* agreement. They should therefore determine what is their own and what is likely to be the other side's BATNA. A BATNA is the 'best alternative to a negotiated agreement' – a concept introduced by Fisher and Ury.[13]

While BATNAs and fall-back or reserve positions are similar in many respects, they are not the same. For example, if you are trying to outsource your catering function, the BATNA may be to continue to provide this facility in-house.

15.5.6 Strategy and tactics

Strategy is the overall plan that aims to achieve, as nearly as possible, the objectives of the negotiation as seen from the perspective of each participant. A *tactic* is a position, manoeuvre or attitude to be taken or adopted at an appropriate point in the negotiation process. Among the tactics to be decided are the following:

- The order in which the issues to be negotiated shall be dealt with.
- Whether to speak first or allow the other side to open the negotiations. Galinsky[14] states that 'substantial psychological research suggests that, more often than not, negotiators who make first offers come out ahead' and suggests that 'making a first offer is related to one's confidence and sense of control at the bargaining table.' The same writer, however, suggests that making the first offer may not be advantageous when the other side has much more information about the item to be negotiated or the relevant market or industry than they do. This situation can be remedied by information gathering prior to the negotiation so that a more level playing field is achieved.
- Whether to build in recesses for discussion. Recesses may cause a negotiation to lose its momentum. Conversely, recesses provide opportunities for reflection on the negotiation so far, for devising new or alternative proposals and sometimes for 'cooling down' and face-saving.
- What concessions to make should the need arise? Some writers suggest that negotiators should only make concessions in return for trade-offs – that is, they should seek to get something in return for everything they concede.
- The timing of concessions.
- What issues can be linked, such as price and quality.
- What the other party's likely reaction will be to each tactic you're thinking of using.
- What tactics the opponent is likely to adopt and how these can be countered.

15.5.7 Rehearsal

Before an important negotiation, it is advisable to subject all arguments, tactics and overall strategies to critical scrutiny. The negotiator will have prepared and indeed may have rehearsed the 'opening speech' which will be made when the negotiation opens. This is a crucial conditioning statement and should include clarity of the benefits of the contract on offer, the fact that the seller must deal with each point as requested and a summary of the contract and its intended operation. The negotiator must prepare and create an environment within which the negotiation will take place. It is possible to create a hostile or relaxed atmosphere, and either party may influence this by actions and words.

15.6 The actual negotiation

15.6.1 Stages

Even with a philosophy of collaborative negotiation, the activities of the participants will change at each stage of the negotiation process. These activities alternate between competition and cooperation. It is useful for a negotiator to recognise this pattern of interaction and the stage that has been reached in a particular negotiation. At this time the following points will be relevant:

- Recap, from time to time, on points that have been agreed and make an appropriate record.
- If there has been a time lapse between negotiations, the negotiator must make a resume of action points outstanding from the last meeting. If information has not been generated by the other side as agreed, that must be sought, ideally prior to the meeting.
- The negotiator must ensure that there has been no major change in the other party's circumstances since the last meeting. This will require some due diligence and research.
- If the other party tables new information, or retracts previously agreed points, a recess must be called to evaluate the new position but only when the detail is understood.
- If any costs or prices change the buyer must check the new calculations. The seller's interpretation must not be accepted without checking and confirming
- Take the initiative by making proposals for the other side to consider. If the seller takes the initiative be mindful that it has happened and make counter demands.
- Whenever the buyer makes a concession its value to the other party must be calculated. It should be noted that the value to the other party is not necessarily the cost to the buyer.
- Try to link previously unconnected points. If the seller seeks a contractual concession, the buyer should look for the corresponding price change.
- Know your walk-away point, where you are prepared for the negotiations to cease. This cannot be a bluff!
- If the negotiation is failing with the seller's negotiators, it may be necessary to request a change in personnel to make progress. This can be done by escalating the negotiations to a higher level in the sellers' business.
- Control your emotions at all times. If a negotiation becomes personal there is a danger that there will be a lack of focus.
- Try to recognise when the seller is bluffing and entering into brinkmanship.
- Acknowledge positively concessions made and allow a loss of face. This behaviour may motivate more concessions.
- Be mindful of unwittingly creating contractual agreement.

The stages that occur during negotiation are indicated in Figure 15.7.

15.6.2 Techniques

Specialist books of negotiation usually list a number of techniques available to negotiators. It is not possible to detail these in this book, although a more detailed description of Fisher and Ury's approach is given in section 15.10. Some general findings include the following:

- In framing an agenda, ensure that the more difficult issues appear later, thus enabling some agreement to be reached early in the negotiation on less controversial matters, smoothing the way to agreement on less straightforward points.

Figure 15.7 **The stages in the negotiating process**

Introductions, agreement of an agenda and rules of procedure

Ascertaining the 'negotiating range'
This means the issues that the negotiation will attempt to resolve
With *adversarial* negotiations, this may be a lengthy stage as the
participants often overstate their opening positions
With *collaborative* negotiations, 'openness saves time'

*Agreement of common goals that must be achieved if the negotiation is to reach
a successful outcome*
This will usually require some movement on both sides from the original
negotiating range, but the movement will be less or unnecessary in
partnership negotiations

*Identification of and, when possible, removal of barriers that prevent
attainment of agreed common goals*
At this stage there will be:
- problem solving
- consideration of solutions put forward by each
- determination of what concessions can be made

It may also be useful to:
- review what has been agreed
- allow a recess for each side to reconsider its position and make
  proposals or concessions that may enable further progress to be made
If no progress can be made, it may be decided to:
- refer the issues back to higher management
- change the negotiators
- abandon the negotiations with the least possible damage to relationships

Agreement and closure
Drafting of a statement setting out as clearly as possible the agreement(s)
reached and circulating it to all parties for comment and signature

- Questions are a means of both eliciting information and keeping pressure on an opponent and can also be used to control the pattern and progress of the negotiation.

- Concessions are a means of securing movement when negotiations are deadlocked. Research findings show that 'losers' tend to make the first concession and that each concession tends to raise the aspirational level of the opponent, so buyers should avoid a 'pattern of concession' in which they are forced to concede more and more. The convention is that concessions should be reciprocated. While flexibility is essential, there is no compulsion to make a counter-concession and the aim should be to concede less than has been obtained. The outcome tends to be more favourable when the concessions made are small rather than large. An experienced negotiator will often 'throw a sprat to catch a mackerel.'

- Negotiation is between people, so it is essential to be able to weigh up the personalities of one's opponents and the drivers that motivate them, such as achievement, fear and similar factors.

15.6.3 Deadlocked negotiations

Negotiations sometimes come to an impasse when both sides see no prospect of further movement or concessions. Techniques for resolving such deadlock include those suggested by Fisher and Ury's concept of principled negotiation (see section 15.10).

Other approaches to such situations include:

- taking a break for each party to refocus
- lightening the atmosphere by the use of humour
- breaking down an issue into sub-issues
- agreeing to 'agree in principle' – if the parties agree in principle, they also agree on objectives
- considering the consequences of non-agreement for the parties concerned
- obtaining third-party assistance as they can listen objectively to arguments, clarify issues and, where required, adjudicate.

The degree of third-party involvement can vary. Susskind and Cruikshank[15] provide a useful model of this, expressing their involvement as lying along a continuum and depending on whether the final decision is made by the parties to the negotiation or an adjudicator. This model is shown in Figure 15.8.

Figure 15.8 The dispute resolution continuum

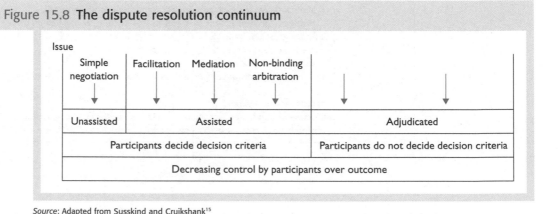

Source: Adapted from Susskind and Cruikshank[15]

Not every situation can be negotiated. For example, the decision of a contractor to refuse to work in situations that might put them in breach of Health and Safety Regulations or expose their employees to physical danger, such as from violent protests or terrorists, has to be accepted.

15.6.4 Negotiating behaviour

All negotiations involve interpersonal skills. The negotiating styles that are applicable vary according to the specific situation. Training in negotiation should, therefore, include training in behaviour analysis, which should lead to an understanding of the responses likely to be evoked by particular behaviour. For example, shouting usually causes the other person to shout back, while humour may diffuse a tense situation.

Table 15.2 Types of behaviour and likely responses to them

Types of behaviour	Likely response
Proposing behaviour Such as suggesting actions: 'Shall we look at sub-contracting?'	Usually elicits either development behaviour in the form of support or reasoned negative behaviour in the form of difficulty solving
Development behaviour Such as building on or supporting proposals made by others: 'Having decided to sub-contract, who shall we approach?'	Usually leads to further development behaviour or, perhaps, a question in return, asking for further explanation
Reasoned negative behaviour Such as disagreeing with others in a reasoned way, stating difficulties with their ideas: 'Price is likely to be a difficulty because their material costs don't attract our quantity discounts'	Tends to evoke similar negative behaviour in response, leading to a downward spiral in terms of communications and emotions. This spiral can be avoided by stating difficulties and identifying differences as reasonably as possible, perhaps by asking further questions
Emotional negative behaviour Such as attacking others, being critical, defending against attacks in the same way: 'Rubbish'	In general, attack begets either attack or defence. It can make resumption of constructive negotiation difficult
Clarifying behaviour Such as checking whether or not people understand, summarising previous discussion: 'As I see it, this is what we agreed'	Tends to lead to supportive development behaviour, although there can be disagreement
Seeking information behaviour Such as seeking facts, opinions, ideas: 'How much discount if we doubled the quantity?' 'What if . . .'	This almost always results in information being given. The certainty of response makes this a powerful shaping behaviour
Giving information behaviour Such as giving facts, opinions, ideas: 'We need to reach a decision today'	This is usually a response to other behaviour, especially seeking information. It is uncertain in its effect, as it depends largely on the content of the statement

Lee and Lawrence[16] have identified seven categories of behaviour, all of which may be encountered in negotiations (see Table 15.2).

15.6.5 Effects of behaviour on other parties

The main fact that the negotiator can learn from the generalisations given in Table 15.2 is that our outward behaviour must be arranged to have the desired effect on those with whom we are negotiating. The desired effect depends on the negotiator's goals. Thus, development behaviour is more likely than emotional disagreement to persuade the other party to accept our viewpoint. Providing and giving information is indispensable to influencing a group. Sometimes it is better to begin a negotiation by asking questions than giving information about the subject matter.

15.6.6 Ploys

A *ploy* is a manoeuvre in a negotiation aimed at achieving a particular result. This is a complex aspect of negotiation, requiring specific application to meet the needs of a particular negotiation. This section deals with some common issues.

1 Priority of demands

Having decided the range of demands there is a key decision to be made regarding which one shall be made first. It could be argued that demanding a rather simple concession which does not carry great financial burden will persuade the seller to make that concession, whereas if a large concession is sought first this will motivate resistance and, possible, intransigence. If there are absolute 'must haves' these should be raised first because if these cannot be agreed everything else is a relative waste of time.

2 Managing timescales

There will inevitably be situations where timescales are tight. The buyer must make a decision about the negotiation sequencing. In some circumstances it would be better to insist that once the negotiations have commenced they will continue until agreement is reached. If this is not the case then there will be a number of 'breaks' which can work against the buyer's interests by having the ending of 'quotation validity' as a closing pressure. In many negotiations it is better to finish negotiations in one go, even if this means spreading them over more than one day.

3 Use of jargon

Every profession has its jargon and sellers will use it to test the buyer's knowledge. It can also be used to undermine confidence. It is therefore a quite deliberate tactic. If jargon is used and the term is not known, clarification must be sought, although the more times this is done by the buyer the more credibility is being lost.

4 Use of figures

The seller's tactics may include a quite deliberate use of numbers to confuse the buyer. Whenever the numbers change the buyer must recalculate and work out their full impact on the contract value.

5 Handling objections

The seller will have prepared standard responses to buyer demands. These will come in the form of objections. The ideal counter from the buyer is a range of tactics which use logical persuasion as the basis for a request, where each demand can be explained in a business-like manner.

6 Use of silence

This will cause problems to the inexperienced negotiator. The skilled seller will, on receiving a demand which he does not wish to accept, fail to respond. The silence can be overwhelming and embarrassing. The danger is that the buyer will break the silence and change the subject. This relieves the seller of a responsibility to respond and weakens the buyer's case. The buyer must therefore maintain the discipline of silence.

Part of a negotiator's skill is being able to appraise people and situations quickly. Learn to discern the hidden meanings in the other person's words. Evaluate statements against what you know. Be patient and be aware of the 'pace' of the negotiation. Often a little stubbornness and conscious competence can yield high returns.

15.6.7 Planning points at concluding stage of negotiations

Depending upon the length of time the negotiations have been in progress, at this time the negotiator may be tired and in danger of lapses of concentration. This is a risk because it is precisely now, that concentration and evaluation facilities must be at their highest. The following points are relevant:

- Make sure that progress is related to the objectives that you set. Ensure that the buyer's resolve has not waned due to the seller's conditioning with such tactics as blocking and refusing to concede major points.
- Determine the financial implications of all actions and agreements reached.
- Summarise the total agreement and test this on the other side. If there is a disagreement of fundamental points they must be debated and resolved.
- Maintain pressure on the other party for remaining concessions that you require.
- Listen for attempts to 'close the sale' by the seller. This takes courage on their part and usually means they are confident that no more concessions are required.
- Be prepared to make additional demands if an opportunity presents itself, even if they had not been planned.
- When it is appropriate (this is a matter of judgement) make a statement of the buyer's final position.
- Explain the contract award process from that point onwards.
- Explain to the other party that all agreements and changes to quotations/tender documents must be evidenced in writing.
- Agree the basis of contract reporting and monitoring.
- File hard and electronic copy of notes of negotiations.
- Arrange for later debriefing of unsuccessful tenderers.
- Undertake a personal evaluation of opportunities lost, successes and mistakes made in the negotiation.
- List the benefits obtained and evaluate if they could apply to other buyers or sellers.

15.7 Post negotiation

This involves:

- drafting a statement detailing as clearly as possible the agreements reached and circulating it to all parties for comment and signature
- selling the agreement to the constituents of both parties – that is, what has been agreed, why it is the best possible agreement and what benefits will accrue
- implementing the agreements, such as planning contracts, setting up joint implementation teams performance review and continuous improvement events
- establishing procedures for monitoring the implementation of the agreements and dealing with any problems that may arise.

15.8 What is effective negotiation?

15.8.1 Characteristics

An effective negotiation may be said to have taken place when:

- substance issues are satisfactorily resolved – that is, an agreement has been reached that is satisfactory to all parties
- working relationships are preserved or even enhanced.

Fisher and Ury[17] have identified the following three criteria for an effective negotiation:

- the negotiation has produced a *wise agreement* – one that is satisfactory for both sides
- the negotiation is *efficient* – no more time-consuming or costly than necessary
- the negotiation is *harmonious* – fosters rather than inhibits good interpersonal relationships.

15.8.2 Negotiation post-mortems

Many organisations hold post negotiation meetings for the purpose of discussing:

- *negotiating strategies and tactics* – the extent to which they were satisfactory and how they might be improved
- *negotiating costs* – the number and duration of negotiating sessions and how these might be reduced
- *negotiating methods* – tools such as e-mail and video conferencing enable more rapid and frequent communication exchange, both of which are key components in the negotiation process
- *the whole procurement process prior to negotiation* – investing time and resources in optimising the process aspects, such as those identified at the introduction to this chapter will result in less necessity for negotiation.

15.9 Negotiation and relationships

15.9.1 Situational and institutional approaches

Ertel[18] states that only rarely do companies think about their negotiating activities as a whole:

> Rather they take a situational view, seeing each negotiation as a separate event, with its own goals, its own tactics and its own measures of success. That approach can produce good results in particular instances, but it can be counterproductive when viewed from a higher, more strategic plane. Hammering out advantageous terms in a procurement contract may torpedo an important long-term relationship with a supplier.

15.9.2 Changing from a situational to an institutional approach

Ertel, therefore, advocates treating negotiation as an institutional capability rather than a series of discrete events. He identifies four changes instituted by companies that had moved away from a situational view of negotiation to a corporate approach concerned with long-term relationships:

- *Creation of a company-wide negotiation infrastructure* – this implies that the outcome of a negotiation does not rely solely on the skill of an individual negotiator. Such negotiators can be supported by databases providing better information to negotiators, drawing lessons from past negotiations, guidance in strategy selection, examples of creative bargaining approaches and evaluation of outcomes. Such an infrastructure not only improves negotiating results but also breaks down the assumption that every negotiation is 'unique and immune to coordination and control.'

- *Broadening the measures used to evaluate the performance of negotiators beyond matters of cost and price:*

  To be judged successful, negotiators have to show, for example, that they explicitly discussed several creative alternatives, used objective criteria to choose among the alternatives and that the final deal fulfils not only the company's interests but the other parties' as well.

Such an approach forces negotiators to think more broadly and creatively about negotiations, both when strategies are initially established and as the bargaining develops.

- *Recognition of the distinction between deals and relationships* – too frequently, negotiators confuse the deal with the broader relationship. To improve a strained relationship, they may offer a price concession. To gain a price concession, they may threaten to terminate the relationship. Such approaches, however, are counterproductive in that they create an adversarial climate in which both parties withhold information to protect their bargaining positions, thereby creating enhanced suspicion, which may adversely affect both the present deal and long-term relationships. If there is a previously established climate of trust, in which the terms of a deal can be discussed without prejudice to long-term relationships, this facilitates the free exchange of information and enhanced creative and collaborative problem-solving, leading to more valuable deals and stronger trading relationships.

- *Understanding of when to walk away from a deal* – successful and unsuccessful negotiations are usually evaluated respectively in terms of deals completed or uncompleted. Completion of deals, however, usually involves concessions on the part of one or both parties that may be in the interests of neither. When, however, a deal is struck that is unattractive to the purchaser, seller or both, the possibility arises that less time and effort will be invested in working together and relationships will be strained. Companies should therefore encourage their negotiators to see their role not as producing *agreements* that may be mutually unsatisfactory, but, rather, as making good *choices*. Prior to meeting, the negotiators of each side should have established their respective BATNAs or the objective hurdles that any negotiated agreement has to clear. Neither should accept an agreement that is not at least as good as their BATNA. To do so is likely to have an adverse effect on relationships. Before concluding a deal, purchasers should consider whether or not a prospective supplier can possibly meet quality, delivery and other requirements, such as the price. If not, they should reject the deal and seek other supply sources. Negotiators should be made aware of the fact that, rather than arrive at a deal on the basis of concessions that would take the agreement below their BATNA, it is better to walk away. Ertel points out that not only do executives have to send the right messages internally, they also need to be aware of how external communications may affect negotiations and quotes the following example:

  In an interview published in a widely read magazine the CEO of a large computer company stated that when he was a sales representative he never lost a customer. . . . Imagine how the statement was interpreted by the company's sales force. The CEO was in effect telling the sales representatives that they could never say no and signalling customers that they held all the leverage. The negotiators' BATNAs were instantly rendered inconsequential with one public statement.

15.10 Negotiation ethics

Negotiation ethics is an aspect of the wider subject of purchasing ethics, considered in Chapter 17, and relationships, covered above. This topic is considered here because ethical perspectives largely determine whether or not a particular negotiation is adversarial or integrative.

Fisher and Ury[19] distinguish between positional and principled negotiation.

15.10.1 Positional negotiation

Positional negotiation views negotiation as an adversarial or conflict situation in which the other party is the enemy. It is based on four assumptions:

- we have the correct and only answer to a particular problem
- there is a 'fixed price'
- opposite positions equal opposite interests
- it is not our responsibility to solve the problems of the other party.

Positions and interests are closely related. Often negotiators will not move from a fixed position because of psychological pressures or needs. A leader of a negotiating team may refuse to consider alternatives for fear of losing face or being seen by team members as backing down.

Positional negotiation has at least two drawbacks:

- it is win–lose – it has only two ways to go, which are forwards to victory or backwards to defeat
- from an ethical standpoint, positional negotiation leads to such questionable tactics as:
  - misrepresentation of a position
  - bluffing (see section 17.10.3)
  - lying or deception
  - only providing selected information or being economical with the truth
  - threatening
  - manipulating.

15.10.2 Principled negotiation

Principled negotiation is fundamentally different from positional negotiation. The very term 'principled' has an ethical connotation. Fisher and Ury criticise positional negotiating on four grounds:

- *arguing about positions produces unwise agreements* – compromising, for example, involves both parties giving up something, so neither is completely satisfied with the outcome

- *arguing about positions is unwise* – time is wasted in trying to reconcile extreme positions
- *ongoing relationships are endangered* – anger and resentment result when one side sees itself as being forced to bend to the rigid will of the other
- *positional bargaining is worse when there are many partners* – it is harder to change group or constituency positions than those of individuals.

Fisher and Ury also see principled bargaining as an alternative to 'hard' or 'soft' bargaining. Soft bargainers may make concessions to cultivate or maintain relationships. Hard bargainers demand concessions as a condition of the relationship.

15.10.3 The Fisher and Ury principles

Apart from 'Don't bargain about positions', Fisher and Ury lay down four elements that parties must follow to obtain an ideal settlement:

1 Separate the people from the problem

This involves viewing the problem as the central issue to be resolved rather than regarding the other person as an adversary. Failure to do so can lead to antagonism between the parties. Fisher and Ury put forward 18 propositions under the 4 headings of perception, emotion, communication and prevention, of which the following are typical.

- *Perception*
  - put yourself in the other party's shoes
  - don't blame the other party for your problem
  - discuss each other's perceptions
  - look for opportunities to act inconsistently with their perceptions.
- *Emotion*
  - first, recognise and understand emotions – theirs and yours
  - allow the other side to let off steam
  - don't react to emotional outbursts.
- *Communication*
  - listen actively and acknowledge what is being said
  - speak about how you feel, not how you feel about them.
- *Prevention*
  - where possible, build pre-negotiation relationships that will enable parties to absorb the knocks incurred in the actual negotiation.

2 Focus on interests, not positions

Positions are symbolic representations of a participant's underlying interests. Each side has multiple needs. To find out about interests, ask 'Why?' and 'Why not?' questions.

3 Invent options for mutual gain

Again, Fisher and Ury classify their approaches under five headings – diagnosis, prescription, broadening options, searching for mutual gain and facilitating the other party's decisions.

■ *Diagnosis*

This includes avoiding:

– premature judgements

– searching for a single answer

– assuming a 'fixed price'.

■ *Prescription*

– separating inventing from deciding

– engaging in brainstorming, including brainstorming with the other party.

■ *Broadening options*

– look through the eyes of different experts

– invent agreements of different strengths, such as substantive versus procedural, permanent versus provisional and so on.

■ *Searching for mutual gain*

– identify shared interests

– dovetail differing interests.

■ *Facilitating the other party's decision*

– help the other party to sell a decision to his/her constituency

– look for precedents

– provide a range of options.

4 Insist on using objective criteria

This requires:

■ fair standards, such as objective criteria, including market value, professional or moral standards, legal criteria, custom and practice

■ fair procedures for resolving conflicting interests

■ reasoning and openness to reasoning

■ never yielding to pressure, only to principle.

15.10.4 Criticisms of principled negotiation

A number of criticisms have been made of principled negotiation, some of which Fisher and Ury recognise. Thus, where the other party has some negotiating advantage, they suggest that the answer is to improve your BATNA. The only reason we negotiate is to produce something better than the results we could obtain without negotiating. BATNAs offer protection against accepting terms that are too unfavourable and rejecting terms that it would be beneficial to accept.

Where the other party will not play or uses dirty tricks, the answer is to insist on principled negotiation in a way that is most acceptable to the competitor. Thus, principled negotiators might ask about the other party's concerns to show that they understand such concerns and ask the competitor to recognise all concerns.

Where the other party refuses to respond, two techniques to try are those of 'negotiation jujitsu', in which, instead of directly resisting the force of the other party, it is channelled into exploring interests, inventing options and searching for independent standards, and using outside intervention or mediation.

McCarthy[20] offers two main criticisms of the Fisher and Ury approach. The first is that it does not provide an adequate analysis of the role of power. The concept of negotiation jujitsu, for example, does not actually turn power back on the other party, but encourages both to ignore dirty tricks and minor power plays. McCarthy holds that the balance of power between the two parties is the key element in determining the limits of a mutually acceptable settlement and concludes 'in the area of collective bargaining at least I know of no set of maxims or principles that will enable any of us to escape from the limits set by a given power situation.'

McCarthy's second point is that Fisher and Ury assume rather than argue that the factors that make for effective negotiation in widely differing situations from domestic quarrels to international disputes are the same. There may be situations in which positional is preferable to principled negotiation.

15.10.5 Can negotiation be ethical?

Arguments that negotiation cannot be completely ethical include:

- it is commonly believed that success in negotiation is enhanced by the successful use of deceitful tactics, such as bluffing and outright misrepresentation

- negotiators have the responsibility of obtaining the best results for those they represent

- what is ethical is affected by cultural factors, such as bribery and deception that may be acceptable in some global negotiations, that 'When in Rome, do as the Romans do'

- self-interest is the most powerful of all motivations – few negotiations can be wholly altruistic

- ethical negotiation is an idealistic concept that does not work in practice

- sharing information may put a negotiator at a disadvantage.

Crampton and Dees[21] list a number of reasons for it being possible to gain from deceptive tactics:

- information asymmetry is great – the greater the information disparity between the two parties, the greater the opportunity one has for profitable deception

- verification of such details as long-term maintenance costs and performance is difficult

- the intention to deceive is difficult to establish – it is hard to distinguish it from a mistake or an oversight

- the parties have insufficient resources to adequately safeguard against deception

- interaction between the parties is infrequent – deception is more likely in one-off relationships

- ex-post redress is too costly – the deceived party may, however, prefer to make an effort, even when the costs exceed the expected compensation

- reputable information is unavailable, unreliable or very costly to communicate

- the circumstances are unusual in a way that limits inferences about future behaviour and deceptions are unlikely to damage future negotiations because they occur in distinctly different circumstances

- one party has little to lose (or much to gain) from deception – a negotiator may not be concerned about the prospect of being caught, providing that it does not occur before the deal has been closed.

Crampton and Dees state that they cannot recommend a single strategy that will work effectively to promote honesty in all negotiations, but they make the following suggestions:

- *Assess the situation* – this involves considering the incentives for deception. What incentives are there for suppressing or misrepresenting information? What is known about the principles of the other side? What is the competence and character of the other side?

- *Build mutual trust* – in most cases, the incentive for deception in negotiation is defensive. It arises from the fear that the other party will unfairly exploit any weakness. This also involves building mutual benevolence, creating opportunities for displaying trust and demonstrating trustworthiness.

- *Place the negotiation in a long-term context. Caveat emptor* is reasonable advice for negotiators. Select negotiating partners wisely, verify when you can, request bonds and warranties, get important claims in writing and, where applicable, such as in IT and outsourcing negotiations, it may be advisable to hire a skilled intermediary.

Ethical negotiation can only take place in a climate of trust. Ascertaining whether or not such a climate exists requires negotiators to answer two questions – 'Can the other party trust us?' and 'Can we trust them?' Each party can answer the first question with some certainty, although they should be aware of self-deception. Not until both sides have established a working relationship can a certain answer be given to the second question. In the interim, both sides should show diligence in obtaining information to provide assurance that the other party will negotiate ethically.

Case study

Negotiating the NTL Contract

For the past 18 months your company has been using NippiTransport Ltd (NTL) to make very urgent deliveries of important business documents to existing clients and potential new clients. The documents include, tenders for new work (a failure to deliver on time will result in exclusion from the tendering process), design drawings and highly confidential contractual documents. There is no contractual agreement in place, everything is verbal. NTL charge £1.50 per mile for delivery, plus a flat rate of £50 per delivery, plus VAT. The service from NTL has been excellent. Their managing director has now asked you, as head of procurement to sign his contract. He explains that he is requesting this 'to get his own house in order'. You have read the contract and three clauses cause you difficulty and, accordingly, you now intend to negotiate the detail with NTL. The relevant clauses read:

Clause 8

Limit of liability. Our liability shall be limited to the cost of delivery and we shall bear no responsibility for direct or indirect losses incurred by the customer as a result of our failure to meet our obligations.

Clause 11

Price. We reserve the right, at any time, to increase our price without prior notification to the customer.

Clause 14

Sub-contracting. We reserve the right to sub-contract any or all of the courier services without seeking customer's approval.

Tasks

1 Assuming you have a desire to negotiate in a positive manner, how would you initially respond to the NTL managing director?

2 Draft a response to Clauses 8, 11 and 14 based on your ideal wording for the clauses.

3 If the NTL managing director told you that he is not prepared to negotiate and you 'must take it or leave it', how would you respond?

4 What would be your BATNA?

Discussion questions

15.1 In a negotiation, each party knows that the other has some power to influence the outcome. What powers have:
   (a) trade unions and employers in a pay negotiation?
   (b) an international airline buying aviation fuel?
   (c) a monopoly seller and a customer in a price negotiation?

15.2 If you were asked to negotiate a contract to purchase IT software what would be your top five 'must haves' in terms of contractual obligations on the supplier?

15.3 A supplier refuses to provide a 'fixed price' for a piece of equipment. They insist on an 'ROM' (Rough Order of Magnitude) price that will be finalised when the equipment has been manufactured. How would you plan for this negotiation?

15.4 Many writers confuse consultation with negotiation. What is the difference between the two concepts?

15.5 Who is the best negotiator you know? What are their distinguishing personal qualities?

15.6 How may time affect your negotiating position with regard to price, quality, negotiating style and future seller relationships?

15.7 You have been asked to negotiate with the lowest priced supplier in a tender process. Their sales director attends the meeting and immediately says, 'Do not even mention the price because we will not change it.' What are your options and choice of tactics?

15.8 Using 'power and coercion' is a negotiation strategy. Under what circumstances could you see it being used?

15.9 Suggest five ways in which to resolve an apparent deadlock in a negotiation.

15.10 Discuss the following statements:
- (a) 'Once you consent to some concession, you can never cancel it and put things back the way they were'
- (b) 'We cannot negotiate with those who say "What's mine is mine, what's yours is negotiable"' (John F. Kennedy)
- (c) 'Flattery is the infantry of negotiation' (Lord Chander)
- (d) 'Always define your terms' (Eric Partridge).

15.11 There are many 'public' negotiations where trade unions and employers put their positions or postures to the media. Why do they do this?

15.12 Name six reasons why negotiations fail when there is a significant contractual dispute. Why do many disputes end up in court?

Past examination questions

1 (a) Describe the difference between a supplier's interests and positions in a negotiation, giving an example to support your answer.
  (b) Explain why it is important for a buyer to understand a supplier's interests and positions.
  (c) Personal power can be used to influence a negotiation. Identify **three** types of personal power, and give **one** example of how each might be used in a negotiation.
  (d) Explain the importance of **four** different roles of team members during negotiation.

CIPS, *Effective Negotiation in Purchasing & Supply*, November 2009

2 A large Internet retail company is about to negotiate with three potential suppliers for its cardboard packaging requirements. Business is growing by 20 per cent year on year as the home purchase market increases. The company has a good reputation in the market for having a strong brand and innovative marketing, but it has a poor credit rating for paying suppliers late. The single supplier order will be for simple cardboard packaging with ten sizes and one colour print. Deliveries will be weekly because stockholding space is limited. Cardboard will be delivered in full truckloads all year round, with extra seasonal deliveries in November and December when sales volumes significantly increase. The negotiations will take place with suppliers from outside the buyer's own country.
  (a) State **three** sources of price information that the buyer can use to benchmark current prices.
  (b) Complete a SWOT diagram representing the above situation which could used to prepare for negotiations with the potential suppliers.
  (c) Describe **two** major differences that might be expected when negotiating with organisations based in other countries.

CIPS, *Effective Negotiation in Purchasing & Supply*, May 2009

3 The composition of the negotiation team is an important part of negotiation strategy planning.
  (a) State **four** typical team member roles that may be required.
  (b) Indicate where final decision-making authority normally lies within the team.

CIPS, *Effective Negotiation in Purchasing & Supply*, November 2008

4 Negotiation planning involves analysing a supplier. A purchaser will also need to identify the people who will be involved in any negotiation meetings or discussions.
  (a) Describe why understanding the types of people and their behaviour patterns is important and how they might affect the outcome of a negotiation.
  (b) Provide a definition for each of the **four** types of people styles in negotiations.

(c) Choose **one** style of negotiation and state how you might deal with them in a negotiation.
(d) Explain how over-reliance on this type of assessment and preparation may affect the purchaser's performance in a negotiation meeting.

CIPS, *Effective Negotiation in Purchasing & Supply*, May 2008

References

1 Aljian, G. W., *Purchasing Handbook*, 4th edn, McGraw-Hill, 1982, section 11, p. 11.5
2 Rubin, J. Z. and Brown, B. R., *The Social Psychology of Bargaining and Negotiation*, Academic Press, 1975
3 Gottschal, R. A. W., 'The background to the negotiating process' in Torrington, D., *Code of Personnel Management*, Gower, 1979
4 Lysons, C. K., Modified version of definition in *Purchasing*, 3rd edn, Pitman, 1993
5 Fisher, R. and Ury, W., *Getting to Yes*, Penguin, 1983
6 Cooper, C. L. and Makin, P., *Psychology for Managers*, British Psychological Society in association with Macmillan, 1988, p. 58
7 Berne, Eric, *Games People Play*, Penguin, 1968
8 Harris, T. A., *I'm OK – You're OK*, Pan Macmillan, 1986
9 Ashcroft, S.G., 'Commercial Negotiation Skills', *Industrial and Commercial Training Journal*, 2004
10 McCall, J. M. and Norrington, M. B., *Marketing by Agreement: A Cross-cultural Approach to Business Negotiations*, Wiley, 1986
11 Cox, A., Win-win, Earlsgate Press, 2004
12 Pena-Mora, F. and Tamaki, T., 'Effect of delivery systems on collaborative negotiations for large-scale infrastructure projects', *Journal of Management in Engineering*, April, 2001, pp. 105–21
13 As 5 above
14 Galinsky, A. D., *Negotiation Strategy: Should You Make the First Offer?* Harvard Business School, 2004
15 Susskind, L. and Cruikshank, J., *Breaking the Impasse*, Basic Books, 1987
16 Lee, R. and Lawrence, P., *Organisational Behaviour: Politics at Work*, Hutchinson, 1988, p. 182
17 As 5 above
18 Ertel, Danny, 'Turning negotiation into a corporate capability', *Harvard Business Review*, May–June, 1999, pp. 55–70
19 As 5 above
20 McCarthy, W., 'The role of power and principle in getting to yes', in Breslin, J. W. and Rubin, J. Z., *Negotiation Theory and Practice*, Cambridge University Press, 1991, pp. 115–22
21 Crampton, P. C. and Dees, J. G., 'Promoting honesty in negotiation', *Journal of Business Ethics*, March, 2002, pp. 1–28

Support tools

This chapter aims to provide an understanding of:

- tendering or competitive bidding
- costing techniques and their application to purchasing
- budgets and budgetary control
- learning curves and their application
- scheduling tools, Gantt charts and networks
- project management
- operational research.

- Types of tenders and tendering procedure.
- Post tender negotiation (PTN).
- Lifecycle costing.
- Target costing.
- Absorption costing.
- Activity-based costing and management.
- Standard costing.
- Purchasing budgets.
- The learning curve theorem.
- Types of projects.
- Gantt charts.
- Network analysis.
- CPM and PERT.
- Operational research and suppliers.

16.1 Tendering

16.1.1 Definitions

A *tender* or *bid* is a formal offer to supply goods or services for an agreed price. From a procurement perspective, tendering (or competitive bidding), is:

> A purchasing procedure whereby potential suppliers are invited to make a firm and unequivocal offer of the price and terms on which they will supply specified goods or services, which, on acceptance, shall be the basis of a subsequent contract.

In some instances tenders will be based on a specification of requirements and contractual terms and conditions provided by the buying organisation. There are occasions when the buyer's needs require innovative solutions on special terms to be agreed. In these cases, tenders will be sought requesting proposals to deliver an acceptable solution for an agreed price and adopting tailored contractual terms and conditions. Tendering is based on the principles of competition, fairness and accessibility, transparency and openness and probity. The process of obtaining tenders should also aim at obtaining the best value and not necessarily the lowest price.

16.1.2 Types of tender

- *Open tenders* – prospective suppliers are invited to compete for a contract advertised in the press or on the Internet – the lowest tender generally being accepted, although the advertisers usually state that they are not bound to accept the lowest or any tender.

- *Single tenders* – by invitation to one firm/contractor only.

- *Selective tenders* – prospective suppliers are invited to tender by public notice (ad hoc list) or where invitations to tender for a contract are limited to those organisations that are on a pre-determined list compiled and maintained for that purpose.

- *Serial tenders* – prospective suppliers are requested on either an open or a selective basis to tender for an initial scheme on the basis that, subject to satisfactory performance and unforeseen financial contingencies, a programme of work will be given to the successful contractor, the rates and prices for the first job being the basis for the rest of the programme. Advantages claimed for this system include:
  - contractors are given an incentive to maintain a high performance level
  - savings in cost and time by eliminating one-contract negotiations for each stage of a programme
  - teams of employees and plant can be moved to successive jobs without disruption
  - supplier security of contract should enable purchasers to negotiate keener prices.

- *Negotiated tenders* – a tender is negotiated with only one supplier so that competition is eliminated. This type of contract is unusual. In the case of a local authority, it would require the waiving of standing orders, and the assurance that EU Regulations are being complied with.

- *Restricted tenders* – a two-stage approach in which interested parties are invited to undergo a pre-qualification assessment before inviting a selected number to tender.

16.1.3 The application of tendering

Tendering is used extensively in public and private sector organisations. The reasons for tendering are fundamentally the same as shown in Table 16.1.

Table 16.1 Reasons for tendering

- To obtain a legally binding offer
- To confirm that technical solutions are available
- To expose the cost drivers behind the contract price
- To determine the contractual terms and conditions
- To identify the quality standards that will apply
- To establish a defined programme of work
- To expose the buyer's and supplier's obligations
- To demonstrate an equitable process and value for money

In the public sector, tendering is, by necessity, a very formal process to ensure conformity to the principles of public accountability, including openness, transparency of decision making, avoidance of a conflict of interest and recognition that 'a public office is a public trust'.

- Most European law on public-sector purchasing is contained in UK regulations or statutory instruments. The Public Contracts Regulations 2006 (SI2006 No 5) which came into force on the 31 January 2006, for example, sets out details, including:
  - procedures leading to the award of a public contract
  - selection of economic operators
  - award of a public contract
  - specialised contracts, e.g. design contests.
- UK Law, Section 135(3) of the Local Government Act 1972, for example, states:

  Standing orders made by a local authority with respect to the supply of goods or materials for the execution of works shall include provision for securing competition for such contracts and for regulating the manner but may exempt from any such provisions contracts for a price below that specified in standing orders and may authorise the authority to exempt any contract from such provision when the authority is satisfied that the exemption is justified by special circumstances.

  Part 1 of the Local Government Act 1999 (which repeats Part III of the Local Government Planning and Land Act 1980; Part 1 Section 3.2 Schedule 6 of the Local Government Act 1988 and Sections 8–11 Schedule 1 of the Local Government Act 1992) imposes a duty on 'best value authorities' to make arrangements to secure continuous improvement in the way that their functions are exercised having regard to 'economy, efficiency and effectiveness'. In addition to local authorities, 'best value authorities' include police, fire, waste disposal, transport, National Parks and Broads authorities.

- European directives on public-sector purchasing recognise three forms of tendering procedure:
  - *open tenders* – all suppliers that respond to the contract notice are invited to tender

- *restricted tenders* – only those suppliers that have been invited by the contracting authority may submit tenders, but restricted procedures will only apply where:
  - the contract value does not justify the procedural costs of an open tender
  - the product required is highly specific in its nature
- *negotiated tenders* – these allow the terms of the contract to be negotiated with one or more suppliers without prior publication of a tender notice, but the negotiated procedure is only available in certain defined circumstances, such as:
  - where, because bids were irregular or unacceptable, no suitable supplier has been found by open or restricted tender procedures
  - where such procedures have resulted in no tender being received
  - where the required product is manufactured purely for research and development or experimental purposes
  - where, for technical or artistic reasons or the existence of exclusive rights, there is only one supplier.

16.1.4 Tendering procedures

General procedures

In public purchasing, procedures will be set out in Standing Orders or Departmental Procurement Regulations. In general, the procedure for open tenders involves:

1 the issue of a public advertisement(s) inviting tenders (OJEU, Trade Press, Consortia websites for example – depending on the nature and value of the purchase)

2 the issue of an invitation to tender (ITT) which will normally include:
   - instructions to tenderers
   - conditions of tender
   - relevant conditions of contract
   - special conditions of contract (if appropriate)
   - specification
   - collusive tendering certificate
   - details of the tender evaluation scoring and weightings
   - form of tender
   - price schedule
   - tender return envelope
   - special sections such as equal opportunities, health and safety and environmental.

3 on the date arranged for the opening of tenders, appointed individuals to attend (after a period where tenders have been held in safe custody); the individuals may include procurement, internal audit, finance or other independent departmental heads

4 tenders will be initialled, listed and entered on an analysis sheet or spreadsheet showing details of prices, rates, carriage charges, delivery, settlement terms and other information necessary for their evaluation

5 tenders will be evaluated on an agreed basis, such as lowest bid or most economically advantageous tender (MEAT), but the public body is under no obligation to accept the lowest or any of the tenders received

6 the successful tenderer will be notified

7 unsuccessful tenderers will also be notified, although, they will not automatically be given reasons for their tender not being accepted – this information should be made available if it is requested.

e-tendering

An electronic tendering solution facilitates the complete tendering process from the advertising of the requirement through to the placing of the contract. This includes the exchange of all relevant documents in electronic format.

The business benefits include:

- reduced tender-cycle time
- fast and accurate pre-qualification and evaluation
- faster response to questions and points of clarification during the tender period
- reduction in labour intensive tasks, receipt, recording and distributing tenders
- reduction in the paper trail
- improved quality of tender specification
- provision of quality management information.

16.1.5 Auditing the tender process

Tender processes can be manipulated. It is good practice to subject the processes to audit. This may examine:

- Were late additions made to the tender list?
- Were any contractors given an advantage by extending a deadline?
- Was any contractor given private briefings?
- Was the budget disclosed to a selected contractor?
- Was the award criteria manipulated to favour one contractor?
- Were changes permitted to one specific tender?
- Was one of the tenderers permitted to write the specification?
- Was appropriate due diligence conducted on all tenderers?
- Was the tender evaluation panel subjected to pressure by anyone?
- Is the audit trail complete?

16.2 Debriefing unsuccessful tenderers

The purpose of the debriefing session is to help unsuccessful tenderers submit more competitive and professionally responsive tenders in the future by identifying the strengths and weaknesses in the tender that was submitted. It is a fact that many buyers are reluctant to engage in a face-to-face debriefing, preferring instead to provide a written rejection with sparse information. This latter approach, while time effective, does very little to engender trust and to improve relationships with tenderers.

A leading firm of consultants[1] has the following guidelines for conducting a debrief:

- explain the tender evaluation model
- describe the evaluation panel members and their roles
- directly relate the feedback to the evaluation model criteria
- be wholly familiar with the detail of the tender
- position the contractor vis-à-vis the competition
- do not disclose competitors confidential information
- identify strengths and weaknesses
- point out any technical errors and contradictions
- point out inadequate, evasive and misleading statements
- make detailed notes of the meeting, attendees, times, issues arising, likely complaints/ possible appeals against the decisions and the contractors' response to the debrief.

The likely benefits from the debriefing include:

- an enhanced reputation for the procurement process
- tenderers may in future submit enhanced value-for-money tenders
- improved completeness of offer from tenderers
- giving unsuccessful tenderers some return on the time and money spent in preparing offers
- improved quality of tenderer's future offers.

16.3 Post-tender negotiations (PTN)

This is, traditionally, an emotive facet of procurement. PTN is defined by the CIPS[2] as:

> Negotiation after the receipt of formal tenders and before the letting of contract(s) with the supplier(s)/contractor(s) submitting the lowest acceptable tender(s) with a view to obtaining an improvement in price, delivery of content in circumstances which do not put other tenderers at a disadvantage or affect their confidence or trust in the competitive tendering system.

PTN is defined by the OGC[3] as:

> Negotiation after receipt of formal bids or tenders and before the letting of contract(s) with those companies submitting tender(s) offering the best value for money with a view to obtaining an improvement in content in circumstances which do not put the other tenderers at a disadvantage, distort competition or affect adversely trust in the competitive tendering process.

PTN, in the public sector, must only take place where permitted (for example, it is not permitted using the 'competitive dialogue'). The potential range of issues for PTN is vast. To illustrate some, not uncommon issues, we outline below examples:

1. Charges for consultants' per diem time. In one situation the tenderer said their rates were based on 150 days per annum chargeable time. This is unproductive and a more common basis would be 200–220 days.
2. The costs of IT licenses based on the numbers of users, rather than the lower license fees for a corporate license.
3. An initial refusal to provide either a 'performance bond' or 'parent company guarantee'.

4 An initial refusal to provide the necessary amount of insurance cover for professional indemnity insurance.

5 An attempt to get the buyer to pay for writing technical material but the supplier retains the intellectual property rights.

6 An initial refusal to comply with the buyer's drug and alcohol testing regime when contractor's staff were working on the buyer's site.

7 A request for payments against achievement of a milestone but not prepared to pass Title to the buyer, nor to let the buyer deduct a retention amount.

8 A request for advance payment at award of contract.

9 An objection to the buyer's right to change key personnel for contractual non-performance

10 A request for an annual uplift in service charges 'at the sellers' discretion'.

16.4 Application of costing techniques

No purchasing professional can afford to be unaware of the various cost accounting approaches to make-or-buy decisions, negotiation, price appraisal and purchasing performance, to mention just four such applications. Relevant approaches include lifecycle costing, target costing, absorption costing, activity-based costing (ABC) and standard costing. Marginal cost as applied to make-or-buy decisions is considered in section 11.14.2.

16.5 Lifecycle costing

The concept of lifecycle analysis with its stages of development, growth, maturity, decline, and withdrawal was introduced in section 2.13.2. As stated in section 13.4.1 lifecycle costing is an important factor when making decisions relating to capital expenditure.

16.5.1 Definition

Lifecycle costing has been defined by the OGC[4] as:

> Lifecycle Costing (LCC) also called Whole Life Costing is a technique to establish the total cost of ownership. It is a structured approach that addresses all the elements of this cost and can be used to produce a spend profile of the product or service over its anticipated life-span.

It has been defined by the Chartered Institute of Management Accountants (CIMA)[5] as:

> The practice of obtaining over their lifetime the best use of the physical assets at the lowest cost to the entity (Terotechnology). This is achieved through a combination of management, financial, engineering and other disciplines.

The term 'Terotechnology', coined in 1970, is derived from the Greek verb *tereo* and means literally 'the art and science of caring for things'. Lifecycle costs are therefore those associated with acquiring, using, caring for and disposing of physical assets, including feasibility studies, research, development, design, production, maintenance, replacement and disposal, as well as the associated support, training and operating costs incurred over the period in which the asset is owned.

16.5.2 The importance of lifecycle costing

Unless lifecycle implications are taken into consideration, there is a danger that initial cost on delivery will be used as the sole criterion when selecting a physical asset. This simplistic approach can, however, have detrimental implications for the total lifecycle cost of the item.

Lifecycle costing is of particular importance for products liable to rapid technological or style changes. From the standpoint of producers, rapid technological change may mean that revenue from sales may be insufficient to make the original investment in design and development worthwhile. From the buyer's viewpoint, the asset may, to a greater or lesser extent, be obsolete before the amount invested in its purchase has been recouped.

Purchasing executives concerned with the acquisition of capital items are therefore advised to:

- ensure that specifications include reference to factors that have a bearing on the cost of ownership of an asset, such as maintenance and the availability of spares
- create a communication bridge with the supplier regarding developments in the particular field
- treat initial costs as only one of many factors that will contribute to their total lifecycle costs
- ensure all factors that may have implications for the total lifecycle costs are given due consideration before recommending the purchase of a particular asset.

16.5.3 Application of lifecycle costing

Apart from the purchase of capital equipment, lifecycle costing can be applied to:

- *acquisition control* – estimating the future costs of large-scale acquisitions
- *optioneering* – comparing the returns on a number of expenditure options
- *pricing* – ensuring that, in addition to direct and general overhead costs (not including depreciation), an interest charge is included that reflects the overall cost of capital required to satisfy all capital providers so that the annual equivalent cost of fixed assets will recover both depreciation and a profit margin that satisfies all providers
- *project analysis* – measurement of the cost of a project against its targets
- *product design* – provision of data that will enable designers to modify or improve designs that will improve consumer satisfaction and give a product greater cost advantage over those of competitors
- *replacement decisions* – as the cost of using and repairing physical assets increases with age, lifecycle costing can indicate when it is more beneficial to dispose of an asset and purchase a replacement than it is to meet increasing maintenance costs
- *supplier support* – provision by suppliers of comparative lifecycle estimates for their products.

Figure 16.1 **Lifecycle costing breakdown structure**

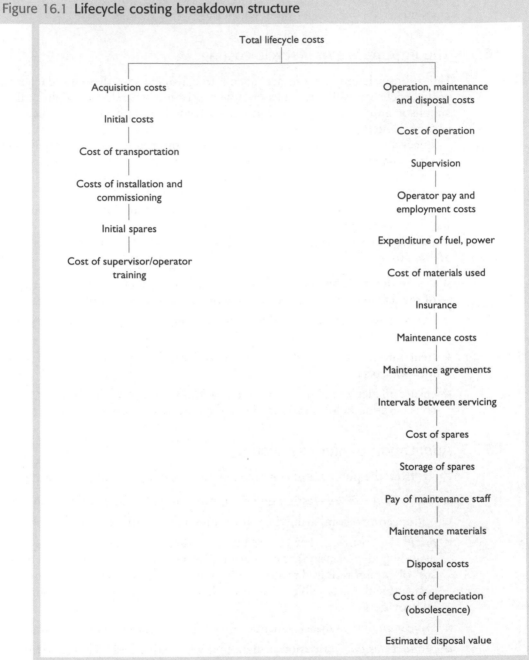

16.5.4 Lifecycle costing methodology

The lifecycle costing methodology involves the following four basic steps:

1 Identify all relevant costs. As shown in Figure 16.1, these are initially broken down into acquisition and operation, maintenance and disposal costs, and then broken down further under each heading.

2 Calculate the costs over the anticipated life of the asset of all the elements identified above. Such costs may be:

  - known rates, such as operator pay, maintenance charges
  - estimated rates based on historical figures or other empirical data
  - guesstimates based on informed opinion.

3 Use discounting to adjust future costs to apply to the present – that is, the time when the purchase decision is made. This reduces all options to a common base, thereby ensuring fair comparison. Discounting was discussed in section 13.9.3.

4 Draw conclusions from the cost figures obtained by the above procedure.

In its simplest form, lifecycle costs (LCC) are:

> Initial cost
> + Operating/maintenance costs over life of item
> + Energy costs
> + Disposal costs or salvage value

The United States Department of Defense (DOD)[6] used a communications system acquisition profile which shows that just prior to production or operations, 95 per cent of the cumulative LCC has been committed. This is shown in Figure 16.2. The situation goes into even starker contrast when you realise that some 60–66 per cent of LCC is in the operation and support phases. This is shown in Figure 16.3.

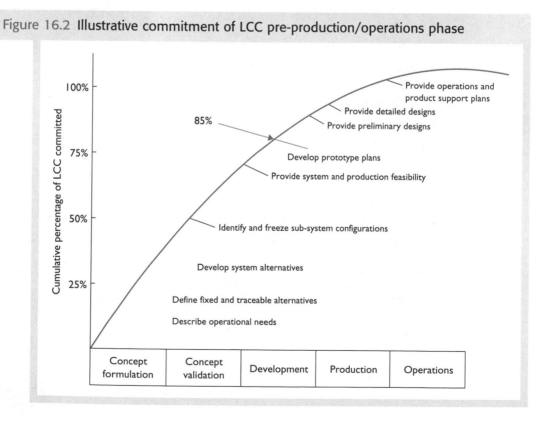

Figure 16.2 **Illustrative commitment of LCC pre-production/operations phase**

Figure 16.3 LCC profile at key milestones

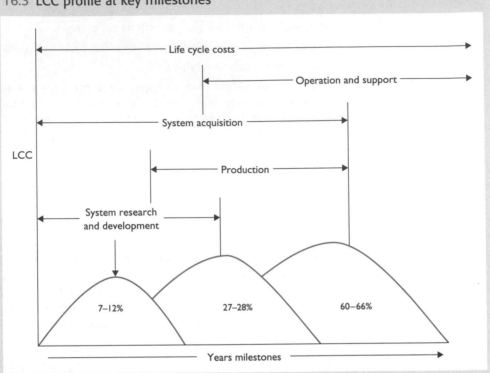

Example 16.1

Lifecycle costs (1)

This example is for a simple rectangular mixing tank. The requirement is for a 20-year tank life. The design brief requested evaluation of three alternative materials:

1 mild steel with applied fiberglass lining
2 stainless steel – austentitic Type 304
3 stainless steel – duplex Type 2205

	Mild Steel	Type 304	Type 2205
Material costs	1646	4060	4432
Fabrication costs	1280	1280	1280
Other installation costs	1500	0	0
Total initial costs	**4426**	**5340**	**5712**
Maintenance costs	2523	321	321
Replacement costs	4651	−290	−229
Cost of lost production	0	0	0
Material related cost	0	0	0
Total operating costs	**7174**	**31**	**92**
Total LCC cost	**11600**	**5371**	**5804**

Example 16.2

Lifecycle costs (2)

This example relates to a situation where a plant engineer is experiencing problems with a Fluid Control Valve that fails due to erosion caused by captivation. There are four options under consideration:

A A new control valve can be installed to accommodate the high pressure differential.

B The pump impeller can be trimmed so that the pump does not develop as much head.

C A variable frequency drive can be installed and the flow control valve removed.

D The system can be left as it is, with a yearly repair of the fluid control valve.

Assumptions

1 The initial investment monies would be borrowed and repaid at the end of year 8

2 All costs are subject to inflation after year 1. *Note*: this is compounded.

3 The inflation rate is used as the discount factor to calculate the present value.

The comparison was:

	Option A	Option B	Option C	Option D
Initial investment cost	5,000	2,250	21,500	0
Energy price (present) per KWh	0.080	0.080	0.080	0.080
Weight average power of equipment in KW	23.1	14.0	11.6	23.1
Average operating hours/year	6,000	6,000	6,000	6,000
Energy cost/year	11,088	6,720	5,568	11,088
Maintenance cost/year	500	500	1,000	500
Repair every 2nd year	2,500	2,500	2,500	2,500
Other yearly costs	0	0	0	4,000
Life time in years	8	8	8	8
Interest rate (%)	8.0%	8.0%	8.0%	8.0%
Inflation rate (%)	4.0%	4.0%	4.0%	4.0%
Present LCC value	**105,505**	**70,561**	**81,683**	**137,505**

16.6 Target costing

16.6.1 Definition

Target costing is defined by CIMA[7] as:

> A product cost estimate derived from a competitive market price. Used to reduce costs through continuous improvement and replacement of technologies and processes.

16.6.2 Target costing in practice

The authors are indebted to CIMA[8] for their permission to use the following extracts from a challenging discussion paper. They observe that a fundamental shift in performance often needs a radical change in the way an organisation is managed. They continue by arguing that a response to the mixed financial performance of NHS Trusts must be the finance community bringing to the table better approaches to managing NHS organisations to improve their understanding and management of costs of services and their effective delivery.

The logic of target costing can, of course, apply to many environments. The basic stages of target costing are the establishment of targets for market price, volume and profit, from which a target production cost is derived. Cost analysis is carried out to determine an actual cost and identify the extent of, and develop plans for, the cost reduction required to target cost. Many organisations have found the real strength of target costing is an overall framework for cost improvement and efficiency within which a range of different techniques for analysis and re-engineering are used.

Target costing has great relevance for procurement and presents a significant opportunity to make a contribution. Target costing is a technique which develops in the early 1970s in Japan's manufacturing industry as consumer demand for more diversified products and shorter product lifecycles made the development and planning stages of new products more important.

16.6.3 The target costing process

Gagne and Discenza[9] identified a number of stages in the process of target costing:

1 Establish a selling price for the new product and estimate sales volume from an analysis of the market, and a target profit.
2 Determine the target cost by subtracting the profit from the selling price.
3 Perform functional cost analysis for individual components and processes.
4 Determine the estimated cost for the product.
5 Compare estimate with target.
6 If estimated cost exceeds target cost, repeat cost analysis/value engineering to reduce estimated cost (an iterative process).
7 Make the final decision whether or not to introduce the product once cost estimate is on target.
8 Manage costs during production of the product.

16.6.4 Cost management techniques relevant to target costing

These include:

- value analysis
- value engineering
- just-in-time
- total quality management
- material requirements planning
- *kaizen*
- lean manufacturing
- activity based costing and management
- cause-effect analysis.

16.6.5 Target costing and procurement

Target costing is primarily associated with the search for competitiveness by product manufacturers and service providers. It is, however, an approach that can be utilised by purchasing, particularly in relation to negotiation, in such ways as the following:

- providing suppliers with a target price that the purchaser is prepared to pay
- identifying, in association with a supplier, the means by which the target price may be achieved, including a fair profit
- incorporating improvements into the product or price at agreed intervals or when a contract is due for renewal
- providing suppliers with an estimate of the lifecycle of parent products in which bought-out components or assemblies will be incorporated – it is then possible to estimate the total demand that a supplier may expect to receive over a defined period of time and this can be used to negotiate quantity discounts, price reviews and learning allowances.

16.7 Absorption costing

16.7.1 Definition

Approaches such as lifecycle and target costing are concerned with price comparison and price control and reduction rather than day-to-day costing methods. Probably the simplest and best understood method of ascertaining costs is absorption costing, defined by the CIMA[10] as:

> A principle whereby fixed as well as variable costs are allotted to cost units and total overheads are absorbed according to activity level. The term may be applied where (a) production costs only or (b) costs of all functions are allotted.

16.7.2 The elements of cost

Cost is the amount of expenditure incurred on a given thing. Costs can be classified in several ways, according to the purpose for which they are required. The most usual classifications are into:

- *direct costs* – direct pay, materials and expenses that can be allocated to specific cost units or centres
- *indirect costs* – expenses such as indirect pay, materials and expenses that cannot be allocated but which can be apportioned to or absorbed by cost units or centres.

Costs can also be classified as:

- *fixed* – a cost that tends to be unaffected by variations in volume of output
- *variable* – a cost that tends to vary directly with variations in volume of output
- *semi-variable* – a cost that is partly fixed and partly variable.

16.7.3 Price composition

The price quoted will include the following and *may* also include provision for such matters as, contingency, negotiation allowance, the cost of providing performance bonds and special insurance requirements and corporate central management/infrastructure overheads.

Direct costs	Materials, labour and expenses	Prime cost
Indirect costs	Works or factory expenses	Work costs
	(Production overheads)	
	Office and administrative expenses	Cost of production
	(Establishment overheads)	(Gross cost)
	Selling and distribution expenses	Cost of sales
	(Selling overheads)	(Selling cost)
Net profit		= Selling price

When the buyer is conducting a scrutiny of suppliers' pricing and seeking to build up an estimate of cost, the assistance of specialist product/service personnel will be required. This is an essential precursor to negotiation. When presented to a supplier it puts them in a position of refuting the estimate on a line-by-line basis.

The questions that the buyer might raise in analysing prices quoted by suppliers will be particular to the specific purchase. Outlined below are some examples of questions that may be applicable to each of the elements that may constitute selling prices.

16.7.4 Material costs

Material costs are arrived at by the following sum:

$$\text{Quantity of material} \times \text{Purchase price of material}$$

- What material is used, that is, would an alternative material reduce costs?
- What standardisation is possible?
- Is it possible for the buyer to purchase materials on behalf of the vendor at a cheaper cost?
- What weight of material has been allowed for?
- What scrap allowances are included?
- Has scrap any resale value?

16.7.5 Labour costs

These can be calculated by multiplying time by the rate of pay.

- What time allocations have been made?
- Has any allowance been included for idle time?
- What element of overtime is included?
- Has any allowance for 'learning' been included? (See section 16.11.)
- What production methods will be used?

16.7.6 Indirect costs

All material, labour and expense costs that cannot be identified as direct costs are termed indirect costs and are usually separated into:

- *production overheads* – indirect production *materials*, such as lubricating oil and spare parts for machinery, indirect *labour*, such as supervisory and maintenance pay, and indirect *expenses*, such as factory rates and insurance
- *administration overheads* – management, secretarial and office services and related expenditure, for example
- *selling overheads* – costs incurred in securing orders, such as salespeople's salaries, commissions and travelling expenses, while overheads may be:
  - *allocated* – charged against an identifiable cost centre or unit – a *cost centre* being a location, function or item of equipment for which costs may be ascertained and related to cost units for control purposes, such as the drawing office or the purchasing department
  - *apportioned* – spread over several cost centres on an agreed basis – rates and lighting may be apportioned on the basis of floor area or space occupied respectively, for example
  - *absorbed* – charged to cost units by means of rates separately calculated for each cost centre – in most cases the rates are predetermined.

16.7.7 Production overhead costs

Production overhead costs are usually absorbed in one of six ways, shown by the following example:

Total overhead for period	£24,000
Total units produced in period	180
Total direct labour hours for period	3200
Total direct pay	£6,400
Total direct material used	£12,000
Total machine hours	4,800

From the above, the following overhead absorption rates (OAR) can be calculated:

- Cost Unit OAR $= \dfrac{£24,000}{180} = £133.33$ overhead per unit produced

- Direct labour OAR $= \dfrac{£24,000}{3200} = £7.50$ per labour hour

- Direct pay OAR $= \dfrac{£24,000}{£6,400} = £3.75$ per £ of pay or 375%

- Direct material OAR $= \dfrac{£24,000}{£12,000} = £2$ or 200% of materials

- Machine hours OAR $= \dfrac{£24,000}{4,800} = £5$ per machine hour

- Prime cost OAR $= \dfrac{£24,000}{(£6,400 + £12,000)} = £1.30$ per £ of prime use or 130%

16.7.8 Non-production costs

These are typically absorbed on an arbitrary basis, such as:

$$\text{Administration overhead} = \frac{\text{Administration costs}}{\text{Production cost}}$$

$$\text{Selling overheads} = \frac{\text{Selling } + \text{ Marketing costs}}{\text{Sales value or production cost}}$$

Price analysis in relation to overheads should therefore involve asking the following kinds of questions:

- What is the basis on which indirect costs are allocated, apportioned or absorbed?
- To what extent can the fixed overhead element per unit be reduced by increased quantities?
- What is the vendor's break-even point per item or contract?
- What is the proportion of selling and administrative overhead as a proportion of production cost?

Attention should also be given to marginal and activity costing approaches, as described in sections 11.14.2 and 16.8 respectively.

16.7.9 Profit

The supplier's attitude to profit will be determined by many factors. For example, when work is in short supply the supplier may forgo profit simply to gain contracts and keep a labour force together. If, in contrast, there is little competition high profits are likely to be sought. The following seven points should be considered when analysing a vendor's anticipated profits:

- *competitive price* – the supplier who offers the lowest price should be allowed what profit can be made, providing this is not excessive
- *initial orders* – a large profit may need to be allowed on initial orders to persuade the supplier to undertake the risks of a new line or production
- *size of order* – a bigger profit may be justified on a small order
- *amount of value added to a product* – suppliers that produce all the components incorporated in a product generally make larger profits than assemblers of purchased parts
- *management expertise required* – with products requiring a high degree of designer production expertise, large profits may be required to keep suppliers interested in the buyer's business, while subcontracted items usually require less skill and therefore the profit should be smaller
- *risks assumed by supplier* – the greater the risk the greater the allowable profit
- *efficiency of supplier* – a supplier that has demonstrated reliability with regard to quality and delivery should not be lost because the process does not allow that supplier adequate profit.

16.8 Activity-based costing (ABC) and management

16.8.1 Definition

Activity-based costing is:[11]

> A cost attribution to cost units on the basis of benefit received from indirect activities, e.g. ordering, setting up, assuring quality.

16.8.2 Activity management and Activity-based costing

Activity-based costing (ABC) is an aspect of activity-based management (ABM). ABM has been defined as:[12]

> A discipline that focuses on the management of activities as a route to improving the value received by the customer and the profit achieved by providing this value.

ABM is based on the principle that 'activities consume costs'. Whereas traditional cost systems focus on the 'worker', ABM systems focus on the work. The field of ABM covers the following activities:

- activity analysis
- activity-based budgeting
- activity-based costing
- benchmarking
- business process re-engineering
- cost driver analysis
- continuous improvement
- operational control
- performance evaluation.

16.8.3 The distinction between absorption-based and ABC costing

Within traditional absorption costing, overhead costs are assigned to products, services, labour or other cost objects using one of the approaches indicated in section 16.7 above. Overhead costs are allocated in proportion to production volume. With ABC, an overhead is allocated to cost objects according to the activities and resources consumed.

16.8.4 Terminology

The following key terms are used in relation to ABC:

An *activity*, in this context, is a repetitive action performed in fulfillment of business functions, such as designing, purchasing, production set-up, assembly, quality control, packaging and shipping.

Activities can be classified as shown in Figure 16.4. Time, for example, can be classified as production or service inspection, transfer time and idle time such as storage or waiting for materials. Only production or service time add value. The other categories of time should be reduced to a minimum or eliminated.

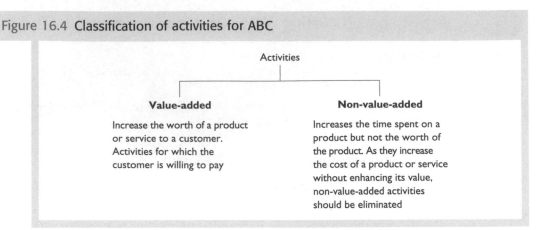

Figure 16.4 **Classification of activities for ABC**

A *resource* is a cost or costs that support activities. The purchasing activity, for example, incurs costs in the form of salaries and benefits, office space, computer time, travelling, training and so on. Thus, as Lapsley *et al.*[13] state:

> Activities consume resources
> and
> Products (or services) consume activities

A *cost object* can be almost anything that incurs costs, such as products, services, units, batches, jobs, customers, sales territories and so on.

A *cost driver* is a factor that has a direct cause–effect relationship to a cost. Activities creating cost drivers may be either:

- resource drivers
- activity drivers.

Resource drivers assign costs to activities, thereby forming activity costs pools, each containing their appropriate shares of resource costs. A number of cost pools can be assigned to an activity cost centre.

For each activity or resource one or more cost drivers must be identified – these are activity drivers. Cost drivers set activity levels. The cost driver for creating a purchase order, for example, may include the number of orders processed or the number of suppliers.

In general, the appropriate cost driver – that is, activity or resource driver – is the one that represents the primary output of the activity. Usually, a cost driver that captures the *number* of activity transactions is preferable to drivers based on the time duration or monetary amount of the activity transaction because it is readily available, easy to understand and apply and motivates people to act in ways likely to achieve organisational goals.

As Cooper and Kaplan[14] point out:

> A company that wants to reduce the number of unique parts that it processes in order to simplify activities such as vendor selection, purchasing, inspection, maintenance of the bill of materials, storage and accounting may decide to apply the costs of these activities using 'number of part numbers' as the cost driver. Then by evaluating and rewarding product

designers according to their ability to design low-cost products, they will be motivated to design products with fewer part numbers.

An *activity cost centre* is a segment of the production or service process for which management wants to separately ascertain the costs of the activities performed, such as purchasing, production, marketing. Activity centres should be created where a significant amount of overhead cost is incurred and several key activities are undertaken.

Direct costs inputs, as with traditional costing, consist of direct labour and direct material and, sometimes, direct technology.

16.8.5 A simple example of ABC

Activity-based costing involves the following steps:

1 Total overhead costs for a given period are computed either prospectively from budgets or retrospectively from departmental and general ledger records.

2 A project team is formed by top management to plan and implement the ABC system. The team – normally led by the management accountant – may be comprised of representatives of the design, production, purchasing/logistics, marketing and financial accounting functions.

3 The estimated or actual total overheads will be divided into service and production categories. Functional managers will then be interviewed and asked questions, such as the following:

■ What activities does your function undertake?

■ What activities are undertaken by each member of staff in the function?

■ What are the outputs of each activity?

■ What equipment and supplies are used for each activity?

■ What overtime is worked?

■ Why does idle time occur?

This activity analysis describes what is done by the enterprise and each function within the enterprise – that is, how resources, including time and effort, are spent and what inputs and outputs are involved.

4 The team will then assign resource costs to activity cost centres and cost pools using first-stage resource drivers, as shown in Figure 16.5 (for simplicity, only three resources – salaries, office costs and computers – are shown here).

5 Second-stage activity drivers, such as the number of purchase orders, items stored, deliveries made, will be chosen. These will normally be outputs and are used to assign the cost pools to cost products, as shown in Figure 16.5.

6 A bill of activities will be prepared for each product, as shown in Table 16.2. This enables the unit cost of each product to be ascertained using ABC.

16.8.6 The application of ABC

Burch[15] states that ABC is especially appropriate in companies where:

■ competition is high

■ product mix is diverse in terms of batch sizes, physical sizes, degree of complexity and raw material characteristics

Figure 16.5 Allocation of service resources to cost pools

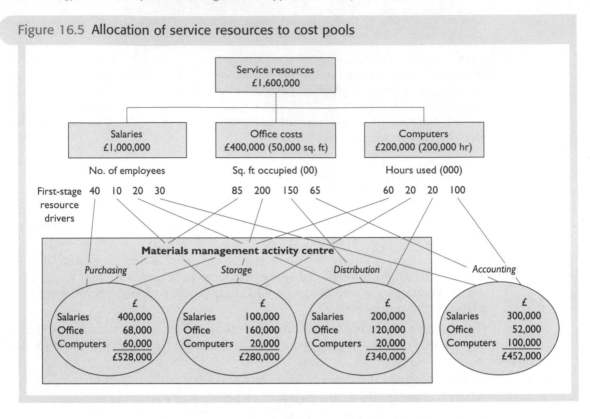

- product lifecycles are short – of three years or less
- collection and manipulation of data are performed by an integrated computer-based information system (ICBIS).

16.8.7 Activity-based costing and Purchasing

Barker[16] states that purchasing is 'a key activity for using ABC' and points out that 'much of the literature uses the purchasing and supply function to illustrate how to apply ABC'. Barker identifies a number of ways in which ABC can be implemented within purchasing, including:

- the attribution of purchasing function costs to products
- the provision of information that can be utilised in relation to make-or-buy and sourcing decisions, such as Ness and Cucuzza's[17] observations that the introduction of ABC at Chrysler showed the actual costs of some low-volume parts were as much as 30 times greater than the stated costs, which made it clear that the company would be better off outsourcing these parts and making more high-volume parts
- analysis of the total acquisition cost of purchased items 'may give buyers the information to prove what they have long suspected: paying more often costs less'.

ABC can also:

- highlight procurement activities that do not add value to products, such as inspection and storage, and which activities should be cut

Table 16.2 Bill of activities for products X and Y for the 52 weeks ending 31 March

	Pool driver rate	Product X = 20,000 units			Product Y = 12,000 units		
		Second stage	Activity cost		Activity driver	Activity cost	
		Driver quantity	Activity cost	Unit cost	Quantity	Activity cost	Unit cost
Purchasing	£264 per order	800	£211,200	£10.56	1200	£316,800	£26.40
Storage	£200 per item stored	600	£120,000	£6.00	800	£160,000	£13.33
Distribution	£1062.50 per delivery	200	£212,500	£10.63	120	£127,500	£10.63
Accounting	£200 per a/c	904	£180,800	£9.04	1356	£271,200	£22.60
Factory administration	£1000 per factory hour	1100	£1,100,000	£55.00	1500	£1,500,000	£125.00
Set-ups	£2000 per set-up	100	£200,000	£10.00	200	£400,000	£33.33
			£2,024,500			£2,775,500	
Activity costs per unit				£101.23			£231.29
Direct materials cost per unit				£65.00			£127.50
Direct labour cost per unit				£25.00			£46.20
Total costs per unit				£191.23			£404.99

With traditional absorption costing, the overhead rate per unit produced would be £4,800,000/32,000 = £150 per unit. The costs would therefore be:

	Product X	Product Y
Direct materials	£65.00	£127.50
Direct labour	£25.00	£46.20
Overheads	£150.00	£150.00
	£240.00	£323.70

- identify ways in which savings in procurement costs can contribute to the competitive advantage of the enterprise, such as a reduction in the number of suppliers and transactions, elimination of unnecessary purchasing documentation, improved design with fewer and standardised parts
- control of the overall procurement function by regarding it as an activity centre in which all purchasing activity-related cost pools are aggregated, which may provide data on drivers and rates that allow comparisons to be made across functions and with potential external suppliers
- have the potential to make a significant contribution to TQM as costs are a key factor in any decision.

16.9 Standard costing

16.9.1 Definition

Standard costing is defined by the CIMA[18] as:

> A control technique which compares costs and revenues with actual results to obtain variances which are used to stimulate improved performance.

Standard costing is therefore a technique of comparisons – the actual with the standard. This approach is used mainly in companies engaged in repetitive production and assumes the use of materials or components the design, quality and specifications of which are standardised. The standard cost of materials is made up of the following elements.

16.9.2 Quantity

Normally this is derived from technical and engineering specifications, frequently as indicated in the bill of materials. Standard quantities normally include an allowance for normal losses due to factors such as scrap, breakages, evaporation and the like.

16.9.3 Price

Prices used are the forecast expected prices – normally the latest prices for the item from approved sources in the quantities estimated for the relevant budget period. Another approach – which takes into account that an item may have to be bought from several suppliers – is to base prices on the average expected to be paid over the period under consideration.

16.9.4 Variances

The difference between the standard and actual cost is termed a *variance*. The most important material variances are those relating to price and usage, which are calculated by using the following formulae:

- *direct materials price variance* – the difference between the standard price and actual purchase price for the actual quantity of material, which can be calculated at the time of purchase or the time of usage – generally the former is preferable – using the formula:

$$\text{(Actual purchase quantity} \times \text{Actual price)} -$$
$$\text{(Actual purchase quantity} \times \text{Standard price)}$$

■ *direct materials usage variance* – the difference between the standard quantity specified for the actual production and the actual quantity used, at standard purchase price, calculated by using the formula:

$$\text{(Actual quantity used for actual production} \times \text{Standard price)} - \text{(Standard quantity for actual production} \times \text{Standard price)}$$

■ *direct materials total variance* – the sum of the usage and price variances, calculated as follows:

$$\text{(Standard direct materials cost of the actual production volume)} - \text{(Actual cost of direct materials)}$$

Example 16.3

Worked examples of price variance formulae

Assume the *standard* quantities and prices of the direct materials used for product X are 75 kg at £3.75 per kg. The *actual* usage and price were 74 kg at £3.85 per kg.

The direct materials price variance is:

$$(74 \text{ kg} \times £3.85) - (74 \text{ kg} \times £3.75) = £284.90 - £277.50$$
$$= £7.40$$

making an adverse variance of £7.40

The direct materials usage variance is:

$$(74 \text{ kg} \times £3.75) - (75 \text{ kg} \times £3.75) = £277.50 - £281.25$$
$$= £3.75$$

making a favourable variance of £3.75

The direct materials total variance will therefore be:

$$\text{(Averse direct materials total price variance)} -$$
$$\text{(Favourable direct material usage variance)}$$
$$= £7.40 - £3.75 = £3.65 \text{ (adverse)}$$

It is also possible to calculate the *direct materials yield* and *mixed variances* for production processes involving the mixing of various materials. Information on these variances and their calculations can be found in any cost accounting text.

16.9.5 Causes of material price variances

Such variances can occur because:

■ actual prices are higher or lower than budgeted

■ quantity discounts may be lost or gained by buying smaller or larger quantities than expected

■ prices paid may be affected by buying higher or lower qualities than anticipated

■ buying substitute materials from stockists due to the non-availability of the planned material.

16.9.6 Causes of material usage variance

These variances can be due to:

- the actual production yield from the material being greater or not as great as planned
- the amount of scrap or shortage being more or less than expected.

Standard costing is an application of the management principle of exceptions. Where a variance exceeds a prescribed level, it will be analysed with a view to identifying controllable and uncontrollable factors. Particularly with regard to prices, standard costs provide a widely used measure of purchasing effectiveness.

16.10 Budgets and budgetary control

16.10.1 Definitions

The CIMA[19] provides the following definitions:

Budget: A plan quantified in monetary terms, prepared and approved prior to a defined period of time, usually showing planned income to be generated and/or expenditure to be incurred during that period and the capital to be employed to attain a given objective.

Budgetary control: The establishment of budgets relating the responsibilities of executives to the requirements of a policy, and the continuous comparison of actual with budgeted results, either to secure by individual action the objective of that policy or to provide a basis for its revision.

16.10.2 Purchasing budgets

These are derived from sales and production budgets and will be divided into:

- A *materials budget* based on:
  - whole units of products to be completed in the budget period converted into individual direct material requirements expressed in terms of physical quantities and monetary expenditure
  - the company's end inventory policy based on the availability of materials and components
- A *purchasing department's operating budget* covering projected expenditure for the budget period on salaries, training, computer time, travelling, entertainment, office space occupied, stationery and so on.

Although budgetary control and standard costs are interrelated, the former can be operated in enterprises where the latter is difficult to apply. The value of budgeting is, however, enhanced when it is used with standard costing.

16.11 Learning curves

16.11.1 Definition

A learning curve (sometimes termed a 'skill acquisition or experience curve') is:

a graphical representation of the rate at which skills or knowledge is acquired over a period of time.

16.11.2 The basis of the learning curve

'Skill to do comes by doing.' A task is performed more quickly with each subsequent repetition until a point is reached where no further improvement is possible and performance levels out. In industry, cost reductions arising from 'learning' are due to the following factors:

- less time required for the operative to weigh up the job
- improved speed and proficiency in performing the actual operations
- reduction in scrap and rectification
- improved operational sequences
- improved tooling as a result of production experience
- the application of value engineering and analysis
- larger lot sizes with reduced setting-up costs.

Learning curves are therefore developed on the basis of the following assumptions:[20]

- the direct labour required to product the $(n + 1)^{th}$ unit will always be less than the direct labour required for the nth unit
- direct labour requirements will decrease at a steeper rate as cumulative production increases
- the reduction in time will follow an exponential curve.

16.11.3 The learning curve theorem

The learning curve theorem is that each time the number of production units is doubled, the cumulative average labour hours per unit figure declines by a specific and constant percentage of the previous cumulative average.

If the learning rate is 80 per cent and the number of items made doubles, the average time per unit is reduced to 80 per cent of its previous value. This is illustrated in Table 16.3. To make one unit required one day but to make two units required 1.6 days. Thus, the average time taken per unit has fallen to 0.8 days – 80 per cent of its original value. As you can see from Table 16.3, this does not mean that the second item took 0.8 days.

If the number of units produced is doubled from two to four and then doubled again to eight, the average time per unit should fall to:

$$80\% \times 80\% = 64\%$$

Table 16.3 Reduction in the average time taken to produce 1 unit

Units produced	1	2	3	4	5	6	7	8	9	10	11	12
Time of last unit produced	1.00	0.60	0.51	0.45	0.42	0.39	0.37	0.35	0.34	0.33	0.32	0.31
Total time so far	1.00	1.60	2.11	2.56	2.98	3.37	3.74	4.09	4.43	4.76	5.08	5.39
Cumulative average time	1.00	0.80	0.70	0.64	0.60	0.56	0.53	0.51	0.49	0.48	0.46	0.45

of the average time per unit when only two were produced, and then to:

$$64\% \text{ of } 0.8 = 0.512 = 0.51$$

of the initial average time per unit. As you can see from the table, this does not mean that the eighth unit took 0.51 days to produce.

It can be shown mathematically that the equation for the learning curve is:

$$y = ax^b$$

where:

y is the cumulative average time per unit
x is the number of units produced so far
a is the time taken to produce the first item
$$b = \frac{\log(\text{learning rate})}{\log(2)}$$

It should be noted that learning curves vary according to:

- the complexity of the operation – the learning rate for simple products is less pronounced than for more complicated items because the opportunity to improve work is greater with the latter
- the opportunity to reduce labour hours in machine-paced operations is limited because the output rate is controlled by the machine
- learning will be affected by the introduction of automation or improved equipment, so, because of this variability in learning rates, it is necessary when several operations are involved in manufacturing a part, to prepare an aggregate learning curve by multiplying the percentage of the total task for a given operation by the learning rate for that operation – the learning rate for all the operations involved will then be aggregated.

Example 16.4

The learning curve theorem applied to a process with several operations

The manufacture of a product involves four operations.

Operation	Improvement rate	Percentage of task
1	90%	30%
2	90%	20%
3	85%	20%
4	80%	30%

The aggregate learning curve slope will be:

$$(0.90 \times 0.30) + (0.90 \times 0.20) + (0.85 \times 0.20) + (0.80 \times 0.30)$$
$$= 0.27 + 0.18 + 0.17 + 0.24$$
$$= 0.86$$

16.11.4 Drawing the learning curve

The cumulative average hours per unit could be plotted on graph paper, when they would appear as shown in Figure 16.6.

Figure 16.6 **Learning curve**

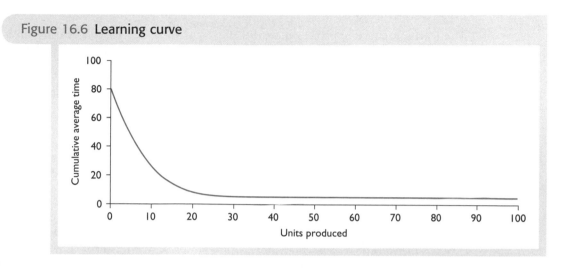

In practice, log-log paper is used (see Figure 16.7) because it has the following advantages:

■ all lines will be approximately straight
■ the cumulative total can be plotted within the confines of the paper
■ for forecasting, a ruler can be laid on the actual line and the results read off.

Figure 16.7 **An 85 per cent learning curve on log-log scale**

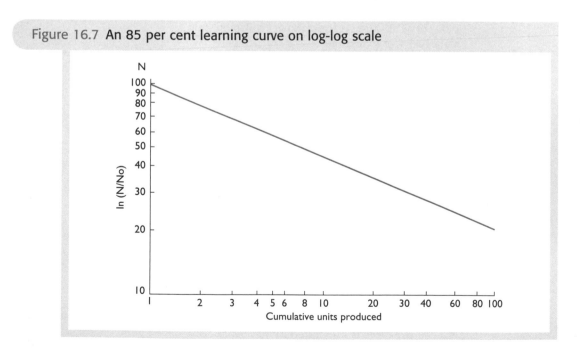

16.11.5 The application of learning curves

The greatest potential for savings resulting from learning curve analysis lies in high-cost items, those with a high direct labour content and those at the beginning of the curve.

Price determination

The learning curve approach indicates the areas in which to concentrate on a price analysis in order to obtain the greatest savings. The method of using learning curves to renegotiate the price for a repeat order is shown in Example 16.5.

Example 16.5

Using learning curve analysis to gain cost savings

Let us say that 200 items were purchased at £100 each. A repeat order for an additional 200 items is under negotiation.

Analyse the supplier's costs based on the following information: £2000 was spent on tools, half of which was written off on the first order. Raw material costs per item were £40 for the first order, but will now be £45. The supplier has given a 10 per cent pay rise to his workforce. Direct labour costs amounted to £50 for the first order.

The supplier made no profit on the first order and considers that he is entitled to a profit of at least 10 per cent. Assuming a 90 per cent learning curve, what should the new price be?

Solution

	£
Original price per item	100.00
Deduct tooling cost	10.00
	90.00
Deduct cost not subject to learning – raw materials	40.00
Balance subject to learning	50.00
Add pay rise of 10 per cent	5.00
	55.00
90 per cent of £55	49.50
Add half cost of tooling	5.00
Add material costs	45.00
	99.50
Add 10 per cent profit	9.95
Price per item for repeat order	109.45

Make-or-buy decisions

When comparing the costs of making and buying, the effect of learning on each production run should be determined and taken into consideration as well as the planned quantity.

Delivery times

Knowledge of the learning curve principle can enable a supplier to offer improved delivery times. The principle is illustrated by Example 16.6.

Example 16.6

Using learning curve analysis to promote delivery times

A contract is placed for 100 units of a component. By allocating 7200 labour hours, the manufacturer expects to produce 10 units in the first month. Assuming that an 80 per cent learning curve applies, how long should it take to complete the order?

Solution

The contract should take just under five months – not ten months as might be expected from a constant output of ten units, which would be the case if no learning took place.

Month	Capacity (labour hours)	Cumulative average values (80% learning curve, from tables)	Units produced	Cumulative total
1	7200	1.00	10	10
2	7200	0.80	16	26
3	7200	0.70	21	47
4	7200	0.64	25	72
5	7200	0.60	30	102

16.11.6 When not to use learning curves

Learning curves are not useful in the following cases:

- when learning is not constant, that is, where a straight line cannot be fitted to the data reasonably accurately
- where the direct labour content of the job is small
- where the cost or volume does not justify the expensive periodic time studies or job costing required to obtain the data from which the learning curve is constructed
- when production is largely automated so that human input is relatively small.

16.12 Project management

16.12.1 Definitions

In the present context, a project may be defined as:[21]

> an activity (or usually, a number of related activities) carried out according to a plan in order to achieve a definite objective within a certain period of time and that will close when the objective has been achieved.

Project management is:[22]

> the function of evaluating, planning and controlling a project so that it is finished on time, to specification and within budget.

16.12.2 Types of project

Lock[23] classifies projects under four headings:

1 *Civil engineering, construction, petrochemical, mining and quarrying projects* – these are normally undertaken at a site, exposed to the elements and remote from the contractor's office

2 *Manufacturing projects* – aimed at the production of a piece of equipment or machinery, ship, aircraft, land vehicle or some item of specially designed hardware

3 *Management projects* – operations involving the management and coordination of activities to produce an end result that is not identifiable principally as an item of hardware or construction, such as the relocation of offices or installation of a new computer system

4 *Research projects* – aimed at extending the boundaries of current scientific knowledge that are high risk because the outcomes are uncertain.

16.12.3 The contribution of purchasing to delivering a project

Purchasing has a significant role to play by contributing to ensuring that a project is 'finished on time, to specification and within budget' in such ways as the following:

- identifying the possible risks associated with the supply chain and, for each risk, determining an acceptable risk mitigation strategy

- liaising at each stage with appropriate members of the project's organisation, such as the project manager, architects, designers, consultants, quantity surveyors, site engineers, concerning the specification, procurement and scheduling of materials, equipment and service required for the contract

- conducting procurement in the most effective manner whether that be through the client's, contractor's or independent agency's procurement facility

- designing a detailed cost model and affordability envelope for consideration at the tender stage

- assistance in preparation of specifications and identifying weaknesses that may, later, generate price change requests

- identifying how the supply chain meets each project milestone need

- issuing pre-qualification questionnaires and invitations to tender

- designing the detailed evaluation models for PQQs and ITTs

- negotiating the terms of the contract and other detail, including price

- establishing and maintaining positive supplier relationships

- conducting effective contract performance meetings

- controlling free issue/customer furnished equipment

- ensuring payments are only made when appropriate

- ensuring performance bonds and insurances remain in place.

16.13 Scheduling

Of the above contributions, one of the most important is that of ensuring that materials and equipment are on site as needed to obviate delays in meeting the scheduled times for the completion of each part of the project.

Two useful scheduling tools are Gantt charts and networks.

16.13.1 Gantt charts

Devised by Henry L. Gantt in 1917, Gantt charts depict the occurrence of the activities comprising a project across time. An example of a Gantt, or bar, chart is shown in Figure 16.8.

Figure 16.8 **Gantt Chart**

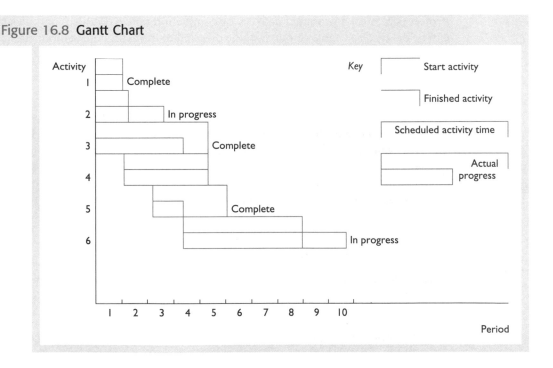

Gantt activity progress charts perform several functions:

- They show at a glance how project activities are progressing, so, in Figure 16.8, for example, activities 2 and 6 are behind schedule, activities 1 and 4 are on time and activities 3 and 5 are ahead of schedule.

- They can facilitate the coordination of activities and labour as activities represented by overlapping bars can be performed concurrently to the degree that they overlap, while activities shown by non-overlapping bars must be performed in the sequence indicated, so activity 4 in Figure 16.8 cannot be started until the completion of activity 1, but can be performed concurrently with activities 3 and 5.

- They are most useful in scheduling a series of unrelated activities, but where many activities must be correlated, network analysis (see next section) is more appropriate.

591

16.13.2 Network analysis

BS 6079-2 defines network analysis as:

> A group of techniques for presenting information to assist the planning and controlling of projects. The information . . . includes the sequence and logical interrelationships of all project activities.

There are two common types of networks:

- critical path analysis (CPA)
- program evaluation and review techniques (PERT)

16.13.3 Critical path analysis (CPA)

Like Gantt charts, CPA is used to plan the tasks that must be completed on time if the whole project is to meet a promised delivery or completion date. CPA also identifies tasks that can be delayed to enable resources to be diverted to more urgent requirements. A further benefit of CPA is that it indicates the minimum time in which a project can be completed.

16.13.4 CPA and sequencing

CPA is similar to Gantt charts in that it is based on the concept that some activities cannot start until others have been completed. Thus, with building, walls cannot be constructed until the foundations have been prepared and roofing cannot take place until the walls have been built. The foundations and walls are thus critical and on the critical path.

Other activities, such as making window frames, are not dependent on the completion of other tasks. Therefore each can be done either before or after a certain *milestone* in the project has been reached. These are non-dependent, or *parallel*, tasks.

16.13.5 CPM/PERT terminology

Some basic terms are shown in Table 16.4.

All the above can be shown in one node as depicted in Figure 16.9.

Figure 16.9 A node, representing an activity with its key schedule details completed

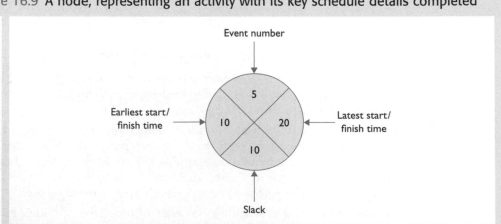

Table 16.4 Key terms used in network analysis

Term	Explanation
Activity	A task or job requiring resources, such as digging foundations. An *activity* is represented by an arrow $\longrightarrow$
An event	A point in time at which an activity or a number of activities start or finish. An *event* is represented by a circle, or *node*, in which the number of the event appears
Path	A sequence of events that leads from the starting node to the finishing node. Thus, the sequence 1, 2, 3, 4, 5, 6 is a *path*. The length (of time) of any path can be determined by adding the estimated times for the activities on that path. The longest path governs the completion time and so is referred to as the *critical path*
Duration	The estimated time in hours or days needed to perform the activity
Earliest start (ES)	The earliest time (measured from the start of the project) when an activity can begin. An activity cannot begin until all the necessary preceding activities have been completed
Earliest finish (EF)	The sum of its earliest start time and duration
Latest finish (LF)	The latest time (measured from the start of the project) when an activity may be completed without delaying any activity that immediately follows it and thereby delaying the completion of the project
Latest start (LS)	The latest finish time minus its duration
Slack	The amount of leeway allowed in either starting or finishing an activity. *Slack* can be calculated as either LS − ES or LF − EF

16.13.6 Network conventions

A precedence diagram indicates the sequence in which activities must be completed. Thus, in the A–C diagram in Figure 16.10, activity A must be completed before activity B can begin and activity B before C.

Figure 16.10 A precedence diagram

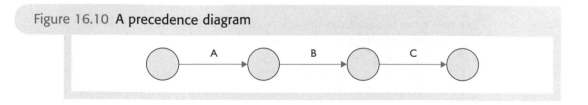

If two activities – A and B – have to be completed before activity C can begin, the diagram would be as shown in Figure 16.11.

A and B can, however, be performed simultaneously and independently of each other.

Figure 16.11 **Non-dependent activities that need to be completed before the next**

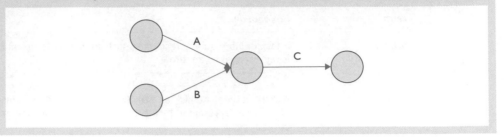

If a number of activities enter a node, it means that each activity must be completed before the activity beginning at that node can commence (see Figure 16.12).

Figure 16.12 **Several activities need to be completed before the next two can start**

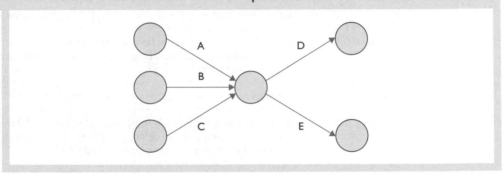

Thus, activities A, B and C must be completed before either activity D or E can start.

Two activities may not, however, share the *same* tail and head event as this would imply that the two activities have the same duration, which may not be the case. A diagram such as Figure 16.13, therefore, is not allowed.

Figure 16.13 **Two activities cannot share same head and tail events**

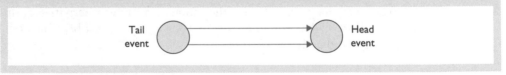

The above can be avoided by using a so-called *dummy node*. The dummy node or activity is used to preserve the separate identities of each activity. An example of a dummy node is shown in Figure 16.14.

Dummy nodes are indicated by dotted lines. In the activities shown in Figure 16.14, activities A and B must be completed before C can be started. Dummy activities have a time activity of zero.

For reference purposes, nodes are numbered from left to right. Each activity must have a preceding 'tail' event and a subsequent 'head' event. Many activities may have the same tail event or same head event (but not both). Activities that do not have a tail are not allowed. Such activities are known as *danglers*. Further, a series of activities that

Figure 16.14 **A dummy node**

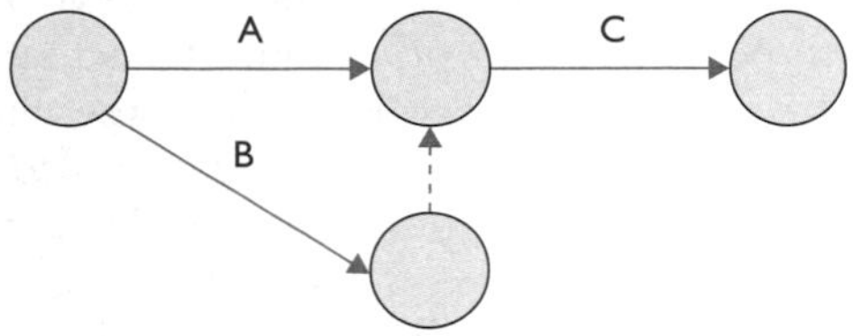

Figure 16.15 **Loops are not allowed**

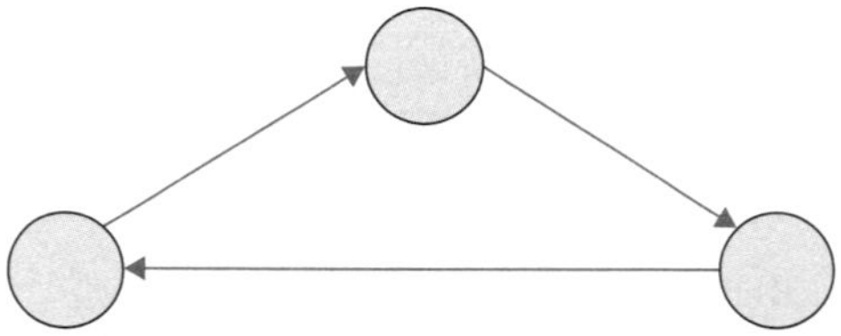

lead back to the same event are termed *loops*. Loops such as that shown in Figure 16.15 are not allowed.

16.13.7 CPM/PERT project scheduling procedure

This involves the following steps:

1 Identify and list the activities that comprise the project.
2 Identify the immediate predecessor activity for each activity in the project.
3 Estimate the duration (time from start to finish) for each activity.
4 Draw a network depicting the activities and their immediate predecessors identified in steps 1 and 2.
5 Using the network and the estimated activity times, calculate the earliest start and earliest finish times for each activity by making a forward pass through the network – the earliest finish time for the last activity in the project identifies the total time required to complete the project.
6 Using the project completion time arrived at in step 5, make a backwards pass through the network to identify the latest start and latest finish times for each activity.
7 Use the difference between the latest start time and the earliest start time for each activity to identify the slack time available for that activity.
8 Find the activity or activities with zero slack – these are the critical path activities.
9 Use the information from steps 5 and 6 to develop the activity schedule for the project.

16.13.8 Network analysis and cost

Time is not the only consideration associated with project management. The cost is of equal importance.

What is known as PERT/Cost is a technique used to plan, schedule and control project costs and ensure adherence to a specified budget. Essentially, it involves identifying all the costs associated with a project and then developing a schedule of when the costs are expected to occur. As with other budgets, actual costs are compared with what was budgeted at prescribed intervals, such as the end of each activity, and appropriate action taken. Attention to critical activities also indicates how, by the introduction of additional resources, it may be possible to shorten completion times. The cost of introducing such resources has to be weighed against the projected savings. If, for example, a project has high daily fixed costs, it may be profitable to take on extra labour, buy or hire equipment or subcontract part of the work to reduce the completion time.

Example 16.7

Network analysis

Steps 1, 2 and 3

A project is comprised of the following activities and their estimated duration times. You are asked to draw the critical path network and ascertain the duration of the critical path and slack times for all the activities.

Activity	Immediate predecessor	Estimated duration (days)
A	–	4
B	A	2
C	B	2
D	C	4
E	C	10
F	D, E	10
G	F	2

Step 4 Draw the network

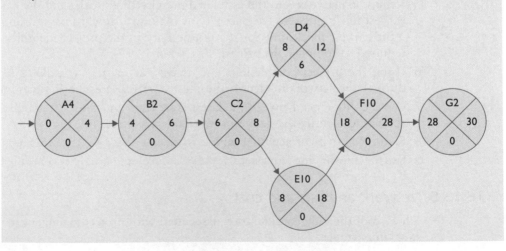

Step 5

Determine the earliest start and earliest finish times and insert them in the nodes as above:

Time required to complete the project = 30 weeks

Steps 6 and 7

Determine the latest starts and latest finish times by working backwards from the completion date. The latest finish time for an activity entering a particular node is equal to the smallest of the latest start times for all activities entering the node.

Slack time = Latest start (LS) – Earliest start (ES)

or

= Latest finish (LF) – Earliest finish (EF)

Activity	Latest start	Earliest start	Slack
A	0	0	0
B	4	4	0
C	6	6	0
D	12	18	6
E	8	8	0
F	18	18	0
G	28	28	0

Insert slack times into nodes.

Step 8

Activities with zero nodes are A + B + C + E + F + G. This forms the critical path.

Step 9

We are now able to state:

- the total time to complete the project, which is 30 weeks
- the scheduled start and completion times for each activity
- which activities are critical and must be completed exactly on time to keep the project on schedule
- how long non-critical activities can be delayed before they cause a delay to the project's completion.

16.13.9 CPM and PERT

Both CPM and PERT use much of the same terminology and techniques. Both aim to show the logical sequence of activities in a project. CPM, however, was developed mainly for use in industrial projects where activity times could be estimated with reasonable accuracy. In contrast, PERT was devised in the late 1950s in connection with the Polaris missile project where the times could not be forecast because the associated activities had not been previously encountered. Unlike CPM, which provides only one time estimate for each activity, PERT provides three – namely:

- *normal (n)* – the most realistic assessment of the time required, without allowing for unforeseen contingencies

- *pessimistic (p)* – the longest times that will be required, allowing for all foreseeable contingencies

- *optimistic (o)* – the shortest duration within which the activity can be accomplished if all circumstances work out favourably.

These three times are used to calculate expected time on the basis of the following weighted average:

$$\text{Expected time} = \frac{(o + 4n + p)}{6}$$

In practice, the estimate would normally be based on the most likely time.

The differences between CPM and PERT have, however, now largely disappeared and the two terms tend to be used interchangeably as a generic term to embrace the whole network planning and control process.

Computerised scheduling

A large project involves many activities, so manual calculations for CPM and PERT would be both tedious and require considerable checking. Computer-generated CPM graphs and schedules, however, can show the relationships between project tasks, identify contingencies and conflicts, anticipate resource needs, permit the updating of networks and allow project managers to easily project the impacts of alternative schedules. Many software packages are currently available for project scheduling and control using network analysis techniques.

Resource constraints

So far, CPM has only been discussed in relation to the time aspect of project management. In practice, managers may wish, or be required, to reduce the duration of a project for several reasons, such as to receive incentive payments for early completion or release resources committed to the project for use on other contracts. This shortening of completion times, which can normally be achieved only by adding resources such as labour, overtime or subcontracting is referred to as *crashing*. Crashing can therefore be defined as the process of reducing the time it takes to complete an activity by adding resources. The aim is to ascertain which activities should be crashed and at what cost. To describe crashing and other CPM/PERT techniques is outside the scope of this book.

16.13.10 Network analysis and purchasing

- Generally, network analysis is applicable to large, complicated, long-running projects, such as construction contracts, and subcontracted work.

- Network analysis provides purchasing with an overview of the complete project and the significance of the contribution of purchasing to its successful completion.

- Network analysis is a team activity to which purchasing contributes essential information, such as the availability of materials and the duration of lead times.

■ The network enables purchasing to compare actual with promised deliveries and take early expediting action on 'slippage' to prevent delays in delivery having a cumulative effect on the whole project.

■ Purchased items can be scheduled for delivery in the right sequence and to the right location, for instance, materials for construction projects can be delivered direct to site immediately before use, thus reducing the possibility of loss from theft or deterioration.

■ In subcontracted work, progress payments can be linked to the completion of specified events.

■ Networks can be used to control expenditure with long-running contracts. Computer printouts can show:

  – actual costs incurred at a given date

  – estimated costs for the rest of the project

  – statements of future expenditure, such as purchase orders still outstanding.

16.14 Operational research (OR)

16.14.1 Definition

Operational research (OR) is defined by the UK Operational Research Society as:

> The application of the methods of science to complex problems arising in the direction and management of large systems of men, machine, materials and money in industry, business, government and defence. The distinctive approach is to develop a scientific model of the system incorporating measurement of factors, such as chance and risk, with which to predict and compare the outcomes of alternative decisions, strategies or controls. The purpose is to help management determine its policy and action scientifically.

In this context, 'research' has the narrower meaning of the application of new mathematical models, methods and techniques to the solution of business or other problems. The above definition emphasises that:

■ OR is concerned with problems of organisation and the allocation of resources, which are labour, machines, materials and money, to achieve a specified objective

■ a model or system can be built

■ OR is a service to management

■ alternative decisions can be evaluated against some measure of effectiveness.

16.14.2 OR procedures

The application of quantitative techniques to management practice is known as operational research. The major phases of an OR project have been identified as being:

■ stating the problem for which a solution is required

■ constructing a mathematical model as an analogue (a symbolic model or simulation) of the real system – generally taking the form:

$$E = f(x_1 y_1)$$

where E represents the effectiveness of the system, and x and y the controllable variables and non-controllable variables in the system respectively

- deriving an optimum solution from the model either *analytically* – that is, by the manipulation of the mathematical model – or *numerically* – which is when a large number of iterations of possible values of the variables are created and the equation solved repetitively
- testing the model and the solution
- establishing controls over the solution – that is, indicating changes in the values of the uncontrollable variables or the relationships between variables that would render the solution invalid
- implementation – translating the tested solution into a set of operating procedures capable of being understood and applied by those who will be responsible for their use.

16.14.3 OR and supplies

Some reference to applications of OR techniques have been made earlier in this book, namely:

- elementary inventory control (sections 10.4 and 10.5)
- network analysis (section 16.13.2 above)
- materials requirements planning (sections 10.16 and 10.17)
- replacement theory and capital expenditure evaluation (section 13.9).

Many supplies problems can be solved by the application of techniques from such OR fields as linear programming, queuing theory and probability theory. The application of OR to supplies work has been assisted by computerisation, which can deal easily with a large number of variables, such as many different items of stores in inventory control. In fact, with the increasing use of computers and availability of specialist software, many OR studies can now be performed by purchasing staff without the need for specialist assistance. In addition to the approaches referred to above, some other applications of OR are given in Table 16.5.

16.14.4 Limitations of OR

Decision making is the process or activity of selecting a future course of action from a number of possible alternatives. Decisions can be grouped into different categories, such as strategic, operational and administrative, and into those that are programmable and non-programmable. Programmable decisions can be worked out by computer as all the variables are quantifiable and the decision rules or constraints clearly defined. Non-programmable decisions cannot be quantified and require the exercise of human judgement. It is important therefore to recognise that OR is limited in its effectiveness, working best in situations where the analysis and comparison of relationships between controllable and uncontrollable variables can be expressed in terms of a mathematical model.

There are times when the subjective judgement of the decision-maker must act contrary to the OR recommendation. OR, for example, can indicate the EOQs and most economic inventory levels for raw materials and components, but these recommendations may be disregarded by the purchasing function if it is known that a threatened strike will seriously disrupt production unless sufficient supplies can be obtained to ensure continuity of output, at least in the short term.

Table 16.5 Applications of OR

Aspect of OR	Typical supplies applications
Linear programming (LP) A mathematical technique for determining the optimum allocation of resources, such as capital, raw materials or labour, or plan to obtain a desired objective, such as minimum cost of operations or maximum profit when there are alternative uses of the resource in question. LP can also help to analyse alternative objectives, such as the economics of alternative resources	■ Analysis of quotations from several suppliers that, because of limited resources, can accept only certain combinations of the business offered. Linear programming can indicate the combination of quotations that will minimise purchasing expenditure ■ Determining the relative advantages of a low price and a high probability of late delivery against a higher price with a better chance of achieving ideal delivery time
Queuing theory Mathematical analysis and solution of problems in which items requiring or providing service stand idle and when optimising either the arrival rate or service rate or both is required	■ Sequencing and scheduling arrivals of parts or components to achieve minimum costs ■ The most economical staffing of stores to provide the minimum waiting time
Games theory A mathematical technique or decision-making tool in competitive situations in which the outcome depends not only on the actions of a manager but also on those of competitors. The aim of the game is to devise a strategy that maximises returns and minimises losses	■ *Negotiation* Decisions are based on the assumption that the rival is shrewd and will always play to minimise the opponent's gain
Decision trees A decision tree is a type of flow chart or visual aid that summarises the various alternatives and options available in a complicated decision process. Decision trees consist of three parts: – the initial decision point – the branches representing various outcomes – the paths, which may consist of several branches representing the various probabilities and events of a particular outcome. The whole tree represents the decision problem. The object of decision trees is not to find optimum solutions, but instead represent visually a wide range of alternatives that can apply to specific policies and procedures	■ Virtually any supplies problems that can be reduced to: – a set of mutually exclusive decisions – for each decision, a set of possible outcomes, together with an assessment of the likelihood of each outcome occurring – revenues or costs for each outcome
Forecasting The process of estimating future quantities required, normally by using past experience as a basis. OR methods of forecasting include: – exponential smoothing – moving averages – trend analysis – multiple regression analysis – curve fitting	■ Any supplies problem involving the prediction of future requirements, such as stock levels, purchasing expenditure, stores space, purchase of sensitive commodities in various market conditions
Probability theory An aspect of forecasting based on mathematical techniques for establishing the likelihood of particular events taking place. The probability of an event ranges from 0 to 1 (0 = event will certainly not occur; 1 = event is certain)	■ The application of statistical techniques, such as sampling, as a means of controlling quality ■ Determining the life expectancy of materials and components ■ Predicting the probability of stock outs at given levels of inventory

Case study

The Motomes Group manufactures a high-quality range of caravans. Seven months ago, it recruited a new engineering design manager who initiated a design review of the whole range of caravans. This has led to significant changes to the bills of materials for each product within the range.

At a recent trade show at the Birmingham International Exhibition Centre, the new range was shown to trade buyers. The demand has been exceptional and the current year's sales are already showing an increase of 24 per cent. This has led to the five-year business plan being revised. Year-on-year, sales are predicted to carry on rising by at least 15 per cent.

The managing director called a senior management meeting, which included you as procurement manager. The meeting dealt with the increase in production and its impact on existing skills and manufacturing facilities and the discussion focused on procurement issues. The engineering design manager voiced the view that, given the increase in quantities, the purchase prices should 'come tumbling down'. He mentioned the learning curve as being very relevant and proposed that your department immediately undertake an investigation into how the purchase prices could be dramatically reduced. In that he was supported by the managing director.

The manufacturing director then said that some existing manufacturing lines would have to be outsourced because he could not create the necessary facilities in the available time. The Motomes Group has never previously outsourced anything.

You have promised that, within a week, you will have a list of all the items to be outsourced. It is likely to include ten lines, each with considerable sub-assembly work being needed, prior to assembly.

The managing director has asked you to prepare a project plan to deal with the outsourcing actions. These parallel actions will be a major challenge for you and your department.

Tasks

1 What techniques are available to you to deal with the pricing issue?

2 What actions would you include in the project plan to ensure that you deliver the outsourcing strategy, on time?

Discussion questions

16.1 Turner[24] records that when Neil Armstrong was being interviewed about the Moon landing, he was asked to state the most frightening moment. Was it as the Moon Lander came down and he thought it might crash? Was it as he stepped off the ladder? Was it when they came to blast off from the Moon and he thought that the rockets might not be powerful enough? No, the most frightening moment was being on the launch pad at Cape Canaveral and under him were 2000 components, every single one of which had been bought on minimum price tender! One of them did indeed fail in 1986.

(a) List the possible dangers of accepting the lowest tender.

(b) If you must accept the lowest tender, how might you seek to ensure that quality or performance does not fall below specified standards?

16.2 The public sector engages in formal tendering whereas the private sector is generally less formal in its approach to obtaining quotations from the supply market. Do you agree with this distinction? If you do agree, how would you account for the contracting approaches?

16.3 Can you identify six positive influences that EU Regulations have had on the way in which public expenditure is committed on long-term contracts?

16.4 It is good practice to debrief unsuccessful tenderers who have engaged in a procurement competition. Accordingly:
(i) What content should be included in a debrief?
(ii) What information would you reveal about other firm's tenders?
(iii) What benefits should accrue from the debrief?

16.5 The following figures show the monthly percentages of all deliveries that have been received on time over a period of 12 months:

90 92 94 93 93 94 95 94 92 93 94 95

(a) Compare a three months' moving average forecast with an exponential smoothing forecast using $a = 0.2$
(b) Which of the two averages provides the better forecast?
(c) What is the forecast for the next month?

16.6 Tenders have been received from three firms in respect of a major price of equipment. The tendered prices are:
1 £254,360
2 £460,899
3 £215,753
Your technical people have made it clear that they want firm 1, but their price must be under £200,000. What actions would you now take?

16.7 The XYZ Co. Ltd incurred the following overhead costs.

	£
Depreciation of factory buildings	2000
Repair and maintenance of buildings	1200
Factory administrative costs (treat as production overheads)	3000
Depreciation of machinery	1600
Insurance of machinery	400
Heating	780
Lighting	200
Canteen	1800

Information relevant to the factory production and service departments is:

Detail	Production A	Production B	Service C	Service D
Floor space (square metres)	2,400	3,200	1,600	800
Volume (cubic metres)	6,000	12,000	4,800	3,200
Number of employees	60	60	30	30
Machinery at book value	£60,000	£40,000	£20,000	£40,000

How do you suggest the overhead costs should be apportioned for departments A, B, C and D?

16.8 Match the terms on the left with the concepts and definitions on the right.

(a) Activity-based costing	(1) Something that increases the worth of a product or service
(b) Lifecycle stages	(2) Expected selling price less desired profit
(c) Value-added activity	(3) The process of attaching costs based on activities
(d) Target cost	(4) Idle time, transfer time, storage time
(e) Non-value-added activities	(5) A principle whereby fixed as well as variable costs are allotted to cost units and total overheads are absorbed according to activity level
(f) Variance	(6) Development, introduction, growth, maturity, decline
(g) Absorption costing	(7) Difference between standard and actual prices and quantities
(h) Cost driver	(8) Something that causes or influences costs

16.9 What is the 'learning curve'? Does it have any practical application in the twenty-first century?

Past examination questions

1 Explain how an organisation can use the product lifecycle as part of its strategy.
CIPS, *The Business Environment for Purchasing and Supply*, May 2009

2 SkyFly is a medium-sized executive charter airline which specialises in providing flexible travel solutions to business users. SkyFly owns a number of medium-sized aircraft. It also leases other aircraft as required.

The directors of SkyFly have recently been considering the acquisition of another smaller company, EvacuFly. This company specialises in providing emergency evacuation services to large corporations which operate in difficult or remote locations that are often subject to civil and social unrest.

Business volumes within SkyFly have decreased over the last two years as a result of competition from larger international companies. SkyFly is now having to fly to more remote locations to retain its market share. EvacuFly already services some of these higher-risk and more remote locations.

SkyFly's profitability is under constant pressure due to increasing energy and operating costs. SkyFly's purchasing challenge is always to obtain premium-quality service offerings (for example, catering, aircraft, flexible departure timings) but at the best commercial terms. Recently SkyFly has also been considering leasing arrangements instead of outright ownership of its fleet of aircraft. The procurement manager at SkyFly has been asked to consider other cost-cutting measures which could improve profitability without compromising on quality.

Tasks

(a) Describe **four** macro environmental factors which impact on SkyFly's operation.
(b) Explain **three** benefits to SkyFly of getting ahead with the acquisition of EvacuFly.
(c) Explain **two** advantages for SkyFly of leasing its fleet of aircraft.

(d) Explain **one** disadvantage for SkyFly of leasing its fleet of aircraft.

(e) Describe **two** ways in which the procurement manager of SkyFly could reduce costs without compromising on quality.

CIPS, *An Introduction to Purchasing Strategy*, May 2009

References

1   Brian Farrington Limited: www.brianfarrington.co.uk

2   CIPS, 'Practice position statement: tendering and post tendering negotiation': www.cips.org

3   OGC, 'Negotiation after receipt of formal bids or tenders and before . . .', www.ogc.gov.uk/briefings_post_tender_negotiation.asp, 13 Jul 2009

4   OGC, Life Cycle Costing (LCC), www.ogc.gov.uk/implementing_plans_introduction_life_cycle_costing_.asp, 13 Jul 2009

5   Chartered Institute of Management Accountants, 'Management accounting official terminology', CIMA, revised 1991, p. 44

6   http://www.directives.doe.gov/pdfs/doe/doetext/neword/430/g4301-1chp23.html

7   As 5 above, p. 49

8   CIMA NHS Working Group, 'Target costing in the NHS – Reforming the NHS from within', October 2005

9   Gagne and Discenza, 'Target costing', *Journal of Business and Industrial Marketing*, 1995, Vol. 10, No. 1, pp. 16–22

10 As 5 above, p. 26

11 As 5 above, p. 90

12 Raffish, N. and Turney, P. B. B. (eds), 'Glossary of activity-based management', *Journal of Cost Management*, fall, 1991, pp. 53–63

13 Lapsley, J., Llewellyn, S. and Falconer, H., *Cost Management in the Public Sector*, Longman, 1994, p. 90

14 Cooper, R. and Kaplan, R. S., 'How cost accounting systematically distorts product costs', in William, J. B. (ed.), *Accounting and Management Field Study Perspectives*, Harvard Business School, 1987, Paragraph D–15

15 Burch, J., *Cost and Management Accounting*, West Publishing, 1994, p. 458

16 Barker, J., 'How to achieve more effective purchasing through activity-based costing', paper presented to Second PSERG Conference, University of Bath, 1993

17 Ness, J. A. and Cucuzza, T. G., 'Tapping the full potential of ABC', *Harvard Business Review*, July/August, 1995, pp. 130–8

18 As 5 above, p. 38

19 As 5 above, p. 58

20 Karjewski, L. J. and Ritzman, I. P., *Operations Management*, Addison Wesley, 1990, p. 208

21 French, D. and Saward, H., *Dictionary of Management*, Pan, 1975, p. 333

22 Lock, D., *Project Management*, Gower, 1994

23 As 22 above, pp. 3–4

24 Turner, J. R., *The Handbook of Project-based Management*, 2nd edn, McGraw-Hill, 1999, p. 234

Chapter 17

Purchasing research, performance and ethics

Learning outcomes

This chapter aims to provide an understanding of:

- purchasing research and its contribution to business change and efficiency
- evaluating purchasing performance
- benchmarking
- purchasing ethics
- purchasing and fraudulent activity
- environmental aspects of purchasing.

Key ideas

- Areas, organisation and methods of purchasing research.
- Quantitative and qualitative approaches to purchasing performance, evaluation and measurement.
- Purchasing audits and benchmarking.
- Principles of personal and global ethics.
- Ethical issues relating to suppliers.
- Ethical codes, training and decisions.
- The nature and indications of fraud and fraud prevention.
- Environmental legislation.
- Environmental purchasing policies and management.
- Screening suppliers for good environmental performance.

17.1 Purchasing research

17.1.1 Definition

Purchasing research has been defined by Fearon[1] as:

> The systematic gathering, recording and analysing of data about problems relating to the purchasing of goods and services.

The importance of purchasing research has been enhanced by the following:

- rapid changes in technology and economic circumstances are increasing the complexity of purchasing

- much purchasing is undertaken in conditions of uncertainty so that strategic decisions have to be made involving individuals, organisations and events outside the direct control of the purchasing company

- electronic data processing provides the facility to store and process vast quantities of data that, when processed, can improve decision making

- the increased outsourcing of non-core business functions

- the new focus on partnering and evaluation of the benefits

- e-procurement facilitating real-time ordering and payment by line employees

- purchasing as a function is increasingly required to quantify its contribution to profitability and its strategic function in the supply chain.

17.1.2 Areas of research

In selecting topics for research, it should be remembered that the greater the expenditure on an area, the greater is the potential for significant cost savings. Among the most important areas of research are the following:

- *materials and commodities*
  - trends in the requirements of the company for specific materials
  - price and cost analysis
  - substitute materials or items
  - specifications and standardisation
  - value analysis, value engineering
  - usage analysis
  - use of learning curves

- *purchasing policies and procedures*
  - whether or not any policies are in need of revision
  - if it is more economical to make in rather than buy out or vice versa
  - whether or not any opportunities exist for the consolidation of purchasing requirements
  - purchasing contributions to competitive advantage
  - forms design, distribution and elimination
  - the application of activity-based costing to the purchasing function
  - how the information made available by EDP can be used more effectively
  - whether or not the purchasing organisation for materials can be improved by regrouping the purchasing, stores and other related subsystems, such as by means of materials or logistics management approaches
  - to what extent operational research methods can be applied to purchasing
  - internal and external customer satisfaction with the purchasing function

- *suppliers*
  - supplier appraisal
  - supplier performance
  - the possibilities for supplier development
  - contracting simultaneously with two suppliers to design and build
  - supplier reviews – how often suppliers are changed and how new suppliers are found
  - supply chain – analysis of at least one level back
  - purchasing consortium
  - price monitoring after contracting
  - outsourcing the procurement process
  - global sourcing
- *staff*
  - staff responsibilities
  - staff turnover, absenteeism, morale
  - what overtime, if any, is worked
  - staff succession
  - staff training and development
  - staff remuneration, facilities and incentives
- *miscellaneous*
  - purchasing applications of IT
  - expert systems and artificial intelligence
  - transportation of bought-out items
  - securing supplies in conditions of uncertainty
  - disposal of scrap and obsolete stores equipment
  - terms and conditions of purchase
  - the measurement of purchasing performance
  - purchasing ethics
  - identification and management of supply chain risk.

17.1.3 Organisation for research

Some research is undertaken by all purchasing departments, even though this may be only rudimentary, such as consulting trade directories or the Internet to locate possible suppliers of an item not previously bought. A willingness to initiate research is essential to the development of the status of purchasing. Unless such an initiative is taken by purchasing, the research role will be assumed by other functions, such as design, marketing and production. Purchasing research may be formal or informal.

- *Small business units* – these may be unable to allocate resources such as personnel and finance to establish a formal purchasing research section. Staff should nevertheless be encouraged to keep up to date by meeting supplier representatives, attending trade exhibitions, attending appropriate short courses, having access to and opportunities for studying journals and other relevant literature, as well as networking with other purchasing staff at meetings of professional bodies, such as the CIPS.

■ *Research sections* – systematic research requires time and freedom from other distractions. These conditions can be best provided when the organisation is large enough, by establishing a special purchasing research section as a centralised staff activity to provide assistance to line members of the purchasing function. Experience has shown that companies with formal purchasing research arrangements:

- engage in more research projects
- do so in greater depth
- make a significant contribution to profitability and operational effectiveness.

■ *Other approaches* – when a specialised research section is not feasible, formalised purchasing research may be undertaken by the following groups:

- *Project teams* concerned with a specific problem or range of problems – probably including staff from outside the purchasing function, such as design, production, finance and marketing, as in a value research or engineering project.
- *Supplier associations.*
- *Research consortiums.*
- *Use of specialised outside research facilities*, such as the Commodities Research Unit of the International Monetary Fund.
- *Collaboration with universities* – this may be 'contract' or 'collaborative' research. In contract research, the agenda for a project is set by the industrial partner with a university providing a research service at a commercial price on the same basis as any other supplier, while collaborative research's goals are jointly defined by both company or companies and the university. 'Clubs' or 'networks' are often set up by an individual university or consortium of universities to focus on a particular research topic. Companies wishing to become members usually pay an agreed annual subscription. Thus, the Centre for Research in Strategic Purchasing and Supply at Bath University claims to work, at any one time, with over 100 companies, often organised into 'project clubs'.
- *Support of individuals working for higher degrees* in purchasing and supply chain management.
- *Use of consultants* to investigate a specific matter. Some large consultancies also undertake independent research that is made available to the relevant industries at a cost. An example is the *Purcon Index* – a specialised survey of the salaries and total remuneration packages of purchasing and supplies staff throughout Britain. This index is updated annually in March and September. Similar research is undertaken by Market Focus Research Ltd.
- *Professional institutes* – The Institute of Logistics and Transport maintains a logistics research network – a special interest group of academics with some interested practitioner members. The network produces the *International Journal of Logistics Research and Applications*. The CIPS supports chairs in purchasing at several UK universities. In the USA, the Center for Advanced Purchasing Studies was established in 1986 as a national affiliation agreement between the NAPM (now ISM) and Arizona State University.

17.1.4 Research methodology

As with all other research, the first step in a purchasing or supply chain investigation is to adopt a plan or model of the research, from inception to completion. Sarantakos[2] states that the general assumption made by researchers who employ a research model in their work rests on the belief that:

- research can be perceived as evolving in a series of steps that are closely interrelated and the success of each depends on the successful completion of the preceding step
- the steps must be executed in a given order
- planning and execution of the research is more successful if a research model is employed – a typical one being that shown in Figure 17.1.

Figure 17.1 A purchasing research model

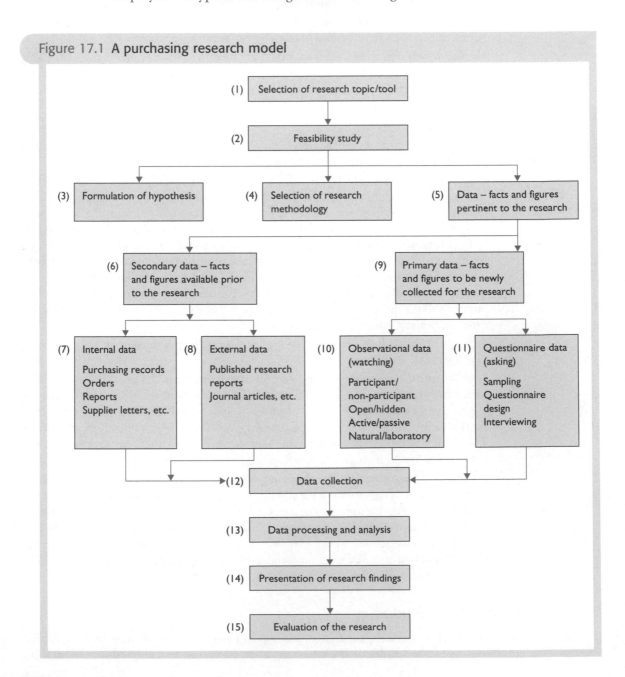

Purchasing performance evaluation

17.2.1 Definition

Purchasing performance evaluation may be defined as the quantitative or qualitative assessment over a given time towards the achievement of corporate or operational goals and objectives relating to purchasing economies, efficiency and effectiveness.

The significant words in this definition are the following:

■ *Quantitative or qualitative – quantitative* assessments are objective and measurable, using such measures as numbers of orders placed, reduction in lead times, price savings and reduced administrative costs, and will tend to be used where purchasing is regarded as a mainly clerical or transactional activity. *Qualitative* assessments use judgemental impressions regarding the contribution of purchasing to suppliers' goodwill, partnership sourcing, value analysis and internal customer satisfaction and is applicable when procurement is regarded as a strategic function.

■ *Performance evaluation – evaluation* is a more accurate term than *measurement*. By definition, 'measurement' implies quantification or the expression of a quality or attribute in numerical terms. Although the performance of purchasing managers is usually assessed by means of objective, quantified measures such as cost/price reductions and contributions to added value or profitability, performance evaluation frequently uses subjective, qualitative assessment approaches.

■ *Over a given time* – evaluations may relate to long-term (over one year) or short-term performance. Long-term objectives frequently extend several years into the future. Periodical reviews look at progress and outstanding actions needing to be undertaken. Progress can only be measured by reference to what was achieved in a past period and targets set for a future period. For this purpose, evaluations should always relate to specific time intervals.

■ *Corporate or operational goals and objectives* – goals or objectives are basic to performance evaluation: 'If we don't know where we are going, we shall not know when we arrive'. *Corporate objectives* will usually be set at board level. Such goals are relatively permanent, expressed in broad terms and derive from the mission statement of an organisation. Today, most corporate objectives relate to the provision of 'customer satisfaction'.

Organisational goals must be 'congruent' – that is, consistent with corporate goals, not only over time but also vertically and horizontally. *Vertically* means that the objectives should be consistent at all levels of the organisation, *horizontally*, that the objectives set for different activities concerned with delivering value to the ultimate customer, as in a supply chain, must be consistent and integrated.

Corporate objectives – usually expressed in broad qualitative terms – must be turned into specifics for operational purposes. Thus, the general strategy of 'delivering a cost-effective procurement service' may, for the next financial year, require purchasing to:

– achieve savings of 10 per cent on purchases

– award contracts for an e-tendering and supplier information database not later than [specify date], subject to availability of funds

- ensure that not less than 70 per cent of purchasing staff are working towards an approved purchasing qualification.

Operational goals, such as those shown above, can be expressed as quantified (SMART) objectives – that is, they should be **S**pecific, **M**easurable, **A**ttainable, **R**esults-orientated and **T**ime-based.

■ *Economies, efficiency and effectiveness* – *economies* means minimising the cost of resources acquired without loss of quality, which is achieved by spending less. Important tools in achieving economy are value engineering and value analysis.

Efficiency covers the relationship between the output of goods or services and the resources used to produce them, which means spending well. Efficiency and productivity are related as productivity is measured by the following ratio:

$$\text{Productivity} = \frac{\text{Outputs produced}}{\text{Inputs consumed}}$$

Effectiveness covers the relationship between the intended and the actual results of projects and programmes – that is, spending wisely. Economy, efficiency and effectiveness – commonly referred to as the three Es – constitute value for money (VFM). Securing and improving VFM is an important corporate objective and responsibility for its achievement lies primarily with operational managers. The terms efficiency and effectiveness will occur again in this text, but, from the standpoint of performance evaluation, some further aspects include the following:

- Organisations, functions, processes and the people concerned may be efficient but not effective – being the lowest-cost producer of products or services that no one wants is efficient but not effective and, as Kydos[3] observes:

  Nothing is more wasteful than doing with greater efficiency that which is totally unnecessary.

- Conversely, we can be effective without being efficient – using a steam hammer to crack the proverbial nut is effective, but not efficient.

- Managers can delegate efficiency, but must deal personally with effectiveness.

- Efficiency and effectiveness are not mutually exclusive – acceptable performance may reflect a combination of efficiency and effectiveness.

17.2.2 Some difficulties in measuring purchasing performance

Van Weele[4] has identified four 'problems' that, he states, 'seriously limit an objective and accurate assessment of the purchasing function':

■ *lack of definition* – concepts such as purchasing performance, efficiency and effectiveness are often not clearly defined or are used interchangeably

■ *lack of formal objectives and performance standards* – the problem, as we see it, however, is not the lack of standards – which receive considerable attention in textbooks and academic articles – but that many purchasing practitioners are either unaware of such standards or unwilling to apply them

■ *problems of accurate measurement* – Van Weele rightly states:

  Purchasing is not an isolated function; purchasing performance is the result of many activities which, due to their intangible character, are difficult to evaluate. In general, direct input–output relationships are difficult to identify; this seriously limits the possibility of measuring and evaluating purchasing activities in an accurate and comprehensive way.

- *differences in the scope of organisational purchasing* – purchasing is not a homogenous activity and with such factors as status, responsibilities, organisation, policies and procedures, it differs widely from one enterprise to another and those differences preclude the development of uniform measurement systems, so they also detract from the attention given to purchasing performance evaluation.

As stated above, a major problem when evaluating purchasing performance is the heterogeneous nature of the purchasing activity. In a USA study of the absence of a consistent system for measuring purchasing performance, Fearon and Bales[5] report that:

Anyone who wants a single group of performance measures for purchasing activities at every organisation is going to be disappointed. The measures that are important to the individual organisation may not be important to another. Therefore, the measures for purchasing performance have to be customised for virtually every organisation.

Measurement of purchasing performance is, however, important for all organisations as:

- if an activity cannot be measured, it cannot be effectively managed, nor can continuous and sustainable improvements be made
- measurement is critical for maintaining the competitive edge of companies in an increasingly crowded global marketplace.

17.2.3 Approaches to performance measurement

These may be grouped under five main headings:

- accounting approaches, namely:
  - profit centres
  - activity-based costing
  - standard costing and budgetary control
  - EVA (see section 17.3.4)
- the purchasing management audit approach
- comparative approaches
  - benchmarking and ratio
  - integrated benchmarking, such as EFQM and balanced scorecards (see sections 17.6.1 and 17.6.2)
- management by objectives (MBO) (see section 17.7)
- miscellaneous approaches, such as SERVQUAL (see section 17.8.2) and Six Sigma (see section 9.9.3).

17.3 Accounting approaches

17.3.1 The profit centre approach

In this approach, the purchasing function or activity is regarded as the part of the company that controls assets and is responsible not only for expenditure but also income.

The aim of this approach is to demonstrate that the purchasing function is a profit rather than a cost centre.

The profit centre approach involves establishing a centralised purchasing organisation that controls assets. The profitability of this centralised purchasing function is generated by an internal accounting transfer of items and services procured by purchasing to other functions at a price above their actual direct cost. In effect, purchasing sells to other functions at what is termed a *transfer price*. The executive in charge of purchasing is therefore expected to base any decisions, where applicable, on profit criteria and performance is measured in terms of the profits generated by the function. An example of the profit centre approach is given in Example 17.1.

Example 17.1

A purchasing department treated as a profit centre

		£
Value of assets controlled by the supplies manager		
Inventory		1,500,000
Purchasing function's floor space and equipment		250,000
Stores' floor space and equipment		750,000
		2,500,000
Annual rate of return required by the company		
on assets employed	15%	375,000
Estimated annual operating expenses		
Purchasing	£150,000	
Stores	£475,000	625,000
Total expenses and return (a)		1,000,000
Total purchases for year (b)		20,000,000
(a) + (b)		21,000,000

Transfer cost of supplies to user function
(i.e. internal customers) will therefore be 5%, i.e.

$$\frac{£1,000,000 \times 100}{20,000,000}$$

Assume notional supplies profit (1%)
Therefore profit on turnover of £20,000,000 — 200,000

$$\text{Return on assets controlled by supplies} = \frac{(£200,000 \times 100)}{£2,500,000} = 8\%$$

To reach the expected return of 15 per cent, other than by increasing the notional profit, the supplies function will either have to reduce the investment in inventory or operating expenses.

This approach is theoretical rather than practical, although it is advocated on the grounds that it:

- provides a measure of the efficiency of the supplies function
- allows supplier managers to control their budgets and spend to save money
- enhances the status of the supplies function by providing measurable objectives.

17.3.2 Activity-based costing

ABC costing, the basics of which have been described in section 16.8, contributes to performance measurement in the following ways:

■ *Distinguishing between value-adding and non-value-adding activities* – ABC management stresses that the non-value-adding activities must be reduced or eliminated and replaced with those that add value. JIT, while different from ABC management, has similar aims in that both approaches seek to eliminate all wasteful activity by using fewer suppliers, improved reliability, minimal paperwork, reduced inventory and so on.

■ *Analysis of cost drivers* – a cost driver is an activity that creates a cost. ABC highlights the fact that complicated products require enhanced negotiation expenses, more suppliers and purchase orders, increased administrative costs and similar cost drivers. The following measures indicate the opportunities for cost savings by simplifying supplier-driven activities.

– Number of suppliers per product $= \dfrac{\text{number of suppliers}}{\text{number of products}}$

Assuming 200 suppliers and 10 products, this will be:

$$\frac{200}{10} = 20 \text{ suppliers per product}$$

– Number of orders per product $= \dfrac{\text{Purchase orders}}{\text{Number of products}}$

$$\frac{1000}{10} = 100 \text{ purchase order per product}$$

Cost savings can be made by:

■ reducing the complexities of bought-out items by means of standardisation
■ reducing the amount of negotiation and number of suppliers by the introduction of single sourcing or an approved supplier list
■ improved design using standard, simplified or fewer parts
■ elimination of unprofitable products.

– *Allocation of overheads to products* – if an ABC analysis shows that product X requires the purchase of items from 12 suppliers while product Y only involves purchasing from two suppliers, it is clear that product X will incur a considerably higher proportion of the purchasing cost than product Y. This should be reflected in the allocation of purchasing function costs to products, which takes place with ABC, but not traditional, costing.

17.3.3 Standard costing and budgetary control

These are described in sections 16.9 and 16.1, but it is worth noting briefly here that *standard costing* can monitor performance by variance analysis, while *budgetary control* assists performance measurement by:

■ defining the results to be achieved by functions and their staff for the purpose of realising overall objectives

- indicating the extent to which actual results have exceeded or fallen below those budgeted
- establishing the extent and causes of budget variations
- appraising budgets to correct adverse trends or take advantage of favourable conditions
- exercising centralised control in circumstances of decentralised activity
- providing a basis for future policies and, where necessary, the revision of current policies.

17.3.4 Economic value added (EVA)

Economic value added (EVA) is a value-based financial performance measure. The basic process for calculating EVA is:

1 calculate the net operating profit after tax (NOPAT)
2 identify the organisation's capital
3 determine a reasonable capital cost rate (CCR)
4 calculate the organisation's economic value added (EVA).

Thus, the information required to calculate EVA can be obtained from the organisation's profit and loss account and balance sheet.

Unlike traditional accounting, however, EVA treats expenditure on such things as salaries, information processing, rent and supplies as capital assets that should directly contribute to added value. Thus, in addition to capital expended on assets such as land, buildings, machines and the like, for internal purposes, EVA regards amounts spent on operations as capital investments. EVA, therefore, is net operating profit minus an appropriate charge for the opportunity cost of all capital invested in an organisation or, alternatively, the amount by which earnings exceed or fall short of the required minimum return investors could get by investing in other organisations offering a comparable risk.

It is claimed that EVA reduces all financial performance to a single measure – 'how do we improve EVA?' This can be done in such ways as:

- improving returns with little or only minimal capital investment
- investing new capital only in processes or equipment that will at least recover their capital cost, while avoiding investments with lower than capital cost returns
- identifying and eliminating processes or operations where the return is below capital cost and where there is no possibility of improving the returns.

The EVA concept is relevant to purchasing as supplies and their procurement are important operating costs. A reduction in such costs by reducing prices, more effective procedures or outsourcing will increase profitability.

17.4 The purchasing management audit approach

17.4.1 Definition

An *audit* may be defined, inter alia, as a check or examination. The term *purchasing management audit* has been defined by Scheuing[6] as:

> A comprehensive, systematic, independent and periodic examination of a company's purchasing environment, objectives and tactics to identify problems and opportunities and facilitate the development of appropriate action plans.

Scheuing states that the operative words in this definition are:

- *comprehensive* – the audit should cover every aspect of purchasing
- *systematic* – a standard set of questions should be developed and used respectively
- *independent* – purchasing personnel should not evaluate themselves
- *periodic* – audits yield the greatest value if they are performed periodically – annually – thus facilitating comparisons, checks and balances and an evaluation of progress.

17.4.2 The purpose of purchasing management audits

A review of some standard purchasing texts by Evans and Dale[7] indicated that purchasing audits serve four main purposes. They:

- police the extent to which the purchasing policies laid down by senior management are adhered to
- help to ensure that the organisation is using techniques, procedures and methods that conform to best working practice
- monitor and measure the extent to, that resources are used effectively
- assist in the prevention and detection of fraud and malpractice.

17.4.3 Who should carry out the purchasing management audit?

Such audits can be carried out by:

- external auditors
- internal auditors
- a central purchasing function
- a purchasing research function
- external management consultants.

Two principles are suggested to govern who should carry out the audit:

- the auditors should be external to the function or department that is the subject of the audit
- the auditors should have an in-depth knowledge of the purchasing function, which will enable them not only to monitor adherence to policies and procedures but also to understand purchasing perspectives and problems and make recommendations as to how policies, procedures and practice can be improved, and, if external with specialist knowledge and experience, are likely to carry greater authority and provide greater objectivity in relation to purchasing audits.

17.4.4 The content of purchasing audits

Suggested headings and typical items for a management – as distinct from a financial – audit of the purchasing function are as follows:

- *Purchasing perspectives, problems and opportunities*
  - What are the perceptions of a sample of purchasing staff of their:
    - status in the organisation
    - involvement in strategic decision making
    - contribution to profitability and competitive advantage?
  - What are the job satisfactions and job dissatisfactions identified by the purchasing staff interviewed?
  - What are the main problems encountered by purchasing staff in doing their job? To what extent are these problems related to:
    - management
    - colleagues
    - internal customers
    - suppliers
    - information
    - resources
    - other internal or external factors?
  - What is the level of morale in the purchasing function?

- *Purchasing organisation*
  - To whom does the person in charge of the purchasing function report?
  - What aspects of purchasing are centralised/decentralised?
  - Would any centralised aspects of purchasing benefit from decentralisation or vice versa?
  - With what other functional activities does purchasing interrelate?
  - What are the formal mechanisms for the coordination of purchasing activities with other functions?
  - What is the assessment of purchasing function performance by its internal customers?
  - On what interfunctional/departmental committees is the purchasing function represented or could be represented?
  - How might the internal organisation of the purchasing function be improved?
  - How might the integration of purchasing with other related functions be improved?

  This information can be obtained from organisational charts and formal/informal interviews.

- *Purchasing personnel*
  - How many members of staff are employed in the purchasing function?
  - What are their grades, qualifications and respective lengths of service?
  - Has every member of the purchasing function an appropriate job description?
  - How do actual duties carried out relate to the job descriptions?
  - Which staff are over/underdeployed?
  - Is an attempt made to 'empower' purchasing staff?
  - What training and development opportunities are provided for purchasing staff?

- How do salaries and remuneration packages compare with those in similar enterprises/industries?
- What is the staff turnover as measured by the formula:

$$\frac{\text{Number of leavers in function for a specified period (usually 1 year)}}{\text{Average number of employees in function during the same period}} \times 100$$

- What is the stability of employment in the function as measured by the formula:

$$\frac{\text{Number of staff with 1 year's service or more}}{\text{Number employed 1 year ago}} \times 100$$

- What staff will reach retirement age within the next five years?

This information can be obtained from job descriptions or specifications, training documents, human resource plans and formal or informal interviews.

■ *Purchasing policies*
- What written/unwritten policies apply to the purchasing function?
- Is there a purchasing manual? How and how frequently is this updated?
- What guidance is provided to purchasing staff about:
  ■ the value an individual at a particular grade can commit the enterprise to spending
  ■ supplier relationships, such as disputes, prompt payment
  ■ conflicts of interest, such as gifts and entertainment
  ■ buying from abroad
  ■ environmental policies
  ■ reciprocal, local and intra-company purchasing?
- What machinery exists for the investigation and enforcement of reported departures from policy compliance?

This information can be obtained, in the main, from relevant documents, manuals, memoranda, instructions and so on.

■ *Purchasing procedures*
- From what sources are requests to purchase obtained?
- How quickly are such requests processed?
- What procedures are laid down for such operational activities as requesting and evaluating quotations, issuing purchase orders, receipt of goods and payment for supplies?
- Are all appropriate procedures computerised?
- To what extent does the purchasing function make use of EDI and e-procurement?
- How are small orders processed?
- What procedures/activities add value and which others do not add value?
- How might purchasing documentation be improved, simplified or eliminated?
- How much time does purchasing staff spend on seeing supplier representatives and engaging in relationship management?
- What are the procedures for capital purchases?
- What e-purchasing security methods are in place to prevent fraud?

Much of this information can be obtained from trailing a sample of purchase orders through from the receipt of the requisition to receipt of goods and payment of the suppliers and from formal and informal interviews.

■ *Purchasing reports*
- What reports are prepared by the purchasing function?
- Who prepares each report?
- At what intervals is each report prepared?
- What is the cost of preparing each report?
- To whom is each report sent?
- What use is made of each report by the receiver?
- Is the report really necessary?

Much of this information can be obtained by trailing reports through from their inception to storage or disposal.

■ *Purchases, suppliers and prices*
- What is the purchase budget – in quantities and value – for the period under review?
- What are the principal purchases?
- Who are the principal suppliers?
- What attempts have been made to achieve single and partnership sourcing?
- How and by what criteria are suppliers appraised?
- Are the results of appraisals communicated to suppliers?
- How do prices paid for samples of purchases compare with what is obtainable in the market?
- In what ways does the purchasing function seek to obtain value for money?
- How and by whom are specifications prepared? Is there any purchasing involvement?
- What environmental purchasing policy/policies are in existence and how successfully are these implemented?
- What savings have been achieved in the period under review and how have these been achieved?

Much of this information can be obtained from the examination of a sample of orders and other purchase documentation and formal and informal interviews.

■ *Inventory*
- Does the company make use of ABC analysis?
- How much inventory is carried, i.e. strategic items, bottleneck items, leverage items and non-critical items?
- What is the rate of turnover of a sample of items under each category?
- What items of inventory have been in stock for more than one year?
- What procedures are in place for the identification of obsolescent, slow-moving or damaged inventory and for the prevention of pilfering?
- What procedures are in place for the disposal of surplus stock, obsolete or scrap supplies or discarded capital items?

– What stockouts have been experienced in the period and why?

– What attempts have the purchasing/supplies function made to reduce inventory investment?

Much of this information can be obtained from an investigation of stores records, the physical inspection of inventory and stores procedures and formal and informal interviews. From the above, it can be seen that the main 'tools' used in purchasing performance audit include:

– formal or informal interviews

– sampling

– trailing a procedure or document through from its inception to its end or storage or disposal

– observation.

These 'tools' can be supported by such procedures as benchmarking and ratio analysis.

17.4.5 Purchasing management audit reports

On compiling the findings into a report with summarised recommendations and supporting reasons, the audit should be presented to senior management. When preparing such reports, auditors should:

■ highlight policies, procedures and personnel where efficiency and effectiveness can be improved

■ commend good practice and performance

■ think beyond simple quantitative measures of performance and consider the full consequences, side-effects and reactions likely to occur when these recommendations are presented

■ support constructive proposals made by purchasing staff that may receive greater attention if made by an outside source.

17.5 Benchmarking and ratios

17.5.1 Benchmarks

A benchmark may be defined as:

> a measured 'best in class' achievement – a reference or measurement standard for comparison that is recognised as the standard of excellence for a specific business process.

As shown in Figure 17.2 benchmarking may take four main forms.

17.5.2 The benefits and criticisms of benchmarking

Benchmarking offers the following benefits:

■ provision of a 'gap analysis' tool – that is, the gap between where we are and 'best in class' organisations

■ the opportunity to creatively incorporate the best practice from any industry into an organisation's operations

Figure 17.2 **The four main forms of benchmarking**

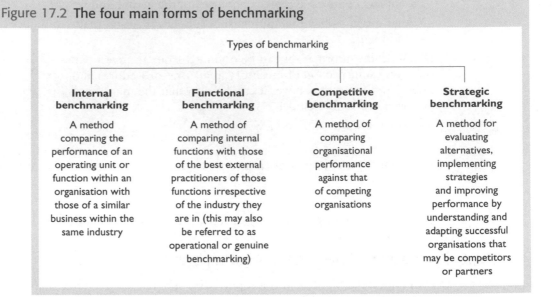

- decision support for setting objectives and a basis for cost–benefit analysis
- it is motivating as it identifies objectives that have been achieved by others
- resistance to change can be diminished when ideas for improved performance come from external sources
- innovations and technical breakthroughs from other industries can be identified earlier and their applicability assessed
- the experience and knowledge bases of employees can be enhanced.

The importance of benchmarking as a basis of comparison is indicated by examples given by Business Link:[8]

- in the top 25 per cent of firms, only 0.5 per cent of suppliers are substandard, whereas those in the lower quartile have six times as many substandard suppliers
- the top 25 per cent of organisations appear to be getting an average of 97 per cent of supplies on time, while in the lower quartile, only an average of 66.5 per cent of supplies are delivered on time
- the upper quartile performers use one ninth (or less) of the number of suppliers used by lower-quartile performers
- the bottom 25 per cent of firms reported an average of eight stock turns per year compared to 32 stock turns achieved by the top 25 per cent of firms in the sample.

There are, however, four main criticisms of benchmarking. These are that:

- benchmarking implies there is only one best method of performing, but there may be approaches other than those chosen as benchmarks that can be better ways of resolving an issue or improving performance
- benchmarking may indicate yesterday's solutions to tomorrow's problems
- price comparisons may be difficult because customised specifications may be unique to the buying institution

- price drivers, such as volume, procurement practices and terms and conditions, may further complicate comparisons.

17.5.3 The benchmarking process

This involves the following steps.

Step 1: Form a benchmarking team

This should consist of between 6 and 12 members, with representatives from both management and employees. Separate teams may be assigned to different benchmarking projects. Each team should have a leader to ensure that the benchmarking exercise is successfully completed.

Step 2: Decide what to benchmark

Almost anything can be the subject of a benchmarking exercise. In general, four prime considerations should be borne in mind when selecting subjects for benchmarking.

- Does the activity have a significant influence on internal and external satisfaction?
- What activities have the greatest potential for differentiation or providing competitive advantage?
- What activities offer the greatest potential for improvement?
- What activities absorb the highest percentage of cost?

The following aspects of purchasing offer considerable opportunities for benchmarking:

- Price and cost comparisons of supplies and services purchased.
- Purchasing processes and management comparisons of purchasing methods and procedures.
- Purchasing personnel comparisons of numbers, competences and training. Care should be taken in the use of such measures and they should not be used in isolation for example. In Table 17.1 three organisations' personnel costs are compared to the purchasing spend to calculate a ratio. We have to assume they are buying the same products with the same number of people, and with only the resulting outturn total purchase cost and remuneration being different. Normally when using ratios you are looking for the highest (e.g. Return on Capital Employed) or the lowest (e.g. PPM defects) to determine the 'best'. However, if one looks at the total expenditure of these three organisations neither the highest or lowest ratio gives the total lowest cost

Table 17.1 Comparison of personnel costs to purchasing spend

	Purchasing Team		
	Group A	Group B	Group C
Wage cost (W)	£100,000	£200,000	£350,000
Purchasing spend (P)	£10,000,000	£8,000,000	£7,900,000
Total cost to organisation	£10,100,000	£8,200,000	£8,250,000
Ratio (W:P)	1:100	1:40	1:22.57

of acquisition. That is not to say trend analysis over time for comparing the same department is not beneficial.

- Internal and external customer satisfaction with purchasing services.

- Supplier performance, in terms of quantity and delivery, because, as stated earlier, in general the satisfaction provided by purchasing to both internal and external customers derives from the performance of suppliers.

- Miscellaneous aspects, including comparisons of environmental or ethical policies and inventory management.

Step 3: Establish performance measures for the key activities identified in step 2

These measures will normally take the form of *ratios*. A ratio may be defined as:

The relationship between two quantities of which the quotient is the measure.

For the purpose of comparison, ratios are expressed as percentages. It would be impracticable to list all the possible ratios applicable to the benchmarking of purchasing activities here – the American Center for Advanced Purchasing Studies, for example, has produced a list of 78 such ratios just for public utilities. Because of this, the following are only a few examples of benchmarks that might be included under each of the six headings listed in step 2.

Price and cost comparisons

Without access to relevant and accurate data on price movements and price comparators effective supplier management is not possible.

$$\frac{\text{Average price paid for commodity or service in period}}{\text{Average market price for commodity or service in period}}$$

$$\frac{\text{Transportation cost on inward supplies}}{\text{Total expenditure on inward supplies}}$$

$$\frac{\text{Selected groupings expenditure such as production supplies, services, capital items}}{\text{Total expenditure}}$$

Purchasing processes and management

$$\frac{\text{Number of small orders (that is, under a specified amount)}}{\text{Total number of orders placed}}$$

$$\frac{\text{Number of purchasing transactions by purchase cards}}{\text{Total number of purchase transactions}}$$

$$\frac{\text{Purchasing operating costs}}{\text{Total organisational expenditure}}$$

Purchases (by number and value) made via:

- a centralised, automated system
- some form of e-commerce
- corporate credit cards.

In relation to total non-pay expenditure:

$$\frac{\text{Number of suppliers used in present period}}{\text{Number of suppliers used in previous period}}$$

Purchasing personnel

$$\frac{\text{Number of purchasing personnel}}{\text{Total number of administrative personnel}}$$

$$\frac{\text{Total expenditure on purchased supplies}}{\text{Total expenditure on purchasing personnel}}$$

$$\frac{\text{Purchasing personnel with approved purchasing qualifications}}{\text{Total purchasing personnel}}$$

$$\frac{\text{Expenditure on training of purchasing personnel}}{\text{Expenditure on employment of purchasing personnel}}$$

$$\frac{\text{Number of days training on purchasing}}{\text{Total number of days worked by purchasing staff}}$$

Internal and external customer satisfaction with purchasing services

Number of complaints made to purchasing from internal customers found to have substance.

Number of complaints made to purchasing from external customers or suppliers found to have substance.

Supplier performance regarding quality and delivery

$$\frac{\text{Number of suppliers with BS ISO 9000 certification}}{\text{Total number of suppliers}}$$

$$\frac{\text{Value of supplies rejected}}{\text{Value of supplies received}}$$

$$\frac{\text{Value of orders received over X days late}}{\text{Value of orders placed}}$$

$$\frac{\text{Number of units received from a supplier in period}}{\text{Number of units promised by supplier in period}}$$

Miscellaneous aspects

$$\frac{\text{Number of suppliers with ISO 14001 certification}}{\text{Total number of suppliers}}$$

$$\frac{\text{Average aggregate inventory value in a given period}}{\text{Total value of all items held in inventory in a given period}}$$

$$\frac{\text{Average annual sales (at costs)}}{\text{Average aggregate inventory value}}$$

It is easy to construct similar ratios according to the requirements of the particular organisation. Such ratios facilitate comparisons with other organisations.

Ratios, however, must be used intelligently. Three ratios often quoted are:

$$\frac{\text{Operating cost of purchasing department}}{\text{Total cost of purchases}} \times 100 = \text{Ratio of operating to procurement cots}$$

$$\frac{\text{Operating cost of purchasing department}}{\text{Number of orders placed in period}} \times 100 = \text{Average cost of orders}$$

$$\frac{\text{Value of purchase savings reported}}{\text{Value of purchase orders placed in period}} \times 100 = \text{Percentage of purchase savings reported of total purchases}$$

In using such ratios, it is important to remember that:

■ the second and third ratios directly above show average values that can be distorted by one abnormally large order

■ the first and second ratios directly above can be improved by increasing the numerator, though the aim should be to reduce the total value of purchases and number of orders placed and a fall in the number of orders may not be attributable to purchasing.

■ with the third ratio directly above, the value of savings reported by purchasing may not be wholly attributable to the efforts of the members of the purchasing staff, who may enhance their alleged savings and omit to offset these with reports of mistakes and losses, but a study by the American Management Association[9] noted six areas in which reported savings can be credited to purchasing:

– more economical savings on supplies developed by buyers

– specification changes at a buyer's suggestion in order to obtain a lower price, longer life or reduce inventory and installation costs

– improved order practices resulting in obtaining a lower price, such as combining orders to obtain bulk discounts

– negotiation of lower prices by the buyers

– reduction of costs other than material price, such as handling or storage costs

– increased returns from the sale of damaged, obsolete or surplus material and scrap.

Many ratios give no indication of sound purchasing judgement.

Step 4: Identify those organisations that achieve world or 'best in class' performance in the areas selected for benchmarking

These can be discovered by means of:

■ databases

■ supplier associations

■ reputation

■ cooperative information-sharing agreements – the members of such agreements may or may not be competitors and may or may not be in the same industry

■ out-of-industry organisations.

Step 5: Obtain information on the performance of the organisations selected in step 4

This may be achieved by visiting the companies and having discussions with their managers and other employees. The key questions to which answers should be sought are the following:

- How do you do it?
- Why do you do it better than we do?
- How can we do it better?

With steps 3, 4 and 5, much help can be obtained from a number of organisations, including the following:

- *Benchmarking Index* – this is the first truly national benchmarking service in the UK for small-sized to medium-sized enterprises (SMEs) – that is, those with fewer than 250 employees. Its objective is to bring high-quality benchmarking information and advice within easy reach of SMEs for the first time. A company completes an assessment, covering financial management and excellence measures. This information is then compared with Benchmarking Index's central database. Company performance can be compared locally, nationally or for a particular sector. A report is then generated that analyses company performance in detail, focusing attention on areas of the company where there is room for improvement. This chargeable service is provided via Business Link partnerships, which include training and enterprise councils (TECs) in England and appropriate authorities in Scotland, Wales and Northern Ireland.[10]

- *The European Benchmarking Network (EBN)* provides information on benchmarking within the European Union and assists in finding benchmarking partners within EU countries.

- *The Corporate Partnership Programme* in partnership with the Chartered Institute of Purchasing and Supply.[11]

- *Pricetrak and Servicetrak and Benchmarker* – these three services are provided by Purchasing Index (UK) Ltd.[12]

  Pricetrak provides a continuous and confidential exchange price benchmarking service. Comparisons are available with all Pricetrak contributors and with 'like users' (such as those in healthcare or higher education).

  Servicetrak is complementary to Pricetrak but more broadly based, including both narrative and quantitative data that highlight key features and processes, such as policies, procedures, performance, score, range, costs, projection and other dimensions of management concern aimed at identifying best practice.

  Benchmarker shows at a glance how supply chain operations in a member company compare to others in terms of cost, service levels and much else.

Again services such as these are useful where a reasonable number of contributors are present and procurement is not that critical to profits. These services would not be appropriate where core products are procured in a market of few large buyers as each buyer is protective of their cost information. As a potential competitive advantage it is not desirable to alert the competition to advantageous deals that they may not be aware of.

Step 6: Identify the lessons to be learned from world-class or 'best in class' organisations

Once identified, the team can consider how these can be implemented into their own company.

Step 7: Make recommendations on the lessons learned

Then the recommendations distilled from the benchmarking exercise can be taken to top management and approval obtained for the implementation of suggested improvements. When such approval has been obtained, the ideas can be 'sold' to employees.

Step 8: Review and monitor

Regularly review and monitor performance.

Summary of steps

The above steps can be summarised as:

- *plan* – select functions and so on for benchmarking, identify benchmarks, appoint a benchmarking team, decide where, when and how to collect data
- *analyse* – compare the organisation with 'best in class' organisations, perform a gap analysis of the differences in performance, ascertain reasons for the gap and how the gap can be closed
- *develop* – set new performance objectives/standards, develop action plans to achieve goals, secure acceptance of the action plan by top management
- *improve* – implement specific actions and integrate them into the business process
- *review* – monitor the results and improvements, review the benchmarks and the ongoing relationship with the 'best in class' organisation.

17.5.4 Benchmarking and continuous improvement

Benchmarks are not static. Benchmark performance tends to be driven to ever higher levels of achievement by competitive market forces. The original target set is therefore a moving target and must be subject to continuous reassessment. Superior performance – or *dantotsu* in Japanese – means 'striving to be the best of the best'.

17.6 Integrated benchmarking

A number of 'frameworks' have been devised to provide a holistic means of evaluating organisational performance and promoting continuous improvement by means of effective and integrated benchmarking. Two of the best-known frameworks are the European Foundation for Quality Management (EFQM) model and balanced scorecards.

17.6.1 The EFQM model

The EFQM model – shown in Figure 17.3 – consists of nine elements, classified into *enablers* and *results*. As a tool for self-assessment, the model allocates 1000 points on a weighted basis between the nine elements, of which 500 points are allocated to enablers

Figure 17.3 **The EFQM business excellence model**

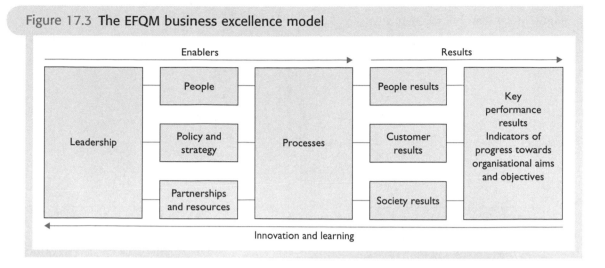

and 500 to results. The *enabler elements* are *how* the organisation approaches the criteria of each element. The *results elements* are *what* the organisation has achieved, and, is likely to achieve. The degree of excellence in the results, the extent to which the results are being achieved and the degree to which they address all relevant facets of the criteria all form the basis for the assessment of results.

17.6.2 The balanced scorecard

The balanced scorecard shown in Figure 17.4 was developed in the early 1990s by Robert Kaplan and David Norton of the Harvard Business School. They describe the innovation of the balanced scorecard as follows:

> The balanced scorecard retains financial measures, but financial measures tell the story of past events. An adequate story for industrial-age companies for which investments in long-term capabilities and customer relationships were not critical for success. These financial measures are inadequate, however, for guiding and evaluating the journey that information-age companies must make to create future value through investment in customers, suppliers, employees, processes, technology and innovation.

As shown, the balanced scorecard is not only a measurement system but also a framework that enables organisations to clarify their vision and strategy and translate them into action. The balanced scorecard approach suggests that we view the organisation from four perspectives: customer, financial, internal business processes and learning and growth. For each of these perspectives, the scorecard suggests that we should develop metrics and collect and analyse data.

The advantage of the scorecard is that it presents many of the seemingly disparate elements of an organisation's agenda in a single report. It also encourages managers to consider all relevant operational measures at the same time.

The *performance prism* is a development of the balanced scorecard developed by Andy Neeley of the Cranfield School of Management and Chris Adams of Anderson Consulting.

For reasons of space, it is not possible to provide a detailed description of EFQM, balanced scorecards and performance prism approaches here. Further information on

Figure 17.4 The balance scorecard

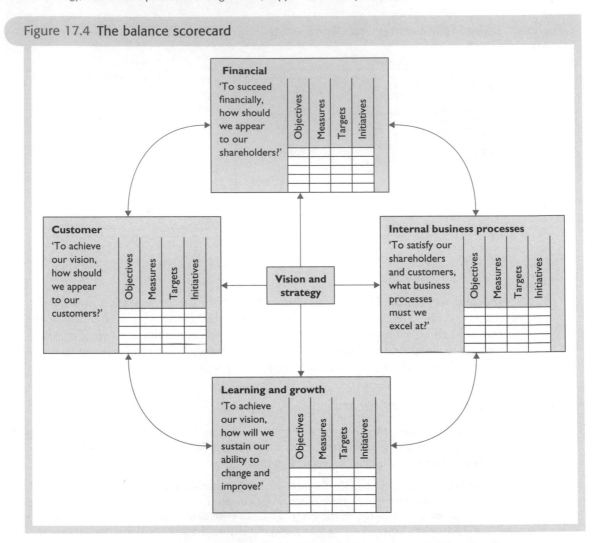

the EFQM model can be obtained from the British Quality Foundation.[13] The foundation also publishes *Assessing for Excellence: A Practical Guide to Self Assessment* and *The EFQM Excellence Model*.

Much has been published on the balanced scorecard. A good place to start is with the books by R. Kaplan, D. Norton and A. Lowes – *The Balanced Scorecard: Measures that Drive Performance, Putting the Balanced Scorecard to Work* and *Using the Balanced Scorecard as a Strategic Management System*.[14]

Two other useful books are Paul R. Niven's, *Balanced Scorecard Step-by-Step*[15] and M. C. S. Bourne and P. A. Bourne's, *Understanding the Balanced Scorecard in a Week*.[16]

The Balanced Scorecard Software Report, published by the Centre for Business Performance, Cranfield University, provides evaluations of 28 existing software packages relating to the selection of balanced scorecard software.

The pioneering book on the performance prism is by A. Neeley, C. Adams and M. Kennerley, *The Performance Prism: The Scorecard for Measuring and Managing Business Success*.[17]

17.7 Management by objectives (MBO)

The aim of MBO is to identify the objectives that a manager or function should be expected to achieve within a given time, at the end of which the actual performance will be compared with the desired results. The objectives will also be compared with the desired results. The objectives will be agreed by the head of the function in consultation with his or her superior. One approach to MBO – known as *key results analysis* – requires functional heads to identify their key tasks, performance standards and control information with a view to suggesting how their individual performance and the performance of their function can be improved.

This analysis forms the basis of discussions with both their immediate superiors and subordinates. The discussions with superiors are to agree functional objectives. When these have been agreed, discussions with subordinates are held to determine what objectives each must achieve if the functional/departmental objectives are to be attained. In this manner, overall objectives are cascaded down through the organisation, as shown in Figure 17.5.

As, however, functions and individuals participate in the setting of their objectives, MBO also works from the bottom up as well as from the top down.

Figure 17.5 Objectives cascade down organisation

17.7.1 Types of objectives

Three main types of objectives can be identified:

- *improvement objectives* – seeking to improve performance in specific ways in relation to specified factors, such as 'to reduce the prices paid for all costings used in the assembly of conveyor rollers by 5 per cent by the next review period', which may be achieved by negotiating with existing suppliers regarding ways in which to reduce the price, such as substituting aluminium for zinc, value analysis or finding new sources from which to purchase
- *personal development objectives* – relate to personal growth objectives or the acquisition of expanded job knowledge, skills and experience, such as 'to commence by the next review an approved course of study leading to the examinations of the Chartered Institute of Purchasing and Supply'
- *maintenance objectives* – formally express intentions to maintain performance at its current level, such as 'to maintain the present zero defects level of component X, purchased from supplier Y'.

The elements of MBO are therefore objectives and feedback.

17.7.2 Objectives and feedback

There is evidence that hard or difficult objectives produce stronger motivation and better individual performances than do easy objectives.

Feedback should:

- be fair
- distinguish between controllable and uncontrollable reasons for failing to meet objectives
- be constructive, leading to better performance
- include performance-based awards, if objectives have been achieved.

17.8 Miscellaneous approaches applicable to measuring purchasing performance

These include Six Sigma and SERVQUAL. Reference to Six Sigma has already been made in section 9.9.3.

17.8.1 Six Sigma

As explained in section 9.9.3 the term 'sigma' is used to describe variability and Six Sigma is a technique for measuring how far a given process deviates from total satisfaction. The central idea behind Six Sigma is that if you can measure how many defects you have in a process, you can systematically devise means for their elimination, thereby approaching, as closely as possible, the concept of zero defects. A Six Sigma quality level is said to equate to 3.4 defects per million opportunities. Six Sigma, however, goes beyond defect reduction to emphasise business process improvement in general, which includes cost reduction, cycle time improvement, increased customer satisfaction and any other measurement important to the company. One objective of Six Sigma is the elimination of every source of waste that can be found in an organisational process.

17.8.2 SERVQUAL

The five determinants of the SERVQUAL approach to service quality evaluation – tangibles, reliability, responsiveness, assurance and empathy – are particularly useful for the evaluation provided to internal customers by purchasing staff.

17.9 Purchasing ethics

17.9.1 Definitions

Purchasing ethics is a subdivision of business ethics, which in turn is the application of general ethical principles in a commercial or industrial context. Purchasing ethics are also related to professional ethics.

- *Ethics* as a general field of study may be defined as:

    The principles of conduct governing an individual or group; concern for what is right or wrong, good or bad.

- *Business ethics* is just the application of the above definition to the workplace and business relationships specifically.
- *Professional ethics* are guidelines or best practice that embody ideals and responsibilities that inform practitioners as to the principles and conduct they should adopt in certain situations.

17.9.2 Principles

The main principles of professional ethics are:

- impartiality or objectivity
- openness and full disclosure
- confidentiality
- due diligence, competency and a duty of care
- fidelity to professional responsibilities
- avoiding potential or apparent conflicts of interest.

These principles are to be interpreted in the light of the wider fields of personal and global ethics shown in Figure 17.6.

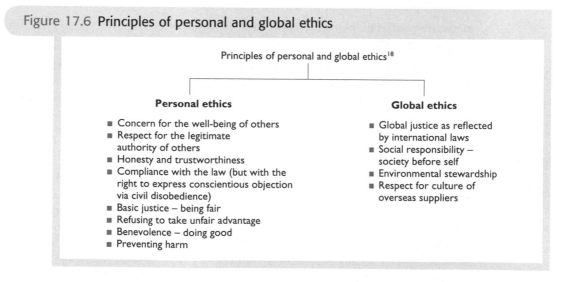

Figure 17.6 **Principles of personal and global ethics**

The range of corporal and individual issues relating to business ethics that might be considered under the above headings is infinite. Some aspects of global and negotiation ethics have been referred to in sections 14.4 and 15.10 respectively. Fraud and environmental issues will be considered in sections 17.13 and 17.14. Reasons of space prevent more than a brief reference to the following organisational issues that are of particular relevance to purchasing.

17.10 Some ethical issues relating to suppliers

These are the provision of practical help and advice, prompt payment, honesty and openness, e-ethics and courtesy to supplier representatives.

17.10.1 Provision of practical help and advice

This can take such forms as:

- helping suppliers to procure their own supplies more effectively and economically
- assistance in finding alternative customers to prevent too great a reliance on a single source
- provision of feedback on unsuccessful tenders
- collaboration on design and production
- supplier development
- placing a proportion of orders with local suppliers, thus assisting the prosperity of the community in which the purchasing organisation is located.

17.10.2 Prompt payment

The organisation should help suppliers maintain their cash flow by:

- paying invoices on time
- ensuring that both finance and purchasing departments are aware of the organisation's prompt payment policy and adhere to it
- dealing with complaints as expeditiously as possible so that payments are not needlessly deferred.

Under the UK Late Payments of Commercial Debts (Interest) Act 1998, which is based on an EU directive, bills must be paid within 30 days. The act provides that, after 30 days, small businesses (those with 50 or fewer employees) can claim interest retrospectively.

17.10.3 Honesty and openness

Honesty and openness are the opposite of deception, as defined by Robertson and Rymon:[19] 'one party's intention to create or perpetuate a false belief in another party'.

The same writers identify four types of 'bluffing' that some purchasing agents may adopt on the premise that, in negotiations, their responsibility is to obtain the best possible price, quality and delivery and that deception and manipulation of the supplier is an acceptable means of achieving the desired end.

The four examples of deception instanced by Robertson and Rymon are giving a false impression to suppliers that:

- other vendors are aggressively competing for a particular contract
- time limits for the completion of negotiations apply
- a competitor is offering a better deal
- the selling firm is in danger of losing the contract.

From their research, Robertson and Rymon reported that:

- to 29 per cent of their respondents admitted to having deceived the seller
- the suggestions that there were other vendors and that the vendors might lose the contract were, respectively, the most and least common forms of deception

- deceptive behaviour is likely to be the outcome of organisational pressure to perform or lack of clear guidance regarding what is permissible, so there is 'ethical ambiguity'
- deception may be a recognised negotiating ploy: 'the buyer may be selling a false deadline but the seller knows that the deadline is false'.

The writers also suggest that the replacement of short-term, arm's length by long-term collaborative purchasing arrangements is likely to be conducive to the development of cooperation, interdependence and trust between buyers and suppliers.

17.10.4 E-ethics

The CIPS[20] suggests that the Internet 'is creating a new environment in which unethical behaviour has far greater implications for companies than was previously the case'. In particular, the balance of power in e-trading, as exemplified by e-auctions, is shifting in favour of the purchaser. A typical code of ethics for e-auctions is that of Dow Chemicals:[21]

Initiate the auction with the intent to award the business. Do not use an online auction as a prospecting tool. Do not solicit, negotiate or accept offline offers once invitations have been sent to auction participants or upon completion of the auction.
Ensure bidders have a clear understanding of what to expect before, during and after the auction: develop and distribute clear auction rules and specifications.
Provide bidders time to prepare for the event, including strategic development and training.
Document and distribute the business criteria that will be used to award business.
Train bidders prior to action:

- ensure bidders are comfortable with the online e-auction tool
- inform all participants of auction results in a timely fashion.

Only invite bidders to participate if they can meet your auction requirements.
Do not allow phantom bidding.

The CIPS further suggests that, with B2B e-commerce, the issues of trust, access, identity, security, privacy, property and confidentiality take on new dimensions.

17.10.5 Courtesy to suppliers' representatives

There is evidence that sales representatives often have a poor opinion of buyers. This is likely to be enhanced where sales representatives are kept waiting unnecessarily. It should be appreciated by purchasing staff that, allowing for travelling time and discussions, a sales representative has a relatively short working day in which to fit calls. Unsolicited sales calls tend to be unwelcome before 9.30am, between 12.15pm and 1.30pm and after 4.30pm. If kept waiting, the salesperson's whole programme of visits in a particular area may be disrupted. Other factors to bear in mind when receiving sales representatives should include:

- using a suitable room for interviews
- giving information regarding the times between which representatives will be seen
- providing them with honest information.

While purchasing staff should be open to information about new products and suppliers, they should be frank, but courteous, about informing a representative, if there is no possibility of business, to avoid making future calls. Above all, a buyer should never be patronising, rude or supercilious. Such behaviour demeans both the representative and the buyer and is clearly not conducive to establishing supplier goodwill. While there must clearly be an exchange of pleasantries, it should be remembered that 'time is money', for both the purchaser and the supplier.

Kennedy[22] instances 22 different tactics used by unscrupulous buyers when dealing with representatives. Not only are such tactics unprofessional, but they also negate a golden rule – always treat others as you would like them to treat you.[23] This rule is unambiguous and easy to understand. The motives for endorsing it may be altruistic, but are actually a reflection of precautionary, defensive self-interest.

17.10.6 Business gifts and hospitality

Policies with regard to the receipt by members of the purchasing staff of gifts from suppliers, especially at Christmas, and hospitality at other times vary widely. The three most common policies are that members of the purchasing staff:

- are forbidden to accept gifts of any kind and those received must be returned
- may retain gifts that are clearly of an advertising nature, such as calendars, diaries, pencils and so on
- are allowed to decide for themselves whether a proffered gift of hospitality is an appreciation of a cordial business relationship or an attempt at commercial bribery.

Our considered view is that the third of the above policies is the best as it regards staff as responsible individuals, capable of distinguishing a gift or hospitality from a bribe. There is also the fact that the first two policies encourage subterfuge, such as having gifts sent to the buyer's home address. There is, however, the danger that younger, less experienced, lower-paid members of staff are likely to be flattered to receive gifts, the implications of which are not always recognised. For this reason, it is useful for all members of the purchasing staff to receive guidance on ethical practice from professional and organisational ethical codes and ethical training.

17.11 Ethical codes and training

In Chapter 1, it was stated that one of the essentials of a profession is 'adherence to a code of conduct'. Professions as diverse as medicine, law, accountancy and architecture have issued codes of conduct. The codes of conduct issued by the Chartered Institute of Purchasing and Supply (CIPS) in the UK and Institute of Supply Management (ISM) in the USA are reproduced in Appendices 1 and 2, respectively.

There are also national and international codes. A good example of a national code is the UK government's *Procurement Code of Good Practice for Customers and Suppliers*. An example of an international code is the *Global Compact*, introduced by the United Nations' secretary general in 1999. This challenges world business leaders to help build the social and environmental pillars required to sustain the new global economy and covers ten principles under four headings on which companies are asked to act.

- **Human rights**
  - *Principle 1* – businesses should support and respect the protection of internationally proclaimed human rights
  - *Principle 2* – make sure that they are not complicit in human rights abuses.

- **Labour**

  - *Principle 3* – businesses should uphold the freedom of association and the effective recognition of the right to collective bargaining

  - *Principle 4* – the elimination of all forms of forced and compulsory labour

  - *Principle 5* – the effective abolition of child labour

  - *Principle 6* – the elimination of discrimination in respect of employment and occupation.

- **Environment**

  - *Principle 7* – businesses should support a precautionary approach to environmental challenges

  - *Principle 8* – undertake initiatives to promote greater environmental responsibility

  - *Principle 9* – encourage the development and diffusion of environmentally friendly technologies.

- **Anti-corruption**

  - *Principle 10* – businesses should work against corruption in all its forms, including extortion and bribery.

Other international codes are those of the *Ethical Trading Initiative (ETI)* and the *International Labour Organisation (ILO)*.

The ETI is an alliance of companies, non-governmental organisations (NGOs) and trade union organisations. The ultimate ETI goal is to ensure that the working conditions of workers producing for the UK market meet or exceed international labour standards.

The ILO's *Declaration on Fundamental Principles and Rights at Work*, adopted in 1998, covers four areas:

- freedom of association and the effective recognition of the right to collective bargaining

- the elimination of all forms of forced or compulsory labour

- the effective abolition of child labour

- the elimination of discrimination in the respect of employment and occupation.

17.11.1 The benefits of ethical codes

Karp and Abramms[24] suggest that both professional and organisational codes are useful in:

- *providing a basis for working together* – most codes require that people treat each other with respect

- *setting boundaries as to what constitutes ethical behaviour* as determined by organisational human rights and professional values, examples of which are declarations of interest, confidentiality of information, competition, business gifts and hospitality

- *providing a safe environment for all subscribers* – without the guidance provided by a code of ethics, employees are always subject and accountable to the value system of anyone in a higher position

- *providing a commonly held set of guidelines* enabling what is right and wrong in a given situation to be judged on a consistent basis, so they help to dispel 'ethical ambiguity'.

17.11.2 Some criticism of codes

Probably most purchasing people think of ethical codes as being remote from the real world. This may be because work often leaves little time for reflection. The requirement to maintain an unimpeachable standard of integrity in all business relationships is fine until one questions the meaning of integrity and to whom the duty of integrity is due. The most prominently cited obstacle to managing ethically is when there is a conflict between employees' own or their profession's ethical code and the ethics of their organisation or their immediate superior, employees may have to choose between remaining silent or speaking out and facing the consequences of being seen as disloyal. They may even have to face termination of employment, which, under conditions of redundancy and restructuring, is not to be lightly contemplated. Some comments from Brigley's[25] respondents include:

- high unemployment affects your ethics – cynical but true
- what people say and what people do are very different
- people suppress their own ethical values in order to be generally accepted and get on in business
- the more senior you are, the easier it is to maintain an ethical stance.

The ISM's code of conduct, for example, lays down that subscribers must denounce all forms or manifestations of commercial bribery. What do you do, though, knowing full well what happens to whistleblowers, if you discover that your boss or colleague is receiving bribes? In summary, it seems that, to be effective, both organisational and professional codes need to be made more relevant to those they apply to and be supported by administrative procedures designed to assist in creating an ethical culture. This in turn means that, to be effective, purchasing ethics require appropriate training and education.

17.11.3 Ethical training

Ethical training sessions for purchasing staff can provide a number of benefits. They reinforce the organisation's ethical codes and policies, remind staff that top management expects participants to consider ethical issues when making purchasing decisions and clarify what is and what is not acceptable. Such training can include the following:

- the field of ethics
- the feasibility of ethics in business
- how people may rationalise their unethical behaviour
  - 'I was only doing what I was told'
  - 'It's not really illegal'
  - 'It's in everyone's interest'
  - 'Everybody does it'
  - 'No one will ever know'
  - 'The company owes me this because it doesn't pay me enough'
- factors to be considered when receiving a gift or the offer of hospitality, including:
  - the motive of the donor – whether a gift is a token of appreciation or a bribe
  - the value of the gift or the hospitality – when it exceeds what is permissible
  - the type of gift or the nature of the hospitality

- the manner in which the offer is made – openly or surreptitiously
- what strings, if any, are attached
- what impressions the gift or hospitality will make on superiors, colleagues, subordinates, bearing in mind the human propensity to think the worst
- what the employer's reaction would be if the matter was brought to his or her attention
- whether the buyer can honestly be satisfied that the gift will not influence his or her objectivity when dealing with suppliers.

If the buyer has doubts about any of the above, the gift or hospitality should be refused.

- double standards – some companies offer gifts to customers' buyers, but refuse permission to their own staff to receive gifts, for example
- what members of the purchasing staff should do if they discover a superior, colleagues or subordinates acting contrary to the company's ethical code
- whistleblowing
- what the possible penalties are for unethical behaviour
- fostering ethical standards:
  - dealing with ethical suppliers
  - management support for ethical behaviour.

Badaracco and Webb,[26] in a study of organisational ethics as perceived by younger managers, conclude that ethics as 'viewed from the trenches' is very different from that viewed from the 'general's headquarters':

> The younger managers believed that, in effect, the people who pressured them to act in sleazy ways were responding to four powerful organisational commandments. First, performance is what really counts so make your numbers. Second, be loyal and show us that you're a team player. Third, don't break the law. Fourth, don't overinvest in ethical behaviour.

The researchers also point out:

> In short, a clear pattern of implicit norms and values had taken shape in the minds of many of these younger managers. This pattern is what we have called the fourth commandment. In only a minority of cases did ethics seem to pay. Middle managers who pressed subordinates for sleazy or illegal behaviour went unpunished. Whistleblowing was often a professional hazard and sleazy behaviour didn't hurt or even seemed to accelerate career advancement especially in the short run and sometimes in the long run too.

Two important conclusions from this research are:

- codes of ethics can be helpful, though not decisive, particularly if they are specific about acceptable and unacceptable behaviour
- codes are more likely to be credible if they are enforced and violations of the code are punished.

Brigley[27] considers that codes are easier to introduce and implement in larger organisations. Smaller companies generally prefer an informal approach to ethical issues. Brigley also reports that, within organisations, senior management's attitudes and tactics and conflicts of values with senior management are mainly concerned with pressures arising from harshly competitive climates and the need for a good bottom-line performance.

17.12 Ethical decisions

While professional associations issue codes of ethics and companies statements of corporate ethical policy, it is a fact that, as Dubinsky and Gwin[28] suggest, business-people tend to employ two sets of ethical standards – a personal set and a business set – and may well have stricter personal than business ethical standards.

How an individual will react with regard to a particular ethical dilemma depends on many factors, including:

- family and cultural influences
- religious or humanistic values
- the behaviour of superiors
- the behaviour of peers
- the prevailing norms and values of society
- the fear of the consequences of discovery of unethical behaviour.

Consider the following questions propounded by Nash:[29]

- What is my intuition and gut instinct – does the decision stink?
- Could I disclose it to my child, a respected mentor or the public?
- Is it right, honest and consistent with my values?
- Is it legal and should the law be obeyed anyway?
- Does it promote trust?
- How does it treat others? Am I hurting anyone?
- Does it add to the good reputation of myself and the organisation?
- Does it put myself or the organisation first?
- Is it fair and beneficial to my organisation's stakeholders?
- What value am I creating?
- Have I considered all the facts?
- Am I blinded by arrogance or saved by humility?
- Will the decision stand scrutiny one, two or three years ahead?
- Would it look good if repeated 20 times over?
- Would it be different if I had ten times more time to make the decision?
- Can I increase the time for its implementation?

17.13 Purchasing and fraud

17.13.1 What is fraud?

Fraud is defined by the CIMA[30] as:

> Dishonestly obtaining an advantage, avoiding an obligation or causing loss to another party.

The term 'fraud' commonly includes activities such as theft, corruption, conspiracy, embezzlement, deception, bribery and extortion.

The World Bank has identified the following violations that should be referred to their Department of Institutional Integrity:

- contract irregularities and violations of the bank's procurement guidelines
- bid rigging
- collusion by bidders
- fraudulent bids
- fraud in contract performance
- fraud in an audit enquiry
- product substitution
- defective pricing and parts
- cost/labour mischarging
- bribery and acceptance of gratuities
- solicitation and/or receipt of kickbacks
- misuse of bank funds or positions
- travel fraud
- theft and embezzlement
- gross waste of bank funds.

The possibility of procurement fraud is of great concern to all organisations. The three essential ingredients of fraud are intent, capability and opportunity. This situation creates a need to maintain effective communication of accepted behaviour and codes of conduct, thereby clarifying what is and is not acceptable behaviour. Purchasing guidelines should always be clearly communicated to all staff, contractors and suppliers.

17.13.2 Distinction between fraud and error

The basic distinction between fraud and error is that of the intention. Any error is unintentional – that is, the person committing the error does not do so knowingly. Errors are accidental and may arise due to negligence, genuine misunderstanding or incompetence. With fraud, however, it is intentional. The person committing fraud does so knowingly, wilfully and with the motive of gaining advantage or benefit by cheating or causing loss or injury to others, acting alone or in collusion with one another.

17.13.3 Indicators of procurement fraud

There are many indicators of potential procurement fraud. They include:

- excessive supplier hospitality to selected staff
- new suppliers continually facing entry 'obstacles'
- budget holders pressurising buyers to place work with named suppliers
- a buyer's lifestyle changing dramatically
- pricing schedules being completed in pencil
- suppliers and contractors being very familiar with senior staff
- specifications favouring a particular supplier

- supplier payments going unchallenged
- the absence of supplier approval data
- no supplier visits or audits.

As indicated in Table 17.2, opportunities for fraud occur at every stage in the procurement process.

17.13.4 E-purchasing and fraud

E-procurement clearly provides many opportunities for both input and output fraud. *Input fraud* can take such forms as the opening of accounts for non-existent suppliers who are paid electronically, the payments going into an account designated by the fraudster, over-stating or understating inventory amounts, deleting inventory records, copying of credit card numbers and so on.

Output fraud tends to be comparatively rare. One example is that of sending unauthorised e-mails with intentionally false information.

17.13.5 The prevention of fraud

The threat of fraud can be reduced in four ways.

- *Establish a culture of integrity* – Casabona[31] points out that 85–90 per cent of computer fraud is the result of an insider job. Some computer experts therefore claim that the most effective security system is the integrity of company employees. Much fraud can be eliminated by careful employee selection. Organisations that communicate and support a commitment to integrity will create environments hostile to fraud. When employees leave, organisations should immediately delete all access information of the former worker and inform all relevant people of the termination.

- *Be alert to giveaway signs* – giveaway signs of fraud include:
  - unfolded invoices that have not come through the post
  - too many orders to one supplier, except where single-sourcing applies
  - loss of supporting documentation
  - sudden, unexplained affluence
  - unwillingness of the employee to take holidays or accept a transfer or promotion to other work.

Evans and Maguire[32] state that the commonest source of discoveries of fraud is outside information. This includes the reporting of fraudulent practices by colleagues and disgruntled mistresses.

- *Take appropriate e-security measures* – technological concerns in e-commerce are usually divided into two broad categories – client server security and data and transaction security. *Client server security* uses various authorisation methods, such as passwords and firewalls, to ensure that only valid users have access to databases. *Data and transaction security* involves ensuring the privacy of electronic messages by using encryption.

- *Recognise the importance of audits* – audits may be internal or external. *Internal audits* in relation to purchasing were described in section 17.4. *External audits*, by members of a recognised professional accountancy body approved by the Department

Table 17.2 Fraud at different points in the procurement process

Phase of procurement process	Possible fraudulent activity
1 Establishing need for goods or services	■ Maintaining excessive stock levels to justify purchases ■ Declaring serviceable items as excess or selling them as surplus while continuing to purchase ■ Purchasing in response to aggressive sales activities ■ Estimates prepared after RFQs requested ■ Failure to develop alternative sources
2 Development of specifications	■ Defining specifications to fit capabilities of a single contractor ■ Defining specifications to fit a single product ■ Advanced release of information to favoured contractors ■ Selective release of information to favoured contractors ■ Breaking up of requirements to allow rotation of bids ■ Vague specifications that make comparisons of estimates complicated
3 Pre-solicitation	■ Unwarranted sole source justifications ■ Erroneous statements to justify sole source ■ Justification of sole source signed by managers with no authority ■ Technical personnel providing advance information to carefully selected suppliers ■ Invalid restrictions in RFQ documents to limit competition
4 Solicitation	■ Restriction on procurement to prevent/obstruct qualified suppliers ■ Limiting time for submission of tenders so that only those with advance information can respond ■ Improper social contact with supplier representatives ■ Conducting bid conferences in such a way that bid rigging or price fixing is facilitated ■ Discussions with personnel about likely employment with a supplier or sub-contractor ■ Rendering special assistance to a supplier in preparing their bid
5 Bid acceptance	■ Improper acceptance of a late bid ■ Falsification of documents or receipts to get a late bid accepted ■ Change in the bid after other bidders' prices are known ■ Falsification in supplier's qualifications, financial capability, successful completion of previous jobs and so on ■ Submission of the bids by one bidder in a different party's name ■ False certificates, such as insurance ■ Rejection of bids without any valid reason ■ Deliberate loss of bids ■ Exercising favouritism towards a particular supplier during the evaluation process ■ Using biased individuals on the evaluation panel ■ Failing to forfeit bid bonds when a supplier withdraws improperly
6 Post contract award	■ Certifying goods without conducting inspections ■ Action not taken for the non-compliance with terms and conditions ■ Double payments for same items/services ■ Contract files are incomplete ■ Substitution of specified goods with used or inferior products ■ Time sheets signed for hours not expended ■ Expenses paid when not incurred ■ Essential spares not delivered but invoiced ■ Invoices settled earlier than contract requires ■ Payment for non-delivered goods/services ■ Unsubstantiated cost growth ■ Charges for skills levels below those contractually agreed

of Trade and Industry, are a statutory requirement under the UK companies acts. Contrary to popular belief, it is not an auditor's primary duty to prevent fraud, but, rather, make an independent examination of the books, accounts and vouchers of a business for the purpose of reporting whether or not the balance sheet and profit and loss account show a 'true and fair view' of the affairs and profit (or loss) of the business according to the best information and explanations obtained. An audit may include a physical verification of assets, such as inventory, and the auditors may also make recommendations that can make the business less susceptible to fraud by its customers, suppliers and employees. Where a fraud is discovered, the auditor has a duty to prove that fraud to its full extent, regardless of the amount in question.

17.13.6 Bribery

At the time this book was being finalised, the Bribery Act 2010 had been planned to come into force in the United Kingdom in April 2011. The implementation was delayed pending the issue of guidelines. The guidelines were issued by the Secretary of State for Justice in March 2011. At first sight the guidelines appear to have softened on the provision of hospitality bringing one response to the effect that 'the sigh of relief in the corporate world will certainly be palpable'. The Act will repeal and replace England's old, much-criticised, laws on bribery with a new comprehensive anti-bribery code. There were a number of Acts repealed or revoked, including:

- Public Bodies Corrupt Practices Act 1889   The whole Act
- Prevention of Corruption Act 1906   The whole Act
- Prevention of Corruption Act 1916   The whole Act
- Scotland Act 1998   Section 43
- Government of Wales Act 2006.   Section 44

The full list can be found in Schedule 2 'Repeals and Revocations' of the Bribery Act 2010.

There are far reaching consequences of the new Act and these obviously have direct relevance to procurement activities. There are two general offences as follows:

- Paying bribes: it will be an offence to offer or give a financial or other advantage with the intention of inducing that person to perform a 'relevant function or activity' 'improperly' or to reward that person for doing so.

- Receiving bribes: it will be an offence to receive a financial or other advantage intending that a 'relevant function or activity' should be performed 'improperly' as a result.

'Relevant function or activity' includes any function of a public nature and any activity connected with a business. The person performing that activity must be expected to perform it in good faith or impartiality or be in a position of trust.

There is a controversial new offence which can be committed only by commercial organisations (companies and partnerships). It will be committed where:

- a person associated with a relevant commercial organisation (which includes not only employees, but agents and external third parties) bribes another person intending to obtain or retain a business advantage; and

■ the organisation cannot show that it had adequate procedures in place to prevent bribes being paid.

There are practical steps that organisations should consider to demonstrate that they have 'adequate procedures'. These steps may include:

■ procurement issue guidance to all suppliers and sub-contractors; publish a code of conduct and then monitor and revise it

■ establish an internal anti-corruption committee

■ corruption training and testing for staff

■ prohibitions on facilitation payments

■ clear policies on corporate hospitality

■ robust screening processes for third-party payments

■ conduct due diligence around selection and appointments of suppliers and sub-contractors

■ disciplinary measures and remedial action arising from unethical behaviour.

The Bribery Act 2010 raises the maximum jail term for bribery by an individual from seven years to ten years. A company convicted of failing to prevent bribery could receive an unlimited fine.

Figure 17.7 shows the impact on firms of the UK Bribery Act and Figure 17.8 shows an overview of the Bribery Act 2010.[33]

Figure 17.7 UK Bribery Act: Impact on firms

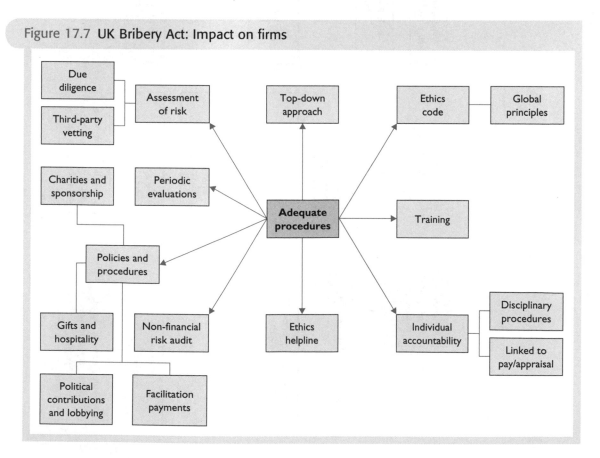

Figure 17.8 UK Bribery Act 2010: An overview

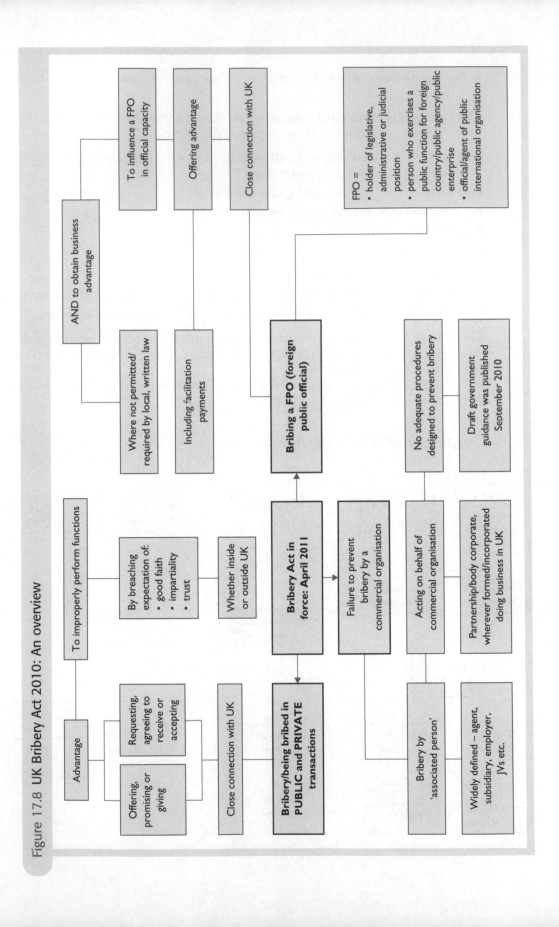

17.14 Environmental aspects of purchasing

17.14.1 Being responsible towards the environment

Being responsible towards the environment is one aspect of the social responsibility of business and should be a consideration when devising strategies.

According to the UK's Environmental Protection Act 1990:

> The environment consists of all or any of the following media, namely, the air, water and land; and the medium of air includes the air within buildings and the air within the natural or man-made structures above or below the ground.

Important areas of environmental concern include the following:

■ *More efficient use of raw materials in manufacturing operations* – this applies especially to timber and minerals. Consumer concern about rainforests has had a direct impact on the demand for tropical hardwoods, which has affected timber producers, wholesalers and users. Of about 80 minerals used by industry, some 18 – including lead, sulphur, tungsten and zinc – are in relatively short supply. Such materials will be subject to rising prices and demands for recycling.

■ *Pollution and waste* – pollution is defined by the Environmental Protection Act 1990 as:

> Pollution of the environment due to the release (into an environmental medium) from any process of substances which are capable of causing harm to man or any other living organism supported by the environment.

■ *Energy savings* – energy to power industry is provided by the environment from such sources as wood, fossil fuels, water, sunlight, wind and uranium.

17.14.2 Legislation

Environmental purchasing may be defined as:[34]

> Purchasing involvement in supply chain activities in order to facilitate recycling, reuse and resource reduction.

It is subject to a 'vast range of international and national environmental legislation and directives'.

International legislation

Most international law is enforced by means of national processes, although EU laws can be enforced via the European Court of Human Rights.

A large number of EU environmental directives have been issued relating to quality, water, waste, chemicals and packaging and packaging waste. European legislation represents the minimum environmental demands and is legally binding for all EU member states. A current list of all pertinent legislation is provided by the European Information Service[35] and the European Information Centres.

UK legislation

This includes the Clean Air Act 1993, the Water Act 2003, the Flood and Water Management Act 2010, the Radioactive Substances Act 1993, the Packaging (Essential

Requirements) Regulations 2003, the Waste Electrical and Electronic Equipment Regulations 2006 and amended in 2007 and the Environmental Protection Act 1990. The latter contains important provisions relating to:

- integrated pollution control
- best available technology not entailing excessive cost (BATNEEC), requiring companies using major polluting processes to spend as much on clean technology as they can afford
- air pollution control
- waste disposal and recycling – *waste* is defined in the Act as:
  - any substance which constitutes a scrap material or an efficient or other unwanted surplus substance from the application of any process
  - any substance or article which requires to be disposed of as being broken, worn out, contaminated or otherwise spoiled; anything which is discarded or otherwise dealt with as if it were waste shall be presumed to be waste unless the contrary is proved
- control of dangerous substances and nuisances.

There are also many directives relating to such environmental areas as air, chemicals, energy, land, noise and statutory nuisance, plant protection, pollution, radioactive substances and waste. Details of these are available from the Department of the Environment, Food and Rural Affairs (DEFRA) and websites such as NetRegs – the UK's environmental regulations on the Internet.

The Environmental Agency, which combined HM Inspector of Pollution, the National Rivers Authority and Local Authority Waste Regulators, was established by the Environmental Act 1995 and is responsible for pollution prevention and control in England and Wales.

17.14.3 Environmental purchasing policies and management

DEFRA[36] has stated that:

> The procurement of supplies and equipment is a potent instrument of environmental policy. Careful purchasing gives full weight to environmental considerations in the selection of products and can help improve environmental standards by reducing pollution and waste. It can also, through the natural operation of the market, influence purchasers and suppliers in their pricing policies and product ranges.

The steps required to give effect to these objectives are shown in Figure 17.9. These nine steps are discussed below.

Step 1: Prepare environmental policy

When prepared, the environmental purchasing policy should be:

- endorsed by senior management
- reflect the nature of the business – that is, if the business is a chemical one, it should address the issues associated with chemical production rather than issues relating to, say, recycled paper or lease cars
- form part of the overall corporate strategy.

Figure 17.9 **Nine steps to implementing an environmental purchasing policy**

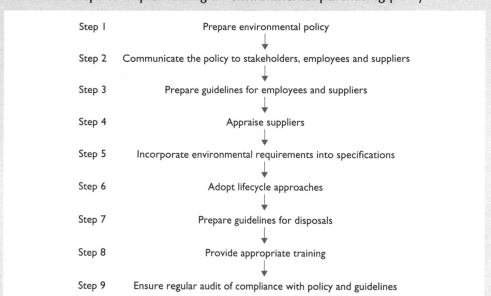

Step 1	Prepare environmental policy
Step 2	Communicate the policy to stakeholders, employees and suppliers
Step 3	Prepare guidelines for employees and suppliers
Step 4	Appraise suppliers
Step 5	Incorporate environmental requirements into specifications
Step 6	Adopt lifecycle approaches
Step 7	Prepare guidelines for disposals
Step 8	Provide appropriate training
Step 9	Ensure regular audit of compliance with policy and guidelines

Step 2: Communicate policy

From the standpoint of employees, the policy communications should be cross-functional to ensure the integration of its implementation throughout the organisation.

Step 3: Prepare guidelines

A good example of guidelines for *employees* – especially purchasing personnel – are those of the Central Purchasing Group of the University of Oxford.[37] In making purchasing decisions, members of staff are instructed to give attention to the following environmental factors:

- ask first if this purchase is really necessary (reduce consumption)
- consider 'whole life' costs and impact when assessing equipment for purchase
- wherever practical, purchase goods and services that may be manufactured, used and disposed of in an environmentally responsible way
- where items are of a similar cost, try to give preference to those that are manufactured with a high recycled content
- wherever practical, specify items that can be recycled or reused
- wherever practical, use suppliers that are committed to environmental improvement
- wherever practical, work with the community at large to progress environmental initiatives and exchange best practice
- can the need be met in another way, by buying used equipment, for example (see section 13.6)
- think whether or not the quantities/quality requested are essential.

In particular, purchasers should consider:

- energy usage, including mains water and drainage water
- waste minimisation and process efficiencies
- reuse and recycling opportunities
- packaging material and how it can best be disposed of
- waste disposal implications
- avoidance of ozone-depleting substances
- reduction of volatile organic compounds
- reduction of materials containing heavy metals
- control of discharges to air, land and water
- noise levels generated by plant and machinery
- eco-toxicity of materials released to land, air and water
- transport choice and pollution.

When comparing environmental with competing products that serve the same purpose, purchasing staff should ensure that environmental products are:

- fit for the purpose and provide value for money
- energy-efficient and resource-efficient
- making the minimum use of virgin materials
- making the maximum use of post consumer materials
- non- (or reduced) polluting
- durable, easily upgraded and repairable
- reusable and recyclable.

An example of guidance for *suppliers* is 'The green supplier guidelines', issued by Toyota Manufacturing North America Inc. Suppliers that provide parts, materials and components directly or indirectly to Toyota are required to complete one or more of the following initiatives:

- obtain ISO 14001 certification
- comply with Toyota's chemical ban list – Toyota has identified 450 chemicals and substances that suppliers of raw materials must phase out from new and/or reformulated materials, beginning 1 August 2000 (this list is regularly updated)
- comply with Toyota's hazardous materials management transportation system.

Step 4: Appraise suppliers

Methods and criteria for the appraisal of actual and potential suppliers are discussed in section 17.14.4 below.

Step 5: Incorporate environmental requirements into specifications

The incorporation of environmental requirements into specifications can be general, as with Toyota's chemical and transportation requirements referred to in Step 3 above or specific to a particular product or application, such as office furniture. The range of such environmental requirements is virtually limitless, but will normally cover such aspects as air, chemicals, energy, land, noise and statutory nuisances, plant protection, pollution and radioactive substances, together with requirements relating to installation, finishing, health and safety, testing and disposal. Reference to some factors in environmentally sensitive design was made in section 8.2.

Step 6: Adopt lifecycle approaches

Lifecycles and lifecycle costing have been discussed in sections 2.13.2 and 16.5 respectively. The terms lifecycle inventory (LCI) and lifecycle analysis (LCA) are also used. Other terms, such as cradle to grave analysis and eco-balancing, cover the same ground. In the case of manufactured products, an LCA involves making a detailed analysis of the costs and environmental impacts of the product, from the mining of the raw materials used in its production and distribution through to its use, possible reuse or recycling and its ultimate disposal. A useful matrix for indicating the environmental impacts of products produced by the International Council for Local Environmental Initiatives is shown in Figure 17.10.

Step 7: Prepare guidelines for proposals

'Surplus' is an omnibus term covering materials or equipment that are in excess of requirements, no longer usable in their original form or have been superseded. Surplus items may still have a value. Many companies have waste-reduction programmes aimed at reducing losses due to scrap or obsolescence.

'Residual' applies to no-value waste resulting from production operations and it must be disposed of in the most efficient manner with regard to environmental directives and pollution and health hazard considerations.

Purchasing can play a major part in waste disposal by doing the following:

- Identifying surplus materials or equipment.

- Arranging for the segregation of scrap, such as into ferrous or non-ferrous metals. Segregation can be facilitated by appropriate colour coding – red for steel, white for cast iron, blue for carbon steel and so on. Scrap should be collected in separate containers for disposal.

- Creating an awareness of the possibilities of salvaging or recycling. 'Salvage' may be defined as 'the realistic value of an asset at the end of its useful life when it is no longer suitable for its original use'. Scrap or spoiled work may possibly be reprocessed or recycled. Reprocessing is the use of scrap to make a different item. This should only be done if it is certain that the cost of salvaging is less than the expenditure on reprocessing. Recycled materials are especially useful to the industries that consume them because they are more cost-effective than the primary variety as none of the initial costs of extracting, processing, transporting or smelting are involved. It has been estimated that every tonne of metal recycled in the UK results in a saving of 1.5 tonnes of iron ore, 0.5 tonnes of coke and, when tin plate is recovered, a 0.3–5-kilogram reduction in the purchase of expensive primary tin. There is also the environmental factor that, when discarded products are allowed to stay out of the recycling system, they may pollute air, land and water and disfigure the countryside. Disposal of scrap – whether metal, wood, paper or other materials – is therefore best

Figure 17.10 International Council for Local Environmental Initiatives: matrix for environmental impacts

Product characteristics	Ecological alternative	Environmental consequences				Action Examples
		Material	Energy	Emissions	Waste	
Material composition	Recycled material	X	X		X	Use recycled toilet and towel papers Procure refuse sacks made of recycled plastics
	Renewable materials	X				Choose recycled concrete or crushed rock rather than gravel as a construction material
	No toxic substance			X	X	Use chlorine-free paper, PCB-free electronics or PVC-free floor coverings
Transport	Short distance		X	X		Buy your fruit and vegetables from local producers
	Transport means		X	X		Make use of rail and boat versus road and plane transport
Manufacturing	Taking into account the environment	X	X	X	X	Choose a producer that has an environmental management system
Packaging	Reduction	X			X	Prefer recyclable, easily returnable or, if possible, no packaging at all
Product use	Durability	X			X	Buy long-term guaranteed carpets
	Repairability/ upgradability	X			X	Choose computers that can be upgraded and do not need to be replaced completely when becoming outdated
	Compatibility with equipment/users' habits	X	X	X	X	When changing to a recycled paper, test its compatibility with copiers and printers before distributing it throughout your organisation
	Energy requirements		X			Choose low-energy lightbulbs to save energy (and reduce your annual costs by up to 70 per cent)
	Safety for users	X	X	X	X	Use alternative pesticides or alternative methods of pest control
End of line	Re-use potential	X			X	Buy refillable toner cartridges for laser and ink jet printers
	Recyclability	X	X		X	When buying white goods, make sure that they can easily be dismantled and their material recycled
	Disposal			X	X	Use biodegradable synthetic vegetable-based hydraulic oil for fleet maintenance

done via a recognised broker affiliated to an appropriate body, such as the British Metals Federation. Better prices may be negotiated if:

- the seller keeps abreast of the current scrap prices – the price of scrap is quoted daily on the London Metal Exchange
- the scrap is segregated according to the buyer's requirements
- scrap is suitably bailed.

Equipment or components may be disposed of by:

- sale via the trade press
- sale to a stockist or dealer
- auction or via trade auctions
- returning them to the supplier – usually this will be at a discount, but stock will have been turned into cash
- sale to employees – especially cars, computers and office equipment
- donating them to schools or charitable organisations.

Step 8: Provide appropriate training

The aim of appropriate training is to enable staff and, possibly, suppliers to learn how to think and act in an environmentally conscious way in the field of purchasing.

Step 9: Ensure regular audit of compliance

Monitoring the environmental purchasing policy and its implementation should form part of the periodical purchasing management audit referred to in section 17.4.

17.14.4 Screening suppliers for good environmental performance

Screening of suppliers can be done via questionnaires, requiring compliance with international standards and the use of specialist assessment tools.

As stated in section 11.8, prescreening suppliers is a good idea and prequalification questionnaires (PQQs) are often used for this purpose, gathering information on a supplier's financial and technical capability, and can be adapted to cover environmental issues, too. A good example is the UK's NHS Supplier Evaluation Performance Evaluation Question Set. The content of this questionnaire has been agreed with NHS representatives, industry and the Office of Government Commerce Buying Solutions and has become the standard for use throughout the NHS and wider government. The questionnaire can, however, be usefully adapted to private-sector use.

Compliance standards

Such standards include EU eco labels and those awarded by the International Organisation for Standardisation (ISO).

Eco labels are an internationally accepted way of differentiating products from an environmental perspective. Although aimed primarily at domestic consumers, the scheme can also be useful for professional purchasers.

The EU eco-labelling scheme uses a product lifecycle approach involving the following stages:

- preproduction
- production

- packaging and distribution
- utilisation
- disposal.

For each stage, environmental effects are considered according to eight criteria:

1 waste relevance

2 noise

3 air contamination

4 water contamination

5 effects on eco-systems

6 consumption of energy

7 consumption of natural resources

8 soil pollution and degradation.

ISO environmental standards

These are a series of reference documents on voluntary standards and guidelines that include eco-labelling, environmental evaluation and environmental aspects in performance standards. The focus on management distinguishes them from being purely performance standards. The aim is to help any country to meet the goals of 'sustainable development and environmental friendliness'. Indeed, many purchasers of products regard certification to ISO 14001 as an assurance of a supplier's commitment to environmental performance and quality.

The main ISO environmental standards are:

- BS EN ISO 14001: 2004: Environmental management systems. Requirements with guidance for use
- BS ISO 14004: 2004: Environmental management systems. General guidelines on principles, systems and supporting techniques
- BS EN ISO 19011: 2002: Guidelines for quality and/or environmental management systems auditing. General principles
- BS EN ISO 19011: 2002: Guidelines for environmental auditing. Audit procedures. Auditing of environmental management systems
- BS EN ISO 19011: 2002: Guidelines for environmental auditing. Qualification criteria for environmental auditors
- ISO 14020: 2000: Environmental labels and declarations – General principles
- BS EN ISO 14040: 2006: Environmental management. Life cycle assessment. Principles and framework
- BS EN ISO 14044: 2006: Environmental management. Life cycle assessment. Requirements and guidelines
- BS ISO 14050: 2009: Environmental management – Vocabulary
- ISO Guide 64: 2008: Guide for addressing environmental issues in product standards.

Organisations seeking ISO certification do so via an accredited certifying body that audits organisations against the requirements of the ISO 14001 standard. The audit involves reviewing policies and procedures, observing operations, interviewing employees and checking records to verify that a system includes all the elements required by ISO 14001 and that these are being effectively implemented.

The eco-management and audit scheme (EMAS)

This is a voluntary initiative, now directed by EC No 1221/2009 which replaced the European Commission Regulation 761/2001.

The aim of EMAS is to recognise and reward organisations that go beyond the minimum legal requirements and improve their environmental performance.

As with ISO 14000 and 9000, EMAS requires a planned, comprehensive, periodic (the minimum frequency is once every three years) audit of an organisation's environmental management system by an accredited EMAS verifier. The environmental policy that all participants must publish provides the initial foundation and direction for the organisation's management system and is more stringently reviewed than a similar ISO 14000 and ISO 9000 policy.

Use of special assessment tools

A danger with questionnaires is that the answers given by suppliers may receive little or no examination by the issuing purchasing organisation. Reliance on environmental standards may also be unsatisfactory. Knight[38] provides an example of a timber supplier that satisfied ISO 14000 requirements because of its methods of wood treatment:

> They had convinced themselves that they were environmentally responsible even though they had never considered where the trees were coming from.

An example of a tool designed to provide both a more precise evaluation against a benchmark set by the purchasing organisation and assist suppliers in meeting the required environmental standards is the environmental vendor evaluation system (EVES), developed by Peter Kileen for Yorkshire Water Services Ltd.[39] his system appraises a supplier's environmental performance against six criteria – namely, design, manufacture, in use, legal, management and measures or controls. Responses to weighted questions provide a score for each of the six areas, forming a profile that can be compared to a benchmark, as shown in Figure 17.11.

The overall environmental performance of a supplier can be categorised into one of six grades, ranging from one (leading, best in class) to six (environmentally unacceptable – do not use). Areas in which the responses fall below the minimum acceptable standard are highlighted, enabling corrective action to be taken between prospective purchasers and suppliers.

Figure 17.11 Overall vendor environmental rating score

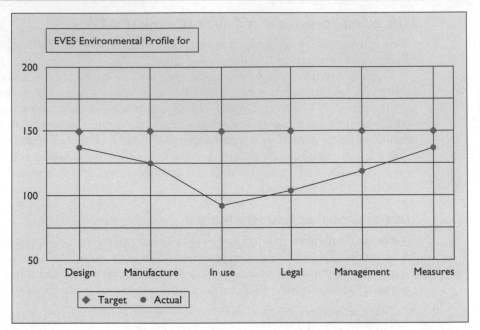

Scores	Design	Manufacture	In use	Legal	Management	Measures	Total score
Max points	150	150	150	150	150	150	900
Actual score	140	125	90	102	120	140	717
Area rates	Design	Construct	In use	Legal	Management	Measures	79.67

Grade 3 – Quite good, but you can still improve use for small- to medium-sized projects

Case study

Purchase Research

Axel Goodwin is a highly qualified marine engineer who has spent two years designing and developing a new system to launch lifeboats in a safer and faster way than is currently possible. Goodwin has five patents 'pending' and is determined to protect his intellectual property rights. Goodwin has spoken to three international shipbuilders located in Germany, Sweden and Japan who are very interested. Goodwin has devised a forward business plan and intends to 'go to market' in six months' time. He does not intend to manufacture and needs to locate a 'partner' or 'partners' to undertake the manufacture, testing of the finished product and delivery to his customers.

Tasks

You are the owner of a small procurement consultancy business and Goodwin has retained you to undertake purchase research to answer the following questions:

1 Where are possible manufacturers located and what initial questions would you ask to determine their apparent suitability?

2 Since there are strategic purchases to be made, including electronics, fabricated items and safety critical supplies, should Goodwin purchase these or let the manufacturers purchase them?

3 How will Goodwin protect his intellectual property rights?

4 How long will it take you to answer the questions outlined above?

You obviously need a detailed plan to deliver your 'project'. Please outline the constituent elements of the plan.

Discussion questions

17.1 You work for an international defence organisation who also manufacture products for the non-defence sector. You have just won a contract in the Far East which requires you to purchase 30 per cent of components/assembles in the local market. Your engineering director has asked that a research study be done on suppliers in Vietnam. If you had to undertake this task how would you:
   (a) plan the research study?
   (b) undertake desk research?
   (c) undertake field research?

17.2 Comment on the following statements:
   (a) Much academic research into purchasing is of little practical benefit to practising purchasing people.
   (b) Much academic research is published in journals that purchasing professionals never read.

17.3 If you were employed as the head of purchasing in a private sector, privately owned power station that could not generate electricity competitively and the chief operating officer wanted 15 per cent saved on the total amount of expenditure:

    1 how would you tackle this task?

    2 would you talk to buyers in other power stations?

    3 what would you say to your strategic suppliers?

17.4   In some procurement situations, suppliers own the intellectual property rights in what they supply, including software source codes and patents. What steps can the buyer take to encourage other suppliers to bid for business?

17.5   Benchmarking of procurement performance is rarely done in either the public or private sectors. Why?

17.6   There is virtually no aspect of purchasing that cannot be the subject of a benchmarking exercise. With reference to organisations known to you, consider the following aspects of purchasing:

- inventory control
- purchasing training and development
- e-procurement.

(a) What organisation does it best?

(b) How does it do it?

(c) What does your organisation need to do to catch up?

17.7   Your head of internal audit has asked you to help her to devise an audit plan to check on the way which purchase prices are agreed and how the process links to accounts payable. What elements of the procurement and payment process would you advise be included in the audit?

17.8   The CIPS policy statement on environmental purchasing suggests that products or services should be selected that 'use or emit fewer substances that damage the environment or health'. How can you do this if you are not a chemist and have no specialised knowledge of the chemical content or disposal difficulties of the products or materials you are buying?

17.9   Consider how, from an ethical standpoint, you would react in each of the following cases.

(a) A sales representative telephones you to say that he has left the employment of a supplier from whom you are currently buying large quantities of a component. He knows the price you are paying and states that his new company can undercut your present price by 20 per cent. You have been dealing satisfactorily with your present supplier for a number of years.

(b) You are negotiating on a one-to-one basis with a small machine shop to carry out operations on 100,000 items to relieve capacity in your own production department. You inadvertently mention that you are very pleased with the price and that, subject to discussion with your own production manager, the sub-contractor is likely to receive an order. He then asks, 'Why not let me increase the price by another £1 – 50p for me and 50p for you?'

(c) You can buy cheaper from an overseas supplier, but you know he has starvation levels of pay and the loss of the local order will cause unemployment.

(d) You have negotiated and signed a contract with a supplier. When you arrive home, you find that an expensive piece of jewellery has been sent anonymously to your wife.

(e) You mention to the sales representative of a steel stockist that you are proposing to build an extension to your home. He says, 'Why not let us supply you with the steelwork at cost price?'

(f) On two occasions, a supplier has delivered sub-standard components that can nevertheless be used. You telephone the supplier's production manager to complain. He says, 'Don't write about it because it might affect a promotion I'm expecting. Let's keep it to ourselves and I will put it right'.

(g) You inform a potential supplier that, on average, your company buys 100,000 units of a certain item each year and, as a result, obtain a substantial quantity discount. You know that the average usage is only 50,000 units.

(h) A supplier asks you, in confidence, to give details of competitive quotes, saying that he will beat any price offered and 'that must be good for you'.

(i) A supplier offers you a bribe, saying, 'We do exactly the same for your boss and he has no worries'.

(j) One of your subordinates tells you that, last night, he took his family to a football match and had the use of a hospitality box (including dinner), provided by a company that you know is seeking a share of your business.

17.10 The procurement department is in an ideal position to be accountable for the value of inventory held in a business. That way, procurement and inventory management would be truly integrated. Do you agree, or is there an alternative approach(es)?

Past examination questions

1 Identify **five** benefits for an organisation of having an environmental policy.
CIPS, *The Business Environment for Purchasing and Supply*, November 2009

2 There are three levels of strategy present in organisations: corporate level, business unit and functional level strategies.
(a) Explain what is meant by each of these three strategies and describe how they are related to each other.
(b) Using examples, briefly explain how the purchasing and supply function could be affected by any **one** of these strategies.
CIPS, *The Business Environment for Purchasing and Supply*, November 2007

3 (a) Identify the type of structure most likely to be associated with each of the following types of organisational cultures.
(i) task culture
(ii) role culture
(iii) power culture
(b) Briefly describe **one** other type of organisational culture.
CIPS, *The Business Environment for Purchasing and Supply*, May 2007

References

[1] Fearon, H., *Purchasing Research, Concepts and Current Practice*, American Management Association, 1976, p. 5

[2] Sarantakos, S., *Social Research*, Macmillan, 1993, p. 91

[3] Kydos, W., *Measuring, Managing and Maximising Performance*, Productivity Press, 1991, p. 17

[4] Van Weele, A. J., *Purchasing Management*, Chapman and Hall, 1995, pp. 201–2

5   Fearon, H. E. and Bales, W. A., *Measures of Purchasing Effectiveness*, Arizona State University, 1997

6   Scheuing, E. E., *Purchasing Management*, Prentice Hall, 1989, p. 137

7   Evans, E. F. and Dale, B. G., 'The use of audits in purchasing', *International Journal of Physical Distribution and Materials Management*, Vol. 18, No. 7, 1988, pp. 17–23

8   Business Link, 'Closing the marketing gap', obtainable from Benchmark Index at Field House, Mount Road, Stone, Staffordshire ST15 8LI (0870 111143) or www.benchmarkindex.com/articles/CTMG.pdf

9   American Management Association, *Evaluating Purchasing*, AMA, 1963

10 Details of the nearest Business Link branch can be obtained by phoning 0845 600 9006 or visiting www.businesslink.gov.uk

11 Details from CIPS at Easton House, Easton on the Hill, Stamford, Lincolnshire PE9 3NZ (01780 756777) or visit www.cips.org

12 Purchasing Index (UK) Ltd, 13–14 Barnard Mews, Barnard Road, Battersea, London SW11 1QU (020 7350 4200) or visit www.pricetrak.com

13 The British Quality Foundation, 32–34 Great Peter Street, London SW1P 2QX (020 7654 5000) or visit www.quality-foundation.co.uk

14 Published by Harvard Business School Press (*Harvard Business Review*: Sept–Oct 1992; Sept–Oct 1993; Jan–Feb 1996)

15 Niven, P. R., *The Balanced Scorecard Step-by-Step*, John Wiley, 2002

16 Bourne, M. C. S. and Bourne, P. A., *Understanding the Balanced Scorecard*, Hodder, 2000

17 Neeley, A., Adams, C. and Kennerley, M., *The Performance Prism: The Scorecard for Measuring and Managing Business Success*, Financial Times Prentice Hall 2002

18 Adapted from Colera, L., *A Framework for Universal Principles of Ethics* at: www.ethics.ubc.ca/papers/invited/colera.html

19 Robertson, D. C. and Rymon, T., 'Purchasing agents' deceptive behaviour: a randomised response technique study', *Business Ethics Quarterly*, Vol. 11, No. 3, 2001, pp. 455–79

20 CIPS, 'E-ethics: position on practice guide', prepared by the CIPS Consulting Group: www.cips.org

21 IPMM Forum at: www.ipmm.ie/ipmm_forum/viewmessages.cfm

22 Kennedy, G., *Everything is Negotiable*, Business Books, 1989, pp. 220–5

23 Matthew 7, verse 12

24 Karp, H. B. and Abramms, B., 'Doing the right thing', *Training and Development*, August, 1992, pp. 37–41

25 Brigley, S., *Walking the Tightrope: A Survey of Ethics in Management*, Institute of Management/Bath University, 1994, p. 36

26 Badaracco, J. L. Jr and Webb, A. P., 'Business ethics – a view from the trenches', *California Management Review*, Vol. 37, No. 2, Winter, 1995, pp. 64–79

27 As 25 above

28 Dubinsky, A. J. and Gwin, J. H., 'Business ethics: buyers and sellers', *Journal of Purchasing and Supply Materials Management*, Winter 1981, pp. 9–16

29 Nash, L., *Good Intentions Aside*, Harvard Business School Press, 1990, quoted in Holden, P., *Ethics for Managers*, Gower, 2000, pp. 82–3

30 CIMA, 'Fraud risk management: a guide to good practice', 2008

31 Casabona, P., 'Computer fraud: financial and ethical implications', *Review of Business*, Vol. 20, Issue 1, Fall, 1988

32 Evans, E. and Maguire, R., 'Purchasing fraud: a growing phenomenon', *Purchasing and Supply Management*, May, 1993, pp. 24–6

33 Included by kind permission of Linklaters

34 Carter, R., Ellram, L. M. and Ready, K. J., 'Environmental purchasing: benchmarking our German competitors', *International Journal of Purchasing and Materials Management*, Fall, 1998, pp. 28–38

35 European Information Service, Local Government International Bureau, Local Government House, Smith Square, London SW1P 3HZ (020 7664 3100) and at: www.lgib.gov.uk

36 Department of the Environment, 'Environmental action guide for building and purchasing managers', HMSO, 1991, p. 6

37 We are grateful to the University of Oxford's Central Purchasing Group for permission to quote from the Group's environmental purchasing policy

38 Knight, A., in a discussion published under the title 'Here today, green tomorrow', *Supply Management*, 11 December, 1997

39 This is described in Kileen, P., 'All about EVES', *Supply Management*, 24 September, 1998. Further details from Peter Kileen, 5 Cedarwood Close, Lytham St Annes, Lancashire FY8 4DP, in whose name the system is copyrighted.

Code of professional ethics – Chartered Institute of Purchasing and Supply (CIPS) (Approved by the CIPS Council, 11 March 2009)

As a member of The Chartered Institute of Purchasing and Supply, I will:

- maintain the highest standard of integrity in all my business relationships
- reject any business practice which might reasonably be deemed improper
- never use my authority or position for my own personal gain
- enhance the proficiency and stature of the profession by acquiring and applying knowledge in the most appropriate way
- foster the highest standards of professional competence amongst those for whom I am responsible
- optimise the use of resources which I have influence over for the benefit of my organisation
- comply with both the letter and the intent of:
  - the law of countries in which I practice
  - agreed contractual obligations
  - CIPS guidance on professional practice
- declare any personal interest that might affect, or be seen by others to affect, my impartiality or decision making
- ensure that the information I give in the course of my work is accurate
- respect the confidentiality of information I receive and never use it for personal gain
- strive for genuine, fair and transparent competition
- not accept inducements or gifts, other than items of small value such as business diaries or calendars
- always declare the offer or acceptance of hospitality and never allow hospitality to influence a business decision
- remain impartial in all business dealing and not be influenced by those with vested interest.

Use of the code

Members of CIPS are required to uphold this code and to seek commitment to it by all those with whom they engage in their professional practice.

Members are expected to encourage their organisation to adopt an ethical purchasing policy based on the principles of this code and to raise any matter of concern relating to business ethics at an appropriate level.

The Institute's Royal Charter sets out a disciplinary procedure which enables the CIPS Council to investigate complaints against any of our members and, if it is found that they have breached the Code of Ethics to take appropriate action.

Principles and standards of ethical supply management conduct (ISM)
(Adopted May 2008)

The following principles are advocated by the Institute of Supply Management (ISM) in the USA:

- Integrity in your decisions and actions
- Value for your employer
- Loyalty to your profession.

From these principles are derived the ISM standards of supply management conduct:

1 PERCEIVED IMPROPRIETY. Prevent the intent and appearance of unethical or compromising conduct in relationships, actions and communications.

2 CONFLICTS OF INTEREST. Ensure that any personal, business or other activity does not conflict with the lawful interests of your employer.

3 ISSUES OF INFLUENCE. Avoid behaviours or actions that may negatively influence, or appear to influence, supply management decisions.

4 RESPONSIBILITIES TO YOUR EMPLOYER. Uphold fiduciary and other responsibilities using reasonable care and granted authority to deliver value to your employer.

5 SUPPLIER AND CUSTOMER RELATIONSHIPS. Promote positive supplier and customer relationships.

6 SUSTAINABILITY AND SOCIAL RESPONSIBILITY. Champion social responsibility and sustainability practices in supply management.

7 CONFIDENTIAL AND PROPRIETARY INFORMATION. Protect confidential and proprietary information.

8 RECIPROCITY. Avoid improper reciprocal agreements.

9 APPLICABLE LAWS, REGULATIONS AND TRADE AGREEMENTS. Know and obey the letter and spirit of laws, regulations and trade agreements applicable to supply management.

10 PROFESSIONAL COMPETENCE. Develop skills, expand knowledge and conduct business that demonstrates competence and promotes the supply management profession.

Electronic versions of the *Principles and Standards of Ethical Supply Management Conduct* and ISM *Principles of Sustainability and Social Responsibility With a Guide to Adoption and Implementation* are available on ISM's Sustainability and Social Responsibility web pages: www.ism.ws.

Definitions, acronyms and foreign words and phrases

Definitions

absorption costing 573
acquisition 154
activity-based costing 577
activity-based management 577
agile production 140
agility 140
audit 616

B2B marketplace 192
balanced scorecard 629
benchmark 621
benchmarking 108
bid 561
bill of exchange 512
budgetary control 584, 615
budgets 584
business ethics 633
buying network 409

capacity 370
capital assets 446
capital equipment 446
capital expenditure 446, 447
capital goods 446
centralised purchasing 164
Codes of Practice 269
collusive tendering 435
components 476
compounding 460
concurrent engineering 241, 246
continuous replenishment programs 351
core process 158
cost-benefit analysis 58
cost of quality 293
countertrade 514
critical success factors 51
cross-functional teams 160

decentralisation 165
decoupling 142
derivatives 464
discounting 460
distribution requirements planning (DRP) 349
downstream supply chain 89
dynamic network 129

e-auctions 195
e-procurement 183, 365
e-sourcing 365

e-supply chain management 182
early supplier involvement (ESI) 248
economic order quantities (EOQ) 331
economic value added 616
effective negotiation 550
effectiveness 21
efficiency 21
efficient customer response (ECR) 351
electronic data interchange (EDI) 185
enterprise resource planning 86
environmental purchasing 647
environmental scanning 45
error 641
ethics 632

failure mode and effects analysis (FMEA) 289
forecasting 324
foreign exchange risks 498
foreign sourcing 494
forwarder 510
fraud 640
freight agents 510
functional analysis 300
futures 464

hedging 60
hub 189

incoterms 500
independent purchasing function 13
innovation 240
integrative purchasing function 13
internal network 128
international sourcing 494
inventory 309–10

just-in-time (JIT) 334–5

Kaizen (continuous improvement) 240
kanban 336

learning curve 584
leasing 453
leverage 19
lifecycle costing 566
logistics 82

management by objectives 631
manufacturing resource planning (MRP II) 345
margin 465
marginal costing 382
market 361

marketplace 190
materials management (MM) 83–4
materials requirements planning (MRP) 341
models 73
moving average 327
multinational sourcing 494

negotiation 526–8
network 89
network analysis 592
network structure 126

opportunity costs 384
organisational buyers 6
organisational change 170–1
organisational culture 172
organisational structure 118
outsourcing 380

partnering 394
passive purchasing function 13
penetration pricing 429
periodic review inventory system 332
personality 533
physical distribution management 84–5
ploy 548
positional negotiation 552
post-tender negotiations 565
postponement 141
pre-negotiation 538
price 418
principled negotiation 552
private sector 46
probability analysis 59
procedure 178
process mapping 145
process-oriented organisations 140
procurement councils 168–9
professional ethics 633
professionalisation 23
professionalism in purchasing 23
profit impact 61
project 589
project management 589
public sector 45
pull strategy 329
purchasing 5–6, 8–9
purchasing consortia 406
purchasing ethics 632
purchasing management audit 616
purchasing performance evaluation 611
purchasing research 606
purchasing task 53
push strategy 329

quality 261
quality control 280
quality system 263

ratio 624
relationship 218
relationship goals 532
reliability 262
retail markets 471
reverse auction 196
reverse logistics 88
right quantity 322
risk analysis 59

satisficing 60
sensitivity 59–60, 327
services 482
sourcing 359
specification 268–9
stable network 128
standard 269
standard costing 582, 615
strategic analysis 44–5
strategic global sourcing 494
strategic supply chain 145
strategy 32–4, 543
sub-contracting 392
substance goals 530
supplier-assisted inventory management 351
supplier-assisted inventory replenishment 351
supplier association 254
supplier development 251
supplier management 7
supplier manuals 205
supplier relationship management 218
supplies 310–11
supply chain 89
supply chain management 98
supply chain optimisation 106
supportive purchasing function 13
sustainable development 407

tactic 543
target costing 571
teams 159
tender 561
tiering 135
time series 326
total quality management (TQM) 263–4
trade-off 85

upstream supply chain 89

value 90, 299
value analysis 295–6
value chain 98
value engineering (VE) 294
vendor-managed inventory (VMI) 351
voluntary sector 46

waste 648
world class purchasing 17–19

Acronyms

ABC (activity-based costing) 577–582

ABCB (Association of British Certification Bodies) 279

ABM (activity-based management) 577

AMS (acquisition management system, MOD) 76

AQL (acceptable quality level) 261

ARR (average rate of return) 459–460

BATNA (best alternative to a negotiated agreement) 542, 551

BATNEEC (best available technology not entailing excessive cost) 648

BEAMA (British Electrotechnical and Allied Manufacturers Association) 436

BOM (bill of materials) 343

BPI (Business Process Integration) 189

BQF (British Quality Foundation) 630

BSI (British Standards Institution) 187, 263

CAD (computer-aided design) 143

CAE (computer-aided estimates) 143

CCL (climate change levy) 473

CCN (contract change notice) 427

CCR (capital cost rate) 616

CE (computer engineering) 143

CEN (European Committee for Standardisation) 294

CER (cost estimating relationship) 424

CFR (Cost and Freight) 501

CFR (customer furnished equipment) 479

CIF (Cost Insurance and Freight) 501

CIMA (Chartered Institute of Management accountants) 566, 571, 573, 582, 584

CIP (Carriage and Insurance paid To) 501

CIPS (Chartered Institute of Purchasing and Supply) 8

CISG (UN Convention on Contracts for the International Sale of Goods) 499, 500

CMRO (consumables or maintenance and repair or operating) 446

COFC (containers on flat cars) 508

CPA (contract pricer adjustment) 427

CPA (critical path analysis) 592

CPC (Customs Procedure Code) 507

CPM (critical path method) 592

CPT (Carriage paid To) 501

CRM (customer relationship management) 93

CRP (capacity requirements planning) 96

CRP (continuous replenishment programs) 351

CSF (critical success factor) 51

CSM (customer service management) 93–94

CT (countertrade) 514–517

DAP (Delivered at Place) 501

DAT (Delivered at Terminal) 501

DBIS (Department for Business, Innovation and Skills) 433, 434, 463

DDP (Delivered Duty Paid) 501

DECC (Department of Energy and Climate Change) 473

DEFRA (Department of the Environment, Food and Rural Affairs) 648

DFD (design for disassembly) 244

DMAIC (define, measure, analyse, improve and control) 284

DPMO (defects per million operations) 283

DRP (distribution requirements planning) 349–351

e-SCM (e-Supply Chain Management) 182–183

EAI (enterprise application integration) 96

EBI (early buyer involvement) 247

ECR (efficient customer response) 94

EDI (electronic data interchange) 185–189

EDIFACT (EDI for Administration, Commerce and Transport) 185

EDRM (Electronic Document and Record Management) 181

EFQM (European Foundation for Quality Management) 76

ENSG (Electricity Networks Strategy Group) 470

EOQ (economic order quantities) 331–332

EPOS (electronic point of sale) 186, 315

ERP (enterprise resource planning) 86

ESI (early supplier involvement) 248–251

ETI (Ethical Trading Initiative) 637

European Benchmarking Network (EBN) 627

EVA (economic value added) 616

EWAM (exponentially weighted average method) 327–328

EXW (Ex Works) 501

FA (functional analysis) 299–300

FAS (Free Alongside Ship) 501

FC & S (Free of Capture and Seizure) 506

FCA (Free Carrier) 501

FFL (fossil fuel levy) 472

FMEA (failure mode and effects analysis) 262

FMS (flexible manufacturing systems) 86

FOB (Free On Board) 501

GEMA (Gas and Electricity Markets Authority) 470

General Accounting Office (GAO, US) 181

ICC (International Chamber of Commerce) 518

IEEMA (Indian Electrical and Electronics Manufacturers Association) 436

ILO (International Labour Organisation) 637

IMP (Industrial Marketing and Purchasing Group) 5

ISM (Institute of Supply Management) 23

ISO (International Organisation for Standardisation) 244, 653

JIT (just-in-time) 17, 139, 254

LCC (life cycle costs) 569
LCH (London Clearing House) 464
LCL (less-than carload) 506
LOC (letters of credit) 513

MBO (management by objectives) 631–632
MES (manufacturing execution systems) 94
MM (materials management) 83–84
most economically advantageous tender (MEAT) 563
MRO (maintenance and repair or operating) 168
MRP (materials and requirements planning) 341–345
MRP II (manufacturing resource planning) 345–347
MTM (many-to-many) 190

NACCB (National Accreditation Council for Certification Bodies) 279
NATO (North Atlantic Treaty Organization) 82–83
NETA (trading arrangements for electricity) 471
NGET (National Grid Electricity Transmission) 470
NGTA (trading arrangements for gas) 471
NHS (National Health Service) 7, 19
NOPAT (net operating profit after tax) 616
NPV (net present value) 461
NTDB (National Trade Data Bank) 363
NTS (National Transmission System) 471

OAR (overhead absorption rates) 575
ODETTE (Organisation for Data Exchange by Tele-Transmission in Europe) 185
OEM (original equipment manufacturer) 102
Offer (Office of the Electricity Regulation) 470
Ofgas (Office of Gas Supply) 470
Ofgem (Office of Gas and Electricity Markets) 434, 470
OFT (Office of Fair Trading) 434, 435
OGC (Office of Government Commerce) 359, 364
OJEU (Official Journal of the European Union) 563
OM (operations management) 94
OPT (optimised production technology) 86
OR (operational research) 599–601

PD (product development) 94, 247–248
PDM (physical distribution management) 84–85
PECL (Principles of European Contract Law) 500
PERT (program evaluation and review technique) 592

PESTEL (political, economic, social, technological, environmental, and legal conditions) 123
PPP (Public-Private Partnership) 390
PQQ (pre-qualification questionnaire) 391
PRO (pricing and revenue optimisation) 106
PVF (price variation formula) 427, 436–438

QAS (quality assessment schedule) 143
QFD (quality function deployment) 287–289
QLF (quality loss function) 284–285
QRM (quick response manufacturing) 94

RBT (resource-based theory) 224–225
RFID (radio frequency identification) 316–317
RFPs (requests for proposals) 270, 485
RFQs (requests for quotations) 179, 270, 430, 485
ROCE (return on capital employed) 460, 623
ROM (rough order of magnitude) 425

SAIM (supplier-assisted inventory management) 351
SAIR (supplier-assisted inventory replenishment) 351
SAVE (Society of American Value Engineers) 293
SBU (strategic business units) 41
SCM (supply chain management) 92–97
SCOR (supply chain operations reference) 76
SGGA (*Supply of Goods and Services Act* 1982) 273
SHETL (Scottish Hydro Electric Transmission Ltd) 470
SITPRO (Simplifying International Trade Procedures Board) 187
SKU (stock keeping unit) 319
SLA (service level agreement) 486–487
SME (small- and medium-sized enterprises) 70
SPC (statistical process control) 254
SPT (Scottish Power Transmission Ltd) 470
SRM (supplier relationship management) 94
SSGA (Supply and Sale of Goods Act 1994) 272, 273
STM (strategic lead time management) 86
SWOT (strengths, weaknesses, opportunities and threats) 35

TCO (total cost of ownership) 20
TCT (transaction cost theory) 223–224
TQM (total quality management) 17, 172
TUPE (Transfer of Undertakings Protection of Employment) 19

ublicly Available Specification (PAS)( )
UCC (Uniform Commercial Code) 499
UNIDROIT (International Institution for the Unifications of Private Law) 209

VAN (value-added networks) 133, 185, 187
VAT (value-added tax) 506

VE (value engineering) 294–295
VFM (value for money) 612
VM (value management) 293–294
VMI (vendor-managed inventory) 90
VOP (variation of price) 427

WBS (work breakdown structure) 423
WEEE (*Waste Electrical and Electronic Equipment Regulations* 2006) 88

Foreign words and phrases

caveat emptor (let the buyer beware) 451
citius, altius, fortius (faster, higher, stronger) 17

dantotsu (striving to be the best of the best) 628

force majeure (events completely outside the control of the contracting parties) 465

Hin Shitsu Ki Ten Kai (how do we understand the quality that our customers expect and make it happen in a dynamic way?) 287

ignorantia juris non excusat (ignorance of the law does not excuse) 208

kaizen (continuous improvement) 240, 572
kanban (ticket) 336
keiretsu (affiliated chain) 40
Kyoryoku Kai (supplier associations) 254

muda (waste) 138

Poka-Yoke (fool proofing) 266

strategia (generalship) 32

tero (art and science of caring for things) 566

Index of names and organisations and some publications mentioned in the text

Abstracts of Statistics 362
Adams, C. 629, 630
Aitken, J. 140, 143
Aljian, G.W. 446
American Management Association 626
American Production and Inventory Control
  Society 334
Ammer, D.S. 418
Anderson Consulting 629
Ansari, A. 337
Applegate Directory 366
Arbulu, R.J. and Tommelein, I.D. 133
Armstrong, V. and Jackson, D. 186
Ashcroft, S.G. 535
Association of British Certification Bodies (ABCB) 279
Atkinson, J. and Meager, N. 387
AT&T 155
Audit Commission 364
Austin Rover 185

Babbage, Charles 10
Badaracco, J.L. Jr. and Webb, A.P. 639
BAE Systems 94
Bank of England Reports (UK) 362
Barclays Bank Plc 202
Barings Bank 467
Barker, J. 580
Bath University 138, 609
Bayer Group 229, 231
BCS 185
Beauchamp, M. 387
Beesley, A.T. 107
Belgian Federal Public Service 192
Benasaou, M. 226, 228
Berne, Eric 533
Beulen, E.J.J. 388
Birmingham, P.A. 229
Birou, L.H. and Fawcett, S.E. 494, 519
Black and Decker 118
Boeing Corporation 94
Bosch 185, 206
Bose Corporation 340
Boshoff, C. 483
Bourne, M.C.S. 630
Bourne, P.A. 630
Bowersox, D.J. 141
Bradford Chamber of Commerce 279
Brian Farrington Ltd 295, 494
Brigley, S. 638, 639
Bristor, J.M. and Ryan, M.S. 409–10
British Electrotechnical and Allied Manufacturers
  Association (BEAMA) 436

British Non-ferrous Metals Federation 463
British Petroleum (BP) 91
British Quality Foundation (BQF) 630
British Standards Institution (BSI) 187, 218, 263
British Standards Online 272
Buffett, Warren 467
Burch, J. 579
Burns, T. and Stalker, G.H. 154
Business Link 622

Calvi, R. 249
Campbell, A. and Yeung, S. 53
Campbell, P. and Pollard, W.M. 232, 233,
  234
Cannon, S. 170, 264
Carnegie Mellon University 69
Carr, A.S., Kaynak, H. and Muthusamy, S. 157
Carr-Saunders, A.M. 23
Carrington, L. 389
Carter, J.R. and Gagne, J. 514
Carter, R. 377
Casabona, P. 642
Cavinato, J.L. 168, 169
Census of Production (UK) 362
Center for Advanced Purchasing Studies 17, 609
Center for International Business Education and
  Research 362
Centre for Constructive Innovation 401
Chandler, A.D. 124
Chartered Institute of Management accountants
  (CIMA) 566, 571, 573, 582, 584, 640
Chartered Institute of Purchasing and Supply (CIPS)
  8, 73–5, 565, 608–9, 627, 636
Chicago and Northwestern Railroad 10
Chisnall, P.M. 411
Choo, C.W. 45
Chopra, S. and Meindl, P. 353
Christopher, M. 91, 142
Christopher, M. and Towill, D.R. 142
Chrysler 580
Citroën 185
Coase, R.H. 223
Collins, D. 173–4
Commission on International Trade Law
  (UNCITRAL) 499
Commodities Research Bureau 463
Commodities Research Unit 463
Competition Appeal Tribunal 434
Competition Commission 434
Cooper, M.C. 89
Cooper, R. and Kaplan, R.S. 578–9
Corporate Partnership Programme 627

Court of Appeal 434
Cox, A. 24, 223, 225–6, 540
Crampton, P.C. and Dees, J.G. 555
Cranfield School of Management 629, 630
Craven, D.W. 128, 130, 133
Crosby, P.B. 261, 267
Cudahay, G. 106, 107
Cyert, K. and March, J. 60

Daft, R.L. 170
David, F.R. 39
Davis, T. 107, 108
Day, A. 229
Day, M. 5
De Marco, A.A. 424
Deccapro 425
Dell Computing 129
Deming, W.E. 264, 266
Denning, Lord 207, 208
Department for Business, Innovation and Skills
    (DBIS) 433, 434, 463
Department for International Development 181
Department of Commerce (USA) 362
Department of Defence (USA) 295, 569
Department of Energy and Climate Change (DECC)
    473
Department of Health 164
Department of the Environment, Food and Rural
    Affairs (DEFRA) 648
Department of Trade and Industry 642, 644
Dow Chemicals 635
Dowlatshahi, S. 246, 251
Downes, L. 47, 49
Dubinsky, A.J. and Gwin, J.H. 640
Duffy, R.J. and Flynn, A.E. 485
Dun and Bradstreet 368

early buyer involvement (EBI) 247
Economic Trends (UK) 362
The Economist 363
Effective Partnering 400
Electricity Networks Strategy Group (ENSG) 470
Ellram, L.M. 402–3
England, W.B. 273, 450
England and Leenders, D.R. 418
Environmental Agency 648
ePedas 365
Ertel, D. 550, 551
Ethical Trading Initiative (ETI) 637
European Association of Metals 463
European Benchmarking Network (EBN) 627
European Commission 434
European Committee for Standardisation (CEN)
    294
European Federation of Quality Management
    (EFQM) 76
European Foundation for Quality Management
    (EFQM) 628

Evans, E. and Maguire, R. 642
Evans, E.F. and Dale, B.G. 617

Fahey, L. and Prusak, L. 35
Farmer, D. 21
Fearon, H. 606
Fearon, M.E. and Bales, W.A. 480, 613
Federation of International Trade Associations 362
Federation of National Associations 294
Feigenbaum, A.V. 266
Fiat 185
Financial Times 363
Fisher, L. 61
Fisher, M.L. 129
Fisher, R. and Ury, W. 529, 542, 544, 546, 550,
    552, 553–4
Ford, D. 5, 127
Ford Motor Company 11, 185, 290
Forker, L.B. 515
Fredriksson and Gadde 377
French, P. Jr. and Raven, B. 23, 122
Futures and Options Exchange 464

Gadde-Lars, E. and Hakansson, H. 110
Gagne and Discenza 572
Galinsky, A.D. 543
Gantt, H.L. 591
Gardner, J.T. and Cooper, M.C. 145
Gartner 347
Garvin, D.A. 261
Gas and Electricity Markets Authority (GEMA)
    470
Gattorna, 87
Gelderman, C.J. and van Weele, A.J. 63, 65
General Electric Company 295, 298
General Motors 185
Giunipero, L.C. and Pearcy, D.H. 24
GKN 185
Goldman, S.L. 140
Grinnel, S. and Apple, H.P. 120
Gullander, S. 254–5
Gunasekaran, A. 143

Hadfield, J.E. 483–4
Hampden-Turner, C. and Trompenaars, F. 498
Handfield, R.R. 250, 253
Handy, Dr. C. 52
Harland, C. 128, 129, 131
Harley-Davidson Inc. 52
Harris, T. 534
Hartley, J. and Jones, G. 251
Hartley, J.L. 304
Haslam, J.M. 273
Hastings, C. 126
Hayes, R.H. and Pisano, G.P. 339
Hiles, A. 486
Hill, J.A. 11
Hines, P. 98, 100, 101, 102

Hines, P. and Rich, N. 146–7, 254
Hoekstra, S. and Romme, J. 142
Hofstede, G. 498
Holmlund, M. and Strandvik, T. 221–2
Honda Company 36, 118
Hughes, R.A. 155
Humbert, X.P. and Passarelli, C.P.M. 393

Ibarra, H. 22, 23
Indian Electrical and Electronics Manufacturers
    Association (IEEMA) 436
Industrial Marketing and Purchasing Group (IMP)
    5
Institute of Logistics and Transport 309, 609
Institute of Purchasing and Supply 24
Institute of Supply Management (ISM) 23, 160,
    487, 636, 638
Institute of Value Management 293–4
Intergraf 195
International Centre for Competitive Excellence 93
International Chamber of Commerce (ICC) 500,
    518
International Court of Arbitration 500
International Federation of Purchasing and
    Materials Management 24
International Institution for the Unifications of
    Private Law (UNIDROIT) 209
International Labour Organisation (ILO) 637
International Monetary Fund 609
International Organisation for Standardisation
    (ISO) 244, 246, 653
International Petroleum Exchange 464
International Wrought Copper Council 463
Ishikawa, K. 267
Izushi, H. and Morgan, K. 255

Jarvelin, A.M. 222
Johnson, G. and Scholes, K. 33–4, 71
Johnson, S. 222
Jones, D. 12
Juran, J.M. 261, 266, 269

Kalakota, R. 93
Kalakota, R. and Robinson, M. 184
Kamann, D. 65, 66
Kanter, R.M. 23
Kaplan, R. 629, 630
Kaplan, R.B. and Murdoch, L. 158
Karp, H.B. and Abramms, B. 637
Kay, J. 224
Kennedy, G. 636
Kennerley, M. 630
Kileeen, P. 655
Killen, K.H. and Kamauff, J.W. 187
Knemeyer, A.M. 395
Knight, A. 655
Kolchin, C. 24
Kotter, J.P. and Schlesinger, L.A. 172

Kozak, R.A. and Cohen, D.H. 376
Kraljic, P. 43, 61, 62, 65, 252, 402, 483
Kreuze, G.J. 514
Kydos, W. 612

Lacity, M.C. and Hirscheim, R. 388, 390
Lakemond, N. 246
Lallatin, C.S. 484
Lambert, D.H. 134, 136
Lambert, D.M. 394
Lamming, R. 7, 25, 110, 128, 129, 130, 135–6
Lapsley, J. 578
Lawrence, E. 32, 35, 52
Lee, H.-C. 182
Lee, R. and Lawrence, P. 547
Leeson, Nick 467
Leighton, D.S.R. 418
Lesem, R. and Neubauer, F. 498
Lewin, K. 172, 173
Lewis, H.T. 10
Liedtka, J.M. 31
Lindblom, C. 36
Local Authority Waste Regulators 648
Lock, D. 590
Lockhead Martin 94
London Clearing House (LCH) 464
London Metals Exchange 464, 653
London Textile Trading House 279
Lowes, A. 630
Lucas 185
Lucas, H.C. and Baroudi, J. 171
Lyles, J. and Payne, R. 166, 168
Lysons, C.K. 486

McCall, J.M. and Norrington, M.B. 537
McCarthy, W. 555
McGinnis, M.A. and Vallopra, R.H. 111
McGregor, D. 121
McKinsey, 124
Manchester Chamber of Commerce 279
Marian, J. 6
Marien, E.J. 95
Marrian, J. 447
Mason-Jones, R. 144
Matsushita 155
Menyzer, J.T. 91, 92
Mercedes Motors 89
Mikkola, J.H. 250
Mileham, A.R. 241
Miles, L.D. 295, 304
Miles, R.E. and Snow, C.C. 41, 42
Miller, J. 299
Minahan, T. 18
Ministry of Defence (UK) 200
    acquisition management system (AMS) 76
Mintzberg, H. 32, 33, 34–5, 36, 118, 122–4
Mitchell, L.K. 232, 233
Moller, C. 267

Monczka, R.M. 388
Monczka, R.M. and Carter, J.R. 187
Morris, N. and Calantone, R.J. 12
Motorola Corporation 129, 155

Nash, L. 640
National Accreditation Council for Certification Bodies (NACCB) 279
National Association of Purchasing Agents 10
National Audit Office 364, 433
National Computing Centre 189
National Economic Development Office 510
National Grid Electricity Transmission (NGET) 470
National Health Service (NHS) 7, 19, 164, 364, 572, 653
National Institute for Manufacturing Management (Australia) 242
National Rivers Authority 648
National Trade Data Bank (NTDB) 363
National Transmission System (NTS) 471
Naylor, J. 108
NEC (Japan) 155
Neeley, A. 629, 630
Nellove, R. and Söderquist, K. 63
Ness, J. and Cucuzza, T.G. 580
Niven, P.R. 630
Norman, G. 187
North Atlantic Treaty Organization (NATO) 82–3
Norton, D. 629, 630
Novack, R.A. and Simco, S.W. 360

Occidental Petroleum 514
Office of Communications 434
Office of Fair Trading (OFT) 434, 435
Office of Gas and Electricity Markets (Ofgem) 434, 470
Office of Gas Supply (Ofgas) 470
Office of Government Commerce (OGC) 359, 364
Office of Rail Regulation 434
Office of the Electricity Market 434, 470
Office of the Electricity Regulation (Offer) 470
Office of the Gas Market 434, 470
Official Journal of the European Union (OJEU) 563
Ohno, T. 335
Operations Research Society 599
Organisation for Data Exchange by Tele-Transmission in Europe (ODETTE) 185
Ostroff, F. and Smith, D. 157
Ouchi, W.G. 233

Pareto, V. 313
Parker, G.M. 161
Partnering Sourcing Ltd. 394, 397, 399
Pena-Mora, F. and Tamaki, T. 541
Pennsylvania Railroad 10
Perkins 185
Perkins, B. 389

Peters, T. 267
Petersen, K.J. 250–1
Philips 155
Pilkingtons 118
Polhig, H.M. 486
Porter, M.E. 4, 41, 47, 49, 56, 90, 98, 99–105, 225, 534
Pragman, C.H. 341
Prahalad, C.K. and Hamel, G. 118
Principles of European Contract Law 500
Probert, D.R. 381
Procter & Gamble 134, 155, 169–70
Public Works and Government Services Canada 202, 245
Purchasing Index (UK) Ltd. 627
Purchasing Research Service 366
Purdy, D.C. 271

Quinn, J.B. 125

Ramsay, J. 402
Raytheon 94
Reck, R.F. and Long, B. 12, 13, 14
Reebok 129
Reilly, P. and Tamkin, P. 390
Renault 185
Rhys, D.G. 339
Richardson, T. 202
Risley, G. 462, 477
Robertson, D.C. and Rymon, T. 634
Rumelt, R.P. 56

Saab 185
Sako, M. 252
Sarantakos, S. 609
Saunders, M. 19
Scheuing, E.E. 616–17
Schonberger, R.J. 17, 280 Shewart, 337, Dr W. 282
Scott, S. 498
Scottish Hydro Electric Transmission Ltd (SHETL) 470
Scottish Power Transmission Ltd (SPT) 470
Shingo, S. 267
Shirley Institute 279
Simplifying International Trade Procedures Board (SITPRO) 187
Simpson, P.M., Sigauw, J.A. and White, S.C. 368
Sitkin, S.B. and Roth, N.L. 233
SKF 185
Snow, C.C. 128, 129
Sobek, I.I. 161
Society of American Value Engineers (SAVE) 293
Solar Energy Market Express 12
Southey, P. 232, 396
Spekman, R.E. 71
Susskind, L. and Cruikshank, J. 546
Sustainable Procurement Action Plan 245
Syson, R. 12, 20–1

Taguchi, G. 267, 284, 286
Technical Indexes Ltd. 272
Tesco 134
Texta N. and Miyamoto, T. 494
Thomas Global Register Europe 366
Toni, A.D. and Tonchia, S. 139
Toshiba 155
Toyota Motors 69, 650
Transfer of Undertakings Protection of
    Employment (TUPE) 19, 234
Treasy, M. 240
Trent, R.J. and Monczka, R.M. 162, 494
Tuns, M. 419
Turner, J.R. 602

UK Institute of Logistics and Transport 98
UK Purchasing and Supply Lead Body 54
UK Trade & Investment International Trade Team
    495
UN Convention on Contracts for the International
    Sale of Goods (CISG) 499, 500
UN Convention on Electronic Communication in
    International Contracts 500
US General Accounting Office 181
US Government Specifications Service 272

Van Hoek, R. 142
van Weele, A.J. 8, 612
van Weele, A.J. and Rozenmeiger, F.A. 154
Verikatesan, R. 380
Vodafone 69

Volkswagen 514
Vollman, T.E. 350
Volvo 162–3, 378

Walmart 134, 169–70
Waller, A. 365
Warwick University 138
Water Services Regulation 434
Waterman, R. 124
Waterman, R.H. 36
Webster, F.E. and Wind, Y.J. 408, 409
Whittington, E. 25
Wilding, R. 107
Williamson, O.E. 223
Wilmott, K. 511
Winkler, J. 418
Winthrop, University 6
Womack, J.P. 138, 139
Woodroffe, G. 274
World Bank 641
World Wide Web 365
Wynstra, F. 246, 247
Wynstra, F. and Ten Pierick, E. 249, 250

Xerox Corporation 515

Yasvas, B.F. and Freed, R. 514
Yorkshire Water Services Ltd 655
Yorkshire Wolds and Coast Primary Care Trust 69

Zaire, M. 265

Subject index

ABC analysis, inventory and 313–15
absorbed overheads 575
absorption costing 573–6
    and activity-based costing 577
    elements of 573
    indirect costs 574–5
    labour costs 574
    material costs 574
    non-production costs 576
    price composition 573–4
    production overhead costs 575
    profit 576
acceptable quality level (AQL) 261
acceptance sampling 282
accounting in performance evaluation 613–16
    activity-based costing 615
    budgetary control 615–16
    economic value added 616
    profit centre approach 613–14
    standard costing 615–16
acquisition costs 317–18
acquisition logistics 82
acquisition of capital equipment 449–50
acquisitions 154
activity 577
activity-based costing (ABC) 577–82
    and absorption costing 577
    in performance evaluation 615
    and purchasing 580–1
activity-based management (ABM) 577
activity cost centre 579
adaptive strategies 41
added value of logistics 86
administration overheads 575
adversarial leverage 225
adversarial negotiation 529, 535
agile characteristics 140–1
agile manufacturing 143
agile production and supply 140–4
    decoupling 142–3
    and lean production 143–4
    postponement 141–2
air transport 509
Air Waybill 505
All Risk 505
allocated overheads 575
anti-corruption issues 637
apportioned overheads 575
arbitrage 465
area planner concept model 169
audits
    eco-management scheme 655
    environmental 654

external and internal 642
    and fraud 642–4
    management 616–21
average rate of return (ARR) 459–60

backward integration 38, 39
backwardation 465
balanced scorecard 629–30
barcoding 315–16
barter 514
batch manufacture chains 90
battle of the forms 207
BCG portfolio 60–1
bear market 467
Benchmarker 627
benchmarking 108, 621–30
    balanced scorecard 629–30
    and continuous improvement 628
    forms of 622
    integrated 628–30
    ratios 624–8
    of supply chains 108
benchmarking index 627
best alternative to a negotiated agreement (BATNA)
        542, 551
best available technology not entailing excessive
        cost (BATNEEC) 648
bid rotation 435
bid suppression 435
bill of exchange 512
bill of lading 505, 512
bill of materials (BOM)
    in MRP 343
bills for collection 512–13
bills of quantities 479–80, 481–2
bottleneck items 63
brand or trade names 273
break-even point 384
breakthroughs in total quality management 264
bribery 644–6
Bribery Act (2010) 644–6
British Standards
    5750 quality management systems 276
    7373-3:2005 Specifications 270
    7850 total quality management 276
    BBS EN 9004:2009 quality systems 278
    BS 6143 economics of quality 276, 293
    BS 11000-1: 2010 Collaborative business
        relationships – Part 1: A framework
        specification 218
    BS EN ISO 9000: 2005 quality systems 280, 290
    BS EN ISO 19011:2002 environmental auditing
        654

British Standards (*continued*)
  BS EN ISO 14020:2000 environmental labels 654
  BS EN ISO 14004:2004 environmental management 654
  BS EN ISO 14040:2006 environmental management 654
  BS EN ISO 14044:2006 environmental management 654
  BS EN ISO 14050:2009 environmental management 654
  BS EN ISO 14001:2004 environmental performance 275
  BS EN ISO 14000 series 278
  BS EN ISO 9000:2005 standardisation 276–9
  BS EN ISO 6433:1995 technical drawing 275
  BS EN ISO 12973:2000 value management 293–4
  ISO Guide 64: 2008 product standards 654
budgetary control 584
  in performance evaluation 615–16
budgeting or cost averaging 468
budgets 584
Bulk Shipments 505
bull market 467
bullwhip effect 328–9
business ethics 633
business gifts 636
Business Process Integration (BPI) 189
Butler Machine Tool Co. Ltd. v Ex-Cell-O Corporation (England) Ltd. 207
buy-back 514–15
buy-side catalogues 193
buy-side exchange 190
buyer
  of capital investments 461–2
  captive 227–8
  and the law 208–9
buyer related pricing 429
buying
  of capital equipment 454–6
  centres, teams and networks 408–12
  network 409–10
  product factors in 411
buying overseas 493–522
  agents 509–11
  capital equipment 517–19
  and countertrade 514–17
  cultural factors 496–8
  customs and excise 506–7
  definitions 494
  foreign exchange risks 498–9
  incoterms 500–4
  information 495–6
  legal difficulties 499
  motive for 494–5
  ocean shipping terms 505–6
  payment methods 512–14
  success factors 519
  terminology 494, 505–6
  transport systems and costs 507–9
  true costs of 517
capacity requirements planning (CRP) 96
capital cost rate (CCR) 616
capital equipment
  acquisition 449–50
  buying 448–9
  buying overseas 517–19
  categories 447
  financing 452–6
  hire purchase 453
  leasing 453–6
  leasing or buying 454–6
  new or used 450–2
  outright purchase 452
  precautions 451–2
  suppliers, selecting 456–8
capital investments 446–63
  and buyer 461–2
  capital assets 446
  capital expenditure 446, 447–8
  capital goods 446
  evaluating 458–61
    average rate of return 459–60
    discounting 460
    forward buying 463
    hand-to-mouth buying 463
    market conditions 463
    net present value 461
    payback 459
    production materials 462
    raw materials 462–3
    sensitive commodities 462–3
captive buyer 227–8
captive supplier 227–8
Carnet 505
centralisation of purchasing 169
centralised activities 168
centralised purchasing 164–5
certification 279
certification authorisations 201
Clean Air Act (1956) 243, 647
climate change levy (CCL) 473
cognitive school of strategy 35
collaboration in tiering 136
collaborative business relationships 218–21
collaborative negotiation 529
collusive tendering 435
combination strategies 40–1
commodities dealing 466–9
  methods 467–9
commodity teams 169
Communications Act (2003) 433
compensation 514–15
Competition Act (1998) 433, 434, 435, 470
competition legislation 433–5
  in UK 433–4

competitive benchmarking 622
competitive strategy 41–2
component make-or-buy 382
component parts and assemblies 476
concentrated supply chains 90
concentric diversification strategies 40
concessions, trading in negotiation 536
concurrent engineering 241–3
configuration school of strategy 34
conformance, cost of 293
conglomerate diversification strategies 40
congruent operational goals 611
consortia, purchasing 406–7
construction supplies 478–9
consumables 477–8
consumables or maintenance and repair or
        operating (CMRO) 446
consumer logistics 83
consumer products 446
Containerisation 505
containers on flat cars (COFC) 508
contango 465
contingency theory 154
contract change notice (CCN) 427
contract management 180
contract price adjustment (CPA) 427
contracts
    battle of the forms 207
    in energy markets 473–5
        market analysis 474
        price structure 473–4
        risks 474–5
    interpretation 209
    legal aspects 206–7
    legally binding 180
    structure 209
contractual relationships 225–6
contractual requirements 219
cooperative planning 85–7
coordination structures 119–21
copyright 404
core competences 224
core processes 158–9
corporate objectives 611
corporate strategy 38
cost analysis 431–2
cost averaging 468
cost estimating relationships (CERs) 424
cost function analysis 300–3
cost management and target costing 572
costing 566–84
    absorption 573–6
    activity-based 577–82
    life cycle 566–71
    standard 582–4
    target 571–3
costs
    of buying overseas 517
    of capital equipment 456

direct 573
drivers 615
fixed 573
of goods sold 58
indirect 573
labour 574
material 574
non-production 576
production overhead 575
of quality 293
semi-variable 573
of services, reducing 487
true, of buying overseas 517
in value chain analysis 103–4
variable 573
counterpurchase 514
countertrade (CT) 514–17
cover bidding 435
Cox model 223–6
critical path analysis (CPA) 592
    procedures 595
    and sequencing 592
    terminology 592–3
critical path method (CPM) 592
    and PERT 597–8
critical success factors (CSFs) 51
cross-functional purchasing 160–1
cross-functional supplier development team 253
cross-functional teams 139
cross-organisational teams 162
CRP
cultural factors (buying overseas) 496–8
cultural school of strategy 35
culture 50
culture, scanning of 50
customer furnished equipment (CFR) 479
customer relationship management (CRM) 93
customer service management (CSM) 93–4
customs and excise (UK) 506–7
Customs Procedure Codes (CPCs) 507

danglers in networks 594
deadlocked negotiations 546
decentralised activities 168
decentralised purchasing 165–6
decision trees 601
decoupling 142–3
defects per million operations (DPMO) 283
define, measure, analyse, improve and control
        (DMAIC) 284
Delphi method 325–6
demand
    forecasting 324–9
        qualitative approaches 325–6
        quantitative approaches 326
    nature of 323–4
demand management 94
Demurrage 505
dependent demand 323, 334

derivatives 464
descriptive school of strategy 34
design
    for disassembly (DFD) 244
    FMEA 290
design FMEA 290
design rights 404
development responsibility in early supplier
        involvement 249
development risk in early supplier involvement
        249–50
differentiation of value chains 104–5
direct cost inputs 579
direct costs 573
direct materials total variances 583
direct materials usage variances 583
direct supply chains 91
directives for sourcing suppliers 363–5
    companies 365
    European Union 363–4
    local and central government 364
discounting capital investments 460
diseconomies of scale 168
distribution requirements planning (DRP) 349–51
    and MRP 350–1
diversification strategies 40
diversionary pricing 430
divestiture strategies 41
divisional purchasing structures 162–4
Documentary Credit 505
dummy node in networks 594–5
Dutch bid auctions 195
Duty 505
dynamic network 129–30

e-auctions 195–6
e-business 181–2
e-catalogues 192–4
e-commerce 154–5, 181
e-ethics 635
e-payment 200–1
e-procurement 17, 183–4
e-purchasing fraud 642
e-sourcing 365
e-Supply Chain Management (e-SCM) 182–3
e-tendering 181, 564
early buyer involvement (EBI) 242, 247
early supplier involvement (ESI) 248–51
    risks 249–50
echelon 349
eco-management and audit scheme 655
economic order quantities (EOQ) 331–2, 463
economic value added (EVA) 616
economics of inventory 317–18
    acquisition costs 317–18
    holding costs 318
    stockout costs 318
economies of scale in purchasing 165

EDI for Administration, Commerce and Transport
        (EDIFACT) 185
effective negotiation 550–1
effectiveness 21, 612
efficiency 21, 612
efficient customer response (ECR) 94, 351
Electricity Act (1989) 470
electricity pricing in energy markets 472–3
electronic data interchange (EDI) 102, 143, 185–9
    standards 185
    transaction in 185
Electronic Document and Record Management
        (EDRM) 181
electronic marketplace 190–1
electronic point of sale (EPOS) 186, 315
encrypted technologies 201
energy markets (UK) 470–6
    consultants and management 476
    contracts, procuring 473–5
        market analysis 474
        price structure 473–4
        risks 474–5
    and energy regulation 470
    pricing 472–3
        electricity 472–3
        gas 472
    retail 471
    supply chains 470–1
    wholesale 471
energy regulation 470
energy savings 647
English bid auctions 195
Enterprise Act (2002) 433, 434, 435, 470
enterprise application integration (EAI) 96
enterprise resource planning (ERP) 86, 347–9
    and MRP 348
entrepreneurial school of strategy 35
Environment Act 1995 648
Environment Protection Act (1990) 243, 647, 648
environmental aspects of purchasing 647–56
    compliance standards 653–4
    legislation 647–8
    policies and management 648–53
    suppliers, screening 653–6
environmental ethics 637
environmental management
    in sourcing suppliers 371–2
environmental scanning 45–9
environmental school of strategy 35
environmental standards 654–5
environmental structure of organisations 123–4
environmental vendor evaluation systems (EVES)
        655
environmentally preferred materials 244–5
environmentally sensitive design 243–6
    green procurement 245–6
    preferred materials 244–5
error and fraud 641

esteem value 296
ethical codes 636–8
ethical decisions 640
ethical training 638–9
ethics
    in negotiation 552–6
    in purchasing 632–40
    of suppliers 633–6
European Foundation for Quality Management
        (EFQM) 628–9
exchange (B2B) 190
exercise price 466
expert systems 325–6
exponentially weighted average method (EWAM)
        327–8
extended supply chains 91
external audits 642
external resource management 7–8

failure mode and effects analysis (FMEA) 143, 262,
        281, 289–92
fixed costs 573
fixed order quantities 330–1, 333
flexible manufacturing systems (FMS) 86
flexible networks 133
Flood and Water Management Act (2010) 647
force majeure 465
forecasting 324–9, 601
    qualitative approaches 325–6
    quantitative approaches 326
foreign exchange risks in buying overseas 498–9
foreign sourcing 494
forward and futures dealing 464–5
forward buying 463
forward integration 38, 39–40
fossil fuel levy (FFL) 472
fraud 640–6
    in e-purchasing 642
    and error 641
    prevention of 642–4
    procurement 641–3
Free Trade Zone 506
freight agents 509–11
full cost pricing 429
functional analysis (FA) 299–300
    costs 300–2
functional benchmarking 622
functional strategies 42–3
fundamental analysis 466–7
futures 464–7
futures contracts 465–6

games theory 601
Gantt charts 591
Gas Act (1986) 470
gas pricing in energy markets 472
General Accounting Office (GAO, US) 181
global competition and TQM 265

global sourcing 155
goods, purchasing 482–3
Gopertz curve 57
green procurement 245–6
growth strategies 38–41

hand-to-mouth buying 463
harvesting strategies 41
Health and Safety in sourcing suppliers
        371
hedging 60, 466
hire purchase of capital equipment 453
HM Revenue and Customs 506
holding costs 318
hollow networks 133
honesty and openness 634–5
horizontal diversification strategies 40
horizontal integration 40
horizontal organisations and processes
        157–9
hospitality 636
hubs 189–90
Hyde v Wrench 207

In Bond 506
incoterms 500–4
    features 501–4
    format 500
    use of 501
incremental acquisitions 449
independent demand 323, 330
independent purchasing function 13
indirect costs 573, 574–5
individual approach to negotiation 539–40
industrial products 446
information
    on market conditions in sourcing 361
    for overseas suppliers 495–6
information technology in purchasing 17
innovation 240–1
    drivers 240
input fraud 642
inspection 281
institutional approach to negotiations 550–2
insurance 370
integrated benchmarking 628–30
integration strategies 38–40
integrative purchasing function 13
intellectual property rights 403–4
intelligence gathering 541
intensive strategies 40
intermodalism 509
internal audits 642
internal benchmarking 622
internal network 128
internal scrutiny 49–51
international sourcing 494
international standards 275–7

intra-company trading 405
intra-organisational integration 119–21
inventory 310–23
    classifications 310–11
    economic order quantities (EOQ) 331–2
    economics of 317–18
        acquisition costs 317–18
        holding costs 318
        stockout costs 318
    fixed order quantities 330–1, 333
    just-in-time 334–41
    management 311–12
    management tools 312–17
        ABC analysis 313–15
        barcoding 315–16
        radio frequency identification 316–17
        software for 317
    performance measures 317–18
    periodic review 332–4
    and purchasing 354
    'push' and 'pull' 329–30
    right quantity 322–3
    vendor-managed 351–3
invitation to tender (ITT) 179, 563

just-in-time (JIT) 17, 85–6, 139, 254
    benefits of 337–8
    definitions 334–5
    in inventory management 334–41
    and JIT II 340–1
    and *kanban* systems 336–7
    and MRP 341
    objectives 335–6
    and purchasing 339–40
    and TQM 266

kaizen 240, 241, 252, 266
kanban and just-in-time systems 336–7
key performance indicators (KPIs) 108, 376
key results analysis 631
Kyoryoku Kai 254

labour costs 574
labour ethics 637
*Late Payments of Commercial Debts (Interest)
    Act* (1998) 634
law and the buyer 208–9
lead times in inventory management 318
leadership 108
lean organisations 138–40
lean production 139, 143–4
learning curves 384–5, 584–9
    application of 588–9
    basis of 585
    drawing 587
    theorem 585–6
learning school of strategy 35
leasing of capital equipment 453–6

legislation
    competition 433–5
        in UK 433–4
    environmental aspects of purchasing 647–8
less-than carload (LCL) 506
letters of credit (LOC) 513
leverage 19–20
    adversarial 225
leverage items 65
life cycle analysis 57, 244, 651
life cycle costs (LCC) 569
life cycle inventory 651
lifecycle costing 566–71, 651
    methodology 568–71
linear programming 601
liquidation strategies 41
local distribution zones (for energy) 471
Local Government Acts (1972, 1988, 1992, 1999)
    562
Local Government Planning and Land Acts (1980)
    562
local suppliers 406
logical persuasion 536
logistics and supply chain 81–116
    distribution management 83–7
    military applications 82
    non-military applications 82–3
    reverse 88–9
    what is 81–2

maintenance and repair or operating (MRO) 168,
    332, 446, 477
make-or-buy 381–6
    cost factors 382–5
    types of 381–2
make-or-buy decisions 588
management by objectives (MBO) 631–2
manufacturing execution systems (MES) 94
manufacturing flow management 94
manufacturing resource planning (MRP II) 86,
    345–7
    and ERP 348
margin 465
marginal costing 382–4
maritime transport 508–9
market conditions
    for capital investments 463
    in sourcing suppliers 361–3
market development strategy 40
market exchange 227–8
Market Focus Research Ltd. 609
market penetration strategy 40
market segmentation model of purchasing 170
marketing and sourcing 404–5
marketplace, electronic 190–1
master production schedule 343
material costs 574
materials budgets 584

materials management (MM) 83–4, 310
materials price variances 583
materials requirements planning (MRP) 86, 341–5
  and DRP 350–1
  inputs and outputs 342–5
  and JIT 341
  terminology 341–2
materials usage variances 583
mechanistic structures 154
Misrepresentation Act (1967) 451, 533
mission statements 53
most economically advantageous tender (MEAT) 563
moving averages 327
multinational sourcing 494

National Economic Development Office 510
National Procurement Strategy for Local Government 6
negotiated tenders 561, 563
negotiation 525–59
  actual 543–9
    behaviour 546–7
    concluding stage 549
    deadlocked 546
    ploys 548–9
    stages 543–4, 545
    techniques 544–5
  adversarial 529, 535
  agenda 539
  approaches to 529
  aspects of 528–9
  BATNAs 542, 551
  business objectives of 536–7
  collaborative 529
  compromise in 535–6
  concessions, trading 536
  content of 529–33
  deadlocked 546
  definitions 526–9
  effective 550–1
  ethics 552–6
  factors in 533–7
    negotiators 533–4
    representatives 534
    strengths and weaknesses 534–7
  individual approach 539–40
  institutional approach to 550–2
  intelligence gathering 541
  legal implications 532–3
  logical persuasion 536
  objectives, determining 541–2
  ploys in 548–9
  positional 552
  post-mortems 550
  post-negotiation 549
  post-tender 565–6
  pre-negotiation 538–43
  principled 552–5
  process 537–8
  relationship goals of 529, 532
  relationships 550–2
  situational approach to 550–2
  strategy and tactics 543
  substance goals of 529, 530–2
  team approach 540
  time, impact of 537
  venue 540
negotiators as representatives 534
net operating profit after tax (NOPAT) 616
net present value (NPV) 461
net profit margins 58
network sourcing 225
networks 126–7
  basics 127–8
  buying 409–10
  classification 128–32
  configuration 132–3, 134–7
  conventions in scheduling 593–5
    danglers 594
    dummy node 594–5
    loops 595
  internal 128
  optimisation 134
networks analysis
  and cost in scheduling 595–7
  and purchasing 598–9
new buy phase in pricing 419
new or used capital equipment 450–2
non-conformance, cost of 293
non-critical items 63
non-production costs 576
non-value-adding activities 615
novation 464

offset 405
  in countertrade 515
Olympic Delivery Authority 135
open account payments 512
open tenders 561, 562
openness 634–5
operational logistics 82
operational objectives 611
operational research (OR) 599–601
  applications 601
  limitations 600
  procedures 599–600
  and supplies 600
operational risk 475
operational sourcing 359
operations management (OR) 94
opportunity costs 384
optimised production technology (OPT) 86
options 466
options contracts 466
organic structures 154

organisational buyers 6–7
organisational change in purchasing 170–4
    implementation of 172–4
organisational strategy 37
organisational structures 118–25
original equipment manufacturers (OEMs) 102
output fraud 642
outright purchase of capital equipment 452
outsourcing 156, 380–91
    benefits of 388–9
    drivers of 388
    handling 390–1
    of manufacturing 381–6
    problems of 389–90
    purchasing 387
    of services 386–7
    types of 388
overdesign 228
overhead absorption rates (OAR) 575

Packaging (Essential Requirements) Regulations
        (2003) 647–8
Pareto analysis 313
Pareto diagram 315
partnering 5, 155, 393–403
partnership sourcing 393–403
    drivers 396
    effectiveness 400–1
    failure 402–3
    implementation 398–400
    relationships 225, 397
passive purchasing function 13
patents 404
pattern, strategy as 33
payback 459
payment
    in advance 513
    prompt 634
penetration pricing 429
performance evaluation
    budgetary control in 615–16
    profit centre approach in 613–14
    in sourcing suppliers 375–8
performance prism 629–30
performance specification 274
Perils of the Sea 506
periodic review inventory system 332–4
perspective, strategy as 33
physical distribution management (PDM) 84–5,
        310
pipelines 508
plan, strategy as 32–3
ploys
    in negotiations 548–9
    strategy as 33
Poka-Yoke 266
political, economic, social, technological,
        environmental, and legal conditions
        (PESTEL) 123

pollution and waste 647
portals 190
portfolio planning and analysis 60
position, strategy as 33
positional negotiation 552
post-mortems in negotiation 550
post-tender negotiations 565–6
postponement 141–2
power 122–3
power school of strategy 35
pre-negotiation 538–43
pre-qualification questionnaire (PQQ) 180, 391
precedence diagram 593
preferred suppliers 225
prescriptive school of strategy 34
prestige pricing 430
Prevention of Corruption Acts (1906, 1916) 644
price
    buyer's control of 432–3
    buyer's role in, pre-tender 418–26
        cost estimating 419–24
        parametric cost estimating 424–6
        procurement cost reduction 426
    in standard costing 582
    supplier's decisions 426–8
    what is? 418
price analysis 430–1
price composition in absorption costing 573–4
price variation formula (PVF) 427, 436–8
Pricetrak 627
pricing
    in energy markets 472–3
        electricity 472–3
        gas 472
    new buy phase in 419
    re-buy phase in 420
pricing and revenue optimisation (PRO) 106
principled negotiation 552–5
Principles of European Contract Law (PECL)
        500
proactive variety reduction 279
probability analysis 59
probability theory 601
process control 282
process FMEA 290
process links 137
process map 146
process-oriented programmes 252
procurement
    green 245–6
    and intellectual property rights 403–4
    purchasing as 6
    and target costing 573
Procurement Code of Good Practice for Customers
        and Suppliers 636
procurement cost reduction 426, 428
procurement councils 168–9
procurement fraud 641–3
procurement process 180

procurement teams 409
product development (PD) 94, 247–8
product factors in buying 411
product innovation strategy 40
product quality *see* quality
production logistics 83
production overhead costs 575
production overheads 575
professional ethics 633
professionalisation 23
professionalism in purchasing 23–5
profit centre approach to performance evaluation
    613–14
profit in absorption costing 576
profitability analysis 58–9
program evaluation and review technique (PERT)
    592
    and CPM 597–8
    procedures 595
    terminology 592–3
project management 589–601
    purchasing in 590
    scheduling 591–9
    types of project 590
promotion pricing 430
Public Bodies Corrupt Practices Act (1889) 644
Public Contracts Regulations (2006) 562
Public-Private Partnership (PPP) 390
public sector buyers 275
Public Supply Contract Regulations 180
Publicly Available Specification 11000 (PAS)
    218
pull inventory strategy 329–30
purchases, low-value 202–3
purchasing 4–9
    and activity-based costing 580–1
    cards 202
    and change 16–17
    as a discipline 5
    economies of scale 165
    environmental aspects 647–56
        legislation 647–8
        policies and management 648–53
        suppliers, screening 653–6
    evolution of 9–15
    and fraud 640–6
    goods 482–3
    and inventory 354
    and just-in-time systems 339–40
    legal aspects 206–9
    manuals 203–5
    market segmentation model of 170
    networks analysis in 598–9
    perspective on 4–5
    petty cash 203
    as problem-solving 5
    procedures 178–213
    as process 4
    as procurement 6

and product development 247–8
    as a profession 5
    professionalism in 23–5
    in project management 590
    as relationship 5
    as resource management 7–8
    self-billing 203
    services 480–3
    and standardisation 278
    standing orders 203
    stockless 203
    as supplier management 7
    in supply chain 4–5
    supply chains and 109–12
        development 111–12
        rationalisation 111
    and value analysis 304
purchasing and supply management (PSM)
    19–25
purchasing budgets 584
purchasing consortia 406–7
purchasing department 4
purchasing department's operating budgets 584
purchasing design 153–77
purchasing ethics 632–40
purchasing function 4
    development of 13
purchasing management audit approach 616–21
purchasing orientation 246–8
purchasing performance evaluation 611–32
    accounting 613–16
        activity-based costing 615
        budgetary control 615–16
        economic value added 616
        profit centre approach 613–14
        standard costing 615–16
    management audit approach 616–21
    measurement difficulties 612–13
purchasing portfolio management 61–7
purchasing relationships 218
purchasing research 606–10
purchasing risk 475
purchasing strategy 42–4
purchasing structure and design 153–77
    centralised purchasing 164–5
    cross-functional purchasing 160–2
    cultural change 172
    decentralised purchasing 165–6
    divisional structures 162–4
    environmental factors 154–6
    evolving structures 169–70
    as functional department 156–7
    horizontal organisations and processes 157–9
    in multi-plant organisations 166–9
    organisational change 170–4
    structural change 171
    teams 159
Purcon Index 609
push inventory strategy 329–30

qualitative assessments 611
quality 260–308
  assurance 279
  costs of 293
  definitions 261
  dimensions of 261–2
  failure mode and effects analysis (FEMA) 262
  gurus 266–7
    Crosby 267
    Deming 266
    Feigenbaum 266
    Ishikawa 267
    Juran 266
    Moller 267
    Peters 267
    Shingo 267
    Taguchi 267
  management of (TQM) 263–8
  reliability and 262
  systems 263
quality assessment schedule (QAS) 276–7
quality assurance 280
quality control 280–92
quality function deployment (QFD) 143, 287–9
quality loss function (QLF) 284–5
quantitative assessments 611
quantity in standard costing 582
queuing theory 601
quick response manufacturing (QRM) 94

radio frequency identification (RFID) 316–17
Radioactive Substances Act (1993) 243, 647
rail transport 508
ratios 624–8
re-buy phase in pricing 420
  modified 421
reactive purchasing 6
reactive variety reduction 279
reciprocity and sourcing 404–5
Reefer 506
registered designs 404
relationship formation hierarchy 221–2
relationship goals of negotiation 529, 532
relationship purchasing 218
reliability 262
requests for proposals (RFPs) 270, 485
requests for quotations (RFQs) 179, 270, 430, 485
resale products 446
research organisations 608–9
research sections 609
resource 578
resource-based theory (RBT) 224–5
resource drivers 578
resources, scanning of 49–50
restricted tenders 561, 563
resulted-oriented programmes in supplier
    development 251
retail and distribution supply chains 90

retail energy markets (UK) 471
retrenchment strategies 40–1
return analysis 58
return on capital employed (ROCE) 460, 623
returns management 94
reverse auctions 196–200
reverse-bid auctions 195
reverse logistics 88–9
risk analysis 59–60
risks
  in buying overseas 498–9
  in early supplier involvement 249–50
  in energy markets 474–5
  to supply chains 97–8
road transport 507–8
robust design 256, 285–7
rough order of magnitude (ROM) cost estimates
    425

safety stocks 319–22
Sale of Goods Act (1979) 272, 451, 452
sampling 281
  specification by 273–4
satisficing 60
scenario planning 57–8
scheduling 591–9
  critical path analysis 592
  Gantt charts 591
  network analysis 592
  network conventions 593–5
  program evaluation and review technique 592–3
sealed-bid auctions 195
secrecy 403
segmentation of services 483–5
selective tenders 561
sell-side exchange 190
selling overheads 575
semi-variable costs 573
sensitive commodities 462–3
sensitivity analysis 59–60
sequencing and CPA 592
serial tenders 561
service chains 90
service level agreements (SLAs) 486–7
service levels in inventory management 318,
    319–22
services 446
  cost of, reducing 487
  nature of 482
  purchasing 480–3
  segmentation of 483–5
Servicetrak 627
SERVQUAL 632
Shipping Conference 506
Simplifying International Trade (SITPRO) 512, 513
single sourcing 225
single sourcing relationships 225
single tenders 561

situational approach to negotiations 550–2
Six Sigma 283–4, 632
skimming pricing 429
small- and medium-sized enterprises (SMEs) 70,
        165, 368, 627
small business units 608
sourcing 358–416
    buying centres, teams and networks 408–12
    decisions 408–10
    directives 363–5
    e-sourcing 365
    finance 368–9
    information 361
    insurance 370
    intellectual property rights 403–4
    intra-company trading 405
    local suppliers 406
    market conditions 361–3
    and marketing 404–5
    offset 405
    operational 359
    outsourcing 380–91
    partnering 393–403
    policies 378–9
    process 360–1
    purchasing consortia 406–7
    reciprocity in 404–5
    strategic 359–60
    sub-contracting 392–3
    supplier base 379–80
    suppliers
        approval of 374–5
        assessment of 366–74
        environmental management of 371–2
        locating 365–6
        performance evaluation 375–8
        productive capacity of 370–1
        quality of 371
        visits 373–4
    sustainability 407–8
    tactical 359
    what is? 359–60
    where to buy decisions 410–12
specialisation structures 118
specification 268–72
    alternative method of specifying 273–4
    alternatives to individual specifications 272–5
    content of 270–1
    definitions 268–9
    existing specifications 272–3
    and public sector buyers 275
    purchasing and 268
    purpose of 269
    sample by 273–4
    types 269
    writing 271–2
spot price 466
stability 40–1

stable network 128
stable networks 128
standard costing 582–4
    in performance evaluation 615–16
standardisation 275–9
    application 275–6
    BS EN ISO 9000:2005 276–7
    purchasing and 278
    purpose 275
    subject matter 275
statistical process control (SPC) 254, 282
statistical quality control 281–3
Statutes (UK)
    Bribery Act (2010) 644–6
    Clean Air Act (1956) 243, 647
    Communications Act (2003) 433
    Competition Act (1998) 433, 434, 435, 470
    Electricity Act (1989) 470
    Enterprise Act (2002) 433, 434, 435, 470
    Environment Act (1995) 648
    Environment Protection Act (1990) 243, 647,
        648
    Flood and Water Management Act (2010) 647
    Gas Act (1986) 470
    Late Payments of Commercial Debts (Interest)
        Act (1998) 634
    Local Government Acts (1972, 1988, 1992,
        1999) 562
    Local Government Planning and Land Acts
        (1980) 562
    Misrepresentation Act (1967) 451, 533
    Packaging (Essential Requirements) Regulations
        (2003) 647–8
    Prevention of Corruption Acts (1906, 1916) 644
    Public Bodies Corrupt Practices Act (1889) 644
    Public Supply Contract Regulations 180
    Radioactive Substances Act (1993) 243, 647
    Sale of Goods Act (1979) 272, 451, 452
    Supply and Sale of Goods Act (1994) (SSGA)
        272, 273
    Supply of Goods and Services Act (1982) (SGGA)
        273
    Trades Description Act 451
    Utilities Act (2000) 470
    Waste Electrical and Electronic Equipment
        Regulations (2006) 88, 648
    Water Act (2003) 647
stock cover 319
stock keeping unit (SKU) 319
stock turn rates in inventory management 319
stockout costs 318
stockouts 319
strategic analysis 44–5
strategic benchmarking 622
strategic business units (SBU) 41
strategic drift 37
strategic global sourcing 494
strategic lead time management (STM) 86

strategic make-or-buy 381
strategic management 44
strategic partnerships 227–8
strategic purchasing 42–3
strategic purchasing and supply chain models 73–6
strategic sourcing 359–60
strategic supplier alliances 226
strategic thinking 31–2
strategy 32–4
    characteristics of 33
strategy development 34–7
strategy formulation 51–6
strategy implementation 67–71
    post-implementation review 71–3
strengths, weaknesses, opportunities and threats
        (SWOT) 35
strike price 466
structures
    control 121–2
    coordination 119–21
    determinants of 122–4
    evolving (purchasing) 169–70
    networks 126–34
    power 122–3
    specialisation 118
sub-contracting 392–3
substance goals of negotiation 529, 530–2
supplier
    benefits of e-SCM 182–3
    captive 227–8
    management 7
    manuals 205–6
    pricing decisions 426–8
    pricing strategy 428–30
    selection and evaluation 229–31
supplier-assisted inventory management (SAIM)
        351
supplier-assisted inventory replenishment (SAIR)
        351
supplier associations (SA) 254–6
supplier development 251–3
supplier factors in buying 411
supplier relationship management (SRM) 94, 218,
        229–31
    model for 230
supplier relationships 217–38
    models of 223–9
    optimisation of 231
    termination of 232–4
suppliers
    of capital equipment, selecting 456–8
    environmental screening of 653–6
    ethics 633–6
    local 406
    management of in sourcing
        approval of 374–5
        assessment of 366–74
        environmental management of 371–2
        Health and Safety 371

locating 365–6
performance evaluation 375–8
productive capacity of 370–1
quality of 371
visits 373–4
preferred 225
representatives, courtesy to 635–6
Supply and Sale of Goods Act (SSGA) (1994) 272,
        273
supply chain management (SCM) 92–7, 310
    enablers 95–7
    inventory systems 349
    and logistics 98
    as management processes 93–4
supply chain networks 127
supply chain operations reference (SCOR) 76
supply chain process models 73–6
supply chains 89–92
    characteristics 91
    in energy markets 470–1
    mapping 144–7
    optimisation of 106–9
    and purchasing 109–12
        development 111–12
        rationalisation 111
    risks to 97–8
    types of 90–2
    vulnerability of 97–8
supply manager concept model 169
supply networks 131–2
    optimisation of 134
Supply of Goods and Services Act (SGGA) (1982)
        273
support tools 560–605
supportive purchasing function 13
sustainability
    and sourcing 407–8
sustainable development 407–40
swaps 514
switch trading 515
SWOT analysis 35, 55–6
systems FMEA 290

tactical make-or-buy 382
tactical purchasing 6
tactical sourcing 359
target costing 571–3
    and procurement 573
target pricing 430
team approach to negotiation 540
teams
    commodity 169
    cross-organisational 162
    purchasing 159
technical analysis 466–7
tendering 561–6
    application of 562–3
    collusive 435
    post-tender negotiations 565–6

tendering (*continued*)
  procedures 563–4
  types 561
  unsuccessful 564–5
tenders
  negotiated 561, 563
  open 561, 562
  restricted 561, 563
  selective 561
  serial 561
  single 561
termination of supplier relationships 232–4
  legal considerations 234
  process 233
  timing 233
terotechnology 566
test marketing 325–6
third-party catalogues 193–4
tiering 135–7
  and linking 136–7
time budgeting 468
time series 325–6
total cycle time reduction 17
total quality management (TQM) 17, 102, 172,
    263–8
  benefits 267–8
  and costs 582
  criticisms of 268
  development of 265–6
  kaizen and 240
  principles 264–5
total systems management 85
trade names 273
trade-offs 85
trademarks 404
Trades Description Act 451
trading arrangements for electricity (NETA)
    471
trading arrangements for gas (NGTA) 471
training, ethical 638–9
transaction cost theory (TCT) 223–4
transaction exposure 498
transaction in EDI 185
transactional analysis 533
transactional linkages 130–1
transactional purchasing 6, 218, 219
transactional response 533–4
transactional stimulus 533
transfer price 614
transformation school of strategy 34
transformational acquisitions 449
true costs of buying overseas 517
turnaround strategies 41

UK Integrated Tariff 506
UK Purchasing and Supply Lead Body 54
ultimate customer 90
ultimate supply chains 91
uncertainty in supply chain analysis 107–8
Uniform Commercial Code (UCC) 499
unsuccessful tendering 564–5
Utilities Act (2000) 470

Valuation Clause 506
value-added networks (VANs) 133, 185, 187
value-added tax (VAT) 506
value-adding activities 615
value analysis 295–9
  and functional analysis 299–300
  and purchasing 304
value chain analysis 103–5
  cost drivers 103–4
  differentiation 104–5
  steps in 105
value chains 98–103
  mapping 144–7
  mapping tools 146–7
  optimisation of 106–9
value engineering (VE) 139, 294–5
  change proposals 295
value for money (VFM) 612
value management (VM) 293–4
value risk 475
value stream mapping 146–7
variable costs 573
variances in standard costing 582–3
variation of price (VOP) 427
variety reduction 279–80
vendor-managed inventory (VMI) 351–3
vertical integration strategies 38
vertical organisations 158
virtual networks 133
vision statements 52–3
volume risk 474–5
volume timing of purchases 468–9

War Risks 506
waste 647, 648
*Waste Electrical and Electronic Equipment
    Regulations* (WEEE) (2006) 88, 648
Water Act (2003) 647
Wharfage 506
wholesale energy markets (UK) 471
work breakdown structure (WBS) 423
world class purchasing 17–19

Yorkshire Purchasing Organisation 406